THE QUEST FOR POWER

The Lower Houses of Assembly
in the
Southern Royal Colonies
1689-1776

The Institute of Early American History and Culture is sponsored jointly by the College of William and Mary and Colonial Williamsburg, Incorporated. Publication of this book has been assisted by a grant from the Lilly Endowment, Inc.

THE QUEST FOR POWER

*THE LOWER HOUSES OF ASSEMBLY
IN THE SOUTHERN ROYAL COLONIES
1689 - 1776*

By

Jack P. Greene

PUBLISHED FOR THE
Institute of Early American History and Culture
AT WILLIAMSBURG, VIRGINIA

BY THE UNIVERSITY OF NORTH CAROLINA PRESS · CHAPEL HILL

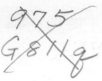

PRINTED BY THE SEEMAN PRINTERY, DURHAM, N. C.

Manufactured in the United States of America

For
Sue

Preface

THE rise of representative government in the British colonies in America during the seventeenth and eighteenth centuries was a factor of enormous importance in the development of both the American political system and the British Commonwealth of Nations. Through their lower houses of assembly the colonists achieved a considerable degree of home rule in the eighteenth century; and it was the lower houses that took the lead in defending American rights and liberties when they were challenged by Crown and Parliament after 1763 and served as a training ground for that remarkable group of political leaders who guided our nation through the crises of its first quarter century. Following the loss of her American colonies, Britain continued her policy of insisting that each of her colonies have its own representative assembly. In the following century these legislatures in the Canadas, Nova Scotia, Prince Edward Island, and New Brunswick led the movement for responsible government. Their victories paved the way for the development of a British Empire with a common monarch and co-ordinate legislatures and eventually for the evolution of a group of independent Commonwealths linked by a common political heritage and allegiance to a mutual sovereign. One can scarcely exaggerate the importance of the existence of representative political systems in the United States and the British Commonwealth in the twentieth century.

The emergence of the lower houses as the dominant element in colonial government has been the grand theme of American colonial history. For nearly a century after 1776 historians interpreted it as a prelude to the American Revolution. In the 1780's George Chalmers saw it as the early manifestation of a latent desire for independ-

ence, an undutiful reaction to the mild policies of the mother country.[1] In the middle of the nineteenth century the American national-
ist George Bancroft, although more interested in other aspects of
colonial history, looked upon it as the natural expression of American
democratic tendencies, simply another chapter in the progress of
mankind.[2] The reaction to these sweeping interpretations set in
during the last decades of the nineteenth century, when Charles M.
Andrews, Edward Channing, Evarts B. Greene, Herbert L. Osgood,
and others began to investigate in detail—and in context—developments from the Restoration to the end of the Seven Years' War.
Under Osgood's direction a whole corps of Columbia University graduate students produced a series of institutional studies of the several
colonies in which the evolution of the lower houses was a central
feature. But this necessarily piecemeal approach, as well as the
excessive fragmentation that characterized the more general narratives
of Osgood and Channing themselves, tended to emphasize the differences rather than the similarities in the rise of the lower houses and
in any case failed to produce a general analysis of the common
features of their quest for power.[3] Among later scholars, Leonard
W. Labaree in his excellent monograph *Royal Government in America* presented a comprehensive survey of the institutional development
of the lower houses in the royal colonies and of most of the specific
issues involved in their struggles with the royal governors, but he did
not offer any systematic interpretation of the general process and
pattern of legislative development.[4] Charles M. Andrews promised
to tackle this problem and provide a synthesis in the later volumes

---

1. George Chalmers, *An Introduction to the History of the Revolt of the American Colonies*, 2 vols. (Boston, 1845), I, 223-26, II, 226-28, especially, for statements
of Chalmers's position.

2. George Bancroft, *History of the United States*, 14th ed., 10 vols. (Boston,
1854-75), III, 1-108, 383-98, especially.

3. Edward Channing, *A History of the United States*, 6 vols. (New York, 1905-
25), II; Evarts B. Greene, *The Provincial Governor in the English Colonies in
North America* (N. Y. and London, 1898); Herbert L. Osgood, *The American
Colonies in the Seventeenth Century*, 3 vols. (N. Y., 1904-7), and *The American
Colonies in the Eighteenth Century*, 4 vols. (N. Y., 1924-25).

4. Leonard W. Labaree, *Royal Government in America* (New Haven, 1930),
172-311, particularly. Two other illuminating studies by Labaree's contemporaries
are Arthur B. Keith, *Constitutional History of the First British Empire* (Oxford,
Eng., 1930), which is legalistic in emphasis, and John F. Burns, *Controversies
Between Royal Governors and Their Assemblies in the Northern American Colonies* (Boston, 1923), which fails to tie together in any satisfactory way developments in the four colonies it treats.

of his magnum opus *The Colonial Period of American History,* but he died before completing that part of the project.[5]

As a result, some fundamental questions have never been fully answered. No one has satisfactorily worked out the basic pattern of the quest; analyzed the reasons for and the significance of its development; explored its underlying assumptions and theoretical foundations; or assessed the consequences of the success of the lower houses, particularly the relationship between their rise to power and the coming of the American Revolution. This book attempts to get at these questions by studying the rise of the lower houses in the four southern royal colonies—Virigina, North Carolina, South Carolina, and Georgia—in the period between the Glorious Revolution and the American War for Independence. I decided to concentrate on one area of the empire in order to achieve a more thorough understanding of a limited number of lower houses in a roughly similar economic and social milieu. The southern lower houses seemed to be the best choice both because earlier historians had given less attention to them and because they afforded the opportunity to compare developments in the oldest royal colony—Virginia—with those in the youngest of the colonies that revolted in 1776—Georgia—as well as between colonies—Virginia and Georgia—whose legislative experience had been almost wholly under the Crown with those—North Carolina and South Carolina—whose lower houses had already acquired strong traditions and habits under proprietary regimes before coming under royal control. Moreover, an extensive reading in the secondary literature on the lower houses of the middle, New England, and West Indian colonies clearly indicates that, although there were many local variants, the general process and pattern of development were the same.

On the theory that it is impossible to understand what it was that Americans were defending in the debate with Great Britain between 1763 and 1776 until we have a clearer notion of what their constitutional position was on the eve of the contest, I have attempted in the first three quarters of the book to sort out the specific powers acquired by the lower houses and to measure the extent of their

5. Charles M. Andrews, "On the Writing of Colonial History," *William and Mary Quarterly,* 3d Ser., 1 (1944), 29-42. The line of interpretation that Andrews would probably have followed is briefly developed in his brilliant *The Colonial Background of the American Revolution* (New Haven, 1924), 3-65.

authority at the close of the Seven Years' War. Against this background, I have examined in the remainder of the book the British challenge to the power of the lower houses in the years of the debate itself. From this perspective it becomes clear both that the threat to assembly rights was of enormous importance in the coming of the Revolution and that the Declaration of Independence was a more realistic analysis of the causes of the Revolution than has generally been supposed. Its list of charges against George III was a fairly accurate statement of grievances as the signers saw them, and its wholesale indictment of George III was less a clever ruse to gain support for the Patriot cause by personifying the adversary than an expression of what by that time had become patently obvious—that the Crown and its ministers were an equal and perhaps even a greater threat to American legislative power than was Parliament.

Originally, I had hoped also to consider the economic and social motivations of the members of the lower houses, analyzing the structure of politics in each colony as well as the foundations of power within each of the assemblies. But this task proved much too large for a single volume, and the present study deals only incidentally with these matters. Hence, it is essentially an institutional and constitutional rather than a political study. The nature of available sources has made it impossible to offer any adequate assessment of many shadowy individuals who played important roles. In any case, institutional momentum was primarily responsible for the emergence of the lower houses. Although the topical organization results in some fragmentation and repetition, it has the advantage of providing a clearer idea of the specific areas in which the lower houses sought to extend their authority.

Several matters of mechanics require explanation. In quotations from manuscripts and printed documents I have expanded all abbreviations but have retained the original spelling without the use of *sic* and the original capitalization and punctuation. I have not converted Old Style dates to New Style, although I have treated January 1 as the beginning of every year.

My obligations are legion. The staffs of libraries and archives in which I did my research were both helpful and courteous. I am indebted for financial assistance to the United States Educational Commission in Great Britain, the Duke University Commonwealth-

Studies Center, and Western Reserve University. I wish especially to thank Professor John R. Alden, who directed this study in its early stages and has continued to be an unfailing source of counsel and inspiration. Other graduate professors, in particular William B. Hamilton, as well as colleagues and friends offered helpful criticisms, and the staff of the Institute of Early American History and Culture assisted me in a variety of ways of which they are probably still quite painfully aware. I am particularly indebted to Professors W. W. Abbot, M. Eugene Sirmans, Thad W. Tate, Jr., and James M. Smith, each of whom read and criticized the entire manuscript at some stage of the writing. David E. Van Deventer and Joanne Kaufman helped with the computations for Appendix III, and Robert M. Calhoon with the index. My wife Sue was helpful at every stage.

J. P. G.

San Marino, California
August 22, 1962

Table of Contents

PART V

CONTROL OVER EXECUTIVE AFFAIRS

PART VI

THE FRUITS OF POWER:
1763-1776

THE QUEST FOR POWER

The Lower Houses of Assembly
in the
Southern Royal Colonies
1689-1776

PART I

BACKDROP TO POWER

From the great religious and Civil indulgences granted by the Crown to encourage Adventurers to settle in America, the Government of the Colonies has gradually inclined more to the democratical than regal side.
—South Carolina Lieutenant Governor
William Bull II, December 1769

The Assembly think themselves entitled to all the Priviledges of a British House of Commons and therefore ought not to submit to His Majesty's honorable Privy Council further than the Commons do in England, or to submit to His Majesty's instructions to His Governor and Council here.
—North Carolina Governor Arthur Dobbs,
August 1760

In the second quarter of the seventeenth century, Crown officials committed themselves to a policy of establishing representative government in the English plantations in North America and the West Indies. This policy gave rise to the representative assemblies—miniature imitations of the House of Commons in each colony. Not content to play a minor role in the affairs of their respective colonies, these assemblies sought to increase their authority at the expense of both the colonial executives and the London government. Their success was striking, and their quest for power became the most important single feature of colonial political and constitutional development, eventually comprising a significant element in the Revolutionary movement that produced the dismemberment of the first British Empire.

I

Process and Pattern

T HE rise of the representative assemblies was one of the most significant political and constitutional developments in the history of Britain's overseas empire before the American Revolution. Crown and proprietary authorities had obviously intended the governor to be the focal point of colonial government with the assemblies merely subordinate bodies called together when necessary to levy taxes and ratify local ordinances proposed by the executive. Consequently, except in the New England charter colonies, where they early assumed a leading role, the representative bodies were dominated by the governors and councils for most of the period down to 1689. But after the Restoration and especially during the years following the Glorious Revolution, the lower houses engaged in a successful quest for power that increasingly restricted the authority of the executive, undermined the system of colonial administration laid down by imperial and proprietary authorities, and made them paramount in the affairs of their respective colonies.

Any student of the eighteenth-century political process will sooner or later be struck by the fact that, although each of the lower houses developed independently and differently, their stories were similar. The elimination of individual variants, which tend to cancel out each other, discloses certain basic regularities, a clearly discernible pattern —or what the late Sir Lewis Namier called a morphology—common to all of them. They all moved along like paths in their drive for increased authority, and, although their success on specific issues differed from colony to colony and the rate of their rise varied from time to time, they all ended up at approximately the same destination. They passed successively through certain vaguely defined phases of political development. During most of the seventeenth century the lower houses were still in a position of subordination, slowly groping for the power to tax and the rights to sit separately from the council and to initiate laws. Sometime during the early eighteenth century most of them advanced to a second stage at which they could battle on equal terms with the governors and councils and challenge even the powers in London if necessary. At that point the lower houses began their bid for political supremacy. The violent eruptions that followed usually ended in an accommodation with the governors and councils which paved the way for the ascendancy of the lower houses and saw the virtual eclipse of the colonial executive. By the end of the Seven Years' War, and in some instances considerably earlier, the lower houses had reached the third and final phase of political dominance and were in a position to speak for the colonies in the conflict with the imperial government that ensued after 1763.

By 1763, with the exception of the lower houses in the corporate colonies of Rhode Island and Connecticut, which had virtually complete authority, the Pennsylvania and Massachusetts houses of representatives were probably the most powerful. Having succeeded in placing its election on a statutory basis and depriving the Council of direct legislative authority in the Charter of Privileges in 1701, the Pennsylvania House under the astute guidance of David Lloyd secured broad financial and appointive powers during the administrations of Daniel Gookin and Sir William Keith. Building on these foundations, it gained almost complete dominance in the 1730's and 1740's despite the opposition of the governors, whose power and prestige along with the Council's declined rapidly.[1] The Massachusetts House, having been accorded the unique privilege of sharing in the selection of the Council by the royal charter of 1691, already

1. Developments in Pennsylvania may be traced in William R. Shepherd, *History of Proprietary Government in Pennsylvania* (New York, 1896); Benjamin Franklin, *An Historical Review of Pennsylvania* (London, 1759); Roy N. Lokken, *David Lloyd, Colonial Lawmaker* (Seattle, 1959); Sister Joan de Lourdes Leonard, *The Organization and Procedure of the Pennsylvania Assembly, 1682-1772* (Philadelphia, 1949); Winfred T. Root, *The Relations of Pennsylvania with the British Government, 1696-1765* (Phila., 1912); and Theodore Thayer, *Pennsylvania Politics and The Growth of Democracy, 1740-1776* (Harrisburg, 1953). On Rhode Island and Connecticut, see David S. Lovejoy, *Rhode Island Politics and the American Revolution, 1760-1776* (Providence, 1958), and Oscar Zeichner, *Connecticut's Years of Controversy, 1750-1776* (Chapel Hill, 1949).

had a strong tradition of legislative supremacy inherited from a half century of corporate experience. During the first thirty years under the new charter, first the benevolent policies of Sir William Phips and William Stoughton and then wartime conditions during the tenures of Joseph Dudley and Samuel Shute enabled the House, led by Elisha Cooke, Jr., to extend its authority greatly. It emerged from the conflicts over the salary question during the 1720's with firm control over finance, and the Crown's abandonment of its demand for a permanent revenue in the early 1730's made possible an accommodation with subsequent governors and the eventual ascendancy of the House under Governor William Shirley after 1740.[2]

The South Carolina Commons and New York House of Assembly were only slightly less powerful. Beginning in the first decade of the eighteenth century, the South Carolina Commons gradually assumed an ironclad control over all aspects of South Carolina government, extending its supervision to the minutest details of local administration after 1730 as a succession of governors, including Francis Nicholson, Robert Johnson, Thomas Broughton, the elder William Bull, and James Glen, offered little determined opposition. The Commons continued to grow in stature after 1750, while the Council's standing declined because of the Crown policy of filling it with placemen from England and the Commons' successful attacks upon its authority.[3] The New York House of Assembly began to demand greater authority in reaction to the mismanagement of Edward Hyde, Viscount Cornbury, during the first decade of the eighteenth century. Governor Robert Hunter met the challenge squarely during his ten-year administration beginning in 1710, but he and his successors could not check the rising power of the House. During the seven-year tenure of George Clarke beginning in 1736, the House advanced into the

2. Useful studies on Massachusetts are Robert E. Brown, *Middle-Class Democracy and the Revolution in Massachusetts, 1691-1780* (Ithaca, 1955); Martin L. Cole, The Rise of the Legislative Assembly in Provincial Massachusetts (unpubl. Ph.D. diss., State University of Iowa, 1939); Thomas Hutchinson, *The History of the Colony and Province of Massachusetts-Bay*, ed. Lawrence S. Mayo, 3 vols. (Cambridge, Mass., 1936); John A. Schutz, *William Shirley: King's Governor of Massachussetts* (Chapel Hill, 1961); and Henry R. Spencer, *Constitutional Conflict in Provincial Massachusetts* (Columbus, 1905).

3. The best previously published study on South Carolina is W. Roy Smith, *South Carolina as a Royal Province, 1719-1776* (N. Y., 1903). Also useful are David D. Wallace, *The Life of Henry Laurens* (N. Y., 1915), and M. Eugene Sirmans, "The South Carolina Royal Council, 1720-1763," *William and Mary Quarterly*, 3d Ser., 18 (1961), 373-92.

final stage of development. Following Clarke, George Clinton made a vigorous effort to reassert the authority of the executive, but neither he nor any of his successors was able to lessen the power of the House.[4]

The lower houses of North Carolina, New Jersey, and Virginia developed more slowly. The North Carolina Lower House was fully capable of protecting its powers and privileges and competing on equal terms with the executive during the last years of proprietary rule and under the early royal governors, George Burrington and Gabriel Johnston. But it was not until Arthur Dobbs's tenure in the 1750's and 1760's that the Lower House, meeting more regularly, asserted its primacy in North Carolina politics under the guidance of Speaker Samuel Swann and Treasurers John Starkey and Thomas Barker.[5] In New Jersey the Lower House was partially thwarted in its spirited bid for power during the 1740's under the leadership of John Kinsey and Samuel Nevill by the determined opposition of Governor Lewis Morris, and it did not gain superiority until the administrations of Jonathan Belcher, Thomas Pownall, Francis Bernard, and Thomas Boone during the Seven Years' War.[6] Similarly, the Virginia Burgesses vigorously sought to establish its control in the second decade of the century under Alexander Spotswood, but not until the administrations of Sir William Gooch and Robert Dinwiddie, when first the expansion of the colony and then the Seven Years' War required more regular sessions, did the Burgesses finally succeed under the effective leadership of Speaker John Robinson.[7]

4. Developments in New York can be followed in Carl L. Becker, *The History of Political Parties in the Province of New York, 1760-1776* (Madison, Wis., 1909); Milton M. Klein, "Democracy and Politics in Colonial New York," *New York History*, 40 (1959), 221-46; Lawrence H. Leder, *Robert Livingston, 1654-1728, and the Politics of Colonial New York* (Chapel Hill, 1961); Beverly McAnear, Politics in Provincial New York, 1689-1761 (unpubl. Ph.D. diss., Stanford Univ., 1935); Irving Mark, *Agrarian Conflicts in Colonial New York, 1711-1775* (N. Y., 1940); William Smith, *The History of the Late Province of New-York . . .*, 2 vols. (N. Y., 1829); and Charles W. Spencer, *Phases of Royal Government in New York, 1691-1719* (Columbus, 1905).

5. Useful analyses of North Carolina are Charles L. Raper, *North Carolina; A Study in English Colonial Government* (N. Y., 1904), and Desmond Clarke, *Arthur Dobbs, Esquire, 1689-1765 . . .* (Chapel Hill, 1957).

6. New Jersey developments can be traced in Donald L. Kemmerer's excellent study, *Path to Freedom: The Struggle for Self-Government in Colonial New Jersey, 1703-1776* (Princeton, 1940).

7. Among the more useful secondary works on Virginia are Percy S. Flippin, *The Royal Government in Virginia, 1624-1775* (N. Y., 1919); Bernard Bailyn, "Politics and Social Structure in Virginia," in James M. Smith, ed., *Seventeenth-*

Among the lower houses in the older colonies, only the Maryland House of Delegates and the New Hampshire House of Assembly failed to reach the final level of development in the period before 1763. The Maryland body made important advances early in the eighteenth century while under the control of the Crown and aggressively sought to extend its authority in the 1720's under the leadership of the older Daniel Dulany and again in the late 1730's and early 1740's under Dr. Charles Carroll. But the proprietors were usually able to thwart these attempts despite a concerted effort by the Delegates during the last intercolonial war under the administration of Horatio Sharpe.[8] In New Hampshire, the House had exercised considerable power through the early decades of the eighteenth century, but Governor Benning Wentworth effectively challenged its authority after 1740 and prevented it from attaining the extensive power exercised by its counterparts in other colonies.[9] However, the lower houses in Maryland and New Hampshire were in no sense impotent and, along with their more youthful equivalent in Georgia, they gained dominance during the decade of debate with Britain after 1763. Of the lower houses in the continental colonies with pre-1763 political experience, only the Nova Scotia Assembly had not reached the final phase of political dominance by 1776.[10]

The lower houses gained their dominance in large part by securing certain fundamental powers in four general areas. First, in the realm of finance, they attempted in imitation of the seventeenth-century House of Commons to impose their sole authority over every

Century America: Essays in Colonial History (Chapel Hill, 1959), 90-115; Lucille Blanche Griffith, The Virginia House of Burgesses, 1750-1774 (unpubl. Ph.D. diss., Brown Univ., 1957); Ray Orvin Hummel, Jr., The Virginia House of Burgesses, 1689-1750 (unpubl. Ph.D. diss., Univ. of Nebraska, 1934); David J. Mays, *Edmund Pendleton, 1721-1803,* 2 vols. (Cambridge, Mass., 1952); Charles S. Sydnor, *Gentlemen Freeholders; Political Practices in Washington's Virginia* (Chapel Hill, 1952); Thomas J. Wertenbaker, *Give Me Liberty; The Struggle for Self-Government in Virginia* (Phila., 1958); and David Alan Williams, Political Alignments in Colonial Virginia, 1698-1750 (unpubl. Ph.D. diss., Northwestern Univ., 1959).

8. On Maryland, see two excellent studies, Charles A. Barker, *The Background of the Revolution in Maryland* (New Haven, 1940), and Aubrey Land, *The Dulanys of Maryland . . .* (Baltimore, 1955).

9. New Hampshire developments can be followed in William H. Fry, *New Hampshire as a Royal Province* (N. Y., 1908), and Jeremy Belknap, *The History of New-Hampshire,* 3 vols. (Boston, 1791-92).

10. On Georgia, see William Wright Abbot, *The Royal Governors of Georgia, 1754-1775* (Chapel Hill, 1959), and Albert B. Saye, *New Viewpoints in Georgia History* (Atlanta, 1943). John Bartlet Brebner, *The Neutral Yankees of Nova Scotia . . .* (N. Y., 1937), is the best study of developments in that colony.

phase of raising and distributing public revenue. They began by claiming the exclusive right to initiate and amend money bills. Having acquired that, they were in an excellent position to secure still more extensive financial authority, including power to audit accounts of all officers handling public money, to control expenditures both by appropriating them specifically and by appointing special officers to dispose of them, and to emit paper money to remedy the chronic American need for a medium of exchange. Second, in the area of the civil list, they refused to provide permanent salaries for royal officials and attempted to control their incomes by establishing and regulating their fees by law. Third, they endeavored to render themselves as independent of the executive as possible. They tried to secure power to regulate their memberships by setting qualifications for both members and voters, establishing constituencies and apportioning representation, and determining both who had been elected and who were proper to sit as members. Authority to regulate the frequency of elections and sessions and to have a completely free hand in their internal proceedings also helped to guarantee their independence. Fourth, they sought to push their power even beyond that of the British House of Commons by acquiring a share in handling executive affairs. They aimed at securing the rights to nominate and appoint all public officials concerned in collecting local revenues as well as supervisors of all public works and services and colonial agents in London. In addition, they sought to influence military and Indian affairs by formulating policy and occasionally even by appointing officials to regulate Indian trade or to supervise spending of military appropriations. They attempted also to limit executive authority in ecclesiastical matters by shifting the patronage in church affairs from the governors to the local vestries and in judicial affairs by assuming the powers to erect courts and to regulate the tenure of judges.

The similarities in the process and pattern of legislative development from colony to colony were not entirely accidental. The lower houses faced like problems and drew upon common traditions and imperial precedents for solutions. They all operated in the same broad imperial context and were affected by common historical forces. Moreover, family, cultural, and commercial ties often extended across colony lines, and newspapers and other printed materials, as well as individuals, often found their way from one colony to another. The result was at least a general awareness of issues and practices in neighboring colonies, and occasionally there was even a conscious borrowing of precedents and traditions. Younger bodies such as those of Georgia and Nova Scotia were particularly indebted to their more mature counterparts in South Carolina and Massachusetts Bay.[11] On the executive side, the similarity in attitudes, assumptions, and policies among the governors can be traced in large measure to their all being subordinate to the same central authority in London, which pursued a common policy in all the colonies.

Before the Seven Years' War the quest was characterized by a considerable degree of spontaneity, by a lack of awareness that activities of the moment were part of any broad struggle for power. Rather than consciously working out the details of some master plan designed to bring them liberty or self-government, the lower houses moved along from issue to issue and from situation to situation, primarily concerning themselves with the problems at hand and displaying a remarkable capacity for spontaneous action, for seizing any and every opportunity to enlarge their own influence at the executive's expense and for holding tenaciously to powers they had already secured. Though conscious of the issues involved in each specific conflict, they were for the most part unaware of and uninterested in the long-range implications of their actions. Virginia Governor Francis Fauquier correctly judged the matter in 1760. "Whoever charges them with acting upon a premeditated concerted plan, don't know them," he wrote of the Virginia burgesses, "for they mean honestly, but are Expedient Mongers in the highest Degree."[12] Still, in retrospect it is obvious that throughout the eighteenth century the lower houses were engaged in a continuous movement to enlarge their sphere of influence. To ignore that continuity would be to miss the meaning of eighteenth-century colonial political development.

One is impressed with the rather prosaic manner in which the lower houses went about the task of extending and consolidating their authority, with the infrequency of dramatic conflict. They gained much of their power in the course of routine business, quietly and simply passing laws and establishing practices, the implications of which escaped both colonial executives and imperial authorities

11. On this point, see Abbot, *Royal Governors,* and Brebner, *Neutral Yankees.*
12. Fauquier to Board of Trade, June 2, 1760, Colonial Office Papers, 5/1330, ff. 37-39, Public Record Office, London.

and were not always fully recognized even by the lower houses themselves. Precedents thus established soon hardened into fixed principles, "undoubted rights," or "inherent powers," changing the very fabric of their respective constitutions. The notable absence of conflict is perhaps best illustrated by the none too surprising fact that the lower houses made some of their greatest gains under those governors with whom they enjoyed the most harmony, in particular Keith in Pennsylvania, Shirley in Massachusetts, Hunter in New York, and the elder and younger Bull in South Carolina. In Virginia the House of Burgesses made rapid strides during the 1730's and 1740's under the benevolent government of Gooch, who discovered early in his administration that the secret of political success for a Virginia governor was to reach an accord with the plantation gentry.

One should not conclude that the colonies had no exciting legislative-executive conflicts, however. Attempts during the middle decades of the eighteenth century by Clinton to weaken the financial powers of the New York House, Massachusetts Governors Samuel Shute and William Burnet to gain a permanent civil list, Benning Wentworth to extend unilaterally the privilege of representation to new districts in New Hampshire, Johnston to break the extensive power of the Albemarle counties in the North Carolina Lower House, Dinwiddie to establish a fee for issuing land patents without the consent of the Virginia Burgesses, and Thomas Boone to reform South Carolina's election laws each provoked a storm of controversy that brought local politics to a fever pitch. [13] But such conflicts were the exception and usually arose not out of the lower houses' seeking more authority but from the executives' attempts to restrict powers already won. Impatient of restraint and jealous of their rights and privileges, the lower houses responded forcefully and sometimes violently when executive action threatened to deprive them of their rights. Only a few governors, men of the caliber of Henry Ellis in Georgia and to a lesser extent William Henry Lyttelton in South Carolina and Bernard in New Jersey, had the skill to challenge estab-

13. The details of these disputes can be traced in Smith, *History of New York*, II, 68-151; Hutchinson, *History of Massachusetts-Bay*, 163-280; Leonard W. Labaree, *Royal Government in America* (New Haven, 1930), 180-85; Lawrence F. London, "The Representation Controversy in Colonial North Carolina," *North Carolina Historical Review*, 11 (1934), 255-70; Jack P. Greene, ed., "The Case of the Pistole Fee," *Virginia Magazine of History and Biography*, 66 (1958), 399-422, and "The Gadsden Election Controversy and the Revolutionary Movement in South Carolina," *Mississippi Valley Historical Review*, 46 (1959), 469-92.

lished rights successfully without raising the wrath of the lower houses. Clumsier tacticians—Pennsylvania's William Denny, New York's Clinton, Virginia's Dinwiddie, North Carolina's Dobbs, South Carolina's Boone, Georgia's John Reynolds—failed when pursuing similar goals.

Fundamentally, the quest for power in both the royal and the proprietary colonies was a struggle for political identity, the manifestation of the political ambitions of the leaders of emerging societies within each colony. There is a marked correlation between the appearance of economic and social elites produced by the growth in colonial wealth and population on the one hand and the lower houses' demand for increased authority, dignity, and prestige on the other. In the eighteenth century a group of planters, merchants, and professional men had attained or were rapidly acquiring within the colonies wealth and social position. The lower houses' aggressive drive for power reflected the determination of this new elite to gain through the representative assemblies political influence as well. In another but related sense, the lower houses' efforts represented a movement for autonomy in local affairs, although it is doubtful that many of the members recognized them as such. The lower houses wished to strengthen their authority within the colonies and to reduce to a minimum the amount of supervision, with the uncertainties it involved, that royal or proprietary authorities could exercise. Continuously nourished by the growing desire of American legislators to be masters of their own political fortunes and by the development of a vigorous tradition of legislative superiority in imitation of the imperial House of Commons, this basic principle of local control over local affairs in some cases got part of its impetus from an early unsatisfactory experience with a despotic, inefficient, or corrupt governor such as Thomas, Lord Culpeper, or Francis, Lord Howard of Effingham, in Virginia, Lionel Copley in Maryland, Sir Edmund Andros in Massachusetts, Seth Sothel in North Carolina, or the infamous Cornbury in New York and New Jersey. Clearly, the task of defending men's rights and property against the fraud and violence of tyrannical executives fell most appropriately to the representatives of those whose rights and property demanded protection.

But the quest for power involved more than the extension of the authority of the lower houses within the colonies at the expense of the colonial executives. After their initial stage of evolution, the lower houses learned that their real antagonists were not the governors but the proprietors or Crown officials in London. Few governors proved to be a match for the representatives. A governor was almost helpless to prevent a lower house from exercising powers secured under his predecessors, and even the most discerning governor could fall into the trap of assenting to an apparently innocent law that would later prove damaging to the royal or proprietary prerogative. Some governors, for the sake of preserving amicable relations with the representatives or because they thought certain legislation to be in the best interest of a colony, actually conspired with legislative leaders to present the actions of the lower houses in a favorable light to Whitehall. Thus, Jonathan Belcher worked with Massachusetts leaders to parry the Crown's demand for a permanent revenue in the 1730's, and Fauquier joined with Speaker John Robinson in Virginia to prevent the separation of the offices of speaker and treasurer during the closing years of the Seven Years' War.

Nor could imperial authorities depend upon the colonial councils to furnish an effective check upon the representatives' advancing influence. Most councilors were drawn from the rising social and economic elites in the colonies. The duality of their role is obvious. Bound by oath to uphold the interests of the Crown or the proprietors, they were also driven by ambition and a variety of local pressures to maintain the status and power of the councils as well as to protect and advance their own individual interests and those of their group within the colonies. These two objectives were not always in harmony, and the councils frequently sided with the lower houses rather than with the governors. With a weakened governor and an unreliable council, the task of restraining the representative assemblies ultimately devolved upon the home government. Probably as much of the struggle for power was played out in Whitehall as in Williamsburg, Charleston, New York, Boston, or Philadelphia.

Behind the struggle between colonial lower houses and imperial authorities were two divergent, though on the colonial side not wholly articulated, concepts of the constitutions of the colonies and, in particular, of the status of the lower houses. To the very end of the colonial period, imperial authorities persisted in the views that colonial constitutions were static and that the lower houses were subordi-

nate governmental agencies with only temporary and limited lawmaking powers—in the words of one imperial official, merely "so many Corporations at a distance, invested with an Ability to make Temporary
By Laws for themselves, agreeable to their respective Situations and
Climates."[14]   In working out a political system for the colonies in the
later seventeenth century, imperial officials had institutionalized these
views in the royal commissions and instructions.   Despite the fact that
the lower houses were yearly making important changes in their respective constitutions, the Crown never altered the commissions or
instructions to conform with the realities of the colonial political
situation but continued to maintain throughout the eighteenth century that they were the most vital part of the constitutional structure
of the royal colonies.   The Pennsylvania and to a lesser extent the
Maryland proprietors were less rigid, although they also insisted upon
their theoretical constitutional and political supremacy over the lower
houses.

Colonial lower houses had little respect for and even less patience
with such a doctrinaire position, and whether or not royal and proprietary instructions were absolutely binding upon the colonies was
the leading constitutional issue in the period before 1763.   As the
political instruments of what was probably the most pragmatic society
in the eighteenth-century Western world, colonial legislatures were
not likely to be restrained by dogma divorced from reality.   They
had no fear of innovations and welcomed the chance to experiment
with new forms and ideas.   All they asked was that a thing work.
When they found that instructions from imperial authorities did not
work in the best interests of the colonies, that they were, in fact,
antithetic to the very measures they as legislatures were trying to
effect, they openly refused to submit to them.   Instructions, they argued, applied only to officials appointed by the Crown.   "Instructions
from his majesty, to his governor, or the council, are binding to them,
and esteemed as laws or rules; because, if either should disregard
them, they might immediately be displaced," declared a South Carolina writer in 1756 while denying the validity of an instruction that
stipulated colonial councils should have equal rights with the lower
houses in framing money bills.   "But, if instructions should be laws

14. [Sir William Keith], A Short Discourse on the Present State of the Colonies
in America with Respect to the Interest of Great Britain, 1729, in CO 5/4, ff.
170-71.

and rules to the people of this province, then there would be no need of assemblies, and all our laws and taxes might be made and levied by an instruction."[15]   Clearly, then, instructions might bind governors, but never the elected branch of the legislature.

Even though the lower houses, filled with intensely practical politicians, were concerned largely with practical political considerations, they found it necessary to develop a body of theory with which to oppose unpopular instructions from Britain and support their claims to greater political power.   In those few colonies that had charters, the lower houses relied upon the guarantees in them as their first line of defense, taking the position that the stipulations of the charters were inviolate, despite the fact that some had been invalidated by imperial courts, and could not be altered by executive order. A more basic premise, which was equally applicable to all colonies, was that the constituents of the lower houses, as inhabitants of British colonies, were entitled to all the traditional rights of Englishmen. On this foundation the colonial legislatures built their ideological structure.   In the early charters the Crown had guaranteed the colonists "all privileges, franchises and liberties of this our kingdom of England . . . any statute, act, ordinance, or provision to the contrary thereof, notwithstanding."[16]   Such guarantees, colonials assumed, merely constituted recognition that their privileges as Englishmen were inherent and unalterable and that it mattered not whether they stayed on the home islands or migrated to the colonies.   "His Majesty's Subjects coming over to America," the South Carolina Commons argued in 1739 while asserting its exclusive right to formulate tax laws, "have no more forfeited this their most valuable Inheritance than they have withdrawn their Allegiance."   No "Royal Order," the Commons declared, could "qualify or any wise alter a fundamental Right from the Shape in which it was handed down to us from our Ancestors."[17]

One of the most important of these rights was the privilege of

15. *South-Carolina Gazette* (Charleston), May 13, 1756.
16. For instance, see the provision in the Maryland charter conveniently published in Merrill Jensen, ed., *English Historical Documents: American Colonial Documents to 1776* (N. Y., 1955), 88.
17. S. C. Commons Journals, June 5, 1739, James H. Easterby and Ruth S. Green, ed., *The Colonial Records of South Carolina: The Journals of the Commons House of Assembly* (Columbia, 1951——), *1736-1739*, 720; hereafter cited as *S. C. Col. Recs.*

representation, on which, of course, depended the very existence of the lower houses. Imperial authorities always maintained that the lower houses existed only through the consent of the Crown,[18] but the houses insisted that an elected assembly was a fundamental right of a colony arising out of an Englishman's privilege to be represented and that they did not owe their existence merely to the King's pleasure. "Our representatives, agreeably to the general sense of their constituents," wrote New York lawyer William Smith in the 1750's, "are tenacious in their opinion, that the inhabitants of this colony are entitled to all the privileges of Englishmen; that they have a right to participate in the legislative power, and that the session of assemblies here, is wisely substituted instead of a representation in parliament, which, all things considered, would, at this remote distance, be extremely inconvenient and dangerous."[19] The logical corollary to this argument was that the lower houses were equivalents of the House of Commons and must perforce in their limited spheres be entitled to all the privileges possessed by that body in Great Britain. Hence, in cases where an invocation of fundamental rights was not appropriate, the lower houses frequently defended their actions on the grounds that they were agreeable to the practice of the House of Commons. Thus in 1755 the North Carolina Lower House denied the right of the Council to amend tax bills on the grounds that it was "contrary to Custom and Usage of Parliament."[20] Unintentionally, Crown officials encouraged the lower houses to make this analogy by forbidding them in the instructions to exercise "any power or privilege whatsoever which is not allowed by us to the House of Commons . . . in Great Britain."[21]

18. This view was implicit in most thinking and writing about the colonies by imperial authorities. For the attitude of John Carteret, Lord Granville, an important figure in colonial affairs through the middle decades of the 18th century, see Benjamin Franklin to Isaac Norris, Mar. 19, 1759, as quoted by William S. Mason, ed., "Franklin and Galloway: Some Unpublished Letters," American Antiquarian Society, *Proceedings,* New Ser., 34 (1924), 245-46. Other examples are Jack P. Greene, ed., "Martin Bladen's Blueprint for a Colonial Union," *Wm. and Mary Qtly.,* 3d Ser., 17 (1960), 516-30, by a prominent member of the Board of Trade, and [Archibald Kennedy], *An Essay on the Government of the Colonies* (N. Y., 1752), 17-18, by an official in the colonies.

19. Smith, *History of New York,* I, 307.

20. Lower House Journals, Jan. 4-6, 1755, William L. Saunders, ed., *The Colonial Records of North Carolina,* 10 vols. (Raleigh, 1886-90), V, 287; hereafter cited as *N. C. Col. Recs.*

21. Leonard W. Labaree, ed., *Royal Instructions to British Colonial Governors, 1670-1776,* 2 vols. (N. Y., 1935), I, 112-13.

Because neither fundamental rights nor imperial precedents could be used to defend practices that were contrary to customs of the mother country or to the British constitution, the lower houses found it necessary to develop still another argument: that local precedents, habits, traditions, and statutes were important parts of their particular constitutions and could not be abridged by a royal or proprietary order. The assumptions were that they could alter colonial constitutions by their own actions without the active consent of imperial officials and that once the alterations were confirmed by usage they could not be countermanded by the British government. They did not deny the power of the governor to veto or of the Privy Council to disallow their laws but argued that imperial acquiescence over a long period of time was tantamount to consent and that precedents thus established could not be undone without their approval. Thus in 1770 the South Carolina Commons asserted that its vote of funds without executive approval to the Bill of Rights Society in Britain was "agreeable to the usage and practice both ancient and Modern of the Commons House of Assembly of this Province."[22] "There are some old-fashioned People too," declared Arthur Lee in defense of the same vote, "who will be constant in thinking, that what has prevailed from the Beginning of the Colony, without Question or Controul, is Part of the Constitution."[23] The implication was that American legislators saw their constitutions as living, growing, constantly changing organisms, a theory which was directly opposite to the imperial view. To be sure, precedent had always been important in shaping the British constitution, but Crown officials were unwilling to concede that it was equally so in determining the fundamental law of the colonies. They willingly granted that colonial statutes, once formally approved by the Privy Council, automatically became part of the constitutions of the colonies, but they officially took the position that both royal instructions and commissions, as well as constitutional traditions of the mother country, took precedence over local practice or unconfirmed statutes.[24] This conflict

22. Aug. 29, 1770, S. C. Commons Journals, XXXVIII, 432, South Carolina Archives Department, Columbia.

23. [Arthur Lee], *Answer to Considerations on Certain Political Transactions of the Province of South Carolina* (London, 1774), 46.

24. For a classic statement of the imperial argument by a modern scholar, see Lawrence H. Gipson, *The British Empire Before the American Revolution* (Caldwell, Idaho, and N. Y., 1936——), III (rev.), 275-81.

of views persisted throughout the period after 1689, becoming more and more of an issue in the decades immediately preceding the American Revolution.

If imperial authorities would not grant the validity of the theoretical arguments of the lower houses, neither after 1689 did they make any systematic or concerted effort to force a rigid compliance with official policies. Repressive measures, at least before 1763, rarely went beyond the occasional disallowance of an offending statute or the official reprimand of a rambunctious lower house. General lack of interest in the routine business of colonial affairs and failure to recognize the potential seriousness of the situation may in part account for this leniency, but it is also true that official policy under both Walpole and the Pelhams called for a light rein on the colonies on the assumption that contented colonies created fewer problems for the administration. "One would not Strain any point," Charles Delafaye, secretary to the lords justices, cautioned South Carolina's Governor Francis Nicholson in 1722, "where it can be of no Service to our King or Country." "In the Plantations," he added, "the Government should be as Easy and Mild as possible to invite people to Settle under it."[25] Three times between 1734 and 1749 the ministry failed to give enthusiastic support to measures introduced into Parliament to insure the supremacy of instructions over colonial laws.[26] Though the Calverts were insistent upon preserving their prerogatives, in general the proprietors were equally lax as long as there was no encroachment upon their land rights or proprietary dues.

Imperial organs of administration were in fact inadequate to deal effectively with all the problems of the empire. Since no special governmental bodies were created in England to deal exclusively with colonial affairs, they were handled through the regular machinery of government—a maze of boards and officials whose main interests and responsibilities were not the supervision of overseas colonies. The only body sufficiently informed and interested to deal competently with colonial matters was the Board of Trade, and it had little authority, except for the brief period from 1748 to 1761 under the presidency of George Dunk, Earl of Halifax. The most useful device

25. Delafaye to Nicholson, Jan. 26, 1722, in Papers Concerning Governorship of South Carolina, 1720-27, bMS Am 1455, Item 9, Houghton Library, Harvard Univ., Cambridge, Mass.

26. For a discussion of these measures, see Bernhard Knollenberg, *Origin of the American Revolution: 1759-1766* (N. Y., 1960), 49.

for restraining the lower houses was the Privy Council's right to review colonial laws, but even that was only partly effective, because
the mass of colonial statutes annually coming before the Board of
Trade made a thorough scrutiny impossible.   Under such arrangements no vigorous colonial policy was likely to develop.   The combination of imperial lethargy and colonial aggression virtually guaranteed the success of the lower houses' quest for power.   An indication
of a growing awareness in imperial circles of the seriousness of the
situation was Halifax's spirited, if piecemeal, attempt to restrain the
growth of the lower houses in the early 1750's.   Symptomatic of this
effort was the attempt to make Georgia and Nova Scotia model royal
colonies at the beginning of royal government by writing into the
instructions to their governors provisions designed to insure the continued supremacy of the executive and to prevent the lower houses
from going the way of their counterparts in the older colonies.   However, the outbreak of the Seven Years' War forced Halifax to suspend
his activities and prevented any further reformation until the cessa-
tion of hostilities.

Indeed, the war saw a drastic acceleration in the lower houses' bid
for authority, and its conclusion found them in possession of many
of the powers held less than a century before by the executive.   During
the early 1760's Crown officials and Parliament, no longer faced with
the necessity of pacifying the colonies to obtain their support for
the war effort, inaugurated a stricter and more vigorous policy aimed
directly at remedying "abuses" in the colonial constitutions which
the lower houses had been painstakingly endeavoring to make integral
parts of those constitutions over the previous century.   Between 1763
and 1776 one imperial measure after another threatened to deprive
the lower houses of powers they had in many cases enjoyed for a long
time.   Their response was to meet the challenge head on, and the
old conflict assumed new and more serious dimensions, eventually
culminating in armed rebellion and the disruption of the old empire.

The Configuration of Politics

THE eighteenth century was a period of phenomenal material expansion for the British colonies in North America. The population rose from less than three-quarters of a million in 1689 to over two and a half million in the decade immediately preceding Independence. Wealth, trade, and production of a wide variety of commodities from the soil, forests, and sea rose proportionately. Nowhere was the progress greater than in the southern royal colonies, stretching from the Potomac south to the Altamaha. When William III acceded to the English throne in 1689, the population of the southern colonies, excluding Indians, was scarcely 80,000. Of these, 70,000 lived in Virginia, where after nearly a century of occupation enterprising planters and yeomen had, despite James I's pessimistic forebodings, built an economy based on "smoak." By 1689 they had taken up most of the rich lands of the Tidewater and were pushing up the great rivers into the Piedmont. The valleys of the James and the Potomac were the scenes of deepest penetration as settlers were already occupying lands immediately beyond the fall lines. But almost the entire Piedmont and all of the still little-known Shenandoah Valley and tramontane region lay before the prospective settler.

For that matter, so did the entire region to the south. Low-country Georgia with its salt marshes and pine barrens would wait another forty years for permanent settlement; the Carolina Proprietary contained less than 10,000 inhabitants. Two-thirds of these lived in the southern part of the province, gradually coming to be known as South Carolina. Founded just two decades earlier by Barbadians and Englishmen, Charleston was already the largest settle-

ment in the southern colonies. But it was still confined to a small
area along the Cooper River between Broad and Water Streets, and
the profitable rice cultivation and valuable furs and skins brought by
Carolina traders from southern Indian nations were only just beginning to boost it into one of America's leading ports. Away from the
immediate vicinity of Charleston, population was sparse. Five years
earlier a group of Scots had gone into the area south of the Stono to
establish an outpost near Port Royal only to see it destroyed by Spaniards in 1686, and a group of French Huguenots had settled in the
area north of Bull's Bay, though their numbers were still few. Farther
north was the even less prosperous Albemarle settlement. Governed
by a deputy from Charleston, the entire area held fewer than 3,000
people, for the most part small planters and yeomen farmers clustered
about the streams that emptied into the sound from which the settlement took its name. North Carolina, as this region was to be called,
had no towns and little direct trade with the outside world, sending
its tobacco overland to the James River and Chesapeake landings in
Virginia. Nowhere in Carolina had settlement proceeded beyond the
Tidewater, and the vast Piedmont had been penetrated only by the
more adventurous Indian traders.

    The scene in 1775 was markedly different. By then there were
four colonies instead of three, Georgia having been founded forty
years earlier by James Oglethorpe and his associates as a buffer province between South Carolina and Spanish Florida and as a haven for
imprisoned debtors. All four colonies were now royal. South Carolina had become royal after its inhabitants had overthrown the proprietary government in 1719. North Carolina had followed in 1728,
when the Crown purchased the rights of the proprietors, and Georgia
in 1752, when the trustees surrendered their charter less than a year
before it was to expire. During the past three-quarters of a century
population figures had soared, rising nearly six times in Virginia,
seventeen in South Carolina, and ninety-two in North Carolina.
Youthful Georgia had well over 30,000 settlers. Thousands of Scotch-
Irish, German, Highland Scot, and English immigrants had joined
with scions of earlier settlers to fill the entire backcountry of Virginia
and the Carolinas and to raise Georgia from a run-down frontier
outpost to a prosperous plantation colony on the threshold of great
expansion. Carolinians were already pushing over the Appalachians

into Tennessee and Kentucky, and Virginians had for over two decades been crossing the Blue Ridge to the headwaters of the Great Kanawha to vie with Pennsylvanians for the rich land and furs of the Ohio Valley.

The affluence of the southern royal colonies was reflected in the ever-growing number of Negro slaves, who constituted a fourth of North Carolina's inhabitants, a third of Virginia's, nearly half of Georgia's, and almost two-thirds of South Carolina's. The valuable staples that the four colonies produced had turned them, along with Maryland, into Britain's most prized possessions on the continent, and their direct trade with London and other British ports bound them more closely than their northern neighbors to the mother country. Tobacco was still the lifeblood of Virginia and, for that matter, of the Albemarle section of North Carolina. Rice culture had long since displaced the Indian trade as South Carolina's leading economic activity, spreading from the swampy bottoms of the Ashley and Cooper Rivers over all the Carolina low country north into North Carolina's Cape Fear Valley and south into coastal Georgia. Second only to rice was indigo. Eliza Pinckney's experiments with that crop in the 1740's had proven successful, and the promised bounty from the mother country had made it profitable enough to be cultivated on nearly every plantation. Also under the aegis of an imperial bounty, naval stores production had become an important occupation in the southern colonies. Large quantities of tar, pitch, turpentine, and rosin, coming especially from the North Carolina pine forests but also from those of South Carolina and Georgia, supplied Britain with almost enough of these materials to keep her vast navy and merchant marine afloat. As a whole, the region bore a rural aspect, but there were a few prospering urban settlements. Charleston was the most opulent commercial center south of Philadelphia and perhaps the most elegant city in British North America. Much less impressive, though yearly increasing in size and trade, were Savannah, Georgia; Wilmington and Brunswick, North Carolina; and Norfolk, Virginia. Williamsburg was the cultural and political center of Virginia, containing both the capitol and the College of William and Mary, the only institution of higher learning in the south. New Bern, North Carolina's capital, was the site of the most handsome "government house" in the British continental colonies, Tryon's Palace.[1]

Coinciding with this extraordinary material progress was a gradual maturing of social and political institutions within the colonies. In Virginia by the close of the seventeenth century, society had in large part attained the form that would characterize it through the eighteenth century. Repeated attempts to achieve a diversified economy had failed, leaving tobacco the chief staple in an overwhelmingly agricultural economy. Slavery was already supplanting indentured servitude as the prevailing system of labor, and the large plantation was rapidly becoming the dominant economic and social unit, although it would continue to be surrounded by a multitude of smaller farms tilled by yeomen farmers and their families and perhaps a few slaves or indentured servants. Originally, these smaller units had produced most of the tobacco, but the "jovial weed" quickly exhausted the soil. The constant demand for new tobacco ground made the acquisition of large tracts of land inevitable and was one of the major factors in the development of the plantation system. Tobacco and land, then, were the twin pillars of the Virginia economy, and the plantation was rapidly becoming the ideal of Virginia society.[2]

The great planters, the men who owned and managed the plantations, set the tone of Virginia society. This remarkable group emerged mainly out of the second generation of immigrants who began

1. This discussion of the economic progress of the southern royal colonies is based largely on the following secondary sources: Evarts B. Greene and Virginia D. Harrington, *American Population Before the Federal Census of 1790* (N. Y., 1932); Thomas P. Abernethy, *Three Virginia Frontiers* (Baton Rogue, 1940); Philip A. Bruce, *The Economic History of Virginia in the Seventeenth Century*, 2 vols. (N. Y., 1896); Thomas J. Wertenbaker, *Virginia under the Stuarts, 1607-1688* (Princeton, 1914); Samuel A. Ashe, *History of North Carolina*, 2 vols. (Greensboro, 1908-25); Charles C. Crittenden, *The Commerce of North Carolina, 1763-1789* (New Haven, 1936); Hugh T. Lefler and Albert R. Newsome, *North Carolina; The History of a Southern State* (Chapel Hill, 1954); Edward McCrady, *The History of South Carolina under the Proprietary Government, 1670-1719* (N. Y., 1897), and *The History of South Carolina under the Royal Government, 1719-1776* (N. Y., 1899); Robert L. Meriwether, *The Expansion of South Carolina, 1729-1765* (Kingsport, Tenn., 1940); David D. Wallace, *South Carolina, A Short History, 1520-1948* (Chapel Hill, 1951); Abbot, *Royal Governors;* and E. Merton Coulter, *A Short History of Georgia* (Chapel Hill, 1933).

2. Wesley Frank Craven, *The Southern Colonies in the Seventeenth Century, 1607-1689* (Baton Rouge, 1949), 138-82, 394-415; Thomas J. Wertenbaker, *The Planters of Colonial Virginia* (Princeton, 1922).

coming to Virginia in the late 1630's and early 1640's. Mostly of middle-class origins, they were younger sons of English gentry or commercial families. They usually brought with them some initial advantages—capital, claims to land arising from their families' earlier investments in the Virginia Company, or political influence in either England or Virginia. But an unusual combination of ambition, ability, hard work, and luck was necessary for economic and social advancement. In emulation of the English gentry they acquired sizable estates, built large and occasionally elegant manor houses, and sought to establish their predominance in county and colony politics. To secure their families' position, they seated each of their sons on handsome estates and married their daughters to scions of families of equal fortune and rank. By the turn of the century most of the great families that would dominate Virginia for the next hundred years were already well established and intimately associated with a particular region: the Hills, Harrisons, Blands, Allens, Carys, Ludwells, Byrds, and Randolphs on the James River; the Burwells, Digges, Pages, Corbins, Robinsons, and Whitings on the York; the Wormeleys, Carters, Beverleys, and Tayloes on the Rappahannock; the Lees, Masons, and Fitzhughs on the Potomac; and the Custises on the Eastern Shore.[3]

The sons of these immigrants just beginning to come into prominence in the decade of the 1690's consolidated the position of the gentry in Virginia affairs. Represented by such men as Robert "King" Carter, Richard Lee II, William Byrd II, William Randolph of Turkey Island, and Robert and Peter Beverley, they greatly increased their holdings in land and slaves, acquired extensive interests in the overseas tobacco trade, extended the social and economic patterns of the Tidewater into the Piedmont, and obtained vast tracts of western lands for their numerous progeny and for speculation. They built even larger houses, equipped them with excellent libraries and furnishings from England, and occasionally sent their sons to England for their education.[4]

Based largely upon wealth, this native aristocracy was never a closed social group; social lines remained fluid throughout the eight-

3. See the excellent discussion in Bailyn, "Politics and Social Structure in Virginia," Smith, ed., *Seventeenth-Century America*, 90-115.
4. Carl Bridenbaugh, *Myths and Realities; Societies of the Colonial South* (Baton Rouge, 1952), 1-53; Louis B. Wright, *The First Gentlemen of Virginia* (San Marino, Calif., 1940).

eenth century. Newcomers or older settlers who gained wealth were
readily accepted by established families. Merchants such as Thomas
Nelson, John Norton, and George Braxton entered the aristocracy
almost immediately upon their arrival. But there were still other
avenues to wealth and social position. Some new arrivals like Dr.
George Nicholas or John Lomax married into established families.
Others such as John Clayton, George Eskridge, John Holloway, John
Mercer, and James Power found entrance through their knowledge of
the law. Still others rose out of the yeomanry or the ranks of the
small planters, either like George Wythe, Patrick Henry, or Dr. Thomas Walker by their own initiative or like Edmund Pendleton or Benjamin Waller through the sponsorship of a prominent family. This
constant replenishing of the gentry was an important factor in maintaining its vigor and helped to offset a general tendency towards decline among the fourth and fifth generations of the original families.
Indeed, the genius of the Virginia gentry was its remarkable capacity
for absorbing new talent.[5]

Unquestionably, the plantation gentry supplied the bulk of social
and intellectual leadership. The Massachusetts lawyer Josiah
Quincy, Jr., found in 1773 an "aristocratical spirit and principle"[6]
pervading the colony, an observation that would have been only
slightly less applicable half or three-quarters of a century earlier. The
desire to enhance one's family name, obtain a landed estate, and
acquire status and wealth in the community were goals not only of
the gentry but of all ambitious Virginians, and the emphasis on hard
work and a rigorous personal independence permeated the entire
society. The gentry's drive for improvement was accompanied by
a high regard for education and mental achievements that produced
an unusually high cultural level for an agricultural society. But most
important, the tradition of gentry leadership was a vital element in
the plantation ethos.

As the social and economic leaders of their communities and the
colony, the emerging plantation elite naturally sought political influence. As a result, political leadership was early identified with
social and economic leadership, and there emerged a remarkably

5. See Jack P. Greene, "Foundations of Political Power in the Virginia House
of Burgesses, 1720-1776," *Wm. and Mary Qtly.*, 3d Ser., 16 (1959), 485-506.
6. Entry of Apr. [?], 1773, Mark A. DeWolfe Howe, ed., "Journal of Josiah
Quincy, Jr., 1773," Massachusetts Historical Society, *Proceedings*, 49 (1916), 467.

stable political environment in which government was dominated at every level by the plantation elite. Public affairs could open doors to public lands, special business advantages, or lucrative government posts. But the gentry also sought office out of a deep sense of public responsibility, embracing the concept of *noblesse oblige* and diligently serving in the county courts, the parish vestry, and the House of Burgesses, for which they received but scant remuneration. Landon Carter was not alone in urging his son to study the laws of the colony in preparation for the day when he would be "in a Capacity to lend a hand towards their improvement or support." Carter assured his son that he would find the service of "advising" others "delightfull," observing that "it is really natural for a thinking Mind . . . to desire to amend error and preserve that which appears to be reasonable."[7] Sons of the gentry were constantly exposed to discussions of public affairs and early acquired an intimate knowledge of the workings of Virginia governmental institutions and the kind of political *savoir-faire* that fitted them for all sorts of responsibilities and gave them a distinct advantage over men from less politically orientated environments. There was, it appeared, a clear connection between political talent on one hand and wealth and family on the other. Moreover, other groups in society, most of which had similar interests and less time to devote to politics, willingly accepted the gentry's leadership, finding it quite natural to return their wealthier and more successful neighbors to represent them or to acquiesce in their decisions on the county bench.[8]

Nothing could have been more natural than the process by which the gentry acquired its extensive interest in politics. The large planters were the most important figures in their communities. Governors appointed them to the county courts; congregations selected them for the parish vestry. Moreover, because the governors were instructed to recommend men of good estates for positions on the Council and because those planters who produced the most tobacco were likely to be the best known in London, it was almost inevitable

7. Dedication of Landon Carter to Robert Wormeley Carter, 1753, in *A Collection of all the Acts of Assembly, Now in Force, in the Colony of Virginia* (Williamsburg, 1733), Library of Sabine Hall, Warsaw, Va.

8. On these points, see Sydnor, *Gentlemen Freeholders;* Bridenbaugh, *Myths and Realities*, 1-53, and *Seat of Empire; The Political Role of Eighteenth-Century Williamsburg* (Williamsburg, 1950); Daniel J. Boorstin, *The Americans; The Colonial Experience* (N. Y., 1958), 99-143; and Greene, "Foundations of Political Power," *Wm. and Mary Qtly.*, 3d Ser., 16 (1959), 485-506.

that most councilors would be drawn from the more substantial members of the plantation group. Sir William Berkeley, who was governor for over a quarter century between 1642 and 1677, was himself a great planter. One of the chief architects of Virginia society, he chose men from the rising gentry for political preferment. By the end of his tenure this group was in firm control of both local institutions and the Council and had great influence in the House of Burgesses. Under the guidance of the gentry the Council became a powerful political unit, assuming a role in Virginia government greater than that of the Burgesses and at times even than that of the governor.

The Council was at the height of its political power during the three decades beginning in 1690. Insisting on local control of Virginia affairs, it made life difficult for governors who challenged its authority. First Sir Edmund Andros, who served as governor between 1692 and 1698, and then the impetuous Francis Nicholson, who after a successful stint as lieutenant governor from 1690 to 1692 and a tour of duty in Maryland succeeded Andros as governor from 1698 to 1705, lost their posts in part because they did not work harmoniously with the Council. Between the death of Lieutenant Governor Edward Nott in 1706 and the arrival of Alexander Spotswood in 1710, the Council exercised complete control over the political fortunes of the colony. Despite a vigorous attempt, Spotswood was unable during his twelve-year administration to break the Council's power or to shore up the Crown's authority in the colony. The best he could do was to reach an accommodation with the Council, establishing a state of political equilibrium between royal authority and local interests. In effect, the governor and Council succeeded in neutralizing each other. In the process, Spotswood discovered the secret of political success. To govern Virginia one had to reach an accord with the plantation gentry—a course followed in large measure by all of Spotswood's successors.[9]

Although Virginia had a long tradition of representative government, the House of Burgesses had never been a consistently powerful force prior to Spotswood's administration. Virginia could claim the

9. See Leonidas Dodson, *Alexander Spotswood: Governor of Colonial Virginia, 1710-1722* (Phila., 1932); Williams, Political Alignments in Colonial Virginia, 1-222; Richard L. Morton, *Colonial Virginia*, 2 vols. (Chapel Hill, 1960), I; Wertenbaker, *Give Me Liberty*, 160-76; and Jack P. Greene, ed., "The Opposition to Lieutenant Governor Alexander Spotswood, 1718," *Va. Mag. of Hist. and Biog.*, 70 (1962), 35-42.

singular distinction of having enjoyed in 1619, while it was still under the control of the Virginia Company, the first representative assembly in the English colonies. After the surrender of the company charter in 1624, the colonists persuaded the Crown to establish representative institutions on a regular basis. At first, the elected delegates were distinctly subordinate to the executive and until the middle of the century did not constitute a separate body but sat in joint session with the governor and Council, who introduced almost all legislation. However, in 1651 or slightly earlier, the legislature became bicameral, the elective branch or lower house eventually taking the name House of Burgesses. With its surrender to the Parliamentary forces in 1652 during the Commonwealth era, the colony became virtually self-governing. The governor and Council exercised their powers by a grant of authority from the Burgesses. Royal control was reimposed on the colony in 1660, but the status gained by the Burgesses during the Commonwealth was not altogether lost. Councilors continued to sit in an advisory capacity with Burgesses on most important committees up to at least 1667, and Governor Sir William Berkeley exercised a strong influence upon legislative proceedings between 1660 and 1677.

Nevertheless, it was during Berkeley's tenure that the Burgesses consolidated its hold on the right to initiate legislation. The only serious invasion of that right came in the wake of Bacon's Rebellion when London authorities sent three bills to the colony in 1680 with Thomas, Lord Culpeper, newly appointed governor, for passage by the Virginia legislature. At the same time they also attempted to apply Poyning's Law—which required the Crown's prior approval of all laws passed by the Irish Parliament—to Virginia by requiring Culpeper to forward drafts of necessary legislation to the Crown for approval before submitting it to the Burgesses. This attempt threatened to undermine completely the Burgesses' right to the initiative, but it failed when the distance between Jamestown and London made enforcement impracticable. By the end of the century the Burgesses had gained considerable political and constitutional authority, having firmly established its exclusive right to tax and having gained extensive control over its membership and internal proceedings, including guarantees of certain important fundamental privileges. Still, it was not so powerful as some of its much younger counterparts in other colonies.[10]

A variety of factors combined to retard the development of the Virginia Burgesses. For one thing, its grant in 1681 of a permanent revenue made the executive less dependent upon it for money, so that it did not meet so frequently as lower houses in other colonies. Also the county courts had jurisdiction on the local level and handled many functions that might otherwise have fallen within its purview. Furthermore, the Council was so powerful and active in representing local interests that it overshadowed the Burgesses in Virginia political life. Although the Burgesses had occasionally shown some disposition to enlarge its sphere of authority, especially in the 1680's under Francis, Lord Howard of Effingham (1683-89), and in the first decade of the eighteenth century during the second Nicholson administration, it did not make a spirited bid for power until the tenure of Alexander Spotswood (1710-22). Urged on by the Council, the Burgesses in 1715 and 1718 fought Spotswood to a standstill in a battle over his Indian and tobacco regulation policies and tried to extend its own authority by acquiring several new powers. When the deadlock between Spotswood and the Council created a political vacuum, the Burgesses was ready to step in to fill it. For the next twenty-five years during the benevolent governments of Hugh Drysdale (1722-26) and Sir William Gooch (1727-49) the Burgesses grew steadily in stature and influence under the successive leadership of Speakers John Holloway (1720-34), Sir John Randolph (1734-37), and John Robinson (1738-66).

During the same period the gentry consolidated its control over the House. Since the Restoration it had played an important role in the House, but smaller planters and yeomen had been numerous and occasionally influential up to the 1720's. As the size of the gentry increased and families became well enough established to take a greater interest in politics, it became clear that the Council was not large enough to hold everyone with political ambitions. Hence, more and more members of the gentry sought their political fortunes in the Burgesses. The result was the emergence during the 1740's and 1750's of an outstanding group of political leaders in the House:

10. Craven, *Southern Colonies in the Seventeenth Century*, 134-36, 159-65, 262-68, 396-97; Labaree, ed., *Royal Instructions*, I, 125; Instructions to Culpeper, 1679-80, CO 1/47. See also Wertenbaker, *Give Me Liberty*, 1-132.

Richard Bland, Charles and Landon Carter, Archibald Cary, Benjamin Harrison V, Richard Henry Lee, Robert Carter Nicholas, Edmund Pendleton, James Power, Peyton Randolph, Benjamin Waller, Beverley Whiting, and George Wythe. These men provided the House and the colony with continuous able leadership down to the American Revolution.[11]

That the Burgesses under the leadership of the gentry had become a powerful political body became apparent in the early 1750's when Lieutenant Governor Robert Dinwiddie (1752-58) attempted to establish without its consent the pistole fee for signing and putting the seal to patents for land. The Burgesses' determined opposition persuaded Dinwiddie to act more circumspectly for the remainder of his administration. During the Seven Years' War the Burgesses further increased its authority as the demand for defense appropriations required more frequent sessions. In the late 1750's and early 1760's it sought to acquire powers long held by legislatures of other colonies including authority to nominate and appoint a London agent and to put itself upon a statutory foundation. Dinwiddie's successor, Francis Fauquier (1758-68), found it more important to retain the friendship of Speaker John Robinson than to obey explicit orders from the Crown. By the end of the war the Burgesses was the most powerful branch of Virginia government.[12]

Perhaps the most striking characteristic of Virginia politics between 1689 and 1763 was its tranquillity. Only Spotswood's attempt to expand Crown authority during the opening years of his government and Dinwiddie's unhappy effort to establish the pistole fee interrupted the steady and quiet tempo of political life. With the exception of Nicholson during his second administration and perhaps John Murray, Earl of Dunmore (1771-76), the men sent to govern Virginia were an able lot. Drysdale, Gooch, Fauquier, and Norborne Berkeley, Baron de Botetourt (1768-70), achieved an extraordinary popularity by allying themselves with the gentry and governing with prudence and moderation. Moreover, there was in Virginia, unlike other colonies, no serious rivalry between the Council and the House. Members of the two houses were bound by close family and social

11. For a list of the leaders of the Burgesses from 1688 to 1776, see Appendix III.
12. See Greene, "Opposition to Alexander Spotswood," *Va. Mag. of Hist. and Biog.*, 70 (1962), 35-42; "The Case of the Pistole Fee," *ibid.*, 66 (1958), 399-422; and "The Attempt to Separate the Offices of Speaker and Treasurer, 1758-1766," *ibid.*, 71 (1963), 11-18.

ties, and, although the Burgesses eclipsed the Council in practical
political power after 1750, the Council's influence and prestige remained high. Nor were there any important sectional divisions. The
social and economic patterns of the Tidewater were extended all the
way to the mountains. Not only did family ties cut across geographi-
cal lines, but there was a remarkable homogeneity in economic activity, religion, and national origins. Only with the settlement of the
Shenandoah Valley and tramontane regions at mid-century were
heterogeneous elements introduced, and they were not a serious divisive force before the Revolution. Indeed, there is no evidence of
any major dissatisfaction with gentry leadership or of any group intent upon challenging it in the years before 1763. Although there
was some personal rivalry over western lands between the planters
in the Northern Neck under the leadership of the Lees and another
group in the James and York River section under the Randolphs
and Robinsons, there were neither political parties nor permanent
factions.[13] There were often disagreements on specific issues, but,
as St. George Tucker later suggested to William Wirt, these were
"only such as different men, coming from different parts of our extensive Country might well be expected to entertain." Tucker had
never witnessed anything in the Burgesses "that bore the appearance
of *party spirit.*"[14]

Under these conditions it is not surprising that the gentry developed a vigorous tradition of personal independence. The whole
society encouraged it. "The public or political character of the
Virginians," reported Andrew Burnaby in the late 1750's, "corre-
sponds with their private one: they are haughty and jealous of their
liberties, impatient of restraint, and can scarcely bear the thought of
being controuled by any superior power."[15] The dimension of this
impatience and independence was revealed in the 1750's, first in the
Burgesses' excited opposition to the pistole fee and then in the
colony's objections to the Crown's disallowance of the Two-Penny
Acts, by which the House had sought in a year of extremely short

13. Williams, Political Alignments in Colonial Virginia, 328-38. For later
manifestations of these splits, see Jackson T. Main, "Sections and Politics in
Virginia, 1781-1787," *Wm. and Mary Qtly.,* 3d Ser., 17 (1955), 96-112.
14. Tucker to William Wirt, Sept. 25, 1815, *Wm. and Mary College Qtly.,* 1st
Ser., 22 (1914), 253.
15. Andrew Burnaby, *Travels through the Middle Settlements in North-America, in the Years 1759 and 1760* (London, 1775), 20.

crops to enable people to pay their public obligations in money instead of tobacco.[16] Both incidents might have been sufficient warning that Virginia, for over half a century almost a model colony, would be at the forefront of opposition to British measures if its liberties were challenged. After 1763 the colony faced for the first time since the days of Nicholson and Spotswood a serious political issue—whether Parliament or the Burgesses had jurisdiction over its internal polity. Moreover, this issue arose at the same time that Speaker John Robinson's death in 1766 disclosed that he had loaned liberal amounts to members of the gentry from public funds under his care as treasurer.[17] The Robinson affair seriously divided the planter group and gave rise to a new impulse which demanded restraints to prevent power of such magnitude from again falling into the hands of one group. The interaction between this impulse and the Revolutionary movement determined the course of Virginia politics for the last decade of the colonial period.[18]

Although South Carolina never reached so high a level of maturity as Virginia during the colonial period, it early developed a thriving economy. Beginning in the 1670's a flourishing trade with the southern Indian nations produced the nucleus of a wealthy mercantile community, and Charleston, as the entrepôt for the trade, became a bustling port. From the first settlement of the colony a majority of the inhabitants had been engaged in agriculture, and in the last decades of the seventeenth century the cultivation of rice provided a valuable staple crop. Like tobacco, rice could be grown profitably on plantations using slave labor, and during the first decades of the eighteenth century slavery became the prevailing system of labor, and the plantation the dominant economic and social unit. By the 1720's the West Indies and the countries of southern Europe were annually buying huge quantities of Carolina rice, and affluent planters were taking their places with Charleston merchants as the economic and social leaders of the colony. Charleston became the center of a vast plantation trade that soon superseded the traffic with the Indians as

16. For extended discussions of these disputes, see Greene, "The Case of the Pistole Fee," *Va. Mag. of Hist. and Biog.*, 66 (1958), 399-422, and Morton, *Colonial Virginia*, II, 751-819.

17. Mays, *Edmund Pendleton*, I, 174-208, 358-85.

18. This idea will be explored at length in my portion of a study of Virginia politics from 1763 to 1789 with Keith B. Berwick.

its principal economic function. In the 1740's the planters added indigo as an important staple, second only to rice as a source of agricultural wealth.[19]

Trade and planting, then, were the chief avenues to wealth in early South Carolina, many of the more enterprising individuals participating in both. Relations between merchants and planters were unusually harmonious, except for the period between 1725 and the late 1730's when they disagreed over paper currency needs, and together they dominated South Carolina society. Like members of the Virginia gentry, they were mostly of middle-class origins. Many of the first immigrants had already made a successful start in the West Indies at Barbados, the Leeward Islands, or Jamaica. Most of them had some initial advantages such as capital, commercial connections in England, grants from the proprietors, or political influence in either England or South Carolina. As in Virginia, however, ambition, hard work, and good fortune were necessary for the acquisition of sizable estates and the permanent establishment of a place for themselves and their progeny. Members of the merchant-planter group intermarried, and by the 1720's recent mercantile families such as the Wraggs, Bees, Pringles, Savages, Barnwells, Eveleighs, and Brewtons had combined with older West Indian immigrants like the Broughtons, Johnsons, Godfreys, Middletons, Draytons, Elliotts, Fenwicks, and Moores; French Huguenots such as the Mazycks, Mottes, and Manigaults; and families that had come directly from England including the Blakes, Izards, and Smiths to form a budding aristocracy.[20]

Between 1720 and 1750 these families developed into a homogeneous group that, though of more recent origin, was in many respects comparable to the Virginia gentry. They made huge fortunes, investing their profits in lands and slaves, expanding their interests in overseas trade and shipping, and extending the social and economic patterns of the Charleston area over the entire low country. Like the Virginia gentry, they began in the 1730's to build fine houses, sometimes on their plantations but more often in Charleston, most of them preferring the advantages of an urban society. Indeed,

19. Verner W. Crane, *The Southern Frontier, 1670-1732* (Durham, 1928); Wallace, *South Carolina, A Short History*, 37-80.

20. McCrady, *South Carolina under Proprietary Government*, 327-28; Arthur H. Hirsch, *The Huguenots of Colonial South Carolina* (Durham, 1928), 90-103, 165-95, 239-60.

although much of their wealth was tied up in agriculture, their society was more urban than rural, and Charleston early dominated all aspects of South Carolina life. Both rice and indigo could be cultivated best on small plots with a few slaves and an overseer, freeing the large planters to spend much of their time in Charleston.

Also like the Virginia gentry, the South Carolina aristocracy was based almost wholly upon wealth. Hence, it too was open and probably even somewhat more fluid than that of Virginia throughout the eighteenth century. Less successful older families and newcomers alike made their fortunes in the years between 1725 and 1765 and easily circulated among the older elite. A significant portion of the celebrated plantation-mercantile gentry at the time of the American Revolution was of comparatively recent arrival. The son of a saddler who immigrated to South Carolina around 1715, Henry Laurens became one of the most opulent merchants in the colony after 1750. Joseph Allston, who started out with a small fortune and five slaves just a few years earlier, had by 1773 acquired five plantations with a hundred slaves on each and accumulated substantial economic holdings. Perhaps the easiest route into the gentry after 1730 was the unusually lucrative professions. Charles Pinckney, a descendant of one of the less prominent earlier immigrants, made a fortune in law in the 1730's and established a family dynasty that ranked with the oldest in the colony. Similarly, the two Rutledge brothers, Andrew, the lawyer, and John, the doctor, came from Ireland about 1730, made advantageous marriages, and acquired wealth and social position. James Parsons, James Michie, John Rattray, and Rawlins Lowndes were other lawyers who followed a similar path. As late as the Revolution, South Carolina was a fertile field for the talented and ambitious.

Their society resembled that of the West Indies more closely than it did that of Virginia. With their estates in the hands of overseers, South Carolinians, like West Indian planters, had more leisure time than the Virginians and were, if we can believe countless observers, less devoted to the ethic of hard work. "State, magnificence and ostentation, the natural attendants of riches," as well as "Cards, dice, the bottle and horses," Josiah Quincy found in 1773, engrossed "prodigious portions of time and attention," though he also discovered a broad range of more formal cultural activities. Their concentration within a small area in and around Charleston plus constant and extensive contact with the culture of the mother country produced a society which was more cosmopolitan than that of Virginia; the South Carolina gentry was constantly borrowing the appurtenances of English culture, and after 1730 it was common for sons of the gentry to go to England for their education.[21]

Quincy's charge that Carolinians had "no great passion" to "shine and blaze in the forum of a senate"[22] was certainly not descriptive of the entire plantation-mercantile elite. Although this group was considerably less oriented towards politics than its Virginia equivalent, it nonetheless exercised leadership at every level of government. To be sure, the majority of the planters were only casually interested in politics, but the merchant-professional segment of the elite participated actively. Out of this group came a number of individuals who, along with a few planters, were deeply interested in politics and whose sense of public responsibility almost equaled that of the Virginia gentry. The younger Bull reported in November 1770 that in South Carolina perhaps more than in any other province there was "a gratuitous execution of many branches of Power under a desire of shewing a public spirit and easing the public expences." Members of the Commons House, he wrote, had always "disdain[ed] taking any pay for their attendance" and members of the gentry supervised all public works and services without remuneration.[23]

From the 1680's on the planter-merchant group dominated the government of the colony. More than a few of their number, including Thomas Smith (1693-94), Joseph Blake (1694-95, 1696-1700), James Moore I (1700-1703), Sir Nathaniel Johnson (1703-9), Robert Gibbes (1710-12), Robert Daniel (1716-17), Robert Johnson (1717-19, 1730-35), James Moore II (1719-21), Arthur Middleton (1725-30), Thomas Broughton (1735-37), William Bull I (1737-43), and William Bull II (1760-61, 1764-66, 1768, 1769-71, 1773-75), acted as chief executive of the colony for over forty-five of the eighty-five years between 1689 and 1776; and two other governors, James Glen (1743-56) and

21. Bridenbaugh, *Myths and Realities,* 54-118; entry of Mar. 25, 1773, Howe, ed., "Quincy Journal," Mass. Hist. Soc., *Proceedings,* 49 (1916), 455.

22. Entry of Mar. 25, 1773, Howe, ed., "Quincy Journal," Mass. Hist. Soc., *Proceedings,* 49 (1916), 455.

23. Bull to Lord Hillsborough, Nov. 30, 1770, Transcripts of Records relating to South Carolina in the British Public Record Office, XXXII, 375, 404-5, S. C. Arch. Dept., Columbia; hereafter cited as S. C. Pub. Recs.

Thomas Boone (1761-64), whose administrations covered almost another two decades, were connected through marriage with the local elite. Moreover, that elite furnished most of the members of the Council down into the 1750's and of the Commons House of Assembly for the entire colonial period. Through the Commons it also handled almost every detail of administration at the local level. Until the late 1760's, there were no courts in the colony other than in Charleston; and except for the church wardens of the parishes, who performed a few minor duties such as supervising elections, and the provost marshals, who handled routine matters of law enforcement, commissioners appointed originally by the Commons carried on all tasks of local administration. Because of this centralized control and because Charleston residents frequently even sat as representatives for outlying districts, South Carolina by the 1720's was virtually a city-state with all power radiating out from Charleston.

In the 1690's South Carolina began to develop a strong tradition of representative government. The proprietary charter ensured Carolinians a voice in legislation by forbidding the passage of laws without the "advice, assent and approbation, of the freemen . . . or the greater part of them, or of their delegates." In establishing civil governments in the Ashley River settlement in 1670, the proprietors willingly complied with that stipulation. They even granted the representatives the unique privilege of choosing half of the Council. But from the beginning the proprietors endeavored to restrict the representatives' power by requiring them to meet with the governor and Council in a single-house assembly and by denying them the right to initiate legislation or to debate or consider any matter "but what is proposed to them by the Councill."[24] Finally, after the Glorious Revolution in England had given added impetus to the movement to bring the proprietary colonies under royal control, the proprietors, hoping to save their charter by keeping the colony quiet, made the legislature bicameral, the lower house taking the name Commons House of Assembly. In 1693 the proprietors conceded to the Commons the right to initiate laws.[25]

From that date until the American Revolution, the most con-

24. Craven, *Southern Colonies in Seventeenth Century*, 325-54; Proprietor's Instructions to Governor and Council at Ashley River, Dec. 16, 1671, South Carolina Historical Society, *Collections*, 5 (1896), 367; Carolina Charter, June 17, 1665, *N. C. Col. Recs.*, I, 104-5.
25. Wallace, *South Carolina, A Short History*, 45-57.

spicuous feature of South Carolina political development was the
ever expanding power of the Commons House. The colony did not
have an established revenue with which to pay for routine governmental expenses, and the demand for money for such matters as well
as for major expenditures to cover Indian relations and defense—
perennial subjects of attention for South Carolina politicians—
necessitated frequent sessions. Beginning in 1692 the Commons met
annually and sometimes semi-annually and after 1730 as many as five
or six times each year. Such frequent sessions meant that it developed much more rapidly than did the Virginia Burgesses. The
Commons spearheaded the opposition to the proprietors after 1690
and acquired broad financial powers in the process. Between 1703
and 1709, during the administration of Sir Nathaniel Johnson, it
asserted its authority over the Indian trade and claimed the power
to nominate all officers receiving a salary from the public. Over the
next decade under Governors Edward Tynte (1709-10), Robert
Gibbes, Charles Craven (1712-16), Robert Daniel, and Robert Johnson the Commons quietly tried to strengthen its hold on these powers.
When the proprietors attempted to curtail its authority by vetoing
several important measures in 1718, the Commons led a revolution
against them, overthrowing Johnson in 1719, electing James Moore II
governor, and inaugurating the movement which eventually brought
South Carolina under the Crown.

Royal government began in South Carolina in 1721, but it was
another eight years before the Crown acquired clear governing rights
by purchasing the colony from the proprietors. In the meantime,
the Commons took advantage of the temporary confusion to consolidate its authority. At the first royal legislative session in 1721 it
pushed through important laws establishing its power to share in the
appointment of all revenue officers, to supervise the Indian trade, to
nominate and appoint an agent in London, to establish courts by
statute, and to fix the constitution of the legislature and regulate
elections by law. From these important beginnings, it proceeded
over the next three decades to increase its authority still further
under a series of able speakers, including James Moore II (1721-24),
Thomas Broughton (1725-27), John Lloyd I (1731, 1731-32), Paul
Jenys (1733-36), Charles Pinckney (1736-40), William Bull II (1740-
42, 1744-47, 1748-49), and Benjamin Whitaker (1742-44). The royal

governors seemed no more able than their predecessors under the proprietors to cope with the Commons. Both his advanced age and the uncertain state of negotiations over the fate of the colony prevented Francis Nicholson (1721-25), the first royal governor, from even trying. By opposing the Commons' efforts to increase the amount of paper currency in the colony in defiance of the royal instructions, Arthur Middleton, who succeeded Nicholson, threw the colony into chaos. General rioting and attempts by paper money advocates to intimidate Middleton and the Council followed a legislative deadlock over this issue, and for three years, from 1727 to 1730, the colony was on the verge of civil war. Governor Robert Johnson arranged a satisfactory compromise between imperial authorities and the Commons over the paper money issue and restored harmony in the colony, but he never challenged the Commons' power. Indeed, Johnson and his three successors—Thomas Broughton, William Bull I, and James Glen—repeatedly had to make concessions to the Commons in order to obtain money for defraying both ordinary governmental expenses and after 1737 defense expenditures required by the last two intercolonial wars. During this period the Commons acquired a wide range of powers and became the dominant element in South Carolina politics. Despite his determined efforts, William Henry Lyttelton (1756-60) was unable to carry out Board of Trade recommendations designed to check the Commons' power; and when Governor Thomas Boone challenged the authority of the Commons to determine the elections of its own members in 1762 during the Gadsden election controversy, he was driven from office. By returning to the policy of co-operation, the younger Bull, who had earlier been speaker of the Commons, maintained amicable relations during his several stints as chief executive in the 1760's and 1770's. But neither Lord Charles Greville Montagu (1766-68, 1768-69, 1771-75) nor Lord William Campbell (1775) had successful administrations, mostly because the crisis in British-American relations forced them into direct opposition to the Commons.[26]

Although there were close family, social, and economic ties between the Council and the House down to the 1750's, there was a

26. See Jack P. Greene, ed., "South Carolina's Colonial Constitution: Two Proposals for Reform," *South Carolina Historical Magazine*, 62 (1961), 72-81, and "Gadsden Election Controversy," *Miss. Valley Hist. Rev.*, 46 (1959), 469-92; McCrady, *South Carolina under Royal Government*, 560-773.

long-standing rivalry between the two bodies that was one of the most important features of South Carolina politics during the colonial period. The Commons' insistence upon absolute control over finance—an issue of the first magnitude from 1725 to 1755—and the recurring battles between the two houses over the Council's claim to a share in framing money bills and supervising expenditures resulted in victory for the Commons and the decline of the power of the Council. As the Crown began to fill the Council with placemen after 1750, that body lost almost all influence in South Carolina politics.[27] Unlike the Virginia Burgesses, which had remarkable continuity in leadership throughout the eighteenth century, the South Carolina Commons experienced a rapid turnover in both membership and leadership, especially during the first decades of royal government. This change can be explained in part by the facts that members of the Commons received no salary for their services and that it met so often that few could afford the time for such constant attendance. But even though individual members changed, the nature of the membership remained the same, being drawn almost entirely from the local governing elite. After 1750 the leadership of the Commons became more stable. Men like Speakers Henry Middleton (1747, 1754-55), Andrew Rutledge (1749-52), James Michie (1752-54), Benjamin Smith (1755-63), Rawlins Lowndes (1763-65, 1772-75), and Peter Manigault (1765-72) as well as other able individuals such as Charles Pinckney, James Parsons, Henry Laurens, William Wragg, Christopher Gadsden, Thomas Lynch, John Rutledge, and John Rattray provided the Commons with a hard core of interested and able leaders in the last decades before Independence.[28]

Except for the battles between the Council and the Commons and the brief challenges to the Commons' authority by Governors Lyttelton and Boone, the political life of the colony was relatively tranquil after 1730. There were no party divisions, and few elections centered on political issues. Nor were there important sectional rifts until after 1750, when the vast Piedmont finally began to be filled by streams of immigrants from the north and Europe and developed an economic system quite different from that of the low country. In

27. Sirmans, "The South Carolina Royal Council," *Wm. and Mary Qtly.*, 3d Ser., 18 (1961), 373-92.

28. For a list of the leaders of the Commons from 1692 to 1775, see Appendix III.

contrast to the situation in Virginia, the two regions were quite heterogeneous, and serious discord developed after 1760 as the western section demanded a court system, local government, and adequate representation. It was these demands that were in large part behind the vigilante rising of the Regulators in the backcountry in the late 1760's. Although low-country leaders willingly granted the first two demands, they were reluctant to consent to an extension of representation, especially when British policy restricting the size of the Commons after 1767 meant that it could be done only by a general reapportionment in which the low country would lose some of its seats. This demand was not satisfied until 1775, when the South Carolinians set up an extralegal government. Even then, however, low-country leaders continued to dominate politics, apparently without objection from western middle-class representatives, who seem to have recognized the superior political experience and talent of the Charleston group.[29]

In many respects North Carolina society was a composite of those of Virginia and South Carolina. This fact is not surprising because most of the settlers came not directly from abroad but from the adjacent colonies. The first settlers in the 1650's and 1660's were Virginians spilling over into the region around Albemarle Sound. They brought with them so many social and economic patterns that the Albemarle section, stretching south as far as Pamlico Sound, was in many respects an extension of the Virginia Tidewater. A mixture of plantations and farms, concentrating on tobacco cultivation but also producing considerable quantities of naval stores and provisions, this region was inhabited by a large number of independent yeomen. By the first decades of the eighteenth century, however, a group of families including the Swanns, Pollocks, Moseleys, Harveys, Dawsons, and Blounts—in many cases closely connected with the Virginia gentry —had acquired large estates and had established a local aristocracy. Beginning around 1715 another group of families, many of whom were already well established in South Carolina, moved north to settle the area around the Cape Fear River. With this immigration came the Moores, Ashes, Harnetts, Howes, and Drys, who carved out

29. See the introduction to William E. Hemphill and Wylma Anne Wates, eds., *Extracts from the Journals of the Provincial Congresses of South Carolina, 1775-1776* (Columbia, 1960), i-xxxiv; see also Richard M. Brown, *The South Carolina Regulators* (Cambridge, Mass., 1963).

large rice plantations for themselves and established a society similar to that of the South Carolina low country. Like their Albemarle neighbors, they found the extensive pine barrens of the Cape Fear region suitable for producing naval stores. By the 1730's the Albemarle and Cape Fear families were beginning to intermarry. Some of the Albemarle families, for example the Swanns, even transferred the seat of their activities to the southern area, and the two societies merged in the region around Pamlico Sound.

Despite the development of close ties between the Albemarle and Cape Fear groups, North Carolina society was never the kind of homogeneous monoculture found in either Virginia or South Carolina. Property was more evenly distributed, and there was a much higher proportion of yeomen farmers. Moreover, there was a wide range of religious groups, the colony having attracted large numbers of dissenting elements almost from the beginning. The immigration of Scotch Highlanders into the upper Cape Fear River Valley after 1730 and of Scotch-Irish and Germans into the Piedmont and Blue Ridge areas after 1740 introduced even greater variety into the colony. This economic and social diffuseness was complicated by the colony's not having a central port such as Charleston or even a cultural capital such as Williamsburg to draw the various groups together. There were, in fact, no good ports in the entire colony. Edenton on Albemarle Sound as well as Bath and New Bern on Pamlico Sound were, because of the shallow waters of the sounds, difficult of access to boats with large draughts. Wilmington and Brunswick on the Cape Fear River were somewhat better situated, but a treacherous sandbar at the mouth of the river rendered them somewhat less than ideal ports. Hence, North Carolina was both more rural and more isolated than either Virginia or South Carolina. The variety in North Carolina society was accentuated by the fact that the ties of the Piedmont area ran north and south into Virginia and South Carolina rather than east into the older settled regions of the colony. Thus Piedmont producers often preferred either Charleston in the south or Baltimore or Philadelphia in the north over Wilmington or Edenton as an outlet for their commodities.[30]

Although the local gentry never dominated North Carolina to the extent that its counterparts did in Virginia and South Carolina, it

30. See Bridenbaugh, *Myths and Realities, passim;* Lefler and Newsome, *North Carolina,* 106-21.

did assume the major role in politics. Because of the colony's rapid growth after 1715, however, the degree of social fluidity exceeded that in either of its neighbors. Although the older families continued to supply the core of political leadership, comparatively large numbers of recent immigrants rose quickly to the status of the older gentry during the last fifty years of the colonial period. Through the middle decades of the eighteenth century, men with talent and political ambitions—lawyers like John Hodgson or Robert Jones, Jr., planters like John Starkey, or merchants like Thomas Barker—could take their places beside the Swanns, Harveys, Ashes, Howes, Harnetts, and Moores. A large percentage of the important North Carolina politicians after 1760 were, in fact, first generation immigrants, including lawyers Edmund Fanning, Richard Caswell, William Hooper, Alexander Martin, and Abner Nash and merchant Joseph Hewes. As in South Carolina, a knowledge of the law seems to have been a quick and easy avenue to political power.[31]

North Carolina's isolation meant that it was relatively inaccessible to the ultimate seat of authority in England, under both the proprietors and the Crown. This fact may help to account for the extreme turbulence of its politics during both the proprietary period and the first two decades of royal government as well as for its reputation as a center of discontent and lawlessness. By the early decades of the eighteenth century a tradition of opposition to authority was firmly rooted in the habits and ideology of the colony. "The inhabitants of North Carolina, are not Industrious but subtle and crafty to admiration, always behaved insolently to their governours," Governor George Burrington (1724-25, 1731-34) reported to the Crown in 1732; "some they have Imprisoned, drove others out of the Country, at other times sett up two or three supported by Men under Arms. . . . All the Governors that ever were in this Province," he observed, "lived in fear of the People . . . and D[r]eaded their Assemblys."[32] The colony's history to a great extent demonstrates the truth of this observation. On several occasions under the proprietors North Carolinians had risen in rebellion: in the 1670's during Culpeper's Rebellion against the enforcement of the Navigation Acts, in 1689 against the arbitrary measures of a proprietor himself, Governor Seth

31. For a list of the leaders of the North Carolina Lower Houses from 1725 to 1775, see Appendix III.

32. Burrington to Board of Trade, Feb. 20, 1732, *N. C. Col. Recs.*, III, 338.

Sothel (1682-89), and in the first decade of the eighteenth century during Cary's Rebellion against the attempt to exclude the Quakers from politics. Taking over the administration in 1714, Governor Charles Eden (1714-22) was the first of the proprietary governors to achieve order. Under him the General Assembly in 1715 codified the colony's laws. But this tranquillity was upset by the discovery that men close to Eden had probably been co-operating with the pirate Blackbeard; and Eden's successors, George Burrington and Richard Everard (1725-31), were unable during the last years of proprietary rule to restore harmony, the former because of his unfortunate disposition and the latter because of Burrington's opposition to him. The result of this discord was that the colony never developed the same settled traditions of representative government and legislative dominance during the proprietary period that South Carolina did. The Albemarle settlement had obtained from the proprietors the privilege of a representative assembly in 1664, six years before the Ashley River settlement, and the North Carolina Lower House had secured the right to sit separately from the Council and to initiate legislation in the early 1690's at the same time as the South Carolina Commons. Still, the North Carolina Lower House, although it frequently played a major part in politics under the able direction of men like Speakers Edward Moseley (1708-11, 1715-23, 1731-34) and John Baptista Ashe (1725-26), was neither so mature nor so powerful as was its equivalent in South Carolina.[33]

Moreover, turbulence during the first two decades after the Crown purchased the colony from the proprietors in 1729 tended to retard the development of the House even further. The chief matters in dispute were the question of land tenure and the somewhat clumsy and characteristically intemperate attempts by Burrington, who was the first royal governor, to make North Carolina political practices conform with his instructions from the Crown. Largely because of his penchant for controversy, Burrington was removed in 1734, but the debate over land tenure continued throughout the long administration of Gabriel Johnston (1734-52). This issue involved both the terms on which quitrents should be paid to the Crown and the validity of a large number of blank patents for land issued by Richard Everard during the period between the Crown's purchase of the col-

33. Lefler and Newsome, *North Carolina*, 47-49.

ony in 1729 and the arrival of Burrington to assume control of the government in 1731. The Crown demanded payment in specie in return for the remission of earlier arrears in rents. But the Lower House, pointing out that it was South Carolina not North Carolina which had large arrears and that the Crown's concession was of little value to North Carolina, insisted upon payment in commodities or paper money according to local custom. The blank patents—grants unrestricted to place or time—enabled the grantees (mainly the Moseleys, Moores, and other influential families) to carve out large sections of land at whatever choice spots they might find in the future.

Burrington objected strongly to these patents, but Johnston and some of his chief associates, in particular London merchant Henry McCulloh, made an even more intensive effort to have the Crown officials declare them invalid to make way for their own wholesale speculations. Thus, there developed two rival factions over the land question: the McCulloh land speculators and a loose and amorphous association of the older planters who opposed them. The latter group operated mainly through the Lower House, while the former included Governor Johnston and his successor, Arthur Dobbs (1754-65), and many members of the Council. This split influenced North Carolina politics during the first three decades of royal government. After his failure to collect the rents without the consent of the Lower House, Johnston found that political peace could be restored only by compromise. In return for authorization to prepare a rent roll, he agreed to permit payment of the rents on House terms and to confirm the validity of the blank patents. Regarding the governor's action as a betrayal of their partnership in speculation, McCulloh tried to prevent confirmation of the blank patents by persuading imperial authorities to disallow the compromise measure in 1741, thus reopening the controversy.

In the 1740's the quitrent question became entangled with a sectional dispute between the northern and southern counties over representation in the Lower House. Opposition to royal policy on quitrents was strongest in the Albemarle counties, each of which had from three to five representatives, while those in the south had only two. The population of the southern counties expanded at a greater rate than that of Albemarle, and they began to demand more representatives. Governor Johnston took advantage of this situation and threw his support behind the southern demands in an attempt to secure support for his policies. In 1746 he called the legislature to meet at Wilmington in the southern part of the province. As he had anticipated, the northern members stayed home, and the southerners passed a measure to equalize representation, thus provoking a bitter controversy that lasted for eight years. During this lengthy dispute the northern members refused to attend the legislature and contested the validity of the new law in London. McCulloh, by this time openly at odds with Johnston, supported the northern members, and the matter was settled in their favor in 1754 after Johnston's death in 1752 had led to the appointment of Arthur Dobbs, McCulloh's partner in his North Carolina land schemes.[34]

This settlement paved the way for the solution of the quitrent issue in the early years of Dobbs's administration, but it did not satisfy the demands of the southern counties for equal representation. The north-south split flared up occasionally during the next decade as the Albemarle members tried to retard efforts to create new counties in the south, but its seriousness should not be exaggerated. There were strong family ties between the two regions, and leadership in the Lower House seems to have been equally distributed between representatives from both. Moreover, despite the opposition of the Albemarle section, the number of southern members gradually increased after 1755 as the growth of the southern section necessitated the creation of new counties. Furthermore, the north-south division was overshadowed after 1760 by a more serious split between east and west which culminated in the late 1760's and early 1770's in the Regulator movement, in large part a western protest against eastern control of politics.

With the quitrent and representation question settled, the early years of Dobbs's administration were tranquil; but toward the end of the Seven Years' War Dobbs ran into increasing difficulty. After 1745, under the leadership of Speaker Samuel Swann (1743-54, 1756-61) and Thomas Barker, John Starkey, Robert Jones, and others, the Lower House grew more powerful as North Carolina's political life quieted down. As the Council, filled with placemen and individuals

34. See Beverley W. Bond, Jr., *The Quit-Rent System in the American Colonies* (New Haven, 1919), 287-317; London, "Representation Controversy," *N. C. Hist. Rev.*, 11 (1934), 255-70; Charles G. Sellers, Jr., "Private Profits and British Colonial Policy: The Speculations of Henry McCulloh," *Wm. and Mary Qtly.*, 3d Ser., 8 (1951), 535-51.

connected with the McCulloh-Dobbs speculating interests, steadily declined in power in the 1750's, the Lower House attained the upper hand in North Carolina politics. Dobbs's attempt to challenge the power of the House after 1758 produced a series of controversies over its rights to appoint public treasurers and London agents, audit accounts, fix judicial tenure during good behavior, and appropriate money voted by Parliament to reimburse the colony for its expenses in the war. From most of these controversies Dobbs emerged second best.[35] The Lower House retained its extensive power, and William Tryon (1765-71), who became governor after the death of Dobbs, restored political order only by working in close harmony with it. When imperial pressure forced Tryon's successor, Josiah Martin (1771-75), to oppose the House's authority, he was no more successful than Dobbs, and his whole administration was marked by political turmoil.

Royal Georgia was largely an extension of low-country South Carolina. Constantly threatened by Indians in the west and Spaniards in the south and lacking a profitable staple, it had not prospered in the twenty years under the trustees. Their insistence upon establishing a society of small farmers without slave labor and their failure to introduce representative government had retarded settlement. After the Crown took over the colony in 1754, the prospect changed rapidly. The introduction of rice and indigo cultivation, the large plantation system, and slavery inaugurated a period of great economic expansion and prosperity; the Crown's successful management of Indian affairs and the removal of the Spanish menace in Florida after 1763 accelerated the progress. Established families, such as the Habershams, Joneses, and Milledges, prospered quickly under the new regime, forming the basis for a plantation gentry similar to that in South Carolina. After 1755 Georgia was perhaps the most mobile society on the mainland, and immigrants from older Carolina families —like the Gibbons, Bullochs, Mulrynes, Bryans, and Elliotts—as well as from Britain—such as merchants John Simpson and Richard Cunningham Crooke or lawyer Alexander Wylly—quickly acquired wealth and social position. William Ewen, potter and servant, was only one of several individuals who rose from a background of moder-

35. On these disputes, see Clarke, *Arthur Dobbs*, 122-208.

ate means to become a successful and wealthy planter. By 1775 the
more successful among both the new and older families were coming
to constitute an economic, social, and political elite, although it was
neither so homogeneous nor so experienced as that of South Carolina
or Virginia.[36]

The most important characteristic of Georgia politics during the
royal period was the dominance of the governor. To avoid the difficulties caused by the rise of the lower houses elsewhere in the colonies,
the Crown had taken particular pains when instituting royal government to insure that the governor and Council would retain the upper
hand in Georgia politics. Georgia's lack of experience with representative institutions gave the Crown an important initial advantage.
More important, the royal governors, with the exception of the first,
Captain John Reynolds (1754-57), whose reckless and arbitrary behavior finally caused his removal after only about two years in office,
were capable men. Henry Ellis (1757-60), who succeeded Reynolds,
was one of the two or three most able governors in the southern
colonies during the entire period between 1689 and 1775. The prestige Ellis brought to the office Governor James Wright maintained for
most of his long administration from 1760 to 1775.

The great influence of the governor plus the comparative inex-
perience of the politicians who sat in the Georgia Commons House
of Assembly prevented that body from playing a major role in
Georgia government before the American Revolution. As the colony
began to prosper economically, however, the pace of political development quickened. Georgia packed into just two decades experiences
and developments that had taken a century or more in older colonies.
During the early 1760's there began to emerge in the Georgia Commons a group of able politicians who were becoming increasingly
aware of the Commons' potential role in Georgia affairs and its possible function as an agency through which they could fulfill their political as well as their economic and social ambitions. Unusually active
in shaping its proceedings in the years after 1763 were prosperous planters like Sir Patrick Houston, Joseph Gibbons, and John Milledge;
enterprising merchants such as John Simpson, Richard Cunningham
Crooke, and Edward Telfair; and professional men with interests in

36. See James R. McCain, *Georgia as a Proprietary Province; the Execution
of a Trust* (Boston, 1917); Saye, *New Viewpoints*, 51-133; and Abbot, *Royal Governors*, 3-33.

planting like the three speakers, lawyers Alexander Wylly and Archibald Bulloch, and physician Noble Wymberly Jones. Inspired by the example of the South Carolina Commons—one of the most powerful of colonial lower houses—and stimulated by the debate with Britian after 1765, which emphasized the necessity of a strong representative assembly, these men looked forward to the Commons' becoming the center of political power in Georgia. Under their leadership the Commons repeatedly tried to enlarge its sphere of influence. After 1765 it put forth claims to many of the powers gained by other legislatures earlier in the century, and, although it enjoyed only indifferent success, it demonstrated its ability to cope effectively with Governor Wright, battling him to a draw in an important fight over the governor's right to reject the speaker in the early 1770's. Wright's careful supervision prevented it from attaining the power acquired by lower houses elsewhere in the colonies, however, and only with the Revolution did the representative element in Georgia finally attain political dominance.[37]

By the decade of the 1760's each of the southern royal colonies had been through a series of common economic, social, and political experiences. The emergence of advanced economic institutions had been accompanied both by the rise of social and political elites and by the development of mature political systems. The extent, degree, and particular nature of these developments varied from Virginia, the oldest overseas colony, to Georgia, the youngest pre-1763 continental establishment, but in all four colonies the over-all pattern was similar. The central feature of their increasing political maturity was the rising power and prestige of the lower houses of assembly, which had, gradually in Virginia and the Carolinas and quite suddenly in Georgia, come to occupy the center of the political stage and to serve as the vehicles through which the local elites advanced their interests and the welfare of the colonies.

37. Abbot, *Royal Governors*, and "The Structure of Politics in Georgia: 1782-1789," *Wm. and Mary Qtly.*, 3d Ser., 14 (1957), 47-65. For a list of the leaders of the Commons from 1755 to 1775, see Appendix III.

PART II

CONTROL OVER FINANCE

We the only representatives of the Inhabitants of this Province will never Submitt to any encroachment upon their Sacred, and most Valuable Rights. They have Constituted us the sole Judges and delegated to us alone the power of determining what Taxes Assessments or Impositions they are able to bear, this fundamental and inherent right, we can never Suffer You to break in upon nor permit any Addition to be made to or Diminuation from the Matter manner or time We find expedient to fix upon.

—South Carolina Commons House of Assembly
to Council, June 1761

It has been a Policy of the Subtle People of North Carolina never to raise any money but what is appropriated, to pretend and insist that no Publick money can, or ought to be paid, but by a Claim given to, and allowed by the House of Burgesses.

—North Carolina Governor George Burrington,
February 1732

CONTROL over finance was the cornerstone of legislative power in the British colonies in America. From their inception the representative assemblies had enjoyed the power to tax and, because governors were unable to govern without money, early found they could grant that money on their own terms, extracting important concessions from their governors in the process. The terms they dictated were designed to extend their authority. They demanded the sole

power to frame all money bills, denying the right of both governors
and councils either to initiate such measures or to propose amendments to them; by adhering strictly to this policy, they succeeded in
depriving the executives of any share in the taxing power other than
the mere formality of finally accepting or rejecting the revenue
bill.   They insisted upon auditing accounts of all officers who
handled public money, thereby acquiring a measure of control
over executive officers and insuring against misappropriation of public funds.   They obtained power to determine how public money
should be spent by strictly appropriating all taxes and occasionally
even appointing committees to supervise the expenditure of particular sums.   Finally, they sought with less success authority to issue
paper money both to meet financial demands upon emergencies and
to provide their colonies with a sufficient circulating medium.   The
attainment of these powers gave the lower houses in the southern
royal colonies an almost ironclad control over financial matters that
enabled them to extend their authority into still other areas of colonial administration.

3

Money Bills

Power to tax was the most important possession of the lower houses. The Virginia legislature claimed it as early as 1624, and in subsequent years the Crown freely extended it to elective houses in all British colonies.[1] The official attitude as stated by Attorney General Philip Yorke and Solicitor General Clement Wearg in 1724 was that "a Colony of English Subjects . . . cannot be Taxed but by the Parliament of Great Britain or by and with the Consent of some Representative Body of the People . . . properly Assembled by the Authority of the Crown."[2] Because Parliament did not undertake to tax the colonies directly before 1764, authority to tax fell to the lower houses. Early in their histories, the representative assemblies in the southern royal colonies tried to strengthen their hold on the taxing power by claiming the sole right to frame money bills. Seeking to limit the power of the governors and councils to either accepting or

1. W. W. Hening, ed., *The Statutes at Large: Being a Collection of All the Laws of Virginia . . .* , 13 vols. (Richmond, 1809-23), I, 124; hereafter cited as Hening, ed., *Va. Statutes*. Although it repeatedly asserted its right, the Virginia Burgesses did not secure an exclusive power to tax until 1666. For a discussion of the controversy, see Elmer I. Miller, *The Legislature of the Province of Virginia* (N. Y., 1907), 157-59; William Z. Ripley, *The Financial History of Virginia* (N. Y., 1893), 93-97; Virginia Council, "Account of the Government of Virginia," May 4, 1683, CO 1/51, No. 105; Additional Instructions to Lord Howard, Dec. 3, 1683, CO 5/1356; Lord Howard to Lords of Trade, Feb. 10, 1685, CO 1/59, No. 17; Nicholas Spencer to Lords of Trade, Feb. 2, 1687, CO 1/61, No. 58; Instructions to Jeffrey Jeffries, May 22, 1691, CO 5/1306; May 24, 1684, Henry R. McIlwaine and John P. Kennedy, eds., *Journals of the House of Burgesses of Virginia*, 13 vols. (Richmond, 1906-15), *1660-93*, xlix-l, 252; hereafter cited as *Va. Burgesses Journals*.

2. Jamaica was under consideration. Extract of Yorke and Wearg's report to the Board of Trade, May 18, 1724, Shelburne Papers, LXXIV, 79-80, William L. Clements Library, Ann Arbor, Mich.

rejecting such measures in their entirety, they demanded an exclusive right to initiate all revenue bills and denied the power of the upper houses to propose amendments to them.

The lower houses had English precedents for the exercise of this right. Before the end of the sixteenth century the House of Commons had claimed the exclusive authority to frame money bills, because, in theory at least, it represented all inhabitants of the realm except members of the House of Lords and the royal family. Despite vigorous protests from the Lords, the Commons managed to establish that claim in the years between the Restoration and the Glorious Revolution, leaving to the Lords only the power to accept or reject the completed revenue measure. The Commons could and through Queen Anne's reign occasionally did tack measures unpopular with the Lords to money bills and refused to permit the Lords to amend them. The Lords had either to pass the measure or to reject the entire revenue law. To decrease further the power of the Lords, the Commons interpreted the term money bill very broadly to include both general taxes for governmental expenses and local levies for private benefit, such as the taxes collected by turnpikes and parish levies.[3]

The Crown sought to prevent a similar development in the colonies by instructing its governors to deny the lower houses the sole right to frame revenue measures.[4] Imperial authorities preferred for governors to prepare an estimate of expenses to form the basis for levying taxes. In the event that tax bills originated in the legislature (as was the case in every colony), they instructed the governors to insist upon the equal right of the council to initiate them, thereby hoping to establish and maintain executive influence in modeling tax legislation. To prevent such influence, the lower houses opposed this instruction, steadfastly adhering to the view that the electors, as the South Carolina Commons declared in 1761, had "Constituted us the sole Judges and delegated to us alone the power of determining what Taxes Assessments or Impositions they are able to bear."[5] In Virginia, North Carolina, and Georgia, the lower houses won the

3. A brief account of the Commons' winning control over money bills is in Sir William Searle Holdsworth, *A History of English Law*, 12 vols. (Boston, 1903-38), X, 586-87.

4. Labaree, ed., *Royal Instructions*, I, 112-13.

5. June 13, 1761, S. C. Commons Journals, CO 5/479, p. 142.

exclusive right to frame money bills with little opposition from either the governors or the upper houses; but the South Carolina Commons secured it only after a spirited thirty-year contest with the Council.

The right of the Council to share in preparing tax measures was probably the most divisive issue in South Carolina politics during the middle decades of the eighteenth century. The Commons House took the initiative in formulating such laws early in the proprietary years and introduced nearly all revenue bills throughout the colonial period. Beginning with the establishment of royal government in 1721, however, the Council claimed equal rights in such matters on the basis of the royal instructions which stipulated that the two houses should enjoy the same privileges in framing money bills. Although the Commons never acknowledged the right of the Council and always rejected its tax bills upon the rare occasions when it did initiate them, the Council managed to play a significant role in framing tax legislation for most of the first two decades under the Crown. Until the mid-1730's, councilors participated with members of the Commons in drafting such laws, and the Council itself occasionally exercised the right of amendment, although the Commons objected as early as 1725. Not until after 1735, when the Commons began to develop a greater awareness of its own importance and consciously sought to enlarge its sphere of authority during the administrations of the elder William Bull and James Glen, did it make a concerted attempt to deprive the Council of its privileges. Success came only after a prolonged and severe struggle.

For the first fifteen years of royal government joint committees of the two houses handled all of the preliminary steps in drafting tax legislation. A committee on petitions and accounts examined and reported on all claims against the public for services performed during the preceding year.[6] After the Commons had considered and amended this report, it referred it to a second committee, which tabulated the claims that had been allowed and formed an estimate. A third committee then examined the treasurer's accounts to determine the amount of money remaining in the treasury from the year before, subtracting that sum from the estimate. Finally, a fourth committee prepared a tax bill to provide for the difference. The first three committees were joint committees, and councilors partici-

6. Beginning in 1732 South Carolinians worked on credit and were paid ex post facto, a system also followed in North Carolina and Virginia.

pated both in allowing claims and in forming the estimate—the two initial steps in creating the tax bill.[7]

In the 1730's the Commons took steps to exclude the Council from these committees. By February 1737, and possibly two years earlier, the Commons was appointing its own committees and intentionally forgetting to invite the Council to participate. For a time the Council did not protest, but in February 1737 it asked for a conference on that year's tax bill. The Commons gave a preview of its future policy by replying that it could not "be justified by the Usage of Parliament in appointing a Committee of this House to confer with the Council on Supplies granted to his Majesty." But the councilors persisted, accusing the Commons of attempting to deprive it of its long-standing *"right* in *altering* and *amending* the Estimate." The Council's arguments carried little weight with the representatives. They argued that their exclusive right to initiate money bills derived "from the ancient and fundamental Constitutions" of England. Asserting that no lower house had the power "to alienate or surrender any of the just Rights and Privileges of the People they represent," they denied that any local precedents or customs could deprive them of their rightful privileges—a position strikingly similar to that taken by later royal governors, who, turning the argument around, declared that colonial customs could not deprive the Crown of its rights. Although the Council would not concede the validity of the Commons' claim, it finally agreed to pass the tax bill without conferring on the estimate in order to prevent a legislative impasse. Thereafter the Commons used this affair as a precedent and refused to permit the Council to share in the committee on petitions and accounts, thereby excluding it from any part in preparing tax bills.[8]

A longer and more bitter contest developed over the Commons' attempt to deprive the Council of the right to amend money measures. Under the proprietors and during the first years of royal government, the Commons repeatedly allowed the Council to amend and alter such bills as a matter of course.[9] Not until December 1725 did the Commons first raise constitutional objections. Its refusal to

7. Smith, *South Carolina as a Royal Province*, 280-82, gives a good description of the procedure for passing money bills.

8. Commons Journals, Feb. 24, 1737, *S. C. Col. Recs., 1736-39*, 245, 249-51.

9. Feb. 23, Oct. 5, 1723, S. C. Commons Journals, CO 5/426, pp. 97-103, CO 5/427, p. 16; Smith, *South Carolina as a Royal Province*, 289-91.

accept a number of the Council's amendments to the annual tax bill produced a deadlock between the two houses that ultimately led to a short prorogation. At the next session, the Commons tried to strengthen its position by putting the argument on constitutional grounds and denied the Council's right of amendment. When the Council replied that Governor Nicholson's thirty-fifth instruction guaranteed it that right, the Commons declared that the undoubted right solely to frame all money bills enjoyed by the representatives of the people of England could not be denied the representatives of the people of South Carolina. In attempting to reconcile the existence of this right with the royal instructions, the Commons speciously argued that the term money bill as used in the instructions applied only to paper money bills and not to tax measures. Crown officials later repudiated the Commons' contentions, but the Council, because of the urgent need for money, backed down and passed the measure without amending it.[10]

Seven years later the Commons went still further and refused even to confer with the Council upon proposed amendments. When the Council suggested several amendments to the 1732 tax bill, the Commons declared sharply "that it is the undoubted priviledge of this house to frame alter and Amend all Tax bills with out the Consent of his Majesty's Council" and adopted the rule "that for the future this house will not Conferr with his Majesty's Council or a Committee thereof on any tax bill that Shall be brought into this house or upon any part or paragraph of any bill for the explaining or amending any Such Tax Bill."[11]

Despite its adamant stand, however, the Commons partially relaxed this rule in May 1733. Although still declining to confer formally with the Council on money measures, it did agree to hear the Council's proposals for amending both the estimate and the tax bill. The Commons rejected three of the proposals—the most important of which was one to pay the annual salary of Chief Justice Robert Wright, who had previously incurred the Commons' wrath by violently opposing its act to suspend the writ of habeas corpus in cases of parliamentary privilege[12]—but accepted four others. Thus

10. Ralph Izard to Newcastle, Dec. 26, 1725, CO 5/387, ff. 192-93; Smith, *South Carolina as a Royal Province*, 291-94.
11. Feb. 12, 1732, S. C. Commons Journals, CO 5/433, p. 15.
12. Smith, *South Carolina as a Royal Province*, 42-48.

the Commons had once again permitted the Council to suggest amendments to a revenue bill. But five days later, when the Council asked for another conference to consider the three proposals the Commons had rejected, the Commons again took a firm stand, refusing to give up "the Priviledge Constantly claimed by this House of Framing Tax-Bills." On this occasion the Commons conveniently used constitutional principles to avoid paying an unpopular chief justice.[13]

The Council would not immediately abandon its attempt to pay Wright's salary. In March 1735 it dispensed with the formality of a conference and added to that year's tax bill an allowance of £2,100 currency for Wright. The Commons promptly rejected the tax bill and, to justify its action, adopted a vigorous set of resolutions that would have done justice to a seventeenth-century English House of Commons. Claiming for its constituents "all the Libertys and Privileges of Englishmen," the Commons argued that it possessed the same rights in "introducing and passing Laws for imposing Taxes on the People of this Province as the House of Commons of Great Britain have in introducing and passing Laws for imposing Taxes on the People of England." The Commons also outlined its future position by resolving "that after the Estimate is closed and added to any Tax Bills no Addition can or ought to be made thereto, by any other Estate or Power whatsoever but by and in the Commons House of Assembly."[14] When the legislature met again after a short prorogation, the dispute flared up anew. The Council once more claimed the power of amendment by virtue of Nicholson's thirty-fifth instruction and, for additional support, cited the 1721 election act, which, it argued, confirmed Nicholson's instructions concerning the legislature. The Commons replied that it had never consented to the Council's exercise of that power and contended that any reference which the election law had to Nicholson's instructions could not deprive the House of a fundamental right. Unable to surmount the Commons' opposition, the Council eventually gave up the point and passed the tax bill without providing for Wright's salary.[15] The

13. May 25, 30, 1733, S. C. Commons Journals, CO 5/433, pp. 61-64.
14. Mar. 28, 1735, *ibid.*, p. 45.
15. Apr. 23, 1735, *ibid.*, pp. 49-50. Not until May 1736, after the governor had presented the Commons with a royal warrant commanding it to pay Wright, did it agree to allow him £700 salary for his last three years. That sum was only a fifth of the total amount due, but the Commons repeatedly refused requests for a larger amount. Smith, *South Carolina as a Royal Province*, 301.

Council's surrender in this instance, coupled with its temporary relinquishment in 1737 of the customary practice of appointing some of its members to meet with those from the Commons on the joint committee on petitions and accounts, seemed to indicate that it had abandoned all claims to rights in forming money bills.

Any delusions which the Commons held to this effect were of short duration, however, for the Council resumed its claims early in 1739 and provoked a dispute which continued for almost a year. Preliminary skirmishes began in February 1739, when the Council requested the appointment of a joint committee to review petitions and accounts according to pre-1735 practice, only to be refused by the Commons.[16] This interchange laid the groundwork for a turbulent controversy. The following April the Council tried to force the issue by amending two money bills, the first to keep and maintain a watch in Charleston and the second to place a duty on Negroes, liquor, and merchandise. The Commons passed over the first measure, expressing confidence "that the Amendments made by your House were made in the Hurry of Business and without considering this Bill as a Tax Bill," but when the Council amended the second bill the Commons promptly defended its privileges. By 1739 the resolutions of 1735, originally conceived as an expedient to avoid paying Chief Justice Wright, had hardened into constitutional principles which had become an end in themselves. The Commons steadfastly refused to relinquish its "undoubted Right and Privilege" to have the "Commencement and sole modelling of all Laws for imposing Taxes." Both houses revived the arguments they had used in 1735, and the ensuing deadlock was broken only by a temporary adjournment.[17]

Upon reconvening in May, the two houses fell into the same dispute. Contention now revolved around the annual tax bill. At the beginning of the session, the Council censured the Commons for having adjourned without solving the chronic problem of preventing the desertion of slaves to St. Augustine in Spanish Florida and accused it of having neglected its real duty of protecting the property of its constituents because it "could not agree with us about your own imaginary Privileges as a House." The Council also refused to proceed further with the tax bill until it had examined all accounts and vouchers relating to the estimate, observing that the "People have

16. Commons Journals, Feb. 8-9, 1739, *S. C. Col. Recs., 1736-39,* 622-24.
17. Commons Journals, Apr. 5-13, 1739, *ibid.,* 689, 695-704.

no other Check or Controul upon their Representatives making too free with their Pockets." The Council's charges enraged the Commons, which appointed a committee to draw up reasons to support its privileges and vindicate its conduct.[18]

The committee's report, adopted by the Commons on June 5, 1739, is one of the clearest and most forceful assertions of the rights of the legislative body and its constituents made in the southern royal colonies in the eighteenth century. The Commons' position had over the years become both more firm and more elaborate. The basic assumption in its report was that colonists brought the rights of Englishmen and the fundamental principles of the British constitution with them when they migrated to America. That the taxing power should reside in the hands of the people's representatives and that the exclusive right of framing money bills should be vested in the House of Commons were among the most important of those principles. "His Majesty's Subjects coming over to America," the report declared, "have no more forfeited this their most valuable Inheritance than they have withdrawn their Allegiance." Nor, the report continued, could any precedents or royal instruction deprive them of the benefits of the British constitution, which they derived "from the very Essence and Frame of it, and not from any Charter of Concession from the Crown." Arguing that instructions were "Directions only, to guide the Judgement and Discretion of the Governour," and not "absolute Edicts," it categorically denied that "a Royal Order" could "qualify or any wise alter a fundamental Right from the Shape in which it was handed down to us from our Ancestors." "The Power of raising and levying . . . Money is of the many Privileges we enjoy; the most essential; and upon which all the rest seem to depend," the report declared. "If that Corner Stone is once removed, the Superstructure of Course will fall to the Ground." Despite its eloquence, the Commons' report did not convince the Council, and on June 7 the legislature adjourned until September without reaching any agreement on the tax bill. After the adjournment, Lieutenant Governor William Bull I dissolved the Commons and called for new elections.[19]

The new Commons House that assembled in Charleston the following November was no less tenacious of its privileges than the old

18. Commons Journals, May 30-31, 1739, *ibid.,* 706-7, 710-11.
19. Commons Journals, June 5, 1739, *ibid.,* 717-23.

one. At the previous session, the Council had waived at least temporarily its claim to the right to participate in the committee on petitions and accounts.[20] Now it once more insisted upon participating
in that committee as well as committees on the treasurer's and powder
receiver's accounts. Again the Commons adamantly refused to agree
to such an arrangement, sending the petitions and accounts to the
Council only after its committee had finished examining them and
prepared its report. The pressing need for a tax bill finally induced
the Council to forego again the privilege of participating in the petitions and accounts committee, but it declared that it would not admit
this instance "as a Precedent for any future Proceedings in the like
Case."[21]

The dispute over the Council's right to amend money bills was
also reopened at this session. After a month of heated debate, both
houses agreed to appoint committees to confer jointly on the method
of passing bills. This conference reached a temporary solution: the
Upper House could send down to the Commons along with the tax
bill a schedule of amendments. If the Commons approved them, it
would incorporate them into the bill before returning it to the Upper
House for final passage. This arrangement was a convenient compromise. It allowed the Council to suggest amendments but reserved
to the Commons the actual process of adding them. Both houses
viewed the agreement as temporary. Each declared that it should
not constitute a precedent and offered the urgent need for money as
the excuse for accepting it. The Council asserted that the agreement
did not abridge "the just Claim which this House hath to amending
Money Bills in the usual Manner," while the Commons resolved that
"the Privileges of this House in regard to the sole Right of introducing, framing, altering and amending subsidy Bills ought to remain
sacred and inviolable not-withstanding the said Example." Nevertheless, the agreement proved satisfactory. Both the duty bill and
the tax bill, which included provisions to maintain the watch in
Charleston, were adopted, ending the year-long controversy.[22]

Although both houses viewed the 1739 rules of procedure as temporary, they followed them for nearly a decade. Once, in April 1740,

20. Commons Journals, June 1-2, 1739, *ibid.*, 713-14.
21. Commons Journals, Nov. 22, 27-28, Dec. 8, 1739, *ibid.*, *1739-41*, 41-42, 52,
57-58, 60-61, 135-36.
22. Commons Journals, Dec. 8-18, 1739, *ibid.*, 90-93, 97-98, 122, 131-43.

during an emergency, the Commons House agreed to amendments made directly by the Council to a bill providing money for Oglethorpe's abortive expedition against Florida, taking care to reassert its privileges and declared that its action should not serve as a precedent.[23]   Usually, however, the Commons sent a message to the Council at each session allowing it to submit a schedule of amendments to the tax bill according to the agreement of 1739.   The Commons accepted some of these amendments, although it usually denied the right of the Council to suggest them, and rejected others.[24]   Thus, even when the Commons permitted the Council to submit amendments, it effectively curtailed the Council's power to amend money bills, making it entirely dependent upon the will of the Commons.

This arrangement persisted until 1748, when the Commons finally took steps to strip the Council of its privilege to suggest amendments. In accepting four out of fourteen amendments proposed to that year's tax bill, the Commons declared in June that henceforth it would absolutely refuse to consider amendments from the Council.[25]   The Commons made few exceptions to this policy during the remainder of the colonial period, and its effect was to deprive the Council of any part in the amendment of money bills.   Although the Council repeatedly proposed amendments through the 1750's and 1760's, the Commons consistently rejected them with no major objection from the Council.[26]

Just as the Commons after 1739 succeeded in depriving the Council of the privilege to amend money bills, so after that date did it also deny the Council any share in initiating them.   The Commons refused upon all occasions to entertain any proposal from the Council that involved appropriating money.   When the Council suggested a conference between committees of the two houses upon an estimate of expenses of certain Indian affairs in April 1747, the representatives agreed to confer but ordered its committee not to discuss "any Esti-

    23. Commons Journals, Apr. 5, 1740, *ibid.,* 301-2.
    24. The Commons accepted such amendments in Mar. 1741 and Mar. and May 1743 and rejected others on six different occasions between Mar. 1741 and June 1747.   Commons Journals, Mar. 23, 1741, *ibid., 549-50;* Mar. 5, 1742, *ibid., 1741-42,* 470-72; Dec. 1, 1742, May 3, 1743, *ibid., 1742-44,* 80, 424-26; May 25, 1744, May 23, 1745, *ibid., 1744-45,* 180-81, 540-42; June 13, 1747, *ibid., 1746-47,* 390-91.
    25. Commons Journals, June 27-29, 1748, *ibid., 1748,* 365-91.
    26. See Mar. 16-17, May 2, 1750, S. C. Commons Journals, CO 5/460, pp. 149-50, 156-57, 180-81; May 11, 1751, *ibid.,* CO 5/463, pp. 183-84.

mate of Expence" with the committeemen from the Upper House.[27]
The Commons not only refused to consider revenue bills introduced
by the Council, but it also eventually deprived the Council of the
privilege of examining the petitions and accounts that provided the
foundation for the annual tax bills. As noted earlier, the Commons
abandoned the practice of reviewing petitions and accounts in a joint
committee of members from both houses at least as early as 1737, and
after 1739 the Council, although it objected frequently, was forced
to content itself with examining them only after the committee of
the Commons had passed them and formed an estimate. This arrangement was not without its disadvantages, however. It provided
the Council with an opportunity to raise questions whenever articles
in the estimate were not properly supported by vouchers in the accounts, which it did repeatedly throughout the 1740's and early 1750's,
despite the declaration of the Commons in 1742 denying the right
of the Council "to demand Reasons from the Lower House, why they
give Supplies to his Majesty, for the Support of his Majesty's Government." These questions often consumed considerable time and were
a constant source of annoyance to the Commons. Still, for nearly
fifteen years the Commons followed the practice of sending accounts
to the Council for perusal while it was considering the tax bill.[28]

Not until 1755 did the Commons resolve to deprive the Council
of the privilege of examining the accounts. Again a constitutional
principle evolved out of practical necessity. In March 1755 a contest
developed between the two houses over the payment of the salary and
disbursements of James Crokatt, the colony's London agent, whom
the Commons had continued in office despite the Council's opposition. When the Council asked for the accounts in order to evaluate
Crokatt's service, the Commons, after considering "the many delays,
and how greatly the Public Business had been formerly retarded by
these Means," passed a resolution designed "to put an end to the
Custom of sending the Public Accompts" to the Council—an "improper and unparliamentary" custom, it declared, that could not "be
supported by the authority of a single Precedent from the practice of
Parliament in Great Britain." The Council had no intention of

27. Commons Journals, Apr. 14, 1747, *S. C. Col. Recs., 1746-47,* 220.
28. Commons Journals, May 6, 1740, Mar. 23, 1741, *ibid., 1739-41,* 331, 548-49;
Mar. 2-5, 1742, *ibid., 1741-42,* 453, 464, 470-72; May 23, 1744, *ibid., 1744-45,* 168;
May 17, 1750, S. C. Commons Journals, CO 5/460, p. 215.

acquiescing and continued to insist upon its right to examine the accounts. Twice that spring it refused its assent to bills, including provisions to pay Crokatt, without first viewing the accounts. At the insistence of Governor Glen, however, the Council finally agreed to a third bill containing the obnoxious provisions because it was needed to raise money to aid Virginia in the Seven Years' War. Thereafter, the Commons strictly adhered to the resolution it adopted at this time—"that for the future no Account petition or other Paper that shall be presented to or laid before this House of for or concerning any Claim or Demand whatever for any matter or thing done or to be done for the service of the Public shall be sent to the Council for their Inspection."[29]

When in April of the following year the Council demanded the accounts, the Commons made this resolution a standing order of the House. But the Council refused to proceed with the tax bill until it had examined the accounts. Governor Glen, interested in a hasty passage of the bill, which would have granted funds for him to build a fort in the Cherokee nation, counseled "temper and moderation" and advised a "mutual yielding, a willingness to meet one another halfway." But neither house would yield. The Commons contended that no precedents of the mother country justified its sending accounts to the Council and agreed to acquiesce only if the Council could show an instance in which the House of Commons had laid accounts before the House of Lords. The Commons admitted that accounts had previously been sent to the Council "some times privately, and at other times openly" but declared that "it is now time to put a stop to this encroachment, since the Council seem to claim it as their right." Glen at first sided with the Council and urged the representatives to give in. He contended that no harm had come from the Council's examining the accounts and begged the Commons not to "draw immediate and real Evils upon our Selves for fear of distant, perhaps imaginary Dangers." But Glen's plea fell on deaf ears. Adhering to its resolution, the Commons replied that permitting the Council to review accounts and vouchers was not a trivial matter, but on the contrary involved "the undoubted and most valuable rights and liberties of all His Majesty's loyal and dutiful Sub-

29. Mar. 21, 1755, Apr. 29, 1756, S. C. Commons Journals, CO 5/472, pp. 85, 113-15; William Henry Lyttelton to Board of Trade, June 19, 1756, CO 5/375, ff. 136-41.

jects the good People of this Province, from which the House hath
no power to depart."[30]

After a week of further delay, the Commons tried to cajole Glen
into siding with it. In a remonstrance of April 29 it reviewed the
controversy and appealed to Glen, as the "one in this Government
who knows the British Constitution" best, to dissolve the Commons
if it had assumed any powers not exercised by the House of Commons
in England or if it had in any way been backward in granting aids. If,
however, the Council was responsible for retarding the public business because of its unjust claims, it asked him to "suspend such of
them as have been the Occasion thereof, and appoint other Men who
have the Service of His Majesty, and the Security and Welfare of the
Province, more at Heart." Glen fell prey to the Commons' blandishments. He replied that the Council had erred in delaying the tax
bill, having chosen, it seemed to him, a poor time "for disputing
Questions about Rights and Privileges," and observed that "Such
Points ought not to be pressed, when the Delays and Difficulties that
are occasioned by moving in such Matters must draw us into imminent Danger, and may prove fatal to us." He further maintained
that the Council could not lose any "real Rights" by temporarily
abandoning its demand to examine accounts: a "yielding to the
Times for the preservation of the Province; a suspending the exercise
of certain Rights that they claim; a postponing Points of Priviledges to
a more convenient Season, could never be interpreted to be a ceding
or departing from their Rights." The Council yielded under Glen's
pressure, but another dispute prevented the passage of the tax measure. The Commons had refused to proceed to business without an
apology from the Council for keeping the legislature so long in session
over the tax bill, and when the Council refused its request, Glen
gave the Commons leave to adjourn until October.[31]

The controversy aroused considerable interest in the colony and
provoked a penetrating examination of the Council's function in
legislative affairs. On May 13, 1756, an article by "T——s W——t,"
tentatively identified by the historian Edward McCrady as Thomas
Wright, son of the former chief justice,[32] appeared in the *South-Caro-*

30. Apr. 2, 15, 21-22, 1756, S. C. Commons Journals, CO 5/472, pp. 92, 104-9.

31. Apr. 29, 30, May 3-4, 1756, *ibid.,* pp. 113-15, 119-24; Lyttelton to Board of
Trade, June 19, 1756, CO 5/375, ff. 136-41.

32. McCrady, *South Carolina under Royal Government,* 285.

lina Gazette. Siding with the Commons, the author questioned even the Council's right to sit as an upper house. It seemed odd to him "that one day they can be freemen, voting for representatives; the next day, representing themselves, as peers; and the third day, metamorphosed into a council of state, to approve or disapprove of what they had determined the morning or day before as an upper house." The implications in this passage are clear. As long as the Council continued to exercise legislative and executive functions—to handle the functions performed in Britain by both the Privy Council and the House of Lords—the South Carolina constitution would not be an accurate model of the British constitution. Moreover, the writer pointed out, even if the Council were admitted to be an upper house, it "would have no right to meddle in money matters, which can be made appear, from many precedents in the journals of the house of commons." Therefore, the demand of the Council to see the accounts when it could neither "lessen nor augment any sum" reminded him of the "novel of the curious impertinent in *Don Quixote*." He further demonstrated that if "the council should take upon them to shorten or increase any sum, provided in a schedule to the estimate, it would lead the assembly into a preplexing review of all the accounts again, who have examined them already with the eyes and judgments of the counsellors, as their representatives."[33]

This declaration in South Carolina of the inconsistency of the Council's acting as an upper house—conceived to justify the Commons' stand on the accounts—was a harbinger of things to come. Fifteen years later the long struggle between the Commons and the Council over finance would culminate during the great controversy over the Commons' power to send money to the supporters of the English radical John Wilkes in the Commons' demand that the Council be deprived of its legislative powers altogether. For the moment, however, the Commons confined its objections to the Council's privilege of examining the accounts.

On June 1, 1756, less than a month after the adjournment, South Carolina welcomed the arrival of a new governor, William Henry Lyttelton, appointed to succeed Glen. In view of the impending war with France, Lyttelton called the legislature back into session at the end of June. The Commons greeted the new governor with a liberal

33. *S.-C. Gazette* (Charleston), May 13, 1756.

aid bill containing all the provisions of the tax bill that had died in the legislative hassle the previous May. Again, when the bill came before the Council, it asked for the accounts, and the Commons once more refused to send them on the grounds that it "would be contrary to a standing Order of the House." When the old dispute seemed likely to be re-enacted, Lyttelton, realizing that the passage of the aid bill was urgent, persuaded the Council to accept it and relinquish the privilege of examining the accounts for the time being.[34] The Commons, however, regarded the Council's action as a precedent and never again sent it accounts for perusal; it had finally succeeded in stripping the Council of its last vestige of power in framing money bills.

Nevertheless, this long and bitter controversy continued to agitate South Carolina politics for the rest of the colonial period. Although the Commons managed to thwart all subsequent attempts by the Council to share in framing tax legislation, it sometimes had to resort to drastic expedients to do so. In the summer of 1761 it succeeded in denying the Council power of amendment only at the cost of two important bills.[35] The Commons had less difficulty in preventing a similar attempt in May 1762 and in stopping the Council's effort to initiate a money bill in September 1764.[36] But in August 1764 it again ran into trouble when the Council temporarily refused to pass the annual tax bill without a clause to pay Governor Boone £7,000 in back salary withheld by the Commons during the Gadsden election dispute.[37] More important, the Council also attempted in 1770 to delete an article for £1,500 sterling voted by the Commons to support the Bill of Rights Society in London, which was collecting money to aid radical John Wilkes, and thus initiated a prolonged and bitter contest over that article.[38]

34. June 25, 30, 1756, S. C. Commons Journals, CO 5/472, pp. 7, 10; Lyttelton to Board of Trade, July 19, 1756, CO 5/375, ff. 132-34; Lyttelton to Sir George Charleston, July 19, 1756, Newcastle Papers, Additional Manuscripts, 32866, f. 227, British Museum, London.

35. The two bills were the duty bill and the bill to continue the South Carolina regiment. June 13, 16, July 8-9, 22, 27, Aug. 4-6, 1761, S. C. Commons Journals, CO 5/479, pp. 142, 148, 180-84, 204-6, 210-11, 216-18.

36. May 28-29, 1762, S. C. Commons Journals, CO 5/480, pp. 133-36; Sept. 22, 1764, S. C. Commons Journals, XXXVI, 260-61, S. C. Arch. Dept.

37. Aug. 23, 25, Sept. 24, Oct. 3, 6, 1764, S. C. Commons Journals, XXXVI, 245-46, 250, 261, 266, 275, S. C. Arch. Dept.

38. See William Bull II to Lord Hillsborough, Apr. 15, 1770, S. C. Pub. Recs., XXXII, 256-59, S. C. Arch. Dept.

Elsewhere in the southern colonies the exclusive right of the lower house to frame money bills never constituted a serious issue. In Virginia neither the governors nor the Council attempted to initiate a money bill after 1689. The Council demonstrated its attitude in 1703 when it refused to express an opinion on raising money to aid New York before the Burgesses had acted, asserting that "in all grants of money, for the Council to declare their opinion before the House of Burgesses give their answer about them, is contrary to the practice and proceedings of Assemblys."[39] Still, the procedure followed in preparing money bills permitting the Council to exercise some influence in their formation. In Virginia, as in many colonies, the government operated on a deferred payment basis. Excepting military expenses, for which funds were allocated in advance, claims for goods or services rendered to the province during the tenure of one legislature were paid by the next. Each year before elections, individuals submitted their claims to the county courts, which certified and then transmitted them to the House of Burgesses. From at least 1684 on, these claims were reviewed by a standing committee which reported them to the House, recommending payment of those considered valid. The House debated, amended, and passed the report, eventually sending it to the Council for its approval. The Council could propose additions or amendments and, if the representatives accepted them, could add them to the report. Claims allowed by this procedure were paid by a poll tax proportioned among the counties by the Burgesses' committee on the public levy.[40]

In addition, the Virginia Council occasionally amended revenue measures, though the Burgesses never conceded its right to do so.[41] During much of the eighteenth century, relations between the Burgesses and the Council were so harmonious that the Burgesses was quite willing to confer with the Council over bills and usually accepted amendments without objection. Only twice during the entire period did any serious disagreements develop over this issue. In 1711, when the Burgesses objected strongly to several major amendments proposed by the Council to a bill to impose duties for paying expenses

39. Minutes of Virginia Council, Mar. 30, 1703, William N. Sainsbury *et al.,* eds., *Calendar of State Papers: Colonial Series* . . . (London, 1860——), *1702-3,* 302-3.

40. Taking the year 1728 as typical, this procedure can be traced in Feb. 2-Mar. 29, 1728, *Va. Burgesses Journals, 1728-40,* 6, 29, 34, 43, 45-46, 51.

41. See the incident in May 22-23, 1706, *ibid., 1703-12,* 199-203.

of the Tuscarora Indian War, the Burgesses denied the Council's request for a conference on the grounds that it was contrary to its "undoubted Right and priviledge . . . to Levy taxes and to grant Aids
and to direct the method of Levying the same." Similarly, in 1754
the Burgesses refused the Council's proposal to delete from a military
aid bill a rider providing for payment of the Burgesses' special agent
Peyton Randolph, whom the Council had opposed sending to England the previous year to present the Burgesses' case against Lieutenant Governor Robert Dinwiddie and the Council in the pistole
fee controversy. On both occasions the Council responded by rejecting the measures in question.[42] Obviously, the Virginia Council
played a significant part in forming money bills, but at no time did
it amend such measures or, for that matter, the book of public claims
without first obtaining the Burgesses' consent.

In North Carolina the story was much the same. Beginning in
1692 the North Carolina Lower House claimed and exercised without
much opposition the right to initiate money bills. Neither the governors nor the Council seems to have challenged that right. In fact,
the Council appears to have introduced only one such bill during the
entire colonial period: in 1762 it initiated a measure to appoint a
public printer and levy a tax to pay his salary. Promptly rejecting
the bill, the Lower House declared "that by the Antient undoubted
and Constitutional right and Privilege of this House all Bills by
which any Tax is laid ought to take their rise in this House."[43] As
in Virginia, however, the process of settling public claims enabled
the Council to play some part in shaping tax legislation. Rather
early in the colony's history, members of the Council sat with representatives on a joint committee of public claims—an arrangement
peculiar to North Carolina. Representatives were in a heavy majority on this committee, and since decisions were made by majority
vote, councilors had but a minor voice. The committee's duty was
to review public claims and report them to the House. After the

42. Dec. 17, 19, 21, 1711, Jan. 30, 1712, *ibid.*, 337-39, 345-47, 356-57; entries of
Dec. 15, 19, 1711, Louis B. Wright and Marion Tinling, eds., *The Secret Diary
of William Byrd of Westover, 1709-1712* (Richmond, 1941), 453-56; Dinwiddie to
James Abercromby, Sept. 1, 1754, Robert A. Brock, ed., *The Official Records of
Robert Dinwiddie*, 2 vols. (Richmond, 1883-84), I, 298-301; hereafter cited as
Brock, ed., *Dinwiddie Papers.*
43. Lower House Journals, Nov. 16, 1762, *N. C. Col. Recs.*, VI, 909.

report had been examined and perhaps amended by the House, it was sent to the Council for approval. The Council's concurrence was usually automatic; only rarely did it propose amendments. Since the taxes necessary to discharge public claims were usually prepared in the House, the Council's power to influence tax measures was distinctly limited.[44]

The North Carolina Lower House also denied the Council's right to amend money bills, though not always successfully. When the Council proposed several amendments to an aid bill in 1755, the Lower House at first took a strong stand, accusing the Council of acting "contrary to Custom and Usage of Parliament" and attempting "to Infringe the Right and Liberties of the Assembly who have always enjoyed uninterrupted the Priviledge of Framing and modelling all Bills by Virtue of which Money has been Levied on the Subject." But the Council insisted upon its amendments, and the House eventually accepted one of them, thereby weakening the strength of its assertion.[45] Again, in 1757 the House permitted the Council to amend an aid bill,[46] but thereafter it adopted a firmer policy. In 1759 it adamantly refused to allow the Council to delete from an aid bill a rider to appoint an agent for the colony, despite the fact that the Council ultimately rejected the bill.[47] Similarly, in 1773 the House would not permit the Council to insert allowances for the chief justice and attorney general in the tax bill and declared the attempt "an infringement upon the rights of the people and an open infraction of a fundamental principle in our Constitution."[48] By taking a stronger stand the Lower House had by the mid-1760's firmly established its exclusive right to frame money bills.

Similarly, the Georgia Commons House of Assembly asserted its exclusive right in drawing up money bills at its inaugural session in 1755 by initiating a tax bill without conferring with the Council.[49]

44. See Lower House Journals, Sept. 27, 1755, Dec. 20-23, 1758, *ibid.*, V, 523, 1086, 1098-99.
45. Lower House Journals, Jan. 4-6, 1755, *ibid.*, 287-89.
46. Lower House Journals, May 25-26, 1757, *ibid.*, 857-61.
47. Upper House Journals, May 16-17, 1759, *ibid.*, VI, 92-93; Arthur Dobbs to William Henry Lyttelton, May 25, 1759, Lyttelton Papers, Clements Lib.; Dobbs to William Pitt, May 18, 1759, Gertrude S. Kimball, ed., *The Correspondence of William Pitt,* 2 vols. (N. Y. and London, 1906), II, 108-9.
48. Lower House Journals, Dec. 20, 1773, *N. C. Col. Recs.,* IX, 781.
49. Commons Journals, Feb. 15, 1755, Allen D. Candler, ed., *The Colonial*

By this action the Commons established precedents that it should originate revenue measures and that the Council should not participate in any phase of the process. The procedure of framing tax legislation was similar to that followed in South Carolina. After a committee of the representatives had examined the treasurer's accounts and reported to the House, the Commons appointed two committees, one to prepare the tax bill and another to form an estimate of the public debt for the ensuing year. Upon completion of their tasks, the respective committees submitted reports to the House, which considered them, annexed the estimate to the tax bill, and after its third reading and passage sent it to the Council for approval or rejection.[50] This arrangement prevailed under the administration of Georgia's first royal governor, Captain John Reynolds, but his successor, Henry Ellis, modified it radically after his arrival in 1757. Ellis restored executive authority in framing money bills by persuading the representatives to accept his estimate of public expenses as the basis for its annual tax bill.[51] Ellis thus took over the function previously performed by a committee of the Commons. As author of the estimate the governor could exert great influence on the initial make-up of the tax bill. Ellis's system was followed until the Revolution.

The Commons nevertheless retained considerable control over money bills. Although the governor prepared the initial estimate, the Commons could amend it. In 1761 the Commons refused to provide salaries for public officers after Chief Justice William Glover testified that most of the officers were receiving adequate stipends from the Crown. Faced with remonstrances from both the governor and the Board of Trade, the Commons altered its stand the following year. But it did not forfeit its right to amend the governor's estimate[52] and retained the privilege to prepare and initiate actual tax legislation and all other money measures. Governor James Wright reported in 1767 that neither the governor nor the Council had ever

---

Records of the State of Georgia, 25 vols. (Atlanta, 1904-16), XIII, 56; hereafter cited as *Ga. Col. Recs.*

50. See Commons Journals, Jan. 15, June 30-July 7, 14, 19, 1757, *ibid.,* 113, 190-200, 211-12, 220. Unlike the lower houses in the other three colonies, the Georgia Commons voted money for the coming fiscal year, thereby providing for expenses before they were incurred.

51. Commons Journals, Dec. 12-13, 1758, *ibid.,* 341-43.

52. Commons Journals, Apr. 14, 1761, Oct. 26, 1762, *ibid.,* 512-16, 703-5. The Crown removed Glover for his part in this affair.

attempted to abridge that privilege.[53] Only once, in fact, does it appear that the Georgia Council tried to amend a money bill. In March 1767 the Commons, by two items in the tax bill, provided for the payment of Charles Garth, whom it had chosen to act as London agent without the Council's consent. Because the Council had not agreed to Garth's appointment, it proposed to strike out the items. The Commons refused to consider the proposal and declared that the Council's request for a conference on the matter was "contrary to the known Custom and Usage of Assembly." Unable to persuade the Commons to recede from that position and not wishing to bear the responsibility for weakening the public credit of the colony by rejecting the entire tax bill, the Council passed the measure without the desired amendments.[54] Thus, the Commons succeeded in repulsing the Council's sole attempt to amend a money bill, and the Council never again raised the issue.

By the end of the Seven Years' War all of the lower houses had to a considerable degree been successful in their quest for the exclusive right to frame money bills. Although the English House of Commons had won that right in the last half of the seventeenth century, London authorities had not extended it to the lower houses in the American colonies. Rather, they instructed royal governors to require the lower houses to share this right with the councils. Without exception the lower houses either ignored or opposed that instruction, and in South Carolina a long and intense controversy ensued between the two houses that lasted for over thirty years. In the end the South Carolina Commons secured exclusive authority over all revenue measures by depriving the Council of the right either to initiate or to amend any bill that levied a tax. In the other southern colonies the authority of the lower houses was not nearly so absolute, but it was still extensive. Neither the Virginia Burgesses nor the North Carolina Lower House tolerated any attempts by the councils to initiate money bills, although they occasionally allowed the councils to suggest amendments. They permitted the councils to participate in the committees that reviewed the public claims upon which the tax bills were based; but the councils' influence was not great, for in both colonies

53. Wright to Shelburne, Apr. 6, 1767, unpublished Colonial Records of Georgia, XXXVII, 183, Georgia Department of Archives and History, Atlanta.
54. Upper House Journals, Mar. 19-20, 1767, *Ga. Col. Recs.*, XVII, 363-68.

the lower houses held a majority on these committees and dominated their proceedings. In Georgia Governor Henry Ellis obtained for the executive some measure of influence in the initial make-up of the annual tax bills by establishing his authority to prepare the original estimates upon which the bills were based; but the Georgia Commons exercised an exclusive right to initiate all money bills without contest, and in 1767 easily resisted the Council's one attempt to amend such a measure.

The exclusive right to frame money bills was one of the most important elements in the lower houses' power to tax and perhaps the most important right won by the lower houses in the southern royal colonies. No political unit can exist without money, and as long as the lower houses' consent was required to raise money, they were certain to occupy a prominent place in the framework of government. Indeed, it was by an ingenious use of their control over finance that the lower houses were enabled to enlarge their powers so greatly in the years before 1763. After that date Parliamentary measures—in particular the Sugar Act, Stamp Act, and Townshend Acts—threatened to deprive them of or at least seriously to curtail their power over money. The lower houses met the threat with vigorous protests and resolute actions. For if they lost the exclusive power to tax, they could look forward only to the dismal prospect of losing as well all of the other rights and powers that they had gained and so carefully preserved in the years before 1763.

4

Accounts

W HILE the lower houses in the southern royal colonies were striving
to gain the exclusive right to frame money bills, they began to exercise the power to examine accounts of funds they had appropriated.
At first they used this power as a device to check on officers handling
colony revenues and to prevent misappropriation of public money,
but soon they realized that it was essential to control over finance.
The English House of Commons had secured it under the later
Stuarts and William III,[1] and the Crown tried to prohibit this development in the colonies. As early as 1680 instructions to governors
required that all money raised by colonial legislatures be given in the
King's name and audited by the auditor general of the plantations
in London or his deputy in America,[2] but they did not expressly deny
to the lower houses the privilege of examining or reviewing accounts.
As a result, the fine line between the privilege to examine and the
power to audit accounts was gradually erased by the lower houses
in all the southern royal colonies except Georgia, where, nonetheless,
the royal instructions regarding accounts never were precisely obeyed.

Among the lower houses in the southern royal colonies, only the
North Carolina Lower House encountered any serious difficulty in
asserting and maintaining its power to audit accounts. An intermittent conflict, which assumed serious proportions at the advent of
royal government under the administration of Burrington and again
in the 1750's and 1760's during the last years of Dobbs's tenure,

1. Holdsworth, *English Law*, VI, 175-76, X, 588.
2. Labaree, ed., *Royal Instructions*, I, 132, 172, 174-75.

centered around the perennial question of whether a royal instruction could supersede either colonial law or colonial practice and ultimately resulted in victory for the Lower House.

Under the proprietors the Lower House had exercised the power without contest and in 1715 had put the matter on a statutory foundation by passing a law to require all treasurers "to account to the Assembly for all Moneys received by authority of Assembly." On the basis of this law and earlier practice the House developed a system by which a joint committee, composed of from six to nine representatives and from two to three councilors, inspected and settled accounts of all public officers at each legislative session, submitting its report to both houses for approval. Because the majority in the committee made decisions, control was securely in the hands of the representatives.[3]

By the time the Crown assumed administration of the colony in 1729 this system was already a well-established feature of North Carolina legislative practice. A conflict developed when Burrington, on the assumption that his instruction took precedence over both the 1715 law and established practice, took steps to deprive the Lower House of power to audit accounts. When the Lower House in its customary manner ordered the public treasurer to lay his accounts before it for auditing in April 1731, Burrington objected and insisted that it apply to him when it desired to "Inspect" the accounts, thus implying that the legislature could do no more than examine accounts. Ignoring this attempt to channel its contact with public officers through the governor, the House contended that its right to audit accounts was firmly established by the 1715 law. It argued that it had "in conjunction with the Governor and Council . . . a larger Right than only to view and examine the Publick Accounts" and proceeded to pass the treasurer's accounts in the usual manner.[4] The question came up again at a subsequent session in 1733 with much the same result. When the Lower House ordered the powder receivers to submit their accounts to it in July, Burrington again contended that it should first ask him "to give Orders to the several

3. George Burrington's Remarks on North Carolina Acts of 1715, [1731], *N. C. Col. Recs.*, III, 188; Lower House Journals, Apr. 11-13, 1726, Apr. 20, 1731, Apr. 2, 1752, *ibid.*, II, 612-21, III, 293, IV, 1331; Upper House Journals, Sept. 28, 1736, *ibid.*, IV, 233; Report of Committee on Public Accounts, Dec. 13, 1757, *ibid.*, V, 793-805.
4. Lower House Journals, Apr. 26, 1731, *ibid.*, III, 299-301.

Receivers of the Powder Money (if they desire to inspect their Accounts) to attend at a time appointed for that purpose, and not to Vote it should be done." The Lower House reminded Burrington that the 1715 law required that anyone handling public funds should "at all times be hereafter accountable to the General Assembly or to such Commissioners as shall or may be appointed by the Authority of the Same and to no other person or persons whatsoever." The implication was that the right of the legislature to audit accounts was confirmed by law and could not be abridged by a royal instruction. Burrington would not admit the validity of the House's claim. He denied that it had any "Power to call for any Accounts but by Application first made to Your Governour" and boldly declared that he would not comply with laws that were contrary to the "King's Instructions." But he did consent to have the powder receivers submit their accounts to the House and did not during his brief tenure succeed in diminishing the control of the Lower House over officers' accounts.[5]

Gabriel Johnston, Burrington's successor, apparently preferred to ignore his instructions regarding accounts. During the first years of his tenure he was chiefly concerned with reaching a suitable quitrent settlement and did not object to the legislature's methods of passing accounts. On the contrary, he officially recognized them in February 1740 when he conceded, while pleading for an aid bill, "that no Colony under His Majesty's Dominions, had so much encouragement as this, to raise the necessary supplies, for the publick service . . . you may appropriate the sums you raise by the strictest Clauses you can invent, the Sheriffs, Receivers and every person concerned in collecting the Publick Revenues are of your own chuseing or recommending and are accountable to you, so that there is a moral certainty, that the money raised by any Law you pass, must be applyed according to the intention of that Law."[6]

Neither Burrington nor Johnston sent any officer's accounts to Britain and the Board of Trade complained in 1751 that it had never received any accounts from North Carolina. Johnston admitted that no accounts had ever been sent "either before my coming to the

5. Lower House Journals, July 11-13, 1733, Jan. 21, 1735, *ibid.*, III, 583-86, 594-95, IV, 121.
6. Upper House Journals, Feb. 7, 1740, *ibid.*, IV, 471-72.

Government or since" but promised to send them in the future.[7] He never fulfilled his promise, however; in 1755 Council President Matthew Rowan acknowledged that the "Treasurers Account has never been sent home" but assured the Board of Trade that newly appointed Governor Arthur Dobbs would "soon be able to regulate that matter."[8]

Indeed, with Dobbs's appointment imperial authorities took steps to bring North Carolina more closely under the influence of the Crown. Among other things, they attempted to undermine the colony's accounting system by disallowing the 1715 law making public treasurers accountable to the General Assembly on the grounds that it was "injurious" to the Crown's "rights and prerogative" and contrary to the royal instructions.[9] Along with the usual instructions regarding accounts, Crown officials gave Dobbs specific orders to inquire into the accounts of public officers and receivers since 1716 and to report his findings to the Treasury and Board of Trade.[10]

But Dobbs did not at first try to carry out his orders. Soon after his arrival in North Carolina he discovered that the Lower House was "much against the Auditors being Concerned in passing accounts."[11] Intent upon preserving harmony with the legislature, he resolved for the time being not to interfere with the traditional system of auditing accounts. He did, however, make an unsuccessful attempt to collect back accounts for transmission to England. To Dobbs's request for a statement of the books and accounts of public money, Alexander McCulloh, the Crown's deputy auditor in the province, replied that such books had never been kept and that "no Accounts of publick Money have ever been produced to me to be audited." The only accounts he had seen were those of Crown revenues submitted by the receiver of the quitrents; "all other Accounts have been passed in the Assembly without ever having been audited by me."[12] For nearly four years thereafter Dobbs carefully refrained from questioning the House's accounting methods.

7. Secretary of Board of Trade Thomas Hill to Johnston, Apr. 12, 1751, CO 5/323, p. 179; Johnston to Board of Trade, Sept. 16, 1751, *N. C. Col. Recs.*, IV, 1075.

8. Rowan to Board of Trade, Oct. 22, 1754, *N.C. Col. Recs.*, V, 144d.

9. Board of Trade to Crown, Mar. 14, 1754, *ibid.*, 107; Order in Council, Apr. 8, 1754, CO 5/297, f. 151.

10. Instructions to Dobbs, June 17, 1754, CO 5/324, pp. 86-88.

11. Dobbs to Alex McAulay, Mar. 17, 1755, DOD 162, f. 72, Northern Ireland Public Record Office, Belfast.

12. McCulloh to Dobbs, Dec. 24, 1754, *N.C. Col. Recs.*, V, 160-61.

Serious trouble between Dobbs and the Lower House over accounts did not develop until 1758. Upset because one of the treasurers had refused to reimburse him for some of his expenses in sending military expresses to New York, Dobbs denounced the accounting
system in a message to the Lower House, objecting to its appointing to its committee on accounts treasurers and other revenue officers.
Sharply rebuking Dobbs for attempting to interfere with its free
choice of appointment to committees, the House replied that it appointed the treasurers to the committee not because of their office
but because they were "unexceptionable" gentlemen.[13] Dobbs did
not intend to drop the matter, but before proceeding further, he
sought support from imperial authorities, suggesting to the Board of
Trade in May 1759 that the colony's public treasurers be replaced by
officers appointed by himself and the Council "who should account
with the Government here and with the Treasury in England."[14]

What began as a minor altercation arising out of Dobbs's pique
with the treasurers developed into a major controversy after 1760 as
Dobbs, increasingly irked by the treasurers' enormous influence in
the Lower House and by the House's lax methods in keeping accounts, vigorously tried to curtail its power over accounts. Although
he had received no encouragement from home, he renewed his attack
on the colony's accounting system in April 1760. Now he took exception to the treasurers' presenting their accounts without passing
them before the governor. The Lower House dismissed his complaints and pointed out that this method was "agreeable to Law"
and to the "uninterrupted usage" of the colony. Dobbs countered
that his instructions required that the accounts be audited and sent
home. But the House did not then have any more respect for royal
instructions than it had had under Burrington. It resolved that "the
Method Observed by the Treasurers in stating their Accounts" was
"agreeable to the direction of . . . several Laws of this Province . . .
And Consonant to Constant and uninterrupted usage" and denied
the validity of the instructions by declaring that the "method Proposed by His Excellency is unprecedented and repugnant to Law."
To add insult to injury, the House refused to grant Dobbs further
aid to carry on the war until he submitted accounts of funds it had
previously entrusted to him.[15]

13. Lower House Journals, Dec. 22-23, 1758, *ibid.*, 1096-99.
14. Dobbs to Board of Trade, May 18, 1759, *ibid.*, **VI**, 32-33.
15. Lower House Journals, Apr. 28-29, May 5, 1760, *ibid.*, 371, 373-74, 380-81.

In December 1760 Dobbs again complained to the Board of Trade about the "manner of passing the Treasurer's Accounts." The representatives, he reported, had taken their accounts "out of the governors and Councils Inspection and will not allow the auditor or Lords of the Treasury to interfere in their accounts but pass them as they please with or without Vouchers, and keep all their Accounts in the Clerks hands which ought to be kept in the Auditor's Office."[16] The Board of Trade agreed that "the Mode of passing the publick Accounts . . . appear . . . not only derogatory to the honor of the Crown but subversive of every principle of Policy which the wisdom of the Legislature here has prescribed by numberless Laws, for the security of the Subject in a matter so essential to his interest." Moreover, the Board wrote, "His Majesty's Instructions by which the mode of passing Accounts is directed, is founded upon the principle and practice of the Mother Country to which the constitution of the Colonies is to assimilate as near as different circumstances will admit." Although these words constituted an endorsement of Dobbs's position, they had little practical effect because the Board neither adopted nor suggested any course of action to change the situation.[17]

While Dobbs was unsuccessfully appealing to the Board of Trade for support to weaken the House's power over accounts, a serious disagreement between the councilors and the representatives over their respective rights in passing accounts clearly revealed that the Council played only a small role in auditing accounts. That disagreement involved the account of James Abercromby, whom the Lower House without the consent of either Dobbs or the Council had appointed London agent in 1758 during a dispute over what the colony should do with its share of a £50,000 Parliamentary grant to reimburse Virginia and the Carolinas for their war expenses. Because the number of representatives on the joint committee on accounts always exceeded by five to seven the number of councilors, the representatives always had a majority on all decisions. Neither Dobbs nor the Council was happy with this arrangement,[18] and, when in

16. Dobbs to Board of Trade, Dec. 12, 1760, *ibid.*, 320.
17. Board of Trade to Dobbs, Apr. 4, 1761, *ibid.*, 540.
18. See Dobbs's charge in Dec. 1760 that the Lower House members so dominated the accounts committee that they "made the Committee of the Councils attendance nugatory" and the Council's complaint in 1751 that its members had not even been consulted in preparing the committee's report. Dobbs to Board of Trade, Dec. 12, 1760, *ibid.*, 320; Lower House Journals, Oct. 10, 1751, *ibid.*, IV, 1295-96.

December 1762 the representatives pushed Abercromby's account through the joint committee, the Council took the unprecedented action of refusing to approve that item when the committee's report came before it. Recognizing that a Council veto of particular items in the report would seriously weaken its power over accounts, the Lower House took the position that a dissent to one item constituted a rejection of the entire report and ordered the treasurer to "have no regard to the said Accounts nor pay any Ballances which may thereby appear to be due." The House thought that the Council would not reject the whole report simply to prevent payment of Abercromby's account; but the Council did precisely that, and similar circumstances in December of the following year produced the same result.[19]

Taking the offensive in April 1762, the Council, probably with Dobbs's encouragement, intensified the dispute when it attempted to gain more influence in the accounting process. Refusing to participate in the joint committee where it was outnumbered, the Council insisted upon appointing its own committee to act separately. When the Lower House objected, the Council declared that it was its "undoubted and Constitutional right to allow or disallow the Public Accounts" and contended that the custom of a joint committee did not mean its committee was "not seperate and equal in their Rights with yours, or that they have not a right to meet, debate, and report, seperately." Taking the position that the Council could not unilaterally change a traditional practice of the legislature, the Lower House branded the Council's action "a new Invention" seemingly "calculated to Introduce a new unknown Constitutional power in the Council, Derogatory to the rights of this House." How this argument was resolved is not clear because there is no report of the committee on accounts for 1762; but almost certainly it was the Council that eventually gave in, for at the next session the legislature resumed the practice of passing accounts in joint committee.[20]

Throughout this dispute Dobbs continued complaining to the Board of Trade, finally submitting a copy of the treasurer's accounts in February 1763 after they had been audited by the joint committee.[21] His complaints were not without foundation, and imperial

19. Lower House Journals, Apr. 23, Dec. 11, 1762, *ibid.*, VI, 696, 964.
20. Lower House Journals, Apr. 27, 1762, Upper House Journals, Nov. 6, 1762, *ibid.*, 826-27, 841-42.
21. Dobbs to Board of Trade, Feb. 23, 1763, *ibid.*, 967.

authorities instructed William Tryon upon his appointment as lieutenant governor in 1764 to persuade the Lower House to conduct a
strict examination of accounts of public funds even though they
could not at that late date hope to deprive the Lower House of its
power to audit officers' accounts. Shortly after Tryon's arrival in
November 1764 Dobbs and the Council tried not only to execute but
also even to exceed this instruction by ordering the treasurers to submit their accounts to the secretary by June 1 of the following year for
a thorough examination by the clerk of the Council. But the treasurers appear to have ignored the order.[22]

Tryon attempted unsuccessfully to comply with this instruction
during his administration.[23] He wrote the Earl of Shelburne in 1767
that he had taken every public and private opportunity to recommend a "stricter examination of the Treasurers' receipts and disbursements" but that all of his efforts had come to naught.[24] Apparently
there were also internal political pressures that prompted Tryon to
continue his efforts. One observer reported that the remissness of
the treasurers in keeping accounts was an important cause of the
Regulator uprising, and in 1768 the Council suggested the appointment of a special committee to audit the accounts in order "to quiet
the minds" of the people.[25] In October 1769 Tryon presented the
House with an elaborate plan for keeping accounts and strongly
recommended that it appoint a standing committee to meet twice
yearly to examine and audit them. The House did not accept Tryon's
plan, but it did appoint the Council's long-time clerk, John Burgwin,
to prepare a statement of the accounts from 1748. Burgwin's report
revealed that substantial sums were due the colony in back taxes, in
particular from sheriffs who had been either remiss or fraudulent in
collecting taxes. To remedy this situation, the House in January
1771 finally required the treasurers to account more thoroughly, but
it did not alter the method of auditing accounts.[26] To the end of
the colonial period the legislature continued to settle accounts in the

22. Council Journals, Nov. 28, 1764, *ibid.*, 1088-89.
23. See Upper House Journals, May 3, 1765, Tryon to Board of Trade, Aug.
15, 1765, *ibid.*, VII, 42, 107.
24. Tryon to Shelburne, July 4, 1767, *ibid.*, 497.
25. Extract of a letter from a Carolinian to a Pennsylvanian, May 17, 1771,
Boston Gazette, Aug. 12, 1771, *N. C. Col. Recs.*, VIII, 637; Upper House Journals,
Dec. 2, 1768, *ibid.*, VII, 917-18.
26. Upper House Journals, Oct. 31, 1769, Lower House Journals, Nov. 6, 1769,
Jan. 24, 1771, *N. C. Col. Recs.*, VIII, 93-97, 139, 459-60.

representative-dominated joint committee. Both Burrington and Dobbs had failed to comply with their instructions to send accounts to England for auditing, and the Lower House's power over officers' accounts was as extensive in 1775 as it had been in 1731.[27]

Elsewhere in the southern royal colonies the right of the lower houses to audit accounts was neither a serious nor a persistent issue. In Virginia, the executive regularly transmitted accounts of the permanent Crown revenues—the quitrents, fines and forfeitures, and two-shilling-per-hogshead tax on tobacco[28]—to imperial authorities for auditing. All three revenues were under the direct supervision of the governor and Council, although the Burgesses attempted several times near the end of the seventeenth century to bring them under its control. In early 1688 the Burgesses unsuccessfully asserted its right to inspect the accounts of all fines and forfeitures collected in the colony, and during the next ten years frequent reports of the mismanagement of the revenue from the two-shilling tax on tobacco prompted suggestions, one by deposed councilor Philip Ludwell in 1689 and another by philosopher John Locke a short time later, that the Burgesses be extended that right. But imperial authorities largely ignored these suggestions, and the Burgesses could never win the power to examine the accounts of that revenue, quitrents, or fines and forfeitures.[29]

With regard to accounts of moneys voted by the Burgesses, the story was different. Throughout the eighteenth century the Burgesses freely exercised the power to examine these accounts. In 1691 it adopted the practice of appointing a public treasurer to oversee the collection, care, and disbursement of all moneys voted by the House. The treasurer was accountable to the House, and by 1700 it had become customary for the Burgesses at each session to appoint a committee to examine his books and report to the House. If the report was satisfactory, the Burgesses sent it up to the Council, whose con-

27. See Lower House Journals, Dec. 8, 1770, *ibid.*, 308.

28. The two-shilling-per-hogshead tax on tobacco was a perpetual tax voted by the General Assembly of 1680. The revenue arising from it was used to pay salaries of the governor and Council and to defray other executive expenses.

29. Nicholas Spencer to Lords of Trade, May 17, 1688, CO 1/64; Ludwell's Petition to the Crown, Sept. 19, 1689, and Howard's Answer, CO 5/1305; Benjamin Harrison's Memorial on Illegal Trading in Virginia, received July 11, 1698, CO 5/1309; Locke's Essay toward Remedys of Grievances of the Virginia Constitution, *ca.* 1698, Locke MSS, c. 9, Bodleian Library, Oxford Univ.

currence was usually a formality, for disagreements between the two houses over accounts were infrequent.[30] This method of passing accounts was followed during the entire royal period. The Burgesses also required all other officers charged with collecting taxes or duties arising from local laws to submit their accounts for inspection. These officers regularly accounted with the treasurer, who in turn accounted with the Burgesses, although the Burgesses often asked them to present to it accounts of revenues collected since last passing their accounts with the treasurer.[31] The Burgesses also rigidly supervised the accounts of any group, including royal officials, to whom it entrusted funds.[32]

For nearly thirty years after 1691 Virginia governors occasionally transmitted general statements of the treasurers' accounts to imperial authorities in compliance with royal instructions. Francis Nicholson did so yearly and sometimes half-yearly,[33] but his successors neglected this task until 1713, when the Board of Trade reminded Spotswood that it expected him to submit a "constant Account of the Receipts and Issues of the publick Revenues made up every half Year."[34] But even when governors sent statements of accounts home, the actual auditing remained in the hands of the Burgesses. The governors' statements were so general that it would have been impossible to conduct a detailed audit, and there is no evidence that Crown authorities ever tried to do so. Spotswood's successors altogether abandoned the practice of sending statements home, thereby ignoring the royal instructions and allowing the Burgesses to audit the accounts without interference from the executive or supervision from London.

30. Hening, ed., *Va. Statutes*, III, 92-94; Dec. 20, 1700, *Va. Burgesses Journals, 1695-1702*, 227; June 7, 1757, *ibid.*, *1752-58*, 490. The procedure in passing accounts may be traced in Feb. 19-Mar. 21, 1728, *ibid.*, *1728-40*, 23, 30, 37-38, 43.

31. For examples of such requests see Aug. 26, Sept. 25, 1734, Aug. 11, 1736, *Va. Burgesses Journals, 1728-40*, 178, 215, 252.

32. See Hening, ed., *Va. Statutes*, V, 401-4, VI, 435-38, 453-61, 521-30, VII, 9-25; Feb. 15-Mar. 8, 1728, July 2, 1730, *Va. Burgesses Journals, 1728-40*, 21-23, 32-34, 100-101.

33. These accounts may be found scattered through CO 5/1312, 1313, and 1314. See also Aug. 23, 1704, Oct. 12, 1705, *Journal of the Commissioners for Trade and Plantations*, 14 vols. (London, 1920-38), *1704-9*, 38, 168; hereafter cited as *Board of Trade Journals*.

34. Board of Trade to Spotswood, July 20, 1713, CO 5/1363; Spotswood to Board of Trade, July 26, 1712, Robert A. Brock, ed., *The Official Letters of Alexander Spotswood*, 2 vols. (Richmond, 1882-85), I, 164. Accounts sent by Spotswood are scattered through CO 5/1317 and 1318.

The South Carolina Commons' power to audit and review accounts of public officers was also extensive, although initially not so exclusive as that of the Virginia Burgesses. From 1707, when the Commons temporarily established its right to appoint a public receiver, until the end of the proprietary period, it had exercised this power in conjunction with the Council. During the royal period a 1721 law which brought all of the public officers under the control of the General Assembly confirmed the right of the two houses to audit accounts.[35] In execution of this law the legislature developed a system similar to the one followed in North Carolina by which joint committees examined and passed accounts of all officers handling colony revenues—including the public treasurer, powder receiver, commissary general, commissioners of Indian trade, comptrollers of country duties, commissioners of public works, and committee to correspond with the colony's agent in England. Although the Commons allowed the Council to participate in these committees in the first few decades of the royal period, the Commons always controlled them because it appointed the majority of their members.[36] The legislature followed this system of settling accounts with few exceptions until 1755.

Proprietary governors probably submitted accounts to the proprietors after they had been audited by the legislature,[37] but none of the royal governors tried to deprive the legislature of its power to settle accounts or seriously endeavored to comply with the royal instructions requiring them to send accounts to England for auditing. Governor Robert Johnson made a halfhearted attempt to execute those instructions in 1735 by requesting the Commons to state in the annual tax bill that money arising therefrom be accounted for "unto his Majesty, or the Lords Commissioners of his Majesty's Treasury, or the Lord High Treasurer." But the Commons refused the request by politely, if speciously, pointing out that the instructions did not require such a positive statement but merely implied that no revenue bills should "be passed wherein any Negative Words shall be inserted, not to have the same made liable to be accounted for unto his Majes-

35. Thomas Cooper and David McCord, eds., *The Statutes at Large of South Carolina*, 10 vols. (Columbia, 1836-41), II, xii, III, 148-49; hereafter cited as Cooper and McCord, eds., *S. C. Statutes.*

36. See Dec. 5, 1733, S. C. Commons Journals, CO 5/433, p. 11.

37. See Instructions to Governor Charles Craven, June 6, 1711, S. C. Pub. Recs., VI, 44, S. C. Arch. Dept.

ty, and to the Lords Commissioners of his Majesty's Treasury."[38]
Subsequent governors ignored the matter altogether, and, although
in the sixties and seventies some of them sent home copies of accounts
of South Carolina revenues for perusal by imperial authorities,[39] none
ever sent them for auditing.

If governors hesitated to upset the status quo, the Commons certainly did not. In the early months of 1739, while it was most actively engaged in winning the exclusive right to frame money bills, the
Commons attempted with temporary success to exclude the Council
from its share in auditing accounts. In response to the Council's
proposal for the appointment of the usual joint committee on treasurer's accounts in February 1739, the Commons replied that it no
longer intended to participate in such a committee, adding that it
had already appointed its own and suggesting that the Council do
likewise. The Commons' scheme was obvious. That the Council
had a legal right to share in auditing officers' accounts under the 1721
public officers' law it did not deny, but it hoped to undermine that
right simply by having its committee settle the accounts first, making
a second examination by the Council's committee unnecessary. For
the moment the Council was silent, but it recognized the implications
of the Commons' action and when the issue came up again the following May it appealed to the representatives to resume the practice of
auditing accounts in a joint committee. The Council vigorously
denied that the 1721 statute gave either house "a Right not only to
examine, but finally to adjust and settle . . . Accounts, by itself,
exclusive of the other House." "For to what Purpose," it argued,
"shall the other House, in such Case, examine them at all, afterwards?" The Commons ignored the Council's appeal, but the following November a newly elected House in a more conciliatory mood
switched its position, accepting an invitation from the Council to
appoint committees on both treasurer's and powder receiver's accounts to meet in a joint session with committees from the Council.[40]
The Commons thus temporarily abandoned its attempt to exclude the

38. Apr. 24, 1735, S. C. Commons Journals, CO 5/433, p. 51.
39. See July 9, 1764, *Board of Trade Journals, 1764-67*, 95; Report of Committee on Treasurer's Accounts, 1770-72, *Manuscripts of the Earl of Dartmouth*, II
(Historical Manuscripts Commission, *14th Report, Appendix, Pt. X* [London,
1895]), 119; hereafter cited as *Dartmouth MSS.*
40. Commons Journals, Feb. 9, May 31, 1739, *S. C. Col. Recs., 1736-39*, 623-24,
710-11; Nov. 22, 29, 1739, *ibid., 1739-41*, 41-42, 63.

Council from a share in examining accounts, and the legislature continued to settle accounts in joint committee for another fifteen years.[41]

Eventually, in 1755, the Commons succeeded in depriving the Council of its influence in auditing accounts. During a dispute over the appointment of an agent, the Commons resolved not to send any accounts to the Council for inspection in the future.[42] Thereafter, only a committee of the Commons audited all officers' accounts, although the Council could require officers to submit their accounts for its perusal.[43]

The situation in Georgia was much different from that in the other three colonies. The Commons House there had only limited authority over accounts except for a brief period near the end of Reynolds's administration, when it exercised broad powers in that area. Reynolds's successor, Henry Ellis, reported upon his arrival early in 1757 that in an attempt to embarrass the new administration Reynolds and his cohort, William Little, had instigated the "Assembly to usurp the power of Auditing the Accounts and Issuing the publick money." That "Measure," Ellis wrote, "at one stroke put our Assembly on the footing of that of Carolina, and subverted that check which ought to subsist for curbing the proceedings of that body."[44]

A skillful tactician, Ellis immediately set about to restore the right to audit accounts to the executive. In April 1757 he inaugurated the practice of the Council's calling in and examining the accounts, and the following June he persuaded the Commons to be

41. Commons Journals, Dec. 2, 1741, *ibid., 1741-42*, 281; Feb. 23, 1744, *ibid., 1744-45*, 8; Nov. 26, 1746, *ibid., 1746-47*, 52; May 13, 1749, Mar. 22, 1755, S. C. Upper House Journals, XVI, Pt. II, 26, XXIV, 45-46, S. C. Arch. Dept. See also entry of May 11, 1754, Treasurer's Ledger B, 49, S. C. Arch. Dept.

42. Mar. 21, 1755, S. C. Commons Journals, CO 5/472, p. 85; Edmund Atkin's Wrong Practices, 1755, in Greene, ed., "South Carolina's Colonial Constitution," *S. C. Hist. Mag.,* 62 (1961), 76.

43. May 6-10, 1758, S. C. Upper House Journals, XXVII, 89-92, S. C. Arch. Dept. There is no record of a meeting of a joint committee on accounts after 1755. Entries of 1756-59, *ibid.,* XXIV, XXVI, XXVIII, *passim.*

44. Ellis to Board of Trade, May 5, 1757, CO 5/646. According to Ellis, Reynolds allowed the Commons to assume these powers with the design of embarrassing Ellis's administration. Ellis to Board of Trade, Mar. 11, 1757, *ibid.;* Ellis to William Henry Lyttelton, June 22, July 8, July 21, 1757, Jan. 21, 1758, Lyttelton Papers, Clements Lib.

satisfied with merely inspecting the accounts.[45] So successful was Ellis that in August 1757, after he had been in the province only a little over six months, he could inform the Board of Trade that he had restored the "right of Auditing the Accounts . . . to the Governor and Council to whom it properly belongs."[46] Only once thereafter, in 1773, after the taxes for the past several years had fallen short of the sums appropriated, did the Commons, upon the recommendation of the acting governor, James Habersham, conduct a strict examination of the treasurer's accounts.[47] On all other occasions, the governor and the Council audited those accounts, submitting them to the Commons for its inspection at each session of the legislature.[48] After the governor and Council had finished with the accounts, the Crown's deputy auditor in Georgia also audited them.[49]

Although its power over the treasurer's accounts was limited, the Georgia Commons seems to have exercised considerable authority over accounts of other revenue officers to whom it had entrusted funds. Georgia statutes required most revenue officers to account with the General Assembly.[50]

By 1763 the lower houses in North Carolina, Virginia, and South Carolina had exercised for many years the power to examine and audit the accounts of all public officers charged with the care of provincial revenues. That power had been won by the English House

45. Council Journals, Apr. 20, 1757, Commons Journals, June 30, 1757, *Ga. Col. Recs.*, VII, 545, XIII, 190.

46. Ellis to Board of Trade, Aug. 1, 1757, CO 5/646. Ellis's success was possible in part because Georgians were so relieved to be rid of Reynolds that they were willing to take a conciliatory position toward Ellis. See Thomas Rasberry to Samuel Lloyd, Nov. 1, 1758, Lilla M. Hawes, ed., *The Letter Book of Thomas Rasberry, 1758-1761* (Georgia Historical Society, *Collections*, 13 [1959]), 18.

47. See Upper House Journals, Dec. 10, 1772, *Ga. Col. Recs.*, XVII, 668-69; Commons Journals, Dec. 18, 1772, Aug. 10, 1773, *ibid.*, XV, 353, 489-91; Habersham to Hillsborough, Apr. 30, 1772, unpubl. Ga. Col. Recs., XXXVII, 635, Ga. Dept. of Arch. and Hist.; Habersham to James Wright, Dec. 4, 1772, *The Letters of the Hon. James Habersham, 1756-1775* (Ga. Hist. Soc., *Collections*, 6 [1904]), 217; hereafter cited as *Habersham Letters*.

48. Council Journals, Apr. 1759-Dec. 1762, *Ga. Col. Recs.*, VIII, 11, 319, 342, 586, 594, 598, 600, 619, 648, 687, 711, 718, 722, 756, 776; Commons Journals, Dec. 12-13, 1758, Nov. 13, 1764, *ibid.*, XIII, 341-43, 594.

49. Commons Journals, Feb. 16, 1762, *ibid.*, 675-76; Treasurer's Accounts, 1761-65, unpubl. Ga. Col. Recs., XXVIII, Pt. II-A, 52-53, 71, 447-48, 450-51, Ga. Dept. of Arch. and Hist.; Wright to Shelburne, May 15, 1767, *ibid.*, XXXVII, 208-9.

50. See Commons Journals, Nov. 1760-Nov. 1761, *Ga. Col. Recs.*, XIII, 451, 455, 463, 503, 541, 598, 604; Statutes, *ibid.*, XVIII, 159-60, 472-79.

of Commons at the end of the seventeenth century, but the Crown had not conferred it upon American lower houses. In fact, royal instructions required that all officers' accounts be audited by the auditor general of the plantations or by his deputy. Contrary to these instructions, no officers' accounts were audited in these three colonies by the auditor general. In North Carolina efforts by Governors Burrington and Dobbs to enforce these instructions were unsuccessful, and the accounts were audited by a joint committee from both houses of the legislature. Control of that committee rested with the Lower House, which appointed the majority of the members. In neither Virginia nor South Carolina did the governors make any attempt to force a compliance with the instructions, and in the latter throughout the royal period and in the former after 1755 accounts were audited by a committee of the Lower House. Only in Georgia did the Lower House not acquire authority over officers' accounts. There the Commons reviewed and inspected the accounts, but the deputy auditor of the plantations audited them.

After 1763 the Crown's new colonial policy did not include a direct assault upon the lower houses' power to audit accounts. When the Crown took over Georgia it had been careful to preserve that power for the governor and Council, but its actions toward other colonies, in particular North Carolina in the 1760's and 1770's, indicated a willingness to concede that power to the lower houses. Indeed, in January 1766 the Board of Trade, in a report to the House of Commons, readily accepted the fact that "Officers being appointed by the Assemblies of the Colonies respectively and accountable only to them; are not subject to the Controul either of Office here or His Majesty's Governors there and therefore do not in ordinary and regular Course transmit their accounts to us."[51] Even so, power to audit accounts was contingent upon power to tax; and British measures after 1763 did challenge the lower houses' power to tax and ultimately their power over officers' accounts.

51. Board of Trade to House of Commons, Jan. 29, 1766, CO 323/19.

5

Expenditures

Power to determine how public taxes should be spent was a natural corollary to the authority to tax, and it became an important element in the lower houses' control over finance. Taking their cue from the British House of Commons,[1] most colonial lower houses assumed that power early in the eighteenth century first by appropriating all revenues in detail and later by appointing special officers to dispose of particular sums. When the Jamaica Commons House of Assembly resolved in October 1753 that it was "the inherent and undoubted Right of the Representatives of the People to raise and apply Monies for the Service and Exigencies of Government,"[2] it was forcefully and categorically asserting the representatives' right to stipulate how each farthing of the public money should be spent. That assertion might well have been made by any of the lower houses in the southern royal colonies during the same decade had their executives seriously challenged their equally "inherent and undoubted" right.

Crown officials had taken extensive precautions to prevent that power from falling into the hands of the lower houses. To keep the lower houses from making specific appropriations, they prescribed that all money be granted in general sums, leaving its final disposition to the colonial executives. Further, they issued instructions first to Jamaica in 1678 and later to all royal colonies requiring that all taxes be given in the name of the Crown and that no money be issued out of colonial treasuries without the governor's warrant.[3] But

1. See Holdsworth, *English Law*, X, 588.
2. *N.C. Col. Recs.*, V, 758-59.
3. Labaree, ed., *Royal Instructions*, I, 203-4; Labaree, *Royal Government*, 274-75.

governors found these regulations difficult to enforce. When called upon to grant supplies, lower houses insisted upon appropriating them in detail, and later, when the colonial wars and the increased activity of the colonial governments required larger and more frequent grants, they occasionally insisted upon appointing commissioners or extrasessionary committees—committees meeting while the legislature was not in session—to dispose of them. By the end of the colonial period the lower houses in the southern royal colonies were so powerful that they could order money from the treasury without executive consent. Governors were powerless to curb these developments. They had to have money to run the government, and the lower houses would provide it only upon their own terms. Those terms included a rigid scrutiny of every detail of governmental administration and operation—matters which in the eyes of imperial officials properly belonged to the governors and councils.

Among the lower houses in the southern royal colonies, the South Carolina Commons had the most extensive control over expenditures. Not only did it insist upon appropriating all public money in detail and reviewing accounts, but through legislative-appointed commissioners it even controlled much of the machinery for applying it. The Commons also used extrasessionary committees to assist the governor and Council in applying moneys when it was not in session until Lyttelton stopped that practice in the mid-1750's. Finally, after 1750 the Commons exercised the power to order money from the treasury without the consent of governor or Council, thus eliminating the executive from any effective authority in the colony's financial affairs.

The Commons adopted the practice of appropriating all taxes in detail early in the proprietary period. To each annual tax bill it attached an estimate of the sum to be raised. A detailed calculation by a legislative committee of anticipated expenses before 1732 or of the public debt after that date, the estimate specified the exact purposes for which that sum was to be spent, thereby preventing the executive from applying it to any other use.[4] For nearly thirty years after the transfer of South Carolina to the Crown, the Commons continued to annex an estimate to each annual tax act without ob-

4. For an example of an estimate, see Cooper and McCord, eds., *S.C. Statutes,* IV, 63-73.

jection from London.   But in 1750, as a part of the general restrictive
policy adopted under the presidency of the Earl of Halifax, the Board
of Trade ordered Governor James Glen to stop that practice because
it gave the Commons a share in disposing of the public money, a function which the royal commission assigned to the governor and Council.   By then, however, the practice was such an integral part of the
colony's legislative procedure that Glen was powerless to effect a
change.   Neither he nor his successors ever attempted to obey the
Board's order.[5]

The South Carolina Commons also appropriated specifically most
extraordinary revenues, such as sums raised for military expenses and
Indian presents.   Thus, in February 1740 when General James Oglethorpe requested funds to finance an expedition against St. Augustine
during the War of Jenkins' Ear, the Commons refused to vote them
unless it knew precisely what they were going to be used for.   The
Council insisted that the matter was purely an executive affair, but
the Commons forced the Council to participate in a conference which
decided upon the details of the expedition, including the number of
officers and men to be raised, their rate of pay, and the total sum required.   When General Oglethorpe came to Charleston in March,
the Commons required him to appear before a legislative committee
and to submit an itemized estimate of proposed expenditures.   Both
houses finally agreed to provide funds for the expedition, but the
Commons insisted that Lieutenant Governor William Bull I make it
clear to Oglethorpe that they could be used only for the exact purposes stated in the appropriating law.[6]   By these proceedings the
Commons through its power of appropriation actually shared in
formulating executive policy concerning the details of the expedition.

For most of the royal period South Carolina's public treasurers
customarily paid money out of the treasury only upon the Commons'
prior resolutions with the governor's and Council's consent.   Governors rarely spent money without first obtaining the Commons' consent.   Most of them respectfully followed the advice of the Commons'
committee, which warned in 1742 that it would "think it of ill Conse-

5. Board of Trade to Glen, Nov. 15, 1750, CO 5/402, pp. 233-70. Any effort of
Glen's to carry out the Board's order must have been made privately with individual members.   He did not submit the matter to the Commons for official
consideration.

6. Commons Journals, Feb. 9-10, Mar. 29-31, 1740, *S.C. Col. Recs., 1739-41*, 191-
93, 198-202, 273-78.

quence to have any Expences determined or resolved upon without the previous Consent of the Assembly, during the sitting of the House."[7]   These arrangements were contrary to the stipulations in the royal commission that money should be issued out of colonial treasuries only upon the governor's warrants with the Council's advice.   Indeed, in February 1750 the Commons even went so far as to deny completely the Council's right "at any Time to point out or direct the Issue of any Money out of the Treasury."[8]

So strong was the South Carolina Commons' power over disbursements that it could force a governor to accept measures he opposed. To prevent South Carolina slaves from running away to St. Augustine, the Commons in May 1749 requested Governor Glen to order out some scout boats, which the colony had frequently employed to capture runaway slaves and to keep a lookout for hostile warships. Glen did not honor the Commons' request because the boats were in bad repair and because imperial authorities had already sent word that they were ordering three ships to the colony for that purpose. But the Commons would not see its request ignored.   It asserted that the representatives were the "only proper Judges of any Expence that shall be necessary to be entered into" and, when the governor did not immediately accede to its demands, ordered commissary general John Dart, an appointee of the House, to purchase two scout boats.   Glen protested that the Commons' assertion seemed "to convey an Idea of an Exclusion of all others from interfering with, or ever judging of the Propriety of, any Measures which your House may recommend." Claiming "at least, an equal Right" in such matters, he argued that to admit the validity of the Commons' position would "destroy the very Being of the other Branches of the Legislature, and, consequently, the whole Frame of Government."   But Glen knew that any attempt to prevent Dart from carrying out the Commons' order would raise a storm of protest from the representatives and in order to maintain the appearance of the royal prerogative directed him to provide the boats.   Having demonstrated their power, the representatives were not disposed to argue over principle and conceded that they were not the only judge of expenses.[9]

The South Carolina Commons also refused to reimburse officers

7. Commons Journals, May 22, 1742, *ibid., 1741-42*, 517-18.
8. Commons Journals, Feb. 7, 1750, *ibid., 1749-50*, 397.
9. Commons Journals, May 15, 16, 24, 1749, *ibid.*, 93, 110-11, 185-87.

for expenses incurred in serving the public unless they first submitted accounts with "proper vouchers." The Commons revealed its attitude in February 1738 when it required Council clerk Jesse Bladenhop to lay the Council journals before one of its committees to be used as vouchers for his account. Bladenhop at first refused on the grounds that such an action would constitute a breach of trust, but the Commons, asserting that it was "contrary to the Law and Usage of Parliament and the Practice of the Lower House of Assembly of South Carolina to grant any Sum to be levied on the People . . . for past Services . . . without making a full Examination and Enquiry into the Nature of such Services," eventually forced Bladenhop to comply.[10]

The Commons even required governors to submit accounts. Choctaw Indian trader Charles McNaire complained to the Board of Trade in 1751 that Glen had directed him to give presents to the Indians in 1747 but that when the House called Glen to account he denied having given the order because he knew that it would not pay for presents distributed without its prior consent.[11] In March 1754 the Commons declined to pay Glen for several expenses until he had submitted accounts for examination by a House committee. The resolution adopted at that time, "that this House will not for the future make Provision for payment of any Account for expences incurred for the public service, unless such Accounts shall be first laid before this House to undergo the usual examination," became a a standing rule of the House.[12]

Glen's successor, William Henry Lyttelton, tried to induce the Commons to modify this rule. At the beginning of his administration he persuaded the Commons to grant him a general unstipulated fund to use at his own discretion for contingent expenses. With such a fund Lyttelton planned to curtail legislative interference in executive affairs and to reduce the governor's dependence upon the House. But the Commons would not abandon any part of its extensive control over finance, and in May 1757, when Lyttelton failed to submit vouchers for all of his expenditures from the contingent fund, the Commons served notice that it intended to subject that fund to

10. Commons Journals, Feb. 3, Mar. 4, 1738, *ibid., 1736-39,* 458-59, 508.
11. Feb. 26, 1751, *Board of Trade Journals, 1750-53,* 280. For a similar incident, see July 6, 1756, S.C. Commons Journals, CO 5/472, p. 20.
12. Mar. 15, 1754, S.C. Commons Journals, CO 5/472, p. 83.

the same rigid scrutiny applied to other appropriations by warning him that future accounts would have to be properly supported by vouchers.[13] Nor was it long before the Commons began to question the wisdom of voting any contingent fund whatever. It turned down Lyttelton's request for a further grant of contingencies in June 1757, informing him that "as that Service has always, hitherto, been provided for by the Schedules to the Tax-Bills; this House do not think proper to make Provision for the same in any other Manner."[14]

Not only did the Commons insist upon reviewing Lyttelton's use of the contingent fund; it even went so far as to reject an account drawn by the governor on that fund. In 1757 Lyttelton employed James Laurens and Company to furnish supplies to Fort Frederica in Georgia, but, when the account came before the House, it rejected the account on the grounds that it was improper for South Carolina to pay for transporting materials to Georgia for defending that colony. Ignoring the Commons' action, Lyttelton ordered the payment of Laurens and Company out of the contingent fund. In December 1758 the Commons once again voiced its disapproval of the Laurens account and indignantly observed that "paying accounts before they have been Audited and Agreed to in this House . . . may be of hurtful Consequences, as the right and authority of this House to judge of the propriety and Legality of Demands against the Public may thereby be eluded and abridged; and the good People of this Province Taxed toward a Service which may be thought by their Representatives very improper." "Paying such Accounts after they had undergone the Solemn Consideration of the House, and been rejected," the House declared, "is unusual unprecedented and an extraordinary procedure." To insure against similar occurrences, the Commons reduced the annual grant for contingencies to £1,800 Carolina currency, barely enough to meet the cost of sending expresses and other incidental expenses of government. Smarting under such a sharp rebuke, Lyttelton broke off correspondence with the House for at least four months, but it may safely be assumed that he was more careful thereafter to avoid taking measures which would not meet with the Commons' approval.[15]

13. May 3, 1757, *ibid.*, CO 5/473, pp. 77-78.
14. July 6, 1757, S. C. Commons Journals, XXXI, 155-56, S. C. Arch. Dept.
15. Dec. 8, 1758, S. C. Commons Journals, CO 5/475, pp. 22-24; Lyttelton to Board of Trade, Apr. 14, 1759, CO 5/376, ff. 81-86.

The Commons also used its power over disbursements to conduct inquiries into executive affairs. The best known and most important inquiry was the Commons' examination in 1740-41 of Oglethorpe's abortive expedition in 1740 against St. Augustine. A joint committee composed of eleven assemblymen and three councilors conducted that inquiry in part to clear South Carolina of charges of remissness circulated in London. The committee's report, eventually published in both Charleston and London, absolved South Carolina's forces from any major responsibility for the expedition's failure, but found the conduct of General Oglethorpe and his independent forces reprehensible.[16]

Indeed, by a broad use of its appropriation powers the South Carolina Commons extended its authority into almost every area of the colony's affairs; by appointing commissioners to dispose of many of its grants it stretched that authority even further. These commissioners were appointed by statute usually upon the nomination of the Commons, and the power given them was considerable. Intended to supervise and execute some specific task, they were authorized to draw orders on the public treasury without the governor's warrant and to fill vacancies in their number. Their tenure was usually unlimited.[17] The Commons used the commissioner system occasionally under the proprietors and during the royal period extended it to most areas of administration. How far it extended this system was indicated by Glen's complaint to the Board of Trade in October 1748 that "much of the executive part of the Government and of the Administration, is by various Laws lodged in different setts of Commissioners, Thus we have Commissioners of the Market, of the Work house, of the Pilots, of Fortifications, and so on, without number." The utter impotence of the royal governors was revealed by Glen's further observation that "most of the Commissioners are named by the General Assembly, and are answerable and accountable to them only, and let their ignorance and mistakes be never so gross, let their neglects and mismanagements be never so flagrant, A Governor has no power either to reprove them or remove them, and indeed it were to little purpose to tell them, he is displeased with them, when he

16. *The St. Augustine Expedition of 1740*, intro. by John Tate Lanning (Columbia, 1954), xii-xvi, xxv.
17. See Journal of the Commissioners of Fortifications, 1755-1770, South Carolina Historical Society, Charleston.

cannot displace them." "Thus by little and little, the People have got the whole administration into their Hands," he complained, "and the Crown is by various Laws despoiled of its principal flowers and brightest Jewells."[18] Certainly, the commissioner system usurped many powers and duties conferred on the governors by their commissions, but, despite Glen's and other governors' dissatisfaction with it, they were unable to curtail its use. The Commons' refusal to provide funds without commissioners to dispose of them made the perpetuation of the system inevitable.

The Commons encroached still further upon the royal prerogative when from time to time it appointed extrasessionary committees from its own members to meet with the governor and Council after its adjournment or prorogation to direct the application of particular grants. It first employed such a committee in the spring of 1737 under the elder Bull. In early February it voted £6,000 to guard against incursions by Spaniards and Indians on the southern frontier and provided that the money be applied "by the Treasurer on Orders drawn for the same by his Honour the Lieutenant Governour, his Majesty's Honourable Council and a Committee of the Commons House of Assembly jointly and not otherwise." To execute this provision the Commons resolved that during its prorogation all members residing in Charleston or those who happened to be in Charleston should constitute a committee of the Commons to meet with Bull and the Council to apply the £6,000. Accordingly, between March 7 and April 2, 1737, during the legislature's recess, there were five meetings in which from five to fourteen assemblymen met with the governor and Council, entering into several resolutions to apply the £6,000 and signing orders for issuing the money out of the treasury.[19] Such proceedings, as the Council observed some eight years later when reviewing the Commons' past conduct, were "without precedent here or in England, and contrary to his Majesty's Instructions, whereby his Governor was directed to take care that no Money should be issued but by Warrant under *his* hand." The Council also noted that by these proceedings "the Assembly at last actually got into a share of the Administration of Government, and the three Estates in the Legislature were . . . brought to Act together in *One*."[20]

18. Glen to Board of Trade, Oct. 10, 1748, CO 5/372, ff. 80-87.
19. Commons Journals, Feb. 7, Mar. 5, 1737, *S. C. Col. Recs., 1736-39*, 220, 286; Mar. 7-Apr. 2, 1737, S. C. Council Journals, CO 5/438, pp. 118-24.
20. May 7, 1745, S. C. Upper House Journals, CO 5/453, pp. 118-45.

Several times during the administration of Glen similar extrasessionary committees met with him and the Council to direct the distribution of Indian presents. In August 1753 and November 1754, while the Commons was recessed, it empowered its committee on Indian affairs to join Glen and the Council to allot Indian presents it had voted.[21]   Earlier, in June 1749 and May 1751, Glen had even permitted the Commons to appoint such extraordinary committees to share in dispensing Indian presents provided by the Crown.[22]   By appointing such committees the Commons seriously encroached upon the executive's powers.   That the Commons actually took a hand in applying Indian presents granted by the Crown is a good illustration of the extent of its fiscal authority, which in this instance, at least, reached beyond provincial revenues to those of the Crown.

William Henry Lyttelton put a stop to the practice of the Commons' appointing such committees early in his administration.   In February 1757 he requested funds to provide presents for some Cherokee Indians in Charleston.   The Commons, as it had been accustomed to doing under Glen, resolved to "provide for defraying the expence of a proper Reward to be given to the . . . Indians by the Governour, in Council, with the consent of a Committee to be appointed by this House for that purpose."   But Lyttelton argued that this provision was "not agreable to the usage of your House; and not free from Constitutional Objections," and urged the Commons to reconsider it. After checking its journals for precedents and finding none before 1749, the Commons voted presents on the basis of the governor's estimate of expense.[23]   But it was not yet ready to abandon the extrasessionary committee altogether.   Less than two months later the Commons agreed to provide for Indian presents up to the value of £2,500 Carolina currency while it was recessed but stipulated that they be given only if consented to by "a Majority of such Members of this House as shall be in Town, to consist of Thirteen at least."   In cases where sums over £2,500 were involved, the Commons asked to be reconvened.   Contending that such stipulations might put him "under very improper Restraints that . . . might be incompatible with

21. Aug. 24, 1753, S. C. Commons Journals, XXVIII, 594, S. C. Arch. Dept.; Nov. 16, 1754, S. C. Commons Journals, CO 5/472, p. 9.

22. Commons Journals, June 1, 1749, *S. C. Col. Recs., 1749-50,* 273-74; May 18, 1751, S. C. Commons Journals, CO 5/463, p. 201.

23. Feb. 3-5, 1757, S. C. Commons Journals, CO 5/473, pp. 21, 26-27.

the safety of the Province," Lyttelton persuaded the Commons to soften the terms of its grant. As a result the Commons agreed to provide for any presents not exceeding £2,500 that Lyttelton might give to the Indians between sessions, but still insisted upon being reconvened when larger sums were required.[24] Because of Lyttelton's firm opposition in this instance, the Commons gave up the practice of appointing extrasessionary committees to assist the governor and Council in their executive duties.

By gaining power to order money from the public treasury without the consent of either the governor or Council, the Commons deprived the executive of its last check upon the colony's financial affairs. During the early years of royal government both the executive and the legislature complied with Crown instructions that money be issued from colonial treasuries only upon warrants signed by the governors, and the treasurer advanced money from the colony's treasury only upon a resolution passed by governor, Council, and Commons or upon the Commons' order and the governor's requisition.[25] Thus executive approval was necessary before public funds might be expended. But after 1750 the Commons increasingly resorted to the practice of borrowing money from the treasury for some particular service without executive consent and repaying the money later by an appropriation in the annual tax bill.[26] This practice enabled the Commons to order money from the treasury by its single authority, which the governor and Council could prevent only by rejecting the entire tax bill that contained the appropriation to repay the treasurer for the sum advanced. That action would almost certainly have put the colony in severe financial straits and provoked a serious political dispute. Consequently, as long as the Commons ordered money out of the treasury only for routine services, both royal governors and the Council wisely chose to let the matter pass without comment. Not until after 1770, when the Commons blatantly displayed its power by voting funds to the English radical John Wilkes, did Crown officials discover that the Commons had acquired it or attempt to deprive the Commons of it.

24. Mar. 31, Apr. 2, 27-29, 1757, *ibid.*, pp. 61, 67, 72-76; Lyttelton to Board of Trade, May 24, 1757, CO 5/375, ff. 203-7.
25. See William Bull II to Earl of Hillsborough, Sept. 8, 1770, S. C. Pub. Recs., XXXII, 320-30, S. C. Arch. Dept.
26. S. C. Committee of Correspondence to Charles Garth, Sept. 6, 1770, "Garth Correspondence," *S. C. Hist. and Geneal. Mag.*, 31 (1930), 246-53.

No less extensive was the North Carolina Lower House's authority over expenditures. It employed all the devices used by the South Carolina Commons except the extrasessionary committee. Long before North Carolina became a royal colony, the Lower House had won control over finances by appropriating all tax revenues in detail and requiring all officers handling public revenues to account with it. When he assumed control of the colony for the Crown in 1731, George Burrington found that the House's power in this area severely limited his authority. "It has been a Policy of the Subtle People of North Carolina," he complained to the Board of Trade in February 1732, "never to raise any money but what is appropriated, to pretend and insist that no Publick money can, or ought to be paid, but by a Claim given to, and allowed by the House of Burgesses; insomuch that upon the greatest emergency there is no coming at any money to fitt out Vessells against a Pirate, to buy Arms, Purchase Ammunition, or on any other urgent occasion."[27] But neither Burrington nor his successors could induce the House to abandon that policy during the royal period.

As Burrington lamented, the House insisted that no money be paid out of the treasury without its prior approval. All claims for money for services performed for the colony had to pass the committee of claims; and after the public creditors were paid the House appropriated those sums remaining in the treasury to particular purposes.[28] Only during the Seven Years' War did the House soften its policy. In order to permit Governor Arthur Dobbs to handle defense exigencies without calling the legislature into session, the House empowered him to spend military funds without its consent. But the House insured that Dobbs would not misapply those funds by stipulating in the appropriation bills the general purposes for which they were to be spent and by requiring him to submit for its examination accounts of every sum expended. When the House accused Dobbs in May 1760 of injudiciously applying those funds, Dobbs underscored the effectiveness of its control by pointing out that "there was not a single sum granted and paid by my warrants but what has been scrutinized and passed before the Committee of Accounts, and afterwards approved of by the House."[29] The House never again gave a

27. Burrington to Board of Trade, Feb. 20, 1732, *N. C. Col. Recs.*, III, 336.
28. See Lower House Journals, Apr. 10, 1753, *ibid.*, V, 73.
29. Dobbs's answers to Lower House's resolutions, Aug. 3, 1760, *ibid.*, VI, 281.

governor such wide latitude, and, when Dobbs contended in November 1764 that he could with the Council's consent expend surplus money without the approval of the Lower House, it ordered the treasurers not to "pay any Money out of any Fund by order of the Governor and Council without the Concurrence or direction of this House" and thereby prevented Dobbs from putting his intention into execution.[30]

Like the South Carolina Commons, the North Carolina Lower House occasionally exercised the power to order money from the treasury without the consent of either governor or Council. Despite the protests of Dobbs, who cited the royal instructions specifying that money should be paid out of the public treasury only upon his warrants, the two public treasurers—one for the northern half of the colony and the other for the southern—invariably complied with the House's orders because they were assured that their transactions would be approved by the joint committee on accounts, which was controlled by the Lower House. Thus Dobbs complained to the Board of Trade in December 1760 that in consequence of his refusal "sometimes to ratify or grant Warrants" approved by the joint committee "the northern Treasurer had made payments to his favourites without my Warrants, and the Assembly this Session have ordered their Southern Treasurer to pay Publick money without any order from me to pay their Sergeants fees for Members in Custody to secure the Members in the Junto's interest."[31]

Also like the South Carolina Commons, the North Carolina Lower House frequently appointed commissioners after February 1740 to build bridges, public buildings, and churches and to collect and apply money appropriated to the Crown for military supplies. The North Carolina system was much like that of South Carolina; it is highly probable, in fact, that it was consciously borrowed. Nominated by the Lower House, the commissioners were appointed by statute to supervise the execution of some specific task. They were empowered

30. Upper House Journals, Lower House Journals, Nov. 27, 1764, *ibid.*, 1253-54, 1318.

31. Dobbs to Board of Trade, Dec. 12, 1760, *ibid.*, 320. See also Dobbs's objection in November 1764 to the House's ordering money out of the treasury without his warrant. Upper House Journals, Lower House Journals, Nov. 27, 1764, *ibid.*, 1253-54, 1318.

to receive money voted for their particular task and had to account to the House unless their duties were purely local in nature.[32]

The North Carolina Lower House not only strictly controlled all provincial revenues but also insisted in the 1750's upon supervising the disposition of North Carolina's portion of the two Parliamentary grants of £50,000 to the southern colonies and £200,000 to all the continental colonies for their expenses in the Seven Years' War. In neighboring South Carolina and Virginia the governors readily allowed the lower houses to assert their authority over their portions of those grants.[33] But Dobbs, who especially resented his financial dependence upon the Lower House, was determined to prevent North Carolina's share from falling into its hands. His efforts produced a serious controversy that lasted more than five years.

In December 1758 the Lower House passed a measure directing how North Carolina's share of the money should be received and applied. Anticipating opposition from Dobbs, House leaders attempted to obtain a *quid pro quo* by offering to pass a bill to establish the colony's capital at New Bern—long one of Dobbs's pet schemes —in return for his assent to its measure. Dobbs was delighted at the prospect of obtaining the capital bill, but he was determined to prevent the passage of the other. Accordingly, he carefully refrained from expressing his sentiments on either of the bills until both had passed the Lower House and had been sent to the Council for its final concurrence. He then persuaded the Council to reject the application bill but to pass the capital bill. Understandably, the House was in "a flame" because it had been outwitted by Dobbs, but it would not give up its efforts to obtain control over North Carolina's share of the Parliamentary money. It appointed James Abercromby to serve as its agent in London with a salary of £150 per year out of the colony's portion of the grant and ordered him to obtain imperial consent to its scheme for receiving and applying the money from the grant. Although Dobbs objected to the House's appointment of Abercromby without either his or the Council's consent, he was, for the moment at least, powerless to prevent it.

To counter Abercromby's activities and to justify his opposition

32. Laws, Walter L. Clark, ed., *The State Records of North Carolina*, 16 vols. (Goldsboro, 1895-1905), XXIII, 136-41, 151-57; hereafter cited as *N. C. St. Recs.*
33. May 20, 29, 1760, S. C. Commons Journals, CO 5/473, pp. 73, 80; May 19, 1760, *Va. Burgesses Journals, 1758-61*, 171-72.

to the application bill, Dobbs wrote the Board of Trade that five members of the House, including the two treasurers and the speaker, had designed that measure to "get our proportion . . . into their Custody under the direction of the Assembly which they ruled, and so apply it as they thought proper without His Majesty or the Governor and Council's interfering in it." Dobbs proposed instead that "the disposal of the money . . . should be under the direction of the Governor and Council, and to have the accounts audited by the Auditor and transmitted to Britain according to my Instructions to be laid out as His Majesty shall direct and approve of." The only alternative to his proposal was "to give up all accounts of money to the Assembly who will neither pay nor allow the Auditor to audit the accounts and keep the Vouchers, by which means they endeavour to engross all power, as they endeavour from time to time to increase it." The time had come, Dobbs argued, "to stop their schemes of their power." He also objected to the House's plan to bring the money to North Carolina in specie. Instead, he proposed to put the money in a London bank "to remit it as wanted to this Province."[34]

In May 1759 the Lower House again attempted to assert control over the Parliamentary money. To a military aid bill it attached a rider to appoint Abercromby agent to receive the Parliamentary money and remit it to a House committee of correspondence to be applied towards the redemption of paper currency. But the Council would not pass the aid bill so long as it contained the rider.[35]

Meanwhile, Abercromby was serving the interests of the Lower House well. In July 1759 he informed the committee of correspondence that the imperial authorities would probably allow the legislature to dispose of the Parliamentary money and privately assured Speaker Samuel Swann that he would be able "to prevent this Money becoming subject to the Governor's Will and Pleasure."[36] Abercromby's prediction proved correct. In August the Board firmly rejected Dobbs's proposals, declaring that the "appropriation by Act of Legislature of the Money granted by Parliament for a compensation to the Province unless otherwise directed by His Majesty is doubtless a very regular and proper method of proceeding."[37]

34. Dobbs to Board of Trade, Jan. 22, 1759, *N. C. Col. Recs.*, VI, 1-5.
35. Dobbs to Board of Trade, May 18, 1759, *ibid.*, 32-34.
36. Abercromby to N. C. Committee of Correspondence and to Samuel Swann, July 20, 1759, Abercromby Letter Book, 165-69, Virginia State Library, Richmond.
37. Board of Trade to Dobbs, Aug. 1, 1759, *N. C. Col. Recs.*, VI, 54-56.

Despite the Board's declaration, Dobbs continued to oppose the Lower House's schemes to apply the money, and the dispute dragged on for another four years, the money remaining in the hands of the agent in London. In December 1761 Dobbs again protested to London against the House's plan to bring the money to North Carolina in specie, maintaining that much of the money "would be lost by Commission Freight and Insurance" as well as in the "Treasurers Fees for receiving and paying it." He also argued that if the sum were allowed to fall into the hands of the treasurers there would certainly be ample opportunity for fraud.[38] Again the Board of Trade disagreed with Dobbs. Denying his contention that "buying up the paper currency with Bills drawn upon the Agent here, will be a more beneficial Method than the remitting the money in specie," it pointed out that if specie were sent over and "substituted in place of paper notes" there would be "a Circulation of Cash, the want whereof has ever been the plea for a paper currency." Nor did the Board agree that Dobbs's scheme was any "less liable to fraud than the other."[39] But not until after the Board specifically ordered him to accept the Lower House's proposals in December 1763 did Dobbs surrender and permit the Lower House to dispose of the Parliamentary money.[40] With that victory the House firmly established its control over disbursements; no governor again attempted to challenge it.

By the middle of the seventeenth century, the Virginia House of Burgesses was already exercising some control over expenditures. As early as 1629 it began making detailed appropriations,[41] and for the remainder of the colonial period it insisted that all ordinary tax revenues be used only to defray expenses allowed by its claims committee. After 1691 the public treasurer, appointed by statute upon the Burgesses' nomination, handled public taxes, paying only those sums allowed by the committee. The Burgesses also appropriated in detail all special aids, such as the £5,000 granted during the War of Jenkins' Ear for the campaign against the West Indies in 1740.[42] In

38. Dobbs to Board of Trade, Dec. 1761, *ibid.*, 598-99.
39. Board of Trade to Dobbs, June 10, 1762, *ibid.*, 725.
40. Jouvencal's representation to Board of Trade, May 16, 1763, Board of Trade to Dobbs, Dec. 15, 1763, *ibid.*, 983-89, 998.
41. See Hening, ed., *Va. Statutes*, I, 142-43, 171, 196.
42. Aug. 25-28, 1740, *Va. Burgesses Journals, 1728-40*, 439-42; Hening, ed., *Va. Statutes*, V, 121-23.

response to South Carolina Governor James Glen's proposal for a meeting of governors to determine each colony's share in the campaign against the French in 1754, Lieutenant Governor Robert Dinwiddie declared that such a plan "would have no Weight with my Assembly, as they are too headstrong to be under any Direction but from their own Opinions and Arguments." To get a supply from the Burgesses, he continued, he had to content himself with "arguing on the necessity and leaving the Quantum to them." Dinwiddie wrote to Maryland Governor Horatio Sharpe that "if a Governor of this Dominion should direct the Assembly in regard to raising Men or Money, [it] would be the infallible way of being disappointed of both."[43]

The treasurer usually issued money only upon the Burgesses' resolution, the Council's approval, and the governor's warrant,[44] but a few times he acted upon the resolve of the Burgesses only. The Burgesses sent Philip Ludwell in 1688 and William Byrd II in 1718 to London as agents to appear for the House against Governor Howard and Lieutenant Governor Spotswood respectively. In both instances the governor and Council refused to assent to the Burgesses' original order for paying the agent, although some years later they agreed to the payment of each agent by the normal procedure. But very likely the auditor paid Ludwell and the treasurer paid Byrd solely upon the order of the Burgesses long before the governor and Council had given their consent.[45] Similarly, in 1753-54 Speaker-Treasurer John Robinson paid Peyton Randolph £2,500 for going to England to represent the Burgesses in the pistole fee dispute, despite the Council's refusal to agree to a resolution authorizing payment and Dinwiddie's vow that he would never sign a warrant for the sum nor permit it to "be allowed" in Robinson's "Accounts."[46]

This question agitated Virginia politics for nearly a year. The

43. Dinwiddie to Glen, Apr. 15, 1754, to Sharpe, May 1, 1754, Brock, ed., *Dinwiddie Papers*, I, 128, 145.

44. Mar. 29, 1728, Aug. 28, 1740, *Va. Burgesses Journals, 1728-40*, 50, 442; Apr. 12, 1746, *ibid., 1742-49*, 221.

45. May 12, 1688, May 7-20, 1691, *Va. Burgesses Journals, 1659-93*, 329, 351, 363-66; Nov. 27, 1718, May 10, 1722, *ibid., 1712-26*, 237-38, 323; William Blathwayt to Francis Nicholson, Jan. 5, 1692, Blathwayt Papers, XV, No. 2, Colonial Williamsburg, Inc., Williamsburg, Va.; Spotswood to Board of Trade, June 24, 1718, Brock, ed., *Spotswood Letters*, II, 277-79.

46. Dec. 17, 1753, *Va. Burgesses Journals, 1752-58*, 168-69; Dinwiddie to Board of Trade, May 10, 1754, Brock, ed., *Dinwiddie Papers*, I, 160.

following August the Burgesses attempted to force Dinwiddie and the Council to confirm Robinson's action by adding a clause to pay Randolph to a military aid bill—a bill which had the strong support of both Dinwiddie and the Council. But the Council refused to pass the measure, sharply reprimanding the Burgesses for adding a foreign clause to a money bill.[47] A compromise decision by Crown officials on the pistole fee dispute during the summer of 1754 paved the way for the payment of Randolph in October. Dinwiddie and the Council passed Robinson's accounts—which included the article to pay Randolph—in return for a bill to appropriate £20,000 for the war. By agreeing to Randolph's payment, the Council sanctioned the Burgesses' power to order money from the treasury without executive consent.[48]

Beginning in the eighteenth century the Burgesses also used the commissioner system to dispose of particular sums. Virginia commissioners did not have the far-reaching powers enjoyed by their counterparts in the Carolinas, for they had to have the governor's warrant in order to draw money from the treasury. But they did have full power to dispose of all money placed in their hands, and the Burgesses could insure against misappropriation by requiring commissioners to submit their accounts to it.[49]

During the last two intercolonial wars the Burgesses also appointed commissioners to supervise the application of military appropriations. In King George's War, when Lieutenant Governor Gooch's poor physical condition prevented him from attending to the detailed expenditure of funds granted for an expedition against Canada in July 1746, the Burgesses appointed nine commissioners, any five of whom could act as a quorum, to expend the money.[50] The Burgesses thereby established a precedent that it tenaciously adhered to there-

47. Dinwiddie to James Abercromby, Sept. 1, 1754, Brock, ed., *Dinwiddie Papers*, I, 298-301. See also Burgess Landon Carter's important, though indirect, challenge of the validity of royal instructions requiring executive consent to issue money out of the treasury, where he argues that "the fixing a Negative Voice in the Council, in every Disposal of the Public Treasury, should this Country be ever so unhappy as to be under the Government of an avaricious and designing Delegate, countenanced by either a pusillanimous, a lording, or an influenced Council, there will be no Means left for the People to carry their Complaints home to England." *Maryland Gazette* (Annapolis), Oct. 28, 1754.

48. Landon Carter's Minutes of the House of Burgesses, 1754, Sabine Hall Collection, Alderman Lib., Univ. of Virginia, Charlottesville.

49. Hening, ed., *Va. Statutes*, III, 213-15, VI, 197-98.

50. *Ibid.*, V, 401-4.

after. During the Seven Years' War it repeatedly refused to make appropriations unless it was allowed to appoint commissioners to supervise their application.   In early 1754 Dinwiddie objected strenuously to the Burgesses' including in a military tax bill a clause "giving a Power to a Committee . . . to order the Application of the Money." That clause, he complained, divested him of "his un-doubted [right] of directing the Application of all Monies raised for the Defense and Security of the Country." But because of the urgent need for money to combat the French along Virginia's western and northern frontier, Dinwiddie finally accepted the measure on the Burgesses' terms, although he did persuade the House to include four councilors among the commissioners. That law required all officers purchasing provisions or spending money for any other purpose to account with the commissioners, who, Dinwiddie complained, "had the sole Power of adjusting and liquidating the Accounts." The commissioners in turn accounted with the legislature. The Burgesses also employed commissioners to apply funds voted by four subsequent laws between October 1754 and April 1757.[51]

The Board of Trade found the Burgesses' use of such commission-ers particularly objectionable. It reported to Secretary of State Wil-liam Pitt in January 1757 that by the Virginia military supply bills "the Disposition and Application of the Money was . . . *put into the hands of Committees therein named, without any obligation upon them to account for the same,* but only to produce an Account of their proceedings to the Assembly, when required."[52] Although the Board's objection did not produce restrictive action on the part of imperial authorities, the Burgesses considerably revised the commis-sioner system in aid bills granted after June 1757. It abandoned its former practice of giving the commissioners absolute authority and empowered them merely to assist the governor in expending the moneys. This change was due not to the Board's objections but—as Dinwiddie suggested in March 1757—to the extraordinary expense of the system.[53]

51. Dinwiddie to Board of Trade, Mar. 12 and May 10, 1754, to Adam Stephen, Aug. 11, 1755, Brock, ed., *Dinwiddie Papers,* I, 98-99, 160-62, II, 149-50; Hening, ed., *Va. Statutes,* VI, 435-38, 452-61, 521-30, VII, 9-25, 69-87.

52. Board of Trade to Pitt, Jan. 24, 1757, CO 5/1367, pp. 295-312.

53. Hening, ed., *Va. Statutes,* VII, 75, 173, 257, 359, 371; Apr. 14, 1757, *Va. Burgesses Journals, 1752-58,* 413-14.

The Georgia Commons House of Assembly also won considerable power over disbursements, although never so much as its counterparts in the Carolinas and Virginia. It did not, for instance, attempt before 1763 to issue money from the treasury without executive approval. Nevertheless, it made a limited use of the commissioner system and specifically appropriated all funds that it raised, although after 1757, when Governor Henry Ellis persuaded the Commons to accept his estimate as the basis for its annual levies, Georgia governors played an important role in determining how money should be spent.[54]

For a brief period near the end of John Reynolds's administration, the Commons strengthened its control by gaining the right to pass upon all orders to issue money from the public treasury. At its first session in January 1755 the Commons, following the example of its South Carolina equivalent, applied to the Crown for permission to pass a law providing "that the Issuing [of] Money from the Public Treasury, that is raised by the general Assembly, may be applied and issued by their Order only."[55] The Board of Trade rejected this application, expressing concern "that this Assembly have laid in such early claims to privileges and powers, which, though of long usage enjoyed by some other assembly, are inconsistent with all Colony Constitution whatever, contrary to the practice of the Mother Country in like Cases, and to the express directions of His Majesty's Commission, by which alone that Assembly is constituted."[56] Despite the Board's ruling, Henry Ellis found upon his arrival in Georgia in 1757 that his predecessor, Reynolds, had in an effort to embarrass him instigated "the Assembly to usurp the power of Auditing the Accounts and Issuing the publick money." In less than six months, however, Ellis reported to the Board that he had restored "the right of Auditing the Accounts, and issuing the publick Money to the Governor and Council to whom it properly belongs."[57] But Ellis's success was not complete. In relinquishing the power to issue public money, the Commons had carefully stipulated that in the future it would not provide "for the Payment of any Accounts, over and above the Charges of the Courts of Oyer and Terminer, and the Setting of

54. Statutes, *Ga. Col. Recs.*, XVIII, 66-73, 240-47, 337-50, 392-408.
55. Commons Journals, Jan. 29, 1755, *ibid.*, XIII, 41-42.
56. John Pownall to Reynolds, June 5, 1755, CO 5/672, pp. 341-49.
57. Ellis to Board of Trade, May 5 and Aug. 1, 1757, CO 5/646.

General Assembly's, But such as may be approved of by this House"—a clear declaration that it would not make appropriations to cover sums issued from the treasury without its prior approval.[58]

Because Parliament provided for most of Georgia's expenses, the Commons was never required to raise large sums of money; consequently, it had much less opportunity to employ the commissioner system than did the lower houses of the other three colonies. Whenever the Commons did grant money for public works, however, it appointed commissioners to supervise the expenditure and required them to account with it. But Georgia commissioners were less thoroughly legislative in character than those in the other southern royal colonies because the governor usually served as one of the commissioners or maintained close supervision over them.[59]

By 1763 the lower houses in Virginia and the two Carolinas were playing a major role in disposing of public money, and the Georgia Commons was ready to extend its power in that area during the final decade of the colonial period. All four lower houses strictly appropriated all taxes and with the exception of the Georgia Commons audited accounts of all officers applying those taxes. In some respects their power to determine how public money should be applied was greater even than that of the British House of Commons. They frequently appointed commissioners to dispose of many of their appropriations, and during the 1740's and 1750's the South Carolina Commons designated extrasessionary committees to assist the executive in disposing of particular sums after the adjournment or prorogation of the legislature. More important, the lower houses in the three older colonies had demonstrated their ability to order money out of the treasury without the approval of the governor or council.

In the years after 1763 imperial officials made no concerted attempt to interfere with the lower houses' exercise of these powers. Indeed, they encouraged the use of specific appropriations; and by the late 1760's the commissioner system was already too well established even in Georgia to be tampered with. Colonial officials disapproved of the lower houses' ordering money from the treasury without executive consent, but they conveniently overlooked instances in which both the North Carolina Lower House and the

58. Commons Journals, July 12, 1757, *Ga. Col. Recs.*, XIII, 207.
59. See Commons Journals, Nov. 1760-Nov. 1761, *ibid.*, 444, 455, 463-65, 598.

Georgia Commons exercised that power in the final decade of the colonial period. Only when the South Carolina Commons sent money to the Bill of Rights Society in London did imperial authorities take any repressive action. That one action had serious consequences, evoking stubborn and sustained resistance from the South Carolina Commons and constituting an important issue in the years immediately preceding the Revolution.

6

Paper Money

Paper currency issued under government auspices was an American innovation. It originated in the colonies near the end of the seventeenth century, and its use became widespread during the eighteenth century. Paper notes of business houses and wealthy individuals had long been an unofficial medium of exchange in England, but the government there had never resorted to paper money. Until recently it was customary to explain the colonies' issuance of paper currencies as part of a conspiracy of American debtors to defraud their British creditors, a view that gave rise to the almost doctrinaire opposition of the British merchants to colonial paper currencies. But it is now generally held that colonists resorted to paper money because of their need for a medium of exchange. They had no other dependable or satisfactory source of money. Imperial authorities forbade exportation of specie from England to the colonies, and the specie that the colonies obtained from southern Europe and the West Indies was quickly drained off to redress an unfavorable balance of trade with the mother country. This scarcity of hard money stimulated the search for a substitute to fulfill the demands of internal trade. Commodities proved unsatisfactory because of their bulk and the possibility of spoilage. The colonies' only recourse was paper money. Paper currencies were also needed to meet frequent military expenses. The colonies were at war for thirty-four of the seventy-four years between the first emission of paper bills in Massachusetts in 1690 and the prohibition of further issues by Parliamentary statute in 1764. On many occasions paper money issues were the only method to obtain the cash needed for military expeditions. Thus, it was both to supply the needs of trade and to meet the demands of war that paper currencies became instruments of government finance in eighteenth-century America.[1]

Influenced as they were by British merchants, imperial authorities generally opposed and attempted to regulate strictly the issuance of paper currencies in the colonies. In 1720 they sent a circular instruction to governors of ten colonies forbidding them to approve laws to issue such currencies without a suspending clause, and they eventually so instructed all the governors.[2] Despite the Crown's insistence on a strict adherence to this instruction, governors often ignored it during emergencies, and opponents of paper currencies began to demand Parliamentary action. In 1741 Parliament passed a statute prohibiting societies like the Massachusetts Land Bank, established the previous year, and the following year it contemplated placing strict regulations on the currencies of all the colonies. In 1751 Parliament forbade the governors of Rhode Island, Connecticut, Massachusetts, and New Hampshire to assent to new issues of paper or to extend the time limit on paper bills already issued except in extreme emergencies. Although this prohibition did not apply to the southern colonies, their governors, even when they recognized the need for more currency, regarded it as the standard for their conduct when the legislatures insisted on putting out additional currency. Eventually, in 1764, Parliament restricted all the colonies from making paper money legal tender in the payment of debts.[3] Because of the imperial authorities' close supervision of the colonial currencies, the American lower houses never secured the legal power to emit paper money. Nevertheless, when the colonies urgently needed money, the authorities were powerless to prevent them from issuing it. Usually the councils and often the governors sided with the lower houses, and in all the southern royal colonies the legislatures frequently passed laws before 1764 to emit paper bills.

The first southern royal colony to issue paper money was South Carolina. In 1703 its legislature voted to issue £4,000 in non-legal

1. Leslie V. Brock, The Currency of the American Colonies, 1700-1764: A Study in Colonial Finance and Imperial Relations (unpubl. Ph.D. diss., Univ. of Michigan, 1941), vii, 4-16, 528-47.

2. Labaree, ed., *Royal Instructions*, I, 218-19.

3. Brock, Currency of American Colonies, 236, 507-8; Heads of Act to regulate British American Currencies, read by Board of Trade, Mar. 11, 1742, CO 323/11, ff. 23-26.

tender bills to pay for an expedition against St. Augustine during Queen Anne's War. The expedition proved more expensive than the legislature had expected and four years later it provided for the emission of another £8,000, half to be exchanged for the 1703 issue and half to be used to pay the debts remaining from the expedition and to fortify Charleston. The legislature made the entire amount legal tender. An expedition against Savannah River Indians in 1708 caused it to issue another £3,000, and later the same year £5,000 more, £2,000 of which was to be exchanged for mutilated bills already in circulation. None of the earlier issues having been retired, the total amount of bills in circulation after the emissions of 1708 was £14,000. The legislature did not print paper money again until March 1711, when pressing financial obligations forced it to add another £2,000; the following November, an expedition against the Tuscarora Indians in North Carolina called for another £4,000, bringing the total amount of paper currency to £20,000.[4]

In 1712 the legislature put its paper currency on a sturdier foundation and satisfied the need for a larger circulating medium by establishing a land bank and printing £52,000 legal tender currency, £16,000 of which was to be exchanged for all bills issued before the Tuscarora emission. It retired these bills promptly at the rate of £4,000 per year according to the original plan, but in 1715 and 1716 during the Yamassee War it was forced to vote £50,000 additional currency. By the end of the war there was about £90,000 circulating. Before the close of the proprietary period, the revolutionary government made two small emissions of £15,000 in 1719 and £10,000 in 1720. When the Crown took over the colony in 1721, therefore, the amount of currency outstanding was a little over £100,000, with an exchange rate in relation to sterling of approximately five to one. With the exception of the 1712 land bank currency, which was put forth mainly to serve the needs of commerce, the paper money issued under the proprietors was largely intended to pay for military expeditions or to meet the colony's pressing financial obligations.[5]

When South Carolina became a royal colony, imperial authorities instructed the governor not to pass laws to emit paper money with-

4. Cooper and McCord, eds., *S. C. Statutes*, II, 206-12, 302-7, 320-23, 324-27, 352-54, 366; Brock, Currency of American Colonies, 116-18.

5. Cooper and McCord, eds., *S. C. Statutes*, II, 389, 627-33, 634-41, 682-83; Brock, Currency of American Colonies, 119-21.

out a suspending clause.[6] The circulating currency was sufficient for nearly a year and a half after the arrival of the first royal governor, Francis Nicholson; but by November 1722 the needs of trade had produced a demand for additional paper. Despite opposition from the Council and some of the Charleston merchants who feared depreciation, the Commons pushed through a bill in February 1723 to print £120,000 legal tender currency. Of this amount, £80,000 was to be used to retire the old bills, and £40,000 was to be added to the circulating currency. Although the law did not contain a suspending clause, Nicholson assented to it, thereby disobeying his instructions.[7] Strong complaints by both Charleston and British merchants brought about the disallowance of the act in August 1723. For passing the measure without a suspending clause, Nicholson received a severe censure from the authorities, who instructed him to retire the currency issued under the law as quickly as possible.[8] Disappointed over the disallowance, the Commons reluctantly adopted a bill to sink the £55,000 already issued. By 1727, however, only £13,500 had been retired.[9]

Between 1726 and 1729 the Commons urged President of the Council Arthur Middleton to issue more paper money. Middleton, supported by the Council, which hesitated to violate the royal instructions, strongly resisted this pressure and attempted to block the Commons' attempts to avoid retiring the 1723 issue by diverting funds appropriated for that purpose to other uses. The currency issue so strained relations between Middleton and the Commons that effective civil government broke down for nearly five years.[10]

The seriousness of this dispute necessitated a solution to the currency question. Curiously, British merchants advanced the most satisfactory answer. Realizing that at least £100,000 currency was needed in South Carolina to accommodate commerce, they proposed that the

6. Labaree, ed., *Royal Instructions*, I, 218.

7. Nov. 23, 30, Dec. 6-15, 1722, S. C. Commons Journals, CO 5/426, pp. 10-13, 20-21, 25-47; Cooper and McCord, eds., *S. C. Statutes*, III, 188-93.

8. Order in Council, Aug. 27, 1723, CO 5/359, ff. 3, 5-6; Board of Trade to Nicholson, July 18, 1723, CO 5/400, pp. 170-72; Board of Trade to Crown, July 26, 1723, CO 5/381, ff. 26-27.

9. Brock, *Currency of American Colonies*, 121; S. C. Commons to Board of Trade, Nov. 15, 1723, CO 5/359, ff. 103-4; Dec. 4, 1723, S. C. Commons Journals, CO 5/427; Cooper and McCord, eds., *S. C. Statutes*, III, 219-21.

10. See Middleton to Nicholson, May 4, 1727, CO 5/387, f. 258; and to Duke of Newcastle, [Dec. 1728], CO 5/360, ff. 94-95; S. C. Council to Crown, Dec. 1728, *ibid.*, ff. 105-49.

old currency be called in and replaced by a new issue, that the law appropriating money to sink the 1723 emission be suspended for seven years, and that the money arising from that law be used to encourage the settlement of poor Protestants. Newly appointed Governor Robert Johnson endorsed the merchants' proposals, pointing out that the planters' debts were "all due and payable in the present paper Bills" and that if "the present paper Currency be lessened and become thereby nearer in Value to Sterling it would ruin at least 19/20 of the Inhabitants." In July 1730 imperial authorities formally approved the merchants' proposals and wrote them into Johnson's instructions. In addition, they empowered him to assent to laws to establish a new paper currency as the situation required, providing, of course, that such laws contained suspending clauses.[11] This arrangement seemed to portend the adoption of an enlightened attitude on the part of both British merchants and imperial authorities, but it was only a temporary relaxation of their doctrinaire opposition to American paper currencies. Upon Johnson's recommendation, the Commons readily agreed to the merchants' proposals and passed a measure to exchange the £106,500 in old paper bills for new ones, temporarily solving South Carolina's currency problem. In November 1731 Johnson reported to the Board of Trade that the "want of more Paper Currency is very great" and that "the Assembly is very desirous of having more," but the Commons did not immediately pass a bill to establish a new currency. When it did try in June 1733, the Council rejected the attempt.[12]

Eventually, the Commons with the support of both the royal governors and the Council passed two acts, one in 1736 and another in 1746, in accordance with Johnson's instructions, but neither was ever confirmed by the Crown. The 1736 act provided for the emission of £210,000, including £100,000 to be exchanged for bills then in circulation and £110,000 new currency. Despite strong opposition from

11. Merchants trading to S. C. to Board of Trade, Feb. 4, 1730, and merchants' answers to queries relating to S. C. bills of credit, received by Board of Trade, Feb. 13, 1730, CO 5/361, ff. 55-56; Johnson's answer to queries relating to S. C. paper currency, received by Board of Trade, Mar. 7, 1730, and A State of the Paper Currency in South Carolina, Mar. 13, 1730, CO 5/361, ff. 59-61, 76-77; Order in Council, July 21, 1730, CO 5/361, f. 144; Labaree, ed., *Royal Instructions,* I, 231-33.

12. Cooper and McCord, eds., *S. C. Statutes,* III, 305-307; Johnson to Board of Trade, Nov. 14, 1731, CO 5/362, ff. 54-58; June 1, 1733, S. C. Commons Journals, CO 5/433, p. 66.

British merchants, Crown authorities were sympathetic, although several minor objections kept them from confirming the measure. Accordingly, in 1739 the Privy Council informed Governor James Glen that it would consent to the law if the Commons would revise the objectionable clauses.[13] The Commons refused, but in June 1746 it pushed through a similar measure with an additional clause providing for the retirement of the entire sum in twenty-five years.[14] In December 1748 Matthew Lamb, legal counsel for the Board of Trade, objected to the loose construction of the bill, and after a long delay imperial authorities disallowed it in April 1754 in the wake of the Parliamentary statute of 1751 prohibiting the issue of legal tender paper in New England.[15] In 1756, Governor Lyttelton received an instruction more severe than the act of Parliament, requiring the Commons to pass a law to retire the paper currency then circulating and prohibiting passage of further currency bills without the Crown's permission except in emergencies and then only when they made provisions for sinking the currency issued.[16] Although this instruction did not bring about the retirement of the paper money circulating in South Carolina, it did prevent further emission of legal tender currency.[17]

There was no increase in the amount of South Carolina's legal tender paper money after 1723, and the amount in circulation was settled at £106,500 after 1731. Even though the South Carolina Commons did not win the power to issue legal tender currency, it evolved two methods after 1731 to satisfy the currency needs of the colony: non-legal tender public orders and tax certificates.

To pay its creditors the government first issued public orders in

13. Cooper and McCord, eds., *S. C. Statutes*, III, 423-30; Bristol merchants' petition against act of 1736, [1736], CO 5/366, f. 26; Order in Council, Mar. 27, 1739, CO 5/367, ff. 1-2; Joseph Wragg to Isaac Hobhouse, June 9, 1736, Hobhouse Papers, Jeffries Collection: African Slave Trade of Bristol, XIII, Bristol Reference Library, Bristol, Eng.; Labaree, ed., *Royal Instructions*, I, 233-34.

14. Cooper and McCord, eds., *S. C. Statutes*, III, 671-77; Peregrine Fury to John Pownall, Jan. 22, 1748, CO 5/372, ff. 4-5; Eliza Pinckney to George Lucas, Jan. 29, 1745, Eliza Pinckney Papers, Duke University Library, Durham, N. C.; David D. Wallace, *The History of South Carolina*, 4 vols. (N. Y., 1934-35), I, 383.

15. Lamb's observations on S. C. Currency act, Dec. 14, 1748, George Chalmers, ed., *Opinions of Eminent Lawyers . . .*, 2 vols. (London, 1814), II, 89-94, hereafter cited as Chalmers, ed., *Opinions*; Order in Council, Apr. 8, 1754, CO 5/374, f. 230.

16. Labaree, ed., *Royal Instructions*, I, 234-35; Brock, Currency of American Colonies, 455.

17. Brock, Currency of American Colonies, 461-62.

1731 during Middleton's administration, promising to redeem them by a certain date and to receive them for taxes. Somewhat later, the Commons began to use tax certificates—notes issued by the treasury as temporary payment to government creditors until the collection of taxes. To the £104,775 of public orders issued in 1731 the Commons added £35,010 in 1737, £36,508 in 1740, £63,000 in 1742, and £20,000 in 1745. With the exception of the 1731 issue, it issued all of these orders to meet immediate expenses for defense. The Commons retired them promptly, however, and by 1749 only £26,545 of the whole amount issued between 1731 and 1745 was still circulating.[18] During the later years of his administration, Glen strongly objected to the use of public orders, and there were no new issues between 1745 and 1755. He rejected both the Commons' 1748 attempt to print £40,000 to hire troops to patrol the coast and its 1755 effort to emit £40,000 to be used against the French.[19]

Indeed, the Crown tried to prevent the issue of public orders by an instruction in 1755,[20] but the Seven Years' War again forced the Commons to resort to public orders. Between 1755 and 1762 it issued £816,358 of public orders as well as several hundred thousand pounds of tax certificates. During the peak year, 1761, over £867,744 of both varieties was circulating in the province in addition to the £106,500 of paper currency. The emergency public orders and the tax certificates were regularly retired during the war, however, and by 1764 only £295,011 of public orders and £183,736 of tax certificates were outstanding.[21]

Although they were not legal tender, both public orders and tax certificates were receivable for all taxes and duties and therefore served the same purpose as paper money. They passed at the same rate of exchange as paper money, which from 1739 was constantly rated

18. Cooper and McCord, eds., *S. C. Statutes*, III, 334-41, 461-64, 546-53, 577-79, 595-97, 653-56; Brock, Currency of American Colonies, 124-26.

19. S. C. Committee of Correspondence to Peregrine Fury, Mar. 24, 1748, CO 5/372, ff. 46-47; Glen to Board of Trade, Apr. 14, 1748, *ibid.*, f. 40; Glen to Duke of Bedford, July 27, 1748, CO 5/13, ff. 245-47; May 6, 1755, S. C. Commons Journals, CO 5/472, pp. 107-8; Glen to Board of Trade, May 29, 1755, CO 5/375, ff. 49-54; Robert Dinwiddie to Benjamin Smith, John Rattray, and John Savage, May 5, [1755], Brock, ed., *Dinwiddie Papers*, II, 29.

20. Labaree, ed., *Royal Instructions*, I, 234-35.

21. Cooper and McCord, eds., *S. C. Statutes*, IV, 18-19, 34, 45, 103; Brock, Currency of American Colonies, Tables XXVI-XXVII.

at seven and a half pounds of currency to one pound sterling.[22] The Crown stopped the issue of legal tender in South Carolina after 1731, but it could not prevent the issuance of an effective substitute, the public order, in times of emergency, and the Commons exercised the power to issue money, or a reasonable substitute, until Parliament's passage of the Currency Act in 1764.

In North Carolina, as in South Carolina, paper currency had its origins in the proprietary period during time of war. To meet the expenses of the Tuscarora Indian War the legislature voted the first issues of £4,000 in 1712 and £8,000 in 1713. It made both issues legal tender but did not provide for the immediate retirement of either.[23] In 1714 it increased the total amount of currency to £24,000 by providing for the emission of £12,000 in additional currency and £12,000 to replace the Tuscarora issues. The following year the legislature voted to retire the bills at the rate of £2,000 per year. By 1722 £12,000 had been retired, and it replaced the remaining £12,000 with new bills.[24] During the transition from proprietary to royal control, the legislature took advantage of the confusion of authority in 1729 before the arrival of royal Governor George Burrington to induce proprietary Governor Richard Everard to assent to an emission of £40,000 legal tender currency. This act provided for exchanging the £10,000 in old bills then in circulation and for loaning the remaining £30,000 to inhabitants on landed security for fifteen years at an annual interest of 6¼ per cent. It further provided for the annual retirement of one-fifteenth of the principal, so that all of the bills would be sunk in fifteen years' time. Thus, when the Crown assumed control of the colony, there was £40,000 of paper currency in circulation.[25]

As a matter of course, imperial authorities gave both Governors Burrington and Johnston the usual instruction not to assent to paper

22. Brock, Currency of American Colonies, 124-26, 446, 457-58; Account of paper money in S. C., Apr. 16, 1740, House of Lords MSS, 161, House of Lords, London.
23. Governor Thomas Pollock to ————, June 8, 1713, N. C. Col. Recs., II, 50; Account of paper money in N. C., Mar. 5, 1741, House of Lords MSS, 166, No. 2; Burrington to Newcastle, July 2, 1731, N. C. Col. Recs., III, 145-46.
24. Laws, N. C. St. Recs., XXIII, 90-92, XXV, 157-58, 173-75.
25. Act to emit £40,000, 1729, Legislative Papers, I, North Carolina Department of Archives and History, Raleigh; Account of paper money in N. C., Mar. 5, 1741, House of Lords MSS, 166, No. 2; Brock, Currency of American Colonies, 108-10.

currency bills unless they contained a suspending clause.[26] Nevertheless, during the first two decades of the royal period the legislature provided for two additional emergency emissions, even though it retired none of the money issued in 1729. At his first legislative session in March 1735 Governor Johnston consented to the Lower House's proposal to emit £12,500 in paper money to defray pressing government expenses. The House voted a five-year tax and duty on liquors to retire this emission and made it legal tender. Moreover, it passed a measure to stamp £40,000 in new bills to be exchanged for those issued in 1729 and suspended indefinitely the provisions for sinking them because of the large amounts due in quitrents and taxes. The total amount of currency circulating in 1735 was, then, £52,500.[27]

In August 1740 the Lower House failed in an effort to issue more paper money to send North Carolina forces against the Spanish in the War of Jenkins' Ear;[28] it did not try again until 1748. Between 1735 and 1748, however, it retired none of the £52,500 issued earlier. It was supposed to retire £12,500 in 1740 and the remaining £40,000 in 1744, but a disagreement between the Council and Lower House over the methods and time for sinking the bills delayed passage of the law until April 1745, though even this statute proved ineffective.[29] From 1745 to 1748 a decline in the colony's economic fortunes and the need to defend its open coasts from attacks by Spanish marauders created a strong demand for additional paper currency, and in April 1748 North Carolina's long assembly persuaded Johnston to pass a new currency act without a suspending clause providing for the emission of £21,350 in paper bills equal in value to proclamation money —that is, foreign coins at the rates established by royal proclamation in 1704. Of this amount £7,000 was to be exchanged for all old bills then circulating at the rate of one new bill for seven old ones; £6,000 used to build four forts at specified spots on the coast; and the remainder used to pay the public debt. Because it was rated so high,

26. Labaree, ed., *Royal Instructions,* I, 218-19.

27. Account of paper money in N. C., Mar. 5, 1741, House of Lords MSS, 166, No. 2; State of paper currency in N. C., received by Board of Trade, Jan. 23, 1740, *N. C. Col. Recs.,* IV, 418-19; Laws, *N. C. St. Recs.,* XXIII, 117.

28. Lower House Journals, Aug. 22, 1740, *N.C. Col. Recs.,* IV, 557.

29. Lower House Journals, Mar. 5-6, Nov. 29, Dec. 1, 4, 1744, *ibid.,* 727, 729, 746-49, 752; Laws, *N. C. St. Recs.,* XXV, 234-35; Johnston to Board of Trade, Apr. 4, 1749, *N. C. Col. Recs.,* IV, 921-22.

the issue more than tripled the amount of currency in circulation and resulted in considerable inflation.[30]

Immediate opposition to the act came from the residents of the colony's northern counties, which had not been represented in the legislature that passed it. They refused to recognize the legality of the measure or to exchange the old currency for the new, and their agent, Henry McCulloh, and a number of others protested to the Board of Trade. Legal counsel Matthew Lamb also reported unfavorably on the act.[31] But the Board neither recommended disallowance of the law nor censored Johnston for having passed it without a suspending clause.

At the beginning of the Seven Years' War, the North Carolina Lower House would not grant money to send troops on Dinwiddie's Ohio expedition without a paper money issue, which, it contended, was needed not only to meet military expenses but also to satisfy the requirements of the colony's expanding economy. Accordingly, in early 1754 it forced upon President Matthew Rowan an act to issue £40,000 paper currency at the rate of proclamation money, with £12,000 for the Ohio campaign, £2,000 for a fort at Ocracoke Inlet, £1,000 for arms and ammunition for poor inhabitants in Rowan and Anson counties on the frontiers, £800 for producing new bills, £4,200 for contingencies, and £18,000 for future use. The House also made provision for eventual retirement of the bills.[32]

Despite urgent military needs during the Seven Years' War, the 1754 issue was the last legal tender emission until 1760. During the intervening period Governor Arthur Dobbs carefully avoided any new issues, although he did consent to re-issue the 1754 bills, instead of sinking them, to meet pressing military expenses. He also permitted the emission of £3,400 in interest-bearing notes in 1756 and of £14,806 in 1757. These notes served the same function as paper currency, but

30. Johnston to Board of Trade, Apr. 4, 1749, *N. C. Col. Recs.*, IV, 921-22; Laws, *N. C. St. Recs.*, XXIII, 292-96; Charles J. Bullock, *Essays on the Monetary History of the United States* (N. Y. and London, 1900), 151-53; Brock, *Currency of American Colonies*, 111-12.

31. James Moir to Secretary of the Society for the Propagation of the Gospel, May 16, 1750, B MSS, 18, f. 180, Society for the Propagation of the Gospel, London; Jan. 25, 1749, *Board of Trade Journals, 1742-49*, 371; Lamb to Board of Trade, Feb. 7, 1750, CO 5/296, ff. 288-89.

32. Matthew Rowan to Board of Trade, Mar. 19 and Aug. 29, 1754, *N. C. Col. Recs.*, V, 109, 137; Laws, *N. C. St. Recs.*, XXIII, 392-98; Brock, *Currency of American Colonies*, 431-33.

they were not legal tender and did not prove objectionable to either imperial authorities or British merchants.[33]

By 1759, however, British merchants were beginning to complain about both the 1748 and 1754 currency emissions. They objected particularly to the currency's having been made legal tender and charged that they were being forced to accept it at face value in payment for debts even though it had greatly depreciated. Spurred by the petitions, imperial authorities instructed Dobbs to secure amendment of the acts to provide that sterling debts contracted since the emissions should be payable in paper only if the creditor was willing to accept it, and then only at the actual, rather than the legal, rate of exchange. This instruction, a classic expression of the prevailing official attitude towards colonial paper currencies, was intended to nullify the legal tender provisions in the 1748 and 1754 laws and was accompanied by the additional suggestion that North Carolina paper bills not be accepted as legal tender in payment of Crown revenues.[34]

But Dobbs never induced the Lower House to comply with the instruction. Indeed, the need for money to provide aid for South Carolina against the Cherokees forced him to consent to two additional paper currency issues of £12,000 in July 1760 and £20,000 in April 1761. The Lower House made both issues legal tender by refusing to vote money under any other condition.[35] Thus, although the Crown could formally prohibit legal tender currency, royal officials could not prevent the Lower House from issuing it when there was no other money available to meet an emergency. In 1761 there was about £95,335 circulating in North Carolina, including both the paper currency and the interest-bearing notes. After 1764, however, when Parliament prohibited further issues of legal tender paper money, the Lower House complied faithfully with the provisions for retiring the currency, reducing it to £60,106 by 1768.[36]

33. Brock, Currency of American Colonies, 434-35.

34. Mar. 28, 1759, *Board of Trade Journals, 1759-63,* 24-25; Labaree, ed., *Royal Instructions,* I, 229-31; May 31, 1759, W. L. Grant and James Munro, eds., *Acts of the Privy Council of England, Colonial Series,* 6 vols. (London, 1908-12), IV, 414-16.

35. Lower House Journals, Dec. 7, 1759, *N. C. Col. Recs.,* VI, 149-50; Apr. 15, 1761, *ibid.,* 686-88; Upper House Journals, Apr., 23, 1761, *ibid.,* 633-34; Dobbs to Board of Trade, July 21, 1760, *ibid.,* 267; Laws, *N. C. St. Recs.,* XXIII, 516-18, 539-41.

36. Lower House Journals, Nov. 24, 1764, *N. C. Col. Recs.,* VI, 1310-11; Brock, Currency of American Colonies, 445.

Georgia was the third of the southern royal colonies to issue paper money. At its first session the Georgia Commons passed an act with a suspending clause to print £7,000. Because the Crown did not confirm it, the act never was legally in force, but the commissioners appointed to produce the currency emitted £2,987 without waiting for the Crown's decision. Although Governor John Reynolds did not formally sanction that action, neither did he attempt to prevent it because of Georgia's great scarcity of money.[37]   Indeed, with the possible exception of Nova Scotia, Georgia was the poorest Crown colony on the Atlantic seaboard with no significant overseas trade and no ready source of hard money, and it was only a question of time until it established a paper currency. Henry Ellis, Reynolds's successor, immediately recognized the colony's need for paper money, and in July 1757, when it became apparent that the colony had no other means to defray its debts, he readily consented to the emission of £638.[38]

Doubly irritated because the measure contained no suspending clause and made the bills legal tender in payment of taxes and officers' fees, the Board of Trade refused to approve this emission. Reminding Ellis of Parliament's 1751 prohibition against such bills in New England, the Board cautioned him against further emissions. But Ellis briskly defended his action and paved the way for future issues by pointing out that the emission had had beneficial results and that Georgia vitally needed some sort of currency to meet the demands of trade. Even before he received the Board's sentiments on the 1757 issue, Ellis had, in fact, already approved an act in March 1759 to print an additional £799 to build a public magazine and to repair the Tybee Island lighthouse and the Savannah church—all necessities for which there were no other means of paying.[39]

Nor did the Board of Trade's opposition deter Ellis from consenting in April 1760 to an issue of an additional £1,100 for defense. At the same time, he agreed to a bill designed to satisfy the colony's commercial needs. Containing a suspending clause, it provided for

37. Statutes, *Ga. Col. Recs.*, XVIII, 48-64; Matthew Lamb to Board of Trade, Jan. 5, 1756, CO 5/645; Mar. 21, 1758, *Board of Trade Journals, 1754-58*, 390; Brock, Currency of American Colonies, 462.

38. Statutes, *Ga. Col. Recs.*, XVIII, 235-40; Ellis to Board of Trade, May 5, 1757, July 8, 1757, CO 5/646.

39. Board of Trade to Ellis, Apr. 21, 1758, CO 5/653; Ellis to Board of Trade, Apr. 24, 1759, CO 5/646; Statutes, *Ga. Col. Recs.*, XVIII, 308-13.

£7,410, of which £4,437 was to be exchanged for the issues then circulating and the remainder loaned out on mortgaged lands, tenements, and slaves at 6 per cent interest. The act also provided that the currency remain in circulation for seven years as legal tender in payment of all debts. The Board of Trade was at first wary of the measure, particularly because it made the bills legal tender and provided for so long a circulation. But Ellis persuaded it to recommend confirmation of the act by pointing out that the colony did not have any trade which brought in either gold or silver, that it was impossible for a colony of Georgia's small trade, wealth, and population to redeem its currency in shorter time, and that the currency would promote the cultivation and settlement of the colony. In July 1761 the Crown assented to the act,[40] marking the first time since the approval of the South Carolina currency proposal in 1731 that it had formally relaxed its policy and permitted the issuance of a legal tender currency in any of the southern royal colonies.

Although the paper money issued under this act temporarily solved the colony's problems by providing a sufficient medium of trade, Ellis's successor, James Wright, found it necessary to consent to two small additional issues. In June 1761 he passed a bill authorizing £180 to repair a lighthouse and the following December £540 to build a fort and battery on Midway River. With the £7,410 issued under the 1760 act these emissions made a total of £8,230 circulating after 1761.[41] Though not large, Georgia's currency was necessary to facilitate its internal commerce and to defray the cost of public works. Like the lower houses in the Carolinas, the Georgia Commons could not be prevented from passing laws to issue money when circumstances required it.

The last of the southern royal colonies to resort to paper currency was Virginia. As in the Carolinas, commodities, chiefly tobacco, had served as a medium of exchange during its early years, and beginning with Spotswood's administration non-legal tender tobacco notes passed as currency. In normal times these notes satisfied the demands of trade, and the Virginia Burgesses did not turn to paper

40. Statutes, *Ga. Col. Recs.*, XVIII, 420-26, 435-55; June 23, 1761, *Acts of Privy Council, Colonial*, VI, 334-35; John Pownall to Wright, Sept. 7, 1761, CO 5/674, p. 207.
41. Wright to Board of Trade, July 13, 1761, CO 5/648, ff. 189-201; Statutes, *Ga. Col. Recs.*, XVIII, 472-79; Brock, Currency of American Colonies, 463-64.

currency until 1755, when there was no other way to raise money for the Seven Years' War.[42]

Indeed, that war placed increasingly heavy financial burdens upon Virginia from 1755 to 1763. That it was in no condition to bear the load was apparent early in the conflict. The Burgesses defrayed the initial expenses in 1754 by extraordinary taxes, and by mid-1754 the great scarcity of specie was a common subject of complaint. John Mercer, Jr., reported in May that no money was to be had in the colony except at horse races and gaming tables.[43] Perceiving the strain that military appropriations were placing on the colony's finances, Landon Carter in the following August proposed a bill to issue £20,000 paper currency. At the time, Carter's plan "met with few Espousers from the great aversion to Paper money,"[44] but by the following spring a different opinion prevailed in the Burgesses. Money was so scarce that the required funds could not be raised except by an issue of paper. As a result, the Burgesses voted in July 1755 to print £20,000 in bills—Virginia's first legal tender paper money. Less than a month later news of Braddock's defeat forced the Burgesses to vote another £40,000. Lieutenant Governor Dinwiddie apologized to the Board of Trade for consenting to these two emissions. Although the Board wished that "other methods . . . could have been fallen upon," it endorsed Dinwiddie's action, observing that "the necessity and exigency of the Service to be provided for will justify the measure to His Majesty."[45]

The £60,000 issued in the summer of 1755 was only the beginning of paper currency in Virginia. Although the Council rejected the Burgesses' attempt to establish a loan office and to emit £200,000 in November 1755, the following spring Dinwiddie was once more forced to agree to the emission of paper. Throughout the winter and spring

42. Henry Hartwell, James Blair, and Edward Chilton, *The Present State of Virginia, and the College,* ed. Hunter D. Farish (Williamsburg, 1940), 9-10, 14-15; Ripley, *Financial History of Virginia,* 145-53; Extract of letter of William Gooch, Feb. 9, 1740, House of Lords MSS, 166, No. 1; Peter Leheup to Thomas Hill, Jan. 23, 1740, CO 5/1324, f. 180.

43. John Mercer, Jr., to Daniel Parke Custis, May 31, 1754, Custis Papers, Virginia Historical Society, Richmond.

44. Carter's Minutes of the Burgesses, Aug. 1754, Sabine Hall Collection, Alderman Lib.

45. Hening, ed., *Va. Statutes,* VI, 461-68, 521-30; July 9, Aug. 23, 1755, *Va. Burgesses Journals, 1752-58,* 293, 314; Dinwiddie to Board of Trade, Sept. 6, 1755, CO 5/1328, ff. 387-88; Board of Trade to Dinwiddie, Nov. 6, 1755, CO 5/1367, pp 156-57.

of 1756 the scarcity of gold and silver was a recurrent theme in Din-widdie's letters, and Virginians complained about the heavy load of taxes.[46] To meet the cost of the war, therefore, the Burgesses author-ized two additional emissions of paper currency of £25,000 and £30,000 in May 1756. At the same time, the burning of a tobacco warehouse created the need for the printing of another £10,000. In the spring of 1757 the last and largest paper money emission under Dinwiddie came, the Burgesses voting £80,000 in new bills and £99,962 to be exchanged for all bills then circulating.[47] By the end of Dinwiddie's tenure in January 1758 the total amount had soared to £179,962.

Although Matthew Lamb questioned Virginia's first paper curren-cy issues in December 1756 because they were legal tender,[48] imperial authorities raised no serious objection until the 1757 issue of £80,000 in new bills. Like the earlier issues, these were to be legal tender, and British merchants feared that they would depreciate and that the Virginians would force the merchants to take them at face value in payment for debts. In the fall of 1757 Edmund Jenings III, a former Virginia resident concerned in the Virginia trade, protested against the act to the Board of Trade, calling its attention to the Parliamen-tary statute of 1751 prohibiting legal tender currency in New Eng-land. Merchant opposition grew during the winter, and, in the fol-lowing June, London, Bristol, and Liverpool merchants submitted separate petitions against the act to imperial authorities.[49] In July the Privy Council decided that the act should not be disallowed, but ruled that the governor be instructed to induce the Burgesses to amend it so that sterling debts contracted before its passage would be

46. Nov. 4, 1755, *Va. Burgesses Journals, 1752-58*, xxiv, 328; Dinwiddie to Board of Trade, Nov. 15, 1755, CO 5/1328, ff. 393-94; Dinwiddie to Duke of Halifax, Nov. 15, 1755, Dinwiddie Letters, Virginia Misc. MSS, f. 16, Library of Congress, Washington; Dinwiddie to William Shirley, Jan. 24, 1756, Loudoun Papers, 767, Henry E. Huntington Library, San Marino, Calif.; Dinwiddie to James Aber-cromby, Feb. 24, 1756, Brock, ed., *Dinwiddie Papers*, II, 358-59; James Maury to John Fontaine, June 15, 1756, Virginia Papers, Bancroft Collection, I, ff. 43-47, New York Public Library, N. Y.

47. Hening, ed., *Va. Statutes*, VII, 9-20, 26-33, 46-54, 69-87; May 1, 1756, *Va. Burgesses Journals, 1752-58*, 392; Dinwiddie to Board of Trade, Sept. 12, 1757, CO 5/1329, ff. 93-94.

48. Lamb's report to Board of Trade, Dec. 18, 1756, CO 5/1329, ff. 105-7.

49. Jenings to Richard Corbin, Oct. 24, 1757, Edmund Jenings III Letter Book, Va. Hist. Soc.; Abercromby to Dinwiddie, Nov. 3, 1757, to Francis Fauquier, June 23, 1758, Abercromby Letter Book, 54-55, 102-3, Va. State Lib.; Memorials of Lon-don and Bristol merchants, [1758], CO 5/1329, ff. 129, 131-32.

payable only in sterling money and the bills would be legal tender only if the creditor were willing to accept them. Despite this decision, imperial authorities did not issue the instruction until January 1759, six months later.[50]

Even while the British merchants were petitioning against the earlier issues, the Virginia legislature was emitting additional paper. Scarcity of specie and the need to provide for defense prompted John Blair, who served as Virginia's chief executive between Dinwiddie's departure and Fauquier's arrival, to consent to an act to print another £32,000 in April 1758 and Fauquier to pass two other bills—one in the fall of 1758 to print £57,000 and another in the spring of 1759 to print £52,000.[51] On receiving the Crown's instruction of January 1759, Fauquier assured the Board of Trade that he would comply with it, but the Burgesses flatly refused to accept it and between November 1759 and March 1762 provided for four additional issues totaling £92,000 without the required limitations.[52] These issues were the colony's last before the end of the war, bringing the total amount of currency issued during the Seven Years' War to about £440,000. By an act of November 1761 the Burgesses provided for the retirement of all the currency by October 20, 1769.[53]

In 1762 the continued insistence of the Virginia Burgesses that their paper currency should pass as legal tender drew forth additional protests from British merchants in London, Glasgow, and Liverpool,

50. July 28, 1758, *Acts of Privy Council, Colonial*, IV, 389-93; Virginia Burgesses to William Pitt, [1758], Chatham Papers, Gifts and Deposits, 30/8, vol. 96, PRO; Additional Instructions to Earl of Loudoun, Jan. 31, 1759, CO 5/1367, ff. 358-62.

51. Hening, ed., *Va. Statutes*, VII, 163-69, 171-231, 255-65; Apr. 12, 1758, *Va. Burgesses Journals, 1752-58*, 506; Blair to Board of Trade, June 20, 1758, Fauquier to Board of Trade, Jan. 9, 1759, CO 5/1329, ff. 161-64, 229-35. For an unfavorable view of these emissions see Richard Corbin to James Buchanan, Apr. 26, 1758, Richard Corbin Letter Book, Colonial Williamsburg, Inc. For a favorable view see [Landon Carter], *A Letter to a Gentleman in London from Virginia* (London, 1759).

52. Hening, ed., *Va. Statutes*, VII, 331-37, 347-53, 357-63, 495-502; Nov. 21, 1759, Mar. 11, 1760, *Va. Burgesses Journals, 1758-61*, 152, 167; Fauquier to Board of Trade, July 14, 1759, CO 5/1329, ff. 335-37. Several councilors opposed the March 1762 emission allegedly because it did not comply with the 1758 instruction; see the dissenting opinion of William Nelson, Thomas Nelson, Robert Carter, Philip Ludwell Lee, 1762, CO 5/1330, ff. 319-20. But Fauquier charged that they merely wanted to disband the regiment then in the colony's service; Fauquier to Board of Trade, Apr. 8, 1762, *ibid.*, ff. 265-68. See also Fauquier to Board of Trade, July 10, 1762, *ibid.*, ff. 311-16.

53. Brock, Currency of American Colonies, Table XXVIII; Hening, ed., *Va. Statutes*, VII, 465-66; Fauquier to Board of Trade, Feb. 24, 1762, CO 5/1330, ff. 219-22.

who complained that the bills were depreciating rapidly.[54] When their petitions came before the Board of Trade, it adopted resolutions against the Virginia currency and declared "that the legislature of Virginia have been wanting, not only in a proper respect to the Crown, but also in justice to the . . . merchants, in refusing to comply with what was recommended in his late Majesty's additional instructions." The Board also blasted Fauquier for "artfully endeavouring . . . to hang out an Appearance of Obedience to Orders" and for not having "in any one instance used your Endeavours to carry those Orders into Execution, or . . . [having] insisted upon the Amendment, which the Instruction Recommends."[55]

The Board's resolutions were not enthusiastically received in Virginia. Fauquier argued that in issuing legal tender paper money he had done nothing more than Blair and Dinwiddie had done in similar circumstances. In fact, when Fauquier did endeavor to induce the Burgesses to meet the Board's objections, it refused, declaring in May 1763 that "Our Dependance upon Great Britain we acknowledge and glory in . . . but this is not the Dependance of a People subjugated by the Arms of a Conqueror, but of Sons sent out to explore and settle a new World, for the mutual Benefit of themselves and their Common Parent." Flatly refusing to remove the currency's legal tender requirements, it also resolved "that as the present possessers of the Treasury Notes have received them under the Faith of a Law, making them a legal Tender in all payments, except for his Majestys Quitrents, to alter that essential Quality of them now would be an Act of great Injustice to such Possessors, and that as the British Merchants have constantly received, and under the present Regulations of our Laws, will continue to receive such Notes for their Sterling Debts, according to the real difference of Exchange between this Colony and Great Britain at the Time of payment, their Property is so secured as to make such Alteration unnecessary with Respect to them."[56]

54. Richard Corbin to Robert Cary, Aug. 22, 1762, Corbin Letter Book, 100, Colonial Williamsburg, Inc.; James Abercromby to Fauquier, Nov. 10, 1762, Robert A. Brock Collection, Huntington Lib.; Memorials of London, Glasgow, and Liverpool merchants, CO 5/1330, ff. 261-63, 277, 279; Richard Corbin's memorial, read by Board of Trade, Dec. 16, 1762, *ibid.*, ff. 255-57.
55. Feb. 1-7, 1763, *Board of Trade Journals, 1759-63*, 330-34; Board of Trade to Fauquier, Feb. 7, 1763, CO 5/1368, pp. 212-17.
56. Fauquier to Board of Trade, May 24 and June 1, 1763, CO 5/1330, ff. 431-34, 453-59; Va. Committee of Correspondence to Edward Montague, June 16, 1763, "Proceedings of the Virginia Committee of Correspondence, 1759-'67," *Va. Mag.*

Neither the British merchants nor the Board of Trade was pleased by the Burgesses' defiance of the Board's demands. "Any further neglect of the Legislature of Virginia to give redress to the complaints of the merchants," the Board declared in December 1763, "would be neither just or equitable"; "if they any longer refused doing justice to the British merchants . . . the Board should think it their duty to advise his Majesty to lay the matter before Parliament."[57] When the Burgesses stood their ground, imperial authorities did present the matter to Parliament, which passed the restrictive Currency Act in April 1764.

The last of the southern royal colonies to employ paper money, Virginia issued more legal tender currency in the nine years during the Seven Years' War than did any of the others during the entire colonial period. It is significant, too, that these issues took place in spite of vigorous opposition from British merchants and imperial officials. In the conflict between imperial authority and imperious necessity, the Burgesses unqualifiedly chose the latter.

The lower houses in the southern royal colonies never secured the constitutional power to emit paper money as legal tender in the period before 1763. So long as authorities in London opposed emission of paper money in the colonies and retained power to disallow colonial laws, the lower houses were unable to exercise that power freely. However, they did exercise it upon many occasions before the end of the Seven Years' War, and they could not easily be prevented from exercising it in other times of stress; indeed, they had been able to emit enough paper money to meet not only the demands of war but also the needs of trade. But Parliament's passage of the Currency Act in the fall of 1764, a direct outgrowth of the merchants' alarm over the refusal of the Virginia and North Carolina lower houses to comply with imperial directives, threatened to end emissions of legal tender paper money altogether. More important, it posed fundamental questions about the nature of the imperial union between Great Britian and the colonies by pointing up the imperial problem of reconciling central control with local needs.

---

of Hist. and Biog., 11 (1904), 345-49; Burgesses' representation, May 1763, Stevens Transcripts, I, No. 1, Add. MSS, 42257, ff. 128-40, British Museum; May 28, 1763, *Va. Burgesses Journals, 1761-65,* 188-92; Fauquier to Egremont, May 19, 1763, Egremont Papers, Gifts and Deposits, 30/47, vol. 14, PRO.

57. Dec. 8, 1763, *Board of Trade Journals, 1759-63,* 418; Board of Trade to Fauquier, Dec. 9, 1763, CO 5/1368, ff. 245-46.

PART III

CONTROL OVER THE CIVIL LIST

I was not able the last Setting to Induce the Assembly to Settle a fixt Sallary upon me, and his Majestys Officers; that being dispenced with now in New England, has I believe Influenced this Province; they don't absolutely refuse it, but postpone it.
> —South Carolina Governor Robert Johnson,
> June 1732

Liberty and Property and no Pistole.
> —The Reverend William Stith against the
> Pistole Fee, Virginia, 1753

T HAT each colony should pay its own way, including the cost of maintaining its civil officers, was one of the canons of English mercantilism. Those officers derived their incomes largely from two sources: salaries and fees. Imperial authorities early tried to deprive colonial lower houses of control over those incomes by requiring them to establish perpetual taxes to provide permanent salaries and by placing the power to settle fees in the hands of the executive. For the most part, the lower houses refused to accept either of these measures. With the exception of the Virginia Burgesses, all lower houses on the continent declined to establish permanent revenues, preferring either to keep salaries under legislative control by paying them only for short periods or, if possible, to shift the salary burden upon the London government. They also closely regulated incomes by fixing all fees by statute, regarding them as taxes and denying the power of governors and councils to settle them by executive order.

CONTROL OVER THE CIVIL LIST

7

Salaries

In 1679 English authorities adopted the policy of requiring royal legislatures to grant perpetual revenues to be placed permanently under the control of the Crown for the support of governors and other officers on the civil establishment. This policy was calculated to shift a large part of the fiscal burden of colonial administration from the mother country to the colonies and render royal officials independent of local legislatures. Conflict developed when American lower houses refused to accede to the policy, preferring instead either to force the Crown to pay officers out of imperial revenues or, if the Crown insisted that each colony support its officers, to pay them by annual grants, keeping them dependent upon the legislature. Crown officials particularly feared that lower houses by the latter arrangement would exert pressure upon the chief executives by either withholding or increasing their yearly salaries, and, when all of the southern legislatures except the Virginia Burgesses refused to provide a permanent revenue, they were forced to adopt the former arrangement and provide salaries from imperial funds. But even though lower houses had no control over executive salaries, they could exercise considerable influence over governors by tendering presents to them at opportune moments in return for favors. To prevent just that sort of development, imperial authorities after 1702 absolutely prohibited governors from accepting gifts from lower houses.[1] By these measures Crown officials succeeded to a remarkable degree in depriving lower houses in the southern royal colonies of control over

1. Labaree, ed., *Royal Instructions*, I, 239-40. The best study of the salary question is Labaree, *Royal Government*, 312-72.

salaries of royal officials, but only at the expense of paying them out of imperial funds.

Virginia's royal governors never suffered for want of a regular salary. From 1628 until the outbreak of the Civil War, the Crown paid them a salary of £1,000 per annum out of customs duties on Virginia tobacco imported into England. After 1642 the colony paid the governor's salary initially by grants of commodities, usually tobacco, and after 1660 by a two-shilling-per-hogshead export duty on tobacco.[2] For nearly twenty years the legislature provided for this duty by temporary measures, re-enacted from time to time, but in June 1680 it agreed to make the duty perpetual in return for the Crown's pardon of Nathaniel Bacon and his accomplices.[3] Control over the money arising from the duty was vested in the Crown, where it remained until Virginia declared its independence, despite the Burgesses' attempt in 1706 to limit the purposes for which it could be used.[4] For the remainder of the colonial period the duty supplied enough money to pay the governor's salary, so that he was not dependent upon the Burgesses for support. After 1679 the governor's annual salary was £2,000,[5] and perquisites raised his annual income to around £3,000. From 1704 until 1768 the Virginia governorship was a sinecure, and a lieutenant governor administered the colony. Under this arrangement the lieutenant governor and the governor-in-chief divided the income.[6] Other royal officials in Virginia included a secretary, a receiver general, an auditor general, an attorney general, and six naval officers. Both the auditor general and the attorney general received salaries from the funds arising from the two-shillings

2. Hening, ed., *Va. Statutes*, I, 280-82; Flippin, *Royal Government in Virginia*, 74-75.

3. Hening, ed., *Va. Statutes*, II, 130-32, 176-77, 458-69, III, 344-49; The Constitution of Government peculiar to Virginia, submitted with memorial of James Abercromby, read by Board of Trade, Nov 21, 1759, CO 5/1329, f. 351; Robert Beverley, *The History and Present State of Virginia*, ed. Louis B. Wright (Chapel Hill, 1947), 239-40.

4. Robert Quary to Board of Trade, Sept. 1, 1706, CO 5/1315.

5. Flippin, *Royal Government in Virginia*, 75-76; Labaree, *Royal Government*, 313-16.

6. Beverly McAnear, ed., "The Income of the Royal Governors of Virginia," *Journal of Southern History*, 16 (1950), 196-211; William Gooch to Thomas Gooch, June 26, 1739, Gooch Letter Book, 71-72, Colonial Williamsburg, Inc.; Francis Fauquier to Earl of Loudoun, Nov. 20, 1758, Loudoun Papers, 5965, Huntington Lib.

duty, but the others depended for their support upon the fees of their respective offices.[7]

Half of the proceeds of the governorship seems never to have supported Virginia's lieutenant governors adequately, although their share usually amounted to more than governors' salaries in the other continental colonies. The lieutenant governors sent the governors a fixed annual sum, including half of the regular salary and half of the expected perquisites, although the amount of the perquisites fluctuated from year to year. Between 1727 and 1749 Gooch sent £1,300 home every year, with the result that his financial situation was somewhat less than comfortable. He predicted to his brother Thomas, Bishop of Norwich, in 1730 that "if I was to stay here tenn years I should not be able to save £1,000." His prediction was not far from the mark, for some nine years later he had managed to save no more than £2,000.[8] Dinwiddie faced the same problem. Upon Governor-in-Chief Lord Albemarle's death in 1755, he appealed to the Earl of Granville, the president of the Board of Trade, for support in obtaining "the full salary" of the governorship "from the Death of Lord Albemarle till His Majesty thinks proper to appoint another Governor" so he could recoup some of his extraordinary expenses.[9]

In that situation it is not surprising that Virginia lieutenant governors were among the more frequent violators of the Crown restriction against accepting presents from the legislature. At least five times after 1689 the Burgesses voted rather sizable presents to their governors, usually at the beginning of their administrations. But these presents seem to have been granted as tokens of good will rather than as bribes, and there is no evidence that they in any way induced the grantees to accede to any of the Burgesses' particular measures. Before the imperial authorities adopted the rigid prohibition against such presents in 1703, the Burgesses had rewarded Lieutenant Governor Francis Nicholson with grants of £300 in 1691 and £200 in 1692

7. List of Officers in American Colonies . . ., Mar. 11, 1762, Chatham Papers, Gifts and Deposits, 30/8, vol. 95, PRO; Account of Va. Civil Establishment, Apr. 7, 1730, House of Lords MSS, 106, No. 20; Nov. 1, 1744, Henry R. McIlwaine and Wilmer L. Hall, eds., *Executive Journals of the Council of Colonial Virginia, 1680-1754,* 5 vols. (Richmond, 1925-45), V, 166; hereafter cited as *Exec. Journals of Va. Council.*

8. William Gooch to Thomas Gooch, July 24, 1730, June 26, 1739, Gooch Letter Book, 24-25, 71-72, Colonial Williamsburg, Inc.

9. Dinwiddie to Earl of Granville, May 7, 1755, Brock, ed., *Dinwiddie Papers,* II, 32-34.

largely as marks of gratitude during the initial years of his first administration. Crown officials reluctantly permitted him to accept the
gifts, although William Blathwayt informed him that it was "un-
usuall to allow of these presents where there is a setled and competent Salary."[10] But when the Burgesses made a similar offer of £500
to Gooch at the opening of his governorship in 1728, the Duke of
Newcastle, then secretary of state, refused to permit him to accept it,
fearing that it might set a bad precedent. Gooch appealed this decision, but the Privy Council's plantations committee upheld Newcastle. For some reason, however, the committee postponed its report,
which seems not to have received any further attention.[11] Whether
this postponement indicated a tacit acquiescence to Gooch's request
is uncertain, but Gooch probably accepted the presents eventually,
for two years later, complaining to his brother of his poor financial
condition, he wrote that "All that I have got already is no more than
the presents they made me."[12] The Burgesses also gave presents to
Dinwiddie and Fauquier at the beginning of their administrations.
It voted £500 to Dinwiddie in 1752 and £1,000 to Fauquier in 1761.
Both quietly accepted the presents without notifying the home government and so avoided involvement in the difficulties that had beset
Gooch.[13] None of these men appear to have made any special concessions to the Burgesses in return for their presents, although the
Burgesses' gifts may have helped to produce some of the good will
between the House and both Gooch and Fauquier. On the other
hand, presents did not prevent the rise of heated controversies during
both Nicholson's and Dinwiddie's administrations. Indeed, it seems
unlikely that they deprived the governors of any measure of their
independence.

10. Nicholson to Blathwayt, June 10, 1691, and Blathwayt's reply, Jan. 5, 1692,
Blathwayt Papers, XV, No. 2, Colonial Williamsburg, Inc.; Address of Va. Burgesses and Council to Crown, presented Oct. 2, 1691, CO 5/1306; Nottingham to
Nicholson, Oct. 23, 1691, CO 5/1358; Apr. 26, 29, 1692, *Va. Burgesses Journals,
1660-93*, 404, 407-8.
11. Feb. 27, 1728, *Va. Burgesses Journals, 1728-40*, 28; Gooch to Board of Trade,
Feb. 12 and Aug. 9, 1728, CO 5/1321, ff. 22-25, 74-75; Gooch to Duke of Newcastle,
Feb. 14 and July 9, 1728, and Newcastle's reply, Dec. 1728, CO 5/1337, ff. 114-15,
123, 126-27; Board of Trade to Gooch, May 7, 1728, CO 5/1366, pp. 2-5; June 2,
July 31, 1729, *Acts of Privy Council, Colonial*, III, 244.
12. William Gooch to Thomas Gooch, July 24, 1730, Gooch Letter Book, 24-25,
Colonial Williamsburg, Inc.
13. Apr. 18, 1752, *Va. Burgesses Journals, 1752-58*, 96; Apr. 6, 1761, *ibid., 1758-61*,
250.

Georgia governors also were independent. From the beginning of royal government to the end of the colonial period, the Crown paid their stipends out of money annually granted by Parliament for the colony's civil establishment. In the 1750's Georgia was still thinly settled and relatively poor, occupying a strategic position between Spanish Florida and wealthy South Carolina, and Parliament wisely undertook to pay the bulk of the colony's expenses, annually defraying over four-fifths of the cost of administration. The Crown used money from Parliamentary grants to pay not only the governor but the rest of the civil establishment including the chief justice, secretary, attorney general, provost marshal, agent, surveyor of land, and register and receiver of quitrents.[14] To begin with, Governor John Reynolds received an annual stipend of £600, but he found that sum inadequate to meet the demands of his office; and, after several applications, imperial authorities raised the salary to £1,000, at which it remained for the rest of the colonial period.[15]

The Crown instructed Georgia governors to urge the Commons to create a permanent revenue to provide for the colony's civil establishment,[16] but they do not seem ever to have broached the matter with the House. Governor Wright reported in 1768 that he had "never had a Farthing more than the Kings Salary, and the Established Fees."[17] Indeed, as long as Parliament continued to support the colony establishment, the Commons was quite pleased to save its constituents that expense, especially in view of the colony's impoverished condition during much of the early royal period. The Commons did make a few token payments to royal officers including the chief justice, provost marshal, register, and secretary, but it did not furnish a large enough proportion of their support to bring them under its control.[18]

Imperial authorities also provided a salary for South Carolina gov-

14. Charges of Ga. Civil Establishment, June 1754-June 1755, Newcastle Papers, Add. MSS, 33029, f. 122, British Museum; July 6, 1756, *Board of Trade Journals, 1754-58*, 248.

15. Aug. 6, 1754, July 6, 1756, *Board of Trade Journals, 1754-58*, 64, 248; Dec. 22, 1761, *ibid., 1759-61*, 238-39; Reynolds to Board of Trade, Dec. 5, 1754, and to Lord Hardwicke, Sept. 8, 1755, Hardwicke Papers, Add. MSS, 35909, ff. 205, 215, British Museum; Memorial of Reynolds, Jan. 3, 1756, CO 5/645; Board of Trade to Reynolds, May 5, 1756, CO 5/653.

16. Labaree, ed., *Royal Instructions*, I, 189-90.

17. Wright to Board of Trade, Dec. 26, 1768, unpubl. Ga. Col. Recs., XXVIII, Pt. II-B, 686, Ga. Dept. of Arch. and Hist.

18. Statutes, *Ga. Col. Recs.*, XVIII, 66-73, 164-71, 240-47, 337-50.

ernors after the Crown took over the colony in 1721. As early as 1684
the Lords Proprietors had adopted the practice of furnishing their
governors with independent incomes, giving them an annual stipend
of £200 taken from the quitrents.[19] Crown officials decided to continue that practice, and when they appointed Francis Nicholson to
the governorship in 1721 they gave him an annual salary of £1,000
sterling as commander of the independent company of infantry that
accompanied him to the colony.[20] The Crown paid Nicholson's successors in the same way until 1736, when the company was placed
under General James Oglethorpe's command and moved to Georgia.
For the next four years South Carolina governors received nothing
from the Crown, but in 1740 James Glen with the help of his patron
—Spencer Compton, Earl of Wilmington—persuaded authorities to replace the stipend diverted to Oglethorpe with an allowance from the
4½ per cent revenue of Barbados and the Leeward Islands; thereafter
South Carolina governors were paid from that source. To begin with,
the Treasury fixed the annual salary at £800 sterling but sometime
before 1762 raised it to £1,000.[21]

That Crown officials had committed themselves from the outset of
royal government in South Carolina to paying the governor's salary
out of imperial funds did not prevent them from endeavoring to
obtain a permanent revenue from the colony to supplement his income and to maintain the rest of the civil establishment. During the
entire royal period they instructed the governors to persuade the
South Carolina Commons to create such a revenue.[22] But the proprietors had always borne the cost of maintaining the civil establishment, providing yearly salaries out of the quitrents for all of their
officers including the chief justice, secretary, attorney general, naval

19. See Instructions to Robert Quary, Mar. 13, 1684, to John Ely, Aug. 16, 1698,
to James Moore, June 19, 1702, to Nathaniel Sale, Dec. 11, 1708, S. C. Pub Recs.,
II, 42, IV, 68-69, V, 91, 233-34, S. C. Arch. Dept.

20. Labaree, *Royal Government*, 330; Aug. 30, 1729, Aug. 10, 19, 1730, William
A. Shaw, ed., *Calendar of Treasury Books and Papers . . .*, 5 vols. (London, 1897-
1903), *1729-30*, 135-36, 432-33, 441; May 11, 1736, Apr. 11, 1738, *ibid., 1735-38*, 252,
582.

21. James Glen to Board of Trade, [1740], and to Lord Wilmington, Apr. 29,
1740, *The Manuscripts of the Marquess Townshend* (Historical Manuscripts Commission, *11th Report, Appendix, Pt. IV* [London, 1887]), 264-65; Aug. 7, 1740,
Treasury Books and Papers, 1739-41, 260; List of Officers in American Colonies
. . . , Mar. 11, 1762, Chatham Papers, Gifts and Deposits, 30/8, vol. 95, PRO.

22. History of the Salaries of the Governors, presented by Board of Trade to
House of Lords, Feb. 1, 1733, CO 5/5, ff. 17-19; Labaree, ed., *Royal Instructions*,
I, 239-40, 271-72.

officers, receiver general, and surveyor general. The parsimonious Commons, always eager to spare the colony any expenses it could, had no intention of taking over those salaries if it could avoid it. Furthermore, although the Commons had augmented proprietary governors' incomes by yearly grants ranging from £100 in 1697 to £400 in the years immediately preceding the revolt of 1719, it had never made those grants permanent and, indeed, had carefully refrained from establishing any revenue over which it had no control.[23] To have done so under the Crown would have meant the abandonment of one of its traditional policies under the proprietors. If it had to provide a part of the governor's salary, therefore, the Commons insisted upon continuing the proprietary practice of making temporary grants by articles in the annual tax acts. As a result, none of South Carolina's royal governors managed to induce the Commons to vote a perpetual revenue.

For over twenty years, however, Crown appointees persisted in their efforts to obtain such a revenue. In the 1720's Francis Nicholson repeatedly asked the Commons to set up a permanent fund to defray the salaries of royal officials, but it refused. In August 1721 the Commons did agree to give Nicholson £500 sterling, not as a salary, but for a year's house rent and his expenses in making the voyage to the colony, and during the remainder of his administration it continued to vote him a similar amount each year, although it adamantly refused to pay the other royal officers.[24] These grants handsomely supplemented his salary from the Crown, and Nicholson took them without hesitation. Despite the fact that they were the very sort of temporary presents that the Crown had forbidden its governors to accept, imperial authorities never censured Nicholson for accepting them.

Nicholson's successor, Robert Johnson, had the same experience. He first requested a permanent establishment in January 1731 in his inaugural address to the legislature. The Commons evaded the issue by declaring it a new matter which would require its "most serious and Deliberate Considera[t]ion" and the following August absolutely refused Johnson's request. But the Commons did make him a one-

23. See Instructions to John Ely, Aug. 16, 1698, to James Moore, June 19, 1702, S. C. Pub. Recs., IV, 68-69, V, 91, S. C. Arch. Dept.; Smith, *South Carolina as a Royal Province*, 74.
24. Aug. 16, 1721, S. C. Commons Journals, CO 5/426, pp. 52-53; May 17, Nov. 16, 1723, *ibid.*, CO 5/427, pp. 38-43.

year grant of £500 as it had formerly done for Nicholson. When Johnson informed the House that he could not accept a temporary allowance without violating his instructions, it replied that it was merely postponing the salary question and that it would be a pity if he refused to accept the allowance, thereby defeating the tax bill and preventing payment of the public debt. Eventually Johnson accepted the temporary grant, agreeing to defer the matter until the following session. In an optimistic vein he wrote the Board of Trade in November 1731 that he hoped to obtain a permanent revenue at the next legislative session "notwithstanding the aversion all America show to precedents of this Nature, which Influences our People very much."[25]

But the Commons' reaction to Johnson's initial proposal to establish a civil list was a harbinger of its future conduct. Johnson's second attempt the following March encountered a similar fate, and he reported to the Board of Trade that he had again been unable "to Induce the Assembly to Settle a fixt Sallary upon me, and his Majestys Officers." That arrangement "being dispenced with now in New England," he added, "has I believe Influenced the Province."[26] Thereafter, Johnson abandoned his efforts to obtain a permanent revenue and contented himself with receiving his pay from the colony in the form of temporary grants.[27] By the close of his administration in 1735, the practice of the colony's paying the governor an annual salary of £500 sterling by one-year grants in each year's tax bill was well established. This arrangement was followed for the remainder of the colonial period.

The only subsequent governor to broach the matter with the Commons was James Glen. On his arrival in South Carolina in 1743, he pressed the Commons to make his salary permanent. But the intervening decade had not brought any change in the Commons' attitude, and it once again declined the request, voting him instead a one-year allowance of £500 sterling as it had done for his predecessors.[28] The Commons' aversion to a permanent revenue discouraged Glen from

25. Jan. 21, July 29, Aug. 17-18, 1731, *ibid.*, CO 5/432, pp. 1-3, 138-39, 157-59; Johnson to Board of Trade, Nov. 14, 1731, CO 5/362, ff. 54-58.

26. Mar. 3, 1732, S. C. Commons Journals, CO 5/433, p. 22; Johnson to Board of Trade, June 26, 1732, CO 5/362, f. 128. On New England developments, see Labaree, *Royal Government*, 336-72.

27. Mar. 1734, S. C. Commons Journals, CO 5/433, p. 129.

28. Commons Journals, Jan. 11, 19, 1744, *S. C. Col. Recs., 1742-44*, 514-15, 537.

trying again, and in 1752 he reported to the Board of Trade that attempts to establish a civil list were futile.[29]

The Commons' refusal either to create a permanent revenue to defray the cost of the civil establishment or to provide salaries for any of the Crown officers except the governor eventually forced London authorities to follow the proprietors' example and pay those salaries out of the quitrents. During the 1730's they awarded annual stipends out of the rents to the chief justice, attorney general, clerk of the Crown, provost marshal, auditor general, secretary, and receiver general. Supported by their salaries and their fees of office, none of these officers depended upon the Commons for any part of his income.[30]

Because the governor depended on the Commons for one-third of his stipend, it might be expected that the Commons would—according to the traditional textbook interpretation—try to extract concessions from him by threatening to withhold that portion of his salary. That the Commons did just that during Nicholson's administration was the charge of the South Carolina Council. "Neither is there anyone thing in the World that lessens the Royall prerogative so much in these parts," the Council complained in December 1728, "as the respective Governors ever more Temporizing and giving away to the Assemblys, for the Sake of these temporary Gifts and Presents." The Commons' gifts to Nicholson, it charged, "were always made him on passing the Currency Laws or do[ing] something else to Gratify" the Commons and were never given "by way of Salary, but by way of Present, that is to say, in more true and plain termes, that if the Governor would not come into their Measures, they would Give him nothing at all." To remedy this evil, the Council proposed the issuance of "a particular Instruction prohibiting all Succeeding Governors, Absolutely to Accept of any Temporary Gifts or presents from the Assemblys on any pretence whatsoever."[31]

The fact that in February 1723 the Commons voted Nicholson the colony's portion of his salary after he had agreed to an addition to the colony's paper money lends weight to the Council's charges, although it is now impossible to determine if that incident involved a

29. Glen to Board of Trade, Apr. 1753, CO 5/374, ff. 86-89.
30. Apr. 3, 1735, *Acts of Privy Council, Colonial*, III, 458-59; Mar. 7, 1738, *Treasury Books and Papers, 1735-38*, 575; June 26, 1739, *ibid., 1739-41*, 168; Feb. 9, 1742, *ibid., 1742-45*, 211; Bond, *Quit-Rent System*, 346.
31. S. C. Council to Newcastle, Dec. 19, 1728, CO 5/360, ff. 96-100.

quid pro quo between Nicholson and the Commons. But even circumstantial evidence that Nicholson made any other concessions to the Commons in return for his temporary salary is lacking. In fact, Nicholson's relations with the Commons were frequently strained. Yet the Commons never failed to grant his yearly stipend. Of course, it could always refuse to pass the annual tax bill if its demands were not met, as it did in the late 1720's under President of the Council Arthur Middleton when trying to issue more paper money. In that situation Middleton went without the salary normally given by the Commons.[32] But, even more important, the Commons' refusal to levy taxes left him without money to run the government, and the knowledge that they would be unable to administer the colony without money was probably more important in inducing governors to make concessions to the Commons than was the fear of losing the third of their salaries paid by the colony. After all, with over two-thirds of their income guaranteed by the Crown and the normal fees of office, South Carolina governors could afford to be somewhat independent. However much they may have been able to use the extra £500, they could, if matters of great importance were involved, do without it.

Indeed, there appear to have been only two other instances in which the Commons directly tried to bribe a governor by either threatening to withhold part of his income or promising him an additional present. Both occurred in 1751. In June the Commons deliberately neglected to make the usual provision for Glen's house rent because he had vetoed several of its favorite bills. And the following July Glen reported that the Commons had offered him "large sums of money, to . . . be raised under collour of Reimbursing me my Expences amongst the Indians" if he would consent to an additional emission of paper money.[33]

Two later governors did not receive any salary from the Commons for several years because their embroilment in disputes with the House prevented passage of the annual tax bills. During the Gads-

32. The Commons eventually voted Middleton a little over a fourth of the normal salary from the colony for his five-year tenure. Middleton claimed that the House owed him £13,500 Carolina currency, but the Commons would vote no more than £3,000. May 21-28, Aug. 11-14, 1731, S. C. Commons Journals, CO 5/432, pp. 79, 88, 149-50, 154; Mar. 28-29, 1734, *ibid.*, CO 5/433, pp. 145-47.

33. May 9, 1751, *ibid.*, CO 5/463, pp. 165-69; Glen to Board of Trade, July 15, 1751, CO 5/373, ff. 151-64.

den election controversy in the early 1760's, the Commons broke off relations with Governor Thomas Boone and did not pass any legislation for nearly two years with the result that Boone did not receive the normal salary from the colony. Even after Boone had left the colony and the Commons had finally passed a tax measure, it refused to pay Boone, contending that its yearly grant was "not a salary, but a gratuity from the people."[34] On his return to England in 1764 Boone applied to colonial officials for payment of his back salary, amounting to £1,250 sterling, out of South Carolina quitrents. The Privy Council's plantations committee ruled that the Commons' action in withholding Boone's pay was unjust and a precedent that might "operate to the prejudice and discouragement of Your Majesty's Service . . . by awing and deterring . . . Governors from the due and faithful execution of their duty."[35] But not until Crown officials had specifically ordered the Commons to pay Boone's back salary would it make provision for its former adversary.[36] Similarly, during the Wilkes fund controversy in the following decade the Commons' failure to pass a tax bill for nearly five years prevented payment of Lord Charles Greville Montagu's colony salary.[37] That neither Boone nor Montagu acceded to the Commons' demands in these controversies illustrates what an ineffective weapon the Commons' control over the governor's salary was in South Carolina. Assured of two-thirds of their annual pay from the Crown, both could resist the Commons' designs without fear of being starved into submission.

When the Crown took over North Carolina in 1729, it made provisions for paying its officials similar to those it had first adopted in South Carolina. It continued the proprietors' policy of paying the governor out of the quitrents, allowing him £700 sterling per annum.[38] But it abandoned the proprietary practice of paying other royal officials from the same source, requiring instead that the North Carolina Lower House grant a permanent revenue to provide for

34. Aug. 22-23, 1764, S. C. Commons Journals, XXXVI, 244-46, S. C. Arch. Dept.; William Bull II to Board of Trade, Sept. 13, 1764, CO 5/378, ff. 3-4; Smith, *South Carolina as a Royal Province*, 348-49.

35. Boone's memorial to Treasury, Nov. 25, 1765, CO 5/378, ff. 15-16; Feb. 10-26, 1766, *Acts of Privy Council, Colonial*, IV, 743-44.

36. Smith, *South Carolina as a Royal Province*, 348-49.

37. See Chapter XXI.

38. Dec. 24, 1730, *Treasury Books and Papers, 1729-30*, 498; Council Journals, Feb. 14, 1715, May 1727, *N. C. Col. Recs.*, II, 170, 726-28.

those officials and for an addition to the governor's salary. But the
Lower House's refusal to set up a permanent fund and the governors'
inability to collect quitrents combined to keep them in a state of
poverty for the first quarter-century of royal government in the colony.

Indeed, the Lower House's reaction to the proposal to establish
a permanent revenue was entirely negative. It had never complied
with similar propositions from the proprietors and, when Burrington
recommended that matter for its consideration in 1731, it replied that
it did not feel "obliged to pay the Salaries of any Officers" inasmuch
as the colony paid large quitrents and the proprietors had always paid
their officers "out of their Revenue arising by the Quit Rents and the
sale of Land."[39] Neither Johnston nor Dobbs fared any better. Both
applied for the establishment of a permanent revenue at the beginning of their administrations only to be refused, Dobbs complaining
in 1764 that the House would not "settle any Salary upon the Governor . . . nor even pay the rent of a House for the residence of the
Governor, when either an House or the rent of one is allowed in all
the other Colonies whether of the Kings or Proprietary Governments."[40] Nor was the Lower House free in giving presents or other
allowances to the governors. It gave Burrington nothing, and, although it voted Johnston £1,300 North Carolina currency upon his
arrival in consideration of his expenses "in Traveling from Cape
Fear with his Equipage to Edenton and his expences during this
Session," it waited thirteen years before making a second grant. In
1748 it voted him £750 proclamation money "for his extraordinary
expences, during his administration" and presented him with two
further allowances of £100 each in 1750 and 1751.[41] But these four
grants are the extent of the money Johnston received from the colony.
The Lower House was even more parsimonious in its treatment of
Dobbs, making him only one meager grant of £50 in 1764 to cover
"his Extraordinary Expense this Session."[42] Because all of these
grants were given either to reimburse governors for some particular
expenditure or to cover their expenses, they did not involve a direct

39. Lower House Journals, Apr. 21, 1731, *N. C. Col. Recs.*, III, 294-95.
40. Upper House Journals, Jan. 17, 1735, *ibid.*, IV, 79; Lower House Journals,
Jan. 21, 1735, Dec. 14, 1754, *ibid.*, 119-20, V, 236; Dobbs to Board of Trade, Mar.
29, 1764, *ibid.*, VI, 1038-39; Labaree, ed., *Royal Instructions*, I, 189-90.
41. Lower House Journals, Feb. 26, 1735, Oct. 10, 1751, *N. C. Col. Recs.*, IV,
147, 1296; Upper House Journals, Apr. 1, 1748, Apr. 9, 1750, *ibid.*, 910-11, 1063.
42. Lower House Journals, Nov. 27, 1764, *ibid.*, VI, 1316.

violation of the royal instructions forbidding governors to accept legislative presents. Nor were the grants given frequently enough to enable the Lower House to bring any of the governors under its control.

The Lower House's refusal to vote a permanent revenue would not have been so serious if the governors had been able to collect the quitrents in a regular way, but neither Burrington nor Johnston was ever able to do so. Both failed to reconcile differences between the Lower House and imperial authorities over details in collecting the rents. Those differences disrupted the colony's political life for over twenty years and temporarily put an end to payment of the rents. Consequently, they were almost never sufficient to meet the salary of the governors, who, more often than not, were unable to collect much of their annual stipends from the Crown.

Upon assuming control of North Carolina in 1729, Crown officials had tried to work out some effective arrangements for collecting quitrents. They offered to remit arrears of rents if the colony would pass a measure to require registration of land grants and to enforce payment of rents; and they further required the colony to raise the rents from two to four shillings per hundred acres and to pay them only in proclamation money or sterling rather than in commodities, as was the colony's custom.[43] The Lower House found these arrangements almost completely unacceptable. It was South Carolina, not North Carolina, that was so far behind in payment of quitrents, and the Lower House was quick to point out that the Crown's offer was not, therefore, much of a concession. Although it was quite willing to provide for registering future grants of land, it insisted that the rents be paid in commodities at the old rate of two shillings per hundred acres and that collection be suspended for two years.[44] But imperial authorities insisted that the Lower House comply with the terms of their original offer; and, because Burrington was unable to foist these terms upon the Lower House, his administration came to a close in November 1734 without his ever having secured passage of a quitrent

43. Bond, *Quit-Rent System*, 287.

44. The Lower House claimed this rate was set in 1668 by the Great Deed of Grant to Albemarle which gave its inhabitants the right to pay the same rates as Virginians. Lower House Journals, Apr. 21, 1731, *N. C. Col. Recs.*, III, 294-95; Bond, *Quit-Rent System*, 289-90. See also Burrington to Duke of Newcastle, July 2, 1731, Act on quitrents, 1731, *N. C. Col. Recs.*, III, 143-44, 149-50, 157-68.

measure and, consequently, without his ever having collected any of his salary.

It is not surprising, therefore, that Burrington was in financial straits during his entire administration. "Haveing lived in this Province some years without receiving any mony from the King, or the Country," Burrington wrote the Duke of Newcastle in July 1734, "[I] was constrained to sell not only my household goods, but even linnen, plate and Books, and mortgage my Lands, and stocks."[45] Upon his return to England, Burrington petitioned the Board of Trade for the £3,208 sterling in back salary for his four-and-a-half-year tour as governor and for certain additional expenses he had incurred in surveying and sounding the colony's ports and harbors. For reasons that are not entirely clear, the Privy Council's plantations committee rejected the petition; but in August 1736 the Treasury finally paid him at least £200 sterling out of the South Carolina quitrents, though that allowance fell far short of the sum to which he was actually entitled.[46]

Johnston fared little better. Before leaving London, he persuaded imperial authorities to increase his annual salary to £1,000 sterling and to establish yearly allowances from the quitrents for the other Crown officers including the auditor, chief justice, baron of the exchequer, surveyor general, secretary, attorney general, and clerk of the Crown.[47] Indeed, some provision to pay the officers had to be made since the Lower House had flatly refused to provide for them, and Johnston reasoned that if the officers were dependent upon the quitrents for their pay they would be more diligent in collecting them. But he was never able during his eighteen-year administration to secure a quitrent measure that pleased both the Lower House and the imperial authorities.

During Johnston's first four years in office the quitrent problem was a constant source of controversy. Prospects for solving it at his first meeting with the Lower House in early 1735 looked good when he agreed to accept rated commodities in payment for the rents. But a disagreement with the House over values of the commodities and

45. Burrington to Duke of Newcastle, June 1, 1734, N. C. Col. Recs., III, 625.
46. Burrington's petition to Crown, [1736], ibid., IV, 164-66; Apr. 29, May 13, 1740, Acts of Privy Council, Colonial, III, 493; Dec. 1, 1737, Treasury Books and Papers, 1735-38, 349, 392.
47. The total civil establishment amounted to £1,455 per year. Aug. 17, Oct. 25, 1733, Treasury Books and Papers, 1731-34, 397, 410; Thomas Smith to John Pownall, Apr. 18, 1753, N. C. Col. Recs., V, 19-21.

places of payment prevented passage of a suitable measure.[48] For a time thereafter Johnston had to collect the rents by royal proclamation. This maneuver was at first strikingly successful, and by September 1737 the quitrents were yielding over £1,000 per year. But mounting opposition, led by the Lower House and culminating in mob uprisings, sharply reduced the annual totals, and by 1738 almost all payments had ceased. Even when collections were at their peak in 1737 the rents were not sufficient to meet the entire demand of the civil establishment. Johnston complained in April 1737 that "though I have been now Governour of this Colony four years" and "have the name of a Salary of £1,000 sterl[ing] yearly I have not yet been able to command £200 Sterling."[49]

Success appeared imminent when Johnston's repeated endeavors finally bore fruit in December 1738 with the passage of a compromise measure. This act incorporated the House's demand that rents might be paid in commodities but purposely undervalued them so that those who had gold and silver would almost certainly pay in specie in accordance with the Crown's wishes. Under this law total collections of quitrents again soared, and much of the arrears in salary owed to the governor and other officers was discharged. But to Johnston's bitter disappointment the Privy Council disallowed the law in July 1741 because of some minor objections, and quitrent collections once more dropped sharply.[50]

For the next seven years Johnston tried unsuccessfully to pass another quitrent law. Past experience had convinced him and the other officers that it was impossible to collect the rents without legislative approval, and throughout the whole time few rents were collected and the officers' salaries fell further and further into arrears. It was impossible, wrote Johnston to the Board of Trade in December 1741, for "the face or appearance of Government" to be kept up as long as the officers were thus deprived of their salaries.[51] By December 1743 Johnston despaired of ever getting the Lower House to pass another

48. Bond, *Quit-Rent System,* 291-92.
49. Johnston to Board of Trade, May 25 and July 10, 1735, Apr. 30, 1737, *N. C. Col. Recs.,* IV, 8, 15, 250-51; Eleazer Allen to Board of Trade, Mar. 29, 1737, *ibid.,* 247; Abstract of North Carolina quitrents, 1739-42, Lansdowne MSS, 1215, f. 163, British Museum.
50. Bond, *Quit-Rent System,* 295-96; Abstract of North Carolina quitrents., 1739-42, Lansdowne MSS, 1215, f. 163, British Museum.
51. Johnston to Board of Trade, Dec. 21, 1741, *N. C. Col. Recs.,* IV, 585.

quitrent bill, and he prepared a memorial to the home authorities pointing out that unless his salary was paid from some other source he would be unable "to keep up and support the character and dignity of his Majestie's Governor."[52]   If this memorial was ever presented to the Crown officials, it accomplished nothing, for Johnston's situation was still unimproved in 1746.   In June of that year he declared that his pay was over "eight years in arrears, and those of the other Officers in proportion and our fees are but very trifling which makes it impossible for us to remain long in any of the Towns of this Province where small and despicable as they are, living is dearer than at London."[53]

Finally, in April 1749 Johnston succeeded in pushing a quitrent bill through the "reformed Lower House"—the long assembly that was elected under his 1746 managed election law and existed for nearly eight years before it was dissolved.   This bill provided for the establishment of an accurate rent roll and for payment of rents in either proclamation money or inspected tobacco rated at a penny per pound, while another statute made suitable arrangements for collecting back rents.[54]   Johnston was confident the law would insure collection of the vast arrears of quitrents and cover the back salaries of the Crown's officers.   But it did not fulfill his expectations.   Inhabitants of the northern counties contested the long assembly's legality, refused to accept any of its laws, and would pay no quitrents.   Inhabitants of the southern counties followed their example, not wishing to pay any rents avoided by their northern neighbors.   Consequently, the officers failed to collect any more quitrents after the passage of the law than before, and in April 1750 Johnston reported that his salary had "run in arrear almost Twelve Thousand Pounds sterling."[55]   He hoped that imperial authorities would approve the 1746 election law and thereby validate the long assembly's actions, including the 1749 quitrent law.   But unfortunately for Johnston they delayed their decision for an excessively long time.   As late as 1751 the fate of the election

52. Case of Gabriel Johnston accompanying Johnston to [?] Adair, Dec. 3, 1743, Historical Manuscripts Commission, *Report on the Laing Manuscripts Preserved in the University of Edinburgh*, 2 vols. (London, 1914-25), II, 338-40.

53. Johnston to Board of Trade, June 6, 1746, *N. C. Col. Recs.*, IV, 792-93.

54. Upper House Journals, Apr. 14, 1749, *ibid.*, 984; Bond, *Quit-Rent System*, 299-300.

55. Johnston's answer to Henry McCulloh's memorial, June 27, 1750, Thomas Smith to John Pownall, Apr. 18, 1753, Arthur Dobbs's memorial to Board of Trade, 1754, *N. C. Col. Recs.*, IV, 1082-90, V, 19-21, 77-78.

law was undecided, and Johnston and his fellow officers were understandably bitter. In September of that year Johnston protested that he and "the rest of His Majesty's Officers have had a very severe time of it to be kept out of our Salarys so long" and pleaded for a prompt decision.[56] But it was another two and a half years before the authorities decided to disallow both the quitrent law and the election law, and when Johnston died in July 1752 his salary was over £13,000 in arrears.[57]

With no pay from the colony and very little from the Crown during his eighteen-year administration, Johnston was hardly well rewarded. He probably depended almost entirely upon profits he earned as a private planter for his support. It might be suspected that the Lower House's refusal to provide for collecting quitrents according to conditions specified by the Crown was deliberately contrived to deprive Johnston and the other officers of their salaries and thereby render them dependent for their financial support upon the legislature. But such was not the case. The Lower House simply would not agree to pay quitrents on the Crown's terms, and payment of the officers' salaries was obstructed in the process. Never did the Lower House show any interest in either taking over the payment of Johnston's salary or securing his dependence by making him frequent presents. As long as it did not provide for any part of his support, it had little to gain by depriving him of his salary and did, in fact, twice agree to measures representing a suitable compromise to the quitrent question only to have them turned down by the Crown.

When Dobbs succeeded Johnston, he quickly saw that the large arrears of salary owed to Johnston's heirs and the other officers would consume the quitrent revenues for many years to come and petitioned the authorities for an annual allowance from another source. Accordingly, upon the order of the Privy Council's plantations committee the Treasury awarded Dobbs a yearly salary of £1,000 sterling from

56. Johnston to Board of Trade, Sept. 16, 1751, *ibid.*, IV, 1076.

57. H. Walpole's report to Treasury, Apr. 10, 1753, *ibid.*, V, 21-23; Johnston's widow's memorial, Oct. 3, 1752, Treasury Papers, I, 350, PRO. At the time of his death Johnston's arrears of salary amounted to £13,462 7s. 2d. Mar. 26, 1754, *Acts of Privy Council, Colonial*, IV, 238-39. In 1761 the Treasury ordered the arrears paid out of the South Carolina quitrents and eventually all but £2,018 was paid from that fund. The balance was not paid until after 1790. [Janet Schaw], *Journal of a Lady of Quality . . .*, ed. Charles M. and Evangeline W. Andrews (New Haven, 1923), 294-95, 310-12.

the 4½ per cent revenue of Barbados and the Leeward Islands.[58] The authorities made this arrangement permanent, and for the remainder of the colonial period North Carolina governors had an assured source of income from the Crown. But the other officers were less fortunate. They continued to depend upon the quitrents for their salaries, and because neither Dobbs nor his successors were able to achieve a satisfactory quitrent settlement, they were rarely paid, depending almost entirely upon their private incomes and fees of office for support.[59]

By the end of the colonial period the Crown had been able to induce only one of the southern lower houses to vote a permanent revenue to support its civil establishment. In 1680 the Virginia Burgesses complied with the Crown's demands by voting to make the export duty of two shillings per hogshead perpetual, and thereafter Virginia governors and other officials received annual salaries from revenues arising from that duty. But, when the lower houses in the other three colonies refused to establish such a revenue, the Crown simply drew incomes for its officers out of imperial revenues and thereby deprived the lower houses of any control over their salaries. Georgia officials were paid by money annually voted by Parliament. In North Carolina governors received their salaries from the 4½ per cent revenue of Barbados and the Leeward Islands, and the other officials had established salaries from the quitrents. Although the rents rarely proved adequate to meet their salaries, the officers never looked to the Lower House for support, rather depending upon their fees of office. Similarly, South Carolina governors received a fixed income from the Barbados and Leeward Islands revenue while other officials were paid from the quitrents. The South Carolina Commons did provide its governors with an annual grant amounting to one-half of their yearly income from the Crown, but it seems that the House only rarely, if ever, tried to use its control over that grant to exert pressure on its governors. Nor does it appear that any of the lower houses gained any appreciable influence over their governors by voting them occasional presents, although several governors, particularly in Virginia

58. Dobbs's memorial to Board of Trade, 1754, *N. C. Col. Recs.*, V, 77-78; Mar. 26-28, 1754, *Acts of Privy Council, Colonial*, IV, 238-39; List of Officers in American Colonies . . . , Mar. 11, 1762, Chatham Papers, Gifts and Deposits, 30/8, vol. 95, PRO; Labaree, *Royal Government*, 333.

59. Bond, *Quit-Rent System*, 301-17; Statement of Civil List in Board of Trade to Lord Shelburne, Apr. 16, 1767, *N. C. Col. Recs.*, VII, 447-48.

and North Carolina, did accept such presents in violation of their orders from the Crown.

Royal officials in the southern royal colonies were, then, remarkably independent. By the mid-1750's they all had established salaries from revenues beyond the control of the lower houses. Consequently, the threat after 1767 to use the revenue arising from the Townshend duties to render officials independent of the legislature was not an important issue in those colonies.[60]

60. See Oliver M. Dickerson, "Use Made of the Revenue from the Tax on Tea," *New England Quarterly*, 31 (1958), 232-43.

8

Fees

THROUGHOUT the colonial period public officials relied upon their fees of office to supplement their regular salaries. For many of them, income from fees constituted the major portion of their support. In most colonies the lower houses came to regard fees as taxes and claimed the right to establish and regulate them by statute. As long as the statutes were equitable, imperial authorities did not seriously object. Beginning in 1670, however, royal instructions usually empowered governors to settle fees with the consent of their councils.[1] Thereafter, at least in the eyes of Crown officials, fees might be regulated either by legislative enactments or by executive ordinances. But American lower houses denied the governors' authority to levy fees without their consent and almost always resisted any attempt to do so, with the result that few officers' fees were settled solely by executive authority in any of the southern royal colonies except Georgia.

The question was most hotly contested in North Carolina, where royal Governors Burrington, Johnston, and Dobbs tried to prevent the Lower House from exercising the power to establish fees, even though it had frequently done so under the proprietors. As early as 1701 it passed an act to regulate the charges of admiralty court officers, and in 1715 it enacted a general law to settle those of the governor, secretary, public register, provost marshal, clerk of the chancery, clerk of the Lower House, collectors, surveyors, escheators, attorneys, constables, and admiralty court officers. By acts of 1722 and 1723 the House also regulated charges of the comptroller, chief justice, and

1. Labaree, ed., *Royal Instructions*, I, 371-72.

naval officers.[2] But under the Crown the governors challenged the power of the House in this area.

Upon assuming control of North Carolina in 1729, the Crown presented Burrington with the usual instruction empowering him to settle fees by executive ordinance. It also instructed him that all officers' perquisites be paid in proclamation money—that is, foreign coins at the rate settled in 1704 by a proclamation of Queen Anne. With the Council's consent, Burrington took steps to implement these instructions, ordering that fees established by proprietary law be received in either proclamation money or provincial bills at the rate of four to one until further regulation be made by law. Previous to this order, officers' charges had been paid in paper bills at the statutory rates. This order meant, therefore, that officers' fees would be four times higher than those paid under the proprietors.[3]

Burrington's order set the stage for a heated debate with the Lower House. Officers willingly complied with it, and when the Lower House convened for the first time under the Crown in April 1731, it immediately equated fees with taxes and made its stand on the traditional right of Englishmen to be taxed only by their representatives. Proceeding from the assumption that the proprietary charter endowed Carolinians with all the liberties and privileges of Englishmen, the Lower House in a stirring pronouncement declared that it was "the undoubted Right and Priviledge of the People of England that they shall not be taxed or made lyable to pay any sum or sums of money of Fees other than such as are by Law established" and charged that Burrington's order was both an "Oppression of the subjects" and a "great Discouragement" to trade. The House then requested the Council to join in asking Burrington to issue a proclamation "declaring such Practices to be contrary to Law" and "strictly forbidding all Officers to take larger Fees than is by Law appointed, under the Pretence of difference of money untill such time as the Officers Fees shall be regulated by Authority of Assembly."

Neither Burrington nor the Council could be expected to permit such a direct challenge to the validity of the royal instructions to pass without protest. The Council accused the representatives of having "Arrogated and assumed to themselves the sole power of Establishing

2. Laws, *N. C. St. Recs.*, XXIII, 83-87, 107, XXV, 142-48, 179-82, 196-98.
3. Lower House Journals, Apr. 21, May 1, 1731, *N. C. Col. Recs.*, III, 294-95, 304-5; Burrington to Duke of Newcastle, July 2, 1731, *ibid.*, 143-44.

Fees Exclusive of the Governor and Council," of violating the royal instruction and "the Lawes of the English Constitution," and of attempting "to set up and erect some other form of Government than is allowed by the Laws of Great Britain." Burrington bitterly compared Speaker Edward Moseley "to a Thief that hides himself in a house to rob it and fearing to be discovered, fires the house to make his escape in the smoak." In reply, the Lower House asserted its right to complain against all oppressions of the subject, reiterated its stand against officers' taking fees larger than established by law, and pledged that it would not violate the King's instruction.[4] As a proof of its declaration, the Lower House prepared a new statute to provide for payments of officers' fees in either proclamation money or its equivalent in paper bills or commodities. But it ingeniously contrived to keep the fees at the same level as they were under the proprietors by reducing them to a fourth of what they had been before. Burrington vigorously protested against such a reduction, declaring that the Crown's officers "must Abondon their Employments and depart this Province or starve here if they take their Fees in the kind manner you prescribe or desire." The House would not alter its decision, however, and won the support of an influential trio in the Council: Secretary Nathaniel Rice, Chief Justice William Smith, and John Baptista Ashe. The ensuing deadlock forced Burrington to prorogue the House without its having enacted a fee bill.[5]

After the prorogation Burrington sought support for his position from imperial authorities, and local officers, despite the Lower House's objections, continued to take their charges in proclamation money or its equivalent in paper bills. Understandably their actions appeared illegal and oppressive to the Lower House and its constituents, but in fairness to the officers it must be noted that the fees under proprietary laws were not high. Even after the 300 per cent raise that resulted from executive ordinance, Burrington could declare with some truth in February 1732 that "As the officers in this Province take their Fees, they are less in value than in any of the King's Governments in these Parts."[6]

By the summer of 1732 the Board of Trade had decided that all

4. Lower House Journals, Apr. 21, 26, May 1, 1731, *ibid.*, 294-98, 300, 304-6.
5. Burrington to Duke of Newcastle, July 2, 1731, *ibid.*, 143-44; Lower House Journals, May 3, 17, 1731, *ibid.*, 308-9, 324-25; Fee bill, 1731, *ibid.*, 157-68.
6. Burrington to Board of Trade, Feb. 20, 1732, *ibid.*, 335.

fees must be paid only in proclamation money. Burrington questioned the wisdom of this decision and wrote to the Board in May 1733 that "even the Permitting . . . [fees] to be received in Bills at four for one, as an equivalent (which is much less than Proclamation money) has been made the greatest handle to raise Clamours against me among the people."[7] Nevertheless, he submitted the Board's decision to the Lower House when it met the following July. The representatives refused even to consider it seriously, declaring that the previous House had gone "as far as it was possible toward a Complyance with the Royal Instruction concerning . . . Fees; inasmuch as the want of Gold and Silver Currancy is so well known in this Province, and now at this last Election our Principals throughout the province having recommended nothing more earnestly to Us than that We should not consent to burthen them with such payments as are impossible for them to make." Burrington replied that he could not "think Your House in Earnest in pretending this Country Suffers by the Fees now taken, because they are not half the Value of those paid in the Neighbouring Governments," but the House would not accede to the Crown's demands.[8] Despite the representatives' repeated protests, however, Burrington had his way; the House failed to make good its contention that fees could be regulated only by legislative enactments, and officers continued to take their charges at the rates specified by the executive ordinance.

Nor was the House any more successful during the early years of Gabriel Johnston's administration. Johnston not only continued Burrington's policy; he also embarked upon a much bolder course calculated to establish the executive's right to regulate fees. With the Council's advice he established by executive ordinance a new charge of £3 current North Carolina money for registering patents or grants of land in the auditor's office. In addition, he proposed the disallowance of the proprietary fee acts because they gave the legislature too much power over fees and the charges fixed by them were insufficient to support the "Principal Officers of the Crown in any tolerable degree."[9]

To induce the House to vote a suitable quitrent bill, Governor

7. Allured Popple to Burrington, Aug. 16, 1732, Burrington to Board of Trade, May 19, 1733, *ibid.*, 353-54, 482.
8. Lower House Journals, July 6, 17, 1733, *ibid.*, 567-68, 598-600.
9. Council Journals, Dec. 9, 1735, *ibid.*, IV, 74; Johnston's observations on N. C. acts, Dec. 5, 1735, *ibid.*, 26.

Johnston yielded to its demands in September 1736 and encouraged
it to "make some proper regulations of Officers' Fees." He informed
it that, although he had already sent a list of charges to England, he
would assent to "a reasonable Bill for settling all the Fees in the Province." The Lower House promptly prepared a comprehensive measure that settled the fees of nearly all of the colony's officers, providing
for payment in proclamation money or its equivalent in paper bills.
More important, the bill placed penalties on officers taking fees not
established by law or fees higher than those settled by law. But differences between the two houses over quitrents brought the session to an
impasse, and the Council rejected the bill.[10]

Thereafter, the Lower House repeatedly tried to pass a new fee
bill, but it was another decade before it succeeded. The Council
tabled one bill in March 1739 and rejected another in February 1740
after Secretary Nathaniel Rice, one of its number, had complained
that Speaker John Hodgson "had in a most indecent manner, in a
publick room" called him "a damned rascal, and said, also he would
cut off half the said Mr. Rice's fees, and raise some others in the
House of Burgesses."[11] In the meantime officers took their fees at the
rates prescribed by the governor and Council. When Johnston continued to establish new fees by ordinance for both executive and judicial officers, the House resolved in November 1744 that "all Officers
demanding new fees by authority of the Governor and Council for
longer time than till the end of the next General Assembly after such
order is contrary to the Law and a grievance" and "that any Court
appointing new fees is contrary to the Laws of this Province and to
the right of the subject." In April 1745 the Lower House failed to
redress these "grievances" by legislative act, and in June 1746 it resolved "that Officers under colour of their Office having taken new Fees
not warranted by Law, and having extorted greater Fees than allowed
by Law is an Oppression of the subjects and a great grievance."[12]

Finally, in April 1748 Johnston permitted the long assembly to
pass a fee bill. His willingness to give up the point that he had so
stoutly maintained during the first fourteen years of his administra-

10. Upper House Journals, Sept 22, 1736, *ibid.,* 229; Laws, *N. C. St. Recs.,* XXV,
220-28.
11. Upper House Journals, Mar. 5, 1739, Feb. 22, 1740, *N. C. Col. Recs.,* IV,
378, 485.
12. Lower House Journals, Nov. 29, 1744, Apr. 15, 1745, June 13, 1746, *ibid.,*
745, 782, 824.

tion was probably due to his unusually harmonious relations with that House and the fact that his influence over it was strong enough to insure that the allowances would be reasonable. The extensive regulations of the 1748 measure established just and adequate rates payable in either proclamation money or paper bills of credit. But the most significant victory for the House was the provision that no new charges could be created except by "the Authority of the Governor, Council, and General Assembly, any Law, Custom, or Usage, to the contrary, notwithstanding."[13] This provision—in direct opposition to the royal instructions—legally established the principle that fees could be fixed only by statute and not solely by executive authority. Despite repeated objections from Johnston's successor, Arthur Dobbs, this law remained in force for the rest of the colonial period.

Dobbs launched his first attack upon the law in October 1756 by complaining to the Board of Trade that the act was inconsistent with his instructions and that "no other fee whatsoever can be taken without a penalty for services not mentioned in the Act." He questioned the Lower House's right to regulate "the fees for places which the Assembly have not created." For many services the officers received no rewards at all, and Dobbs suggested that establishing fees for those tasks and raising those charges already set by the act would render officers more independent of the legislature. He therefore recommended that the Crown disallow the measure and proposed "that the fees should be regulated and fixed in England and not left to the Council here who will consider their private interests and attachments with the Assembly more than the independency of the Officers."[14]

The Board's response was not what Dobbs had expected. Instead of agreeing with him, it upheld the Lower House's right to regulate fees by statute. Although it conceded that the instructions empowered him to settle fees with the advice of the Council, it pointed out that the instruction had "never been considered as operating to prevent the doing it by Act of Assembly, on the contrary Acts have been passed in almost all the Colonies for this purpose, many of which have been confirmed by the Crown." "It is true indeed that some have been repealed," the Board continued, "but not for being contrary to the King's instructions or from an Opinion that the Legislature had no power to ascertain Fees but upon complaint made that the Fees estab-

13. Laws, *N. C. St. Recs.*, XXIII, 275-84.
14. Dobbs to Board of Trade, Oct. 31, 1756, *N. C. Col. Recs.*, V, 643-45.

lished were improper ones." Finally, the Board observed that even if the act should be repealed it would not be practicable or prudent "to have the Fees fixed and ascertained here." On the contrary, it ruled that in that case fees should be settled by "the discretion of yourself and your Council under the Authority vested in you by your instruction."[15]

The Board's ruling was significant, for it clearly indicated imperial recognition that colonial legislatures had secured the right to regulate fees by law. But it by no means implied that the Crown had accepted the Lower House's contention that charges could not be established by executive authority, for it still maintained the governor's right to fix fees with the Council's advice by authority of the royal instructions. Indeed, Dobbs could have interpreted the Board's letter as a reassertion of executive authority to establish fees.

But the important point that the Board failed to consider was that the statute in question made the regulation of fees by executive authority illegal, and Dobbs was reluctant to violate it by either raising fees or establishing new ones. Yet, in 1759 Dobbs did take advantage of the opportunity to establish with the Council's approval a charge of £5 in paper bills for a completely new service—the granting of royal charters to the counties. The House challenged this action in May 1760 by passing a resolution condemning the fee as "Illegal and Oppressive," and the following December Dobbs rejected a bill to amend the old fee bill probably because it was aimed at regulating the fee on charters. In April 1761 the House considered a bill to prevent exactions of illegal and oppressive fees but never enacted it.[16]

Although Dobbs continued to take the charter fee, the House's violent reaction dissuaded him from establishing other charges, and, notwithstanding the Board's 1757 ruling, he again sought the support of Crown officials in December 1761. Once more he attacked the 1748 fee law as "an Encroachment on the prerogative," complaining that the act made no provision for over half of the services of some officers and pressing the Board for its disallowance. The Board again disappointed him and displayed signs of irritation, expressing surprise

15. Board of Trade to Dobbs, Mar. 10, 1757, *ibid.,* 750.
16. Lower House Journals, May 23, Dec. 3, 1760, Apr. 13, 1761, *ibid.,* VI, 411, 511, 684; Dobbs to Board of Trade, Feb. 28, 1760, Dobbs's comments on May 1760 resolutions of Lower House, Aug. 3, 1760, *ibid.,* 228-29, 288-89.

that "after the late commissioners of Trade had so clearly expressed
their Opinion of the propriety of settling the Fees of Office by provincial Laws you should still continue to state the Law passed for
that purpose in North Carolina as an encroachment upon the Prerogative of the Crown." "It does in no case come within such a description," the Board emphasized, "but on the contrary is not only
justified by the example of like laws in every other Colony but is also
in itself the most reasonable, effectual and constitutional Method of
settling Fees that can be followed." Reiterating its earlier ruling, the
Board explained that the Crown had disallowed colonial fee laws
only when fees were insufficient. Because there had been no complaints about the meagerness of the fees established by the North
Carolina law "by any publick Officer whatever except yourself," the
Board failed to see any justification for its disallowance.[17]

The Board's ruling was significantly different from its earlier one.
In 1757 it had merely upheld the right of colonial lower houses to
regulate fees by statute, reserving, nevertheless, for the governors and
councils a co-ordinate right under the royal instructions. But in 1762
the Board went even further and expressed preference for that method
as "the most reasonable, effectual and constitutional Method of settling Fees that can be followed."[18]

The Lower House's power in this area went unchallenged for the
remainder of the colonial period. In 1767 Governor William Tryon
reported without objection that fees were "for the most part if not
altogether regulated by statute," and in 1771 Governor Josiah Martin
even asked the House to ascertain the fees of the governor by law.
The House willingly complied with Martin's request and during his
and Tryon's administrations passed five other measures to settle
charges for attorneys, inspectors of hemp and flax, and clerks of both
superior and inferior courts.[19]

In South Carolina the fee question never became a serious issue
because the power of the Commons in this area was never seriously

17. Dobbs to Board of Trade, Dec. 1761, Board of Trade to Dobbs, June 10,
1762, *ibid.*, 596-600, 726-27.
18. Board of Trade to Dobbs, Mar. 10, 1757, June 10, 1762, *ibid.*, V, 750, VI,
726-27.
19. Laws, *N. C. St. Recs.*, XXIII, 788-89, 800, 814-18, 859-62, 896-900, 952-55;
Tryon's view of polity, 1767, *N. C. Col. Recs.*, VII, 485; Lower House Journals,
Dec. 6, 1771, *ibid.*, IX, 165.

challenged. As in North Carolina the practice of fixing officers' fees by statute was of proprietary origin. The legislature first passed such acts in 1683 and during the following decade effected extensive regulations by eight additional laws.[20] In 1698 it reduced these early measures into a general law which ascertained the charges of the governor, the provost marshal, the secretary, the clerk of the Crown, the surveyor general, the attorneys, the registers, the sheriffs, certain judges, and a number of other minor officers. The proprietors confirmed the law in 1714, and it formed the basis for the colony's fee system during the remainder of the proprietary period.[21]

When the Crown assumed control of the colony, it provided Francis Nicholson with the usual instruction empowering him to settle fees by executive ordinance.[22] But Nicholson did not try to interfere with the colony's established practice. Instead, he proposed in September 1721 that the Commons settle charges of officers and courts by law according to custom, and the Commons responded by passing the first general fee act since 1698. But this measure expired after two years, and, when it was not renewed, the 1696 regulation again came into force.[23]

Not until 1736 did the Commons again attempt to pass a fee bill. The most extensive regulation to that date, the 1736 measure ascertained the fees of nearly every officer in the colony from the governor to the sextons.[24] Although the Council had complained in 1728 that "Officers Fees are very Shamefull at present, and ought to be augmented, at least double to what they now are,"[25] this measure apparently reduced many older rates. Complaints against the act by South Carolina's patent and warrant officers prompted the Board of Trade to refer it to Francis Fane, its legal counsel. Fane reported that the act took away "three parts in four of the legal Fees of the Patent Offices" without "the least complaint of Corruption or Misbehaviour in their several Offices" and recommended its disallowance. "The practice of lessening the Fees of the Officers appointed by the Crown prevailes so much in the Colonys abroad," he declared, "that

20. Cooper and McCord, eds., *S. C. Statutes*, II, v, viii, 3, 4-6, 18-19, 39-40, 86-92.
21. *Ibid.*, 143-50; Proprietor's order, Sept. 1714, S. C. Pub. Recs., VI, 65, S. C. Arch. Dept.
22. Labaree, ed., *Royal Instructions*, I, 371-72.
23. Sept. 1, 21, 1721, S. C. Commons Journals, CO 5/426, pp. 92-93, 168; An Act for Ascertaining Publick Officers Fees, Sept. 21, 1721, CO 5/412, ff. 93-100.
24. Cooper and McCord, eds., *S. C. Statutes*, III, 414-23.
25. S. C. Council to Newcastle, Dec. 19, 1728, CO 5/360, ff. 96-100.

without your Lordships Interposicon His Majesty's Gracious Intentions in his grants of Offices must be soon entirely defeated." Upon the Board's recommendation, the Privy Council disallowed the act in April 1737 and asserted the executive's right to ascertain fees by ordinance.[26]

Faced with the need for a new law, the Commons considered a regulatory measure at nearly every session for the next few years[27] but did not pass one until May 1743, when it adopted regulations nearly as extensive as those of the previous law. The Commons carefully inserted a suspending clause in order to avoid one of the principal objections against the 1736 law,[28] but its reduction of fees aroused opposition by South Carolina naval officer Alexander Murray and others which prevented prompt confirmation.[29] Indeed, the Crown never formally approved it, the Board of Trade postponing agent James Wright's attempt to secure its confirmation fifteen years after its passage in March 1758.[30] So long as the measure was pending before imperial authorities, the Commons could not legally attempt any further general regulation of officers' charges.

Although the 1698 law was the only statutory regulation in force, William Bull II reported in 1764 and Lord Charles Montagu in 1767 that the only fees taken by the officers were those the Commons had allowed in the acts of 1736 and 1743.[31] These reports illustrate the Commons' extensive control over officers' charges. Even though imperial authorities had disallowed the 1736 measure and had not confirmed the one of 1743, South Carolina officers were in effect bound by those acts, for they knew that if they took fees higher than allowed they might incur the displeasure of the Commons, which could pre-

26. George Morley, James Wedderburn, Thomas Gadsden, William Saxby, Jr., and Samuel Wheatley to Privy Council, [1736], Fane to Board of Trade, Feb. 16, 1737, CO 5/365, ff. 184, 195; Board of Trade to Crown, Mar. 15, 1737, CO 5/385, ff. 235-36; Apr. 6, 21, 1737, *Acts of Privy Council, Colonial*, III, 546-47.

27. Commons Journals, Oct. 8, 1737-Jan. 26, 1738, Jan. 18-26, 1739, *S. C. Col. Recs., 1736-39*, 345, 354, 420-21, 428, 593, 607-8; Feb. 27, 1740, *ibid., 1739-41*, 211.

28. Commons Journals, Jan. 17, May 7, 1743, *ibid., 1742-44*, 141-55, 459.

29. Murray to A. Brett, May 11, 1743, Newcastle Papers, Add. MSS, 32700, f. 121, British Museum; Mar. 14, 1758, *Board of Trade Journals, 1754-58*, 389.

30. Thomas Hill to Matthew Lamb, Jan. 13, 1748, CO 5/402, pp. 141-42; James Wright's memorial, Mar. 14, 1758, CO 5/376, f. 23; Wright to Lyttelton, Nov. 25, 1758, Lyttelton Papers, Clements Lib.; Mar. 14, 1758, *Board of Trade Journals, 1754-58*, 389.

31. Bull's report on S. C. fees, 1764, CO 325/5; Montagu to Earl of Shelburne, Aug. 14, 1767, Shelburne Papers, LVI, 101, Clements Lib.; Bull to Board of Trade, Dec. 21, 1764, S. C. Pub. Recs., XXX, 232-34, S. C. Arch. Dept.

vent the exaction of higher fees in either of two ways. First, it might put pressure on the governor to restrict certain officers who were taking high fees, as it did in the case of the Charles ton customs house officers in 1732, of the secretary in 1735, and of all the colony's officers in 1761.[32] Secondly, it could divert to other purposes or eliminate either partially or entirely an officer's fees by resolution or by a provision in another act. For instance, in 1748 Governor Glen complained that an act to empower two justices and three freeholders to determine actions for debts under £20 Carolina currency took away nearly three-fourths of the emoluments of the provost marshal, and in May 1752 he objected to a Commons resolution that reduced the charges of the secretary as well as the clerk and messenger of the Council for granting land to poor Protestants.[33] What it lacked in theory, the Commons exercised in practice; in the final analysis, it set fees in South Carolina.

Like its counterparts in the Carolinas, the Virginia Burgesses also exercised the power to regulate officers' fees throughout the colonial period, and Governor Dinwiddie's attempt to share that power in the early 1750's produced the important pistole fee controversy, the most serious dispute over the fee question in the four southern colonies. The Burgesses first assumed the power to settle fees by statute early in the seventeenth century. In 1624 it limited charges of surveyors and during the following forty years extended the scope of its regulations to include fees of the secretary, clerks of the legislature and county courts, and sheriffs. In April 1699 it subjected fees of the collectors and naval officers to statutory regulations, and throughout the eighteenth century it periodically passed general fee acts. During the early years of the century these acts settled the fees of only the secretary, clerks of the county courts, and sheriffs, but the Burgesses added those of coroners and constables in 1718 and surveyors in 1734. By the middle of the century the Burgesses had also brought under statutory regulations the charges of the governor and attorney general; the admiralty, customs, and naval officers, and the speaker, sergeant at arms, and clerk of the Burgesses.[34] The Burgesses made few

32. Jan. 27, 1732, Mar. 7, 1735, S. C. Commons Journals, CO 5/433, pp. 7, 34; June 19, 1761, *ibid.*, CO 5/479, p. 152.

33. Commons Journals, Jan. 30, 1748, *S. C. Col. Recs., 1748*, 46-47; May 14, 1752, S. C. Commons Journals, CO 5/466, p. 206.

34. Hening, ed., *Va. Statutes*, I, 125, 176, 201, 220, 265-67, 275-76, 295, 335, 452,

changes in the rates of the established fees after 1700. Spotswood
vetoed its one attempt to reduce the fees in 1715, and it always opposed any attempt to raise them, such as the one made by the Council
in 1728.[35]

Beginning in 1679 the royal instructions empowered Virginia governors to establish fees with the Council's consent,[36] but only once
did a governor attempt to do so before the middle of the eighteenth
century. In the mid-1680's Howard, without the consent of either
Council or Burgesses, imposed fees of two hundred pounds of tobacco
for his fixing the public seal to land patents and other official documents and thirty pounds of tobacco for the secretary's recording surveys of land. The Burgesses objected to these fees at three successive
sessions after 1685 and, when Howard refused to abolish them, appealed to the home authorities through its special agent, Philip Ludwell.[37] The Glorious Revolution delayed a decision on Ludwell's
appeal, but when the Privy Council did hand down a ruling in
September 1689 it was unfavorable to Howard, declaring the fees
illegal because he had not asked the Council's consent in establishing
them.[38] This decision clearly implied that the Burgesses' consent was
unnecessary to establish fees, but none of Howard's successors attempted to establish fees by executive ordinance for over a half century. When Governor Dinwiddie demanded a similar fee in 1752, therefore, he set off the pistole fee controversy—the most bitter constitutional battle in Virginia before 1763.

In every royal colony except Virginia, the governor was allowed a
fee for sealing land patents. Dinwiddie asked the Board of Trade's
permission to take such a fee in August 1751 at the time of his appointment as lieutenant governor. The Board did not act before he

463-65, 490, II, 143-46, III, 195-97, IV, 59-74, 239, 326-55, 492-507, V, 36-54, 246-
47, 326-44, VI, 200; Alexander Spotswood to Board of Trade, Aug. 14, 1718, Brock,
ed., *Spotswood Letters*, II, 286-87; Report on Va. fees, Nov. 23, 1764, CO 325/5;
Fauquier's letter, 1763, Report on State of American Colonies, King's MSS, 205,
ff. 270-73, British Museum.

35. Sept. 7, 1715, *Va. Burgesses Journals, 1712-26*, 167; Mar. 29, 1728, *ibid.*, *1728-
40*, 49.

36. Labaree, ed., *Royal Instructions*, I, 371-72.

37. Howard to Committee, Feb. 10, 1685, CO 1/59, No. 17, f. 87; Nicholas
Spencer to William Blathwayt, May 17, 1688, Blathwayt Papers, Colonial Williamsburg, Inc.; May 9, 1688, *Va. Burgesses Journals, 1660-93*, 316-17.

38. Ludwell's petition, Mar. 25, 1689, Howard's answer to Ludwell, May 23,
1689, Ludwell's second petition, Sept. 19, 1689, CO 5/1305; Sept 9, 1689, *Acts of
Privy Council, Colonial*, II, 142-43.

left for Virginia, but in April 1752, soon after his arrival in Virginia, he obtained the Council's consent to charge a pistole—a Spanish coin equal to about three and one-half Spanish dollars—for sealing land patents.[39] The establishment of this fee by executive ordinance was perfectly legal under the royal instructions, but it was contrary to practice in Virginia, where, since Howard's unhappy attempt in the 1680's, fees had customarily been settled by statute. Consequently, Dinwiddie tried to remove any question about the legality of the fee by submitting the matter to the Board of Trade for its opinion in October 1752. The Board promptly signified its approval, and Sir Dudley Ryder, the King's Attorney and Solicitor General, upheld the executive's power to establish the fee by ordinance, ruling in February 1753 that the Virginia legislature had no right to participate in settling fees for services relating to Crown lands.[40]

While the Board of Trade was sanctioning the establishment of the pistole fee, resistance to it was forming in Virginia. Supported by many powerful land speculators upon whom the fee would weigh most heavily, the opposition was spearheaded by William Stith— Anglican clergyman, historian, President of the College of William and Mary, and chaplain to the House of Burgesses. His toast *"Liberty and Property and no Pistole"* became the slogan of the opposition. Stith, along with Richard Bland—a leading member of the Burgesses and author of a tract on the controversy—and other opponents of the fee, attacked it on two grounds. The most important argument and the one stressed later when the Burgesses appealed the matter to the Privy Council was that no fee was legal unless settled by legislative enactment according to the long-established practice of Virginia. In a letter to the Bishop of London, Stith vigorously and cogently asserted that "Our Laws have clearly settled the Methods of taking up new Lands, and prescribed the several Fees to the several Officers; which certainly implies an Exemption from all other Fees, except those specified by Law; and the Governor might by the same Reason have demanded 10, 20, or 100 Pistoles as one." Similar reasoning led Bland to conclude that Dinwiddie's demand for the

39. Dinwiddie to Board of Trade, Aug. 1751 and Oct. 6, 1752, CO 5/1327, ff. 417, 497-98; Apr. 22, 1752, *Exec. Journals of Va. Council*, V, 385.

40. Dinwiddie to Board of Trade, Oct. 6, 1752, CO 5/1327, ff. 497-98; Board of Trade to Dinwiddie, Jan. 17, 1753, CO 5/1367, pp. 5-7; Ryder's opinion on pistole fee, Feb. 1, 1753, CO 5/1328, f. 83.

pistole was "subversive of the Rights and Liberties of my Country." A royal instruction empowering a governor to establish fees could not, in other words, supersede local law and tradition. Opponents of the fee also argued that it was a tax imposed upon Virginians without their consent; Stith's declaration that "This Attempt to lay Taxes upon the People WITHOUT Law was certainly AGAINST Law, and an evident Invasion of Property" is not unlike colonial denunciations of Parliamentary taxation in the following decade.[41]

By November 1753 resistance to the pistole fee was widespread; when the House of Burgesses convened in that month, six counties presented petitions complaining of the charge. To the Burgesses' query as to his authority for establishing the fee, Dinwiddie replied that it was taken by his direction with the consent of the Council, according to royal instruction, and also with the approval of the home officials. The Burgesses in turn declared the fee a grievance and asked Dinwiddie to discontinue it, asserting that it was "an Infringement on the Rights of the People, and a Discouragement from taking up Lands, and thereby . . . the settling the Frontiers of this Country, and the Increase of his Majesty's Revenue of Quitrents." Moreover, the Burgesses contended that the terms and conditions by which the Crown granted lands to the inhabitants of Virginia could not "be altered or infringed by the Advice of the Council," citing the Privy Council's ruling against Lord Howard in 1689 to support its contention. The pistole fee, Dinwiddie countered, was established to increase Crown revenues from quitrents, and he refused to discontinue charging it, declaring that his right to take it was confirmed by *"unquestionable Authority."* After Dinwiddie's refusal to comply with its request, the Burgesses adopted forceful resolutions which declared that the fee was unconstitutional, that an appeal should be made to the Crown for relief, and that anyone paying the fee should "be deemed a Betrayer of the Rights and Privileges of the People."[42]

In an attempt to effect a compromise between Dinwiddie and the

41. Stith to Bishop of London, Apr. 21, 1753, Fulham Palace MSS, Virginia (Second Box), 13, Fulham Palace, London; Richard Bland, *A Fragment on the Pistole Fee, claimed by the Governor of Virginia, 1753,* ed. Worthington C. Ford (Brooklyn, 1891), 36-37; Mays, *Edmund Pendleton,* I, 68-71; Glenn C. Smith, "The Affair of the Pistole Fee, Virginia, 1752-55," *Va. Mag. of Hist. and Biog.,* 48 (1940), 209-21.

42. Nov. 21-28, Dec. 4, 1753, *Va. Burgesses Journals, 1752-58,* 129, 132, 136, 141, 143-44, 154; Burgesses' resolves, Dec. 4, 1753, CO 5/1328, f. 79; Act to establish pistole fee, Dec. 6, 1753, CO 5/14, f. 15.

Burgesses, the Council introduced a bill on December 6 to establish the fee by statute, but the Burgesses was resolved to carry the case to the Crown and rejected it. On December 15 the Burgesses appointed Peyton Randolph, Crown Attorney General in Virginia and a burgess for William and Mary College, to present an address against the fee in England. It offered Randolph £2,500 sterling and promised him an annual stipend of £300 sterling for life in case he lost his place as attorney general because of his services for the House. When the Council rejected the House resolution to pay Randolph, Speaker-Treasurer John Robinson declared that he would pay him without the customary resolution, and Randolph sailed for England later in December.[43] To counteract Randolph's activities in England, the Council submitted an address in support of Dinwiddie, who wrote the home authorities defending his conduct in the controversy and complaining of the Burgesses' opposition. Dinwiddie selected James Abercromby, an experienced colonial agent, to present his case.

Randolph arrived in England early in February and brought the complaints of the Burgesses to the attention of the Privy Council later that month, but the final hearing was not held until the following June.[44] In the meantime Randolph and Abercromby were active in behalf of their clients. Probably at the instigation of Randolph, notices reporting the dispute in a light unfavorable to Dinwiddie appeared in many English newspapers and periodicals, and the affair stimulated considerable discussion in the London coffee houses. It is quite likely that Randolph also had a hand in arranging for the publication of a pamphlet written by Landon Carter, a leading member of the Burgesses, which argued dispassionately and forcefully that Virginia had inherited "all the Constitutional Rights of *Great-Britain*" and charged that the pistole fee was "subversive of Law and Constitution" and "against the known Laws of the Land, and therefore against the Maxims of a *British* Government." Abercromby, on the other

43. Dinwiddie to Board of Trade, Jan. 29, 1754, CO 5/1328, ff. 93-94; Dinwiddie to James Abercromby, Feb. 9 and Apr. 26, 1754, Brock, ed., *Dinwiddie Papers*, I, 71-73, 140.

44. Va. Council to Crown, Dec. 1753, and Dinwiddie to Board of Trade, Dec. 29, 1753, CO 5/1328, ff. 77-78, 81-82, 85; Dinwiddie to Earl of Holderness, Dec. 29, 1753, CO 5/14, ff. 11-12; Dinwiddie to Treasury, Dec. 29, 1753, Treasury Papers, I, 353, PRO; Dinwiddie to Abercromby, Feb. 9, 1754, Brock, ed., *Dinwiddie Papers*, I, 71-73; Feb. 28, 1754, *Acts of Privy Council, Colonial*, IV, 234.

hand, solicited the support of the various boards that were concerned with colonial affairs.[45]

On June 18, 1754, the Privy Council assembled at the Cockpit to hear the case. As was customary in such hearings learned lawyers represented both parties. William Murray and Alexander Hume Campbell appeared for the governor and Alexander Forrester and Robert Henley, later Earl of Northington, for the Burgesses.[46] The arguments advanced in this hearing clearly outlined the foundation of the long constitutional struggle between colonial lower houses and imperial authorities, revealing two diverging concepts of the status of lower houses and the constitutions of the colonies. The counsels for the governor based their contentions on the assumptions that the lower houses were subordinate lawmaking bodies, that the royal instructions were inviolable, and that the Crown's decisions were supreme in all matters relating to the colonies, colonial practice and usage to the contrary notwithstanding. The counsels for the Burgesses did not deny the Crown's supremacy but argued that no governor even with the consent of his Council, the royal instructions, or an order of the authorities in London, could modify or abridge the usage of the Virginia constitution.[47]

The Privy Council demonstrated little reverence for the Virginia constitution, approving Dinwiddie's conduct in the affair and upholding his right to take the pistole. But the Burgesses took some satisfaction from the ruling that certain patents, including those in the governor's office before the establishment of the fee in April 1752,

45. *Gentleman's Magazine*, 24 (1754), 94; *Whitehall Evening Post* (London), Feb. 23, 1754; *Kentish Post* (Canterbury), Feb. 27, 1754; Dinwiddie to Abercromby, Apr. 26, 1754, Brock, ed., *Dinwiddie Papers*, I, 137-41; [Landon Carter], *A Letter from a Gentleman in Virginia, to the Merchants of Great Britain, Trading to that Colony* (London, 1754), 8, 16, 22.

46. A long-time rival of Pitt, Murray was attorney general to the Newcastle administration and later lord chief justice of the King's bench. See J. M. Rigg *s.v.* "Murray, William, first Earl of Mansfield," in Sidney Lee *et al.*, eds., *Dictionary of National Biography* (London, 1885——); hereafter cited as *DNB*. Campbell was King's counsel, chancellor of the Duchy of Lancaster Chamber, and M.P. for Berwickshire. Gerrit P. Judd IV, *Members of Parliament, 1734-1832* (New Haven, 1955), 140. Henley was also King's counsel and later attorney general in the Devonshire-Pitt administration and lord keeper of the great seal. See G. F. Russell Barker in *DNB s.v.* "Henley, Robert, first Earl of Northington." Forrester was a lawyer of the Middle Temple, author, and later M.P. successively for Dunwich, Okehampton, and Newcastle-under-Lyme. Judd, *Members of Parliament*, 198.

47. Greene, "The Case of the Pistole Fee," *Va. Mag. of Hist. and Biog.*, 66 (1958), 406-22.

those for lands amounting to less than one hundred acres, and those for lands to the west of the Allegheny Mountains, were to be granted upon the usual charges and exempted from payment of the pistole. As a further concession to the Burgesses, the Privy Council ordered Dinwiddie to reinstate Randolph, whom he had replaced with George Wythe, as attorney general.[48] Despite these concessions the Privy Council's decision showed little appreciation for the Burgesses' constitutional objections to the pistole fee. By upholding Dinwiddie's right to establish the fee, the Privy Council confirmed the power of the governor and Council to settle and regulate fees without consulting the Burgesses. Although this method of establishing fees was the one specified in the royal instructions, it was not the one usually followed in Virginia. There fees had normally been settled by statute. When the Burgesses argued that Dinwiddie's establishment of the pistole fee was contrary to the custom of the Virginia constitution, it was defending its right to a very real power acquired over the years to participate, indeed to assume the major role, in establishing and regulating officers' fees. That the Privy Council did not uphold the Burgesses in its exercise of a power it had long enjoyed is one of the many instances in the decades immediately preceding the American Revolution of the inability or unwillingness of British officials to recognize and accept constitutional changes that had taken place in the colonies.

Nevertheless, the Burgesses received the Privy Council decision in October 1754 with almost as much rejoicing as did Dinwiddie. Dinwiddie was obviously happy that his right to take the fee had been upheld; the House of Burgesses was pleased because certain patents had been exempted from the payment of the pistole and because Randolph was to be reinstated as attorney general. Relations between the lower house and the executive were further ameliorated when the Council approved Treasurer Robinson's accounts containing an item to pay Randolph the £2,500 promised him by the Burgesses the previous December for serving as agent.[49]

In theory the Privy Council decision firmly established the power of the governor and Council to settle and regulate officers' fees without the Burgesses' consent according to the method prescribed in the

48. Board of Trade to Dinwiddie, July 3, 1754, CO 5/1367, ff. 94-100.
49. Landon Carter's Minutes of the Burgesses, 1754, Sabine Hall Collection, Alderman Lib.

royal instructions. But the strong opposition exhibited by the Burgesses to the pistole fee was a deterrent to similar attempts in the future,
and the vast majority of fees continued to be settled by legislative
enactments. Dinwiddie himself declared at the conclusion of the
affair that he would have given up the fee entirely had he anticipated
the storm it would raise.[50]

Subsequent governors did not challenge the Burgesses' right to
settle fees by statute. When the House created pilots for the colony's
waterways in 1762, it settled their charges by law,[51] and Fauquier reported in November 1764 that almost all officers' charges were established by legislative enactments. Only the fees of the clerk of the
Council, the pistole fee, and two of the governor's charges, all of
which had been introduced by Dinwiddie, were settled solely by
executive authority.[52] When Dunmore came to the colony in the
early 1770's, he found that fees taken by the governor's clerk for signing commissions for public offices had been established by the governor and were not sanctioned by law. Upon learning that "some
people objected to the paying of them, and questioned the authority
by which they were demanded" and that "they were talked of, in the
light of taxes imposed by a Governors, Single, Authority," he submitted the matter to the Burgesses, asking it to establish them by law
but offering to abolish them if it thought them unreasonable. The
Burgesses expressed its appreciation for his candor in placing the
matter before it but declared that it considered the *"Emoluments of
Government, as by Law established, adequate and amply sufficient"*
to support the *"Honour and Dignity of our Governors"* and asked
him to abolish the fee.

Dunmore complied, but the abolition of the clerk's fees put the
expense of supporting the clerk upon him, and he wrote Hillsborough
in May 1772 applying for an allowance to cover that expense.[53] Hillsborough was sympathetic toward the application but regretted that
Dunmore had laid the matter before the Burgesses in the first place,
pointing out that the fees were legal if they were moderate and if
they had been "established by a regular Order of the Governor and

50. See Hening, ed., *Va. Statutes*, VI, 244, VII, 278-79, 384-86; Dinwiddie to
Abercromby, Feb. 24, 1755, Brock, ed., *Dinwiddie Papers*, I, 511-12.
51. Hening, ed., *Va. Statutes*, VI, 490-94.
52. Report on Va. fees, Nov. 23, 1764, CO 325/5.
53. Dunmore to Hillsborough, May 2, 1772, CO 5/1350; Feb. 18-28, 1772, *Va.
Burgesses Journals*, 1770-72, 173, 185, 200-201.

Council." In his defense Dunmore replied to Dartmouth, Hillsborough's successor, that the Council had not, in fact, consented to fix the fees in question and that even if imperial authorities did recognize the legality of establishing officers' charges by executive ordinance "the people of this colony, whatever may be urged to them, are not disposed to admit it to be so, for they talked of the fees in the light of taxes." Dartmouth appreciated Dunmore's position. He insisted that fees might be settled by the governor and Council but agreed that "in the present moment" it might not "be advisable for them to exercise that Right."[54] Dunmore thus accorded formal recognition to the Burgesses' long-claimed and long-exercised right to regulate all fees by statute, and Dartmouth's approval constituted an admission by the London authorities of the impropriety and futility of interfering with the Burgesses' exercise of that right.

In Georgia the Commons House did not succeed in gaining power to regulate fees by statute in the period before 1763. When the Crown took over Georgia it provided its first governor, John Reynolds, with the usual instruction given to royal governors empowering him to establish fees by executive ordinance. Accordingly, in January 1755, shortly after his arrival, Reynolds met with the Council to settle the charges of the colony's officers.[55] Georgia's first Commons did not oppose this action when it met later in the month, but it did prepare a remonstrance to the King complaining that "fixing and settling of the Fees of the Publick Officers of this your Majesty's Colony being solely in the Power of the Governor and Council without the Concurrence and Consent of the Assembly seems to Us a great hardship and may be attended with Consequences hurtfull to Our Constituents as it puts it entirely out of our Power to procure them any Redress if ever they should have reason." It asked accordingly "that the Fees of the Publick Officers of this Colony may be settled by Act of General Assembly and no[t] otherwise, as is the Custom of all Your Majesty's other Provinces in America."[56]

Reynolds sent this remonstrance to the Board of Trade along with another asking permission to pass a law to settle qualifications of

54. Hillsborough to Dunmore, July 1, 1772, CO 5/1350; Dunmore to Dartmouth, Nov. 16, 1772, and Dartmouth to Dunmore, Oct. 27, 1773, CO 5/1351.

55. Council Journals, Jan. 2, 1755, *Ga. Col. Recs.*, VII, 63-87.

56. Commons Journals, Jan. 29, 1755, *ibid.*, XIII, 41-42; Ga. Commons' remonstrance and address to King, Feb. 21, 1755, CO 5/644.

voters and representatives. The Board's initial reaction was not favorable. Secretary John Pownall wrote Reynolds in June 1755 expressing concern "that this Assembly have laid in such early claims to privileges and powers, which, though of long usage enjoyed by some other Assembly, are inconsistent with all Colony Constitution whatever, contrary to the practice of the Mother Country in like Cases, and to the express directions of His Majesty's Commission, by which alone that Assembly is constituted."[57] Although Pownall was probably referring more to the remonstrance on electoral qualifications than to the one on fees, the Board wrote Reynolds the following August that it would advise the Crown to refuse both remonstrances. Contrary to the Board's advice, however, the Privy Council's plantation committee decided that the Commons might pass a law to regulate fees with a suspending clause. The Board of Trade acquainted Reynolds with the committee's decision in May 1756,[58] but probably because of a change in administration the Commons did not attempt to pass a fee law until November 1761. The Council rejected it and with the governor continued to fix fees by executive ordinances for the rest of the period before 1763.[59]

By 1763 the lower houses in the three older colonies not only had gained the power to regulate officers' fees, but also had effectively denied the executive's authority to exercise that power as directed by the royal instructions. In the two Carolinas all charges were settled by legislative act. After a long struggle with the first two royal governors, the North Carolina Lower House had established its power to regulate fees by an act in 1748; in South Carolina fees were legally fixed by a 1698 statute, although officers took their fees at rates specified in two acts of 1736 and 1743 despite the fact that the Crown disallowed the first and never confirmed the second. The great majority of officers' charges in Virginia were also ascertained by statute. The Burgesses had resisted Dinwiddie's attempt in 1752 to settle the pistole fee solely by executive authority, and, although the Crown

57. Pownall to Reynolds, June 5, 1755, CO 5/672, pp. 341-49.
58. Board of Trade to Reynolds, Aug. 6, 1755, *ibid.*, pp. 357-59; May 5, 1756, CO 5/653; Aug. 26, 1755, *Acts of Privy Council, Colonial*, IV, 311; Nov. 6, 1755, *Board of Trade Journals, 1754-58*, 184-85.
59. Commons Journals, Nov. 24, 1761, Jan. 19, 1762, *Ga. Col. Recs.*, XIII, 603, 638; Wright to Board of Trade, Dec. 11, 1764, unpubl. Ga. Col. Recs., XXVIII, Pt. II-A, 158-59, Ga. Dept. of Arch. and Hist.

upheld his right to settle fees by ordinance, the Burgesses' opposition was so strong that governors established few fees thereafter without its consent. Only in Georgia did the governors and Council settle charges by executive authority. Even there the Crown had expressed its willingness to permit the Commons to assume that power, but it was another decade before the Commons did so.

When imperial authorities adopted the general restrictive policy after 1763, they made no effort to deprive the southern lower houses of their power to regulate fees by statute; the question of who should exercise that power was not, therefore, an issue in the pre-Revolutionary years. Crown officials may have planned some reform in 1764 when they required the governors to send home statements of all fees taken in their particular colonies, but, if that was their intention, they never attempted to implement it. Again in the early 1770's they reviewed the colonial fee system but apparently did not object to the legislatures' settling fees by law.[60] Never did they indicate that they intended to reverse the Board of Trade's 1761 ruling, in the case of North Carolina, that statutory regulations were perhaps the "most reasonable, effectual and constitutional Method of settling Fees that can be followed."

60. See Wright to Board of Trade, Dec. 11, 1764, unpubl. Ga. Col. Recs., XXVIII, Pt. II-A, 158-59, Ga. Dept. of Arch. and Hist.; May 22, 28, 1764, *Board of Trade Journals, 1764-67*, 58, 62; Case of civil officers claiming fees in the colonies, [1774], *Dartmouth MSS*, II, 125.

PART IV

CONTROL OVER LEGISLATIVE PROCEEDINGS

. . . that a Method of enlarging the Number of Assembly Men by Order of Governour and Council is not agreeable to the Constitution, that the Representatives of the People are the proper Judges what Encrease is necessary, nor ought any Encrease to be made without their Assent.
—North Carolina Lower House of Assembly,
July 1733

It is the undeniable fundamental and inherent Right and Privilege of the Commons House of Assembly, of this Province, solely to examine and finally determine the Elections of their own Members.
—South Carolina Commons House of Assembly,
December 1762

THE lower houses of assembly in the southern royal colonies early tried to free themselves from executive interference by establishing their authority over their compositions and proceedings. To obtain exclusive authority over membership, they attempted to acquire the powers to regulate the qualifications for members and the franchise, erect constituencies and apportion representation, determine disputed elections, and expel members. As an adjunct to their control over membership, they also tried to win authority to determine the frequency of elections and meetings of the legislature by passing statutes requiring elections and legislative sessions at stipulated intervals. They endeavored to gain control over internal proceedings by asserting their power to regulate legislative procedure and to appoint and manipulate legislative officers, including speakers and clerks, and by establishing their right to enjoy certain fundamental privileges, such as freedom from arrest during session and freedom of speech and debate.

Had the lower houses attained all of these powers, they would have achieved a remarkable degree of independence from the governors and councils. None of these powers would have deprived the executive of its fundamental authority to convene, prorogue, and dissolve the lower houses, but in combination they would have reduced to a minimum its power to interfere in the houses' internal affairs and curtailed its influence in determining the composition of the representative body or the time and frequency of meetings and elections. In their quest for power, however, the lower houses succeeded only partially in achieving these goals.

9

Membership

AUTHORITY over membership was a fundamental goal in the lower
houses' drive to establish control over their composition and proceedings. As long as governors and councils retained any influence over
the make-up of the representative body, they could mold its character
along whatever lines they desired. Specifically, they could control its
membership by erecting constituencies and apportioning representation, regulating qualifications for voters and legislators, determining
disputed elections, and denying its power to expel members. The
executive could also influence the complexion of the lower houses
through its power to determine the frequency of elections and sessions. That power enabled it to continue an unusually amenable
legislature indefinitely or, if such a body could not be obtained, to
permit long periods to elapse between meetings.

To deprive the executive of such vast influence, the lower houses
in the southern royal colonies sought to extend their authority in
each of these areas. Crown officials conceded to the lower houses
the powers to determine disputed elections and expel members and
did not, as a rule, object to their assumption of the authority to regulate qualifications of members and voters as long as the Crown's instructions to limit the franchise to freeholders were complied with.
On the other hand, they regarded the powers to establish constituencies and apportion representation and to determine the frequency
of elections and sessions as essential parts of the royal prerogative,
assigning them exclusively to the executive. Although the official
attitude toward these two powers was always clear, imperial authorities did not force a rigid compliance with it during the first half of

the eighteenth century; as a result the lower houses usually assumed both of them. For the most part, the lower houses established their authority over membership in the normal course of business without serious opposition from either the Crown or its officials in the colonies. But challenges from later governors occasioned some explosive incidents, in particular North Carolina's representation controversy and South Carolina's Gadsden election dispute. And the attempts of Crown officials to curtail the lower houses' exercise of that power after 1750 constituted an important source of legislative dissatisfaction with imperial policy during the critical years preceding the American Revolution.

Power to establish constituencies and apportion representation was the basic component of authority over membership. Both the royal officials and Carolina proprietors originally intended for it to remain in executive hands, where it could have served as a valuable political weapon. By creating new electoral districts or juggling the apportionment in old ones, governors and councils could secure more tractable legislatures and, to some extent at least, control the composition of the representatives. But the lower houses early insisted that such matters could be settled only by statute. In Virginia and South Carolina the lower houses had established this principle with relative ease during their first half century of development, but in North Carolina and Georgia it was a different story. An executive-legislative struggle over this power was a central feature of North Carolina politics during much of the royal period, and by the time Georgia became a royal colony in the 1750's the Crown had decided to enforce more rigidly the long-standing official policy of reserving that power for the executive.

The Virginia House of Burgesses first assumed the power to set electoral districts and apportion representation by statute in 1645. It confirmed existing constituencies and stipulated that no county should elect more than four burgesses, except James City, which could elect six, five for the county and one for Jamestown. In 1661 and 1662 the Burgesses further limited the apportionment to not more than two for each county and one for Jamestown, and in 1669 it required each county to return two representatives. In revising the colony's laws in 1705, the Burgesses retained this apportionment, which remained unchanged for the rest of the colonial period.   Under the election laws of 1669 and 1705 each new county automatically became a constituency with the privilege of sending two representatives, and between 1689 and 1776 the Burgesses created thirty-eight new counties, faithfully extending representation to the western areas of the colony as they were settled.   In addition, it extended to Williamsburg in 1722 and Norfolk in 1736 the privilege that it had conferred upon Jamestown of sending a borough representative.   During the years before 1763 Crown officials never challenged the Burgesses' right either to erect counties and boroughs or to apportion representation, and thereby relinquished, in effect, the power of the executive to establish constituencies.   The one electoral district not originally established by the Burgesses in the period after 1689 was the College of William and Mary, which beginning in 1693 sent one member by virtue of its charter—a privilege confirmed by the Burgesses in the election act of 1705.[1]

The South Carolina Commons had only slightly more difficulty in establishing its power to erect electoral districts and apportion representation.   The proprietors retained that power without serious opposition until 1716, when the Commons pushed through an act making the parish the unit of representation and specifying the number of legislators each parish might elect.   This step inaugurated a three-year contest with the proprietors, who disallowed this measure as well as a second one, almost identical with the first, passed by the Commons in March 1719.   But the Commons was persistent and in 1721 it took advantage of the uncertain situation at the beginning of royal administration to pass the measure again, and royal authorities permitted it to stand.   The 1721 statute apportioned unequally thirty-six representatives among eleven parishes—St. Philip's of Charleston sending five, four other parishes four each, three parishes three each, and three parishes two each.[2]   Thereafter, the Commons freely created new electoral districts by statute.   Between 1721 and 1770 it established eleven new parishes, and the membership of the House rose from thirty-six to forty-eight.   But the apportionment was by no

1. Hening, ed., *Va. Statutes*, I, 299-300, 545, II, 20, 272-73, III, 236-46, IV, 541-42, V, 205; Julian A. Chandler, *Representation in Virginia* (Baltimore, 1896), 17.

2. Cooper and McCord, eds., *S. C. Statutes*, II, 683-91, III, 50-55, 135-40; Proprietors to Governor and Deputies of Carolina South and West of Cape Fear, Mar. 13, 1685, and Proprietors' Instructions to Col. Philip Ludwell, Apr. 12, 1693, S. C. Pub. Recs., II, 31-36, III, 92-93, S. C. Arch. Dept.

means equitable. The representatives from the older Tidewater parishes used the power of appointment to retain their dominance, with the result that newer western parishes, unlike those in Virginia, were vastly underrepresented, particularly after the end of the Seven Years' War.[3]

Governor James Glen was the only royal official bold enough to contest the Commons' power in this area. Upon his appointment to the governorship in 1739 Crown officials instructed him that each parish with one hundred householders should have the right to send two members to the legislature.[4] Glen did not immediately attempt to execute this instruction, but in the late 1740's he twice sought to persuade imperial authorities to restore the executive's power to establish constituencies and settle apportionment.[5] They paid no attention to his complaints, however, and without support from home he was unwilling to risk provoking a major altercation with the Commons. In April 1751 he did offer a weak challenge to the Commons' right to create electoral districts, vetoing a bill to divide the parish of St. Philip's, Charleston, largely because it granted the new parish of St. Michael's the privilege of electing three representatives. But Glen was unable to sustain the challenge and accepted the measure the following June.[6] Neither he nor his successors again disputed the Commons' power over constituencies and apportionment.

It was in North Carolina that the contest over this power assumed important dimensions, constituting a major political issue throughout the royal period. The proprietors originally intended to divide the colony into counties, each with four precincts. The precinct was to be the electoral unit sending five representatives to the Lower House. Accordingly, Albemarle County was settled on this plan, and its four parishes elected five members each.[7] Subsequently, the governor and Council established additional precincts whenever newly settled regions obtained enough inhabitants to warrant separation from the older precincts, granting them an appropriate number of representa-

3. See William Bull II to Hillsborough, Sept. 10, 1768, and Nov. 30, 1771, S. C. Pub. Recs., XXXII, 37, 366-67, S. C. Arch. Dept.
4. Instructions to Glen, July 19, 1739, CO 5/401, p. 410.
5. Glen to Board of Trade, Oct. 10, 1748, CO 5/372, ff. 80-87; Letter of Glen, 1749, Report on State of American Colonies, King's MSS, 205, ff. 289-90, British Museum.
6. Apr. 24, June 14, 1751, S. C. Commons Journals, CO 5/463, pp. 41-42, 118-20.
7. See Instructions to Capt. Henry Wilkinson, 1681, *N. C. Col. Recs.*, I, 333.

tives. Finally, the Lower House put the whole process under statutory regulation and asserted its power to determine the apportionment in 1715 with the passage of the biennial act. That act confirmed the privilege of all existing precincts to continue to elect the number of representatives they had traditionally returned but provided that precincts created in the future should return only two members. That this provision was calculated to insure the continued supremacy of the Albemarle precincts in the Lower House was clearly indicated during the next decade by the House's willingness to ignore it in cases involving new precincts created in the Albemarle section. Thus, when the Lower House divided Chowan precinct in 1722, it granted the new electoral unit, Bertie, five representatives. Similarly, upon the creation in 1729 of Tyrrell precinct from the area just across the sound from the old Albemarle districts, the House awarded it three representatives.

During the remaining years under the proprietors the Lower House also gained the right to erect constituencies. To be sure, the governor and Council created Carteret precinct in 1722 and granted it the privilege of electing representatives without legislative action, but the Lower House extended similar privileges by statute to both Bertie precinct and Edenton in 1722 and to Tyrrell precinct in 1729, thereby establishing precedents for erecting constituencies by law. In addition, it served notice in 1729 that it intended to exclude the executive from any further share in exercising that power by contesting the attempt by the governor and Council to erect New Hanover into a precinct and refusing to admit representatives from that district until it had been confirmed by statute.[8]

Despite these precedents, the North Carolina Lower House had to fight to retain its powers of erecting electoral districts and apportioning representation during the royal period. Usually, the controversy turned around the overrepresentation of the Albemarle precincts. The Crown's first three governors all traced the vigorous legislative opposition they encountered to Albemarle's dominance over the Lower House and sought ways to effect reforms. Almost immediately after his arrival in the colony in 1731 George Burrington complained that "a Small part of the Province have Twenty Six Representatives

8. Laws, *N. C. St. Recs.*, XXV, 175-78, 212-13; Burrington to Council, Dec. 26, 1732, *N. C. Col. Recs.*, III, 442-49; Nathaniel Rice and John Baptista Ashe to Burrington and Council, [1732-33], *ibid.*, 449-57.

[and] all the Remainder but ten" and suggested "that two representatives are Sufficient for a Precinct [as] the Counties in Virginia send no more."[9]   To remedy the situation Burrington determined to reduce the Albemarle majority by creating three new precincts in the southern portion of the province.

The majority of the Council consented to this step; two councilors, John Baptista Ashe and Nathaniel Rice, opposed it. Contending that "there were very few Inhabitants" in the new precincts, they accused Burrington of "writing and forming some Petitions for such Precincts, and promoting them by much Art and persuasion." More important, they raised the constitutional issue by denying that the executive could create constituencies without legislative approval. Although they conceded that the governor and Council had exercised that power before 1715, they argued that the executive's assent to the biennial act in that year constituted an admission that it could not constitutionally erect electoral districts without approval from the Lower House. If the old precincts "were legally and regularly appointed," they asked, "what need was there of a Law to establish them?" They further asserted that the constitution of the legislature could be changed only by the "Governor, Council and Representatives of the People in a General Assembly" and cited Virginia "where many precedents appear in their printed Laws of such busyness being done by their Governor Council and Assembly." Pleading for the independence of each of the three branches of the legislature, Rice and Ashe advanced the obvious and standard legislative argument that "if a Power of altering the form of Representation, either by adding to or diminishing the Number of Representatives be lodged in the Persons of whom the upper House consists, that then the Lower House, is dependent on and owes it's Being at least the form thereof (which is in effect the same) to the Upper House; by which means the Upper House will be solely (as it were) the whole Legislature." They reasoned that if this power were carried to extremes the governor and a minority of the Council might "think it proper to divide a Precinct whose Inhabitants for some particular ends may be at such Governor and Council's devotion into ten Precincts" and thereby obtain a majority in the Lower House.[10]

9. Burrington to Board of Trade, Sept. 4, 1731, *N. C. Col. Recs.*, III, 207.
10. Rice, John Montgomery, and Ashe to Board of Trade, Nov. 17, 1732, Rice and Ashe to Board of Trade, Apr. 20, 1733, Rice and Ashe's Objections in Council, [1732], Rice and Ashe to Burrington and Council, [1732-33], *ibid.*, 380, 439-42, 449-57.

Burrington, on the other hand, rested his case on precedents established both before and after 1715 of precincts having been erected solely by executive action. He argued that the biennial act merely allowed "those Precincts erected by the Governour and Council to be regularly appointed" and in no way constituted a denial of executive authority in that area. He accused Rice and Ashe of trying "to disquiet and amuse the People, and to shew their zeal for the support and augmentation of the Power and privileges of the House of Burgesses, nay further to carry them to a [point] hitherto unknown and unthought of even in North Carolina."[11]

The Lower House took its cue from Burrington's opponents, refusing to admit the members returned from the three new precincts when it met in July 1733. In justifying its action, it followed Rice and Ashe's arguments and declared that a "Method of enlarging the Number of Assembly Men by Order of Governour and Council is not agreeable to the Constitution, that the Representatives of the People are the proper Judges what Encrease is necessary, nor ought any Encrease to be made without their Assent." The Lower House clearly saw that to permit the governor and Council to exercise that power would make it dependent upon the executive. As far as it was concerned, electoral districts could be created only by statute. To break the resulting deadlock, the Lower House and Council agreed to establish the new precincts by law so "that at the next biennial Election they should return Members to serve in that Assembly." However, before the agreement could be implemented, Burrington dissolved the legislature, censuring it for refusing "to admitt Several Members . . . legally chosen and returned by the proper Officers, pursuant to the Ancient and constant practice of the province" and declaring that "as you are but part of an House, my allowing your Proceedings or Orders would be giving up an undoubted Right of his Majesty, which has never before been contested."[12] A second attempt to establish the three new precincts by statute in November 1734 failed when the session was cut short by the arrival of Burrington's successor, Gabriel Johnston.[13]

The controversy continued under Johnston. In his first session the three new precincts returned members by virtue of executive

11. Burrington to Council, Dec. 26, 1732, *ibid.,* 442-49.
12. Lower House Journals, July 7, 11, 18, 1733, *ibid.,* 575, 583, 611.
13. Lower House Journals, Nov. 11, 1734, *ibid.,* 640.

writs. The Lower House refused to admit them, maintaining "that those Members are not qualified to sit in General Assembly untill these Precincts be Established and Confirmed by the Sanction of a Law." The contest was finally settled when Johnston assented to an act confirming and establishing these precincts, thereby recognizing the House's exclusive power to create constituencies by statute.[14]

Johnston never again challenged the House's exercise of this power, but its composition was a source of constant embarrassment to him, for the chief opposition to his measures, in particular a law to collect quitrents, came from the overrepresented Albemarle precincts. As early as December 1735 he urged imperial authorities to disallow the biennial act. Among other objections he expressed his dislike for the clauses allowing each of the Albemarle precincts to send five representatives to the Lower House and urged that the law be disallowed "by his Majesty in Council in the most express terms, any Law usage or Custom to the contrary notwithstanding." Johnston's repeated remonstrances against the act finally produced its disallowance in July 1737; but the imperial administration did not take steps to remedy the representation problem, and Johnston probably considered it unwise to risk inflaming the colony by attempting any reformation at the provincial level.[15]

The Crown's disallowance of a 1739 compromise quitrent law in 1741 convinced Johnston that he could never secure a rent measure acceptable to both the Albemarle representatives and Crown officials, and he began to search for means to maneuver around the Albemarle group. In September 1741 he convened the legislature in Wilmington, in the southern portion of the colony, hoping that the Albemarle members would not attend. But his designs were thwarted when a sufficient number of them made the journey and managed to block all proposed rent legislation. Despite the failure of this scheme, Johnston recognized its political possibilities. After three relatively fruitless sessions at Bath and New Bern, in the middle area of the colony, between February 1744 and June 1746, he again called the legislature to meet in Wilmington in November 1746. As he had

14. Lower House Journals, Jan. 21, Mar. 1, 1735, *ibid.*, IV, 122, 154-55.
15. Johnston's Observations on N. C. acts, Dec. 5, 1735, Johnston to Board of Trade, Oct. 15, 1736, *ibid.*, 25, 177-78; Johnston's Observations on N. C. acts, [1738-39], CO 5/295, 142-44; May 19, 27, July 21, 1737, *Acts of Privy Council, Colonial*, III, 568.

hoped, the Albemarle members stayed home, thinking that since they constituted a majority, the House would be unable to meet because of the lack of a quorum.

But the Albemarle representatives underestimated the resourcefulness of the southern members, who promptly repudiated the long-established custom that the presence of a majority was necessary to transact business and acted under Johnston's royal instructions, which stipulated that fifteen members should constitute a quorum. Enjoying complete control, they immediately set about to equalize the apportionment, passing a bill limiting to two the number of representatives from each county. At the same time, the House passed another law to establish the seat of government at New Bern—a central point between the two sections. Johnston happily accepted both measures, if, indeed, he did not play the major role in promoting them, and dissolved the House, issuing writs for the election of another under the new law.[16]

The reapportionment scheme precipitated a full-scale controversy. Denying the validity of the new election law, the northern counties refused to reduce their representation to two and sent their usual five members. When the newly elected House convened in February 1747, the southern members seized control, resolved that the Albemarle elections were null and void, and called for new ones. For the next seven years the northern counties refused to return representatives as they fought for the restoration of their traditional privileges.[17]

Ironically, the Albemarle counties, long the staunchest opponents of Crown policies in North Carolina, now found themselves trying to enlist the aid of Crown officials against Johnston and the southern counties. They sent Henry McCulloh and later Thomas Barker and

16. Laws, *N. C. St. Recs.*, XXIII, 251-52; Lower House Journals, Nov. 20, 28, 1746, *N. C. Col. Recs.*, IV, 838, 842; Johnston to Board of Trade, Jan. 20 and Mar. 9, 1747, *ibid.*, 844, 1152-53. In 1739 the legislature passed an act to change the precincts to counties. David L. Corbitt, *The Formation of the North Carolina Counties, 1663-1943* (Raleigh, 1950), xviii.

17. Lower House Journals, Mar. 3, 6, and Oct. 2, 5, 1747, *N. C. Col. Recs.*, IV, 857-58, 860, 863-64; Upper House Journals, Mar. 30, 1749, *ibid.*, 972-73; Johnston to Board of Trade, Mar. 9, 1747, *ibid.*, 1152-53; Corbin Morris's Observations on North Carolina to Duke of Newcastle, [1748], Newcastle Papers, Add. MSS, 32715, f. 172, British Museum; Rev. Clement Hall to Secretary, May 1, 1751, B MSS, 19, p. 125, Society for the Propagation of the Gospel, London; Johnston's speech to the N. C. legislature, Hayes Collection, microfilm, reel 1, folder 22, Southern Historical Collection, University of North Carolina Library, Chapel Hill; London, "Representation Controversy," *N. C. Hist. Rev.*, 11 (1934), 255-70.

Wyriot Ormond to England to lobby for the disallowance of the representation law and insisted on their right to return five representatives on the grounds that there had been less than a majority—the customary quorum in North Carolina—present and that a clause suspending its execution until the Crown had given its assent should have been included as required by the royal instructions in the passage of unusual acts.[18] Johnston defended the act by charging that the Albemarle counties had deliberately "entered into a Solemn Agreement among themselves to Disobey the prorogative" by not attending the legislature, hoping "to make a meeting of Assembly Impossible." "What could I do," Johnston asked, "when the People themselves, that is, Eleven Counties out of Seventeen, and three Boroughs out of four, offered to me a Law for my Assent, which prevented the Governour and Council from continuing Cyphers, which restored the Prerogative of the Crown to its just Weight in the Legislature and secured the People an Equal Representation"—powerful considerations for the confirmation of the law.[19]

But the Albemarle counties had tradition on their side, and the Board of Trade obtained unfavorable legal reports on both the election and seat of government laws from counsel Matthew Lamb in September 1747 and February 1750 and from Attorney General Dudley Ryder and Solicitor General William Murray in December 1750. Ryder and Murray proposed the disallowance of both laws on the grounds that they had been "passed, by management, precipitation, and surprise, when very few members were present, and are of such nature, and tendency, and have such effects and operation, that the governor, by his instructions, ought not to have assented to them, though they had passed deliberately in a full assembly."[20] In spite of these unfavorable reports, the Board of Trade procrastinated, perhaps hoping to find some means of salvaging something for the prerogative. Finally, while preparing instructions for Arthur Dobbs, Johnston's successor, the Board again submitted the matter to Ryder

18. McCulloh's Observations, received by Board of Trade, May 11, 1748, CO 5/296, ff. 91-92; Peter Payne and others' Petition, [1747-48], *N. C. Col. Recs.*, IV, 1158-60.

19. Johnston to Board of Trade, May 17 and Dec. 28, 1748, *N. C. Col. Recs.*, IV, 869-70, 1163-66; Samuel Swann's Deposition, Oct. 10, 1747, CO 5/296, f. 96.

20. Lamb to Board of Trade, Sept. 25, 1747, *N. C. Col. Recs.*, IV, 1155-56; Lamb to Board of Trade, Feb. 7, 1750 CO 5/296, ff. 288-89; Ryder and Murray to Board of Trade, Dec. 1, 1750, Chalmers, ed., *Opinions*, I, 242-44.

and Murray. They recommended in July 1753 that the Albemarle counties be permitted to retain their right to return five members each, declaring that it was not "advisable for the crown to impeach rights heretofore granted and enjoyed," but proposed that the King erect towns and counties "as the province grows more peopled and cultivated . . . and give them the privilege of chusing representatives: and to preserve the king's prerogative, we think it ought rather to be done, in this way, than by act of assembly." By this procedure the Crown could guarantee the ancient rights of the Albemarle counties but at the same time transfer the power to erect constituencies from the Lower House to the executive.[21]

The Board of Trade was eager to restore this power to the prerogative and moved to put the suggestion of Ryder and Murray into effect. In March 1754 it recommended that the Privy Council disallow the 1746 election law and twelve other statutes passed over the years in North Carolina to create electoral districts. It also proposed that the governor be "directed to confirm the rights of the several Towns Precincts or Counties by Charters of incorporation." To remedy any inconvenience arising "from one part of the Province having a larger proportion of Representatives in the Assembly than the other," the Board urged that he "be instructed as the Province grows more peopled to erect such and so many Towns and Counties in the Southern District with the privilege of sending such a number of Representatives to the Assembly as that each different district or division [has] a reasonable and just proportion."[22] The Privy Council accepted the Board's proposals, disallowing the thirteen statutes in April and embodying the other recommendations in Dobbs's instructions in June. For the time being, the Lower House was to consist of sixty representatives: five each from Chowan, Perquimans, Currituck, Pasquotank, and Tyrrell; three from Bertie; two each from the thirteen remaining counties; and one each from the four towns. The executive could add to this number as the colony expanded and it became necessary to create new constituencies. Most important, perhaps, the instructions positively forbade Dobbs to assent to any law altering the number in the House, thereby depriving the Lower House of the

21. Ryder and Murray to Board of Trade, July 20, 1753, Chalmers, ed., *Opinions,* I, 276-95.
22. Board of Trade's Representation to King in Council, Mar. 14, 1754, *N. C. Col. Recs.,* V, 81-108.

power it had enjoyed since 1715 to create constituencies and settle representation and inaugurating a policy that Crown officials would seek to apply to all the colonies in the following decade.[23]

No sooner had Dobbs broken the news of these restrictions to the Lower House than it began working out a plan to nullify them. During the period of harmony at the beginning of his administration it persuaded him to request the Board of Trade to restore the right to establish counties to the legislature. Authorities in England thought the request reasonable and in June 1755 ruled that the Lower House might re-enact all the disallowed laws, provided that "such new Acts" did not "give Power to such Towns or Countys to send Representatives." Accordingly, in October 1755 the House passed a bill to re-establish all the old counties and towns.[24] The implications of this concession had escaped imperial authorities. To be sure, the governor still retained the technical power to establish new electoral districts, because all new counties and towns had to secure a charter from the governor before they were legally entitled to return members to the legislature. But in regaining the right to erect counties the Lower House had, in effect, again acquired the power to establish constituencies, for the governor by custom was obliged to allow each county to return representatives. Thus between 1754 and 1766 the Lower House created ten new counties and four new boroughs by statute, and the governor extended to all of them the privilege of electing representatives.

Events attending the election of a new legislature in 1760 clearly indicated that the House had regained the power to establish electoral districts. Tyrrell County had not taken out a royal charter as required by the royal instructions, so Dobbs refused to send it a writ empowering it to hold an election. Ultimately, he persuaded county authorities to obtain a charter and issued an election writ, but the Lower House boldly resolved that not granting an election writ for the "antient County" of Tyrrell was "a manifest infringement on the rights of the subject, and tenders to endanger the Constitution."[25]

23. Order in Council, Apr. 8, 1754, *ibid.,* 116-18; Instructions to Dobbs, June 17, 1754, CO 5/324, pp. 25-29.

24. Lower House Journals, Jan. 9, 1755, and Oct. 25, 1756, *N. C. Col. Recs.,* V, 301-3, 735; Dobbs to Board of Trade, Jan. 11, 1755, *ibid.,* 326-28; Order in Council, June 24, 1755, CO 5/22, f. 27.

25. Dobbs's Answers to Lower House's Resolutions, Aug. 3, 1760, *N. C. Col. Recs.,* VI, 301-2.

This resolution implied that representation depended upon something more basic than royal charters—the ancient practice and usage of the colony. Attorney General Thomas Child, member of the House's so-called "junto" against Dobbs, gave more concrete expression to this attitude when he questioned the legality of the instructions requiring counties to take out charters and contended that each district had a right to send members without either a charter or the King's writ. Upon Child's recommendation, the House put the whole matter to a test by admitting a member returned from the newly erected town of Halifax, which had held an election without either charter or writ. Rather than contest this point, Dobbs granted a charter to Halifax and issued an election writ. Thus, the Lower House forced Dobbs to grant representation to a constituency of its designation, although it did not establish its contention that royal charters were unnecessary and illegal. That the Board of Trade found the representatives' action "unconstitutional and not warranted by any authority whatever" mattered little. In practice, at least, the Lower House still had great influence in creating electoral districts.[26]

Moreover, the Lower House could deny representation to any area simply by refusing to erect it into a county, because custom prevented the governor from extending representation to any district not formally established as a county or town—a tradition which emphasized the governor's limited role in creating constituencies. Dobbs complained to home authorities in December 1761 that the Lower House, controlled by Albemarle members, refused to divide New Hanover County in order to "Keep down the numbers of the Southern District" but at the same time attempted to divide counties in the "Northern District to add to their Numbers." The House denied the charge, claiming that it postponed dividing New Hanover only "till by an increase of the white Inhabitants it might become less prejudicial to them, and more reasonably necessary."[27] Still, the Board of Trade sided with the governor. In June 1762 it asserted "that the refusal of the Assembly to pass Acts for incorporating any settlement into a township or county, upon petition of the inhabitants setting forth their qualifications . . . is unjust and subversive of the rights

26. Dobbs to Board of Trade, May 28, 1760, *ibid.*, 245-46; Council Journals, Dec. 6, 1760, *ibid.*, 344; June 2, 1762, *Board of Trade Journals, 1759-63*, 282-83.
27. Dobbs to Board of Trade, Dec. 1761, Couchet Jouvencal to Board of Trade, May 16, 1763, *N. C. Col. Recs.*, VI, 598, 985-86.

and liberties of the subject," threatening action by Parliament "if the Lower House of Assembly shall continue to persist in such un-dutifull and unreasonable claims and proceedings." The Board di-rected Dobbs to exercise the authority outlined in his instructions "of erecting towns and counties by Royal Charter."[28]

Despite the Board's threat, the northern members continued in their old course. Dobbs wrote in March 1763 and again in January 1764 that they had refused to establish counties in the south "lest they should loose their power."[29] Thus, despite express instructions from the Crown placing the power to erect constituencies solely in execu-tive hands and threats of Parliamentary action, the North Carolina Lower House, like its counterparts in Virginia and South Carolina, continued to exercise that power.

The Georgia Commons was less successful. The Board of Trade prepared instructions for Georgia's first royal governor, John Reyn-olds, in the spring and summer of 1754 just after its decision in the North Carolina representation controversy. To avoid similar com-plications in Georgia it designated the first constituencies, settled the distribution of representatives, and gave the executive the exclusive power over those matters in the future. It provided also for a legis-lature of nineteen members: four from Savannah; three from Ebenez-er; two each from Augusta and Great and Little Ogeechee; and one from the Sea Islands and each of seven towns.[30]

This apportionment was unsatisfactory to the Georgia Commons, and in 1757 it accused the colony's former trustees of promoting an "unequal and Injurious division of the Colony into Districts" for "Selfish purposes to secure a Majority in the General Assembly." "By the present regulation," it complained, "near three fourths of the Colony in respect to extent of Country or number of Inhabitants"—the area south of Little Ogeechee River—"sends but four Members to serve in General Assembly." This protest anticipated the Commons' attempt in March 1759 to pass an election bill designed in part "to Add some Members to those parts of the Province which have con-siderably increased and improved."[31] Governor Henry Ellis rejected

28. June 2, 1762, *Board of Trade Journals, 1759-63*, 282-83.
29. Dobbs to Board of Trade, Mar. 7, 1763, Jan. 14, 1764, *N. C. Col. Recs.*, VI, 972, 1024-25; Upper House Journals, Dec. 11, 1762, *ibid.*, 891-92.
30. Instructions to Reynolds, Aug. 6, 1754, CO 5/672, pp. 117-22.
31. Commons Journals, Jan. 25, 1757, Mar. 12, 1759, *Ga. Col. Recs.*, XIII, 128-31, 409.

the bill but agreed to send it to the Board of Trade for an opinion. The Board approved his action, objecting particularly to that part of the bill that empowered a "particular place to send Representatives" as "improper and unnecessary." The governor, the Board pointed out, was "not only empowered but directed by His Majesty's Instructions to issue Writs to such places as are properly qualified to send Representatives."[32] The Board's firm stand thwarted the Commons' initial bid for the power to create electoral districts and apportion representation; it did not again attempt to acquire that power in the years before 1763. But the incident did result in Ellis's establishing one new constituency and reapportioning representation along more equitable lines the following year, creating in the process six new seats in the Commons.[33]

Thus, by 1763 only the Virginia Burgesses and the South Carolina Commons were firmly and openly in control of the power to create electoral districts, although the North Carolina Lower House had subverted a royal order designed to deprive it of that power by maintaining its right to establish counties, which were the basic unit of representation. The imperial policy established for North Carolina and Georgia in 1754, a policy designed to prevent their lower houses from creating constituencies by statute, was a harbinger of a wholesale assault in the following decade upon American lower houses' exercise of this power. As part of the general tightening of the reins after 1763, Crown officials sought in 1767 to deprive the lower houses of this power altogether.

A second element in control over membership was the power to determine qualifications of members and voters, and the lower houses in the southern royal colonies early tried to fix those qualifications by statute. Such statutes were adopted in Virginia as early as 1646, in South Carolina in 1697, and in North Carolina around the turn of the century. Nor did Crown officials question the right of the lower houses to pass these measures until well into the eighteenth century. As long as they conformed with the stipulation that the franchise be limited to freeholders—a provision first put forth in an instruction issued to Virginia in 1676 and eventually extended to all royal colo-

32. Board of Trade to Ellis, July 24, 1759, CO 5/673, pp. 242-46.
33. See Wright to Hillsborough, Dec. 26, 1768, unpubl. Ga. Col. Recs., XXVIII, Pt. II-B, 682-83, Ga. Dept. of Arch. and Hist.

nies, including North and South Carolina—Crown authorities did not
object to them and occasionally even encouraged their passage, as it
did in the case of a Virginia statute of 1713.[34]   The forty-shilling
freehold qualification was traditional in England, and the Crown's
insistence that it be adopted in the colonies was understandable. Even
so, the franchise was usually somewhat more liberal in the colonies.
Freemen with neither land nor its equivalent in money were eligible
to vote in Virginia before 1670 and again between 1676 and 1699 and
in North Carolina until 1734.[35]   After 1734, however, the freehold
qualification was adhered to in all of the southern royal colonies except South Carolina, where non-freeholding taxpayers enjoyed the
ballot to the end of the colonial period.[36]   But it is improbable that
the freehold requirement excluded many people from voting.   In
1712 Lieutenant Governor Alexander Spotswood asserted that Virginia's voting laws allowed "every one, though but just out of the Condition of a Servant, and that but purchase half an acre of Land, an
equal Vote with the Man of the best Estate in the County," probably
a fair description of voting arrangements in Virginia; those of the
other three colonies were only slightly, if any, more restrictive.   With
the exception of Catholics, probably almost all free white males could
vote.[37]

    With somewhat less success the lower houses also attempted to
regulate qualifications for members, establishing certain minimum
residence, age, and religious requirements.   For the most part, Crown
officials objected only when such qualifications barred placemen from
membership.   Royal governors found that by conferring offices upon
individual representatives they could greatly increase their influence

34. Labaree, ed., *Royal Instructions*, I, 93; Board of Trade to Alexander Spotswood, Apr. 23, 1713, CO 5/1363.

35. See Hening, ed., *Va. Statutes*, I, 333-34, 403, 411-12, 475, II, 20, 106, 272-73,
280, 356-57, III, 172-75; Cooper and McCord, eds., *S. C. Statutes*, II, ix, 249-51,
683-91, III, 2-4, 50-55; Laws, *N. C. St. Recs.*, XXV, 191, 214; Julian A. Chandler,
The History of Suffrage in Virginia (Baltimore, 1901), 9-11; Philip A. Bruce,
Institutional History of Virginia in the Seventeenth Century, 2 vols. (N. Y., 1910),
II, 410-16; George Burrington to Board of Trade, Sept. 4, 1731, *N. C. Col. Recs.*,
III, 207; Cortlandt F. Bishop, *History of Elections in the American Colonies*
(N. Y., 1893), 273-77; Labaree, ed., *Royal Instructions*, I, 93-94; Arthur B. Keith,
Constitutional History of the First British Empire (Oxford, Eng., 1930), 233.

36. See Atkin's Wrong Practices, 1755, and Short Observations, 1756, in Greene,
"South Carolina's Colonial Constitution," *S. C. Hist. Mag.*, 62 (1961), 76, 80.

37. Spotswood to Board of Trade, Oct. 15, 1712, and Oct. 24, 1715, Brock, ed.,
Spotswood Letters, II, 1-2, 134-35; Joseph Boone *et al.* to Parliament, Mar. 13,
1705, *N. C. Col. Recs.*, I, 639.

in the house. In Virginia, Governor Berkeley used this technique to good advantage in the 1660's and 1670's, and Spotswood viewed with delight the prospect of distributing among the burgesses "forty Agencys" created by a 1713 tobacco inspection law.[38] Similarly, William Byrd II wrote in 1740 that Gooch would "not have the least Influence, with our Assembly, if he can't make Friends by the skillfull distribution, of the Few Places, that have always been in his Gift." "All other Acts of Persuasion are empty and Vain," Byrd continued, "and My Lord may as well send over his Picture, as a Lieutenant Governour who has it not in his Power to gain over men of Figure and Interest in the Country."[39] Henry Ellis reported from Georgia in 1757 that his predecessor, John Reynolds, had attempted to increase his influence with the Commons by appointing eleven of the nineteen members to places of trust.[40]

Attempts by the lower houses to exclude placemen from membership created a minor political issue in the older southern royal colonies, particularly in Virginia. In 1705 and again in 1715 the Virginia Burgesses tried to pass bills "excluding all Officers in places of profit or Trust from Siting in the Assembly" only to have them vetoed by the governors. Similarly, Spotswood vetoed a 1718 attempt to forbid county court clerks from serving in the House,[41] but a 1730 measure to disqualify sheriffs and require sitting members who accepted a place of profit to stand for re-election fared better. Gooch thought it would exclude capable men and thereby lessen the quality of the Burgesses, but assented to it to keep the Burgesses "in good Humour, while matters of greater moment were under their deliberation." Thirteen years later, however, he reported that he had not found it "productive of any Consequence of moment, in any shape whatever."[42] The Burgesses also passed a bill in 1736 excluding tobacco inspectors, and together these measures were remarkably effective in reducing the number of placemen in the House. Between 1730 and

38. Spotswood to Board of Trade, Dec. 29, 1713, Brock, ed., *Spotswood Letters,* II, 49; Wertenbaker, *Give Me Liberty,* 77-78.

39. Byrd to Major Otway, Feb. 1740, "Letters of the Byrd Family," *Va. Mag. of Hist. and Biog.,* 37 (1929), 30.

40. Ellis to Board of Trade, Mar. 11, 1757, CO 5/646.

41. Spotswood to Board of Trade, June 24, 1718, Brock, ed., *Spotswood Letters,* II, 275-80; May 8, 1705, *Va. Burgesses Journals, 1703-12,* 110-11; Sept. 7, 1715, *ibid., 1712-26,* 167.

42. Hening, ed., *Va. Statutes,* IV, 292-93; Gooch to Board of Trade, July 23, 1730, and Feb. 14, 1743, CO 5/1322, ff. 53-66, CO 5/1325, f. 130

1760 it forced approximately forty members to resign their seats for having accepted offices of sheriff, coroner, tobacco inspector, clerk of the courts, collector, surveyor, and other places of profit after their election to the House.[43]

The effort to exclude placemen was neither so sustained nor so extensive in the two Carolinas and Georgia. The North Carolina Lower House did disqualify commodity inspectors; the South Carolina Commons prohibited revenue officers or other officials appointed by the legislature from membership in 1717 and 1721; and the Georgia Commons excluded the provost marshal or anyone authorized by him to manage elections in 1761.[44] But two other attempts failed, the imperial officials disallowing a South Carolina statute of 1745 disqualifying all officeholders with a salary of over £20 proclamation money and Governor Arthur Dobbs vetoing a North Carolina measure of 1757 precluding "several of his Majesty's friends from sitting in future assemblies."[45]

Although Crown officials permitted the lower houses a rather free exercise of the power to establish qualifications for voters and members during the first half of the eighteenth century, they adopted a more rigid policy after 1750. When the Crown established royal government in Georgia in 1754, it settled those qualifications in the royal instructions. In the same year, royal authorities forbade North Carolina's governor, Arthur Dobbs, to pass laws regulating such qualifications unless they contained a suspending clause.[46] Over the next decade this restriction became an important part of imperial policy toward the colonies. Crown officials refused to confirm a South Carolina law of 1759 and a Virginia law of 1762 at least in part because the laws established member and voter qualifications, although they apparently did not object to a North Carolina law of 1760 for the

43. Hening, ed., *Va. Statutes*, IV, 481-82; *Va. Burgesses Journals, 1727-40, 1742-49, 1752-58, 1758-61, passim.*

44. See Cooper and McCord, eds., *S. C. Statutes*, III, 2-4, 148; *Laws, N. C. St. Recs.*, XXV, 313-19; Saye, *New Viewpoints*, 122.

45. Commons Journals, Mar. 1, 1744, *S. C. Col. Recs., 1744-45*, 36; Board of Trade to James Glen, June 15, 1748, CO 5/402, pp. 151-61; Order in Council, June 30, 1748, CO 5/372, f. 50; Cooper and McCord, eds., *S. C. Statutes*, III, 656-58; Dobbs to Board of Trade, Dec. 27, 1757, *N. C. Col. Recs.*, V, 947.

46. Labaree, ed., *Royal Instructions*, I, 108. See also Wright to Hillsborough, Dec. 26, 1768, unpubl. *Ga. Col. Recs.*, XXVIII, Pt. II-B, 682-83, Ga. Dept. of Arch. and Hist.

same purpose.[47] After 1767 they placed upon all the continental
colonies the same restrictions as they had put upon North Carolina in
1754. Because the Crown permitted statutes passed earlier in the
century as well as the North Carolina law of 1760 to stand, there
remained statutory regulations upon the qualifications of voters and
representatives in all of the southern royal colonies except Georgia
for the rest of the colonial period. But the imperial authorities' continued insistence upon rigid compliance with this restriction became
a serious grievance in both Virginia and North Carolina after 1767.

A third ingredient of control over membership was the power to
determine disputed elections. The English House of Commons had
won that power in 1604 in the cases of Goodwin and Fortescue, and
most American lower houses claimed it early in their history. Both
the Virginia legislature and the Georgia Commons exercised it at
their initial meetings. The South Carolina Commons acquired it at
least as early as 1692, and the North Carolina Lower House, the lag
gard among the southern lower houses, wrested it away from the Coun
cil in 1725. Usually exercising this power through legislative committees on privileges and elections, all four lower houses occasionally
denied seats to members because of undue influence, bribery, intimida-
tion at elections, or failure to meet qualifications, although they frequently excused minor violations if the election appeared to have been
freely and openly conducted and if the candidate himself was not responsible for the irregularity.[48] In any case, the decision belonged
exclusively to the lower houses. Virginia Speaker Sir John Randolph
rendered a classic statement of the lower houses' attitude toward this
power in 1736, when, in his address to Lieutenant Governor Gooch, he
claimed for the Virginia representatives the "sole Right of determining
all Questions concerning their own Elections, lest contrary Judgements,
in the Courts of Law, might thwart or destroy Theirs."[49] Authorities
in London never contested the lower houses' claim to this power, but
on two occasions during the decade after 1755 royal governors, first in

47. Hening, ed., *Va. Statutes*, VII, 517-30, VIII, 305-17; Laws, *N. C. St. Recs.*,
XXIII, 523-26. Cooper and McCord, eds., *S. C. Statutes*, IV, 98-101; May 26, 1761,
Board of Trade Journals, 1759-63, 199; Board of Trade to Privy Council, May 29,
1761, S. C. Pub. Recs., XXIX, 112-13, S. C. Arch. Dept.
    48. Mary P. Clarke, *Parliamentary Privilege in the American Colonies* (New
Haven, 1943), 133-34, 140-41, 143; Commons Journals, Jan. 13, 1755, *Ga. Col Recs.*,
XIII, 21.
    49. Aug. 6, 1736, *Va. Burgesses Journals, 1727-40*, 242.

Georgia and later in South Carolina, challenged their exercise of it, provoking intense political controversies in the process.

The Georgia dispute, which occurred a little over a year after the establishment of royal government in the colony, threw the local political situation into turmoil and was an important factor in the Crown's decision to recall Governor John Reynolds. At the conclusion of the first session of the legislature in early 1755 Reynolds upon his own initiative issued writs for the election of three members to fill vacancies occasioned by the appointment of two representatives to the Council and the refusal of another to serve. This action was an invitation to controversy. According to customary procedure in both England and the older American colonies, governors issued such writs only upon the representatives' request. As a result, the Commons did not immediately admit the three newly elected members when it reconvened the following year, referring the matter instead to its committee on privileges and elections. When the committee could not immediately obtain credentials for the three from the secretary, Reynolds grew impatient and adjourned the House for a week. Upon its reconvening Reynolds greeted it with a sharp reprimand, terming its proceedings "an Attack upon the Liberty of the Subject" and "a Contempt of the Authority" of the Crown. To make matters worse, he refused to recognize the legality of any of the Commons' proceedings until the three members had been admitted, and he raised the constitutional issue by ordering the House "to recede from these unwarrantable claims and Pretensions, and immediately admit the members now returned." Clearly, Reynolds was insisting that the three members were duly elected and thereby assuming the power to determine who was properly elected to serve in the Commons.[50]

Accepting Governor Reynolds's challenge, the Commons on the following day resorted to drastic action in order to complete its reply. First, it removed Clerk William Little, Reynolds's chief political ally, when he refused to keep the journal until the new members had been admitted. Then, when Reynolds tried to adjourn the House, some members snatched the adjournment message from the speaker and forced him to remain in the chair for five hours until the House had completed its defense. Under the circumstances, the Commons' reply

50. Commons Journals, Feb. 4, 12, 1756, *Ga. Col. Recs.*, XIII, 88, 91-93; Reynolds to Board of Trade, Mar. 29, 1756, CO 5/645.

was remarkably mild. It explained that it had not refused to admit the members but had merely delayed acting upon the question until they had produced evidence of having taken the proper oaths. Disclaiming any intention of abridging the liberty of the subject or showing contempt for the Crown, the representatives argued "that a Committee to enquire into the Rights of Election is not only the first step in point of form, but also the surest Method of securing to the Subject the essential Privilege of being fairly represented which it is our proper Business to take care of." Nor did the Commons show any inclination to relinquish its right to determine elections, gently but firmly reminding Reynolds "that Writs are never issued in such cases but in consequence of an Application from the House which could not be made during a Recess."[51]

The mildness of the reply did not prevent Reynolds from dissolving the Commons, however, and this hasty action was an important factor in determining the Board of Trade to recommend his removal in July 1756. The Board's objections to Reynolds's conduct ignored the principal question of who should have the power to determine elections, but his subsequent recall and the Commons' refusal to admit the new members until its committee had investigated and weighed their elections resulted in its attaining firm control over that power. Thereafter, no governor violated it.[52]

Coming on the eve of the Revolutionary crisis, the famous Gadsden election controversy in South Carolina had even graver consequences. A vaguely worded clause in the 1721 election law requiring members to take state oaths before the governor or his deputies made it possible for the governor to refuse oaths to members whose credentials he did not approve. By this device a governor could usurp from the Commons the power to determine the validity of elections. Thus, in 1725 Francis Nicholson refused to administer the oaths to James Atkin, elected for the parishes of St. Thomas and St. Dennis, because a bill of indictment against him was pending. The representatives protested that they were "the Sole judges of our own priviledges and of the Qualifications of our own Members," but Nicholson refused to abandon his position unless the Commons could produce a precedent

---

51. Commons Journals, Feb. 13, 1756, *Ga. Col. Recs.*, XIII, 95-98. For the political ramifications of this controversy, see Abbot, *Royal Governors*, 48-49.

52. Commons Journals, Feb. 19, 1756, *Ga. Col. Recs.*, XIII, 99-100; Board of Trade to King in Council, July 29, 1756, CO 5/653.

for its claim from the proceedings of the British House of Commons. The House obliged with an authenticated example from 23 Elizabeth, wherein a member of Parliament indicted for felony was allowed to retain his seat until convicted, so that innocent persons might not be deprived of their seats. Nicholson may not even have acknowledged this precedent, however; for it was nearly a month before he finally gave Atkin the oaths, during which time he may have been acquitted.[53] This incident was not serious, and none of Nicholson's successors attempted to violate the Commons' power to determine the validity of its own elections until 1762.

Indignant because the Commons had ignored his recommendation to amend the 1721 election law, Governor Thomas Boone—already resentful of the Commons' extensive power—waited for an opportunity to demonstrate its defects to the legislature. That opportunity came in September 1762 when Christopher Gadsden was returned for the parish of St. Paul as a result of an election in which the church warden, the officer responsible for conducting South Carolina elections, had not been sworn to a due execution of his task as required by the election act. Although the letter of the law had been violated, the spirit obviously had not, for the election had been carried on without any other irregularity, and Gadsden was the overwhelming choice of the St. Paul electors. Furthermore, in the past the Commons had occasionally admitted members returned from elections in which the church wardens had not been properly sworn. Consequently, the Commons declared Gadsden elected, but Boone refused to administer the oaths to him, charged the Commons with an "undeniable . . . infraction of the Election Act," and abruptly dissolved it, immediately calling for new elections.[54]

When the new Commons House convened in late November, it immediately appointed a committee to consider the proceedings of the previous House and to report "whether by the said proceedings the Election Act hath been violated or infringed." The committee was also to consider "the Liberties and privileges of this House, with regard to the right of determining their own Elections" and Boone's

53. Cooper and McCord, eds., *S. C. Statutes*, III, 135-40; Apr. 16, 1725, S. C. Commons Journals, CO 5/428, pp. 25-28.
54. Boone to ————————, Jan. 17, 1762, Misc. MSS, P/2465, South Caroliniana Library, University of South Carolina, Columbia. Sept. 10, 13, 1762, S. C. Commons Journals, CO 5/480, pp. 154-59; *S.-C. Gazette* (Charleston), Feb. 5, 1763.

speech "at Dissolving the last General Assembly." The Commons accepted the committee's report—a vigorous defense of the Commons' right to determine the validity of the elections of its own members—and presented it along with a remonstrance to Boone. In the report the Commons declared that "it is the undeniable fundamental and inherent Right and Privilege of the Commons House of Assembly . . . solely to examine and finaly determine the Elections of their own Members." Dismissing Boone's charge that it had violated the election law in the Gadsden case, the Commons argued that church wardens were not expressly required to take special oaths for each election because they were sworn to execute the duties of their office at the time of their appointment. Further, the Commons denied that "the existence of the body of the People Representatives, either is, or ought to be owing to the Election Act; much less to a rigid Execution thereof," as Boone had declared in his dissolution speech, and asserted that "the right of the Inhabitants of this Province to be represented in the Legislature, is undeniably founded, not upon that Act, but in the known and ancient Constitution of our Mother Country, therefrom Originally derived, and always to have appertained to, and been exercised by them, as British Subjects"—an unmistakable declaration that the right of representation was one of the traditional rights of Englishmen and as such was an inherent right of the freemen of South Carolina. The Commons concluded its report with four resolutions modeled closely after those of the English House of Commons in the 1702 case of *Ashby* v. *White,* a classic argument in favor of that body's right to determine the validity of elections. The resolutions declared that that right belonged *"SOLELY"* and *"ABSOLUTELY"* to the representatives of the people, that "CONSTITUTIONALLY" the governor could take notice of only such actions of the House as were formally set before him, that Boone's refusal to administer the state oaths to Gadsden after he had been declared duly elected by the Commons "was a breach of . . . Privileges," and "that the abrupt and Sudden dissolution of the last Assembly, for matters only Cognizable by the Commons House, was a most precipitate, unadvised unprecedented Proceedure; of the most dangerous Consequence, being a great Violation of the Freedom of Elections, and having a Manifest Tendency to Subvert and destroy, the most Essential and invaluable rights of the People, and reduce the Power and Authority of the House, to an

Abject dependence on, and Subserviency of the Will, and Opinion of a Governor."[55]

Haughtily refusing to give ground, Boone held that Gadsden had not been elected because the church wardens had not taken the required oaths. He denied the Commons' contention that the church wardens' initial oath of office qualified them to execute the writs of election and pointed out the vast difference between the two oaths. Boone reminded the Commons that it existed only by the election act and that if that act were disallowed the people would be without representation. He also refused to acknowledge that the House had the sole power to determine elections, both because the governor was required by his commission to supervise elections and because a House might determine an election contrary to law. Boone explained that the "last Commons house of Assembly . . . having endeavoured to give Validity to an Election which the law did not warrant, Violated that law, and assumed a power they had no right to," applauded himself "for having checked Constitutionally so dangerous an Usurpation," informed the Commons that it had "a good and gracious Sovereign ever ready to discountenance oppression, and to brush [aside] an arbitrary and imperious Governor that dares to trampel on the people's liberties," and suggested that it prefer its "Complaints to the Royal Ear."[56]

The Commons immediately ordered its committee on privileges and elections to prepare a reply and suspended business until it was drafted. In the reply the Commons reasserted its former contention that Gadsden's election was valid and again denied that the existence of the Commons House depended on the election law. It argued that if the election law were disallowed the Commons House would be elected by the previous election law and so on retrogressively to the proprietary charter. In fact, the Commons maintained that the charter merely confirmed "the natural right of the *FREEMEN* of this Province to be Represented." It also reiterated its right to review elections of its members, observing "that we are far from thinking that Your Excellency has proved the last House guilty

55. Nov. 24-Dec. 6, 1762, S. C. Commons Journals, CO 5/480, pp. 13, 19-33. The House of Commons' resolutions in the case of *Ashby* v. *White* may conveniently be found in Thomas P. Tasswell-Langmead, *English Constitutional History*, 10th ed., rev. and enl. by Theodore F. T. Plunckett (Boston, 1946), 301-2.

56. Dec. 7, 1762, S. C. Commons Journals, CO 5/480, pp. 36-38.

of any, much less a 'Dangerous Usurpation' which we humbly apprehend ought to have been done before Your Excellency could with any Propriety applaud yourself for having Constitutionally checked it." On December 16 the Commons resolved by an overwhelming majority to do no further business with Governor Boone until he had apologized for violating its rights and privileges, and it directed its committee of correspondence to transmit a full account of the dispute to the colony's London agent, Charles Garth.[57]

A spirited newspaper controversy followed over the question of whether the Commons was justified in putting a stop to public business. The Commons' chief defender was Christopher Gadsden. In the *South-Carolina Gazette* he declared that the Commons' action was "absolutely necessary," the "only step that a *free* assembly, *freely* representing a *free* people, that have any regard for the preservation of the happy constitution handed down to them by their ancestors . . . could *freely* take." He built his case on two premises: that representatives ought to be chosen freely by the voters and that election returns ought to be examined freely by the representatives so chosen. Writing that "*free* men . . . have an *inherent* not *permissive* right to be so," Gadsden contended that individual freedom depended upon the freedom of the lower house and that the right to determine elections "is so unalienable and inherent in the people, that they can be no longer denominated a free people when it is parted with; because all their *freedom* as British subjects most essentially depends on it." This right, he argued, was the *"sine qua non"* of the legislative body, conceded to Parliament by the Act of Settlement and brought by English emigrants to America. No free Briton, he declared, would, "like Esau," sell his "birth-right for a mess of potage."

Gadsden's assertions that the dispute could "be constitutionally decided only by a British parliament" and that before British subjects could be deprived of the rights and liberties of their birthright "they must be tried and condemned *by their peers*" seemed, as Boone later interpreted them, "to acknowledge . . . no other authority than the Parliaments" and to "expressly deny . . . the King's power to determine in matters of . . . privilege." At the very least, these assertions suggested a marked reluctance to admit the right of London officials to rule on questions of parliamentary privilege. In addition,

57. Nov. 24, Dec. 9, 16, 24, 1762, *ibid.,* pp. 15-16, 39-49; *S.-C. Gazette* (Charleston), Feb. 5, 1763.

Gadsden proposed that the colonies unite in appointing one general agent to protect the *"natural* privileges" of British subjects in America. Finally, he gave early expression to an attitude his countrymen were to use frequently two years later. By asserting that the right of representation was a "natural right" and that because Americans did not vote for members of Parliament they could be represented only in their own legislative assemblies, he was rejecting the British theory of virtual representation and anticipating the arguments used by Americans during the Stamp Act crisis.[58]

Between December 16, 1762, and April 24, 1764, the Commons was in session six times for periods up to two months, but it strictly adhered to its resolution of December 16, 1762, to do no business with Boone until he had apologized. Despite Boone's urgent appeal for measures to check outrages committed by the Creek Indians, the Commons refused to conduct any business until after Boone had left the province in May 1764. During the interval the controversy came to the attention of authorities in London. The Board of Trade ruled in March 1763 that Boone had dissolved the Commons without sufficient reason, but this decision did not satisfy the Commons. After Boone again violated its power to determine elections in September 1763 by refusing to administer the oaths to several members until he had reviewed the Commons' journals to see that they had properly qualified, the Commons adopted a petition to the Crown asking Boone's removal. In May 1764 even before receiving a letter from the Earl of Halifax ordering him home to give an account of the controversy, the disgruntled governor left the colony.[59] At a hearing before the Board of Trade in July Boone failed to vindicate himself. He had "taken up the matter in dispute with more Zeal than prudence," the Board decided, and in the process he had "been actuated by a degree of Passion and Resentment inconsistent with good Policy, and unsuited to the dignity of his Situation." Although imperial authorities found the Commons' long neglect of public business censurable, they wisely decided upon Boone's removal; to prevent

58. *S.-C. Gazette* (Charleston), Feb. 5, 1763; Boone to Board of Trade, Mar. 29 and Sept. 15, 1763, CO 5/377, ff. 213-14, 233-35.

59. Bull to Board of Trade, May 16, 1764, CO 5/377, f. 433; Halifax to Boone, June 9, 1764, CO 5/390, f. 34; Sept. 10-13, 1763, S. C. Commons Journals, CO 5/478, 25-29. The Commons published the documents relating to this dispute as *A Full Statement of the Dispute Betwixt the Governor and the Commons House of Assembly of His Majesty's Province of South Carolina in America* ([London], 1763).

similar disputes in the future they instructed Boone's successor, the younger Bull, to appoint deputies to administer the oaths.[60] The Board's decision was clearly unsympathetic to Boone's position. Because it did not uphold him in his attempts to usurp the power to determine the validity of elections, this decision represented a victory for the Commons. Thereafter no one questioned its exclusive power to determine the validity of the elections of its own members, and future governors hesitated to revive a dispute which had broken one of their predecessors.

The Gadsden election controversy left no grievances, but it was of the utmost significance to the approaching Revolutionary movement. The techniques and arguments employed by the Commons and its protagonists in this contest would be useful in the following decade, and the controversy provided an opportunity for the representatives to acquire an important type of political experience—the waging of a political war of attrition in defense of a constitutional right. Most important, this bitter and stirring contest attracted the interest and consumed the energies of the most important politicians in South Carolina for nearly two years. Carried on with great intensity, it was responsible for arousing a spirit of opposition and producing a climate of opinion among those leaders conducive to resistance at a critical time. Just as the Gadsden election case was being concluded, authorities in Britian were beginning to tighten the reins and to initiate a policy of Parliamentary taxation of the colonies through the Sugar and Stamp Acts. The Commons' success in this dispute increased its confidence and made it less hesitant to embark upon troubled waters in the future. The hostility toward Boone and the enthusiasm for the defense of constitutional rights and privileges displayed by the Commons between 1762 and 1764 were easily transferred to Parliament and its Stamp Act in 1765. Certainly, the Gadsden election controversy helped to set the stage for the Revolutionary movement in South Carolina.[61]

60. Board of Trade to Privy Council, July 16, 1764, CO 5/404, pp. 226-29. Indications of public resentment at the long interruption of legislative business may be found in Henry Laurens to Dr. John Augustus Shubert, Dec. 31, 1763, and to Christopher Rowe, Feb. 8, 1764, Laurens Letter Book, 1762-66, 89, 100-101, Historical Society of Pennsylvania, Phila.

61. For a full discussion of this dispute, see Greene, "Gadsden Election Controversy," *Miss. Valley Hist. Rev.*, 46 (1959), 469-92.

A fourth component of control over membership was the power to punish or expel members. As in the case of the power to determine validity of elections, imperial authorities did not object to the lower houses' exercise of this power. Nor did any of the governors in the southern royal colonies ever contest it, so that it was never a subject of political controversy. Cases of members' being called to the bar of the house for reprimand or punishment appear frequently in the journals of all four houses. Cases of expulsion were much more rare, although a few occurred in every colony. The grounds for expulsion varied. The Virginia House of Burgesses expelled two members as early as 1652 and five in the eighteenth century for moral and religious reasons. It also expelled Thomas Osborne in 1736 and William Andrews in 1742 for committing misdemeanors as tobacco inspectors, Henry Downs in 1742 for having been convicted of a felony in Maryland twenty years earlier, William Clinch in 1757 for extorting a receipt and release from a debt from an old man, and William Ball in 1758 for counterfeiting treasury notes.[62] The Georgia Commons ejected four members for writing a seditious letter at its inaugural session in 1755 and later in the same session a fifth for failing to take his seat.[63] The South Carolina Commons excluded James Graeme in December 1733 for bringing an action against Speaker Paul Jenys, who had signed a warrant against Rowland Vaughn at the Commons' command.[64] The North Carolina Lower House does not appear to have exercised the power of explusion until 1757, when it ejected James Carter for misappropriating public funds. More famous was its expulsion of Harmon Husband, leader of the North Carolina Regulators, in December 1770.[65] The period of exclusion after expulsion varied from colony to colony. The Georgia Commons excluded the members expelled in 1755 only until the end of the session. In the cases of Graeme in South Carolina and Osborne, Andrews, and Downs in Virginia, exclusion continued until the dissolution of the House that expelled them. Permanent exclusion occurred in Virginia in

62. Clarke, *Parliamentary Privilege*, 195; Aug. 21, 1736, *Va. Burgesses Journals, 1727-40*, 264-65; May 24, 1742, *ibid., 1742-49*, vii, 33-34; Apr. 26, 1757, *ibid., 1752-58*, 436-37; Nov. 9, 1758, *ibid., 1758-61*, 50.

63. Commons Journals, Jan. 27, Mar. 6, 1755, *Ga. Col. Recs.*, XIII, 39, 77.

64. Dec. 8, 1733, S. C. Commons Journals, CO 5/433, pp. 19-20.

65. Council Journals, Dec. 20, 1770, *N. C. Col. Recs.*, VIII, 269.

1757 with William Clinch and in North Carolina in 1758 with the perjurer Francis Brown.[66]

An important adjunct to control over membership was power to determine the frequency of elections and sessions. Crown officials tried to keep this power from falling into the hands of the lower houses by stipulating in the royal instructions that the colonial executives should call, adjourn, prorogue, and dissolve the lower houses at pleasure. But the English House of Commons had attempted to secure statutory guarantees of regular sessions and frequent elections in the Triennial Acts of 1641 and 1694 and the Septennial Act of 1716, and almost all of the colonial lower houses followed its example. The four lower houses in the southern colonies were no exception. Between 1689 and 1763 each of them attempted to pass statutes modeled after the Triennial and Septennial Acts. Except in the case of South Carolina, they were unsuccessful largely because imperial authorities conscientiously tried to disallow such statutes and after 1750 prohibited royal governors from assenting to them.[67]

Among the southern lower houses, those of proprietary Carolina led in the quest to gain this power. In 1694 the South Carolina Commons passed a measure to prevent "inconveniencies happening by long intermission of General Assemblies" that provided for annual sessions and limited the life of the Commons to three years. The Commons made no attempt to alter these arrangements under the proprietors, but at the first royal legislature in September 1721 it passed another statute which continued the triennial provision but required sessions every six months.[68] Governors occasionally violated this requirement, but the Commons insisted upon a strict compliance with the three-year limitation. When in June 1724 Francis Nicholson proposed to continue one House for fifteen more months, the Commons declined to "Revive the Assembly for a Longer time than limitted by Law" and declared itself dissolved.[69]

66. Commons Journals, Jan. 27, Mar. 6, 1755, *Ga. Col. Recs.*, XIII, 39, 77; Dec. 8, 1733, S. C. Commons Journals, CO 5/433, pp. 19-20; Aug. 21, 1736, *Va. Burgesses Journals, 1727-40*, 264-65; May 24, 1742, *ibid., 1742-49*, vii, 33; Sept. 15, Nov. 9, 1758, *ibid., 1758-61*, 5, 50; Lower House Journals, Dec. 5, 1758, Apr. 30, 1760, *N. C. Col. Recs.*, V, 1058, VI, 375.
67. Tasswell-Langmead, *Constitutional History* (1946 ed.), 443-44, 586-87.
68. Cooper and McCord, eds., *S. C. Statutes*, II, 79-80, III, 135-40.
69. June 16-17, 1724, S. C. Commons Journals, CO 5/427, pp. 38-39, 45.

Except for a brief period from 1745 to 1751, the 1721 law was in force for the remainder of the colonial period. In March 1744 the Commons proposed a bill which would have required biennial elections and the following year actually passed a bill requiring annual elections. But many inconveniences arose from annual elections, and in March 1747 the Commons adopted an amending statute to increase the maximum life of each House to two years. Imperial authorities objected to the clauses in both of these measures which limited the duration of the House and required elections at specified intervals. They sharply rebuked Governor James Glen for passing the first and disallowed both of them.[70] With the disallowance of the second in October 1751, the 1721 triennial law was automatically revived. Despite occasional complaints by South Carolina officials,[71] imperial authorities permitted it to stand.

Asserting that "the frequent sitting of Assembly is a principal, safeguard of their People's priviledges," the North Carolina representatives passed a biennial act in 1715. It provided that burgesses were to be elected every second September and were to meet the first Monday in the following November, thus giving statutory confirmation to a practice established under the Fundamental Constitutions.[72] Both of the early royal governors, Burrington and Johnston, urged its disallowance, pointing out that it empowered the voters to assemble on an appointed day and choose burgesses without the King's writs—a patent usurpation of the executive's power to call elections at pleasure. Further, in November 1725 the Lower House had even denied the executive's right to prorogue the legislature beyond the legally appointed meeting day. Another objection was the biennial clause. In 1731 Burrington complained to imperial authorities that "the time of an Assemblies continuance being So Short causes Several well meaning Members to be Timorous fearing they should not be chosen again." Similarly, Johnston wrote in 1736 "that there must be a new election every two years which is too short a time to settle a Country

70. Cooper and McCord, eds., *S. C. Statutes*, III, 656-58, 692-93; May 25, 1748, *Board of Trade Journals, 1742-49*, 289; Commons Journals, Mar. 1, 1744, *S. C. Col. Recs., 1744-45*, 33-36; Glen's Observations on S. C. laws, Oct. 10, 1748, CO 5/372, ff. 88-94; Board of Trade to Glen, June 15, 1748, CO 5/402, pp. 151-61; Orders in Council, June 30, 1748, Oct. 31, 1751, CO 5/21, f. 78, CO 5/373, f. 45.

71. See Atkin's Wrong Practices, 1755, and Short Observations, 1756, in Greene, "South Carolina's Colonial Constitution," *S. C. Hist. Mag.*, 62 (1961), 72-81.

72. Laws, *N. C. St. Recs.*, XXIII, 12-14.

which has been so long in confusion, and men of sense who sincerely mean the Publick good are so much afraid of the next Elections that they are obliged to go in with the majority whose Ignorance and want of education makes them obstruct everything for the good of the Country."[73]

These complaints finally moved the Board of Trade to submit the act to legal counsel Francis Fane. In April 1737 Fane reported unfavorably, objecting to the law's giving "a Power . . . to the Assembly . . . to meet without the Consent of the Crown." "The Charter granted to the Lords Proprietors," he observed, "does not in the least warrant a proceeding so derogatory of the power and Authority of the Crown." Arguing that the "Power of Calling of Parliaments is admitted to be an Inherent priviledge in the Crown," he charged—apparently without recalling Parliament's 1641 Triennial Act—that "this is the first Instance, that such an Attempt has been made to deprive the Crown of it." Acting on Fane's report, the Privy Council disallowed the North Carolina biennial act in July 1737.[74] Thereafter, there were no statutory limitations upon the frequency of elections and sessions in colonial North Carolina, the Lower House making no effort to secure any in the years before 1763.

The Virginia Burgesses also attempted at several times to acquire the power to regulate the frequency of elections and sessions. It had been elected annually until 1659, when it became biennial. But after 1662 Governor Sir William Berkeley adopted the practice of proroguing the House from session to session. Thus, Berkeley permitted the House elected in 1662 to continue for fourteen years before he finally dissolved it, although no subsequent governor ever continued one House more than seven years. Under these arrangements, sessions were held at the executive's pleasure, and on several occasions periods of two to three years passed without one.[75] John Locke's proposal in 1697 that sessions be held annually in the colony appears not to have received serious consideration, and Lieutenant Governor Alex-

---

73. Lower House Journals, Nov. 1, 1725, *N. C. Col. Recs.*, II, 575-76; Burrington's Observations on N. C. laws, 1731, *ibid.*, III, 180-81; Johnston's Observations on N. C. laws, [1734-35], *ibid.*, IV, 25; Burrington to Board of Trade, Sept. 4, 1731, *ibid.*, III, 207; Johnston to Board of Trade, Oct. 15, 1736, *ibid.*, IV, 177-78.

74. Francis Fane to Board of Trade, Apr. 1, 1737, CO 5/365, f. 202; Order in Council, July 21, 1737, *N. C. Col. Recs.*, IV, 251.

75. Bruce, *Institutional History of Virginia*, II, 431-32.

ander Spotswood thwarted the Burgesses' attempt in 1715 to pass a triennial act for *"the frequent meeting and calling Assemblys."*[76]

No further attempt to enact such a law was made until the 1760's, when, according to Richard Henry Lee, the demand arose for a statute to direct "the calling of new Assembly's" and to appoint a "time for the meeting of the representative body when chosen."[77] In response, the Burgesses passed an act in 1762 with a suspending clause that limited the duration of a legislature to seven years and required at least one session every three years. Lieutenant Governor Francis Fauquier accepted the measure but reported to the Board of Trade that its limitations had "been constantly practised agreeably to the Restrictions to which the British parliament is subject" and suggested that "it might . . . be deemed an Incroachment on the Royal Prerogative."[78] Board counsel Matthew Lamb, consistent with recent Crown policy, agreed with Fauquier. He reported that the act limited "the Continuance of the Assembly" and fixed "the times for holding the same" and was, therefore, "an Infringement of his Majesties Prerogative." Noting that these powers were normally exercised by the governor and Council, Lamb ruled that it was "Unnecessary and Improper, that any Law should be Passed, wherein that Power should be Restrained fixed or Altered."[79] Because of this unfavorable report, Crown officials never confirmed the measure, and the Burgesses had still not obtained any statutory limitations upon the frequency of elections and sessions by 1763.

The Georgia Commons first tried to obtain such limitations in 1759. In March it presented Governor Henry Ellis with a triennial bill, threatening to cease all business until he approved it. Ellis privately persuaded the representatives not to take such a violent step, and when the Commons presented him with the measure, he agreed only to "consider of it." The Commons argued that the privilege of passing such a law was enjoyed in other colonies, particularly in South Carolina, and requested Ellis either to recommend it

76. Locke's Essay towards the Remedys of Chief Grievances of Constitution of Virginia, Locke MSS, c. 9, Bodleian Lib.; Sept. 2, 7, 1715, *Va. Burgesses Journals, 1712-26*, 160-67.

77. Richard Henry Lee to Arthur Lee, Dec. 20, 1766, James C. Ballagh, ed., *The Letters of Richard Henry Lee*, 2 vols. (N. Y., 1911-14), I, 20-21.

78. Hening, ed., *Va. Statutes*, VII, 517-30; Fauquier to Board of Trade, Mar. 12, 1763, CO 5/1330, ff. 395-97.

79. See Hening, ed., *Va. Statutes*, VIII, 305-17; Lamb to Board of Trade, May 17, 1763, CO 5/1330, ff. 403-5.

for royal approval or to promise to dissolve the House within three years from the date of the election writs. Ellis chose to send the bill to the Board of Trade, to which he suggested that the term should more properly be limited to five or seven years, observing that "exceptionable as it is in some parts, perhaps there never was a more moderate and innocent one framed by an American Assembly." But the Board was not convinced of the necessity of limiting the duration of the Commons by statute, taking the position that so long as the governor retained the power of dissolution and could use it to put an end to a lower house whenever he deemed it necessary statutory limitations were superfluous. In the face of such strong opposition the Commons temporarily abandoned the attempt.[80]

By 1763 only the South Carolina Commons by its 1721 triennial act had succeeded in placing effective statutory regulations upon the frequency of elections and sessions. The hostile attitude of Crown officials prevented the passage of similar laws in Virginia and Georgia and led to the disallowance of a long-standing North Carolina statute in 1737. But the absence of statutory regulations in these colonies did not mean that these matters were not to a considerable degree controlled by the lower houses. Especially in North Carolina and to a lesser extent in Virginia and Georgia, where an established revenue in the first and an annual grant from Parliament in the second partially defrayed expenses, the control of finance by the lower houses brought with it rather frequent sessions. Particularly after 1740 annual or biannual meetings were usually necessary to provide for ordinary governmental expenses, and in time of emergency or war more frequent sessions were required. Nevertheless, attempts by all three lower houses to pass statutes regulating the frequency of elections and sessions in the two decades preceding the Revolution indicate that they strongly desired well-defined legal guarantees. That Crown officials took pains to prevent the lower houses from obtaining such guarantees was another source of conflict in imperial-colonial relations after 1763.

The extent of the lower houses' control over membership varied from province to province among the southern royal colonies on the

80. Ellis to Board of Trade, Feb. 28, 1759, and Mar. 15, 1759, CO 5/646; Board of Trade to Ellis, July 24, 1759, CO 5/673, pp. 242-46; Commons Journals, Mar. 12, 1759, *Ga. Col. Recs.*, XIII, 407-10.

eve of the Revolution. By 1765 only the South Carolina Commons had acquired all five of the powers involved in that control. All four legislative bodies had established their authority to determine the validity of elections and to expel and punish members without major opposition from either governors or imperial authorities, although the Gadsden election controversy had forced the South Carolina Commons to extreme measures to meet Governor Thomas Boone's challenge to its power to determine elections. Both the South Carolina and Virginia bodies had also quietly and effectively assumed the powers to establish constituencies and apportion representation and to regulate qualifications of voters and members. In North Carolina the Lower House had re-established its authority to settle member and voter qualifications in 1760 after an early statute for that purpose had been disallowed in 1737. The contest over the power to create electoral districts and apportion representation produced the eight-year controversy which ended in the Crown's removing that power from the control of the Lower House and placing it in the hands of the executive. But in practice the Lower House still retained this power, for it continued to exercise the authority to create counties, which by custom automatically became constituencies. In fact, the North Carolina representatives even admitted members from districts to which the governor had not granted representation and so demonstrated its power to recognize the constituent rights of whatever areas it pleased. Only the Georgia Commons had failed to secure either of these powers. Despite occasional efforts by all four lower houses, only the South Carolina Commons succeeded in acquiring the power to regulate the frequency of elections and sessions.

The Crown's rigid policy of reserving for colonial executives the powers to establish constituencies and apportion representation, settle qualifications of electors and elected, and determine the frequency of elections and sessions was largely responsible for the lower houses' failure to acquire those powers. Even more systematically applied after 1763, that policy constituted a serious challenge to the lower houses which had already won those powers, threatening ultimately to reclaim them for the Crown. That policy struck at the very heart of legislative control over membership and was an important source of irritation in all of the southern royal colonies in the decade preceding the Revolution.

IO

Internal Proceedings

In the lower houses' assertion of authority over their composition and proceedings, control over their internal proceedings was an important goal. To exclude the executive from any influence in their internal affairs, the lower houses demanded the power to appoint and manipulate legislative officers, including speakers and clerks; the right to enjoy certain privileges, such as freedom of speech and debate and freedom from arrest during sessions; and the authority to regulate house rules and procedure. But Crown officials were unwilling to permit them an unlimited exercise of power in any of these areas. They did not object to the lower houses appointing minor legislative officers such as committee clerks, chaplains, and sergeants at arms, but they insisted that the choice of the clerk remain in the hands of the executive and that the speaker, though chosen by the representatives, be subject to the governor's approval. Similarly, imperial authorities were willing to grant the lower houses freedom of speech and debate, but objected to their assumption of other privileges, particularly freedom from arrest during sessions. Perhaps colonial officials were most liberal in the realm of rule and procedure, permitting the lower houses a free reign except in the matter of designating how many members were necessary to constitute a quorum.

In view of these attitudes, it is not surprising that several bitter conflicts between lower houses and colonial executives arose over these powers in the southern royal colonies during the eighteenth century. Serious disputes over the right to appoint the clerk developed in Virginia at the end of the seventeenth century and in the two Carolinas during their first years under the Crown. In North Carolina there was an almost continuous controversy over the quorum question throughout the royal period.

A particularly important element in control over internal proceedings was the power to appoint the officers of the house. The extent to which colonial executives could influence affairs in the house depended largely upon the degree of their control over these officers, whom they tried to use to direct legislative proceedings into channels favorable to the executive. For that reason, the lower houses early asserted control over their officers in any one of three different ways. They preferred to nominate, appoint, and pay an officer, thus rendering him entirely independent from the governor and Council. But they occasionally had to settle for an arrangement by which they either nominated and paid an officer appointed by the governor or, in some cases, paid an officer nominated and appointed by the governor. Either arrangement brought the lower houses considerable authority over the officer in question.

The two most important officers in the house were the speaker and clerk. The speaker was the key official. He presided over the house, signed bills after passage, and acted as chief spokesman for the representatives. As a rule, the speaker retained his post until the dissolution of the house, and the office was a place of honor as well as political power and prestige. The office, South Carolina Speaker Peter Manigault declared in 1769, was "An Honour" that he endeavored "to Discharge with Resolution and Integrity." It was much sought after and was filled by many of the most capable colonial leaders: Robert "King" Carter, Sir John Randolph, John Robinson, and Peyton Randolph in Virginia; Edward Moseley, Samuel Swann, John Ashe, and Richard Caswell in North Carolina; Charles Pinckney, William Bull II, Andrew Rutledge, Benjamin Smith, Rawlins Lowndes, and Peter Manigault in South Carolina; and Noble Wymberly Jones, Archibald Bulloch, and William Young in Georgia.[1] The English House of Commons had won complete authority over its speaker in 1679 when it refused to accept Charles II's nominee.[2]

1. Peter Manigault to —————————, [Mar. 30, 1769], Manigault Family Papers, 1330, South Caroliniana Lib. See also Noble Jones to Noble Wymberly Jones, Aug. 20, 1760, Noble Wymberly Jones Papers, Ga. Hist. Soc., Savannah, and William Beverley to James Patton, Aug. 22, 1737, William Beverley Letter Book, 1737-1744, N. Y. Pub. Lib.

2. Josef Redlich, *The Procedure of the House of Commons* . . . , trans. A. Ernest Steinthal, 3 vols. (London, 1908), II, 160-63.

Following the Commons' example, all American lower houses assumed the power to nominate and control their speakers. The Crown insisted upon retaining for its governors the privilege of rejecting the lower houses' choice for the speakership, but no governor in the southern royal colonies attempted to exercise that privilege in the years before 1763.

Next in importance among the officers of the lower houses was the clerk, who was responsible for taking minutes and keeping records. The Crown appointed the clerk of the English House of Commons[3] and, for that reason, insisted upon the right to appoint clerks for colonial legislatures, preferring that the clerk have a settled salary so that he would not be financially dependent upon the lower house. But in each of the southern royal colonies the lower house managed to achieve some degree of control over its clerk.

In Virginia the Burgesses regularly elected its clerk until the mid-1680's. Imperial authorities first challenged the Burgesses' right in 1679 when they instructed Governor Culpeper to remove Robert Beverley from the clerkship for denying the royal commissioners appointed to investigate Bacon's Rebellion access to the Burgesses' papers. Culpeper wisely decided to ignore this instruction, but in 1686 Beverley again incurred the wrath of London officials for contesting the governor's veto power and altering the Burgesses' records. On this occasion, Crown officials summarily dismissed Beverley and commanded Howard to appoint a successor. Thereafter they instructed the governor to appoint the clerk.[4] In 1691 Nicholson allowed the House to nominate the clerk, but his successor, Andros, complied with the Crown's instructions and appointed a clerk before the Burgesses met. When the House convened, it asked Andros to restore the original method of selecting clerks. He replied that he had acted regularly and the House agreed; but it asked him to let it choose its own clerk and to support an application to the Crown for the restoration of its former privilege. Andros refused, and the House gave in, accepting the governor's appointee, who was, however,

3. See Orlo C. Williams, *The Clerical Organization of the House of Commons, 1661-1850* (Oxford, Eng., 1954), 7-14, 16-17, 39-40, 49-53, 68-69, 99-101, 107-8, 192.

4. Hening, ed., *Va. Statutes*, I, 424; Labaree, ed., *Royal Instructions*, I, 120; Instructions to Lord Culpeper, 1679-80, CO 1/47, No. 106; Howard to Comm. of the Privy Council, Feb. 10, 1685, CO 1/59, No. 17; Lord Sunderland to Howard, Aug. 1, 1686, CO 5/1357; Howard, to Lord President of Privy Council, Feb. 22, 1687, CO 1/61, No. 68; Flippin, *Royal Government in Virginia*, 194-95.

the same man it had chosen in the previous assembly. Thereafter, Virginia governors appointed the clerk without question, but they followed Andros's example and always appointed a clerk acceptable to the Burgesses. In addition, the fact that the clerk relied upon the Burgesses for his salary meant that it was not without control over him.[5]

A similar arrangement evolved in Georgia, where the governor appointed the clerk but the Commons paid his salary.[6] The question whether the clerk was to serve the Commons or the governor arose early in the royal period, and it was settled in favor of the Commons. When William Little, appointed clerk by Governor John Reynolds, refused in 1756 to enter and read the minutes until several members returned by the governor's writs had been admitted, the Commons ordered him to withdraw, accused him of contempt, and appointed Matthew Roche in his place.[7] Although this action was partly responsible for Reynolds's dissolving the Commons, future clerks, not wishing to experience Little's fate, were careful not to offend the Commons.

After fifteen years of intermittent controversy under the Crown, the South Carolina Commons managed to retain considerable control over its clerk, although it lost the power of appointment. The Commons appointed its own clerk without contest throughout the proprietary period and for the first years under the Crown, though in February 1723 Nicholson unsuccessfully challenged its power of appointment. Under President Arthur Middleton the Commons again appointed the clerk until January 1728, when Middleton refused to administer the oaths to John Bayley, the choice of the Commons, claiming the power of appointment for the executive. This action evoked a furious response from the House, but Middleton adhered to his position, pointing out that the British House of Commons did not appoint its clerk. When neither side would give in, Middleton dissolved the Commons.[8] Under Governor Robert Johnson this con-

5. Apr. 17, 1691, Mar. 3-6, 8-9, 1693, *Va. Burgesses Journals, 1659-93*, 33, 414-16, 418-19; Francis Fauquier's Answers to Board of Trade's Queries, Jan. 30, 1764, CO 5/1330, ff. 557-65.

6. See Commons Journals, Jan. 22, 1762, *Ga. Col. Recs.*, XIII, 645; Statutes, *ibid.*, XIX, Pt. I, 43, 483-84; Wright's Answers to Board of Trade's Queries, Nov. 15, 1766, unpubl. Ga. Col. Recs., XXVIII, Pt. II-A, 438, Ga. Dept. of Arch. and Hist.

7. Commons Journals, Feb. 13, 1756, *Ga. Col. Recs.*, XIII, 95.

8. July 28, Aug. 16, 1721, Mar. 8, 1722, Feb. 15, 1723, S. C. Commons Journals, CO 5/426, pp. 5, 54-56, 83, 85-86; Aug. 1, 1727, *ibid.*, CO 5/429, p. 209; Jan. 31, 1728, *ibid.*, CO 5/430, p. 1; Smith, *South Carolina as a Royal Province*, 111-12.

test was revived. The Commons again appointed Bayley clerk. Johnson refused to allow the House to exercise the right of appointment but offered to select anyone it recommended. He finally issued a commission to Bayley, but the Commons declined to recognize Bayley as clerk by Governor Johnson's commission, asserting that it was "the Undoubted Right of this house to Choose their own Clerk." Bayley then resigned, surrendering his commission to the governor, and the Commons chose Eleazer Allen, whom Johnson agreed to accept until he received further instructions from England.[9]

Imperial authorities forbade Johnson to allow the Commons to appoint its own clerk on the grounds that the British Commons did not enjoy that privilege. To make sure that their decision was respected, they appointed Isaac Amyand clerk by royal warrant. Johnson himself was unhappy with this decision. He privately agreed with the Commons that it was unjust to deprive the representatives of "a privilege they always enjoyed—under the Proprietors" and he predicted that they had "so worked one another up" that they would not accept Amyand. However, in December 1732 Johnson dutifully sent the warrant commanding him to appoint Amyand to the Commons, which appointed a committee to consider the matter. Reporting that it had been "the constant Practice of the Commons House of Assembly to choose the Clerk officiating in that House," the committee cited instances in which the Commons had been allowed to exercise this power under Nicholson and suggested that the Crown really meant that Amyand should be clerk of the Council. The representatives then informed Johnson that "we can't betray the Trust reposed in us by the People we Represent, in so suddainly parting with a Privilege which we in common with all other his Majesty's Plantations in America have ever enjoyed" and begged him not to "insist that Mr. Amyand be immediately admitted to Act as Clerk in the Commons House of Assembly: but suffer the affairs of this his Majesty's Province to go on in the usual Course" until it had "first addressed his Majesty on this Subject." But Johnson refused to permit the House "to Dispute the King's possitive Commands" and insisted on the immediate admission of Amyand to the clerkship. The opposition of the Commons gave way under Johnson's pressure, and it agreed to accept Amyand after it discovered that the governors ap-

9. Jan. 21-23, Feb. 18, 1731, S. C. Commons Journals, CO 5/432, pp. 4-8, 10-11.

pointed the clerks of the lower houses in both New York and New Jersey.[10]

Henceforth, South Carolina governors appointed the clerk, but because he depended upon the Commons for his salary he remained under its control. In fact, subsequent governors may unofficially have permitted the Commons to nominate the clerk. When Amyand died in 1739, the elder Bull appointed Childermas Croft, a favorite of the Commons, who had previously served it as deputy clerk. Croft held the office until his death in 1761, when the younger Bull appointed Thomas Bromley admittedly "at the Unanimous, but private Recommendation of the Members of Assembly." Thus it would seem that in the cases of both Croft and Bromley the executive appointed a man whom the Commons desired. Paid and privately named by the Commons, the clerk was really under its authority.[11]

The North Carolina Lower House was more successful in a similar contest with the Crown. Like its southern neighbor, the House had appointed its own clerk under the proprietors. At the first royal legislature in 1731, it appointed a clerk as usual, Ayliffe Williams. Governor George Burrington then issued Williams a commission for the office, which the Lower House refused to recognize. In reviewing the journals, the Board of Trade noticed these proceedings and reminded Governor Burrington that he was not to allow the Lower House any greater privileges than the British House of Commons enjoyed and that he was to appoint the clerk.[12] Following these instructions, Burrington, in July 1733, insisting upon his right to appoint the clerk and all other officers except the speaker, commissioned Ayliffe Williams clerk and John Richards sergeant at arms. The Lower House referred the matter to a special committee, which found that "it has been the constant practice of the House to name and appoint all their Officers Such as Clerk, Sargeant, Messenger and Door

10. Johnson to Board of Trade, Mar. 26, 1731, CO 5/362, ff. 36-37; Allured Popple to Johnson, Nov. 18, 1731, CO 5/401, p. 19; Dec. 8, 13-14, 1732, S. C. Commons Journals, CO 5/433, pp. 3-6; Extract of Johnson to Mr. Hutcheson, Oct. 29, 1732, Misc. MSS, P-62/281, South Caroliniana Lib., and Dec. 21, 1732, Wilmington Papers, I, Lib. Cong.

11. Jan. 19, 1733, S. C. Commons Journals, CO 5/433, p. 9; Commons Journals, Mar. 5, 1737, *S. C. Col. Recs., 1736-39*, 321; William Bull I to Board of Trade, Nov. 20, 1739, CO 5/367, ff. 144-45; Warrant appointing Childermas Croft clerk, May 12, 1740, CO 5/384, f. 77; William Bull II to Board of Trade, May 28, 1761, CO 5/377, f. 79.

12. Allured Popple to Burrington, Aug. 16, 1732, Burrington to Board of Trade, May 19, 1733, *N. C. Col. Recs.*, III, 354, 482-83.

Keeper." "Nor can we find," the committee reported, "that the Lords proprietors or their Governours ever attempted to Name or appoint those officers." The committee suggested asking the Crown "to continue to the Assembly such priviledges, as they have hitherto enjoyed and which has never been disputed" and decided that if the governor would "not permitt the Ancient Liberty and Priviledges of this Assembly that in Such case . . . rather than to prejudice or retard the Business of this Session (untill his Majesty's pleasure be known) to admitt of the said Officers appointed by the Governour, saving to this House their Ancient Rights and Priviledges." However, the House never sent a petition to England and appears to have waived its rights temporarily, admitting appointees of Governor Gabriel Johnston in both November 1734 and January 1735. But it was apparently only biding its time until Crown officials had forgotten the issue, for in February 1739 it quietly appointed William Heritage clerk with no objection from Johnston. Heritage filled the post until 1769, and the Lower House chose his successor, James Green, Jr., again without opposition from the executive. Thus, the North Carolina Lower House exercised the right both to nominate and to appoint the clerk except for the brief period from 1733 to 1739. That it also paid his salary meant that he was thoroughly under its control.[13]

By the end of the colonial period only the North Carolina Lower House had gained and maintained complete control over the nomination, appointment, and salary of its clerk, but the legislatures of the other colonies paid the salaries of their clerks and thereby exercised authority over them. They also enjoyed the right of nomination in Virginia and South Carolina.

Crown officials did not object to the lower houses' appointing minor officers of the house. Such officers included a sergeant at arms in Virginia and North Carolina; a messenger in Georgia and South Carolina; a cashier in South Carolina; doorkeepers in North Carolina and Virginia; a chaplain in Virginia; a macebearer in North Carolina; deputy or assistant clerks in North Carolina, South Carolina, and Georgia; and clerks of committees in North Carolina, South Carolina, and Virginia. All of these officers, with the exception of the sergeant at arms in Virginia, who although appointed by the gover-

13. Lower House Journals, July 4, 7, 1733, Nov. 6, 1734, *ibid.*, 566-67, 576, 635; Jan. 16, 1735, Feb. 8, 1739, *ibid.*, IV, 116, 383; Dec. 14, 1757, *ibid.*, V, 925; Oct. 24, 1769, *ibid.*, VIII, 108.

nor's commission was sometimes nominated and always paid by the
Burgesses, were appointed and controlled by the lower houses. There
was some dispute over the appointment of a sergeant at arms in North
Carolina, which resulted in the governor's appointing him by com-
mission in 1733; but thereafter he was appointed by the Lower
House.[14]

A second ingredient in authority over internal proceedings was
the right to enjoy certain fundamental privileges. Since at least the
reign of Henry IV the speaker at the opening of Parliament had
regularly presented to the Crown a petition claiming the ancient
rights and privileges of the Commons, and all of the lower houses in
the southern royal colonies adopted that practice. Such a petition
appeared first in Virginia in 1684, in South Carolina in 1702, in
Georgia at its first royal legislative session in 1755, and in North Carolina in 1760. When such petitions appeared late, as in the case of
North Carolina and Virginia, the lower houses seem to have exercised
the privileges requested for a long time before presenting a formal
petition.

The most important privileges claimed by these petitions were
freedom of speech and debate and freedom from arrest and molesta-
tion for representatives and in some cases their servants during sessions. The English Commons had claimed the former as early as 1541
but did not finally secure it until the passage of the Bill of Rights.
It won the latter in 1604 as a result of Shirley's case, although the
monarchy did not completely recognize it until after the Restoration.
Less important requests by the lower houses were that the representatives be permitted freedom of access to the governor, that the governor put a favorable construction upon the lower house's acts, and that
the speaker's errors not be imputed to the house. For the most part,
Crown authorities allowed the lower houses free exercise of these
privileges. Officials in the colonies occasionally violated them, pro-

14. See Smith, *South Carolina as a Royal Province*, 115; Florence Cook, "Procedure in the North Carolina Assembly, 1731-1770," *N. C. Hist. Rev.*, 8 (1931),
264-66; Flippin, *Royal Government in Virginia*, 197-98; Stanley M. Pargellis, "Procedure of the Virginia House of Burgesses," *Wm. and Mary Qtly.*, 2d Ser., 7 (1927),
79-81; John P. Corry, "Procedure in the Commons House of Assembly in Georgia,"
Georgia Historical Quarterly, 13 (1929), 110-27; Lord Dunmore's Answers to Board
of Trade's Queries, 1774, CO 5/1352. For an application for one of the posts of
committee clerk for the Virginia Burgesses, see Petition of Godfrey Pole, Feb. 27,
1728, Godfrey Pole Papers, Va. Hist. Soc.

voking minor disputes and grandiloquent assertions of privilege by the lower houses in the process, but there were no major controversies over questions of privilege in the southern royal colonies during the eighteenth century.[15]

Freedom of speech and debate was the cornerstone of a free legislative body. Without it nothing could be thoroughly debated, and for that reason the lower houses clung to it tenaciously When President Arthur Middleton of South Carolina objected to his being accused within the Commons of selling judicial posts in 1726, the representatives maintained that if "any Reflections had been made . . . that were unjust and Inconsistent with the liberty of Speech that is Allowed in a Commons house of Assembly the members that made them would have been brought to order" and warned him "that we shall alow nobody but ourselves to be Judges of our debates."[16] Similarly, when Lieutenant Governor Thomas Broughton and the South Carolina Council objected in 1737 to some indiscriminate scribbling on one of the Commons' messages which reflected upon John Hammerton, secretary of the province and councilor, the House observed that whatever was in the message "which in the Course of Debate . . . had been inserted and was afterwards struck out by this House before the Bill was passed and sent up, could not by any Rules of parliamentary Proceedings be taken Notice of by your Honours, since after the Expungement it was no longer Part of the Bill" and resolved that "the Freedom of Speech, Debate or Proceedings in the Commons House of Assembly ought not to be examined or questioned in any Place out of the said House" and that "the Governour of this Province ought not to take Notice of any Proceeding in the said House but when the same is properly laid before him in a parliamentary Way."[17] The Commons also charged Governors Lyttelton and Boone with violating this privilege, the former in February 1760 and the latter in November 1762.[18] Similarly, in May 1760, the North Carolina Lower House threatened to expel members who divulged the contents of its speeches or proceedings. In the same colony, when Governor Arthur Dobbs

15. Clarke, *Parliamentary Privilege*, 61-92; Carl Wittke, *The History of English Parliamentary Privilege* (Columbus, Ohio, 1921), 23-30, 33; Tasswell-Langmead, *Constitutional History* (1946 ed.), 374-75, 426.

16. Feb. 4, 1726, S. C. Commons Journals, CO 5/428, p. 159.

17. Commons Journals, Mar. 2-4, 1737, *S. C. Col. Recs., 1736-39*, 270-71, 279.

18. Feb. 6, 1760, S. C. Commons Journals, CO 5/473, p. 4; Nov. 30, 1762, *ibid.*, CO 5/480, pp. 19-21.

objected to a provision in a treasurer's bill before it had passed the House, the House resolved that "His Excellency's taking notice of any matter or thing transacting in this House before being made acquainted with it by this House, and directing Entries in the Journals thereof is inconsistent with the antient liberties and Privileges of this House."[19]

In order that their debates and proceedings would not be frequently interrupted and their number diminished, the representatives also claimed exemption from arrest. The Virginia legislature enjoyed it from 1624 on, despite its denial by royal instruction between 1728 and 1738.[20] In 1769 the Burgesses attempted to write that privilege into law, but Board of Trade counsel Richard Jackson objected because it had been denied members of Parliament by recent statute, and the measure was not confirmed by the Crown.[21] Nevertheless, no governor ever denied the Burgesses that privilege. Occasional infringements of it provoked special assertions by the South Carolina Commons at least three times before 1775. In 1748, when the provost marshal arrested Representative William Drake while he was on his way to Charleston to qualify as a member of the House, the Commons declared "that whosoever shall Prosecute any Civill Process already Comenced or to be Commenced against any Member of the Commons House of Assembly of this Province in the Court of Common Pleas, Court of Equity or any other Court during the Priviledge of Parliament shall be Deemed a Betrayer of the Rights and Priviledges of this House and shall be Proceeded against accordingly." Similarly, in 1733 the Commons expelled a representative for bringing a legal action against the speaker of the house, and when attorney David Graeme issued a writ against Representative Thomas Wright in 1754 it resolved "that no Representative of the Inhabitants of this Province being a Member of the Commons House of Assembly of this Province is liable to be arrested in his person during the Privilege of Assembly."[22]

The lower houses frequently protected these privileges by com-

19. Lower House Journals, May 23, 1760, *N. C. Col. Recs.*, VI, 409; Dobbs to Board of Trade, Dec. 12, 1760, *ibid.*, 321-22.

20. Hening, ed., *Va. Statutes*, I, 125; Labaree, ed., *Royal Instructions*, I, 114-15.

21. Hening, ed., *Va. Statutes*, VIII, 305-17; Jackson to Board of Trade, June 5, 1771, CO 5/1333.

22. Feb. 10, 1728, Dec. 8, 1733, Mar. 2, 1754, S. C. Commons Journals, CO 5/430, p. 19, CO 5/433, pp. 19-20, CO 5/472, p. 57.

mitting offenders to jail or to the custody of their officers. Imprisoning representatives, outsiders, and even Crown officials for violations of privilege, the houses often abused their power of commitment until at times the real danger was not to the legislature from the governor or others but to the citizens from the legislature. For instance, the South Carolina Commons resolved in 1733 "that it is the Undeniable Privilege of the Commons house of Assembly to Commit into Custody of their Messenger such Persons as they Judge deserve to be committed" and then declared even "that no Person Committed by this House for Breach of Privilege or Contempt of this House ought to be by any Writ of Habeas Corpus made to appear in any other Place or before any other Judicature during that Session of Assembly wherein such person was so Committed," thus suspending the right of habeas corpus in cases of privilege.[23]   Henry McCulloh, receiver general of quitrents for the Crown in the Carolinas, reported a law in North Carolina "that subjects any person to the Pillory who will openly sensure the Conduct of the Governor Council and Assembly";[24] and the South Carolina Commons charged twenty-eight Charleston merchants with libel, committed them, and forced them to pay fees of £1,200 for petitioning against a paper currency bill in December 1722.   Indeed, the lower houses committed many outsiders.   A typical case occurred in Virginia in 1728, when Burgess William Andrews complained that he had been abused by Edward West.   The Burgesses took West into custody, forced him to kneel at the bar of the House while the speaker reprimanded him, and required him to ask pardon of Andrews and the House.   The North Carolina Lower House similarly treated Peter Young in 1731 for having "uttered divers scandalous speeches reflecting generally on the Members of Assembly."   Nor were assemblymen immune from such treatment.   Burgess Thomas Johnson received the standard treatment when he incurred the displeasure of the Virginia House in 1759 for having accused it of "Plots, Schemes, and Contrivances" to squander away the public money.[25]

The lower houses occasionally even committed royal officials.   The South Carolina Commons arrested the provost marshal in April 1726

23. Apr. 6, 1733, *ibid.,* CO 5/433, p. 40.

24. McCulloh to Thomas Hill, Feb. 16, 1745, CO 5/371, f. 71.

25. S. C. merchants to Board of Trade, May 29, 1723, CO 5/358, ff. 244-47; Feb. 13-14, 1728, *Va. Burgesses Journals, 1727-40,* 9-20; Apr. 3, 1759, *ibid., 1758-61,* 114; Lower House Journals, May 15, 1731, *N. C. Col. Recs.,* III, 317-18.

for not heeding an order of the House and Chief Justice Richard Allien in May 1728 for refusing to appear before the Commons. In 1729 it committed the clerk of the Council for insolence, whereupon President Middleton dissolved it; and in 1733 it took James St. John and Benjamin Whitaker, the surveyor and deputy surveyor generals, into custody for contradicting its orders. This last action caused William Trewin, deputy judge of the vice admiralty, to complain and not without some justice that if "a King's Officer" appeared "Zealous for the prerogative or Interest of his Master," he could expect to be "insulted, ridiculed, and affronted."[26] Certainly, the South Carolina Commons had no respect for rank of office in questions of privilege. Nor did the other houses. In North Carolina the Lower House attempted in July 1733 to commit Chief Justice William Little for presenting a libelous petition and took into custody a receiver of the powder money for refusing to submit his accounts to the House.[27] And the Virginia Burgesses committed the public printer, William Parks, in 1749 for printing a libel against the Burgesses in the *Virginia Gazette,* releasing him only after the Council had acknowledged its responsibility for the article.[28] These examples illustrate how far the lower houses would go to protect their rights and privileges.

The third element in control over internal proceedings was authority to regulate house rules and procedure. For the most part, Crown officials readily conceded that authority to the lower houses in the southern royal colonies. They allowed the representatives a free hand in using the committee system, initiating legislation, and establishing house rules of procedure. Only in the Carolinas, where the royal officials disliked proprietary regulations designating the number of members necessary for a quorum, did they attempt to interfere with the lower houses' power to determine their rules and procedure.

In England the House of Commons had assumed the power to determine a quorum in 1641, when it decided that forty members (less than one-tenth of its total number) would be sufficient to transact business.[29] In both Carolinas, however, proprietary regulations speci-

26. Apr. 26, 1726, May 11, 1728, Feb. 21, 1729, S. C. Commons Journals, CO 5/429, p. 181, CO 5/430, pp. 23-25, 101; Letter of William Trewin, May 19, 1733, CO 5/364.
27. Lower House Journals, July 17-18, 1733, *N. C. Col. Recs.,* III, 603-4, 611.
28. W. P. Palmer *et al.,* eds., *Calendar of Virginia State Papers and Other Manuscripts,* 11 vols. (Richmond, 1875-93), I, 241-43.
29. Redlich, *Procedure of House of Commons,* II, 75-76.

fied that a much larger percentage of members was necessary to constitute a quorum. A South Carolina statute of 1716 set the quorum at sixteen, slightly more than half of the total membership of thirty-one. In 1719 the number of representatives was raised to thirty-six and the quorum to nineteen,[30] where it stayed throughout the colonial period despite the fact that the membership of the Commons was eventually increased to forty-eight. But nineteen was nearly 40 per cent of forty-eight—a proportion far larger than that of the British Commons; and South Carolina governors occasionally complained that the quorum was too large. Governor James Glen wrote in 1748 that the size of the quorum often created "many obstructions and delays." "A Party of pleasure made by a few of the Members," he lamented, "renders it often impossible for the rest to enter upon Business, and sometimes I Have seen a Party made to go out of Town purposely to break the House as they call it (well knowing that nothing could be transacted in their absence) and in this manner to prevent the Success of what they could not otherwise oppose."[31] In 1756 the Board of Trade also contended that the size of the established quorum "put it into the power of any one or two factious Member[s] who have an Influence in the Assembly to put a stop to all Business and obstruct His Majesty's Service and the Publick good of the Province by prevailing upon others to absent themselves." The Board suggested that Governor Lyttelton alter the situation,[32] but neither he nor his successors made any effort to do so.

A similar development occurred in North Carolina, but the consequences were much more serious. The biennial act of 1715 provided that a quorum should consist of not less than half of the total members, a provision based on the proprietary charter, which specified that no laws were "to be enacted, but by the advice, assent, and approbation of the greatest part of the Freemen, or their Delegates."[33] Greatly at variance with procedure in the British Commons, this provision was frequently attacked by royal Governor Gabriel Johnston. He charged in 1747 that because the Albemarle members constituted well over half of the total membership they could and did break up

30. Cooper and McCord, eds., *S. C. Statutes*, II, 683-91, III, 50-55, 135-40.
31. Glen to Board of Trade, Oct. 10, 1748, CO 5/372, ff. 80-87.
32. Short Observations, 1756, in Greene, "South Carolina's Colonial Constitution," *S. C. Hist. Mag.*, 62 (1961), 80.
33. Laws, *N. C. St. Recs.*, XXIII, 12-14; Thomas Pollock to Roger Moore, Jan. 15, 1747, Pollock Letter Book, 1710-61, N. C. Dept. of Arch. and Hist.

legislative sessions by withdrawing "Privately and then the Majority of Burgesses being absent, no more Business could be done, so that the very being of Assemblies depended upon their whim and Humour, and not on the Kings Writ; and Governours Proclamation and Prerogation." The result, Johnston lamented, was to make "the remaining Members of no weight in the Legislature."[34] Consequently, Johnston's "managed" election act of 1746 put aside this custom and reduced the number necessary for a quorum to fourteen and the speaker. The Albemarle members, through their agent, Henry McCulloh, objected to the act on the grounds that it had been passed by less than half of the representatives, which was not a quorum under the established customs of the province.[35] When the matter came before the Crown's attorney and solicitor generals in 1753, they questioned whether "a majority of the representatives" was "necessary to constitute a quorum of the assembly" and pointed out that such an arrangement was "very extraordinary, and liable to great inconvenience."[36]

Accordingly, when Arthur Dobbs was appointed governor in 1754, his instructions specified that fifteen members should make up a quorum.[37] For a while the Lower House accepted this alteration without objection, but in April 1758 it resolved that it could not "consistent with the ancient Customs and proceedings in this House, proceed to the Dispatch of farther Business, unless a Majority of the Representatives in the Province were attending." The House adopted a similar resolution in November 1760 and repeatedly violated Dobbs's instruction during the remainder of his administration.[38] Dobbs was powerless to enforce it because the Lower House simply declined to act unless a majority were present. He and his two successors, William Tryon and Josiah Martin, presented this matter on several occasions to the imperial authorities, who supported them; but the Lower House adamantly refused to recognize the governors' instructions, thereby denying royal authority to regulate its internal

---

34. Johnston to Board of Trade, Mar. 9, 1747, *N. C. Col. Recs.*, IV, 1152-53.

35. Laws, *N. C. St. Recs.*, XXIII, 251-52; McCulloh's Observations on the Pretended Acts of North Carolina, received by Board of Trade, May 11, 1748, CO 5/296, ff. 91-92.

36. Sir Dudley Ryder and William Murray to Board of Trade, July 20, 1753, Chalmers, ed., *Opinions*, I, 293.

37. Labaree, ed., *Royal Instructions*, I, 106.

38. Lower House Journals, Apr. 28, 1758, *N. C. Col. Recs.*, V, 1000; Nov. 7, 1760, *ibid.*, VI, 470.

proceedings in regard to a quorum and succeeding in enforcing a provision of its own.[39]

By the late 1760's the lower houses in the southern royal colonies had secured an authority over internal proceedings comparable to and in one instance greater than that exercised by the British House of Commons. Like the imperial body, they all enjoyed the power to nominate their speaker, freedom of speech and debate and freedom from arrest for their members during legislative sessions, and the authority to determine house rules and procedure. Also like the British Commons, the lower houses of Virginia, South Carolina, and Georgia allowed their clerks to be nominated by the representatives of the Crown. But the clerks were dependent upon the lower houses for their salaries in all three colonies and were actually nominated by the lower houses in both Virginia and South Carolina. These arrangements were similar to British practice whereby the Crown appointed clerks agreeable to the Commons—usually from the Commons' clerical staff—and whereby after 1732 the Commons provided part of the clerk's income. But contrary to the British Commons, the North Carolina Lower House not only paid and nominated but also appointed its clerk and, in that respect, exercised a greater power than its British antecedent. With one exception—the Crown's attempt to reject the speaker in Georgia during the early 1770's—none of the elements involved in the lower houses' quest for control over internal proceedings was a serious issue in the years after 1763.

39. See Dobbs to Board of Trade, Dec. 12, 1760, Dec. 1761, Jan. 14, 1764, Mar. 29, 1764, *ibid.,* 319-20, 597-98, 1024-25, 1035-36; Board of Trade to Dobbs, Apr. 4, 1761, June 10, 1762, *ibid.,* 539-40, 724; Couchet Jouvencal to Board of Trade, May 16, 1763, *ibid.,* 983-85; John Pownall to Tryon, July 2, 1764, *ibid.,* 1049; Martin to Dartmouth, Mar. 12, 1773, *ibid.,* IX, 600; Dartmouth to Martin, June 10, 1773, *ibid.,* 665; June 2, 1762, Dec. 9, 1763, *Board of Trade Journals, 1759-63,* 282-83, 419; Dobbs to William Henry Lyttelton, Apr. 28, 1758, Lyttelton Papers, Clements Lib.

PART V

CONTROL OVER EXECUTIVE AFFAIRS

In Virginia, South Carolina, and some other Colonies, Acts of Assembly were, from time to time assented to, which appointed men to executive Offices; and those innovations in the Constitution, passed sub silentia, at the Boards in England; at times when little attention was paid to colony matters.
> —Anthony Stokes, *A View of the Constitution of British Colonies* (London, 1783)

It is the inherent right of this House, to nominate Persons to be appointed to the Office of Public Treasurers of this Province.
> —North Carolina Lower House of Assembly
> December 1760

The Agent being a Person appointed for solliciting the Affairs of this Province we conceive the Province should be understood to be the People; and as the People only are to pay for his services it seems just and reasonable that the Representatives of the People should have the Nomination of their Agent.
> —South Carolina Commons House of Assembly,
> March 1755

COLONIAL lower houses made their most important innovations in the area of legislative handling of executive affairs. Pushing their authority well beyond that of the British House of Commons, they demanded and in many cases obtained a significant share of the traditional powers of the executive. As a corollary to their extensive control over finance, they claimed the right to nominate and appoint all public officials concerned in collecting, handling, and disbursing local revenues. Quite logically, they stretched that claim to include the selection of most public officers, including supervisors of all public works and services, public printers, and colonial agents in London. Their financial authority also enabled them to play a significant part in military and Indian affairs. In return for money to finance those affairs, the lower houses insisted upon a share in determining policy and in some instances upon appointing officials to implement that policy. Finally, the lower houses sought to usurp executive power in church appointments by shifting the patronage from the governors to the local vestries and in judicial matters by establishing their right to erect courts and to settle judicial tenure. In the southern royal colonies, they were remarkably successful in attaining these powers and by the late colonial period were playing an important role in the conduct of executive affairs.

Revenue Officers

ONE of the more important powers gained by American lower houses was that of nominating and appointing officials to collect, hold, and apply funds arising from provincial revenues.[1] In England the House of Commons would not have questioned the Crown's right to appoint these officers, for they were executive officials, whose appointment traditionally belonged exclusively to the Crown. As was so often the case in colonial America, however, there was a wide gulf between imperial theory and experience on the one hand and American practice on the other. Authorities in London had intended for colonial executives to appoint such officers, but their failure to oppose systematically the lower houses' numerous appointments in the late seventeenth and early eighteenth centuries enabled the lower houses to establish precedents that supported their contention that officers who handled money should be appointed by the authority that raised it. "In Virginia, South Carolina, and some other Colonies," Anthony Stokes declared in 1783 in his study of the constitution of the British colonies, "Acts of Assembly were, from time to time assented to, which appointed men to executive Offices; and those innovations in the Constitution, passed sub silentia, at the Boards in England; at times when little attention was paid to colony matters."[2] In its narrowest implications the lower houses' exercise of the power of appointment

1. Provincial revenues included all money raised by the colonial legislatures and should be distinguished from Crown revenues, which included quitrents, imperial customs duties, fines, and forfeitures.

2. Author's annotated copy, Anthony Stokes, *A View of the Constitution of the British Colonies in North America and the West Indies, at the Time the Civil War broke out on the Continent of America* (London, 1783), 23-24, John Carter Brown Library, Providence, R. I.

was merely one manifestation of their extensive financial authority, but in its broadest sense it gave them a significant share in executive affairs. Revenue officials appointed by the lower houses were simply legislative officers performing executive duties. In the south the extent of the lower houses' authority in this area varied from colony to colony. At the two extremes were South Carolina and Georgia.

The South Carolina Commons succeeded in obtaining virtually complete control over all officers concerned in handling revenues arising from South Carolina laws. Glen was by no means exaggerating when he reported to the Board of Trade in 1748 that "besides the Treasurer" the Commons "appoint the Commissary, the Indian Commissioner, the Comptroller of the dutyes . . . the Powder Receiver, (etc.),"[3] and the "etc." included a wide range of minor officials.

The source of the Commons' power to appoint most of these officers can be traced to the proprietary period. The proprietors appointed a treasurer for the Carolinas until 1691, when the Commons adopted the practice of nominating and appointing the treasurer of the southern province by statute. For nearly a decade the House united that office with the speakership. It named Jonathan Amory public receiver to collect a duty on skins and furs in an act of September 1691 and elected him speaker a year later. Amory filled both posts until his death sometime before November 1700, when the Commons abandoned the attempt to combine them. George Logan was receiver by the governor's appointment from Amory's death until the Commons chose Thomas Smith in November 1700, and in April 1703 the Commons selected Logan to succeed Smith. Between 1704 and 1707 Logan was active in behalf of the dissenters in the controversy with Governor Nathaniel Johnson over establishing the Anglican church. Consequently, when the law that appointed Logan treasurer expired in 1707, Johnson opposed Logan's re-election and proposed in his stead Major Alexander Parris. The Commons insisted that Logan be continued as receiver and a bitter controversy ensued, which terminated only when Logan voluntarily relinquished the office.[4] Thereupon the Commons passed an act declaring its right to

3. Glen to Board of Trade, Oct. 10, 1748, CO 5/372, ff. 80-87.
4. Cooper and McCord, eds., *S. C. Statutes*, II, 64-68, 110-12, 200-206, 247-48; Smith, *South Carolina as a Royal Province*, 15-17; Proprietor's Commission to William Saxby, Apr. 17, 1676, S. C. Pub. Recs., I, 41-42, S. C. Arch. Dept.; A. S. Salley,

nominate the public receiver—a right which it had enjoyed since 1691 —and elected Captain George Smith to the office. The House replaced Smith in June 1712 with Alexander Parris, who held the post for the remainder of the proprietary period.[5]

After Logan had voluntarily withdrawn from the contest in 1707, both Johnson and the Council agreed to the measure asserting the Commons' right to nominate the receiver, but they later regretted it. The Commons frequently cited that law as giving it power to nominate not only the receiver but all officers handling provincial revenues. In 1717 the Commons used the law to defend its right to appoint a powder receiver and carried its point in spite of strong opposition from Governor Robert Johnson.[6] Thereupon Johnson submitted the law to the Lords Proprietors, who disallowed it in July 1718, ruling that it was "inconsistent with the safety welfare and good government of the Province . . . and inconsistent with and contrary to the Usage and Custom of Great Britain." But the Commons refused to recognize the disallowance and in February 1720, after the overthrow of the proprietors, declared the act still in force.[7]

The question of who should nominate and appoint revenue officers came up again at the first meeting of the Commons under the Crown in the summer of 1721. The Council contended that the officers should be appointed by the mutual consent of all three branches of the legislature, but the representatives argued that because they were "the Representatives of the whole people, so they are more particularly concerned in raising mony, and Consequently ought to have the

ed., *Journal of the Commons House of Assembly of South Carolina,* 19 vols. (Columbia, 1907-49), Sept. 20, 1692, *1692,* 4; Sept. 15, 1693, *1693,* 33; Mar. 14, 1696, *1696,* Pt. I, 44; Dec. 5, 1696, *1696,* Pt. II, 16-17; Nov. 10, 1697, *1697,* 19; Sept. 13, 1698, *1698,* 33; Nov. 1-4, 14, 1700, *1700,* 6-10, 18; Apr. 24, 1703, *1703,* 68; hereafter cited as Salley, ed., *S. C. Commons Journal.*

5. Cooper and McCord, eds., *S. C. Statutes,* II, xii, 305-6, 656.

6. The legislature created this office in 1687, and the governor first exercised the power of appointment. The legislature assumed that power for a while in the 1690's but relinquished it in 1703 when it assigned the duties of the office to the captain of the battery, an officer appointed by the governor. This arrangement was followed until 1717, when the death of Matthew Porter, long-time powder receiver, precipitated the dispute over the right of nomination between Johnson and the Commons House that resulted in the appointment of the Commons' candidate, Colonel Miles Brewton, to the office. *Ibid.,* II, 20-21, 42-44, 82-84, 150-53, 213-14; Nov. 1, 1700, Salley, ed., *S. C. Commons Journal, 1700,* 7-9.

7. Smith, *South Carolina as a Royal Province,* 17-20; Proprietors to Johnson, July 22, 1718, S. C. Pub. Recs., VII, 143-44, 147, S. C. Arch. Dept.; Cooper and McCord, eds., *S. C. Statutes,* III, 103.

Appointment of the Officers that are accountable for it, it being sufficient for the upper house to have a power of calling such Officers to
an Account." To support its claim the Commons cited the 1707
statute placing the right of nomination in its hands. The Council
conceded that that statute had given the Commons power to nominate
the public receiver but pointed out that the British House of Commons had never tried to name officers to hold and disperse money. It
argued that the act was therefore contrary to the provision in the
royal instructions that forbade Nicholson to allow the South Carolina
Commons any more power than its British counterpart. But the
Commons would not accept this argument. It declared that it was
not claiming a "new Priviledge" but merely asserting an "Ancient
Right" confirmed by a proprietary law. It also pointed out that none
of the royal instructions specifically referred to the question at issue
and that they could "only have reference to Laws to be past for the
future, Subsequent to these Instructions, and not to those that have
been past many Years Since." Here, then, was a clear, if still un
refined, expression at the very beginning of royal government in South
Carolina of the doctrine that instructions could not supersede established statutes or traditions—the first step toward the ultimate conclusion that the instructions were binding only upon royal officials
and not upon the colony as a whole.[8]

Both houses had to give way upon important points before a
compromise was finally worked out. The Commons agreed that revenue officers should be appointed by the entire legislature and that
they should act under a commission from the governor. In exchange
the Council agreed to accept the Commons' nominees for the various
posts and to require the treasurer to sign two bonds, one to be lodged
with the secretary and the other with the speaker of the House.
Further, the Council acceded to the Commons' demand that it be
given the authority to direct the officers to act by the governor's commission. This last concession implied that the officers derived their
power from the Commons even though they acted by virtue of an
executive commission and, along with the Council's consenting to accept the Commons' nominees, gave the Commons the better end of
the bargain. As long as it was allowed to exercise the right of nomination in practice, the Commons was willing to forego a legal assertion

8. Sept. 13-15, 1721, S. C. Commons Journals, CO 5/426, pp. 121-31.

of that right and to agree to an act vesting the appointment in the legislature as a whole.[9]

The treasurer law, passed as a result of this compromise, provided the foundation for the South Carolina Commons' power over executive appointments. It confirmed "the power, right and authority" of the legislature to nominate and appoint all "civil officers which now do or hereafter may receive a settled salary out of the publick treasury," including the treasurer, commissary general, comptroller, powder receiver, and two port waiters. The act named specific people—the nominees of the Commons—to each of these posts, excluded them from membership in the Commons, and made all of them accountable to either house.[10]

The treasurer was the most important of the officers over whom the Commons thus acquired control. The treasurer law and the general duty law—both passed in September 1721—defined the powers, duties, pay, tenure, and other aspects of the office. The treasurer's powers and duties were twofold. In the first place, he was to receive and hold all duties, taxes, penalties, forfeitures, and impositions levied by the South Carolina legislature. Secondly, he was to dispose of money only upon the order of all three branches of the legislature. The Commons strongly impressed the limitations of the second of these duties upon Alexander Parris, the last proprietary and first royal holder of the post in March 1722, when it reprimanded him "for paying Money on Account of the Publick without Orders as the Law directs" and ordered him not to make any further payments without its consent. Accountable to both the Council and the Commons for all money passing through his hands, the treasurer received as a salary 5 per cent of all money collected, 2½ per cent of all money dispersed, and fees. He held office at the pleasure of the legislature and was required to take an oath of office and to post a bond of £5,000 current Carolina money. Members of both the Council and the Commons were excluded from the office, and the governor and Council were empowered to fill vacancies temporarily until the next meeting of the General Assembly.[11]

9. Sept. 18-20, 1721, *ibid.*, pp. 143-45, 155; Cooper and McCord, eds., *S. C. Statutes*, III, 148-49.

10. Sept. 19, 1721, S. C. Commons Journals, CO 5/426, pp. 144-45; Cooper and McCord, eds., *S. C. Statutes*, III, 148-49.

11. Cooper and McCord, eds., *S. C. Statutes*, III, 148-49, 166-69; Mar. 8, 1722, S. C. Commons Journals, CO 5/426, p. 71.

The treasurer act also empowered the legislature to appoint the commissary general, an office created in 1721 to supply the colony's military garrisons and later to pay for surveying lands for poor Protestant settlers and to provide for Indian presents and military tools and supplies.[12] Unlike the treasurer, the commissary was not concerned with collecting taxes.   Rather, he acted as the colony's agent to procure various goods and services, and he was obliged to draw orders on the treasurer for money to pay for them. The Commons periodically required him to submit his accounts for its inspection and paid him an annual salary ranging from £200 currency in 1734 to £400 currency in 1751. In addition, the commissary received 2½ per cent of all sums that he paid out in the colony's service, which annually amounted to around £300 currency.[13] The treasurer also served as commissary, and, when the Commons removed Alexander Parris from the treasurership in 1735, it also deprived him of the commissary's post. At that time, upon Governor Johnson's recommendation, the Commons separated the two offices because of the increase in the commissary's duties in providing for new settlers. Despite the 1746 recommendation of a Commons' committee that the commissary's office again be combined with the treasurership, the two offices remained separate until the end of the colonial period.[14]

The powder receiver and the receivers and comptroller of the country duties were also appointed by the legislature according to the treasurer law. All of these offices were of proprietary origin. The powder receiver collected from each vessel entering the colony a duty of one-half pound of gun powder per ton, which he kept in the magazine to be used to defend the colony. He derived his support from certain legally established fees payable by shipmasters.[15] Before 1736 the treasurer was the only receiver in the colony, and he collected all import and export duties at Charleston. Assisting him and especially

12. Aug. 16, 1721, S. C. Commons Journals, CO 5/426, p. 50; Commons Journals, June 10, 1748, *S. C. Col. Recs., 1748,* 302-3; May 19, 1749, *ibid., 1749-50,* 154; May 15, 1752, S. C. Commons Journals, CO 5/466, pp. 211-12; Mar. 26, 1756, *ibid.,* CO 5/472, p. 84; Mar. 23, 1757, *ibid.,* CO 5/473, p. 84.

13. Mar. 1, 1722, S. C. Commons Journals, CO 5/426, p. 59; Mar. 1734, *ibid.,* CO 5/433, p. 129; Mar. 28, 1735, *ibid.,* p. 45; May 9, 1751, *ibid.,* CO 5/463, pp. 169-75; Jan. 16, 1755, *ibid.,* CO 5/472, pp. 21-22; Mar. 23, 1757, *ibid.,* CO 5/473, p. 57.

14. Aug. 16, 1721, *ibid.,* CO 5/426, p. 50; Commons Journals, Nov. 29, 1746, *S. C. Col. Recs., 1746-47,* 73; Jan. 16, 1755, S. C. Commons Journals, CO 5/472, pp. 21-22.

15. Cooper and McCord, eds., *S. C. Statutes,* II, 20-21, 42-44, 82-84, 150-53, 213-14, III, 588-90, IV, 104.

concerned in granting permits for importing goods into the province, taking entries from shipmasters on oath as to the amounts of cargo to be landed, and keeping records of such landings was the comptroller. He was required to give bond of £1,000 to the governor, and his income came entirely from fees established by statute. The Commons had appointed a comptroller at least as early as 1703 and had defined his duties and obligations and asserted its right of nomination and appointment by laws of 1716 and 1719. The proprietors disallowed the latter law in July 1719, but under the Crown the Commons again established its right to share in the appointment in the 1721 treasurer's act.[16] Until the mid-1730's Charleston handled almost all of the colony's commerce and there was no need for more than one comptroller and one receiver. But the increase in trade to both Beaufort and Georgetown prompted the Commons in 1736 to pass an ordinance to empower those officers to appoint deputies for those ports, and seven years later the Commons assumed direct authority over the deputies, appointing a receiver and a comptroller by statute for both Beaufort and Georgetown. These officers were subordinate to the public treasurer, with whom they were periodically required to account and to deposit money collected for the public.[17]

In addition, the Commons shared in the appointment of a variety of lesser officers. At least from 1716 it appointed officers known as waiters, gaugers, or searchers to assist the receiver and comptroller in collecting duties. There were two such officers for Charleston and after 1743 two each for Beaufort and Georgetown. As in the case of the comptrollers and receivers, the Commons appointed them by legislative ordinances.[18] After 1719 it also named and appointed tax gatherers in the annual tax acts to collect the yearly levies. They deposited their collections with the public treasurer and were accountable to him, but there are instances in which the Commons required them to account directly to one of its committees.[19]

16. *Ibid.*, II, 202, 649-61, III, 56-69, 159-70.
17. *Ibid.*, III, 413, 597-98, 722-23, 755, IV, 14-15, 44, 154.
18. *Ibid.*, II, 654, III, 148-49, 186, 193, 597-98, 776-77; IV, 14-15, 52, 154, 165.
19. Feb. 8, 1722, S. C. Commons Journals, CO 5/426, p. 26; May 9, 13, 1755, *ibid.*, CO 5/472, pp. 116-18; Cooper and McCord, eds., *S. C. Statutes*, III, 82-83, 149-57, 308-17. In addition to the officers treated here, there was a vendue master, who was not technically a revenue officer but merely a supervisor of the sale of goods in the public markets. By a law of 1710 his appointment was given to the governor. *Ibid.*, II, 348-49. In 1748 the Commons tried to repeal that law allegedly for the purpose of depriving the governor of the power of appointment. Glen to Duke of Bedford, July 27, 1748, CO 5/13, pp. 245-47.

Although the treasurer act carefully specified that appointments be made by joint action of the governor, Council, and Commons, the predominant position of the Commons in the legislature inevitably gave it almost exclusive power in this area. For all practical purposes, the Commons made good its pretension to the sole right of nomination.[20] Only three times during the entire royal period did either the governor or Council challenge that right. The most important challenge came when Gabriel Manigault, who succeeded Parris as treasurer in 1735 after the latter had been found remiss in keeping his accounts, resigned in March 1743.[21]

The Council seized this occasion to assert its equal right to the power of nomination. It immediately accepted the resignation and recommended Othniel Beale for the post. But the Commons had its own candidate, Jacob Motte, and was determined to prevent the Council from participating in the right of nominaiton. The resulting deadlock lasted for a month. The Council would not accept the Commons' compromise candidate, William Cattell, Jr., and the Commons was even less likely to have agreed to the Council's proposal to refer the matter to the governor. Before the Commons could act on that proposal, however, the deadlock was broken by a private arrangement between Motte and Beale. The former persuaded the latter to withdraw from the contest in return for a share of the profits of the treasurership "for 3 or 4 years." The Council then agreed to Motte's appointment, although he had first to persuade the Commons that he had not acted unethically in making a private agreement with Beale.[22]

Motte's appointment can hardly be interpreted as a decisive victory for the Commons. His success was due largely to his own efforts rather than to any show of power by the Commons, though the Com-

20. See Cooper and McCord, eds., *S. C. Statutes*, III, 148-49, 450, 595, 685-86, IV, 14-15, 104, 166, 254, 331; Aug. 3, 16, Sept. 19, 1721, S. C. Commons Journals, CO 5/426, pp. 19, 50, 145; Nov. 21-22, 1734, Mar. 6, 28, 1735, *ibid.*, CO 5/433, pp. 9-10, 34, 45; Commons Journals, Nov. 11, Dec. 3, 1736, Mar. 10, 1738, *S. C. Col. Recs.*, *1736-39*, 12, 31, 532-33; May 20, 1742, *ibid.*, *1741-42*, 502-5; Jan. 14-15, Mar. 19, June 11, 1746, *ibid.*, *1745-46*, 37-40, 153-54, 220-21; Jan. 16, 22-23, 1755, S. C. Commons Journals, CO 5/472, pp. 21-22, 27-29; July 9, 1761, *ibid.*, CO 5/479, p. 183.

21. Mar. 24-28, 1735, S. C. Commons Journals, CO 5/433, pp. 39-46; Commons Journals, Mar. 23, 1743, *S. C. Col. Recs.*, *1742-44*, 312.

22. The actual agreement was for Beale to become security for Motte and to pay half of the salary of the treasurer's clerk in return for half of the profits of the office. Commons Journals, Mar. 24-Apr. 9, Apr. 26-May 3, 1743, *S. C. Col. Recs.*, *1742-44*, 315-16, 349-50, 354-59, 382, 384-85, 389, 404-6, 413-15, 422-24.

mons could probably have forced the Council to yield had the matter not been settled by negotiation. The Commons did just that in 1755 when Glen rather feebly challenged its right to nominate a commissary general. Only once, in 1761 in connection with the appointment of a comptroller in Charleston, did the Commons accept a Council nominee, Samuel Prioleau, who had had considerable support in the Commons before the Council proposed him.[23]

From time to time during the royal period Crown officials complained about the Commons' exercise of the power to appoint revenue officers, but they never made a concerted attempt to deprive the House of that power. The Council's request in 1729 that South Carolina governors be instructed not to permit the Commons to share in the appointment of executive officials elicited no response.[24] Henry McCulloh, the Crown's commissioner of quitrents for the Carolinas, attempted to persuade Lieutenant Governor William Bull I to combine the offices of public treasurer and royal receiver general in 1743, but Bull was much too deft a politician to embark upon such a radical course.[25] Glen's complaint in October 1748 that the "Treasurer, the Person that receives and pays away all the Public money raised for his Majesty, is named by them [the Commons], and cannot be displaced but by them" brought the matter to the Board of Trade's attention. The Board replied that the act of 1721 giving the legislature the power of appointment was a "great Encroachment" on the prerogative and would surely be disallowed, but it did not formally recommend proceedings against the law.[26] With Lyttelton's appointment as governor in 1756 the Board again expressed its disapproval of the measure, declaring it to be "inconsistent with the true principles of the Constitution and . . . an open violation of the Rights and Prerogative of the Crown." It ordered Lyttelton to induce the Commons to repeal the the law and threatened to disallow the measure if its order was not carried out,[27] but again no positive action resulted. Nor did the

23. Jan. 16, 23-24, Feb. 1, Mar. 7, 13, 1755, S. C. Commons Journals, CO 5/472, pp. 1-24, 27, 30, 42, 68, 75; May 7, June 3, 27, July 8, 1761, *ibid.*, CO 5/479, pp. 63, 126, 179, 183; Mar. 31, May 20, 1762, *ibid.*, CO 5/480, pp. 63, 113.

24. Stephen Godin's Proposed Additional Instructions to S. C. Governor, July 30, 1729, CO 5/361, ff. 17-21.

25. Mar. 23-25, 1743, S. C. Council Journals, CO 5/444, pp. 41-42, 47-48, 55-56.

26. Glen to Board of Trade, Oct. 10, 1748, CO 5/372, ff. 80-87, July 15, 1751, CO 5/373, ff. 151-64; Board of Trade to Glen, Nov. 15, 1750, CO 5/402, pp. 233-70.

27. Short Observations, 1756, in Greene, ed., "South Carolina's Colonial Constitution," *S. C. Hist. Mag.*, 62 (1961), 81.

imperial authorities take any remedial measure in response to another official's charge in 1763 that the Commons House had "Arbitrarily Claimed and Exercised" the exclusive powers of nominating and appointing the treasurer.[28]

The Commons had not, of course, actually won the sole right either to nominate or to appoint revenue officers. Appointments were made by formal act of all three branches of the legislature. Nevertheless, the Commons did with only one exception nominate all such officers. Had there ever been any determined opposition to its nominees, almost certainly the Commons would have arbitrarily claimed and exercised the rights of nomination and appointment, as it did in the case of the colonial agent in 1754 and 1755.

The Commons' power over revenue officers was increased by the mechanics of the accounting system. The 1721 treasurer act specified that the treasurer be accountable to both the Council and the Commons, and under the system employed before 1755 a joint committee did audit all officers' accounts. But, because the committee's decisions were made by majority vote and the Commons supplied the majority, it controlled the committee. After 1755 the committee was composed solely of members of the Commons. When the Commons was the major voice in passing and auditing his accounts, the treasurer was unlikely to ignore its directions. Secretary John Hammerton complained to the Board of Trade in 1738 that Treasurer Gabriel Manigault refused to comply with the governor's order to pay him for surveying and granting lands in new townships because the Commons had forbidden him to obey the order. Manigault well knew that he had to obey the command of the Commons if his accounts were to be approved.[29] By coupling the power to audit accounts with the power to appoint and to nominate, the Commons exercised almost absolute authority over the colony's revenue officers.

South Carolina revenue officers did not exercise great political power, as did public treasurers in some other colonies. Although serving for a comparable length of time, Jacob Motte never acquired power or influence equal to that of Speaker-Treasurer John Robinson

28. Report on South Carolina Boundaries, 1763, Stevens Transcripts, I, No. 3, Add. MSS, 42257, ff. 434-56, British Museum.

29. Oct. 4, 1738, *Board of Trade Journals, 1735-41*, 253; July 20, 1738, *Acts of Privy Council, Colonial*, III, 614; John Hammerton to Board of Trade, [1738], CO 5/366, ff. 125-26.

in Virginia. This difference may have been due to the South Carolina legislature's excluding treasurers from membership in either the Commons or the Council. There was no opportunity for them to add the prestige of the speaker's office to that of the treasurer's. In addition, the South Carolina Commons' tight control over the treasurers prevented them from exercising much of the power that they might have wielded as custodians of public funds. In spite of Glen's charge in October 1748 that "the present and last [treasurers] were most unexceptionable Men; but the one before [Parris], by making Partys in the Assembly, keep't himself in 'till he broke with great Sums of the Public money in his Hands,"[30] there is no indication that Parris greatly influenced proceedings in the House.

The power of the North Carolina Lower House to appoint revenue officers was not so extensive as that of the South Carolina Commons. There were no equivalents to the offices of commissary general or comptrollers and receivers of the country duties except during the early 1750's, when the Lower House appointed collectors for each county to gather import duties.[31] Nor does it appear that the House ever made any concerted effort to appoint the powder receivers,[32] and, although county treasurers appointed by statute collected taxes for over twenty years after 1720, the House in 1743 assigned that task to the sheriffs, whom the governor selected for each county from three candidates nominated by the county courts.[33] Nonetheless, it did acquire the power to appoint public treasurers, although its right to do so was a serious issue through much of the royal period.

Scanty records make it impossible to be certain, but it appears that the House first appointed treasurers in 1711 at the beginning of the Tuscarora War to collect important export duties levied to meet military expenses. Burrington's statement in 1733 that before this time there were no public treasurers and that the sheriffs collected

30. Glen to Board of Trade, Oct. 10, 1748, CO 5/372, ff. 80-87.

31. Laws, *N. C. St. Recs.*, XXIII, 363-64, 372-73, 530.

32. It is, however, unclear from existing records exactly who had the right of appointment before 1754. See *ibid.*, 45-46, 401-2; Lower House Journals, Apr. 12-13, 1726, *N. C. Col. Recs.*, II, 618-21; July 13, 1733, *ibid.*, III, 593; Feb. 5, 1735, Mar. 2, 1739, *ibid.*, IV, 130-31, 403; Dobbs's Commissions to Thomas Barker and Wyriot Ormond, Jan. 1755, *ibid.*, V, 328-29.

33. Laws, *N. C. St. Recs.*, XXIII, 122-27, 129-30, 210-12, 217-18, 349-50, 424-32, 526-31, XXV, 162-66; Act to emit £40,000, 1729, Legislative Papers, I, N. C. Dept. of Arch. and Hist.

taxes is probably accurate.[34]   When Burrington became royal governor in 1731, Edward Moseley was acting as public treasurer.   A lawyer and a member of the Council for nearly twenty-five years during three different appointments, Moseley was the leader of the Lower House during his tenure as speaker from 1708 to 1711, 1715 to 1723, and 1731 to 1734 and a champion of a legislative supremacy.[35]   The source of and authority for his appointment as treasurer are not clear.   Failure of the 1711 duty law to produce money fast enough to meet the requirements of the war led the House to create a paper currency, and among the commissioners appointed to issue the currency was Moseley.   In 1714 the Lower House put out additional paper and Moseley was reappointed as well as given the task of supervising the process of exchanging the new currency for the old.   Not until 1722, however, was he actually referred to as public treasurer.   By calling him public treasurer, empowering him to receive certain revenues arising from taxes, and requiring him to give security for the office, an act passed at that time to replace old bills with new in effect made Moseley public treasurer and constituted an acknowledgment by the governor and Council that the power to nominate and appoint the public treasurer, at least in this instance, belonged to the legislature. When the legislature emitted additional currency in 1729, the issuing statute again referred to Moseley as treasurer for the emission of 1722 and assigned him the task of exchanging the new bills for the old. The fact that the 1729 law did not specifically refer to him as public treasurer for the new emission but did designate him one of eleven precinct or county treasurers responsible for collecting taxes levied under the law casts some doubt on whether the House intended him to serve as public treasurer after the old bills were exchanged.   However, he was acting in that capacity at the meeting of North Carolina's first royal legislature in 1731.[36]

Throughout Burrington's administration the questions of who had the power to appoint the public treasurer and whether or not Moseley legally held that office were subjects of a heated controversy.   Disregarding the opinion of Board of Trade Secretary Allured Popple

34. Burrington to Board of Trade, May 19, 1733, N. C. Col. Recs., III, 484.
35. Elizabeth G. McPherson, Edward Moseley: A Study in North Carolina Colonial Politics (unpubl. M.A. thesis, Univ. of North Carolina, 1925).
36. Laws, N. C. St. Recs., XXV, 157-58, 173-75; Burrington to Board of Trade, May 19, 1733, N. C. Col. Recs., III, 483-87; Act to emit £40,000, 1729, Legislative Papers, I, N. C. Dept. of Arch. and Hist.

that the Crown's receiver general was the only receiver necessary or proper for the colony, Burrington in April 1731 presented the Lower House with a copy of his forty-seventh instruction, which specified that no officers were to serve in the colony except under a commission from the governor or the Crown, and informed it of his intention to appoint "a fit person" to act as treasurer until the King commissioned someone to fill that office.[37] The House replied that it was "very well satisfied with the Ability and Integrity of the present Publick Treasurer Ed[war]d Moseley Esquire who was appointed to that office in an Act of Assembly by the Governor Council and Assembly" and argued "that such an officer so appointed is not to be removed but by the like Power." In addition, it contended "that the 47th Instruction doth not extend to officers appointed by Act of Assembly as are the Publick and Precinct Treasurers and sundry other officers" and pointed out "that the Publick Treasurers of our Neighbouring Governments are appointed in like manner by the Governor Council and Assembly."

The Council sided with Burrington in answering the Lower House. It questioned whether Moseley's integrity was equal to his ability, denied that he had been appointed by legal authority, and declared that "Nothing can be more clear or Express than the latter part of the 47th Instruction wherein His Majesty declares that no officer whatever shall be appointed but by himself or his Governor which surely excludes the House of Burgesses from any share in the nomination of a Treasurer unless you can prove that the Treasurer is not a Publick officer." The House interpreted the forty-seventh instruction quite differently, however. Implying that instructions could not supersede colonial laws, it argued that that instruction was "never designed by His majesty to Vacate such Authorities as are granted by Act of Assembly but only to prevent all Persons whatever acting by any Commission from the late Lords Proprietors." The House defended Moseley against the Council's reflections on his character and asserted that "his appointment . . . has been by several Acts of Assembly ever since the year 1715."[38]

Caught in the crossfire between Lower House and Council, Bur-

37. Burrington to Popple, Dec. 8, 1730, Popple to Burrington, Dec. 10, 1730, *N. C. Col. Recs.,* III, 89, 90; Instructions to Burrington, Aug. 13, 1730, CO 5/323, pp. 63-64; Upper House Journals, Apr. 22, 1731, *N. C. Col. Recs.,* III, 263.
38. Upper House Journals, Apr. 26-27, May 1, 1731, *N. C. Col. Recs.,* III, 265-69.

rington wrote to the Duke of Newcastle and the Board of Trade in July 1731, complaining that the "Assembly of this Province have all-ways usurped more power than they ought to be allowed" and citing as the prime example its exercises of the authority to name the public treasurer. He also noted that eleven precinct treasurers appointed by the currency act of 1729 "were all in the Assembly" and constituted "so great a Party that they can lead the Assembly as they please." To remedy this situation he urged that "a Treasurer for this Government be appointed by the Lords of the Treasury." Burrington repeated his suggestion in February 1732, reporting that the "settling Treasurers by the Pretended Act in 1729 is taken from the Method in New England" and warning that "if this were suffered here, these men would have such an influence in Elections, that scarce a man could be Chose but by their approbation." But Crown officials were cautious in their response. Secretary Popple asked Burrington in August 1732 for a report "with respect to the power claimed by the Assembly of chusing the public Treasurer of the Province and what has been the constant practise and by what authority Mr. Moseley was originally appointed."[39]

Burrington's reply was a remarkable analysis of the issues involved in the contest over the right to appoint the public treasurer. It demonstrated a clear understanding of both the position of the lower houses and the immediate implications of that position for the constitutional development of the colonies. The representatives, Burrington reported, claimed "it as their Right to appoint the Province Treasurer who is the keeper of the Province Money." They admitted that the Crown could appoint receivers to handle quitrents and other royal revenues, he wrote, but they argued that they should appoint those who handle money raised by the legislature because those who had "the direction of the end" ought also "to have the appointment of the means or the End may be frustrated" and because it had long been the custom both in North Carolina and other colonies for the legislature to appoint treasurers "for receiving the money they raise." But such practice, Burrington recognized, was contrary to the practice of the home government, where the Crown appointed members of the Treasury to handle funds voted by Parliament. To permit colonial

39. Burrington to Newcastle, July 2, 1731, and to Board of Trade, Feb. 20, 1732, *ibid.*, 151, 335; Popple to Burrington, Aug. 16, 1732, *ibid.*, 354.

lower houses to exercise the right of appointment, he implied, would be to allow them to extend their power beyond that of the House of Commons. Certainly, he declared, "it would be very extraordinary for the Colonys to assert or claim a higher right or Privilege than the People of England enjoy," and suggested that "if the Colonys have assumed that Power in any place it may have rather passed unobserved then allowed of or Established."[40]

Despite Burrington's frequent entreaties, Gabriel Johnston, upon his appointment as governor in 1734, found the situation in regard to the public treasurer still unchanged. Perhaps Burrington's unpopularity with the Board of Trade provides a partial explanation for its inaction, but the fact that the Board showed little interest in a similar appeal from Johnston before he went out to the colony leads one to conclude that it simply failed to realize the importance of the treasurership in North Carolina. In the meantime Moseley continued to act as public treasurer at least through February 1735.[41]

Once he was in office, Johnston did not challenge the Lower House's power of appointment, and during his administration the House strengthened its hold on that power. Sometime between 1735 and 1740 the House divided the office, appointing two public treasurers. Moseley, who became for the third time a member of the Council in 1735, was appointed treasurer for the southern counties, and the speakers, William Downing until 1739 and John Hodgson from 1740 to 1748, treasurers for the northern counties.[42] During the same period the Lower House abandoned the institution of precinct treasurers, assigning their duties to the sheriffs in 1740.[43] A law in 1748 substituted as treasurer for the southern counties Thomas Barker for Hodgson, who after 1746 had assumed the leadership of the Albemarle opposition to the long assembly during the representation controversy with Johnston. The same law specifically defined the duties,

40. Burrington to Board of Trade, May 19, 1733, *ibid.*, 483-84. See also Moseley to Burrington and Council, Apr. 3, 1733, *ibid.*, 489-90.

41. Johnston's remarks on his Instructions, [1733-34], *ibid.*, 495-96; Upper House Journals, Feb. 25, 1735, *ibid.*, IV, 102.

42. The separation was probably effected in one of two tax bills passed in 1735, neither of which is extant. Laws, *N. C. St. Recs.*, XXIII, 117, 121. Developments in the treasurership over this period can be traced in *ibid.*, 131, 155, 275; Council Journals, Nov. 20, 1739, Feb. 15, 1740, *N. C. Col. Recs.*, IV, 354, 441; and James Murray to [Mr. Houston], Mar. 25, 1740, Nina M. Tiffany, ed., *Letters of James Murray, Loyalist* (Boston, 1901), 59.

43. Laws, *N. C. St. Recs.*, XXIII, 151-57.

salary, and tenure of the treasurers. They were to receive from the
sheriffs all taxes levied by the legislature, submit their accounts to the
legislature for auditing, and put up a bond of £2,000 sterling. Their
salary was to be 5 per cent of their total receipts, and their term four
years, the governor and Council being empowered to fill vacancies
temporarily when the legislature was not in session.[44]

During Johnston's administration the Lower House also established its exclusive right to nominate the treasurers. Moseley's being
treasurer from his appointment to the Council in 1735 until his death
in 1749 constituted a precedent for one of the treasurers' being from
the Council. The appointment of Eleazer Allen, also a councilor, to
succeed Moseley strengthened the precedent, and upon Allen's death
in 1750 the Council insisted that Councilor George Nicholas succeed
him. But the House nominated John Starkey and, when the Council
continued to insist upon Nicholas, declared that it had always held
the "right to nominate a person for that Office." The Council expressed surprise at the representatives' assertion of "an exclusive right
to the nomination of such person," alluding vaguely to "precedents
to the contrary," and rejected the bill to appoint Starkey. But some
three months later, for reasons not entirely clear, it finally agreed to
Starkey's appointment.[45] From that date on treasurers were members
of the Lower House, which always exercised the right of nomination.

Unlike Johnston, Dobbs seriously challenged the authority of the
Lower House to nominate and appoint treasurers. In December 1754,
at the beginning of his tenure, he assented to a military appropriation
bill that reappointed Starkey as southern treasurer and Barker, who
after his resignation in 1752 had been succeeded by John Haywood,
as northern treasurer.[46] But he later regretted this action and frequently assailed the act as well as the two treasurers.

For nearly three years matters between Dobbs and the treasurers
ran smoothly, but Starkey's leadership of the opposition in the Lower
House, culminating in 1757 in its refusal to accept some of Dobbs's
defense measures, finally moved Dobbs to attack its right to appoint
treasurers. Characterizing Starkey as "a professed violent Republi-

44. *Ibid.*, 273-75.
45. Upper House Journals, Apr. 4-5, 1750, *N. C. Col. Recs.*, IV, 1058-60; Lower
House Journals, July 7-9, 1750, *ibid.*, 1071-72; Laws, *N. C. St. Recs.*, XXIII, 331-32,
349-50.
46. Laws, *N. C. St. Recs.*, XXIII, 378-80, 400.

can," Dobbs accused him in a letter to the Board of Trade in December 1757 of "opposing all taxes that do not turn out to his profit," of "attempting to gain power to the Assembly by encroaching upon his Majesty's Rights," and of "having taken upon himself the payment of the allowance to the Members for their attendance which he can advance or delay as he pleases so that all the low Members who want a supply follow him like Chickens so that he sways the House against the most sensible Members in it." To lessen Starkey's power Dobbs proposed that the Crown disallow the 1754 appropriation bill by which the treasurers had been appointed and issue "an Instruction for the future not to pass any Law for appointing provincial Treasurers without excluding them from being Members of either House." He also urged the Board to consider whether it would not be worth losing the £3,600 in paper bills still circulating from that act to prevent "the Obstruction given to the Kings service here by that Republican Treasurer Starkey." By this action the Crown could deprive the House of the power of appointment which, Dobbs observed, was "an Encroachment upon the Crown."[47]

When the Board did not indicate immediate interest in his proposals, Dobbs launched a concerted campaign to have the treasurers removed. In January 1759 he wrote the Board that Starkey acted "not as His Majesty's Treasurer for his service, but calls himself Treasurer for the Public not accountable to the Crown." Once more he pressed the Board for the disallowance of the law that had appointed the treasurers and emphasized that "an approaching peace, when nothing will be required but for their own benefit will be a proper time to insist upon his Majesty's Prerogative." Reiterating his complaints the following May, he suggested that "his Majesty or Governor and Council here should appoint one or two Treasurers who should account with the Government here and with the Treasury in England."[48]

Finally, in June 1759, the Board submitted his complaints against the treasurers to the Treasury and the following August issued its final opinion on the matter. In an unusually enlightened decision the Board declared that the "practise which has prevailed for so long a time in all the Colonies of appointing Publick Treasurers by Act of Legislature and making them accountable only to the General Assem-

47. Dobbs to Board of Trade, Dec. 27, 1757, *N. C. Col. Recs.*, V, 948-49.
48. Dobbs to Board of Trade, Jan. 22, May 18, 1759, *ibid.*, VI, 6-7, 33.

bly and in some Cases to one branch of it, is certainly irregular and it is to be wished that it had been properly checked in its infancy, but having prevailed and been acquiesced in for so long a series of years, any attempt to set it aside in the present situation of Affairs would in Our judgment be improper and therefore we cannot advise the repeal of the Aid Act passed by You in 1754, especially when We consider that a considerable part of the Taxes thereby to be raised would be lost by such repeal."[49] The decision was an important one, constituting as it did a frank admission by Crown officials of the futility of trying to deprive the Lower House of a long-established power when its support was needed in the war effort. It showed clearly that imperial authorities were prepared, if not to recognize officially, at least to tolerate indefinitely the lower houses' exercise of the power to nominate and appoint public treasurers.

The Board's decision might have left Dobbs with small hope of wresting the powers of nominating and appointing public treasurers from the Lower House. Without prospect of support from the home authorities, he could well have abandoned his efforts entirely. That he did not is a testimony to his tenacity and optimism. He gave up his attempts to obtain immediate reforms, but he took pains to keep the matter fresh in the minds of imperial officials. He suggested to the Board in January 1760 that the clause appointing the treasurers without limitation of time in the 1754 appropriation bill might be disallowed when that law expired in 1763. Simultaneously he submitted a copy of Barker's accounts to illustrate how carelessly they were kept. Moreover, he removed Starkey from his posts as justice of the peace and colonel of the militia for Onslow County in an effort to curb the treasurer's power, which he had come to regard as a serious challenge to his own.[50] He repeated these suggestions and complaints in December 1761, but his continued efforts made little impression on the Board of Trade, which for the most part either ignored them or curtly dismissed them as it did in May 1763 by referring Dobbs back to the "Sentiments and Directions" in the "Mode of appointing Treasurers" that it had set forth in 1759. [51]

49. Board of Trade to Dobbs, June 1, Aug. 1, 1759, *ibid.*, 45, 55-56.
50. Dobbs to Board of Trade, Jan. 19, 1760, *ibid.*, 217-18; Dobbs's reply to May 1760 resolutions of Lower House, Aug. 3, 1760, *ibid.*, 297-98.
51. Dobbs to Board of Trade, Dec. 12, 1760, *ibid.*, 319-24; Dobbs's Answers to Board of Trade's Queries, Dec. 1761, *ibid.*, 619-20; Board of Trade to Dobbs, May 10, 1763, CO 5/325, ff. 113-14.

When the 1754 appropriation bill expired in 1763, Dobbs had no other alternative than to assent to a new treasurer's bill. At the legislative session in February 1764 he offered to accept a bill to appoint treasurers for a short term until the Crown had instructed him how they should be appointed for the future. At first the Lower House denied that the clause appointing the treasurers in the 1754 bill had expired. But Barker, who had been prevented from resigning in November 1760 by Dobbs's maneuvers to appoint his successor,[52] was still pressing the House for leave to resign, and, when both Dobbs and the Council signified their willingness to concur in the matter, the House took the opportunity to put the treasurerships on a more solid legal footing by passing a bill that continued Starkey as southern treasurer and appointed Representative Joseph Montfort to succeed Barker in the northern post. Dobbs did gain one important concession in this bill when he persuaded the Lower House to limit the treasurers' term of office to three years. In reporting upon the act to the Board of Trade, he explained that he had passed it "to put it out of doubt, lest some should refuse to pay the public Taxes to other Treasurers should they have been appointed by the Crown."[53] Dobbs had, in effect, admitted that he was unable to prevent the Lower House from exercising the power to appoint treasurers. He probably still hoped to enlist the aid of imperial authorities in his fight, but at no time after their 1759 decision was there any real possibility that his hopes would be fulfilled. Neither of Dobbs's successors was bold enough even to challenge the Lower House upon the matter, and it continued to appoint treasurers by statute for the remainder of the colonial period.

Although the governors had conceded the power of appointment to the Lower House, the Council was not yet ready to surrender its claim to the right of nomination. John Starkey's death early in 1765 set the stage for an extended controversy between the Lower House and the Council over who should succeed him. When Barker had attempted to resign in November 1760, the Lower House, in order to obtain the Council's consent to a measure appointing a London

---

52. On this incident see Dobbs to Board of Trade, Dec. 12, 1760, *N. C. Col. Recs.*, VI, 319-24; Lower House Journals, Dec. 1-3, 1760, *ibid.*, 502-3, 508; Upper House Journals, Dec. 3, 1760, *ibid.*, 469.

53. Dobbs to Board of Trade, Mar. 29, 1764, *ibid.*, 1035-36; Laws, *N. C. St. Recs.*, XXIII, 618-19; Upper House Journals, Feb. 4, Mar. 5, 1764, *N. C. Col. Recs.*, VI, 1091, 1127-29; Lower House Journals, Feb. 8, Mar. 3, 1764, *ibid.*, 1154a, 1199.

agent, had agreed to accept Councilor John Rieussett as his successor, although it had stipulated that the incident did not constitute a precedent or contravene its "inherent right" to nominate.[54]   Now, however, the Council insisted upon its right of nomination, refused to accept House candidate Richard Caswell, and held out for Councilor Lewis De Rossett.   Neither side would give in, so, to fill the vacancy until the legislature agreed on a candidate, Tryon appointed Speaker Samuel Swann, a popular choice with the House and one that would certainly not destroy his good relations with that body.[55]   When the legislature met again in November 1760, Tryon was unable to prevent another battle between the two houses with the Council once again insisting on De Rossett and the House supporting Assemblyman John Ashe.   Only after the House had agreed that it would not deem the act "as the relinquishing any rights which in your opinion you have to a joint nomination" would the Council finally accept Ashe. But the matter was settled only temporarily, for the 1764 treasurer bill was to expire at the end of 1767.   The Council's declaration in consenting to Ashe that "the appointment of a Provincial Treasurer is a creation of the legislature here, dissimilar from and repugnant to the constitution of the British Government" and that it had "a co-equal right" with the Lower House "both in the nomination and appointment" was a strong indication that the Council would revive the controversy.[56]   But the Council did not again contest the House's right of nomination, permitting it to reappoint Montfort and Ashe in 1766 for a term of five years and to rename Montfort and replace Ashe with Richard Caswell in 1773.[57]

The importance of the Lower House's having control over the treasurers was revealed in the 1770's when they obeyed its order to suspend the collection of taxes voted to retire the colony's paper currency despite Governor Josiah Martin's express orders to the contrary.

54. Lower House Journals, Dec. 1-3, 1760, *N. C. Col. Recs.*, VI, 502-3, 508; Upper House Journals, Dec. 3, 1760, *ibid.*, 469.

55. Upper House Journals, May 16, 1765, *ibid.*, VII, 55-56; Tryon to Board of Trade, Aug. 15, 1765, *ibid.*, 107.

56. Lower House Journals, Nov. 6, 10, 1766, *ibid.*, 348-49, 356; Upper House Journals, Nov. 20, 25-27, Dec. 1, 1766, *ibid.*, 312-14, 324, 327-28, 330-31, 337; Laws, *N. C. St. Recs.*, XXV, 494-95.

57. Tryon to Shelburne, Jan. 31, Mar. 7, July 4, 1767, *N. C. Col. Recs.*, VII, 430-31, 443, 497; Upper House Journals, Jan. 4, 15, 1768, Jan. 25, Mar. 1, 1773, *ibid.*, 597-99, 622-23; IX, 378, 428; Laws, *N. C. St. Recs.*, XXIII, 723-25, 904-6; Martin to Dartmouth, May 30, 1773, *N. C. Col. Recs.*, IX, 657.

Like Dobbs, Martin became convinced that the Crown should take steps to gain the power to appoint the treasurers. The Lower House had "long fatally to the policy of this Country, usurped the nomination of those Officers," he lamented in September 1774, requesting Dartmouth to consider "whether it will not be . . . expedient if it can be done with propriety to vest in his Majesty's Governor the appointment of Treasurers."[58] Martin's request was remarkably similar to Dobbs's requests ten and fifteen years earlier and, like them, failed to win any support at home. The Lower House's power to nominate and appoint public treasurers continued undiminished.

In Virginia, as in North Carolina, the power of the House of Burgesses was limited by the fact that the governor and Council appointed most of the minor revenue officers, including the collectors of special duties on skins, furs, liquors, and slaves and servants; sheriffs, who were responsible for collecting taxes; and commissaries, who purchased and distributed provisions to the Virginia forces during the Seven Years' War. However, with the exception of the collectors of the duty on skins and furs, who were responsible to the College of William and Mary, all of these officers were accountable to the public treasurer, who was nominated and appointed by the House of Burgesses.[59]

The Virginia Burgesses was, in fact, the first of the southern lower houses to gain the power to appoint a treasurer. The Crown had chosen the treasurer in Virginia until April 1691, when Lieutenant Governor Nicholson permitted the Burgesses to nominate and appoint by statute its former speaker, Colonel Edward Hill, to act as treasurer to handle money arising from two revenue acts. But a year later Nicholson appointed Hill to a collectorship, thereby forcing him to resign as treasurer. In his place Nicholson appointed Councilor Henry Whiting. By this maneuver Nicholson hoped to wrest the power of appointment from the Burgesses, and the Council stood behind him, rejecting the Burgesses' attempt in March 1693 to appoint its own nominee. Whiting continued as treasurer until his death in 1694, but the Crown's disapproval in 1693 of the revenue measures

58. Martin to Hillsborough, Jan. 30, 1772, and to Dartmouth, Apr. 2, Sept. 1, 1774, *N. C. Col. Recs.*, IX, 233-34, 960-61, 1051-54.

59. Hening, ed., *Va. Statutes*, III, 23-24, 63-66, 88-92, 123-24, 229-35, 264-67, 344-49, 356-58, IV, 143-50, V, 54-57, 236-37, 310-18, VII, 26-33, 272, 284-85; Robert Dinwiddie to Major John Carlyle, Jan. 27, 1754, Brock, ed., *Dinwiddie Papers*, I, 439-40.

of 1691 removed the need for such an officer. Nevertheless, the Burgesses continued to demand the power to appoint a treasurer and in 1699, after a five-year contest, finally forced Nicholson to accede by refusing to vote money to replace the recently burned capitol unless it was allowed to name a treasurer to receive that money. The Burgesses appointed a former speaker, Robert Carter, and continued to exercise the power to name and appoint the treasurer for the remainder of the colonial period.[60]

Between 1699 and 1738 the duties, salary, tenure, and other aspects of the treasurership took their final shape. The treasurer received from collectors and held all revenues arising from provincial laws, disposed of those revenues upon the Burgesses' order and the governor's warrant, and accounted with the Burgesses.[61] His salary was 4 per cent of all money passing through the office until 1748, when the Burgesses raised it to 5 per cent. Five men held the office during these years. After Carter, the Burgesses appointed Benjamin Harrison, Jr., in 1705, Peter Beverley in 1710, John Holloway in 1723, and Sir John Randolph in 1734.[62] Each of these men had been or was at the time of his appointment speaker of the House, and from 1710 to 1766, except for a seven-year period after 1715 when its altercation with Spotswood prevented it from replacing Beverley with its new speaker, Daniel McCarty,[63] the Burgesses combined the offices of speaker and treasurer, the treasurer holding office until he was succeeded as speaker. In the event of a vacancy between legislative sessions, the governor and Council appointed a temporary replacement to serve until the House met again.[64]

60. Hening, ed., *Va. Statutes*, III, 92-94, 197-99; May 14, 1691, Mar. 24-31, 1693, *Va. Burgesses Journals, 1659-93*, 370, 437-44; Andros's Proclamation, Sept. 1, 1693, CO 5/1308; Locke's Essay toward Remedys of Grievances of Virginia Constitution, *ca.* 1698, Locke MSS, c. 9, Bodleian Lib.; Hartwell, Blair, and Chilton, *Present State of Virginia*, 62-63; Wertenbaker, *Give Me Liberty*, 129; Flippin, *Royal Government of Virginia*, 275-76.

61. Included in these revenues were money from the duties on liquors, slaves, and servants; the public levy; and all special taxes. Hening, ed., *Va. Statutes*, III, 92-94, 197-99, 476-78, 495-96, IV, 135-38, 150-51, 182, 433-36.

62. *Ibid.*, III, 92-94, 476-78, 495-96, IV, 135-38, 150-51, 182, 433-36. The salary varied with the amount of money passing through the office. Fauquier reported in 1758 that it normally amounted to about £300 a year but in wartime rose to £1,000 annually. Fauquier to Board of Trade, June 28, 1758, CO 5/1329, ff. 175-78.

63. For the Burgesses' attempt to appoint McCarty treasurer, see May 21, 29, 1718, *Va. Burgesses Journals, 1712-26*, 200-201, 214; Spotswood to Board of Trade, June 24, 1718, Brock, ed., *Spotswood Letters*, II, 278-79.

64. Hening, ed., *Va. Statutes*, III, 92-94, 197-99, 476-78, 495-96, IV, 135-38, 150-51, 182, 433-36. An instance of the governor and Council's making an interim

By 1738 both the royal governors and the London authorities had at least tacitly admitted the Burgesses' power to nominate and appoint the treasurer. Commenting in 1711 on the act to appoint Peter Beverley to the treasurership, Spotswood observed without protest that such an act passed "of Course every Session of Assembly, where any Duty is laid on publick debts to be paid." Similarly, neither Drysdale nor Gooch objected to subsequent appointments.[65] Nor did London authorities contest the Burgesses' power to appoint the treasurer. In reporting on a 1723 measure to appoint John Holloway to the office, Board of Trade legal counsel Richard West observed with an air of resignation that "it seems to be now a practice in all the American Colonies for their respective Generall Assemblys to assume to themselves the nomination of all Officers Relateing to the Revenue," and West's successor, Francis Fane, did not object to a 1734 law to appoint Sir John Randolph.[66] The Board of Trade could have recommended some repressive action to check the Burgesses' control over the treasurership after West had called the matter to its attention. But it did not, handling the matter in the same casual manner that characterized much of its treatment of colonial affairs during the second quarter of the eighteenth century and permitting the Burgesses to continue nominating and appointing the treasurer.

From 1738 to 1766 John Robinson filled the offices of treasurer and speaker.[67] During his twenty-eight year tenure, Robinson's power in the colony was nearly as great as the lieutenant governor's. Some historians attribute it to his control over Virginia's treasury. Upon his death an examination of his accounts revealed that he had loaned large sums of public as well as private money to burgesses and councilors alike. This revelation gave rise to the assertion that Robinson made opportune loans to gain votes and influence in both chambers of the legislature, although the complete absence of any evidence

---

appointment to fill a vacancy occurred in 1737. Mar. 18, 1737, *Exec. Journals of Va. Council,* IV, 389. Fauquier reported that the motive in attaching the treasurership to the speakership was to provide a recompense for the speaker. Fauquier to Board of Trade, June 28, 1758, CO 5/1329, ff. 175-78.

65. Spotswood to Board of Trade, Mar. 6, 1711, Brock, ed., *Spotswood Letters,* I, 58; Drysdale's Observations on Va. laws, June 29, 1723, CO 5/1319; Gooch to Board of Trade, Nov. 20, 1734, CO 5/1323, ff. 149-58.

66. Reports of West to Board of Trade, Jan. 10, 1724, and of Fane to Board of Trade, Nov. 16, 1735, CO 5/1323, ff. 177-79.

67. Hening, ed., *Va. Statutes,* V, 64-65, 173-74, VI, 195-97, 248-50, VII, 33-35, 242-44, 466-69.

of irregularity in his accounts before 1765 renders the validity of such an assertion doubtful. Indications are that the deficiency in his accounts discovered in 1766 was of recent origin.[68] The real secret of his power would seem to have been his long tenure and his immense popularity.

Both Gooch and Fauquier got along well with Robinson. Gooch voiced no objections to him, and Fauquier described him in 1759 as "a Man of Worth, Probity and Honor, the most beloved both in his public and private Character of any Man in the Colony" and again in 1761 as "the Darling of the Country, as he well deserves to be for his great integrity, assiduity and ability in business." Gooch and Fauquier accepted Robinson's power and worked in harmony with him.[69] On the other hand, Dinwiddie disliked Robinson because of his opposition to the pistole fee in 1753-54. It will be recalled that during the dispute over that fee Robinson proposed to pay Peyton Randolph £2,500 without the consent of the governor or Council for acting as agent for the House. Further, Dinwiddie reported that Robinson had "behaved with great Warmth and ill Manners" to him. From that time on Dinwiddie sought to lessen Robinson's power by trying to separate the offices of speaker and treasurer. He was determined, he wrote James Abercromby in October 1754, "on calling a new Assembly to regulate it [the combined offices of speaker and treasurer] for the Future in a more Constitutional Method."[70]

Robinson's display of power during the Seven Years' War intensified Dinwiddie's dislike for him. The observation by the historian George Chalmers that "in a practical view of government, Dinwiddie ruled on ordinary occasion . . . But Robinson acted as dictator on all emergencies" is accurate.[71] Dinwiddie depended upon the Robinson-dominated Burgesses for supplies and men, and, when the Burgesses reappointed Robinson after the 1756 election, Dinwiddie was forced to consent to the appointment. He had not abandoned his conviction that the offices of speaker and treasurer should be separated, but he

68. George Chalmers, *An Introduction to the History of the Revolt of the American Colonies*, 2 vols. (Boston, 1845), II, 353-54; Mays, *Edmund Pendleton*, I, 176-77, 184.

69. Fauquier to Board of Trade, Apr. 10, 1759, May 12, 1761, CO 5/1329, ff. 303-6, CO 5/1330, ff. 129-35.

70. Dinwiddie to Board of Trade, May 10, 1754, and to James Abercromby, Oct. 23, 1754, Brock, ed., *Dinwiddie Papers*, I, 160-62, 373-76.

71. Chalmers, *History of the Revolt*, II, 353-54.

realized that the necessity of securing a military appropriation and of getting on with the Burgesses during the course of the war precluded any possibility of separating them at that time. But Dinwiddie continued his campaign for separation after he stepped down as lieutenant governor. He brought the matter to the attention of the Board of Trade, which directed his successor, Fauquier, to separate the offices "if it could be done without prejudice to his Majesties Service," although the Board purposely did not make this directive a formal instruction in order to give the new governor some latitude in such a "delicate Affair."[72]

Fauquier never attempted to carry out this directive. Shortly after his arrival in Virginia in June 1758, he submitted it to the members of the Council and to Attorney General Peyton Randolph, all of whom advised him "that this could not be effected without manifest prejudice to his Majestie's Service" and that to attempt it "might throw the Country into a Flame." Not only was the practice of long standing but also Robinson was "the most popular Man in the Country: beloved by the gentlemen, and the Idol of the people." These findings, plus the necessity of keeping the Burgesses in good humor so it would vote money for the war, persuaded Fauquier not to attempt an immediate separation of the two offices. By consulting directly with Robinson, Fauquier established a harmonious spirit that distinguished his entire administration and resulted in Robinson's support of Fauquier's defense proposals.[73] Although the Board of Trade continued to contend that combining the two offices was "both irregular and unconstitutional" and to urge Fauquier to effect a separation, he found to the Board's displeasure that it was more to his advantage to maintain good relations with Robinson than to attempt to implement the Board's directive. Twice, in 1758 and 1761, Fauquier risked the censure of the Board by passing measures to continue Robinson as speaker and treasurer, and he expressed his determination to do so again in 1766 when the dissolution of the legislature made a new law necessary.[74]

72. Hening, ed., *Va. Statutes*, VII, 33-35; Fauquier to Board of Trade, Apr. 10, 1759, CO 5/1329, ff. 303-6.

73. Fauquier to Board of Trade, June 11, 28, Sept. 23, 1758, Apr. 10, 1759, Mar. 13, 1760, CO 5/1329, ff. 171-73, 175-78, 185-90, 303-6, 399-403.

74. Board of Trade to Fauquier, Jan. 18, Nov. 20, 1759, CO 5/1367, pp. 350-54, 397-98, Sept. 10, 1761, July 22, 1766, CO 5/1368; Fauquier to Board of Trade, May 12, 1761, Feb. 24, 1762, CO 5/1330, ff. 129-35, 219-22, June 5, 1765, CO 5/1331;

But Robinson died in the spring of 1766 before the passage of a
new law, and the disclosure that he had loaned large sums of public
money to his indebted friends, including a number of the most prominent politicians in Virginia,[75] convinced the Burgesses of the impropriety of continuing to unite the two offices.   The House solved
Fauquier's problem by voluntarily detaching the treasurership from
the speakership, appointing Robert Carter Nicholas as treasurer and
Peyton Randolph as speaker.   To compensate Randolph for the loss
of income involved in the speaker's losing the treasurer's office, the
Burgesses granted him an annual salary of £500, which was later
raised to £600.[76]   It continued to follow this arrangement for the
remainder of the colonial period, and both Randolph and Nicholas
held their posts until after Virginia had committed itself to the
Revolution.

Unlike the lower houses in the other southern royal colonies, the
Georgia Commons did not before 1763 win the right either to nominate or to appoint any revenue officers except the tax collectors appointed in the annual tax laws.[77]   By the time the Crown took over
Georgia in the 1750's, London officials were thoroughly aware of the
danger to the prerogative from lower houses' appointing and controlling revenue officers.   In Georgia, therefore, the Crown assigned the
duties that the powder receiver performed in South Carolina to one
of its naval office clerks, and the governors appointed the public
treasurer, the only officer concerned to any important extent in handling provincial revenues during the early years of royal government.
Three men—Jonathan Bryan, James Edward Powell, and Noble Jones
—held the office.   Reynolds appointed the first two in May 1755 and

Nov. 14, 1761, *Va. Burgesses Journals, 1761-65,* 26-27; Hening, ed., *Va. Statutes,*
VII, 242-44, 466-69.

75. Mays, *Edmund Pendleton,* I, 174-208, 358-85, gives an excellent discussion
of this affair.

76. Hening, ed., *Va. Statutes,* VIII, 210-14, 394-95, 587-88; Nov. 7, 1766, *Va.
Burgesses Journals, 1766-69,* 11; Robert Carter Nicholas to Col. William Preston,
May 21, 1766, Preston Papers, 2 QQ 97, Draper MSS, State Historical Society of
Wisconsin, Madison; Fauquier to Board of Trade, May 11, 1766, and to Lord
Shelburne, Nov. 18, 1766, CO 5/1331, CO 5/1345; Dunmore's Answers to Board of
Trade's Queries, 1774, CO 5/1352; William Nelson to Edward and Samuel Athawes,
Nov. 13, 1766, William Nelson Letter Book, Va. State Lib.

77. Statutes, *Ga. Col. Recs.,* XVIII, 69-70, 159-60, 167-68, 244, 343, 398-99, XIX,
Pt. I, 36-37, 62, 107-12, 136, 168-72, 453-55, 460-62.

April 1756 respectively, and Ellis appointed the third in May 1760.[78] All three were councilors at the time of their appointment, and only Powell had served as a member of the Commons. They collected all taxes and duties levied by the legislature and held office at the governor's pleasure or until they resigned. Their pay was 5 per cent of all taxes received, which in 1773 usually amounted to about £150 sterling per annum, plus perquisites, which amounted to as much as £83 annually.[79] Although Georgia treasurers were neither nominated nor appointed by the Commons, they were not entirely beyond its control. The first tax act passed under the Crown in 1755 required the treasurer to submit his accounts to the Commons whenever it wanted to inspect them. The Commons followed that practice throughout the royal period and thereby exercised enough control over the treasurer to prevent him from misapplying public money.[80] At no time did the Commons attempt to secure the power to appoint the treasurer. Nor did it initially show any interest in extending its appointive powers, permitting the functions performed by the comptroller in South Carolina to be assigned to the Crown's local comptroller of the King's customs when it first imposed provincial duties in 1762.[81] Not until the mid-1760's did it make a concerted bid to establish its power to appoint a variety of executive officials.

By 1763 the lower houses in the three older colonies were exercising the power of nomination and appointment to important revenue posts, thus depriving the governors of part of their appointive power and in their limited spheres extending their authority beyond that of the British House of Commons, which left the appointment of revenue officers entirely to the Crown. The South Carolina Commons enjoyed the most extensive authority over officials of the revenue. It nominated and appointed by statute the treasurer, commissary general, comptrollers and receivers of the country duties, port waiters, powder

78. Council Journals, May 23, 1755, Apr. 3, 1756, Mar. 26, 1760, *ibid.*, VII, 177, 335, VIII, 266; Reynolds to Board of Trade, Mar. 29, 1756, unpubl. Ga. Col. Recs., XVII, 262, Ga. Dept. of Arch. and Hist.

79. See Statutes, *Ga. Col. Recs.*, XIX, Pt. I, 42; Wright's Answers to Board of Trade's Queries, Nov. 15, 1766, unpubl. Ga. Col. Recs., XXVIII, Pt. II-A, 438, Ga. Dept. of Arch. and Hist.; Wright to Shelburne, May 15, 1767, *ibid.*, XXXVII, 208-9; Report of Sir James Wright on the State of Georgia, Sept. 20, 1773, Ga. Hist. Soc., *Collections*, 3 (1873), 172-73.

80. See Commons Journals, July 7, 12, 1757, *Ga. Col. Recs.*, XIII, 200, 206-7.

81. Statutes, *ibid.*, XVIII, 484-88.

receivers, and tax gatherers.   The North Carolina Lower House
appointed the public treasurers and for a time the collectors of public
duties, and the Virginia Burgesses appointed the treasurer.   By unit-
ing the speakership with the treasurership, the South Carolina Commons between 1692 and 1700, the Virginia Burgesses between 1710
and 1766, and the North Carolina Lower House for much of the
period between 1711 and 1748 went even further and combined the
top legislative post with an important executive one.   Indeed, all
three of them were already nominating and appointing treasurers by
1715 before imperial authorities realized all of the implications involved in the lower houses' choosing and controlling such important
executive officers.   By the time Crown authorities recognized the
seriousness of the situation, they hesitated to try to curb the lower
houses in the exercise of such a long-established power for fear of
raising storms of controversy in the colonies.   However, they did take
steps to prevent the Georgia Commons from seizing the authority to
select revenue officers when they took over that colony in the 1750's
with the result that that body was unable to secure the power to
appoint any officers except the annual tax collectors in the years before 1763.   Nevertheless, they did not modify their policy in regard
to the older colonies, and in 1759 they actually conceded the power
to appoint treasurers to the North Carolina Lower House.   Nor did
imperial officials alter that policy when they adopted a stricter colonial
program after 1763, not once making any effort to deprive the lower
houses in the older colonies of their powers of nomination or appointment.

12

Public Works and Services

Aᴍᴇʀɪᴄᴀɴ lower houses frequently appointed commissioners to direct the construction of public works or to supervise public services. Appointed to execute specific tasks and to apply funds appropriated to those tasks, such commissioners provided lower houses with a convenient device to assume some control over executive affairs. They were almost invariably directly accountable to the lower houses, which in many cases supervised their activities closely. This practice was not peculiar to the colonies. Parliament had followed it as early as 1427 in making statutory provision for sewer commissioners to survey walls, dikes, sewers, bridges, weirs, and other drainage devices and to see that they were kept in repair. By the end of the sixteenth century the sewer commissioners had become an integral part of local administrative machinery and in the later seventeenth and early eighteenth centuries constituted a well-established precedent for Parliament's extending the commissioner system to three other areas: poor administration, road building, and civic improvement. Before the English Civil War Parliament had usually left the nomination of such commissioners to the lord chancellor and other chief officers of the Crown, but after 1660 it quite often named the commissioners in the statutes providing for their offices and thereby usurped the right of nomination from the Crown. After the initial appointment, however, Parliament did not exercise such close control over commissioners as did the American lower houses. Nor did it make such extensive use of the system, rarely appointing commissioners to handle tasks outside the four areas mentioned above and leaving the vast majority of its appropriations to be disposed of by officers of the Crown.[1] In contrast, some American lower houses employed commissioners for nearly every detail of administration. With the exception of the Virginia Burgesses, southern lower houses used them extensively during the eighteenth century.

Legislative use of commissioners to perform executive tasks was most common in South Carolina. Governor James Glen complained to the Board of Trade in October 1748 that "much of the executive part of the Government and of the Administration, is by various Laws lodged in different setts of Commissioners, Thus we have Commissioners of the Market, of the Work house, of the Pilots, of Fortifications, and so on, without number."[2] Glen was not exaggerating. Power was centralized in the Commons, which delegated the authority to perform public works or services, whether purely local or pertaining to the colony as a whole, to "different setts of Commissioners." Indeed, through the commissioner system the Commons extended its authority over nearly every aspect of government from building a church in a parish distant from Charleston to erecting fortifications for the colony's protection. There was almost no division of power between central and local governments.

South Carolina commissioners executed a multitude of purely local tasks. For the parishes they carried on all public works, including building and maintaining bridges, roads, and highways; establishing and regulating ferries; clearing and improving creeks and rivers; and building parish churches. They also performed most public services, such as establishing schools, maintaining the watch and enforcing town ordinances in Charleston, and caring for the poor. In addition, they handled matters which pertained both to some particular locality and to the entire colony, such as erecting parishes with power to send representatives to the Commons.[3]

Commissioners also undertook tasks pertaining to the colony as a whole. From 1696 on pilots and pilot boats in the colony's various

1. Holdsworth, *English Law*, X, 202-20.
2. Glen to Board of Trade, Oct. 10, 1748, CO 5/372, ff. 80-87.
3. Cooper and McCord, eds., *S. C. Statutes*, II, 116-17, 135-36, 236-46, 282-94, III, 9-14, 171-72, 364-66, 378-81, 658-60, 699-700, IV, 8-10, 22-24, 35-37, 162-64, VII, 7-12, 17-22, 22-27, 41-43, 49-60, 74-75, 477-512, IX, 1-246; Records of the Commissioners of the High Roads of St. John's Parish, Berkeley Co., 1760-1798, S. C Hist. Soc.

ports and harbors were under the supervision of commissioners. Likewise the device adopted in 1713 of employing a commissioner to build a lighthouse on Sullivan's Island for the port of Charleston was used later when beacons and buoys were required for the ports of Georgetown and Beaufort. The legislature assigned to commissioners the job of erecting public buildings, including a governor's house in 1712, a state house in 1712 and again in 1751, an exchange and customs house in 1767, district courthouses and jails in 1769, and two new powder magazines in 1770. In 1766 the Commons appointed special commissioners to enforce a law to prohibit temporarily the export of rice from the colony, and a year later it chose others to supervise a colony-wide survey. It is not now possible to determine when or for what purpose commissioners of the market were appointed, but they were inspecting the weights of public scales in Charleston in 1746. Similarly, the Commons employed commissioners—termed inspectors—to execute a series of bounty laws passed in the two decades before the Revolution to promote the production of specific commodities in the colony, including hemp in 1765, flax and linens in 1770, and tobacco and flour in 1771.[4]

All South Carolina commissioners served without pay,[5] but the term and method of their appointment varied from one group to another. Most were temporary, though a few of the more important groups were permanent. Some commissioners were provided for by law but were appointed by the governor. Others originally appointed by statute were authorized to perpetuate themselves by electing new members to fill vacancies. Still others were originally named in the law providing for them, but the governor filled subsequent vacancies. Whatever the variations, the commissioners owed their initial appointments to an act of the legislature in which the Commons was the dominant force.

The commissioner system was so well established in South Carolina that most governors accepted it without protest. But Glen found the system particularly objectionable, and his comments upon a 1751 law to divide St. Philip's Parish offer a glimpse into the ways the

4. Cooper and McCord, eds., *S. C. Statutes,* II, 127-30, 173-76, 191-95, 378-81, 609-11, III, xxx-xxxi, 225-28, 406-8, 678-80, 691, 712-14, 757-63, IV, 28-29, 156-57, 232-33, 236-38, 257-61, 315-17, 319-20, 327-31.
5. See Bull to Hillsborough, Nov. 30, 1770, S. C. Pub. Recs., XXXII, 404-5, S. C. Arch. Dept. Bull thought this willingness to serve without "pay or profit" a manifestation of a truly "laudable spirit."

South Carolina commissioner system encroached upon the Crown's prerogative. He informed the Commons that it was "Customary in Great Britain in Acts of this Nature when Commissioners have been appointed for the purposes in the said Acts that the Nomination of such Commissioners has been left to the Crown and a time has been limited for their Continuance" and complained that the St. Philip's act named the commissioners, empowered them to fill vacancies in their number, and placed no time limitation upon their appointment so that "they would be a sort of corporation having perpetual Succession." Glen also objected to the act's authorizing the commissioners "to draw Orders upon the public Treasurer for all such Sums of Money as shall come into his Hands" to "be applied to building the said Church" as "contrary to His Majestys Instructions by which the Governor is not to suffer any public Money whatsoever to be issued or disposed of otherwise than by Warrant under his Hand by the Advice of the Council." Glen's objections were well founded, but they aroused resentment in the Commons, which quite naturally regarded them as an attack on one of the colony's established institutions of government. In the end, Glen had to abandon his protest, and his successors discreetly avoided raising the issue altogether.[6]

Perhaps the most important commissioners in South Carolina after 1736 were those of fortifications. Erecting fortifications was clearly an executive task over which royal governors were given exclusive power by their royal commissions,[7] but the South Carolina legislature assumed it at an early date. From at least 1703 it was customary for the building, repair, and maintenance of coastal fortifications to be handled by commissioners appointed by statute. Between 1703 and 1719 the Commons passed four laws to appoint commissioners to build batteries, sea walls, breastworks, redoubts, entrenchments, palisades, and other fortifications. In 1719 and 1720 it passed two additional acts providing for commissioners but leaving their appointments to James Moore, its appointee as governor during the revolt against the proprietors, and his Council. Between 1720 and 1736 the Commons does not appear to have passed any formal laws dealing with fortifications, but there were several instances in which it designated persons to conduct specific repairs or constructions of forts and fortifications.[8]

6. Apr. 24, 1751, S. C. Commons Journals, CO 5/463, pp. 118-20.

7. Labaree, ed., *Royal Instructions*, II, 822.

8. Cooper and McCord, eds., *S. C. Statutes*, III, 179-83, VII, 28-33, 43-49, 60-73; Aug. 16, 1721, S. C. Commons Journals, CO 5/426, p. 51; Aug. 4, 1722, *ibid.*, p. 12.

An examination of the Commons' proceedings on fortifications reveals the extent to which the Commons could influence executive affairs through the use of commissioners. Although commissioners for fortifications were required by law to act with the consent of the governor and Council, they were in fact under the direction of the Commons. Fortification laws contained extensive instructions for the commissioners and thereby made the advice of the governor and Council unnecessary for at least major operations. Futhermore, when the Commons appointed persons by simple legislative resolution to repair fortifications, it usually required them to carry out orders specified by a House committee which had inspected the works. Thus, the Commons deprived the governor and Council not only of their power to appoint people to repair fortifications but also of a large share of their authority to direct construction.[9] Moreover, the executive's dependence on the Commons for money made it impossible for it to prevent the Commons from assuming control over the building of fortifications and the appointment of commissioners to carry out its directions. The fact that the commissioners were accountable to the Commons was assurance enough that they would obey its commands.

The first systematic attempt under the royal government to fortify Charleston came in 1736, when the Commons passed a fortifications measure to carry out recommendations of European engineer Gabriel Barnard. Although the commissioners were permanently appointed, they executed little of a rather comprehensive plan. The law providing for them is no longer extant, but the powers, duties, and other aspects of their office may be ascertained from their journal. The Commons named the original commissioners, but vacancies were filled by the governor. It also empowered them to draw money from the public treasurer, for which they were accountable to the House. They were supposed to act under the advice and direction of the governor and Council, but in practice they followed the Commons' orders as specified in its fortifications appropriations. Their range of activity was wide. They were concerned not only with building fortifications in Charleston but also with constructing a magazine at Dorchester, repairing Johnson's Fort, and consulting with the men who were to

9. See Aug. 3, 1721, S. C. Commons Journals, CO 5/426, p. 15; Aug. 4, 1722, *ibid.*, pp. 7, 12; Feb. 1-4, 1726, *ibid.*, CO 5/428, pp. 154-60; Arthur Middleton to Francis Nicholson, Feb. 4, 1726, CO 5/387, ff. 198-99; Robert Johnson to Board of Trade, Mar. 30, 1732, CO 5/364, ff. 223-24.

build forts at places away from Charleston. After 1755 there were usually seven commissioners, and at one time or another from 1755 to 1770 they included the powder receiver, the speaker of the Commons, and several other representatives. From the personnel, it would appear that governors usually filled vacancies with people acceptable to the Commons.[10]

From 1736 until 1752 the fortifications commissioners operated without opposition from either governor or Council. Indeed, far from opposing the commissioners, governors worked with them and encouraged the Commons to participate in supervising them. In November 1736 Lieutenant Governor Broughton recommended that the Commons conduct "a strict Enquiry into the present State of the Fortifications, what repairs have been made to the Old, and how far the New Ones are carried on," and in January 1744 Governor Glen invited the Commons to appoint a committee to join one of the Council to assist him in inspecting the fortifications and determining a site for building a new magazine. During these years the Commons frequently issued directions to the commissioners about the details of their work.[11] But Glen eventually developed serious objections to the Commons' control over the commissioners and in 1752 challenged the constitutionality of such officers.

At least as early as 1748 Glen had come to regard the commissioner system as an infringement of the constitution and a legislative device for usurping executive power. Perhaps because of neglect but more probably because he hoped gradually to abolish the fortifications commissioners, Glen had not filled vacancies as they had occurred. By early 1752 Fort Johnson and the Charleston works were in urgent need of repair, and three times in the first four months of that year the Commons asked Glen to fill the vacancies and to assist the commissioners in making necessary repairs. Glen ignored the first two requests, but he replied to the third that an engineer's advice was needed before the fortifications could be repaired. He also sug-

10. Cooper and McCord, eds., *S. C. Statutes,* III, 436; Smith, *South Carolina as a Royal Province,* 198-99; Journal of the Commissioners of Fortifications, May 10, Sept. 1, 1755, Aug. 25, Sept. 20, 1756, Mar. 10, May 16, Sept. 10, Oct. 26, 1757, Mar. 16, 1758, July 31, 1760, Sept. 13, 1762, S. C. Hist. Soc.; Commons Journals, Sept. 17, 1742, *S. C. Col. Recs., 1742-44,* 27-28; May 14, 1752, S. C. Commons Journals, CO 5/466, pp. 208-10.

11. Commons Journals, Nov. 11, 1736, Dec. 16, 1737, *S. C. Col. Recs., 1736-39,* 9-11, 384; Jan. 21, 1744, *ibid., 1742-44,* 543-44.

gested that the 1736 fortification law might need amending, declaring that "power over all Castles, Forts, Fortifications and places of Strength is inherent in the Crown and the King having by his Commission vested the sole power and Command over the Fortifications of this Province in his Governor, perhaps such Establishments as Commissioners of Fortifications may be thought contrary to the prerogative of the Crown and I have reason to think the Lords Commissioners for Trade and plantations are of that Opinion."

Glen's reply elicited a considered response from the Commons. It expressed concern "that his Excellency should Question whether he is at liberty to act agreeable to the directions of a Law that was passed so long before his being appointed Governor," thus implying that his commission could not supersede colonial laws. If London authorities had considered that law objectionable, the Commons declared, it "could never have existed so long." The Commons also denied that its using commissioners in any way encroached upon the royal prerogative, arguing that they were intended simply to relieve the governor of the details of fortification work, that they acted under the governor's direction, and that the governor was empowered to fill vacancies. Further, the Commons contended "that the Law for establishing these Commissioners is of Force and until it be repealed by His Majesty . . . ought not nor cannot legally be dispensed with" and again urged that Glen fill the vacancies.[12]

But Glen still declined to fill the vacancies, and an adjournment postponed the contest until the following fall. In September a severe hurricane lashed Charleston and almost entirely demolished its fortifications. Glen immediately called the Commons into session and requested an appropriation to repair the damage. The Commons replied that there was already over £12,000 in the fortifications funds that might be used for repairs and once more asked Glen to appoint new commissioners. But Glen continued to refuse to fill the vacancies and seriously questioned the wisdom of using either the fortifications fund or the commissioners for the job. He proposed instead that a competent engineer be hired to be "under the Eye and direction of the Governour and Council who I am persuaded will be very careful how the Money raised for that purpose is laid out." That method,

12. Jan. 22, Mar. 11, Apr. 29, May 5, 14-15, 1752, S. C. Commons Journals, CO 5/466, pp. 66-67, 98, 164-65, 174-77, 208-10, 212.

he argued, was the one "prescribed by the British Constitution." In particular, Glen asked that Gerald De Brahm, an engineer from Georgia, be employed for the task. But the Commons had little use for the British constitution when it was contrary to South Carolina law, and it also objected to De Brahm both upon the grounds that his services cost too much and upon the specious pretext that he was a foreigner and therefore a poor security risk. It continued to insist that the commissioners were perfectly competent to carry out the repairs.

After nearly two months of such wrangling, the Commons decided to take a more forceful stand. In late November it appealed to Glen "for the last Time" to fill the vacancies and in an unusual twist threatened to submit the matter to the Crown if he continued to refuse. In a somewhat softer tone, it declared that it had no intention of permitting Glen and the Council "to burthen themselves with the trouble of purchasing Materials, and contracting with Work-men for building or repairing the Fortifications: which by a Law of this Province the Commissioners only are impowered to do." At that point Glen proposed a compromise solution. He agreed to fill the vacancies and offered to leave the tasks of purchasing materials and contracting with workers to the commissioners but still insisted that an engineer be hired to direct the repairs. The Commons remained adamant in its refusal to employ an engineer, and, when it learned that Glen had without its consent hired De Brahm to prepare a plan for rebuilding the Charleston fortifications, it flatly refused to pay him, declaring that he had "been employed contrary to the advice and disagreeable to the Inclination of the House."[13] So the controversy ended without Glen's having won his point and with the commissioners of fortifications still an important South Carolina institution.

Aside from a few minor repairs by the commissioners, the fortifications remained untouched until the renewed danger of foreign attack in the Seven Years' War again focused attention on the matter over two years later. In March 1755, when the province appeared to be in real danger, the Commons reversed its earlier position and hired De Brahm to undertake the work in conjunction with the commissioners of fortifications, who supplied him with workmen and materials. De Brahm's methods of construction were unsatisfactory, and it was fortunate that he completed only a portion of his rather exten-

13. Sept. 27, 30, Oct. 5, Nov. 25, Dec. 7, 12-13, 1752, *ibid.*, Pt. I, pp. 3-4, 9, 20-21, Pt. II, pp. 9, 20-22, 25-28.

sive plan.[14] Additional work on the fortifications awaited the arrival of Governor Lyttelton in 1756. The Commons was more generous in granting funds for fortifications under Lyttelton. It permitted him with the aid of two engineers from the British forces stationed in Charleston to assume the major role in supervising construction, although it was careful to leave the tasks of providing workers and materials to the commissioners of fortifications, who also participated in directing the work. After 1757 no major construction of coastal fortifications was undertaken until the outbreak of the Revolution, but the commissioners continued to function until at least 1770, making repairs to old fortifications as they were required.[15]

Not all South Carolina fortifications were under the commissioners' direction. Their activities were for the most part limited to coastal defenses, whereas the governors usually supervised the building of frontier forts. By no means, however, did the governors have a free hand in this matter. The Commons invariably imposed certain limitations on its appropriations for those forts, and its power to audit accounts of all appropriations assured respect for its limitations.[16]

Following the South Carolina Commons' example, the Georgia Commons early employed commissioners to carry on public works and services. It first appointed commissioners in 1757 to build forts in six different areas and thereafter delegated almost all major works to such officers. The Commons also assigned them the tasks of repairing these forts and finishing the works around Savannah in 1760 and of building additional forts on Cockspur Island and Midway River in 1761 and at Augusta and Frederica in 1765. Similarly, the Commons used commissioners to provide churches and burial grounds for the six parishes; to build a magazine and guardhouse in Savannah; to repair or rebuild the Tybee Island lighthouse and the Savannah courthouse; to regulate harbor pilots, the Savannah market, and the

14. Mar. 11, May 8-9, 1755, *ibid.,* CO 5/472, pp. 72, 111-12; Journal of the Commissioners of Fortifications, Sept. 1, 1755, S. C. Hist. Soc.; Smith, *South Carolina as a Royal Province,* 206-7.

15. See Smith, *South Carolina as a Royal Province,* 207; June 25, 1756, S. C. Commons Journals, CO 5/472, p. 7; Journal of the Commissioners of Fortifications, 1755-70, S. C. Hist. Soc.; Lyttelton to Earl of Loudoun, Mar. 27, June 13, 1757, Loudoun Papers, 3184, 3672, Huntington Lib.; Abstract of a letter from Lyttelton, July 12, 1757, State Papers Foreign, 109/68, f. 78, PRO.

16. Mar. 9, 1757, S. C. Commons Journals, CO 5/473, p. 43.

hire of slaves by the public; to establish a workhouse and a watch for Savannah; to provide roads and ferries; and to improve rivers and creeks.[17]

Georgia's commissioner system was similar to South Carolina's. As in the older colony, the legislature named the commissioners in the statutes creating their positions. Those appointed to carry on some public work were usually empowered to prepare plans, choose sites, contract for materials, and employ workmen; those employed to provide some public service were authorized to hire people to perform that service. Most of them had to have the governor's warrant to obtain necessary funds from the treasurer, although a few were empowered to issue orders for money directly without the governor's consent. In either case, the Commons required them to account with it. Their terms of office usually lasted only until their project was completed. Vacancies were filled either by direct appointment of the governor and Council or by the remaining commissioners with the governor's approval. Many of the commissioners were members of the Commons, of course, but there were usually some councilors and occasionally the governor himself on all of the various boards of commissioners. Thus, the executive had more influence in Georgia than in South Carolina. But through the power to appoint officers to perform public works by legislative enactments, the Commons deprived the governor of a portion of his appointive power.[18]

From time to time the Virginia Burgesses also employed commissioners or trustees to carry on public works, but it did not use them so extensively as did the Commons of either South Carolina or Georgia. In Virginia the county courts handled all local projects, including the building of courthouses, tobacco warehouses, roads, and bridges, which the South Carolina Commons normally entrusted to commissioners. Before the end of the Seven Years' War about the only local task performed by commissioners, or directors or trustees as they were usually called in Virginia, was the laying out of towns. Occasionally the Burgesses did employ directors to undertake the construction of important public buildings, as in the case of the capitols in 1703 and

17. Statutes, *Ga. Col. Recs.*, XVIII, 202-11, 258-72, 299-303, 350-53, 408-17, 420-26, 472-79, 494-501, 515-25, 558-66, 570-80, 639-48, 717-42, 764-68, XIX, Pt. I, 3-11, 83-89, 147-51, 253-88, 337-45.
18. *Ibid.*, XVIII, 206, 264, 300, 351, 413, 475, 558, 578.

1748, the governor's palace in 1705, a jailer's house in 1722, and a wall around the public magazine in 1755; but it left the building of other public structures and all fortifications and other military installations under the governor's direction. The governor also appointed all tobacco inspectors, although the Burgesses limited him in his selection to the nominees of the county courts.[19]

In the decade after 1765 the Burgesses used the trustee system much more extensively than it had in earlier years. It regularly placed all major public works and services in the hands of trustees. In 1766 it appointed trustees to build a road from the Northern Branch of the Potomac to Fort Pitt and in 1769 named others to establish, equip, and staff a mental hospital in Williamsburg. In 1772 and 1773 it assigned to trustees the task of joining with Maryland commissioners to build a lighthouse on Cape Henry and hire a keeper for it and to place buoys in Chesapeake Bay. Also in 1772, varying the commissioner system, it empowered three different sets of private subscribers to elect trustees to undertake the improvement of navigation or building of canals up the Potomac to Fort Cumberland, around the falls of the James, and from Archer's Hope Creek to Queen's Creek near Williamsburg. At the same time the Burgesses appointed still other commissioners to construct a canal between the head of North River and that of Elizabeth River. The Burgesses used commissioners for a host of lesser projects as well, including selling surplus military stores, determining the value of tobacco damaged at public warehouses by fire or flood, ascertaining the value of certain parish churches, building an addition to the public jailer's house in Williamsburg, and caring for the lands of the Gingaskin Indians. Perhaps most significantly, during the last ten years of the colonial period the Burgesses gradually assumed many of the traditional functions of the county courts by occasionally assigning to trustees tasks formerly handled by the gentlemen justices, such as building bridges, clearing rivers and creeks, and building and repairing roads. But it left the vast majority of local works and services in the hands of the county courts.[20]

19. See Hening, ed., *Va. Statutes,* III, 285, 419-32, IV, 26-28, 32-36, 55-57, 112-16, V, 507, VI, 60-69, 197-98, 396-99, 421-23, 521-30, VII, 33, VIII, 86. See also Albert O. Porter, *County Government in Virginia* (N. Y., 1947), 56-65.

20. Hening, ed., *Va. Statutes,* VIII, 146-50, 252-53, 264-65, 378-81, 390-92, 539-41, 543-53, 556-81, 585-86, 623-25, 652-53, 660-62.

As a rule, Virginia directors, or commissioners, were less thoroughly legislative in character and less powerful than South Carolina commissioners. Particularly during the early period, councilors as well as burgesses served as directors, although the latter usually predominated. They could not order money directly from the public treasury, being required to have the governor's warrants for funds as needed. But like the South Carolina commissioners they were named by statute to perform some particular task and were endowed with the necessary powers to complete it. In addition, the Burgesses required them to account with the House for all sums of money that passed through their hands. But in no instance could they perpetuate themselves indefinitely, holding office only until their project was finished.[21]

The North Carolina Lower House used the commissioner system sparingly both under the proprietors and during the early years of royal government. Before the 1740's it employed commissioners to improve the ports of Roanoke and Bath, to establish and regulate towns, and to build an occasional road or church. Like the Virginia Burgesses it left most local works to the county courts, including the building and care of roads, ferries, and courthouses.[22] But the colony's rapid population growth and expansion during the middle decades of the eighteenth century created a need for more public works, and after 1745 the Lower House assigned a wide variety of projects to commissioners, including the building and maintenance of fortifications, public buildings, churches, ports, towns, rivers, bridges, and roads.

The major attempt to fortify the colony came between 1740 and 1760. In 1745 the legislature appointed twelve commissioners including Governor Johnston and several councilors to build a fort on the Lower Cape Fear River near Brunswick. Because of inadequate funds and mismanagement on the part of the commissioners, the fort was not completed until after 1759, when the Lower House deprived the commissioners of most of their authority and appointed William Dry to finish the project. By a 1748 statute the legislature appointed

21. Ibid., III, 285-87, 421, VI, 197-98, 521-30.
22. Laws, N. C. St. Recs., XXIII, 133-41, XXV, 175-78, 194-96, 201-9, 229-30; Paul M. McCain, The County Court in North Carolina Before 1750 (Durham, 1954), 99-134.

commissioners to build three forts at Bear Inlet, Ocracoke Inlet (later Fort Granville), and Old Topsail Inlet (later Fort Dobbs). But the Bear Inlet fort was never even begun, and it was over a decade before either Fort Granville or Fort Dobbs was completed. During the early stages of the Seven Years' War the Lower House also employed commissioners to build a fort in western North Carolina, although the project apparently never went beyond the selection of a site.[23]

Improving navigation facilities and erecting public buildings were other major projects assigned to commissioners. After 1750 the legislature passed at least five measures designed to render North Carolina ports easier of access. These measures called for commissioners to clear and deepen channels, erect beacons, and establish pilots for Currituck Inlet and the ports of Bath, Beaufort, and Roanoke. The Lower House also appointed commissioners to supervise the construction of public buildings in the two abortive attempts to establish a capital at New Bern in 1746 and at Tower Hill on the Neuse River in 1758, but in neither case did they ever undertake their assignments.[24] When the legislature did finally decide to establish the capital permanently at New Bern in 1766, it left the building of the governor's palace under the supervision of Governor Tryon—the one instance in the years after 1740 when the Lower House did not assign a major public work to commissioners.[25]

After 1740 the Lower House began to appoint commissioners to undertake many local tasks that had formerly been handled by the county courts. A 1745 statute appointed several different sets of commissioners to build and repair all roads, bridges, cuts, and watercourses within their respective districts. The House also made extensive use of commissioners to establish towns and to build churches, courthouses, and jails. These appointments threatened to deprive the county courts of their control over local works, but by the mid-1750's the House reversed the trend and began to assign an increasing number of local projects to the county courts. Thus, when

23. Laws, *N. C. St. Recs.*, XXIII, 229-31, 292-96, 440, 505-6; Lower House Journals, Oct. 21, 1756, May 20, Nov. 28, Dec. 5, 1757, Dec. 19, 1758, Dec. 20, 1759, *N. C. Col. Recs.*, V, 729, 849, 897, 909, 1084-85, VI, 164-65; Matthew Rowan to Board of Trade, Mar. 19, 1754, *ibid.*, V, 108-9; Dobbs to Earl of Loudoun, July 10, 1756, *ibid.*, 594-601, and Oct. 22, 1756, Loudoun Papers, 2064, Huntington Lib.
24. Laws, *N. C. St. Recs.*, XXIII, 252-67, 347-48, 375-78, 483-84, 506-7, 667-72, XXV, 373-78, 460-61.
25. *Ibid.*, XXIII, 664-65; Tryon to Board of Trade, Dec. 3, 1766, and to Shelburne, July 7, 1767, *N. C. Col. Recs.*, VII, 266, 499.

it established an inspection system in each county to keep up the quality of the colony's export commodities, including meat, rice, indigo, naval stores, and lumber products in 1755, tobacco in 1758, and flax, butter, flour, leather, and skins in 1770, it placed the appointment of the inspectors in the hands of the county courts. Similarly, by three statutes passed between 1764 and 1771 the House assigned them exclusive jurisdiction over building roads and bridges, establishing ferries, and improving creeks and rivers.[26]

Thus, the North Carolina system for handling local tasks was a curious blend of the methods of Virginia and South Carolina. It was not so centralized as that of South Carolina, where nearly all such undertakings were directed by legislative-appointed commissioners. Nor was it so decentralized as that of Virginia, where the bulk of such projects was supervised by the county courts. Rather, it was an ill-defined system of concurrent jurisdiction with the Lower House having final authority.

The conditions under which North Carolina commissioners held office varied from one group to another. All were originally appointed by statute to carry out some specific project, but their composition, money powers, and length of terms in office, as well as the manner of filling vacancies among them, were not uniform. Among the commissioners for Fort Johnston, for instance, were the governor and several councilors, but as a rule the commissioners were either members or at least nominees of the Lower House. Similarly, some commissioners' terms were unlimited, others served only until the completion of their project, and still others were restricted to a specified period. Vacancies were usually filled in one of two ways: either by the commissioners themselves or by the governor from two nominees of the remaining commissioners. The House required all commissioners to account with it for any money passing through their hands, and it empowered most of those concerned with major projects to draw money directly from either tax collectors or the public treasurers. In special cases the House even permitted the port commissioners to appoint a receiver of their own choosing.[27]

26. Laws, *N. C. St. Recs.*, XXIII, 133-35, 141-49, 220-29, 231-32, 607-11, 639-54, 728-41, 785-86, 790-801, 851-52, 906-8, XXV, 243-54, 263-64, 268-73, 313-19, 329-30, 348-49, 367-69, 378-89, 403-4, 468-72.

27. *Ibid.*, XXIII, 229-31, 255, 292-96, 347-48, 375-78, 466-67, 483-84, 506-7; Lower House Journals, Oct. 21, 1756, *N. C. Col. Recs.*, V, 729.

By appointing commissioners to supervise the building of public works and the execution of public services, the lower houses in the southern royal colonies assumed control over many important details of executive affairs. The lower houses of the two Carolinas and Georgia assigned all major works to commissioners, including building fortifications, public buildings, lighthouses, churches, canals, and magazines; improving ports and navigation; and establishing and regulating pilots and markets. In the early years of the eighteenth century the Virginia Burgesses permitted the governor to direct the construction of some public works, although it simultaneously appointed commissioners for other projects and after 1760 followed the example of the Carolina lower houses and employed them for all major works. The lower houses of South Carolina, Georgia, and, to a lesser extent, North Carolina also appointed commissioners to perform many local tasks such as maintaining roads, bridges, and ferries, building courthouses and parish churches, and laying out towns, although the lower houses in North Carolina and Virginia assigned most local duties to the county courts. The details of the commissioner systems varied from colony to colony, and before 1765 the influence of the executive was particularly strong in both Virginia and Georgia. But in every case commissioners owed both their appointments and their powers to legislative enactments and were accountable to the lower houses for their conduct. These conditions dictated that the commissioners would to a large extent be controlled by the lower houses and would constitute an effective device by which the lower houses could extend their authority over executive matters.

13

Colonial Agents

ONE of the most significant powers gained by American lower houses in the eighteenth century was that of appointing and controlling the colonial agents. Resident in London, these agents formed an important link in the chain of imperial relations. Just as royal governors were the Crown's representatives in the colonies, the agents were the colonies' emissaries at the seat of empire. Their responsibilities were legion. It was their duty to secure acceptance of colonial legislation; promote the trade of their respective provinces; forward papers, documents, and news from both official and unofficial sources in London to the colonies; protest and lobby against Parliamentary legislation detrimental to the colonies' interests; handle details of appeals from colonial courts to the Privy Council; draft and present petitions; serve as a source of information about the colonies for the various boards of imperial government; and perform a host of lesser assignments. In short, they were to present their respective colonies to London officials in a favorable light and insofar as possible use their influence to insure that the course of imperial government did not run contrary to the interests of those colonies. The closer their connections with the ministry or other important colonial officials the better, because it was important, as young Peter Manigault wrote from London in 1754, that the agent have sufficient "interest with people in power" to "keep fair with the ministry."[1]

Imperial authorities preferred that each agent be appointed by

1. Peter Manigault to Andrew Rutledge, Feb. 26, 1754, Manigault Papers, 2733, South Caroliniana Lib. Ella Lonn, *The Colonial Agents of the Southern Colonies* (Chapel Hill, 1945) gives a full discussion of the colonial agent and the mechanics of his office.

act of all three branches of the legislature in his colony. Rarely was the agent not dominated by one or another of these branches. A glance at his position reveals the advantages of controlling the agent. His attitudes and activities in London were likely to be determined by the body that was responsible for his appointment and his salary. For instance, if he was dominated by the lower house and could be paid only by its vote he could almost certainly be counted on to support it in its disputes with imperial authorities. Thus, there developed a movement by the lower houses to bring the agents under their authority. In most instances the fact that they controlled the purse strings eventually tipped the scales in their favor.

Taking the lead in this movement among the southern lower houses was the South Carolina Commons. Under the proprietors it had employed Abel Kettelby from 1712 to 1716 to secure favorable trading privileges for the colony and to act as agent to solicit the colony's affairs in Great Britain. During the last bitter years under the proprietors the Commons sent first Joseph Boone and Richard Beresford in 1715 to protest to the proprietors against their grant of excessive powers to Chief Justice Nicholas Trott and then John Barnwell in 1719 to assist Boone in petitioning the Crown to assume control of the South Carolina government.[2] Under the Crown the Commons sought to establish its right to name and to assume the major role in directing the agent, but it was not at first completely successful. Although it did gain control of the committee to correspond with the agent by establishing its right to appoint nearly three-fourths of the members, it was unable to secure the exclusive right of nomination. In September 1721 the Council, with Nicholson's support, forced the Commons to agree to the appointment of two agents, John Lloyd and Francis Yonge, the former to represent the Commons and the latter the Council. Similarly, in 1724 the Council's opposition prevented the Commons from replacing Yonge, who had continued as sole agent after Lloyd had returned to South Carolina in the winter of 1722-23. The deadlock between the two houses over the paper money question after 1728 temporarily prevented the appointment of a regular agent, and for the next three years each House

2. Lonn, *Colonial Agents*, 41-46, 67-71; Cooper and McCord, eds., *S. C. Statutes*, II, 600-602, 621-22; S. C. Committee of Correspondence to Boone and Beresford, Nov. 30, 1716, S. C. Pub. Recs., VI, 256-57, S. C. Arch. Dept.

maintained a separate agent, Stephen Godin acting for the Council and Samuel Wragg, who had first been sent by the Commons to assist Yonge in 1725, for the Commons.[3]

During the next quarter century the Commons put the agency on a more regular footing and consolidated its control over the office. The solution of the paper money question in 1731 under Johnson paved the way for the appointment by the two houses of Peregrine Fury of London as agent. Fury held the post from 1731 to 1749, and during his long tenure the Commons assumed almost complete authority over him by virtue of its control of the committee of correspondence. Just how it used its authority to its own political advantage is illustrated by the numerous instances in which the committee gave instructions to Fury solely upon the Commons' order without the Council's prior consent. A striking illustration of such an order occurred in June 1739, when the Commons, locked in a controversy with the Council over their respective rights in framing money bills, ordered the committee to write Fury "to direct him to answer any Misrepresentations which shall or may be made in Great-Britain to the Disadvantage of the Conduct of this House in Vindication of the Rights and Privileges of this House during the late Dispute with the Gentlemen of the Council."[4]

Despite considerable dissatisfaction with Fury and several suggestions from time to time that he be replaced, the Commons continued to reappoint him until June 1749, when it chose James Crokatt, a London merchant formerly resident in South Carolina, to replace him.[5] Crokatt was no stranger to the Commons. It had previously asked him to co-operate with Colonel John Fenwick in seeking favorable action on the currency bill of 1746, and, although he declined to undertake that task, he was later instrumental in getting a bounty on indigo. His appointment began in September 1749, and

3. Sept. 1-2, 5, 7, 20, 1721, S. C. Commons Journals, CO 5/426, pp. 89-96, 104, 149, Jan. 13-Feb. 15, Mar. 23-28, June 15, 1724, *ibid.*, CO 5/427, pp. 35-36; Apr. 17, 1728, *ibid.*, CO 5/428, p. 38; Cooper and McCord, eds., *S. C. Statutes*, III, 157, 183, 251-52, 266-68; Lonn, *Colonial Agents*, 71-73.

4. Cooper and McCord, eds., *S. C. Statutes*, III, 307-8; Commons Journals, June 6, 1739, *S. C. Col. Recs., 1736-39*, 725.

5. See Commons Journals, Dec. 17, 1737, Mar. 11, 1738, *S. C. Col. Recs., 1736-39*, 385-86, 543; Apr. 21, May 17, June 28, 1744, *ibid.*, *1744-45*, 133-34, 153, 214-15; Mar. 20, 1746, *ibid.*, *1745-46*, 165; May 20, 27, June 10-13, 1747, *ibid.*, *1746-47*, 250-51, 292-93, 352, 380-81, 389, 395; June 1, 1749, *ibid.*, *1749-50*, 268, 276; Cooper and McCord, eds., *S. C. Statutes*, III, 490, 723; Lanning, *St. Augustine Expedition*, xiii-xiv.

like his predecessors he was the instrument of the Commons, which continued to dominate the committee of correspondence and repeatedly ordered him to perform tasks to which the governor and Council were opposed. Thus in December 1749, despite Glen's opposition, the Commons directed Crokatt to seek the Crown's approval for an addition to the colony's paper money, and in June 1751, after a dispute with Glen over a bill to divide the parish of St. Philip's, Charleston, the Commons ordered the committee of correspondence to countermand any orders to the agent from the governor and Council on that bill.[6] There was little question that Crokatt was securely under the Commons' control. But between 1754 and 1756 the Council seriously challenged that control.

Crokatt's attempted resignation in early 1754 set off a bitter and significant controversy between the two houses. Although the Commons attempted to persuade Crokatt to stay on, the Council voted to accept his resignation, insisting that he was not legally agent anyway because the ordinance appointing him had long since expired. But the Commons replied that both Crokatt and Fury had served for several years without formal statutory reappointments, argued that a formal ordinance was unnecessary, and proceeded to correspond with Crokatt through its committee until the following September, when the Commons received notice of Crokatt's agreement to continue in the agency. Crokatt's decision did not obviate the Council's objections to the manner of his appointment. When the legislature reconvened in January 1755, the Council again insisted upon making a formal appointment. This time the Commons agreed, but a deadlock ensued when the Council tried to replace Crokatt with Charles Pinckney, a South Carolinian then residing in London. Unable to persuade the Council to accept Crokatt, the Commons continued to regard him as agent, while Pinckney acted in behalf of the governor and Council.[7]

6. Commons Journals, June 17, 1746, *S. C. Col. Recs., 1745-46*, 243-44; May 5, June 1, 1749, *ibid., 1749-50*, 52-53, 276; Dec. 14, 1749, S. C. Commons Journals, CO 5/460, pp. 60-66; June 14, 1751, *ibid.*, CO 5/463, p. 42; Nov. 22, 1749, *Board of Trade Journals, 1742-49*, 462; S. C. Committee of Correspondence to Crokatt, June 17, 1749, CO 5/13; Lonn, *Colonial Agents*, 133.

7. Jan. 26, 31, Feb. 1-2, 7-8, Sept. 3, 1754, Jan. 14-16, 23, 28, Feb. 6, 1755, May 20, 1755, S. C. Commons Journals, CO 5/472, Pt. I, pp. 15, 22-23, 42-45, Pt. II, pp. 19-22, 27-28, 35, 47, 128-29; Feb. 6, 1754, S. C. Upper House Journals, CO 5/470, pp. 97-98; William Henry Lyttelton to Board of Trade, June 19, 1756, CO 5/375, ff. 136-41; Charles Pinckney to Peter Manigault, Apr. 8, 1756, Mani-

The controversy now turned upon the payment of Crokatt's salary and expenses. If the Commons through its exclusive power to frame money bills could pay Crokatt, it could keep him or any subsequent agent of its choosing in office despite executive opposition. In March 1755 the Commons included provision for Crokatt's salary in the annual estimate. When the Council questioned the allowance to Crokatt, the Commons rendered a classic declaration of the lower houses' attitude toward the agency, asserting "that the Agent being a Person appointed for solliciting the Affairs of this Province we conceive the Province should be understood to be the People; and as the People only are to pay for his services it seems just and reasonable that the Representatives of the People should have the Nomination of their Agent: notwithstanding such Agent cannot be appointed by law, but with the Assent of the Governor and the Advice and consent of His Majestys Council." This assertion served notice that the Commons was willing to share the power of appointment with the governor and Council but that it claimed and intended to exercise the exclusive right of nomination. The Council could not, of course, accept the Commons' declaration without forfeiting the last vestige of its control over the agent, and when the Commons refused to permit the Council to amend the tax bill by striking out the provision to pay Crokatt, the Council rejected it entirely. Three subsequent attempts by the Commons to pay Crokatt that spring met a similar fate.[8]

Crokatt continued to serve as agent under the Commons' exclusive direction for another year. In January 1756 the Commons finally moved to replace him. It considered several people, including Charles Pinckney, before finally choosing William Middleton, a member of a prominent South Carolina family then residing in England. The Council readily consented to Middleton's appointment in a new ordinance that named six councilors to the committee of correspondence, an increase of four over the old arrangement. But whatever advantage the Council may have expected to gain from this apparent victory was nullified by the failure of the ordinance to restrict the number of representatives that might serve on the committee. The Commons later appointed its speaker and thirteen other members, so that repre-

gault Papers, 1330, South Caroliniana Lib.; Lonn, *Colonial Agents*, 135; Smith, *South Carolina as a Royal Province*, 165-66.

8. Mar. 20-22, Apr. 9-12, May 1-2, 8-9, 15, 19-20, 1755, S. C. Commons Journals, CO 5/472, pp. 80-86, 89-96, 103-4, 111-13, 121, 127-29.

sentatives outnumbered councilors by over two to one, and, because the presence of only two councilors was necessary to conduct business, the Commons' domination of both the committee and the agent remained secure.[9]

With Middleton's appointment by the Commons' own initiative, the question of whether or not Crokatt should continue as agent was solved; but the matter of Crokatt's salary still had to be determined. His payment would mean that the Council no longer exercised much control over the agent and that the Commons could continue in office and pay that officer without its consent. But in the end the Council was unable to prevent Crokatt's payment. The legislature's failure to pass a tax bill the previous year had brought demands from the colony's creditors for payment, and the need for money to put the colony in a state of defense was pressing. At the urging of Governor Lyttelton the Council finally yielded in May 1756 and passed a tax bill containing provision to pay Crokatt.[10] The Commons thus demonstrated its ability to keep an agent in office without the executive's consent, and for the rest of the colonial period its authority over the agent remained unchallenged.

The Commons nominated and controlled both of the agents that served the colony during the last two decades before the Revolution. Middleton's refusal to accept the agency led to the appointment in November 1756 of James Wright, son of former Chief Justice Robert Wright, for the post. The statute to appoint Wright increased the Council's membership on the committee to eight. But the number of representatives was again left to the discretion of the Commons, which appointed twelve, one fewer than it had named the previous March but still enough to give it a majority. Wright's tenure was comparatively brief. He served only a little over three years before his appointment to the governorship of Georgia in May 1760.[11] The Commons waited two years before it again filled the office, this time with Charles Garth, member of Parliament for Devizes, who served

9. May 20, 1755, Jan. 28, Feb. 12, 18-20, Mar. 20, 1756, *ibid.*, Pt. II, pp. 130-31, Pt. IV, pp. 38, 54-55, 58-59, 78; Cooper and McCord, eds., *S. C. Statutes*, IV, 26-27.

10. Lyttelton to Board of Trade, June 19, 1756, CO 5/375, ff. 136-41; Apr.-May, 1756, S. C. Commons Journals, CO 5/472.

11. Nov. 12, 1756, May 20, 1757, S. C. Commons Journals, CO 5/473, pp. 6, 93; Jan. 17, 1759, *ibid.*, CO 5/475, p. 34; Lyttelton to Board of Trade, Dec. 6, 1756, CO 5/375, ff. 160-61; S. C. Agent act, Nov. 19, 1756, CO 324/60, ff. 261-64; Cooper and McCord, eds., *S. C. Statutes*, IV, 34-35; S. C. Committee of Correspondence to Wright, July 8, 1757, Lyttelton Papers, Clements Lib.

the province until the outbreak of the Revolution. The act to appoint Garth changed the composition of the committee of correspondence considerably by reducing the number of councilors from eight
to four and raising the number of members necessary to constitute a
quorum to nine, none of whom was required to be from the Council.
There was no limitation on the number of representatives that might
act on the committee, and the Commons regularly appointed seventeen.[12] These changes deprived the Council of any influence over
the agent. In the years that followed the Commons exercised an
almost unlimited authority over Garth. Particularly during the
Gadsden election controversy in 1763 and 1764 and the Wilkes fund
controversy beginning in 1770, the Commons demonstrated that it
could use him to present its complaints against royal governors without restraint from either the governor or Council. The South Carolina Commons had succeeded in its quest to secure complete control
over the colonial agent.

North Carolina was the last of the three older colonies to establish
a regular agency, but its Lower House was the second of the southern
royal legislatures to assert its authority over the agent. Beginning as
early as 1676 the colony had been represented in England by a number of special agents and Burrington had emphasized the need for
a permanent agent as early as 1731,[13] but the House showed little
interest in establishing one until 1748. To protest against Governor
Johnston's "managed" election act of 1746, the northern counties sent
Henry McCulloh to England in 1747. McCulloh's appointment served
as a catalyst to the establishment of a regular agency by the House.
To counteract McCulloh's activities, which it feared might lead to
the election law's disallowance, the long assembly, made up exclusively of southern members, passed a statute in October 1748 to appoint
James Abercromby permanent London agent.
    Abercromby served the House for over a dozen years, being re-

12. Cooper and McCord, eds., *S. C. Statutes*, IV, 164-65; Apr. 28, May 7, 24,
Nov. 24, 1762, S. C. Commons Journals, CO 5/480, Pt. I, pp. 77-78, 92-93, 121, Pt.
II, pp. 15-16; Wright to Lyttelton, Dec. 29, 1759, Lyttelton Papers, Clements Lib.;
Sir Lewis B. Namier, "Charles Garth and his Connexions," *English Historical
Review*, 54 (1939), 443-70, 632-52.
    13. See Lonn, *Colonial Agents*, 24-41, 284; Lower House Journals, May 15, 1731,
Feb. 27, 1735, *N. C. Col. Recs.*, III, 315-16, 320, IV, 151; Burrington to Board of
Trade, Nov. 14, 1732, to Newcastle, Nov. 15, 1732, *ibid.*, III, 370-75; Johnston to
Board of Trade, May 17, 1748, *ibid.*, IV, 869-70.

appointed in 1751 and 1754. His original appointment was for a term of two years, beginning in March 1749. The committee appointed to correspond with him consisted of two councilors and three representatives. By appointing the majority of the members to the committee, the Lower House would theoretically be able to control it and through it the agent. But in the early years Governor Johnston seems to have assumed a prominent role in supervising the agent, although the House insisted on reviewing the conduct of the committee and on issuing instructions to Abercromby. Upon the expiration of Abercromby's third appointment, the House decided that the colony could not afford a permanent agent and voted to dismiss him. But he did not sever his connections with North Carolina. Within less than nine months political events in North Carolina were to call him back into service as agent for the Lower House.[14]

A controversy in December 1758 between Dobbs and the Council on the one hand and the Lower House on the other over the methods of disposing of North Carolina's share of the £50,000 Parliamentary grant to reimburse Virginia and the Carolinas for their war expenses touched off a two-and-one-half-year debate over the appointment of an agent. Abercromby had taken the preliminary steps to obtain North Carolina's portion of the grant before he received notice of his dismissal in April 1758. He had recommended to the Board of Trade that the money be used to sink North Carolina's depreciated paper currency and after his dismissal continued to urge the colony's legislative leaders to appropriate the money to that purpose, suggesting also that his salary and expenses for the thirteen-month period between the expiration of his last appointment and his receipt of the notice of his discharge be defrayed by the grant.[15]

Certain leaders of the House including Speaker Samuel Swann and Treasurers John Starkey and Thomas Barker, derisively referred to by Governor Dobbs as the "junto," thought Abercromby's recommendation a good one. When the House met in December 1758, they

14. Laws, *N. C. St. Recs.*, XI, 110-12, XXIII, 362-63, XXV, 266; Lower House Journals, Oct 17, 1749, *N. C. Col. Recs.*, IV, 1020-21; Dobbs to Abercromby, Dec. 28, 1757, *ibid.*, V, 788-89; Abercromby to Sec. of Board of Trade, Apr. 13, 1758, *ibid.*, 928-29; Johnston to Abercromby, Oct. 24, 1748, CO 5/296, f. 104; N. C. agent act, Oct. 1748, CO 324/60, ff. 281-84; Abercromby to Swann, Apr. 13, 19, 1758, and to Dobbs, Apr. 20, 1758, Abercromby Letter Book, 94-97, Va. State Lib.

15. Abercromby to Sec. of Board of Trade, Apr. 13, 1758, *N. C. Col. Recs.*, V, 928-29; Abercromby to Swann, Apr. 19, 1758, and to Dobbs, Apr. 20, 1758, Abercromby Letter Book, 95-96, Va. State Lib.

formed a plan to bring the colony's portion of the Parliamentary grant to North Carolina in specie and entrust it to the public treasurers. They inserted the plan in a multi-purpose bill to grant military aid and to appoint an agent. The agent named was Abercromby, who was to receive a grant for his past services and a yearly salary out of the Parliamentary grant. His term was two years, and he was to be directed by a committee of five representatives and no councilors. Abercromby was to transmit North Carolina's portion of the grant in specie to Treasurers Barker and Starkey. Anticipating opposition to this plan from Dobbs, House leaders tried to arrange a *quid pro quo* by offering to pass a measure to fix the capital at Tower Hill, near New Bern, long one of Dobbs's favorite projects. Dobbs was eager to obtain the capital bill, but he ardently opposed the House's scheme to bring the sum over in specie, fearing that Swann and the rest of the "junto" might turn the money to their own use. He also had serious objections to the representatives' blatant attempt to appoint an agent under its exclusive direction. He therefore outmaneuvered the House by persuading the Council to wait until after the capital bill had been passed a final time before rejecting the military aid bill. Thus Dobbs secured the capital bill without consenting to the House's scheme to dispose of the Parliamentary money.[16]

But Dobbs's victory evoked a violent reaction from the House. Having failed in its attempt to appoint an agent and to pass a law to dispose of the Parliamentary funds through the normal legal channels, the Lower House now determined to act extraconstitutionally by its own authority. First it prudently secured Dobbs's agreement to a resolution to pay Abercromby's arrears of salary from the Parliamentary grant. Then, without the consent of the governor and Council, it appointed Abercromby "provincial agent," responsible solely to the Lower House, to request that part of North Carolina's share of the Parliamentary grant be used to purchase globes and to establish free schools in each county. Dobbs complained vigorously to the Board of Trade and Secretary of State Pitt, and when he met the Council in executive session in March 1758 he concurred with it in appointing Samuel Smith, "Secretary to the Northwest Passage" in London, agent for the governor and Council to counter the Lower House's designs. Thus, North Carolina was in the unique position of being represented

16. Lower House Journals, Dec. 20, 1758, *N. C. Col. Recs.*, V, 1087; Dobbs to Board of Trade, Jan. 22, 1759, *ibid.*, VI, 2-4.

by two agents, neither with legal authority. When the Lower House reconvened the following May, the agency controversy was revived. Called together to provide a military appropriation, the House insisted on including in the appropriation bill a rider to appoint agent Abercromby under its exclusive control. But the Council refused to pass the bill so long as it contained the rider, and the session ended in deadlock.[17]

Meanwhile, Abercromby had accepted the appointment as provincial agent, and Samuel Smith had assumed his duties as agent for the governor and Council. In the eyes of imperial authorities, neither acted under legal authority, but Abercromby had the advantage of valuable experience and connections acquired during his long service as agent for both Virginia and North Carolina. Working for the branch that controlled the purse, he was also more certain that he would eventually be paid for his services. As might have been predicted, Abercromby turned the situation to the House's advantage. The Board of Trade ruled in August 1759 that the right to appropriate the funds granted by Parliament rested with the Lower House and held that Dobbs might properly have passed the agent bill had it not been attached to the aid bill and had members of the Council been included in the committee of correspondence.[18]

In May 1760 Dobbs again summoned the Lower House to grant a military appropriation, but the dispute over the appointment of an agent once more threatened to disrupt proceedings. At the opening of the session the House signified its intention to appoint an agent and brought in a bill for that purpose, not as a rider this time but as a separate measure. The House abandoned Abercromby, despite his faithful service, largely because of the Council's opposition to him, in favor of London merchant Anthony Bacon. But Bacon proved

17. Dobbs to Board of Trade, Jan. 22, May 18, 1759, to Pitt, May 18, 1759, *ibid.*, 2-4, 32-34, 40-41; to Pitt, Feb. 6, 1759, Kimball, *Correspondence of Pitt*, II, 35-36; and to Lyttelton, May 25, 1759, Lyttelton Papers, Clements Lib.; Council Journals, Mar. 3, 1759, *N. C. Col. Recs.*, VI, 76-77; Upper House Journals, May 16-17, 1759, *ibid.*, 92-93; Abercromby to Swann, July 20, 1759, Abercromby Letter Book, 165-66, Va. State Lib.

18. Abercromby to N. C. Committee of Correspondence, July 20, 1759, May 10, 1760, Abercromby Letter Book, 106a-7a, 167-68, Va. State Lib.; Board of Trade to Dobbs, Aug. 1, 1759, *N. C. Col. Recs.*, VI, 54-55. Smith was never paid. The Council asked that he be awarded £1,000 sterling for "five years Agency" in November 1764, but the House flatly refused on the grounds that he "never was appointed Agent for this Province." Lower House Journals, Nov. 27, 1764, *ibid.*, 1316-17.

to be as disagreeable to Dobbs and the Council as Abercromby had been, and the House's refusal to accept a substitute or to allow the Council to appoint some of its members to the committee of correspondence once more resulted in a legislative impasse. Again the House resorted to extralegal methods. It unilaterally appointed Bacon to serve as agent, although it twice tried to formalize his appointment by passing agent bills in 1760. The first failed in the Council, and the second, accepted by the Council after the House had agreed to permit councilors to sit on the committee of correspondence, was vetoed by Dobbs, who objected to the provision requiring Bacon to receive the Parliamentary money and remit it in specie to the committee of correspondence and to the House's attempting to pass the measure as a rider. The House then tried to place the controversy on a constitutional basis by resolving that "it is the Inherent and undoubted right of this House to nominate an agent to be appointed for this Province (in a Bill for that purpose) to sollicit the affairs thereof at the several Boards in England" and by reintroducing the agent bill as a separate measure in direct defiance of the governor. Both houses accepted the new bill, but Dobbs retaliated by dissolving the legislature before the measure came before him.[19]

Dobbs's continued opposition to the Lower House's nominee did not meet with approval at home, however. In one of the clearest statements of the imperial authorities' attitude toward the nomination and appointment of colonial agents in the late colonial period, the Board of Trade wrote Dobbs on April 4, 1761, that it did not consider it "the part of the Crown or its' Officers either in point of Right or Propriety to interfere in the nomination of an Agent so far as regards the Choice of the person, in this respect the Representatives of the people are and ought to be free to chuse whom they think proper to act, in whatever concerns the Affairs and Interest of the Colony here and with whom they and the Council only can correspond, the Governor being very properly restrained by his Instruction from corresponding upon matters of a publick nature relative to his Government with any other persons than those servants of the Crown

19. Lower House Journals, May 5, 23, 26-27, Dec. 5-6, 1760, *N. C. Col. Recs.,* VI, 380-81, 414-16, 429, 433-34, 436, 515-20; Dobbs's Answers to Lower House's resolutions of May 1760, Aug. 3, 1760, *ibid.,* 306-8; Dobbs to Board of Trade, May 28, July 21, Dec. 12, 1760, *ibid.,* 248-51, 267-68, 319-24; Upper House Journals, July 8, Dec. 3, 1760, *ibid.,* 442, 469; Council Journals, Dec. 6, 1760, *ibid.,* 345.

here, in whose department the Affairs of America are placed." The Board's position was clear. As long as the Council was allowed to participate in the committee of correspondence, it would concede the right to nominate the agent to the Lower House. While the Board was issuing this statement, the House was finally forcing Dobbs to consent to a law to appoint an agent, although Dobbs's unflinching opposition to Anthony Bacon forced it to abandon him in favor of Couchet Jouvencal, secretary to William Pitt. Because the agent law was tacked to an aid bill, Dobbs passed it with considerable trepidation. Nor were his fears without foundation, for the Board of Trade was opposed to such a practice and later termed the appointment "irregular and unprecedented," advising Dobbs that upon the expiration of Jouvencal's term an agent law should be passed separately.[20]

After a struggle of nearly two and a half years, North Carolina once again was represented in London by a legally constituted agent firmly under the Lower House's control. The committee appointed to correspond with Jouvencal consisted of three councilors and five representatives. Because of its majority on the committee of correspondence, the Lower House played the leading role in directing him. Dobbs complained in April 1762 that the Council's members of the committee were not consulted about correspondence with the agent and that Jouvencal's letters were addressed to Speaker Swann rather than to the committee as a whole with the result that Swann dominated the committee. When the question of Jouvencal's reappointment came up in March 1764, the Council tried to gain more influence in the committee by proposing that the presence of one councilor be necessary to constitute a quorum. The Lower House turned down the proposal, and the Council rejected the agent bill. The whole agency controversy was reopened as the Lower House again acted on its own by resolving that Jouvencal continue as agent until April 1765 under the direction of five representatives, thus setting the stage for a five-year contest during a critical period in imperial-colonial affairs.[21]

20. Board of Trade to Dobbs, Apr. 4, 1761, *ibid.*, 538-39; Laws, *N. C. St. Recs.*, XXIII, 539-41; George Pollock to Corbin Morris, June 20, 1761, Pollock Letter Book, N. C. Dept. of Arch. and Hist.
21. Lower House Journals, Apr. 22-23, 1761, Apr. 29, 1762, Mar. 7-9, 1764, *N. C. Col. Recs.*, VI, 692, 695, 836-37, 1205-7, 1214; Upper House Journals, Apr. 23, 1761, *ibid.*, 659-60; Feb. 10, 1762, *Board of Trade Journals, 1759-63*, 249-51; Board of Trade to Dobbs, Feb. 17, 1762, *N. C. Col. Recs.*, VI, 702-3.

The last of the lower houses of the older southern royal colonies to gain control over a permanent agent was the Virginia House of Burgesses. Between 1624 and 1690 no fewer than twenty-two special agents appeared before the various boards in England in behalf of the colony, but no permanent agency was established for Virginia until late in the seventeenth century. When the governor and Council did create such an office, it was unique in that the appointment was entirely in the hands of the executive. Owing both his nomination and his salary, which was early set at £100 sterling per annum from the two-shillings-per-hogshead tobacco revenue, to the governor and Council, the agent looked to them for direction and sided with them in cases of controversy between the executive and the Burgesses. But despite the Burgesses' exclusion from control over this officer, he was considered agent for the colony of Virginia.[22]

Although the Burgesses made no concerted effort to share in the appointment or direction of an agent until after the middle of the eighteenth century, it did appoint a number of special agents between 1688 and 1755 mostly to perform fairly routine tasks for the colony. The governor and Council readily consented to most appointments;[23] but four of them resulted from controversies between the Burgesses and the executive, and in each case the Burgesses found it necessary to make appointments without the consent of the governor and Council in order to present its side of the dispute to Crown officials. In 1688 the Burgesses sent Philip Ludwell to England to prefer charges against its governor, Lord Howard of Effingham, who had incurred the representatives' hostility by establishing fees without their consent. William Byrd II played a similar role in 1701 when the Burgesses, despite Nicholson's opposition, selected him to persuade Crown officials to withdraw an order requiring Virginia to contribute money to help New York defend its frontiers against Indian attacks. Significantly, the success of both missions and the fact that both agents were probably eventually paid indicated that the Burgesses could appoint an agent even without the executive's consent.[24]

22. Lonn, *Colonial Agents*, 4-26, 57-61, 140-41, 392-93; Account of Va. Civil Establishment as settled in 1717 and 1726, Apr. 7, 1730, House of Lords MSS, 106, No. 20.

23. See Mar. 28, 1728, June 28, 1732, July 1, 1732, *Va. Burgesses Journals, 1727-40*, 49, 160-61, 167; Apr. 18, 20, 1752, *ibid., 1752-58*, 96-99; John Blair to Bishop of London, Aug. 14, 1732, Fulham Palace MSS, Virginia (First Box), 14, f. 164; Isham Randolph's Petition, Mar. 17, 1732, House of Lords MSS, 115.

24. See May 12, 1688, May 7, 16, 18-19, 1691, *Va. Burgesses Journals, 1660-93*,

In 1718 Byrd again undertook to serve the House without the governor's approval, this time in what appears to have been an attempt by the Burgesses to secure the power to appoint an agent whenever it deemed necessary. Byrd was already in England, and it is likely that his own experience there the year before had prompted the Burgesses to make the attempt. The Board of Trade had refused to receive him as agent for the Council, insisting that all Virginia matters be presented either through the governor or the regular agent, who at the time was Nathaniel Blakiston. Byrd eventually had had to insist upon his rights as a councilor in order to gain an audience with the Board. This transaction convinced Byrd that the Virginia legislature needed to maintain a permanent agent in London, and in October 1717 he suggested to fellow-councilor Philip Ludwell that such an appointment be made. When the Burgesses met in May 1718 it followed Byrd's suggestion and introduced a bill to appoint an agent to present an address to the Crown asking that a recent instruction to prohibit the colonies from passing laws affecting the trade and shipping of Great Britain be revoked and that the governor's power to appoint judges of oyer and terminer be restricted. This bill, as Spotswood later reported, empowered the Burgesses "to name, (barely by a Resolve of their House,) any person to be their Agent; by the like Resolve Change him and put in another, and by the same power to pay such Agents what sums they thought fitt, without any Concurrence of the Governor or Council." Without question, the bill appears to have been designed to secure to the Burgesses the right to appoint an agent without the approval of the governor and Council. This conclusion is reinforced by the Burgesses' subsequent actions. After the Council had rejected its bill, the Burgesses, without the executive's approval, appointed Byrd to present its address, promising him "a suitable gratification for his trouble."[25]

329, 351, 362, 363-65; Aug. 26, Sept. 16-Oct. 2, 1701, *ibid., 1695-1702*, 268, 298-302, 313, 317, 319, 333-34; Sept. 30, 1701, Henry R. McIlwaine, ed., *Legislative Journals of the Council of Colonial Virginia*, 3 vols. (Richmond, 1925-45), I, 321, hereafter cited as *Leg. Journals of Va. Council;* Board of Trade to Crown, May 18, 1702, CO 5/1312. It is impossible to determine with any certainty if Byrd was ever paid, but it seems likely that he received his salary in 1705 after Edward Nott had replaced Nicholson when the Burgesses reimbursed him for other expenses incurred during his agency. Nov. 17, 1705, *Va. Burgesses Journals, 1703-12*, 157.

25. Byrd to Ludwell, Oct. 28, 1717, "Some Colonial Letters," *Va. Mag. of Hist. and Biog.*, 3 (1895), 352-53; Spotswood to Board of Trade, June 24, 1718, Brock, ed., *Spotswood Letters*, II, 277-79; May 19, 27, 30, 1718, *Va. Burgesses Journals,*

When the House met again in November, it charged Spotswood with attempting to subvert the constitution and to deprive Virginians of their "ancient Rights and priviledges." At the insistence of Spotswood's friends in the House, it later softened some of the more serious charges it had leveled against him in a series of instructions to Byrd, but significantly it did not alter its request that Byrd procure an instruction to the governor requiring him to consent to pay any agent the House should send to represent it in England—another clear indication that what the Burgesses was striving for was the freedom to appoint an agent without executive interference. The Burgesses voted Byrd £300 sterling for performing these tasks, but Spotswood insisted that Blakiston was the proper channel through which the House should transmit its address. He was determined not to sanction Byrd's appointment in any way and refused to consent to his payment. Byrd undertook the assignment without assurance of payment, although he was unable to accomplish much. The Board still hesitated to accept him as agent, and he was unable to persuade imperial authorities to take any action against Spotswood. But after his return home in February 1720 Byrd made his peace with Spotswood, and in 1722, as a result of a *quid pro quo* in which the House agreed to pay Spotswood an equal amount for his expenses in his 1717 trip to New York to treat with its governor on relations with the Iroquois Indians, the governor and Council consented to pay him the £300 which the Burgesses had promised him in 1718.[26]

Not until December 1753, during the bitter pistole fee controversy with Robert Dinwiddie, did the Burgesses again attempt to appoint an agent without executive consent. It resolved to send Peyton Randolph, member of the House and Crown attorney general, to England to protest the fee and voted him a salary of £2,500 sterling and in the event that he lost his post as attorney general the sum of

---

1712-26, 198, 210, 216; May 24, 1718, *Leg. Journals of Va. Council*, II, 619; Bill to Appoint an agent, May 21, 1718, in Greene, ed., "Opposition to Spotswood, 1718," *Va. Mag. of Hist. and Biog.*, 70 (1962), 41-42.

26. Nov. 20-21, 27, Dec. 1, 1718, May 10, 23, 1722, *Va. Burgesses Journals, 1712-26*, 228-31, 237-38, 243, 323, 335; Louis B. Wright and Marion Tinling, eds., *William Byrd of Virginia: The London Diary (1717-1721) and Other Writings* (N. Y., 1958), 26-35. The Burgesses' attempt to appoint Byrd for a third time in 1720 to deliver an address to the Crown asking relief from quitrents for western lands failed because of Spotswood's opposition. See *ibid.*, 35-36, 486; Dec. 14, 20-23, 1720, *Va. Burgesses Journals, 1712-26*, 299-300, 308-10, 313-14; Lonn, *Colonial Agents*, 122-23.

£300 per year for life. It also empowered him to appoint a permanent agent for the House at an annual salary of £200. Although Randolph failed to accomplish his mission entirely, the Burgesses insisted that he be paid the full salary promised him, and Dinwiddie and the Council, elated over their victory in the controversy, consented in the fall of 1754. The pistole fee controversy had two important consequences: it demonstrated to the Burgesses the need for a permanent agent under its control, and it aroused an intense dislike in that body for James Abercromby, Dinwiddie's agent during the affair and beginning in 1754 permanent agent for the colony.[27]

Between the summer of 1755 and the spring of 1759 the Burgesses made several attempts to appoint an agent subject to its authority, but Dinwiddie's opposition forced it to abandon the effort temporarily.[28] Speaker John Robinson outlined the Burgesses' position when he wrote in June 1758 to Secretary of State William Pitt: "It is true there is a Person residing in Great Brittain that bears the Character of Agent for this Colony, but when it is considered that his Appointment is from the Governor, or through his Influence, he can not be properly looked upon as the Agent for the Colony, but rather for the Governor, and as it is not uncommon for the Interest of the Colonies and that of their Governors to be very opposite, it will hardly be supposed that a Person so appointed will interest himself in the Affairs of the Colony committed to his Care, how muchsoever they may tend to his Majesty's Service and the Wellfare of the Colony, if they happen to be disagreeable to the Governor or clash with his Interest."[29]

Dinwiddie's resignation in January 1758 was the signal for the Burgesses to renew its efforts to appoint an agent. During the next year the Council rejected two agent bills, one in April during John Blair's administration and the other in October under Fauquier.

27. Dinwiddie to Abercromby, Feb. 9, Nov. 16, 1754, Brock, ed., *Dinwiddie Papers*, I, 71-73, 408-10; May 12, 1755, *Va. Burgesses Journals, 1752-58*, 250-51; Landon Carter's Minutes of the Burgesses, Oct. 17, 1754, Sabine Hall Collection, Alderman Lib.; John Blair to Abercromby, May 30, 1759, CO 5/1329, f. 373; Francis Fauquier to Board of Trade, Sept. 1, 1760, CO 5/1330, ff. 59-65.

28. Aug. 22, 1755, Apr. 29-May 3, 1756, *Va. Burgesses Journals, 1752-58*, 314, 389-93; Dinwiddie to Abercromby, Feb. 18, 1755, May 24, 1756, Brock, ed., *Dinwiddie Papers*, I, 505-8, II, 419; Abercromby to Earl of Loudoun, Aug. 3, 1756, Loudoun Papers, 1410, Huntington Lib.; Jenings to Dinwiddie, Sept. 21, 1754, Edmund Jenings II Letter Book, Va. Hist. Soc.

29. Robinson to Pitt, June 11, 1758, Chatham Papers, Gifts and Deposits, 30/8, vol. 96, PRO.

Fauquier signified that he could not pass the bill without permission from the Crown, whereupon the Council threw it out, declaring "that it was making an Alteration, and introducing a Power that was unknown to the Constitution, that it was striking at the Prerogative of the Crown, and taking from his Governor, who is his Representative: the Exclusive Power." But Blair wrote to Abercromby in January 1759 that he feared the bill would pass when the Burgesses reconvened.[30]

The following April the Burgesses succeeded in its attempt to appoint an agent. It followed the example of the North Carolina Lower House of the previous December, tacking an agent bill as a rider to a military appropriation bill. Fauquier refused to "suffer the Tack" but offered to pass a separate agent bill if it got by the Council. The Burgesses then submitted one to the Council, which it passed by a wide margin after Councilor Peter Randolph had assured it that Fauquier would consent if it did. Fauquier's effort to induce the Burgesses to nominate Abercromby was to no avail. Instead it chose Edward Montague, barrister of the Middle Temple. The act appointed the agent for a term of seven years and designated a committee of correspondence consisting of four councilors and eight burgesses in which the majority made all decisions. It was inevitable that the House would control the committee. Virginia now had two agents, Abercromby for the governor and Council, and Montague technically for the General Assembly but in reality for the House of Burgesses.[31]

The passage of the agent bill gave Abercromby some reason to fear for his job. There was some opposition in the Council to the colony's having two agents, and Abercromby worked diligently to secure the measure's disallowance. Although he obtained an opinion from Charles Pratt, one of the Crown's attorney generals, that the Virginia agent act did not eliminate his position as agent for the governor and Council—thus assuring him that he would probably retain his post—he could not persuade imperial authorities to disallow

30. Apr. 8, 1758, *Va. Burgesses Journals, 1752-58*, 503; Blair to Abercromby, Jan. 15, 1759, CO 5/1329, f. 371; Richard Corbin to Abercromby, Oct. 21, 1758, *ibid.*, ff. 367-68; Philip Ludwell to Gov. D————, Mar. 22, 1759, *ibid.*, ff. 369-70.

31. Fauquier to Board of Trade, Apr. 14, 1759, CO 5/1329, ff. 275-78; Philip Ludwell to Gov. D————, Mar. 22, 1759, *ibid.*, ff. 369-70; Blair to Abercromby, May 30, 1759, *ibid.*, f. 373; Hening, ed., *Va. Statutes*, VII, 276-77.

the agent act.[32] In fact, when the Board of Trade referred the act to legal counsel Matthew Lamb, he reported that the Virginia Burgesses had the same power to nominate an agent as lower houses in other colonies, thereby approving the act in principle. He did object, however, to the clause giving the committee of correspondence power to remove the agent and to select a successor with the approval of *"the Assembly only."* He pointed out that the governor and Council had thereby "put it into the Power of *the Committee of Correspondence and the Assembly alone,* Imediately after to Remove such Agent and to Appoint another, and so to Continue for the Term of Seven Years, without any Controul or Approbation on their Part." Lamb suggested that the act be amended to require that vacancies be filled by act of the whole legislature and "not by any Single Part of it, or any Committee of Persons named." The Board accepted Lamb's suggestion and advised Fauquier that the act would have to be amended accordingly before the Crown would confirm it. Upon Fauquier's recommendation, the Burgesses made the governor's and ultimately the entire legislature's approval necessary for all new appointees of the committee. The agent bill then met with the Board's approval. The Burgesses' efforts to secure control over an agent had finally succeeded.[33]

After 1759 Virginia was represented by two permanent agents in England, Abercromby serving the governor and Council until 1774 and Edward Montague acting for the General Assembly. Dependent upon the Burgesses for his salary and receiving his instructions and directions from the Burgesses-dominated committee of correspondence, Montague was thoroughly the instrument of the House. Upon the expiration of his first appointment in 1765, the Burgesses reappointed him for another term of seven years. But during his second term Junius Americanus, probably Arthur Lee, in a letter to the *Maryland Gazette* raised some serious questions about Montague's conduct as

32. Ludwell to Gov. D————, Mar. 22, 1759, Blair to Dinwiddie, May 29, 1759, CO 5/1329, ff. 369-70, 377-78; Abercromby to Corbin, June 29, 1759, to Blair, July 6, 25, 1759, and to Fauquier, July 26, 1759, Abercromby Letter Book, 152-60, 169-70, 173-77, Va. State Lib.; Abercromby to Loudoun, July 20, [1759], Loudoun Papers, 6125, Huntington Lib.; Abercromby's Memorial, read by Board of Trade, Nov. 21, 1759, CO 5/1329, ff. 343-49; Pratt's report of case of Va. agent, Dec. 24, 1759, Treasury Papers 1/389, ff. 30-31, PRO.

33. Lamb to Board of Trade, May 15, 1760, CO 5/1329, ff. 407-9; Board of Trade to Fauquier, June 13, 1760, CO 5/1367, pp. 405-12; Hening, ed., *Va. Statutes*, VII, 375-77.

agent, charging him with not opposing the Stamp Act in return for certain personal favors. It is impossible to tell if this accusation led to any general dissatisfaction with Montague among the burgesses. It may well have played an important part in the Burgesses' decision to discontinue the agency altogether in March 1772 at the end of Montague's second term. But it is also certain that many burgesses had already reached the conclusion that no agent could have much success in persuading Crown officials to take a more favorable attitude toward the colonies at that time and that the office was therefore, as Lord Dunmore later declared, "inexpedient."[34]

As would be expected, the Georgia Commons was the last of the lower houses in the southern royal colonies to make good its claim to the right of nominating and directing the agent. From 1753 to 1763, during the early years of royal government, Benjamin Martyn, former-ly secretary to the trustees of Georgia and an appointee of the Crown, served the province as agent. Martyn received both his salary and his instructions from the Crown, and his most important duty was to receive and transmit to Georgia its annual Parliamentary grant. That duty necessarily brought him into close contact with the Treas-ury, from which, along with the Board of Trade, he received his directions. His salary was fixed at £350 sterling per year.[35] Martyn was technically agent of the Crown for the colony rather than agent from the colony, but his presence in that office might have seriously retarded the demand for a legislative-appointed agent. That demand was not slow to develop at least in part because of Martyn's long association with the trustees—an association that rendered him un-desirable to the Georgia Commons.

The Georgia Commons moved to appoint another agent for the colony as early as February 1757, when it formally protested to the

34. Hening, ed., *Va. Statutes*, VIII, 113; Lonn, *Colonial Agents*, 359; Richard Henry Lee to Landon Carter, Mar. 7, 1772, Ballagh, ed., *R. H. Lee Letters*, I, 62; Robert Carter Nicholas to John Norton, Jan. 4, 1771, Norton Papers, Colonial Williamsburg, Inc.; Dunmore's Answers to Board of Trade's Queries, 1774, CO 5/1352; "Proceedings of the Virginia Committee of Correspondence," *Va. Mag. of Hist. and Biog.*, 10 (1902), 157-69, 353-64; 12 (1904), 337-56.

35. Lonn, *Colonial Agents*, 51-52; Benjamin Martyn's appointment as Georgia agent, Feb. 14, 1753, CO 324/60, ff. 301-3; Estimate of the Ga. Civil Establishment, June 24, 1754, to June 24, 1755, Newcastle Papers, Add. MSS, 33029, f. 122, British Museum.

Board of Trade against Martyn's acting as "Nominal Agent";[36] but it did not secure an agent of its own choosing for another five years. In February 1762 Governor James Wright agreed to an ordinance to appoint William Knox, Georgia provost marshal, assistant agent to Martyn. Knox's appointment was for one year with a salary of £50 and he was to follow the instructions from the General Assembly or from the committee of correspondence. The committee consisted of five councilors, the speaker, and six representatives, any seven of whom might constitute a quorum provided at least two were from the Council. Through its majority the Commons was able to control the committee, and it insisted on reviewing all transactions with the agent.

Knox served the colony well, sharing the agent's duties with Martyn, and the following year the Commons appointed him full "provincial" agent for one year and raised his salary to £100 sterling over and above his reasonable charges and disbursements. The Commons renewed Knox's appointment in 1764 and 1765, and it appeared that Knox might retain the agency as long as he wished, especially in view of the Board of Trade's ruling in May 1764 that the Crown agent for Georgia should no longer handle any of the colony's affairs "other than what may relate to the Grants of Parliament," thus officially recognizing the Georgia legislature's right to appoint an agent. But Knox's desire to curry favor with the ministry led him to take a stand on the Stamp Act that was unacceptable to the Georgia Commons and resulted in his dismissal. This dismissal inaugurated a long, involved, and at times acrimonious controversy over the agency that seriously disrupted Georgia politics during the next three years and became involved in the wider constitutional debate between Britain and the colonies.[37]

Without exception the lower houses in the southern royal colonies

36. Commons Journals, Jan. 25, Feb. 2, 1757, *Ga. Col. Recs.*, XIII, 129-30, 152; Ga. Commons' Address to Board of Trade, Feb. 2, 1757, CO 5/646.

37. Commons Journals, Feb. 19, Nov. 17, 1762, Jan. 20, Mar. 2, 1763, *Ga. Col. Recs.*, XIII, 680, 729, XIV, 6, 44-45; Statutes, *ibid.*, XVIII, 481-83, 536-38, 580-82; Wright to Board of Trade, Feb. 20, 1762, June 3, 1763, CO 5/648, ff. 265-70, 411-16; Board of Trade to Wright, May 29, 1764, unpubl. Ga. Col. Recs., XXXIV, 542-43, Ga. Dept. of Arch. and Hist.; Ga. Committee of Correspondence to Knox, Apr. 19, 1763, and Habersham to Knox, Mar. 9, 1764, Oct. 28, 1765, *Habersham Letters*, 11, 17, 44-46; Knox to William Henry Lyttelton, Feb. 10, 1762, "Manuscripts of Captain H. V. Knox," Historical Manuscripts Commission, *Report on Manuscripts in Various Collections*, VI (Dublin, 1909), 86.

had succeeded in securing the authority to nominate, appoint, and through a committee of correspondence manipulate a colonial agent by 1763. The South Carolina Commons exercised that right throughout the royal period and in 1754-55 even demonstrated its power to keep an agent in office without executive approval. Both the North Carolina Lower House and the Virginia Burgesses occasionally employed special agents in London during the early eighteenth century, but neither of them moved to establish regular agents under their control until the middle of the century. The North Carolina body first appointed a permanent agent in 1748 and twice, between 1758 and 1761 and between 1764 and 1766, maintained an agent in London despite strong opposition from Governor Dobbs and the Council. The presence in London after 1690 of a regular agent chosen by the governor and Council and paid out of the two-shillings-per-hogshead permanent revenue retarded the development of the demand of the Virginia Burgesses to create an agency under its control. But the pistole fee controversy in 1753-54 convinced it that such an office would be invaluable, and, after several abortive attempts, it finally succeeded in establishing one in 1759. Like the Virginia Burgesses, the Georgia Commons was for a time prevented from appointing an agent because the Crown agent selected to handle the colony's Parliamentary grant had pre-empted the job. But in 1762 it successfully asserted its right to employ an agent of its own choosing.

All four lower houses appointed the majority of the members to the committees of correspondence and thereby maintained strict supervision over the agents, turning them, for all practical purposes, into legislative officers. At no time after 1763 did British officials attempt to interfere with the lower houses' right to name and appoint the agents, at least not so long as all three branches of the legislature concurred in the appointments. Indeed, in the case of North Carolina they even ruled that the right of nomination should rest with the Lower House. Yet in both North Carolina and Georgia, where the governors and councils challenged the lower houses' right of nomination, serious controversies over the agencies developed in the decade before Independence that constituted important issues in the approaching Revolutionary movement.

14

Public Printers

Potentially one of the most important powers sought by lower houses in the eighteenth century was the right to appoint public printers. Beginning in the reign of Henry VII in England, the Crown had regularly designated an official printer to publish the statutes of the realm and occasional state papers, but it had never insisted that its printer have a monopoly on the public business. Consequently, the power to appoint that official never became a serious issue between Crown and Parliament, and in the seventeenth century the House of Commons frequently hired its own printers to publish its journals and some committee reports.[1] In America the story was quite different. A printing press and a newspaper were invaluable to a colony, but in a young colony a printer could scarcely support himself without a government subsidy, and American legislatures found it necessary to offer a salary or a monopoly on government printing to attract printers to the colonies. In the thirty years before 1763 each of the lower houses in the southern royal colonies established the office of public printer either formally by an official legislative act granting a settled salary from the colony or informally by an unofficial promise of an annual sum for handling government printing. In either case the printer was expected to publish the colony's laws, legislative journals, and other government papers and to distribute them to the governor, councilors, representatives, and other public officials.

The printer did far more than merely print government papers. To supplement his income he also published a newspaper, sometimes,

1. Frederick S. Siebert, *Freedom of the Press in England, 1476-1776* (Urbana, 1952), 32-33, 171, 245, 281.

particularly in the years before 1760, the only one in the colony. As
the selector of the materials printed in his paper, he was in a peculiarly favorable position to shape attitudes and opinions, and in time of
conflict he could be of great service to the party he supported. Probably few contests before 1763 generated enough popular interest to
make control over the printer an important issue, but thereafter, during the debate with the mother country over taxation and imperial
policy, the significance of the printer rapidly became apparent. Because the printer owed his appointment, salary, and monopoly on
government printing to the lower house, it would seem likely that that
body would have received favorable treatment in the press and even
have manipulated the complexion of his newspaper in its favor. But
when there were no rival printers in the colony, as was so often the
case in the south before the end of the Seven Years' War, there was
little chance of the printer's losing the public business, and he could
afford to take a neutral position. He might, in fact, come under the
influence of the governor, for whom he would stifle unfavorable comment or keep inflammatory articles out of print. By 1760, however,
rival printers were beginning to appear in nearly every colony, and
the possibility of losing the public business or his government salary
to a competitor was usually sufficient to bring the public printer firmly under the lower house's control.

Virginia was the first of the southern royal colonies to establish
the office of public printer. In 1732 the Burgesses appointed by formal resolution William Parks, who since 1727 had been publisher of
the *Maryland Gazette* at nearby Annapolis, to serve as public printer
to publish its journal and the colony's laws and to distribute copies of
them to each burgess, justice of the peace, and county court. For
performing these services the Burgesses voted Parks an annual salary
of £120. Parks continued in the office for nearly two decades and
beginning in 1736 published the *Virginia Gazette*. Upon his death
in 1750, he was succeeded by his apprentice, William Hunter, who
served continuously as public printer until his death in 1761, when his
apprentice, Joseph Royle, succeeded him. The Burgesses paid its
printers well, raising Parks's annual salary to £280 before he died and
paying Royle £375 after 1764.[2]

2. May 20, June 10, July 1, 1732, Dec. 21, 1738, *Va. Burgesses Journals, 1727-40*,
121, 141-42, 167, 387; June 19, 1742, Oct. 25, 1744, *ibid., 1742-49*, 70, 149; Mar. 12,

All three of Virginia's first printers owed both their appointments and their annual salaries to the Burgesses, which it, would seem, as former Lieutenant Governor Spotswood suggested in 1736, might have held a rather tight control over them. But such was not the case, for there were no rival printers in Virginia competing for their jobs. All of them appear, in fact, to have been closely under the supervision of the royal governors. Thus, in 1754 Hunter would not publish a piece by Landon Carter taking the Burgesses' side in the pistole fee controversy, and in 1765 Lieutenant Governor Fauquier had enough influence with Royle to prevent his printing another essay of Carter's against the Stamp Act.[3] But neither did the printers dare publish anything against the Burgesses, lest they suffer the fate that befell Parks in 1749. In May the Burgesses took him into custody and threatened more severe proceedings because he had printed in the *Gazette* at the Council's direction a paper defending its authority to deny the Burgesses the right to search its legislative journals, which the House considered "a malicious and scandalous Libel, highly and injuriously reflecting on the Proceedings of the House of Burgesses."[4]

But Royle's neutralism in the Stamp Act controversy convinced many burgesses that he was too much under the governor's influence, and they moved to bring the public printer more closely under their control. Thomas Jefferson and others encouraged William Rind to come from Maryland and set up a rival *Gazette* in 1766.[5] In November, when Royle's appointment—held temporarily by his apprentices, Alexander Purdie and John Dixon, after his death earlier in that year —expired, the Burgesses appointed Rind "Public Printer" by a large majority from a field of four candidates. Purdie and Dixon ran a poor fourth behind both William Stark and Robert Miller, both of whom proposed to set up a press in the colony if they could obtain the government business. The fate of Purdie and Dixon was sufficient warning to Rind and his successors that the public printer stood in grave dan-

---

1752, *ibid.*, *1752-58*, 30; Nov. 5, 1761, Jan. 18, 1764, *ibid.*, *1761-65*, 11-12, 214. For a sketch of Parks, see Lawrence C. Wroth, *William Parks: Printer and Journalist of England and Colonial America* (Richmond, 1926). On Hunter, see Ruth Lapham Butler, *Doctor Franklin: Postmaster General* (N. Y., 1928), 43-71.

3. Spotswood to Parks, [1736], Misc. MSS, Mass. Hist. Soc., Boston; *Maryland Gazette* (Annapolis), Oct. 24, 1754; Carter to Joseph Royle, June 3, 1765, Fairfax Papers, Brock Collection, Huntington Lib.

4. May 11, 1749, *Va. Burgesses Journals, 1742-49*, 403-4.

5. Bridenbaugh, *Myths and Realities*, 41-42.

ger of losing his job if he displeased the House. Neither Fauquier nor the Council made any effort to challenge the Burgesses' right to select the public printer on this occasion, and for the remainder of the colonial period the Burgesses continued to exercise that right without contest. When Rind died in 1774 the House chose his wife, Clementina, from a field of three candidates to succeed him; upon her death the following year it passed over two rival printers to appoint Alexander Purdie—by that time firmly committed to the patriot cause. Both of the Rinds and Purdie served the House well, and for their efforts the Burgesses increased the annual salary of the office to £450 after 1770. Their *Gazette* was an invaluable medium of expression for the House in its debate with the mother country in the decade before the Declaration of Independence.[6]

The South Carolina Commons acquired a printer at about the same time that the Virginia Burgesses did. In 1731 it offered a bounty of £1,000 Carolina currency to any printer who would come to the colony and set up his press. Three men—George Webb, Eleazer Phillips, and Thomas Whitmarsh—responded. Webb's death early in 1732 reduced the field of candidates to two, and the Commons awarded Phillips the bounty and selected him to serve as official printer, despite strong opposition from Governor Robert Johnson, who actively supported Whitmarsh. But Phillips's tenure was short. He died late in 1732, leaving the post as official printer to Whitmarsh, who was now the only printer in the colony. In the fall of 1733 Whitmarsh died, and the colony was left without a printer. Within six months, however, a new printer arrived to take Whitmarsh's place. Philadelphia printer Benjamin Franklin had invested heavily in Whitmarsh's Charleston enterprise, and upon Whitmarsh's death Franklin rushed another protégé—the Huguenot immigrant Lewis Timothy—south to carry on the business. Early in 1734 Timothy took over the duties of the official printer and resumed publication of Whitmarsh's newspaper, the *South-Carolina Gazette*. Timothy established what proved to be a family dynasty that continued to handle the vast majority of government printing down to the Revolution.

6. Nov. 7, 1766, *Va. Burgesses Journals, 1766-69,* 17-18; June 21, 1770, *ibid., 1770-72,* 86; May 24, 1774, June 6, 1775, *ibid., 1773-76,* 124-25, 195-96. On the role of the press from 1763 to 1776, see Arthur M. Schlesinger, *Prelude to Independence: The Newspaper War on Britain, 1764-1776* (N. Y., 1958).

When he died in 1738, his wife Elizabeth ran the business until her son Peter reached his majority in 1746. Except for a brief period between March 1772 and November 1773, when he formed a partnership with Thomas Powell and Edward Hughes and turned the bulk of his printing business over to them, Peter Timothy published the *Gazette* and did most of the colony's official printing for the remainder of the colonial period.[7]

Unlike the Virginia Burgesses, the South Carolina Commons never created a formal office of public printer with a regular salary from the colony. But by guaranteeing one printer a monopoly or near monopoly on government printing and voting him annual allowances for his work for the public, the Commons did, in effect, make him official printer. Still, it never gave any of its printers an official title, although it did occasionally refer to Peter Timothy as "printer to the Honourable Commons House of Assembly."[8] Certainly, the official printer could count on a substantial amount of business from the colony every year. In 1734 Lewis Timothy earned £150 Carolina currency from the colony. As the Commons increased the scope of its activities, the annual amount of public printing also increased, with the result that Peter Timothy did over £270 worth of printing for the public in 1764.[9] In 1758 Robert Wells established a rival newspaper and thereafter handled a small portion of the public printing. But Timothy's close relations with the Commons (he had even served as a member of that body from 1752 to 1754) and his willingness to make his newspaper a vehicle for legislative opinion in any conflicts involving the House assured him of the vast majority of government printing jobs. After 1763 Timothy's *Gazette* provided the Commons with an outlet for its contentions in the controversies with Parliament and Crown officials, becoming perhaps the most important patriot paper in the southern colonies.[10]

When the North Carolina Lower House finally got around to seeking a printer for the colony in the middle of the eighteenth century,

7. Hennig Cohen, *The South Carolina Gazette, 1732-1775* (Columbia, 1953), 3-5, 230-45.
8. *Ibid.*, 242.
9. Apr. 18, 1735, Salley, ed., *S. C. Commons Journals, 1734-35*, 170; Aug. 9, 1765, *ibid., 1765*, 167.
10. Cohen, *South Carolina Gazette*, 242-44; Philip Davidson, *Propaganda and the American Revolution* (Chapel Hill, 1941), 232-33.

it followed the Virginia Burgesses' example and formally established an office of public printer with a fixed annual salary from the colony. The necessity of hiring a printer to publish the 1749 revisal of North Carolina statutes prompted the legislature to pass a law to appoint James Davis—who had learned his trade in Williamsburg under William Parks—public printer for a term of five years with an annual stipend of £160 proclamation money.[11] Davis set up his press in New Bern in the same year and almost immediately printed the House journal for the spring session. In 1751 he began issuing the *North Carolina Gazette,* the colony's first newspaper, and during the 1750's he took an active part in local politics, first serving on the Craven County court and from 1755 to 1760 acting as one of the county's representatives to the Lower House. He performed his printing tasks satisfactorily, and the House continued to reappoint him public printer, raising his yearly salary to £200 proclamation money in 1760.[12]

But in the early 1760's some dissatisfaction developed among Governor Dobbs and others over Davis's failure to deliver copies of the printed laws and journals to the western counties according to the terms of his contract. In November 1762 the Council passed a measure to replace Davis with Alexander Purdie—another Virginia printer—only to have it die in the Lower House. But in March 1764 Dobbs added his influence to those who wanted to replace Davis and recommended the appointment of a new printer, declaring that he could "never approve" of Davis "upon Account of His negligence in not Printing the Laws Journals and other Public Orders nor dispersing them in proper numbers for the use of the Province." For once, the majority of House members appears to have agreed with Dobbs. They voted to appoint a committee to find a new printer. Accordingly, the committee contracted with Andrew Stewart of Philadelphia, who proceeded immediately to the colony, setting up his press in Wilmington in June. But when the legislature met the following November, Davis's many friends in the House and those northern members who wanted to keep the public printer at New Bern voted to continue Davis as public printer. On the other hand, the Council insisted that the legislature was obliged to appoint Stewart, who had come to the

11. Lower House Journals, Apr. 6, 1749, *N. C. Col. Recs.,* IV, 990; Upper House Journals, Apr. 14, 1749, *ibid.,* 984; Laws, *N. C. St. Recs.,* XXIII, 314-15.

12. Alonzo T. Dill, *Governor Tryon and His Palace* (Chapel Hill, 1955), 72-75; Laws, *N. C. St. Recs.,* XXV, 266-67, 349, 455-56.

colony assuming that he would get the public post, and, when the House continued to support Davis, the Council flatly rejected the bill providing for his appointment.[13]

The Council's action set the stage for the one vigorous contest in the southern colonies over who had the right to appoint the public printer. Its rejection presented Dobbs with an excellent opportunity to assert the executive's right to appoint the printer. He immediately informed the House that he had with the Council's advice appointed Stewart "printer to his Majesty in this Province" for a term of eighteen months and asked the House to vote him an adequate salary. But the House denied that it knew of any "such office as his Majesty's Printer of this Province; and of no duties, fees, or emoluments annexed or incident to such office" and declared that "the said appointment is of a new and unusual nature, truly unknown either to our Laws or constitution, and . . . a most Extensive stretch of power." In addition, it resolved that Davis should print the laws and journals of the session for the usual salary of £200. To make that resolution more palatable to the Council, the House stipulated that if Davis failed to distribute the documents as required he would forfeit part of his salary and resolved that Stewart be paid £100 proclamation money for his expenses in coming to the colony. The Council consented to pay Stewart, but it rejected the House's resolution to appoint Davis.

In the meantime, Dobbs issued a vigorous defense of his right to appoint a printer. He maintained "that it is his Majesty's undoubted prerogative to nominate and appoint a printer to Publish his Proclamations and orders of Government, and to Publish his Laws" and asserted "that the right of the Commons or lower House of Assembly, is only to appoint a Printer to publish their Votes and Resolutions during their Sessions." But the representatives would not give in. They replied "that the appointing a Printer for the Province, is the inherent right of the People we represent" and insisted that Davis continue as public printer.[14] The session ended without an agreement and with both Davis and Stewart claiming the post. Upon the

13. Upper House Journals, Nov. 13-16, 1762, Mar. 8, Nov. 21, 1764, *N. C. Col. Recs.*, VI, 844-45, 1139-40, 1243; Lower House Journals, Nov. 16, 1762, Mar. 5, 1764, *ibid.*, 908-9, 1200.

14. Lower House Journals, Nov. 21, 24, 26, 1764, *ibid.*, 1301, 1311-14; Upper House Journals, Nov. 26-27, 1764, *ibid.*, 1248-49, 1252.

House's order Davis proceeded to print the laws and journals of the session and continued to print his newspaper at New Bern under a new title, *The North Carolina Magazine; or, Universal Intelligencer.* Acting under Dobbs's commission, Stewart set up his press in Wilmington, also printed the session laws, and established a rival newspaper, *The North Carolina Gazette.*[15]

When the legislature met again in November 1766, the question of who was actually public printer was still in dispute. Dobbs had died since the last session, and his successor, Tryon, had withdrawn Stewart's commission in February 1766 for printing an inflammatory letter against the Stamp Act in his *Gazette.*[16] Stewart was left without any strong support for the printer's place, but the Council still insisted that he be paid for the work he had done under Dobbs's commission. After the Lower House passed a resolution to pay Davis £190 for printing the 1765 laws and journals, the Council hinted that its agreement to that resolution might be contingent upon the House's consent to pay Stewart as well. But the House had not altered its position during the intervening two years. It informed the Council that Stewart's commission was "unknown to the Laws and constitution of our Country" and denied that the colony owed him a salary, but offered to consider "his claim for services rendered the public as a printer" if he would submit it to the House. In the end the Council agreed to pay Davis, but Stewart received nothing beyond the £100 voted him in 1764 to cover his expenses in moving to the colony.[17] By preventing Stewart's payment, the Lower House had denied the executive's right to appoint a Crown printer for the colony. On the other hand, by consenting to pay Davis, the Council had conceded the House's right to designate the public printer. At the same session the House formally reappointed Davis for a term of three years, raising his salary to £250. Stewart continued to publish his newspaper in Wilmington until his death in 1769, when Adam Boyd took over his business and began issuing the *Cape Fear Mercury.* Stewart and Boyd as well as Davis probably favored the legislature in the debates with Britain, but Davis's close association with the House and his long tenure assured him of continuous reappointment as public print-

15. Dill, *Governor Tryon*, 75-76.
16. Council Journals, Feb. 26, 1766, *N. C. Col. Recs.*, VII, 187-88.
17. Upper House Journals, Nov. 29, Dec. 2, 1766, *ibid.*, 334-41; Report of Claims Committee, Nov. 6, 1766, *N. C. St. Recs.*, XXII, 843.

er down to and through much of the War for Independence and guaranteed the House favorable treatment in his newspaper.[18]

Georgia was the last of the southern royal colonies to acquire a printer. Not until 1762 did its legislature appoint a public printer, James Johnston. He had come to the colony from Scotland the year before probably at the urging of his elder brother, Lewis, who was a leading member of the Commons House of Assembly. His arrival was well timed. Georgia was just embarking upon a period of rapid expansion, but it was still without a newspaper or any means to publish government records. The legislature recognized the value of Johnston's services and immediately resolved to help him establish himself in the colony. It guaranteed him a monopoly on all government printing for four years and awarded him an annual sum of £100 for the same period not as a salary but as an "encouragement" to help "defray part of the heavy Charges and Expences attending the procuring of Materials and other necessarys for setting up" his press. Like the North Carolina Lower House, the Georgia Commons made Johnston's appointment by a formal statute that required him to publish and distribute the laws passed at each session and all official proclamations.[19] Johnston began work in early 1763, establishing the colony's first newspaper, the *Georgia Gazette,* in April and during the next four years laying the foundations for a successful business. When his original appointment expired in 1767, the Commons did not formally renew it, although, upon his request, it did grant him an additional £50 to help support him for another year. Thereafter, Johnston, like the South Carolina printer, had no official title nor received any fixed income from the colony but continued to perform all the duties of the public printer, handling all government work and being paid annually according to the quantity of that work.

Johnston's government business kept him in close touch with both the executive and the Commons, but he never came completely under the control of either. Throughout the disputes with Britain he opened the columns of his newspaper to both sides, attempting to maintain an impartial position. Almost certainly his sentiments were with Governor Wright and the Council, to which his brother was

18. Laws, *N. C. St. Recs.,* XXIII, 675, 801, 971; Dill, *Governor Tryon,* 75-78.
19. Statutes, *Ga. Col. Recs.,* XVIII, 488-93; Alexander A. Lawrence, *James Johnston: Georgia's First Printer* (Savannah, 1956), 3-5.

appointed in 1764. But he never showed any inclination to risk losing the public business by refusing to publish patriot pieces; and his newspaper continued to serve the colony's small group of radicals and the patriot-dominated Commons as a vehicle for circulating their opinions until February 1776, when he chose to leave Georgia rather than submit to censorship by the patriot Council of Safety.[20]

By 1763 each of the southern royal colonies had a public printer. In Virginia and North Carolina he was appointed by formal statute or by a resolution passed by the entire legislature, but during the 1760's both the Virginia Burgesses and the North Carolina Lower House successfully asserted their right to nominate him. In South Carolina after the 1730's and in Georgia after 1767, the official printers had no formal appointment but deserved the title because of their virtual monopolies on government printing. The South Carolina Commons exercised very close supervision over its printer, Peter Timothy, who personally favored the House in all disputes and who after 1760 well knew that if he displeased the Commons he would lose the public business to one of his rivals. In Georgia, printer James Johnston had no rival, and the Commons was unable to bring him completely under its control. But his reliance upon the House for government printing contracts and his conception of the printer's role as an impartial one kept him from closing his press to the representatives and assured them of a ready outlet for any materials they wished to put in print.

Significantly, Crown officials made no attempt to deprive the lower houses of their control over the official printers. And in the controversies with Britain that consumed much of the lower houses' energies in the years after 1763 the public printers played an important role. By presenting the houses' side of the controversies to the public, they helped to create a climate of opinion favorable to the lower houses.

20. Lawrence, *James Johnston,* 4-11, 9-18.

15

Military Affairs

CROWN officials conferred all military powers in the royal colonies upon the governors, but from time to time the lower houses shared in the exercise of these powers. As commanders-in-chief of their respective colonies, royal governors were empowered to nominate and appoint all officers of the colony's military establishment; raise, arm, and command the provincial troops; and employ such troops wherever necessary to repel invasions, execute the commands of the Crown, or put down insurrections. But without the support of the lower houses, the governors' military powers amounted to little. Money required to man, equip, and maintain even the smallest military force was forthcoming only upon the vote of the lower houses. In military affairs as in all other matters the lower houses granted money only upon their own terms. Hence, they not only appropriated all military funds specifically but also subjected them to certain limitations by determining the number of men to be employed, their rate of pay, and their place and period of service. In addition, lower houses sometimes granted funds only upon the condition that they be supervised and applied by legislative committees, thus implying the right of those committees to direct or at least to maintain a strict surveillance over operations as well. By threatening to withhold an appropriation, lower houses could also force governors to appoint house nominees as officers or remove officers offensive to them.

In using their power over money to encroach upon the governors' military prerogative, American lower houses were pursuing a well-marked path which the English House of Commons had traversed in the late seventeenth century. Control over the military forces was one of the principal points of controversy between Crown and Parliament after 1640. The House of Commons managed to put the militia under statutory regulation in the 1660's, and under William III it assumed an important share of the Crown's military powers. In appropriating money for military purposes, the Commons stipulated the maximum number of men that might be raised and, by limiting the term of the grants to one year, it made sure that the Crown would not undertake any expensive military operations without its approval, thereby acquiring considerable influence in determining military policy. But the English House of Commons never interfered in military matters so extensively as did the American lower houses during the eighteenth century. Never did it attempt to nominate military officers or to assume the actual direction of a war through Parliamentary committees. [1]

In the southern royal colonies, royal commissions and instructions invested the governors with the power to organize, train, maintain, and call out the militia and to appoint its officers. But during the eighteenth century the lower houses repeatedly limited and defined these powers by statute. The Virginia Burgesses first regulated the militia by legislative act in April 1685, although it did not undertake a general regulation until October 1705. When royal government was established in the two Carolinas, their militias were already operating under laws passed during the proprietary period. The South Carolina Commons passed militia laws beginning in 1703 and the North Carolina Lower House beginning in 1715 or earlier. In Georgia the Commons placed regulations upon the militia in 1755 at the very outset of royal government. Completely disregarding powers given to the governors by the royal commissions and instructions, these laws authorized the governors to organize, train, and muster the militia; to appoint its officers; and to call it into service in times of emergency.[2] The Crown might have been expected to object to colonial militia laws which conferred powers already given, but it made no particular effort to disallow them. Although the Board of Trade

1. Mark A. Thomson, *A Constitutional History of England, 1642 to 1801* (London, 1938), 153-61, 292-97.

2. Labaree, ed., *Royal Instructions,* I, 392-93; Hening, ed., *Va. Statutes,* III, 13-14, 335-42, IV, 118-26, V, 16-24, VI, 112-18, VII, 93-116, 274-75; Cooper and McCord, eds., *S. C. Statutes,* IX, 617-24; Laws, *N. C. St. Recs.,* XXIII, 29-31, 244-47, 518-22, 596-601, XXV, 334-37, 394; Statutes, *Ga. Col. Recs.,* XVIII, 7-47.

did object strenuously to a South Carolina act of 1747 because it conferred upon the governor a "new" power to assemble and arm the
militia and to appoint its officers on the grounds that the governor
already held this power by virtue of his commission, such protests
were unusual.[3]

The militia laws adopted by the southern legislatures strictly
limited the governors' powers. They specified the militia's organization, those eligible to serve, the time and place of musters, the rates
of pay of the militia when called into service, and the powers and
duties of the officers. Among the most important limitations upon
the governors' military authority were the clauses to prohibit the
militia from service outside its particular colony. By their commissions, the governors were empowered to march the militia anywhere,
but the Virginia Burgesses had refused to permit the militia to serve
outside the colony as early as 1701, and the laws of North Carolina
in 1746, South Carolina in 1747, Virginia in 1748, and Georgia in 1755
restricted their militias to service within their respective colonies.[4]
In 1764 the South Carolina Commons refused to comply with the
Earl of Halifax's request for authority to call out part of the South
Carolina militia for the general defense of the colonies against the
Indians, declaring that such a power was "inconsistent with the
Militia Act" and that to send the militia "to the Protection of his
Majesty's other Colonys, would be . . . a means of exposing the Province to every the least inconsiderable Invasion or Insurrection." Objections by imperial authorities to such restrictions were of little avail,
and Governor Glen's report in 1753 that the South Carolina Commons would never "be prevailed upon . . . to assent to the Governour's
power of carrying the Militia out of the Province" summed up the
position of the lower houses in all the southern royal colonies.[5]

Nor could governors call the militia into service for any appreciable length of time without appropriations from the lower houses.
Thus, the lower houses could, as the Virginia Burgesses did in 1754

3. Board of Trade to James Glen, Nov. 15, 1750, CO 5/402, pp. 233-70.
4. See Hening, ed., *Va. Statutes*, III, 335-42, IV, 118-26, V, 16-24, VII, 93-116,
274-75; Cooper and McCord, eds., *S. C. Statutes*, IX, 617-24, 645-63; Statutes, *Ga.
Col. Recs.*, XVIII, 7-47; Laws, *N. C. St. Recs.*, XXIII, 244-47, 518-22, XXV, 334-
37, 394-95; Board of Trade to James Glen, Nov. 15, 1750, CO 5/402, pp. 233-70;
Sept. 29, 1701, *Va. Burgesses Journals, 1695-1702*, 323-24.
5. Glen to Board of Trade, July 20, 1753, CO 5/374, ff. 187-219; July 3, 1764,
S. C. Commons Journals, XXXVI, 101-2, S. C. Arch. Dept.

and the South Carolina Commons in 1757, prevent the governors from calling out the militia. Only the governors' power to appoint militia officers was not seriously curtailed by statute. The North Carolina Lower House in 1746 unsuccessfully tried to make militia colonels accountable to it for all fines they received, and Henry Ellis reported in May 1757 shortly after his arrival in Georgia that he had thwarted an attempt by his predecessor, John Reynolds, to give to the Commons the governor's right of appointing militia officers. In South Carolina the Commons prevented Lyttelton from appointing an adjutant general to review the militia by refusing to provide a salary for such an officer. But the restriction of Virginia in 1757 and North Carolina in 1760 that officers be residents of the counties in which they held their commands was the only real limitation upon the governors' powers of nomination and appointment, and it was not serious.[6]

Another of the governors' military powers that the lower houses encroached upon was that of nominating, appointing, and disciplining both permanent officers, such as commanders of forts, storekeepers, and armorers, and also special officers, such as those in command of the forces raised for participation in the Seven Years' War. Clearly, this power belonged to the governors as representatives of the King in the colonies—a fact which seems not to have been disputed in either Virginia or Georgia. Nor did the North Carolina Lower House make more than one attempt to interfere with its governors' exercise of this power. From 1757 to 1760 it tried to secure the right to nominate a storekeeper for Fort Johnston to care for ordinance supplies and military stores given North Carolina by the Crown by refusing, even in the face of a specific order from Crown officials, to provide a salary for Dobbs's appointee. But in this instance Dobbs's staying power exceeded that of the House, and it agreed in 1760 to allow his ap-

6. See Cooper and McCord, eds., *S. C. Statutes*, IX, 645-63; Hening, ed., *Va. Statutes*, VI, 112-18, VII, 93-100; Laws, *N. C. St. Recs.*, XXIII, 518-22; Francis Fauquier's Answers to Board of Trade's Queries, Jan. 30, 1763, CO 5/1330, f. 547; Lower House Journals, June 26, 1746, *N. C. Col. Recs.*, IV, 831-32; Ellis to Board of Trade, May 5, 1767, CO 5/646; Nov. 20, 1756, Jan. 27, 1757, S. C. Commons Journals, CO 5/473, pp. 12-17. The S. C. Commons refused to permit Lyttelton to make draughts from the militia to serve in the Seven Years' War. Lyttelton to General James Abercromby, May 16, 1758, Abercromby Papers, 258, Huntington Lib. The Va. Burgesses rejected Dinwiddie's proposal "to decimate the Militia, and them the Lot fell on, if they could not go, to get an able Body'd Man in his room." Dinwiddie to Sec. of State Robinson, Nov. 16, 1754, CO 5/15, ff. 7-8.

pointee a sum for storing and handling the supplies, abandoning its attempt to gain the right to nominate him.[7]

If the lower houses in the other southern royal colonies were moderate in their encroachments on the governors' power to appoint military officers, the South Carolina Commons certainly was not. That body never pretended to nominate or appoint military officers as a matter of right, but it rarely passed up a chance to exercise that power. It persistently pursued the maxim that all officers receiving a salary from the public should be nominated or at least approved by the public's representatives. Councilor Edmund Atkin accurately described the situation when he complained to the Board of Trade in 1755 that the Commons "virtually appoint Officers in the Nomination of the Crown . . . by recommending Persons for such Offices to the Governour who for fear . . . of disobliging the Assembly, appoints them accordingly."[8]

Whenever the Commons voted money to raise a military force, it almost invariably nominated the officer or officers in charge of that force. Thus in February 1755 the Commons voted to raise a crew of rangers to protect the colony's frontiers and recommended that Glen appoint William Gray as their commander. But Glen had wearied of accepting the Commons' nominee for every military office and to put a stop to that practice he appointed a Captain Frances instead. When the Commons continued to insist upon Gray, Glen pointed out the irregularity of its "proposing by name a particular person to have the Command," adding that "though this practice of yours, by being often repeated does not seem strange to your selves . . . It is nevertheless matter of wonder to others that You persist in a Course that is not Constitutional." But the representatives assured Glen that "we have no design to arrogate any Authority or assume to ourselves any Power that belongs not of right to the Commons House of Assembly," innocently protesting "that had we not been prompted by a desire to serve our Country, a desire to do the known Will of our Constituents and withal to prevent a misapplication of the Pub-

7. William Gooch's Answers to Board of Trade's Queries, July 23, 1730, CO 5/1322, ff. 68-74; Lord Dunmore's Answers to Board of Trade's Queries, 1774, CO 5/1352; Upper House Journals, May 16, Nov. 22, 1757, *N. C. Col. Recs.*, V, 831, 870; Dobbs to Board of Trade, Dec. 27, 1757, *ibid.*, 949; Lower House Journals, Jan. 9, 1760, *ibid.*, VI, 199; Order in Council, July 7, 1756, *ibid.*, V, 592-93.

8. Atkin's Wrong Practices, 1755, in Greene, ed., "South Carolina's Colonial Constitution," *S. C. Hist. Mag.*, 62 (1961), 77.

lic Money no names would have been mentioned in any of our Messages." This was enough to induce Glen to recall Frances's commission and reissue it to Gray. The Commons had again had its way.[9]

Similarly, the Commons refused to furnish a salary to John Hume, appointed by Lyttelton to care for military stores given to South Carolina by the Crown in April 1759, because it had not concurred in his nomination. Nor could an Order in Council induce the Commons to change its mind. It justified its stand by arguing "that matters of this Nature have from the Infancy of the Province, been under the Management and Superintendency of Commissioners of Fortifications; that there has always been found, Gentlemen of Ability and Integrity, who have readily engaged in Serving the Public in that Station, without any fee Salary or Reward." However, the Commons would probably have provided a salary if Lyttelton had permitted it to exercise the right of nomination.[10]

Once in office, military officers were not removed from the Commons' authority. They were usually dependent upon that body for their salaries and were therefore subject to legislative investigation and, in the event that their services were unsatisfactory, to suspension or removal. For instance, in March 1737 the Commons insisted, though unsuccessfully, that Captain James Sutherland be suspended as commander of Fort Johnson because he was guilty of "a very great Neglect" in keeping the fort. Similarly, the Commons asked the elder Bull to reprimand the commander of Fort Johnson in 1739 because he had declared that he would forcefully turn any legislative committee out of the fort.[11]

The lower houses not only sought to deprive the royal governors of some of their military powers but also insisted upon taking a hand in forming military policy. Every military establishment of provincial troops in the southern royal colonies owed its existence to a colonial legislature. The Crown preferred that military funds be granted by the lower houses without stipulations so that governors

9. Feb. 7, Mar. 1, 4, 6, 1755, S. C. Commons Journals, CO 5/472, pp. 49-51, 58-59, 61-62, 64-66.

10. Dec. 2, 1762, *ibid.*, CO 5/480, pp. 22-24; May 14, 1762, *Acts of Privy Council, Colonial,* IV, 536.

11. Commons Journals, Mar. 1, 1737, Feb. 28, 1739, *S. C. Col. Recs., 1736-39,* 265-66, 650-51.

could apply them in the Crown's best interest. The direction of military affairs was, after all, a question of policy and therefore an executive task. But colonial lower houses had other ideas. Without their appropriations there could be no provincial military establishment at all, and they insisted upon placing specific limitations upon nearly every sum of money granted for military purposes. They usually stipulated the purpose of the appropriation; the number of men and officers to be raised; their distribution and organization, rates of pay, and place and period of service; and the apportionment of supplies. Insofar as these stipulations limited executive discretion in disposing of funds, the lower houses participated in determining military policy and thereby usurped a portion of the governors' military powers.

The Virginia Burgesses seems to have assumed a large part of the responsibility for all military operations within the colony just before Bacon's Rebellion. An act of March 1676 raised five hundred men to defend the colony against the Indians. It specified where the men were to be stationed, named the captains in command of each post, established the rate of pay for each rank, apportioned ammunition, appointed commissioners to impress men and horses and to employ Indians, and, almost as an afterthought, empowered the governor to direct the force. Thereafter bills for military purposes nearly always included similar provisions. From 1691 to 1693 the Burgesses employed a group of rangers to scout at the head of each of the great rivers as a precautionary measure against Indian attacks. The acts providing for them specified that each group consist of a lieutenant, eleven soldiers, and two Indians and settled their pay. Between 1695 and 1740 Virginia had no major military obligations. But acts of 1705 and 1728 took precautionary defense measures empowering the governor to raise the militia at a specified rate of pay in case of invasion or other menace. The year 1740 marked the beginning of Virginian participation in the mother country's imperial wars with Spain and France. In August the Burgesses voted to raise £5,000 towards defraying the expense of supplying and transporting Virginia soldiers serving in an expedition against the Spaniards in the Caribbean. Although it designated the purpose of the appropriation, this act deviated from established practice by leaving the application of the grant to the discretion of Lieutenant Governor Gooch, who was participating in the expedition.[12]

But the Burgesses' abandonment in 1740 of its policy of strictly appropriating military aid was not a harbinger of things to come. Indeed, in 1746, when it voted £4,000 to defray the cost of sending Virginia soldiers on an expedition to Canada, it not only strictly appropriated the sum and specified the conditions under which the soldiers were to be raised as it had done before 1740; it also appointed a committee of nine burgesses accountable to the General Assembly, any five of whom were to apply the money. Introduced because Gooch was in poor health and unable to attend to the routine expenditures connected with the expedition, this committee gave the Burgesses control over the application of its appropriations and provided it with a precedent which it later cited in defense of its efforts to usurp a large share of the actual direction of military operations during the Seven Years' War.[13]

When Dinwiddie called the Burgesses together in February 1754 to obtain money "to take more vigorous measures" against French encroachments along the Ohio River, he found himself saddled with a legacy from his predecessor—a legislative committee to supervise the expenditure of the appropriation. The Burgesses would not vote money for an expedition against the French unless its expenditure were directed by such a committee. With the backing of the Upper House, Dinwiddie objected that such a committee tended "towards an Alteration of a fundamental Part of the Constitution by taking from the Governor his undoubted right of the Application of all Monies raised for the Defence and Security of the Country." Had not Dinwiddie already aroused its distrust by establishing the pistole fee for attaching the seal to land patents, the Burgesses might have yielded to his demands. But it was unwilling to place so large a sum in the hands of one who had so recently seemingly revealed his passion for money by creating a new fee to add to his perquisites. The urgent need for funds to repel the French from the Ohio eventually forced Dinwiddie to give in.

The Burgesses insisted upon appointing similar committees to ad-

12. Hening, ed., *Va. Statutes*, II, 326-36, III, 82-85, 98-101, 115-17, 119-21, 362-67, IV, 197-204, V, 121-23.

13. *Ibid.*, V, 401-4; July 12, 16, 1746, *Va. Burgesses Journals, 1742-49*, xxiv, 227, 231.

minister appropriations voted in October 1754, August 1755, March 1756, and April 1757. With the consent of Dinwiddie, whose signature to all warrants for money was necessary, these committees directed the expenditure of all moneys raised for defense and exerted considerable influence in directing military operations. In addition, they adjusted accounts of all officers charged with purchasing supplies, procuring enlistments, or paying troops. The committee appointed in February 1754 consisted of only fourteen members, ten from the Burgesses and four from the Council. The Burgesses increased the membership to sixteen in 1755 by adding two burgesses and to seventeen in 1756 by appointing another councilor. Any seven members could constitute a quorum, and the committee was accountable to the Burgesses, quite naturally looking to it for direction.[14]

Dinwiddie co-operated with these legislative committees, but he never approved of them. He repeatedly apologized to imperial authorities for passing bills providing for them but excused himself because of the urgent need for money to prosecute the war. Nor did London officials look upon them with favor. The Board of Trade lamented in July 1754 "that the Assembly should have availed themselves of such exigency to have proposed the Bill in a manner inconsistent with His Majesty's Rights and Authority, and the method which he has prescribed for raising money for publick Service." And in January 1757 the Board objected to Pitt's plan to give pecuniary aid to Virginia because the Burgesses had placed the disposition of all money it had raised for the war *into the hands of Committees . . . without any obligation upon them to account for the same,* but only to produce an account of their proceedings to the Assembly, when required." Giving "Sums of Money at large, to be issued and applied under the direction of Provincial Legislatures," the Board observed, "does not appear to Us the most likely method of furnishing a real and effectual Support."[15]

14. Hening, ed., *Va. Statutes,* VI, 112-18, 435-38, 521-30, VII, 9-20, 69-87; Nov. 4, 1755, Apr. 10, 21, 23, 1756, *Va. Burgesses Journals, 1752-58,* 328, 363, 374, 381; Dinwiddie to Governor James Hamilton of Pennsylvania, Jan. 29, 1754, Edward E. Ayer Manuscripts, 952, Newberry Library, Chicago; Dinwiddie to Board of Trade, Mar. 12, May 10, 1754, CO 5/1328, ff. 193-94, 211-13; Dinwiddie to John Robinson, Jan. 24, 1755, and to Charles Dick, Aug. 11, 1755, Brock, ed., *Dinwiddie Papers,* I, 477-78, II, 150-51.

15. See Dinwiddie to Board of Trade, Mar. 12, 1754, CO 5/1328, ff. 193-94; Dinwiddie to Earl of Halifax, Oct. 25, 1754, Brock, ed., *Dinwiddie Papers,* I, 366-69; Board of Trade to Dinwiddie, July 4, 1754, and to William Pitt, Jan 24, 1757, CO 5/1367, pp. 103-9, 295-312.

But it was not the opposition of the governors or the imperial authorities that finally induced the Burgesses to discontinue using committees to apply military appropriations. Such committees had proved expensive. Beginning with the aid bill passed in March 1758 the Burgesses assigned the committees' duties to the governor, although it limited his use of the funds by appropriating the money in detail and by specifying the number of men and officers to be raised, their organization, their rate of pay, and their place and period of service. Furthermore, it appointed three commissioners "to examine, state and settle . . . accounts." But there was a decided difference between these commissioners and the committee formerly employed. Whereas the committee had actually controlled the application of money, the commissioners were merely to assist the governor by auditing all accounts. The new system proved satisfactory, and the Burgesses employed it for the remainder of the Seven Years' War and again in 1764 and 1765 when Fauquier had to call out part of the militia to defend Virginia's northern and western frontier from Indian attack.[16]

To imperial authorities and Virginia governors, clauses in the aid bills passed during the war prohibiting forces from serving outside the colony were nearly as objectionable as the Burgesses' use of legislative committees to dispose of its appropriations. The Board of Trade expressed its disapproval of such clauses in January 1757. Thereafter the Burgesses consented to send troops to South Carolina in 1757 and to the Cherokee country in 1760. In 1758 and 1759 it even gave the governor a discretionary power to send the troops wherever he should direct, but it was primarily concerned with protecting its own frontier and usually limited the troops to service in Virginia.[17]

In both Carolinas the lower houses used devices similar to those employed by the Virginia House of Burgesses to encroach upon the governors' military powers. As early as 1701 the South Carolina Commons stipulated that the public receiver pay out defense money only upon the legislature's order. A 1715 law to raise troops for the Yamassee War is no longer extant, but one can assume that it did

16. Hening, ed., *Va. Statutes*, VII, 69-87, 163-69, 171-231, 251-53, 255-65, 331-37, 347-53, 357-63, 369-72, 381-83, 463-65, 495-502, VIII, 9-12, 124-33; Apr. 14, 1757, *Va. Burgesses Journals, 1752-58*, 413-14.

17. Hening, ed., *Va. Statutes*, VII, 69-87, 163-69, 255-65, 357-63; Board of Trade to William Pitt, Jan. 24, 1757, CO 5/1367, ff. 295-312; Fauquier to Board of Trade, Dec. 17, 1759, CO 5/1329, ff. 395-97.

not differ much from a 1718 statute that empowered the governor to enlist forty-eight men and to appoint officers to defend the frontier. The same act settled the rates of pay for the troops and appointed commissioners to furnish provisions and supplies. Between 1721 and 1735 South Carolina had no cause to raise troops for her defense. Frontier and seacoast were relatively quiet, and during the entire period the Crown had an independent company stationed in the colony.

The threat of a combined Spanish-Indian attack on the colony led the Commons under the elder Bull to appropriate £5,000 in February 1737 to maintain troops and to put the province in a state of defense. But the Commons voted this money with the provision "that all the Members of this House who live and reside in Charles Town, or shall happen to be in Charles Town when any Business is to be transacted by the Committee shall be a Committee of this House to join his Honour the Lieutenant Governor, and the Committee of his Majesty's Honourable Council for drawing Orders on the Treasurer pursuant to the Directions in the Estimate." Accordingly, in March and April 1737, during the legislative recess, from five to fourteen members of the Commons met with the governor and Council in five different sessions, during which "Consultations were held, Resolutions entered into for the Execution of various matters, and in what manner; And orders drawn and signed for Money to be issued out of the Treasury, by the whole in Conjunction." As the Council appropriately noted some years later, the Commons House by these proceedings "at last actually got into a share of the Administration of Government, and the three Estates in the Legislature were more than once brought to Act together in *One*."[18]

But the South Carolina Commons' participation in administering military affairs was only temporary. Never again did it insist or even propose that some of its number assist in directing either military preparations or operations. It voted a grant of £55,000 for an attack on the Spanish at St. Augustine to General James Oglethorpe in 1740 with the understanding that he use the money only for purposes it stipulated and that Colonel Alexander Vanderdussen com-

18. Cooper and McCord, eds., *S. C. Statutes*, II, xxii-xxiii, 182-85, III, 39-41; Commons Journals, Mar. 5, 1737, *S. C. Col. Recs., 1736-39*, 286; Mar. 7-Apr. 2, 1737, S. C. Council Journals, CO 5/438, pp. 118-24; May 7, 1745, S. C. Upper House Journals, CO 5/453, pp. 144-45; Smith, *South Carolina as a Royal Province*, 192-93.

mand the South Carolina forces, but it made no attempt to assume direction of the expedition. Nor did the Commons show any inclination to participate in supervising expenditures of the several military appropriations it made between 1756 and 1761 during the Seven Years' War. But it did take steps to retain adequate control over its grants by appropriating the money in detail; specifying the number of men and officers to be raised, their organization and pay, and their place and period of service; and insisting on auditing the accounts of all expenditures.[19]

North Carolina followed much the same course as its southern neighbor. Aside from the Tuscarora War in 1712, for which there is no legislation preserved, there was little need for a military force in the colony before 1740. In that year the Lower House voted £1,200 sterling to raise and supply a troop of 400 men to be sent with men from Virginia and other colonies upon an expedition against the Spaniards. The House appointed six of its members commissioners to hire vessels and buy provisions and all other necessaries for feeding and transporting the troops. It also empowered them to hold all money appropriated for the expedition, issue it for specified services, and account to the legislature for the entire amount. Thus, their powers exceeded those of the similar Virginia committees, which could handle and issue money only upon the governor's warrants. During the Seven Years' War the House made several military appropriations, although it never again attempted to employ commissioners as it had done in 1740. But like the South Carolina Commons, the North Carolina Lower House made certain that its grants would not be misapplied by appropriating them in detail, making them accountable to the legislature, and specifying with each grant the number of men and officers to be raised and their conditions of service.[20]

19. Cooper and McCord, eds., *S. C. Statutes*, III, 546-53, IV, v-viii, 113-28, 144-48; Commons Journals, Feb. 10, 1740, *S. C. Col. Recs., 1739-41*, 199-207; July 9, 13, 1759, Feb. 10, 13, 1760, S. C. Commons Journals, CO 5/473, Pt. II, pp. 13-14, 24, Pt. III, pp. 10-13; Account of money raised in S. C. for the Crown from Aug. 1756 to Oct. 1757, Treasury 1/370, f. 10; Lyttelton to Board of Trade, Feb. 22, 1760, CO 5/376, ff. 181-84; William Bull II to William Pitt, Apr. 28, 1761, CO 5/20, ff. 241-44. In 1757 Lyttelton rejected a bill empowering him to form an artillery company that he had organized because he conceived that he already held that power by virtue of his commission. Lyttelton to Board of Trade, Dec. 22, 1757, CO 5/376, ff. 39-40.

20. Laws, *N. C. St. Recs.*, XXIII, 151-57, 392-98, 422-24, 440, 475, 483, 485, 503, 516-18, XXV, 331-33, 345-48, 350-52, 361-64, 370-72, 394-95; Lower House Journals,

Because of Georgia's relative poverty, the Commons of that colony made no major military appropriations during the colonial period. Consequently, it had no opportunity to usurp any of the governor's military powers.[21]

During the eighteenth century all of the lower houses in the southern royal colonies exercised some of the military powers which by the royal commissions and instructions were delegated exclusively to the governor. All of them passed laws to regulate the militia, and the lower houses of the two Carolinas even insisted occasionally upon nominating persons to military offices. In Virginia, North Carolina, and South Carolina the lower houses exercised considerable authority over forces raised during the inter-colonial wars through laws passed to provide military appropriations. In addition, the South Carolina Commons in 1737, the North Carolina Lower House in 1740, and the Virginia Burgesses in 1746 and from 1754 to 1757 appointed legislative committees to supervise the expenditures of these appropriations. Through these committees and through the specifications made in the appropriation bills, the lower houses formed military policy. In using legislative committees to apply military grants and in exercising the right to nominate military officers, the lower houses in the southern royal colonies wielded greater authority over military affairs in their respective colonies than did the House of Commons in England.

Apr. 28, 1760, Apr. 15, 1762, *N. C. Col. Recs.*, VI, 369-72, 806; Gabriel Johnston to Newcastle, Nov. 5, 1740, *ibid.*, IV, 421; Dobbs to Board of Trade, May 30, 1757, to William Pitt, Dec. 30, 1757, May 7, 1758, *ibid.*, V, 761-64, 792, 934-35; Dobbs to Pitt, May 29, 1760, CO 5/19, ff. 519-22; Dobbs to Earl of Loudoun, Oct. 30, 1756, May 30, 1757, Dec. 24, 1757, Loudoun Papers, 2121, 3740, 5083, Huntington Lib.

21. Such small appropriations as were made for military purposes were usually given without stipulations. An example is the Commons' grant of £200 to Governor Henry Ellis in 1758. Commons Journals, June 30, 1758, *Ga. Col. Recs.*, XIII, 308-9.

16

Indian Affairs

At one time or another all the English colonies faced the problem of living peacefully with the Indians when traders and settlers were encroaching upon their lands. Because there were no precedents in the mother country, solutions had to be worked out on the spot. Although the Crown assigned Indian relations as matters of diplomacy to the governors and councils,[1] the lower houses in some colonies quite early took an interest in them and often played a major role in their conduct.

Among the southern royal colonies Indian relations were most important to South Carolina. Unlike Virginia and North Carolina, whose immediate frontiers were, after the early years of the eighteenth century, singularly free from menace by strong Indian tribes, South Carolina was constantly threatened by the possibility of attack from the large Indian nations lying to the west of Charleston. First the Catawbas and Cherokees and later the Creeks, Chickasaws, and Choctaws provided South Carolina with valuable sources of trade but at the same time acted both as impediments to her expansion and as threats to her security. By 1700 Charleston had come to dominate the Indian trade on the southern frontier, a position which she enjoyed throughout the colonial period.

With the exception of the Yamassee War in 1715, most of South Carolina's Indian problems previous to the 1740's arose from trade. The security of the colony demanded that the traders be placed under some sort of regulation to prevent, insofar as it was possible, any deceptive or dishonest dealings which might involve the colony in

1. Labaree, ed., *Royal Instructions*, II, 471-78.

war. Hence, the attention given to Indian affairs by the South Carolina Commons was almost entirely devoted to regulating that trade.
But settlers followed traders, and by the 1740's they were beginning
to exert pressure on the Lower Cherokees. Constant westward expansion also alarmed other Indian tribes to the southwest, making
them susceptible to the blandishments of the French and Spanish.[2]
From the beginning of the War of Jenkins' Ear in 1739 to the conclusion of the Seven Years' War in 1763, South Carolina's major Indian problem was to secure alliances or at least promises of neutrality
from the large Indian nations to the west and south.

The South Carolina Commons first took an interest in the Indian
trade during the closing decade of the seventeenth century. First the
proprietors and then the governor and Council had managed the
trade, but the Commons passed minor regulations as early as 1691
and after a long struggle finally pushed through in 1707 a comprehensive law that transferred control of the trade from the governor
and Council to a board of commissioners subject only to the legislature's authority. The nine commissioners named in the act creating
their posts were mostly members of the Commons with experience in
Indian affairs. Their chief duties were supervisory, and they themselves did not participate in the trade. They granted or withheld
licenses that traders were required to purchase annually, issued instructions to traders and their agent, and served as a court of appeal
from their agent's decisions. The agent resided among the Indians
and received a salary of £250 per year. He was to carry out the directions of the commissioners and scrutinize the conduct of the traders.[3]

What the Commons had established was simply a system of public
regulation of private business. But it did not prove entirely effective,
and its weakness was in part responsible for the calamitous Yamassee
War in 1715. Consequently, in 1716 the Commons took the trade
out of the hands of private individuals and gave it in the form of an
absolute monopoly to the Indian commissioners, who were to manage
it "for the sole use, benefit and behoof of the publick." The new
system provided for only five commissioners, each with an annual

2. See Meriwether, *Expansion of South Carolina;* Crane, *Southern Frontier.*
3. Cooper and McCord, eds., *S. C. Statutes,* II, vii, 64-68, 309-16, 359-60; Crane,
Southern Frontier, 137, 140-53; Smith, *South Carolina as a Royal Province,* 213;
William L. McDowell, ed., *Colonial Records of South Carolina: Journals of the
Commissioners of the Indian Trade, September, 20, 1710-August 29, 1718* (Colum-
bia, 1955).

salary of £150 from the public. The Commons appointed the original commissioners by statute, but once appointed they constituted an almost independent corporation with full powers to perpetuate themselves by filling vacancies in their number. Trade was restricted to three posts, or factories, on the frontiers which were presided over by factors, or agents, appointed by the commissioners. All profits went into the public treasury.

Scarcely more than two years after the establishment of the new system, the proprietors disallowed it. In March 1719 the South Carolina legislature re-enacted it with certain modifications, the Indian commissioners still participating directly in the trade but no longer enjoying a monopoly. Private traders could once more engage in the Indian commerce, although they had to have a license from the commissioners and pay a tax of 10 per cent of the value of their purchases. Nor could they trade with Indians within twenty miles of the public factories. The new law also reduced the number of commissioners to three, stipulating that all appointments and removals be in the hands of the House.[4]

During the transition from proprietory to royal government between 1719 and 1721, the Commons again altered the Indian trading system, reverting in general to the conditions that had existed between 1707 and 1716. The government no longer directly participated in the trade. Instead, the three commissioners appointed by the act upon the Commons' nomination were to serve only as supervisors to check abuses of private traders. They could grant licenses and take from traders bonds which met their approval. In addition, the Commons assigned them the task of supervising garrisons established to protect the traders on the Indian frontier. For their services, they each received a yearly salary of £300. Despite an unfavorable report from Board of Trade counsel Richard West and complaints by Virginia traders against having to come to Charleston to take out a license in order to trade in South Carolina, London authorities allowed the act to stand until the South Carolina Commons amended it a year or so after its passage.

To replace the disallowed law the Commons in February 1723 removed the Indian commissioners and vested their powers in the

4. Cooper and McCord, eds., *S. C. Statutes,* II, 677-80, III, 86-96; Crane, *Southern Frontier,* 193-94, 197-99; Proprietors to Johnson, July 22, 1718, S. C. Pub. Recs., VII, 145, S. C. Arch. Dept.

governor and Council in what appears to have been a successful attempt by Nicholson to regain control of the trade for the executive. But managing recalcitrant and irascible Indian traders proved too large a task for him, and within a year he was ready to return the supervision of the trade to the Commons, which adopted a single commissioner system. In February 1724 it appointed Speaker James Moore as Indian commissioner with complete supervisory powers over the trade and a yearly salary of £600.[5] This arrangement proved satisfactory and except for a few months in 1751 remained in use until 1761. The Commons nominated and controlled the commissioner, and, curiously, its dominance over this officer went unchallenged by either Crown or governor for over twenty-five years.

Between 1724 and 1751 seven men served as commissioner. Moore lived only a month after his appointment, and the Commons replaced him with George Chicken. He was followed by John Herbert in 1727, Tobias Fitch in 1733, William Drake in 1734, Childermas Croft in 1739, and William Pinckney in 1747. By 1731 the business of the commissioner had so increased that it was necessary to provide him with a secretary and to appoint a special agent to oversee the trade with the Creeks, although this last office was only temporary. The Commons made no further changes in the system, although in 1742 it did consider a proposal to reduce Indian expenses by excluding private traders and giving the colony a monopoly.[6] It remained for Governor Glen to effect some reforms in 1751.

Glen probably never liked the South Carolina Indian commissioner system. In 1748 he complained to the Board of Trade about an ordinance of the previous year appointing William Pinckney Indian commissioner, observing that he "has a Salary from the Public and has by the Indian Trading Law the power to Licence Persons to Trade with the Indian Nations for which he has also a fee." "Many other Powers," he added, "are by that Law improperly Lodged in His Hands." More than that, Pinckney had refused to honor his order

5. Cooper and McCord, eds., *S. C. Statutes*, III, 141-46, 184-86, 229-32; Crane, *Southern Frontier*, 14-15; Smith, *South Carolina as a Royal Province*, 216-17.

6. Cooper and McCord, eds., *S. C. Statutes*, III, 246, 250, 273, 371-72, 399-402, 517-25, 693; Crane, *Southern Frontier*, 200; Apr. 28, 1733, S. C. Commons Journals, CO 5/433, p. 46; Commons Journals, May 22, 1742, *S. C. Col Recs.*, 1741-42, 517-18; Johnson to Board of Trade, Nov. 14, 1731, CO 5/362, ff. 54-58; A. S. Salley, ed., *Journal of Colonel John Herbert, Commissioner of Indian Affairs for the Province of South Carolina, October 17, 1727 to March 19, 1728* (Columbia, 1936).

not to grant a license to a trader who he had heard was conniving with the French, and he was miffed "that it was not in my power to displace him for his disobedience." Glen noted that "those little insults from inferior Officers set a Governor in a very disagreeable and ridiculous light to the People." But, as was not uncommon in the thirties and forties, the Board of Trade gave Glen's complaint no more than a casual reading and allowed the Indian trading law to stand.[7]

Convinced by the Board's inaction that any change in the trading system would have to come from within the colony, Glen waited for an opportunity to effect some reforms. In May 1751, when the Commons passed a measure to revive the expiring Indian trading law, Glen vetoed it, complaining that the old Indian trading law was contrary to his commission and instructions because it empowered the Indian commissioner to draw orders on the public treasurer. He recommended that the bill be amended, but the Commons' adjournment came almost simultaneously with his veto, thus preventing immediate action. When the Commons reconvened for a brief session the following August, Glen again called the matter to its attention. Because of the intense summer heat, the Commons declined to undertake any extensive or permanent reforms in regard to the Indian trade at that time but agreed to pass an ordinance empowering Glen, the Council, and a committee of seven assemblymen to serve as a temporary board to make orders, rules, ordinances, and bylaws for regulating the trade until a permanent settlement could be reached. This board continued to supervise the trade until the following May.[8]

From March to May 1752 the Council and Commons debated a new Indian trading bill. The Commons was well satisfied with the old system, but the Council insisted upon a number of reforms. Among other things, the Council proposed that the governor have power to restrain undesirable traders from visiting the Indians, that power to license traders be founded on a warrant from the Council, and that the Indian commissioner be deprived of the power to revoke licenses unless he was present when the occasion for such a revocation arose. Repeatedly, the Commons rejected the Council's proposals until May 9, when it agreed to empower the governor and Council to

7. Glen's Observations on S. C. laws of 1747, Oct. 10, 1748, CO 5/372, ff. 88-94.
8. May 9, Aug. 28, 30, 1751, S. C. Commons Journals, CO 5/463, Pt. I, pp. 165-67, Pt. II, pp. 47, 51-54; Cooper and McCord, eds., *S. C. Statutes*, III, 754-55.

revoke licenses of traders whose behavior endangered the colony's security in return for the Council's offer to abandon its other proposals.[9]

Although Glen thus gained the power to revoke licenses of Indian traders, he had failed to destroy the commissioner system. The Commons again appointed William Pinckney as commissioner with powers comparable to those he had enjoyed under the previous law. Except for a brief absence from the province beginning in May 1754, during which time with the consent of the Commons he deputed Childermas Croft to serve in his place, he retained the office until 1761, when the Commons allowed the Indian trading law to expire. The appointment of a royal superintendent of Indian affairs for the Southern Department in 1756 did not diminish Pinckney's authority over the Indian trade, although his jurisdiction was limited briefly by a 1755 ordinance that temporarily empowered Glen, the Council, and a committee of eleven assemblymen to lower prices of Indian goods in the Creek nation.[10]

The expiration of the Indian trading law in August 1761 left the colony without trade regulations. Accordingly, when the legislature convened in February 1762, Governor Thomas Boone earnestly recommended the passage of a new bill. To maintain peace with the Cherokees, he proposed that trade with them be placed under a public monopoly. Despite a heated dispute between the two houses over their respective rights in regard to money bills, they did finally pass such a measure. Interestingly, the arrangement set up by the act was not unlike the one used in the colony from 1716 to 1719 during the Commons' initial search for a satisfactory Indian trading system. Restricted to the Cherokees, the act placed the trade with them under public control, putting it under the supervision of five directors. Trade could be carried on only from Fort Prince George at Keowee. These arrangements succeeded in maintaining peace with the Cherokees, but they were unprofitable. By the time the monopoly was dissolved in 1765 the public had suffered a loss of nearly £400. The dissolution marked the end of the South Carolina Commons' long

9. Mar. 10, 12, 20, Apr. 22-23, 1752, S. C. Commons Journals, CO 5/466, pp. 92, 101-3, 117-18, 138, 144.

10. Cooper and McCord, eds., *S. C. Statutes*, III, 763-71, IV, 19-20; May 11, 1754, Sept. 22-23, 1755, S. C. Commons Journals, CO 5/472, Pt. I, p. 128, Pt. III, pp. 10-13; John R. Alden, *John Stuart and the Southern Colonial Frontier* (Ann Arbor, 1944), 69-70.

domination over the Indian trade. As trading centers got farther away from Charleston, the Commons lost much of its early interest in Indian commerce; between 1764 and 1767 control passed gradually to the royal Indian superintendent and later back to the governor and Council.[11]

Until the mid-1730's Indian diplomacy in South Carolina was centered almost entirely around the Indian trade. But by 1735-36 the French and Spanish had become influential among the Indians on the southern frontier, and the maintenance of agreeable trade relations was no longer sufficient to keep the Indians at peace. Alliances with the Indians or at least assurances of their neutrality became the object of South Carolina diplomacy. It was natural in view of its long experience in regulating the Indian trade that the Commons should participate in conducting Indian diplomacy. As would be expected, it decided when to send special agents to the various Indian nations; nominated, instructed, and paid those agents; and determined all matters of expense in regard to Indian affairs, such as the giving of presents. Governors could not prevent the Commons from exercising these powers because they could send neither agents nor presents to the Indians without funds voted by the Commons, and it was loathe to provide money for projects which were not of its own making. Consequently, the Commons dominated Indian affairs for over twenty years after 1736.

Between 1736 and 1755 the Commons' power to share in the conduct of Indian diplomacy was practically unlimited. Beginning with Thomas Broughton, South Carolina governors regularly placed all accounts and letters concerning Indian affairs before the Commons for its perusal. By March 1750 this practice was so well established that the Commons, upon Glen's failure to submit such papers to it, could indignantly observe that "Your Excellency, as well as former Governors . . . , usually laid before the Commons House of Assembly all Letters and Accounts they at any time received relating to the . . . Indians" and refused to vote funds to promote the colony's interests in a Cherokee-Creek war until it had inspected those papers. Similarly, in March 1752 the Commons protested because Glen had submitted

11. Cooper and McCord, eds., *S. C. Statutes,* IV, 168-73; Alden, *John Stuart,* 177, 207-14, 249; June 1761, S. C. Commons Journals, CO 5/479, p. 162; Feb. 12, May 27-29, 1762, *ibid.,* CO 5/480, pp. 5-6, 129-42; Journal of the Directors of the Cherokee Trade, 1762-65, 152-53, S. C. Arch. Dept.

copies rather than originals of certain Indian papers. It declared that the "Consideration of Indian Affairs was what Generally employed the first attention of the Assemblys of this Province being a matter of the highest Concern to the Peace and safety of the Inhabitants" and imperiously informed Glen that it expected him to "Communicate to this House all the Letters Accounts and Papers of every kind which You lately received concerning Indians, and that in the usual manner by Sending to Us the Original Papers themselves as we conceive there can be nothing in them private or personal to your Excellency, and which we think may not only be proper but necessary to be laid before Us without any Exception or reserve whatever." This was one time when Glen remained firm, however, refusing to supply the original papers and stamping the Commons' declaration as "Unprecedented and Unparliamentary" and inconsistent "with the British Constitution or the just prerogative of the Crown."

Because Glen's position no more conformed to South Carolina practice than did the Commons' declaration to the British constitution, the House struck back forcefully. It pointed out that it had "been the long and usual Custom" of both former governors and Glen to place "all Original Letters Papers and Accounts whatever relating to Indian Affairs" before the House and resolved that it had "a right" to inspect such papers. To deprive the House of that right, the Commons argued, prevented it from "forming a true Judgment of the State of the Indians" and "from assisting his Excellency with their Advice in Affairs of that Importance to the Province." When the Commons could not persuade Glen to alter his position, it stubbornly refused to grant any money for Indian expenses. During the ensuing weeks it refused to pay for sending some Catawbas and their prisoners to New York to settle a feud between them and their northern enemies because it was "still in the dark" about Indian affairs. A little later it declined to act on Glen's recommendation that an agent be sent to the Creeks to prevent a war between them and the Cherokees and observed that it seldom had any accounts of Indian affairs "unless Money is wanted to carry into Execution some matter recommended by his Excellency." Eventually the Commons agreed to pay for the Catawbas' New York trip, but it obstinately refused to interfere in the Creek-Cherokee affair. For his part, Glen did not comply with the Commons' demands for the original papers that session. But the following February, when he had other proposals to make, he carefully avoided a repetition of the controversy by sending the Commons the original Indian papers.[12]

Quite often during the middle years of the eighteenth century South Carolina employed special agents to treat with various Indian tribes, and the Commons invariably insisted upon nominating them. It inaugurated this practice in 1731 when it empowered Governor Robert Johnson to appoint an agent to the Creeks but reserved the nomination for itself. Thereafter the Commons regarded all such nominations as its right. In December 1736 it selected two agents to deal with the Creeks and Cherokees, despite Governor Broughton's insistence on another candidate for one of the posts. Similarly, the Commons named two men, one to deliver presents to the Chickasaws and another to act as Catawba agent, in February 1738, and twice it designated an agent to the Creeks, in January and December 1740. When the occasion arose to send another agent to the Creeks in July 1744, the Commons treated Glen more liberally by permitting him to choose one of its five nominees.[13] Without independent funds to pay such agents, governors were powerless to prevent the Commons from nominating them; for the Commons usually refused to pay agents employed by the governor without its consent. Thus, in May 1750 the Commons rejected James Adair's petition for reimbursements which he claimed Glen had promised him for keeping the Choctaws loyal to South Carolina between 1744 and 1750. Likewise, in the spring of 1753 it turned down Thomas Bosomworth's account because Glen and the Council had not consulted the House before sending him as agent to the Creeks. The House eventually paid Bosomworth, but the treatment received by both him and Adair discouraged the executive from making appointments without the Commons' consent.[14]

The Commons also insisted that no presents be given Indians without its approval. Its instruction to the Creek agent in 1737 that

12. Commons Journals, Mar. 16, 1750, S. C. Col. Recs., 1749-50, 471; Mar. 10, 13, 17, 20, May 1, 7-8, 13, 15, Feb. 27, 1753, S. C. Commons Journals, CO 5/466, pp. 97, 104, 113, 123-24, 169, 184-88, 205, 212.

13. Cooper and McCord, eds., S. C. Statutes, III, 327-34; Commons Journals, Dec. 8-10, 14, 1736, Feb. 1-2, 1737, Feb. 25-27, 1738, S. C. Col. Recs., 1736-39, 53-60, 69, 192, 197-200, 483-88; Jan. 31, Dec. 20, 1740, ibid., 1739-41, 165, 452; July 7, 1744, ibid., 1744-45, 239-41.

14. May 16, 1750, S. C. Commons Journals, CO 5/460, p. 213; Mar. 1, Apr. 16, 18, 1753, ibid., CO 5/466, pp. 56, 89-96; Mar. 15, 1754, ibid., CO 5/472, p. 81.

he distribute presents only "in such Manner and on such Occasion as he shall be instructed from time to time by the General Assembly" was representative of its policy. That the Commons' prior consent was necessary to insure its paying for presents was made amply clear to two Indian traders, Charles McNaire and Thomas Bosomworth. Acting upon instructions from Glen, both had distributed presents to the Indians, the former in 1747 and the latter in 1752, but the Commons initially refused to reimburse them because it had not first approved their gifts.[15]

Beginning in 1749 the Commons began to participate directly in distributing Indian presents, even when they were granted by the King rather than by the Commons. Glen agreed in June that the King's presents should be distributed by an agent appointed and directed by the entire legislature. Because the Commons could not participate in directing the agent after its adjournment, Glen requested it to "think on some Method of those Things being done during the Recess." The Commons responded by empowering its Indian affairs committee to meet with Glen and the Council during the recess to agree "upon Instructions, with such Restrictions and Limitations as shall be thought necessary, to be given to the Agent appointed on the behalf of this Province to see the Distribution of the Presents." Thus was the practice begun of the Commons' appointing a committee of its members to direct the distribution of Indian presents when it was not in session. Subsequently, the Commons empowered its committee on Indian affairs to act in its behalf during recesses on three separate occasions, in May 1751 and in November 1754 in regard to further presents granted by the King and in August 1753 in regard to presents given by the Commons to the Chickasaws. The South Carolina Commons had once again stretched its power well beyond that of its imperial counterpart by assuming a direct share in performing executive tasks.[16]

Not until the last years of his administration did Glen object to the Commons' sharing in the conduct of Indian diplomacy. Called

15. Commons Journals, Dec. 14, 1737, *S. C. Col. Recs., 1736-39*, 374; Apr. 18, 1753, S. C. Commons Journals, CO 5/466, pp. 93-94; May 10, 1754, *ibid.*, CO 5/472, p. 122; Feb. 26, 1751, *Board of Trade Journals, 1749-53*, p. 280.

16. Commons Journals, June 1, 1749, *S. C. Col. Recs., 1749-50*, 273-74; May 18, 1751, S. C. Commons Journals, CO 5/463, p. 201; Aug. 24, 1753, S. C. Commons Journals, XXVIII, 594, S. C. Arch. Dept.; Nov. 16, 1754, S. C. Commons Journals, CO 5/472, p. 9; Mar. 23, 1751, S. C. Council Journals, CO 5/462, pp. 55-60.

together in September 1755 after the Creeks had been reported as sympathetic to the French, the Commons voted to send an agent to persuade the Creek chiefs to come to Charleston to regulate the trade with their nation. As was usual in such cases, the Commons stipulated who should handle the assignment, recommending Henry Hyrne to Glen. If he were appointed, the Commons resolved to pay him £2,000 currency for three months' service and £20 per day thereafter and to furnish him with a clerk, nine men, and two servants. In addition, it agreed to give the Creeks presents worth up to £1,500 currency but stipulated that "if an Agent is appointed, a Committee of this House, aided by a Committee of the Council should be authorized, during the Recess of the House, to agree with the Governor for distributing such of the Indian Presents as shall remain undisposed of: and also to correspond with the Agent, and his Excellency the Governor of Georgia; and in general to negotiate all such matters relative to the said Indian Affairs, as shall be given them in Charge by this House."

Glen objected to both the nature and the spirit of the Commons' measures. The Creek leaders had already assured him that they were coming to Charleston, and he did not therefore think it necessary to send an agent. He also warned the Commons that sending them presents in their villages might lead them to expect greater gifts when they came to Charleston. More important, Glen raised constitutional objections to the Commons' practices of naming the person to serve as agent and of prescribing that its committees should share in directing that agent after it had adjourned. Glen's complaint illustrates how extensive the Commons' power in Indian diplomacy was. "You have so frequently, I may say so constantly recommended Persons to be commissioned by the Governor, on such Events," Glen protested, "that I could have wished you had declined doing it on this Occasion." He particularly objected to the Commons' making Hyrne's appointment a condition for its appropriation. Although he had previously encouraged such a practice, Glen now objected to the Commons' stipulating that its committee "agree with the Governor" on distributing the presents and pointed out that a more constitutional method would be for him to distribute them "with the advice of the Council and Assembly; or, which is the same thing, a Committee of each House." The stipulation, Glen declared, was an assumption of "Powers that neither belong to the one house nor the other, nor to both united, and that were never pretended to belong to the House of Peers or Commons in our Mother Country since the beginning of the English Monarchy except once, A Period that every good Man wished could be struck out of our Annals." To pacify Glen the Commons changed its stipulation, voting that the presents be distributed by the governor with the advice of the Council and the House Indian affairs committee. Still, it contended that an agent should be sent to discover the true state of affairs with the Creeks. But Glen ignored the Commons' contention and soon adjourned it until the fall.

For all Glen's objections, the Commons' power over Indian affairs was still undiminished. The following January it again appointed a committee on Indian affairs and invited Glen and the Council to meet with it to determine how the commissary general should dispose of the King's presents to the Indians which had been found "unfit for that Service." Glen again raised constitutional questions about the Commons' taking the lead in disposing of Indian presents, although he did agree to consider the invitation "as an Advice" and immediately to "give directions, accordingly, if the Council agree to it." But such subtle distinctions mattered little to the Commons as long as its practical power remained intact and its committee participated in disposing of the presents.[17]

Glen's opposition was neither strong nor constant, but Governor Lyttelton proved a more formidable opponent. In February 1757 he asked for presents for some Cherokees then visiting the colony, and the Commons characteristically resolved to pay for "a proper Reward to be given the said Indians by the Governour, in Council, with the consent of a Committee to be appointed by this House for that purpose." But Lyttelton found that the appointment of such a committee was "not free from Constitutional Objections" and asked the Commons to reconsider the matter. This time it was the Commons who backed down. Failing to find precedents for such committees before the late 1740's, it did not insist upon appointing one to share in distributing the presents and provided for their expense according to Lyttelton's estimate.[18]

17. Sept. 16-20, 1755, Mar. 16, 1756, S. C. Commons Journals, CO 5/472, Pt. III, pp. 1-2, 3-4, 6-8, Pt. IV, p. 73.
18. Feb. 3-5, 1757, *ibid.,* CO 5/473, pp. 21, 26-27.

However, the Commons was not yet ready to abandon its powers in Indian diplomacy to the executive. When Lyttelton refused to grant its request for accounts and papers in regard to Indian affairs in March 1757, the Commons informed him that "it hath been usual for the former Governors of this Province (when requested to do so) to communicate to the Assembly such accounts, respecting Indian Affairs, as had been received from any of the Indian Nations." It pointed out that it could not fully consider several demands upon the public for Indian expenses until it was "acquainted with the present situation of Indian Affairs" and again requested Lyttelton to send the papers for its examination. Lyttelton once more denied the Commons' request, and the Commons retaliated by withholding approval of his various Indian expenses. Three weeks later Lyttelton informed the Commons that he had sent Daniel Pepper as agent to the Creeks to distribute presents and requested that it pay for the mission. Still reluctant to provide for expenses without first seeing the Indian accounts and papers, the Commons attempted to gain access to them by requiring the Council's clerk to submit his journals and the Indian books for its perusal ostensibly to enable it to determine his yearly allowance. But Lyttelton foiled the attempt by advising the Council not to allow its clerk to submit his journals to the Commons and persuading the Commons to assign the clerk a regular salary instead of paying him so much per page.[19]

The Commons acceded temporarily to the governor's demands but guarded against a similar problem in the future. It agreed to provide for the Creek presents but made clear that it intended to retain its influence in Indian matters by resolving "that this House will not hereafter make provision for defraying the expense of any Presents that shall for the future be given to any Indians, in the Recess of the General Assembly, unless the same be done with the consent of a majority of such of the Members of this House as shall be in Town, to consist of Thirteen at least." Lyttelton met the challenge head on, arguing that the House's resolution "would lay me under very improper Restraints that in such times as these of great Public Dangers and Emergencies might be incompatible with the safety of the Province." Upon his request, the Commons finally withdrew its resolu-

19. Mar. 9, 17, 29, 31, 1757, *ibid.*, pp. 44-45, 52, 59-61; Lyttelton to Board of Trade, May 24, 1757, CO 5/375, ff. 203-7.

tion, but only after the speaker's vote had broken a tie. That Lyttelton had, however, won only a limited victory was indicated by the House's resolution that it would provide for presents given by him during the recess of the legislature only up to the value of £2,500 current money with the request that it be called into session whenever it was necessary to provide gifts over that amount.[20]

Lyttelton's firm stand against the Commons went a long way toward restoring the executive's power over Indian diplomacy and won him the praise of the Board of Trade. He had successfully resisted the Commons' demands to have all Indian papers and accounts placed before it, and he had induced the Commons to give up the practice of having a committee of its members meet with the Council and governor to distribute Indian presents during recesses.[21]

The Commons temporarily regained some of its powers in Indian diplomacy after Lyttelton left the province to assume the governorship of Jamaica. Under the younger Bull in April 1760 the Commons determined South Carolina policy by refusing to send presents for the Creeks to Georgia Governor Henry Ellis because it feared that to do so would reduce "the Importance this Province has been always industrious to maintain" among the Indians. Further, it granted £7,000 for presents to induce South Carolina's Indian allies to join the colony in its war against the Cherokees and without objection from Bull provided that the presents "be distributed among the said Indians by the Commander in Chief, with the advice of a Majority of a Committee of the Council and a Committee of this House to be appointed for that purpose." Accordingly, the following day Bull requested the Commons to appoint a committee to "assist" him "in the immediate distribution of some Presents to those Indians."[22]

But Bull's successor, Thomas Boone, was no less careful to preserve the prerogative than Lyttelton had been. As the Cherokee War was drawing to a close, the Commons voted in May 1762 that if the Cherokees behaved and delivered up their prisoners it would provide £2,500 "to enable . . . the Governor (with the Concurrence of a Committee of the Assembly during a recess of the House) to give such

20. Mar. 31-Apr. 2, 27-30, 1757, S. C. Commons Journals, CO 5/473, pp. 61-64, 67, 72-73, 75-76.
21. Lyttelton to Board of Trade, May 24, 1757, CO 5/375, ff. 203-7; Board of Trade to Lyttelton, Nov. 9, 1757, CO 5/403, pp. 200-208.
22. Apr. 29-May 1, 1760, S. C. Commons Journals, CO 5/473, pp. 53-56.

presents to them as may shew on our part a reciprocal desire of friendships and Agreement" and appointed a committee of thirteen to meet with the governor. Like Lyttelton, Boone resolved to put a stop to the Commons' using such committees to usurp a share of the governor's power to distribute presents, informing the Commons that "during the recess of Assembly, I can look upon a Committee of your House, in no other light than as private Gentlemen, and as such neither publicly to be consulted upon any matter of Government, or more Intitled to your Confidence that I am." In the face of Boone's opposition the Commons backed down and voted £500 to enable him to present gifts to some Cherokees and Chickasaws then in Charleston and a month later voted additional sums of £7,000 for presents to the Chickasaws and Choctaws to be distributed by the governor's appointee.[23]

Firm stands by Lyttelton and Boone had indeed borne fruit. By the end of the latter's administration in 1764, the Commons' power to participate in Indian diplomacy, which had grown so extensive under the elder Bull and Glen, had been sharply curtailed. But even if the Commons no longer played the leading role in the conduct of Indian diplomacy, it was still important. It could and did exercise considerable authority in all matters requiring appropriations until the Crown assumed complete control over southern Indian affairs in the middle 1760's under royal superintendent John Stuart.

Because of its position as a buffer colony against some of the stronger southern tribes, Georgia was as much concerned with Indian affairs as was South Carolina. Savannah, of course, never occupied a place in Indian trade comparable to that of Charleston, and because of Georgia's sparse population before 1763 it probably did not appear so ominous a threat to the Indians as the faster expanding and more populous South Carolina, which took the lead in diplomacy among the southern Indians throughout the 1740's and 1750's. But the Savannah Indian trade and the security of the colony depended in large measure upon amiable relations with the Indians. Until the establishment of royal government in Georgia in 1754, the trustees regulated the Indian trade; thereafter it was in the hands of the governor. The Georgia Commons seems never to have attempted to

23. May 28-29, June 30, 1762, *ibid.,* CO 5/480, pp. 132-38, 147-48.

assume direction of the trade, although in February 1758 at the instigation of Governor Ellis it did pass an act that required all Indian
traders to take out a license and invested the governor with the "sole
management and regulation of the Indian Trade" in the colony. The
trade remained in the hands of the executive until it passed to the
royal superintendent of Indian affairs in the mid-1760's.[24] Nor did
the Georgia Commons participate much in matters of diplomacy.
Indian presents were regularly provided for by annual grants from
Parliament, and accounts of Indian expenses were audited by the
governor and Council. There was little need for supplementary
grants from the Commons even if the colony had been able to bear
their expense. Except for small appropriations for extraordinary
services, therefore, the Georgia Commons was excluded from participating in Indian diplomacy.[25]

Because of the absence of any large Indian tribes close to the
settled area of Virginia and North Carolina between 1689 and the
late colonial period, their lower houses never took the interest in
Indian affairs that the South Carolina Commons did. During the
seventeenth century the Burgesses had occasionally placed statutory
regulations upon the Indian trade, but it had never manifested any
strong interest in bringing that trade under its direct supervision.
Similarly, for most of the eighteenth century the Virginia Burgesses
left both the enforcement of Indian trade regulations and the conduct of diplomacy in executive hands. In fact, as South Carolina
began after 1690 to engross the lucrative trade with the larger nations
along the southern frontier, the Burgesses steadily lost interest in Indian commerce. At Spotswood's instigation, it attempted in 1715 to
regain some of the commerce by passing a bill to establish a private

24. H. B. Fant, "The Indian Trade Policy of the Trustees for Establishing
the Colony of Georgia in America," *Ga. Hist. Qtly.*, 15 (1931), 207-22; John P.
Corry, *Indian Affairs in Georgia, 1732-1756* (Phila., 1936); Ellis to Earl of Loudoun,
Nov. 28, 1757, Loudoun Papers, 4911, Huntington Lib.; Ellis to Lyttelton, Jan.
21, Feb. 18, 1758, Lyttelton Papers, Clements Lib.; Commons Journals, Feb. 15,
28, 1758, *Ga. Col. Recs.*, XIII, 282, 299-300; Council Journals, July 3, 1761, *ibid.*,
VIII, 522-24; Letter of James Wright, 1766, Report on State of American Colonies,
King's MSS, 205, f. 315, British Museum.

25. Estimate of Ga. Civil Establishment, 1754-55, Newcastle Papers, Add. MSS,
33029, f. 122, British Museum; June 21, 1754, *Acts of Privy Council, Colonial*, IV,
259; July 6, 1756, *Board of Trade Journals, 1754-58*, 248; Dec. 22, 1761, *ibid.*,
1759-63, 238-39; Council Journals, Nov. 18, 22, 1757, *Ga. Col. Recs.*, VII, 671-72;
Commons Journals, July 20, 1757, *ibid.*, XIII, 225.

Indian company with a twenty-year monopoly on Indian trade. But this measure in no way represented an effort to bring the trade under public control, and, when imperial authorities disallowed it in 1717, few burgesses expressed regrets.[26]

Briefly, during the Seven Years' War, the Burgesses did put the public in charge of the trade, passing a law in 1757 to invest the management of the Indian trade for three years in five directors: Peter Randolph, William Randolph, Richard Bland, Archibald Cary, and Thomas Walker—the last four of whom were leading members of the House. Given an original capital stock of £5,000, they were to purchase goods, contract with factors to sell them, and build a fort from which to carry on the trade. By these arrangements the Burgesses hoped to sell goods to the Indians cheaply without profit either to the directors or to the colony. Dinwiddie expected this scheme to be of more service than giving Indians large presents, but it proved both expensive and unpopular with private traders and the Crown's superintendent of Indian affairs. When the act expired the Burgesses abandoned it, ordering the directors to sell their remaining goods and pay the proceeds therefrom into the public treasury. Although the Burgesses briefly revived the public trading company scheme in 1765, it was never keenly interested in it.[27]

If the Burgesses showed little inclination to assume direction of the Indian trade, it showed even less to take an active part in Indian diplomacy. Of course, in matters of expense, such as providing presents or participating in conferences, the Burgesses' consent was necessary. But for the most part Dinwiddie accurately characterized the situation when he wrote that Indian affairs came within the province of the governor and Council.[28]

26. Hening, ed., *Va. Statutes*, I, 126, 173, II, 138-43, 350-51, 410-12, 480, III, 69; Crane, *Southern Frontier*, 171; Leonidas Dodson, *Alexander Spotswood*, 70-111; W. Neil Franklin, "Virginia and the Cherokee Indian Trade, 1673-1752," East Tennessee Historical Society, *Publications*, No. 4 (1932), 3-21; Spotswood to Bishop of London, Jan. 27, 1715, and to Board of Trade, June 24, 1718, Brock, ed., *Spotswood Letters*, II, 89, 281-82.

27. Hening, ed., *Va. Statutes*, VII, 116-18, 354-55; Alden, *John Stuart*, 74-75, 117-18; Dinwiddie to Lyttelton, Aug. 27, 1757, Lyttelton Papers, Clements Lib.; W. Neil Franklin, "Virginia and the Cherokee Indian Trade, 1753-1775," E. Tenn. Hist. Soc., *Publications*, No. 5 (1933), 22-38; Letter of Fauquier, 1763, Report on State of American Colonies, King's MSS, 205, ff. 266-67, British Museum.

28. William Gooch to Board of Trade, July 23, 1730, CO 5/1322, ff. 53-66; Board of Trade to Dinwiddie, July 4, 1754, CO 5/1367, pp. 103-9; Apr. 12, 1746, *Va. Burgesses Journals, 1742-49*, 221; Dinwiddie's Answers to Board of Trade's Queries, no date, CO 5/1328, ff. 323-32.

The North Carolina Lower House was even less interested than the Virginia Burgesses in participating in Indian affairs. It had passed trade regulations as early as 1669 but had always left their enforcement to the governor. Acts of 1715 and 1749 provided for executive-appointed Indian commissioners to settle disputes between Indians and colonists over trade. Neither act appears to have been either stringently enforced or adequate to serve the interests of even North Carolina's small trade. In 1754 Dobbs recommended passage of more extensive regulations, but the Lower House did not respond until 1757 when it passed an act that required all North Carolina traders to take out a license, although it left the licensing power to the royal superintendent of Indian affairs. Like the Virginia Burgesses, the North Carolina Lower House concerned itself with Indian diplomacy only when money was needed to pay for presents or to defray the expenses of attending Indian conferences. Usually the House permitted the executive to distribute presents, but at least twice, in May 1757 and December 1759, it appointed individuals to do so.[29]

The Virginia, North Carolina, and Georgia lower houses never wielded great power over Indian affairs during the colonial period. Each placed statutory regulations upon the Indian trade, but only the Virginia Burgesses for a brief period after 1757 attempted to direct it. As a rule they influenced Indian diplomacy only insofar as they passed upon all matters of expense relating to Indian affairs. On the other hand, the South Carolina Commons played an important role in Indian affairs. It assumed control over the Indian trade early in the eighteenth century and appointed and directed the commissioner employed to supervise that trade. The South Carolina Commons also took a large part in Indian diplomacy by granting money only for projects that met with its approval and by appointing special committees to meet with the governor and Council to shape the course of Indian diplomacy during legislative recesses. But by 1763 Governors Lyttelton and Boone had curtailed even the power of the South Carolina Commons over Indian affairs by refusing to

29. Laws, *N. C. St. Recs.,* XXIII, 87-88, 333, XXV, 121-22, 356-58; Council Journals, Jan. 22, 1732, Oct. 14, 1736, *N. C. Col. Recs.,* III, 414, IV, 224; Lower House Journals, Dec. 14, 18, 1754, Sept. 30, Oct. 15, 1755, Oct. 19, 1756, May 23, 27, Nov. 24, 1757, *ibid.,* V, 235, 241-42, 528, 556-57, 722, 854, 863, 893; Dec. 17, 1759, *ibid.,* VI, 161.

allow it to appoint committees to act with the governor and Council between sessions. In addition, the Commons, decreasingly concerned with Indian problems after the removal of the French and Spanish menace in the 1760's and the decline of the Indian trade as a major element in the economy of South Carolina, did not object to the Crown's taking over the expensive conduct of Indian diplomacy and in 1761 voluntarily abandoned the practice of appointing a commissioner to supervise the Indian trade. Although it appointed directors to take over the Cherokee trade between 1762 and 1765, it never made any concerted effort to reassert its control over the trade.

The fact that none of the lower houses in the southern royal colonies was exercising any considerable authority over Indian affairs following the Seven Years' War meant that they would not regard the Crown's delegation of increased power to royal Indian Superintendent John Stuart as a challenge to their authority. The only real opposition to that step from colonial official quarters came, in fact, from the royal governors, who resented having to take a back seat to Stuart in affairs of Indian diplomacy. But their protests were of little avail, for Stuart retained control over Indian relations until the end of the colonial period. He was less successful in his attempt to assert his authority over the Indian trade. Beginning in 1764 he tried to establish some regulations over southern traders by virtue of authority derived from the Proclamation of 1763, but he had little support from either London or the colonial capitals and no adequate machinery in the Indian country to maintain a very strict enforcement.[30]

For a brief period after Shelburne took over as secretary of state for the Southern Department in the summer of 1766, Stuart's efforts met with greater success. Stuart persuaded imperial officials to strengthen his authority over the trade by disallowing a 1765 Virginia act designed to place the supervision of Virginia's trade with the Cherokees directly in the hands of legislative-appointed directors.[31] With Shelburne's approval, he also put into operation an elaborate regulatory system providing for commissaries resident in the Indian towns to enforce stringent controls over the trade. But this system

30. Alden, *John Stuart*, 207-8, 214. See also Boone to Board of Trade, Apr. 7, 1764, S. C. Pub. Recs., XXX, 133, 137, S. C. Arch. Dept.
31. Hening, ed., *Va. Statutes*, VIII, 114-18; Shelburne to Fauquier, Aug. 7, 1767, CO 5/1374; Alden, *John Stuart*, 251-52.

proved extraordinarily expensive, and in March 1768 Shelburne and other London authorities returned the supervision of the trade to the individual colonies. Thereafter, the governors and councils of the several colonies assumed the direction of the trade, the lower houses, surprisingly perhaps, never attempting in the remaining few years of the colonial period to reassert their authority in that area.[32]

32. Alden, *John Stuart,* 242-61. See also Hillsborough to Tryon, Apr. 15, 1768, *N. C. Col. Recs.,* VII, 707-9.

17

Courts and Judges

In England the establishment of courts and the appointment of judges had always been the prerogative of the Crown. With the exception of the Restoration, when Parliamentary statute was necessary for the revival of some of the prerogative courts abolished by act of the Long Parliament in 1641, Parliament never tried to establish courts by statute. Nor did it attempt to appoint judges, although it did regulate the conditions for their holding office. Before 1689 judges usually held their places during pleasure. But this arrangement was not conducive to an independent judiciary, for if the judges failed to please the Crown they were likely to lose their jobs. Under William and Anne judges held their appointments *quamdiu se bene gesserint,* or during good behavior, and the Act of Settlement in 1701 stipulated in addition that they be removed only upon the request of both houses of Parliament and that their salaries be fixed permanently. Thereafter, the judges' positions were secure, and Englishmen could look forward to a more impartial administration of justice. The final steps in the attainment of an independent judiciary came in 1760, when Parliament declared that judges' commissions were not terminate upon the death of the Sovereign. But these regulations did not encroach upon the Crown's rights of nomination and appointment.[1]

It is not surprising that upon the transfer of political institutions to the American colonies the Crown should delegate the powers of establishing courts and appointing judges to its representatives. After 1661 it empowered its governors with the consent of their councils to

1. Holdsworth, *English Law*, VI, 234-35; Thomson, *Constitutional History*, 140-52, 282-91, 411-20.

establish as many courts, both criminal and civil, within their respective provinces as they should deem necessary and to appoint judges. Subsequently, royal instructions limited the governors' power to establish courts by requiring the Crown's consent for their erection or dissolution. In order that home authorities might be thoroughly informed on the judicial organization of the colonies, the Board of Trade required each new governor to submit a report "of all establishments of jurisdictions, courts, offices and officers, powers, authorities, fees and privileges granted or settled within" his particular colony. Royal instructions also restricted the governors' power to appoint judges. Beginning in 1671 appointments were to be made only with the advice and consent of the councils, and until 1753 they were to be given without limitations of time. This last restriction, when coupled with a further instruction first given in 1672 that judicial officers not be displaced "without good and sufficient cause" to be signified to the Crown, tended to establish tenure for judges during good behavior. But such was not the intention of the imperial authorities, although it seems peculiar that the Crown should deny to the colonial judiciary that security of tenure guaranteed to English judges by the Act of Settlement in 1701. The Crown was unwilling to limit its power of appointing and removing judges in the colonies. In an attempt to arrest the development of a judicial tenure during good behavior in the colonies, Crown officials issued an instruction to new governors after 1753 requiring that judges' commissions be granted during pleasure only. In 1761 they extended this instruction to all royal colonies.[2]

But in judicial affairs, as in other matters, rules worked out for the colonies in England were not always followed on the other side of the Atlantic. One former governor, Thomas Pownall, observed in 1764 that the power delegated to the governor by the Crown to establish courts was "universally" denied by colonials, who maintained that such establishments could be made only by acts of the legislatures. Pownall exaggerated somewhat, but it was nevertheless true that the constant colonial practice of establishing courts by statute for three-quarters of a century before 1750 had given rise to the notion that courts could be created in no other way. Although

2. Labaree, ed., *Royal Instructions*, I, 295-97, 366-69, II, 820-21; Labaree, *Royal Government*, 373-74.

the Board of Trade and its legal counsels usually examined carefully all acts touching upon judicial matters and, if they encroached seriously on the prerogative, occasionally recommended their disallowance, they contributed to the development of this notion by their frequent confirmation of such acts. In general, it was customary in all the southern royal colonies except Georgia for courts to be established by legislative enactments, although the lower houses never really established their right to create courts by statute, for such statutes were always subject to disallowance when they came before Crown authorities.

Colonial lower houses seldom attempted to usurp the power to appoint judges from the royal governors, but most of them did as their imperial counterpart had done before them: they strove to regulate the terms of judicial appointments. They particularly disliked the royal instruction issued after 1753 requiring the appointment of judges during pleasure, arguing that it was not conducive to an independent judiciary because it made a judge's continuance in office dependent upon the whims of a governor. They contended instead that judicial appointments should be during good behavior and in some cases that the removal of judges should be approved by the legislatures. The wide gulf between the Crown's position and that of the lower houses produced serious controversies in several colonies. But among the southern royal colonies such conflicts arose only in the two Carolinas.[3]

In Virginia it was customary throughout the colonial period for the legislature to establish courts and jurisdictions by statute. The legislature inaugurated that custom as early as March 1624 and during the next half century repeatedly passed measures to settle details of the judiciary. The General Assembly, in fact, served as the highest court in Virginia until 1682, when the Crown deprived it of that status by royal order. Thereafter the upper chamber retained a judicial function; but, as the branch of the legislature which usually took the lead in initiating legislation, the Burgesses quite naturally played a major role in shaping the colony's court system and after 1728 had a standing committee on courts of justice.[4]

3. Thomas Pownall, *The Administration of the Colonies* (London, 1764), 53; Labaree, *Royal Government*, 371-419.
4. Hening, ed., *Va. Statutes*, I, 125, 168-69, 185-87, 272-73, 302-5, 345-46, 398-99,

Both the superior and inferior courts in Virginia rested upon a statutory foundation. The general court, consisting of the governor and Council, was the supreme court; and the legislature had subjected it to extensive regulations by acts of 1662 and 1684. Imperial authorities raised no objections to the first of these measures, but they did take exception to provisions in the second fixing the times for holding courts. In 1690 they issued a special instruction to the governor requiring the legislature to alter that act by adding a clause specifying "that the power of appointing courts to be held at any time whatsoever remain in you or the commander in chief of that our said colony for the time being."

Home officials also objected to a comprehensive general court law passed by the Burgesses as part of the 1705 revisal of the laws. Solicitor General James Montague approved the measure, but the Board of Trade regarded its very passage as an infringement of the prerogative. In particular, the Board disliked the clause stipulating that there should be "no Court of Record in Virginia but the General Court and the County Courts" because it derogated "from her Majesty's Royal Prerogative by restraining her Power of Constituting other Courts of Record as may hereafter upon Emergent occasions be found Convenient." To remedy this objection, Spotswood persuaded the Burgesses in 1710 to pass an explanatory act declaring that "nothing in the said act contained, shall be construed, deemed, or taken to derogate from, lessen, or abridge the roial power, prerogative, and authority of her Majesty . . . of granting commission or commissions of *oier and terminer,* or of constituting and erecting such other court or courts of record as her Majesty . . . by her . . . commissions . . . or instructions to her . . . governor . . . shall direct, order or appoint." The issue raised on this occasion was whether or not colonial laws to create courts usurped the executive power to establish still other courts for the same purpose. There was little question in the minds of colonial legislators that they did, but Attorney General Edward Northey ruled in 1717 that they did not.[5]

462; II, 60-72; Feb. 10, 1728, Aug. 6, 1736, *Va. Burgesses Journals, 1727-40,* 16-17, 244-45; Oliver P. Chitwood, *Justice in Colonial Virginia* (Baltimore, 1905), 19-73.

5. Hening, ed., *Va. Statutes,* II, 58-61, III, 287-302, 489-90; Labaree, ed., *Royal Instructions,* I, 163; Spotswood to Board of Trade, Mar. 6, 1711, Brock ed., *Spotswood Letters,* I, 49-50; Board of Trade to Edmund Jenings, Mar. 26, 1707, CO 5/1362; Montague to Board of Trade, Aug. 20, 1707, Shelburne Papers, LXI, 168-69, Clements Lib.; Northey to Board of Trade, Dec. 24, 1717, CO 5/1318.

Imperial authorities did not raise the issue again in regard to Virginia or for that matter any of the other southern royal colonies. Subsequently, the Burgesses passed other laws to regulate the general court in 1727, 1746, and 1749.[6] Imperial authorities seem to have approved the first two, but they disallowed the third not because it encroached upon the prerogative but because it did not clearly distinguish between petty and central jurisdiction. The Burgesses tried to obviate imperial objections in an act of November 1753, but both Lieutenant Governor Dinwiddie and the Board of Trade objected to its provisions for the court's appellate jurisdiction. Finally, however, the Board acknowledged that "the method prescribed . . . has been found by long experience to be attended with no inconvenience" and did not advise the disallowance of the law.[7]

The Burgesses also settled the county courts by statute. Throughout the seventeenth and eighteenth centuries it frequently passed laws to regulate those courts. As a rule, London officials allowed these measures to pass without question, but in 1704 Attorney General Northey objected to one of them because it usurped the executive power to establish courts. "I cannot approve of Erecting Courts in the Plantations by the Acts of the Assembly," he wrote, "that Authority being Lodged in the Governour by Virtue of the Queens Commission." Still, the Board of Trade did not advise the disallowance of the law.[8]

In Virginia, judges' appointments seem always to have been in the hands of the executive. The Crown appointed the councilors, who were judges of both the General Court and the court of oyer and terminer, and the governor with the Council's advice appointed all county court justices.[9] The terms of these appointments probably conformed to the royal instructions, for there was no law requiring that they be given during good behavior.

6. Labaree, *Royal Government,* 375-76; Hening, ed., *Va. Statutes,* IV, 182-97, V, 319-20, 467-88; Apr. 12, 1746, May 10, 1749, *Va. Burgesses Journals, 1742-49,* 220-21, 400-1.

7. Hening, ed., *Va. Statutes,* VI, 325-50; Order in Council, Oct. 31, 1751, CO 5/1327, f. 343; Dinwiddie to Board of Trade, Feb. 10, 1755, CO 5/1328, ff. 319-20; Board of Trade to Dinwiddie, Aug. 6, 1755, CO 5/1367, pp. 151-55.

8. Northey to Board of Trade, Aug. 14, 1704, CO 5/1304; Hening, ed., *Va. Statutes,* I, 272-73, 302-5, 345-46, 398-99, 462, II, 61-75, III, 504-16, V, 489-508.

9. See Dinwiddie's Answers to Board of Trade's Queries, no date, CO 5/1328, ff. 223-32; George L. Chumbley, *Colonial Justice in Virginia* (Richmond, 1938), 81-82.

In South Carolina the Lords Proprietors had retained the power to erect courts throughout the proprietary period, but under the Crown the Commons, like the Virginia Burgesses, regularly established courts by statute. The Commons first undertook to regulate the courts immediately after overthrowing the proprietors in 1719. Important among the causes of the 1719 revolution were Chief Justice Nicholas Trott's abuses of the extensive judicial powers conferred on him by the proprietors. To remedy these abuses, the Commons passed a law in February 1720 to place the courts under extensive limitations. That act diminished the chief justice's power by providing for the appointment by the Crown of five assistant judges. Similarly, it stripped the governor and Council of their major judicial power by forbidding them to serve as a court of chancery, and it gave the General Assembly appellate jurisdiction over cases from the inferior courts involving more than £100. That the act was designed to place legislative checks upon the governor's judicial powers was nowhere more evident than in the section forbidding the governor to suspend or remove judges in any case whatsoever. The Crown did not disallow this measure for nearly thirty years, but many of its more radical provisions were nullified either because the executive did not enforce them or because the Commons modified them by subsequent acts. Certainly, the General Assembly after 1721 never exercised the appellate jurisdiction entrusted to it by that act, and the Commons restored the chancery powers of the governor and Council by a 1721 law.[10]

The act of 1720 was primarily regulatory in purpose, but it did create new jurisdictions and contribute to the development within the Commons of the idea that courts should be established by statute. Accordingly, the Commons created county and precinct courts by acts of 1721 and 1722. Both acts came under the fire of the Council during the period of anarchy from 1728 to 1731. Through Stephen Godin, its London agent, the Council asked the disallowance of all South Carolina court laws, recommending that "such Courts may be Established by Virtue of your Majesty's Royal Comission and Instructions . . . and not by virtue of any Act of Assembly." Later, Godin requested the Board of Trade to include this recommendation in the

10. Lords Proprietors to Philip Ludwell, Nov. 8, 1691, S. C. Pub. Recs., III, 35, S. C. Arch. Dept.; Act to regulate S. C. Courts, Feb. 1720, CO 5/372, ff. 198-202; Cooper and McCord, eds., *S. C. Statutes*, VII, 163-65.

governor's instructions, but Crown officials ignored his requests. Indeed, they apparently did not consider the Commons' establishment of courts as a serious encroachment on the prerogative.[11]

Between 1731 and 1735 the Crown disallowed three different South Carolina acts to regulate the courts of justice, but not because they infringed upon the executives' power to create courts. In 1732 it disallowed a 1727 law which altered the writ in a civil action from a summons left at a man's house to a capias served directly upon the defendant after South Carolina merchants had complained that the capias obstructed their efforts to collect debts from planters. Two more acts met a similar fate in 1755. An act of 1732 required the governor to appoint two or more assistant judges. To begin with, these judges were subordinate to the chief justice in the court of common pleas, but by an act two years later the Commons gave them an equal voice.[12] Both laws tended to reduce the power of the chief justice, the second quite deliberately. Chief Justice Robert Wright had aroused the Commons' wrath two years earlier by opposing its suspension of the habeas corpus act in cases where its privilege of commitment was involved. In retaliation the Commons not only withheld Wright's salary but also attempted to limit his judicial powers in the 1734 law. Wright's protests against these laws prompted the Crown to disallow them in March 1735. Royal officials regarded the clauses requiring the governor to appoint assistant judges as serious encroachments upon the Crown's "undoubted Right of Appointing Judges" because the governor already held those powers by virtue of his commission and instructions. But they were not blind to the colony's need for assistant judges, and they sent an additional instruction to Lieutenant Governor Thomas Broughton directing him to appoint two "in the several courts of law in that province" by his own authority.[13]

11. Cooper and McCord, eds., *S. C. Statutes,* VII, 166-76, 178-83; S. C. Council's Memorial to Crown, received by Board of Trade, July 30, 1729, Godin's Proposed Additional Instructions to S. C. Governor, July 30, Aug. 14, 1729, CO 5/361, ff. 13-16, 17-21, 53-54.

12. Cooper and McCord, eds., *S. C. Statutes,* III, 323-26, VII, 184-89; Board of Trade to Crown, Mar. 7, 1732, CO 5/381, ff. 89-90; Thomas Lowndes to Board of Trade, Dec. 14, 1731, Merchants trading to S. C. to Board of Trade, received by Board of Trade, Jan. 14, 1732, CO 5/362, ff. 50, 81-82.

13. May 9, 30, 1733, S. C. Commons Journals, CO 5/433, pp. 56, 63-64; Commons Journals, Nov. 11, 1736, *S. C. Col. Recs., 1736-39,* 9-11; May 16, 1734, *Board of Trade Journals, 1729-34,* 389; June 10, Aug. 7, 1735, *ibid., 1735-41,* 21, 52-53; Mar. 20, 1734, *Acts of Privy Council, Colonial,* III, 410-12; Labaree, ed.,

The judicial system as established during the first fifteen years under the Crown was not changed in any of its essentials until just before the Revolution. The Commons made only one alteration, placing the court of common pleas on a statutory basis in March 1737,[14] and Crown officials made no concerted effort to change existing arrangements. In 1755 at the time of Lyttelton's appointment as governor the Board of Trade carefully reviewed the Carolina courts. It found "that several of the laws for establishing the principal courts of justice . . . were in many parts defective, improper and inconsistent with the rights and prerogative of the Crown" and instructed Lyttelton to recommend to the Commons that those laws be revised so that the rules and methods of proceedings in South Carolina courts would "be as near as may be agreeable to the rules and methods of proceeding in the courts of law and equity in Great Britain."[15] Questions of defense were paramount at that time, however, and another decade elapsed before the Commons undertook any serious reconstruction of the judicial system.

The question of tenure was not a serious issue in South Carolina in the period before 1763. Except for a clause in the act of 1720 forbidding the removal or suspension of judges by the governor, the Commons made no regulations concerning tenure. In 1749 an assistant judge cited that clause to support his contention that Glen could not suspend him from office, but when the matter came before Board of Trade legal counsel Matthew Lamb, he ruled that the 1720 law was "passed by an usurped authority" and "should not be considered as a law." Thereafter, there were no statutory tenure regulations at all; and in the absence of any statute to the contrary it is safe to assume that judges' appointments were during pleasure in conformity with the royal instructions. This assumption is substantiated by Boone's report in 1763 that the Commons House had never attempted to settle the tenure of judicial officials by act.[16]

In North Carolina the practice of establishing courts by statute

---

Royal Instructions, I, 370-71; Wright to Privy Council, Aug. 12, 1734, CO 5/364, f. 14; Order in Council, Mar. 4, 1735, CO 5/365, f. 76; Report of Privy Council's Plantations Committee, Aug. 14, 1735, CO 5/381, ff. 197-202.

14. Cooper and McCord, eds., *S. C. Statutes*, VII, 189-91.

15. Feb. 20, May 1, 29, 1755, *Board of Trade Journals, 1754-58*, 114, 142, 152.

16. Lamb's Opinion on Usurped Assembly in S. C., May 30, 1750, Chalmers, ed., *Opinions*, I, 354-55; Boone to Board of Trade, June 17, 1763, CO 5/377, f. 221.

originated under the proprietors. As in South Carolina, the proprietors established the earlier courts without the legislature's consent, but in the 1720's the Lower House began to bring the judicial system under statutory regulations, passing acts to regulate the precinct courts and to enlarge their jurisdiction. Under the Crown the House continued this practice. In 1738 it passed an act to set up circuit courts and to enlarge the power of the county courts, and in 1746 it undertook extensive regulations of the colony's whole judicial system. By a law designed to fix the capital permanently at New Bern, Johnston's long assembly set up circuit courts and put all other courts on a statutory foundation. That law was in force until April 1754, when the Crown disallowed it. In proposing disallowance, the Board of Trade ruled that "fixing the seat of Government and establishing Courts of Justice are acts of Sovereignty which belong to Your Majesty alone and therefore ought not to have been done by Act of Assembly." "Nor is it in any degree a justification of this measure that the great inconveniency and confusion occasioned by the want of a seat of Government and of proper Courts of Justice made it absolutely necessary to pass this Law," the Board continued, "since the same thing might have been done by the sole act of the Governor and Council." Accordingly, it suggested "that the Governor be directed to establish such and so many Courts of Justice as shall appear to be necessary and proper for the better administration of justice." The ruling was clear enough. Despite dozens of colonial precedents to the contrary, the Board still adhered to the principle that establishing and regulating courts belonged exclusively to the executive and could not constitutionally be handled by legislative enactments.[17]

The Crown agreed with the Board and issued an instruction to Dobbs at the time of his appointment in 1754 ordering him to establish courts by executive ordinance. Perhaps fortunately for intracolony harmony, however, Dobbs did not follow this instruction closely. Instead, he chose to abide by the precedents of settling courts by statute. In January 1755 he passed two laws, one to fix supreme courts and another to regulate county courts, and in October 1756 he agreed to a statute to amend the supreme court law. For over four years

17. Proprietor's Instructions to Gov. of Albemarle, 1667, to John Harvey, Feb. 5, 1679, *N. C. Col. Recs.*, I, 168-71, 236; Laws, *N. C. St. Recs.*, XXIII, 100-2, 111, 127, 252-67; Board of Trade to King, Mar. 14, 1754, Order in Council, Apr. 8, 1754, *N. C. Col. Recs.*, V, 107-8, 117.

these measures escaped the notice of imperial officials, but in early 1759 Chief Justice Charles Berry and Attorney General Thomas Child brought substantial charges against them before the Board of Trade. They centered their charges upon the supreme court act for usurping a portion of the governor's judicial authority by creating associate judgeships and leaving to the governor "only . . . the form of naming and commissioning them." They also objected to the act's delegating "the whole right of exercising Judicature" to the associates whenever the chief justice was absent or disabled. That right, they declared, could "be only . . . solely delegated by the Crown." They further complained that the act extended the circuit to 1,900 miles a year, a distance so long that the chief justice could attend only half of it. The other half would necessarily be handled by the associates, and the judicial powers of the chief justice would thereby be decreased. Berry and Child's complaints caused the disallowance of these three court acts along with two others, one relating to juries and another concerning orphans' estates, in April 1759.[18]

The disallowance of these measures left the colony without legally constituted courts, and between November 1759 and May 1760 the re-establishment of the judicial system was one of the chief occupations of the Lower House. Two bills proposed by the Lower House in January 1760 failed because of the inability of the two houses to agree on a proper fund for paying the associate judges. The following April the Lower House again framed both an inferior and a superior court bill. The first was perfectly acceptable to all parties, but fundamental constitutional disagreements developed over the second. That law provided for the three associate justices and restricted nominations to attorneys of seven years' practice and at least one year's residence in North Carolina.

Dobbs complained that this restriction largely deprived the Crown of its right of nomination, but he found the clause stipulating that the associate judges were to have tenure during good behavior even more objectionable, for it was directly contrary to his instructions issued in 1754 specifying that judges hold office only during pleasure. Unable to persuade the Lower House to revise the law, Dobbs sought

18. Laws, *N. C. St. Recs.*, XXV, 274-95; Labaree, ed., *Royal Instructions*, I, 299; Lower House Journals, Oct. 25, 1756, *N. C. Col. Recs.*, V, 734-35; Berry and Child to Board of Trade, Feb. 24, 1759, Board of Trade to King, Apr. 12, 1759, Order in Council, Apr. 14, 1759, *ibid.*, VI, 13-15, 25-29; Apr. 3, 1759, *Board of Trade Journals, 1759-63*, 25.

the advice of the chief justice and the attorney general. Because of the colony's need for some sort of judicial machinery, they advised him to violate his instructions and assent to the bill.[19] Dobbs hesitated, hoping to induce the House to alter the exceptionable tenure clause, but it insisted that appointing judges during pleasure "Shews an unreasonable Desire to retain the Power of Appointing Judges for private Views and Partial Ends." Dobbs then assented to the inferior court bill but rejected the superior court bill, deciding to prorogue the legislature for three days to give the Lower House time to reconsider its position. After the prorogation Dobbs met the House with a conciliatory gesture, offering to pass the superior court bill if the House would consent to limit its operation to two years. The House accepted the offer, and the bill passed into law. The settlement was a sensible one. It satisfied the colony's immediate need for courts and at the same time made the law temporary in case imperial officials could not be persuaded to accept its tenure stipulations.[20]

Neither of the court laws fared well in England. The Board of Trade objected to the superior court act because of its tenure provisions and to the inferior court act because it gave the county courts too wide a jurisdiction. As a result, the Crown disallowed both laws in December 1761 and censured Dobbs for passing them. At the same time, it sent a circular instruction not only to Dobbs but to all the colonies positively forbidding the appointment of judges during good behavior.[21]

News of the Crown's disallowance of these acts caused the Lower House to despair of ever passing a court law which would meet with imperial approval. To defend its contention that judges should hold office during good behavior, it pointed to the example of the mother country as well as that of several American colonies. In preparing a new superior court bill, the House at first adhered to its position on

19. Lower House Journals, Jan. 1-7, May 17, 19, 1760, *N. C. Col. Recs.*, VI, 185-95, 402-4; Dobbs to Board of Trade, Jan. 19, May 28, 1760, *ibid.*, 216-20, 243-51; Labaree, ed., *Royal Instructions*, I, 367; Thomas Child's Answers to Dobbs's Queries, May 20, 1760, *N. C. Col. Recs.*, VI, 254-56.

20. Lower House Journals, May 23, 26-27, 1760, *N. C. Col. Recs.*, VI, 416-19, 425, 437; Dobbs to Board of Trade, May 28, 1760, Dobbs's Answers to Board of Trade's Queries, 1761, *ibid.*, 243-51, 622-23.

21. Matthew Lamb to Board of Trade, Nov. 4, 1761, CO 5/299, ff. 179-80; Board of Trade to King, Dec. 3, 1761, and Feb. 1762, *N. C. Col. Recs.*, VI, 587-91, 700-701; Dec. 14, 1761, *Acts of Privy Council, Colonial*, IV, 502-6; Dec. 17, 1761, Feb. 10, 1762, *Board of Trade Journals, 1759-63*, 236, 249-51; Labaree, ed., *Royal Instructions*, I, 367-68.

tenure. It would not, it declared, "run the risque of having Judges Obtruded on us who perhaps may be utter Strangers to our Laws and must . . . hold their appointments on the precarious footing of the pleasure of a Commander in Chief." But in December 1762 the necessity of providing the colony with some sort of judicial machinery forced the House to give in, and it consented to the passage of a temporary two-year superior court bill that was discreetly silent on the tenure question. By this tactic the House avoided acknowledging the Crown's right to appoint judges during pleasure but put no legal obstacles in the way of such appointments. More important perhaps, it left the question open for future debate. The House never again formally raised the issue during the colonial period, but there is no doubt that it was a lingering grievance. Nearly a dozen years later Governor Martin reported that it was "a fixed principle" with the House never to grant the chief justice a permanent salary until the Crown had appointed him during good behavior, and Martin's later letters indicate that the tenure question was vital among North Carolina legislators to the very end of the colonial period. Also in December 1762, the House obtained a new inferior court bill after it had removed the features of the older bill that Crown officials had found objectionable. A third bill to establish courts of oyer and terminer failed in the Council, which argued that such courts could be created by the governor and Council without legislative sanction. The Lower House, taking the opposite point of view, asserted that no courts could be established without its approval—a view that had gradually grown up over the years; and the Council's rejection in no way deterred the House from making a similar attempt whenever a favorable opportunity arose.[22]

The superior and inferior court laws passed at this time proved more permanent than expected. Crown officials were pleased with them and urged Governor Tryon to induce the Lower House to make them permanent. But the House refused. To have done so would have been to abandon entirely the attempt to obtain judicial tenure during good behavior. Until the Crown changed its attitude upon

22. Lower House Journals, Nov. 4, 20, 1762, *N. C. Col. Recs.*, VI, 896-97, 915-16; Couchet Jouvencal to Board of Trade, May 16, 1763, *ibid.*, 986-88; Upper House Journals, Nov. 19, 23, Dec. 11, 1762, *ibid.*, 848-54, 890-92; Laws, *N. C. St. Recs.*, XXIII, 550-74; Dobbs to Board of Trade, Mar. 7, 1763, *N. C. Col. Recs.*, VI, 970; Josiah Martin to Dartmouth, May 5, 1774, and Oct. 16, 1775, *ibid.*, IX, 992, X, 277.

that question, however, the House was willing to renew the measures for short periods. It did so repeatedly until 1773, when yet another question—the right of North Carolina residents to attach the property of foreigners in suits for debts—arose to block a permanent settlement of the colony's judicial system and constituted an important element in the unfolding Revolutionary movement in North Carolina.[23]

From the beginning of royal government in Georgia, the Crown instructed its governors to erect courts by their own authority, and they did so without the consent of the legislature up to the Revolution. Twice in the 1750's the Commons unsuccessfully tried to pass bills relating to the courts. A bill passed in February 1755 to regulate the General Court failed in the Upper House, and a bill to regulate the courts of request got by Governor Reynolds in December 1757 but was later disallowed by the Crown. Nor was there any dispute over the tenure of judges in Georgia. After 1754 its governors appointed judges during pleasure according to their instructions.[24]

Between 1689 and 1763 the lower houses in the older southern royal colonies acquired considerable power over the colonial judiciary. The Crown had early specified in the royal instructions that courts be created by the governor and council, but with the exception of the Georgia Commons all of the southern lower houses customarily established courts by statute. Crown officials seldom objected to such statutes, and the custom became so widespread that the lower houses came to look upon it as a matter of right and denied the executives' power to set up courts without their consent. This development was completely opposite from practice in Britain, where the House of Commons never attempted to interfere with the Crown's right to establish courts. On the question of judicial tenure the lower houses were less successful. In England judges held office during good behavior throughout the eighteenth century, but Crown officials instructed American governors that colonial judges be appointed during pleasure only and in 1761 disallowed a North Carolina statute pro-

23. John Pownall to Tryon, July 2, 1764, *N. C. Col. Recs.*, VI, 1049; Laws, *N. C. St. Recs.*, XXIII, 632-34, 688-703.

24. Labaree, ed., *Royal Instructions*, I, 298, 367-68, Upper House Journals, Feb. 25, 1755, *Ga. Col. Recs.*, XVI, 59; Board of Trade to Crown, Feb. 21, 1759, CO 5/673, ff. 221-31; Order in Council, Mar. 3, 1759, CO 5/647; Henry Ellis to William Henry Lyttelton, Apr. 1757, Lyttelton Papers, Clements Lib.

viding tenure during good behavior for superior court judges. After 1763 the tenure question continued to be an important issue in both Carolinas, but it was eventually overshadowed by the Crown's refusal to accept court legislation designed by the North Carolina Lower House to guarantee its constituents the right to attach the property of foreigners. That action provoked a controversy of major proportions beginning in 1773.

18

Church Offices

In England the right to nominate to church offices usually belonged to the patron or patrons—the individual, group, or institution responsible for establishing or endowing the particular church in which the office was vacant. Almost never was it left to the local congregations. The patron in turn "presented" his nominee to the bishop under whose jurisdiction he was to serve. If the candidate met with his approval, the bishop inducted him into his office. Tenure of church offices was for life, removal being possible only for bad character or denial of the faith. That the Crown should wish to transfer these arrangements to the colonies was to be expected. Nor is it surprising that it wanted to retain the patronage to church offices. Accordingly, after 1680 the Crown placed all ecclesiastical preferments under the authority of the governors through the royal instructions and commissions. Governors were limited in their choices only by the stipulation that all ministers should have a certificate from the Bishop of London, head of ecclesiastical affairs for the colonies.[1] As usual, however, regulations adopted in England were not closely followed in America, and in all of the southern royal colonies except Georgia the lower houses passed statutes to transfer control over church patronage from the governors to the local vestries.

In Virginia as early as 1643 the power of nomination and presentment passed into the hands of the vestries. Previously an instruction to one of the earlier governors to supply ministers for the parishes

1. Elizabeth H. Davidson, *The Establishment of the English Church in Continental American Colonies* (Durham, 1936), 18; Labaree, ed., *Royal Instructions*, II, 484-85, 821.

had not been enforced, and the respective rights of governors and vestries regarding church offices had not been defined. But in March 1643 the General Assembly passed an act to empower the vestries to elect their own ministers and present them to the governor for induction. Neglect and "misbecoming behaviour" were the only grounds for suspension or removal. Suspensions could be made by the governor and Council, but the power of removal was to be exercised only by the General Assembly. In March 1658, during the Interregnum, the legislature passed another act transferring all power over church offices to the vestries, but in March 1662, after the Restoration, it revived the former system.[2]

Actual practice deviated much from the letter of the law. Commonly, the vestries employed their ministers from year to year and never presented them to the governor for induction. As a result, ministers were entirely dependent upon the vestries, who could and did remove them at will. This practice did not meet with the approval of the ecclesiastical authorities in England. The Archbishop of Canterbury labeled it "a very pernicious thing" and pointed out what was already clear to both the vestries and the clergy in Virginia—that a "minister will not know how to preach against any Vice, but some of the Great Men of his parish may fancy the Sermon was made against him, and so make a faction to turn out the Minister."[3] The Bishop of London echoed the Archbishop's sentiments and along with John Locke proposed that the situation be remedied by giving the governor the right to nominate and induct ministers when the vestries failed to do so. In 1703 the Crown's attorney general, Sir Edward Northey, expressed the same opinion. He upheld the right of the vestries to nominate and present their ministers under the laws of 1643 and 1662 but ruled that if the vestries did not present within six months the governor could both nominate, or in the technical language of the church collate, and induct. This ruling was in accord with English practice wherein the patron's right of nomination passed to the bishop if he failed to exercise it within six months.[4] In Virginia

2. Davidson, *Establishment of Eng. Church,* 18; Hening, ed., *Va. Statutes,* I, 240-43, 433, II, 44-47.

3. Dr. James Blair's Memorial concerning Sir Edmund Andros, 1697, and "A true Account of a Conference at Lambeth," Dec. 27, 1697, William S. Perry, ed., *Papers relating to the History of the Church in Virginia, 1650-1776* (Hartford, 1870), 15, 48; hereafter cited as Perry, ed., *Va. Church Papers.*

4. Northey's Opinion, July 29, 1703, Perry, ed., *Va. Church Papers,* 127-28; Bishop of London to Sir Philip Meadows, Aug. 9, 1698, CO 5/1309; Locke's Essay

the effect of Northey's ruling was negligible. Francis Nicholson, governor at the time it was handed down, made no attempt to enforce it and permitted the vestries to continue their old practice of hiring ministers on an annual basis without ever presenting them for induction. A survey of the Virginia clergy by the Bishop of London in 1724 revealed that only six out of twenty-nine ministers reporting had actually been inducted. Thus, over 80 per cent of the Virginia clergy was dependent upon the vestry for temporary employments.[5]

Attempts by royal governors to reform this system met with strong opposition from the leaders in the vestries and in both houses of the legislature. In early 1711 Alexander Spotswood toyed with the idea of asking the legislature to pass a law requiring the vestries to induct their ministers but found the Burgesses "so cold on that Subject" that he feared even to "venture to recommend it in a publick manner." Over the years he became less timorous, however, and the continued urgings of the Bishop of London persuaded him to take more vigorous measures.[6] His commission and instructions clearly empowered him to collate and induct ministers, but the statute of 1622 had transferred the right of collation to the local vestries. In 1718 he challenged that measure by nominating and inducting a minister to a vacancy in St. Anne's Parish, Essex County. The vestry of that parish refused to receive his appointee and hired another minister of its own choosing. Spotswood then cited his commission and instructions to support his pretensions to the exclusive rights of collation and induction. His action alarmed the vestry, which enlisted the aid of Commissary James Blair and Colonel Philip Ludwell in the Council to oppose him openly. The vestry did not deny the governor's right to induct but argued that the congregation through the vestries should have the patronage because they had founded the churches and were, therefore, according to English precedent, the patrons. They further argued that their rights to nominate and present were confirmed by acts of 1643 and 1662 and took the typical colonial position that the

---

towards Remedys of Grievances of Virginia Constitution, *ca.* 1698, Locke MSS, c. 9, Bodleian Lib.

5. James Blair's further affidavit, May 1, 1704, J. Wallace to Dr. Woodford, Apr. 3, 1707, Answers of Virginia Clergy to Bishop of London's Queries, 1724, Perry, ed., *Va. Church Papers*, 132, 185-86, 261-318.

6. See Nott to Board of Trade, Dec. 24, 1705, CO 5/1315; Spotswood to Bishop of London, Oct. 24, 1710, Mar. 6, 1711, Oct. 26, 1715, May 23, 1716, Brock, ed., *Spotswood Letters*, I, 27, 66-67, II, 137, 158.

governor's commission could not supersede colonial laws and practice.[7]

The Burgesses naturally sided with the vestries, and in the fall of 1718 directed its agent, William Byrd, to present Crown officials with complaints against Spotswood's conduct. Specifically, it charged him with acting contrary to Northey's 1703 opinion, which denied the governor's right to collate until the living had been vacant six months. Byrd was unable to interest imperial authorities in the affair, however. The Board of Trade submitted the matter to Crown Solicitor General William Thomson, who upheld Spotswood and reversed Northey's decision, ruling that no Virginia law could deprive the governor of his ecclesiastical power. But the Board made no attempt either to enforce his decision or to rule in favor of the vestry. Eventually, Spotswood agreed to serve as the defendant in a lawsuit with the Bruton Parish vestry over his right to collate its benefice. Both parties agreed to try the case in the General Court and then appeal it to the King in Council. But before that case was decided, the Crown replaced Spotswood with Hugh Drysdale, who perhaps wisely chose not to pursue the matter.[8]

The strong opposition aroused by Spotswood in 1718 discouraged subsequent governors from attempting to secure the patronage to church offices for the Crown. In fact, Gooch readily concurred with the Burgesses in passing an act in 1748 to extend the time the vestries might wait to fill a vacancy before losing the right of nomination from six to twelve months. The Crown confirmed the act, but it soon was attacked, first by Commissary William Dawson and later by Lieutenant Governor Robert Dinwiddie. Dawson questioned the vestries' right to the patronage in a letter to the Bishop of London in July 1751, and Dinwiddie complained not only to the Bishop but also to the Board of Trade and secretary of state, the Duke of Bedford, that the act deprived the Crown of "the Patronage and Presenta-

7. Spotswood to Board of Trade, Aug. 14, 1718, Brock, ed., *Spotswood Letters,* II, 292-93; Spotswood to Vestry of St. Anne's Parish, Essex Co., Sept. 3, 1718, Blair's remarks on Spotswood's letter, 1719, Robert Raymond's Opinion, Nov. 17, 1718, Perry, cd., *Va. Church Papers,* 197-98, 203-8, 236-37.

8. Thomson to Board of Trade, Mar. 5, 1719, CO 5/1318; Nov. 21, 1718, *Va. Burgesses Journals, 1712-26,* 231; Spotswood to Board of Trade, May 20, 1720, Brock, ed., *Spotswood Letters,* II, 335; Blair's Answers to Spotswood's Accusations, 1719, Blair to Bishop of London, July 17, 1724, Perry, ed., *Va. Church Papers,* 233, 321-22; "Church Patronage in Virginia," *Va. Mag. of Hist. and Biog.,* 22 (1914), 401-9.

tion of the Clergy" and urged Bedford to instruct him to amend it.[9] Neither the Board, the Bishop, nor Bedford took any action in the matter, although the Bishop was in essential agreement with both Dawson and Dinwiddie. In his reply to Dawson the Bishop staunchly maintained that the right of appointment was his, and he lamented to Dinwiddie that the act "appears . . . to be a great blow to the Kings Supremacy and right of Patronage, and to leave no room, either for the Governor, or the Bishop, to take care of the Affairs of the Church which is required of them." He realized that as "the People has got this power, they will not easily part with it," but he did suggest that some time it might be found necessary "to qualify it, to prevent the abuse of it." But Dinwiddie could not alter it, as he pointed out to the Bishop in August 1755, without the prior consent of London authorities, for the Crown had formally confirmed it.[10] Nothing further came of this matter under Dinwiddie, but during Fauquier's tenure the clergy itself questioned the right of the vestries to control the patronage to church offices.

Passage of the Two-Penny Act in 1758 set off a controversy which had extensive ramifications. The chief dispute was over the medium of payment of the ministers' salaries, but the vestries' right to the church patronage and the authority of the Virginia Burgesses to alter a law confirmed by the Crown without the Crown's consent were also involved. The Burgesses first set the clergy's annual salaries at 1,600 pounds of tobacco in 1696 and, although the clergy often received the worst of the tobacco, continued this arrangement by laws of 1728 and 1748 to the general satisfaction of most parties concerned. The Crown confirmed the last of these acts, which according to royal instructions could not be altered without permission from home authorities. Nevertheless, the smallness of the tobacco crop in Halifax, Hampshire, and Frederick Counties caused the Burgesses to pass an act in December 1753 to allow those counties to pay their ministers £100 for that year instead of the 1,600 pounds of tobacco usually allowed. The

9. Hening, ed., *Va. Statutes*, VI, 90; Dawson to Bishop of London, July 15, 1751, Perry, ed., *Va. Church Papers*, 377-79; Dinwiddie to Board of Trade, June 5, 1752, CO 5/1327, ff. 461-62; Dinwiddie to Duke of Bedford, June 5, 1752, CO 5/1338, ff. 79, 86.

10. Bishop of London to Dawson, Sept. 21, 1752, Dawson Papers, Virginia Religious Papers, Lib. Cong.; Bishop of London to Dinwiddie, Sept. 19, 1754, Va. Misc. MSS, Lib. Cong.; Dinwiddie to Bishop of London, Aug 1755, Brock, ed., *Dinwiddie Papers*, II, 161-62.

Burgesses granted the same privilege to Princess Anne and Norfolk counties in July 1755 and the following November extended it to the whole colony for one year by the first of the so-called Two-Penny Acts. Dinwiddie readily passed all three acts, even though they amended the 1748 law. The last evoked some protests from the clergy, but the real storm was three years away.[11]

With these laws for precedents, Fauquier did not hesitate to pass an act in 1759 to allow all Virginians to discharge their tobacco debts for the preceding year in money, although he realized that he was violating his instruction. A flurry of complaints among the Virginia clergy followed. At a convention they decided to send the Reverend John Camm, described by Fauquier as "a Man of Abilities but a Turbulent Man who delights to live in a Flame," to England to place formal complaints against the act before imperial authorities. Camm served the clergy well. He attacked the act for being both unjust and unconstitutional[12] and found a strong ally in the Bishop of London, who traced the injustice of the 1759 Two-Penny Act to the 1748 measure giving the vestries the right of patronage to church offices. He declared that "no sooner were they in possession of the Patronages but they wanted also to be absolute Master's of the Maintenance of the Clergy." Although Camm could not deprive the vestries of their right of patronage, with the aid of the Bishop he did persuade the Crown to disallow not only the 1759 measure but also its predecessors of 1753 and 1755. As a result, Crown officials warned Fauquier not to pass any further acts altering a law confirmed by the Crown without a suspending clause and subsequently rejected an appeal from both the Council and Burgesses.[13] By forbidding the Burgesses to alter a

11. Hening, ed., *Va. Statutes*, III, 151-53, IV, 204-8, VI, 88-90, 369-70, 502, 568-69; William Gooch to Thomas Gooch, Aug. 25, 1736, Gooch Letter Book, 54-55, Colonial Williamsburg, Inc.; Va. Clergy to Bishop of London, Nov. 29, 1755, Perry, ed., *Va. Church Papers*, 434-40; Thomas Dawson to Bishop of London, Feb. 25, 1756, Fulham Palace MSS, Virginia (Second Box), f. 13.

12. Hening, ed., *Va. Statutes*, VII, 240-41; Fauquier to Board of Trade, Jan. 9, 1759, CO 5/1329, ff. 229-35; John Camm's Petition to Board of Trade, May 14, 1759, *ibid.*, ff. 263-65; May 14, 1759, *Acts of Privy Council, Colonial*, IV, 420; Virginia Clergy's Representation, Read by Board of Trade, May 23, 1759, CO 5/1329, ff. 271-73; James Abercromby to John Blair, June 30, 1759, Abercromby Letter Book, 162-64, Va. State Lib.

13. Bishop of London to Board of Trade, June 14, 1759, Fulham Palace MSS, Virginia (First Box), f. 54; Order in Council, Aug. 10, 1759, CO 5/1329, ff. 431-32; James Abercromby to John Blair, Aug. 3, 1759, Abercromby Letter Book, 179-81, Va. State Lib.; Aug. 29, 1759, *Acts of Privy Council, Colonial*, IV, 421; Fauquier to Board of Trade, June 30, 1760, CO 5/1330, ff. 41-44; Report to Privy Council on Va. Legislature's Address, May 20, 1761, CO 5/1368, ff. 179-85.

law confirmed by the Crown, the imperial authorities denied its right to tamper with the clergy's salaries. But the right of patronage to church offices remained where the Burgesses had placed it—in the hands of the local vestries.

Indeed, the most important effect of this controversy was to produce for the first time in Virginia a thorough scrutiny of two of the Crown's most important devices for controlling the colonies—the royal instructions and the suspending clause. In two different exchanges of pamphlets with Camm—one in 1760 and the other in 1764—Burgesses Landon Carter and Richard Bland, like the lower houses in both Carolinas over the last four decades, argued that instructions bound only the governor and not the legislature. Moreover, they also questioned the justice and constitutionality of requiring suspending clauses in laws that appeared urgent to local legislators. Thus Carter declared in 1760 that because "Instructions" were "neither Laws of publick Authority, nor Rules of Constitution" they could "only be directory" to the governor and denied that the Crown could require compliance with any rule that would "effect the Ruin of the Community." In the same year Bland conceded that instructions ought to be obeyed whenever possible but contended that because *"salus populi est suprema lex"* instructions could "be deviated from with Impunity" whenever the needs of the people required. Going much further in 1764, Bland anticipated the later American argument that colonial lower houses had exclusive jurisdiction over the internal affairs of the colonies by implying that no power could restrict the authority of the Virginia legislature to do what it thought best for the internal affairs of Virginia. Insisting that instructions were only "Guides and Directions for the Conduct of Governors" and could not "consistently with the Principles of the *British* Constitution . . . have the Force and Power of Laws upon the People," he asserted that the "Legislature of the Colony have a Right to enact ANY Law they shall think necessary for their INTERNAL Government." Coming on the eve of the constitutional debate with Britain that led to the American Revolution, these arguments were especially significant both because they revealed an increasing impatience with imperial checks upon colonial legislative power and because they indicated that Virginians claimed a status for their legislature—or, as Landon Carter referred to it, "Parliament"—that they would not part with easily.[14]

14. [Landon Carter], *A Letter to the Right Reverend Father in God, the Lord*

Like the Virginia Burgesses, the South Carolina Commons divested its governors of their patronage to church offices. In 1704 and 1706 the Commons passed measures to confirm the right of the conforming inhabitants of each parish to elect their own ministers. Thereafter, no one ever seriously challenged that right, despite the fact that royal instructions and commissions stipulated that all ecclesiastical appointments be made by the governor. The clergy in 1722, Governor James Glen in 1748, and the Bishop of London in May 1762 objected to the 1706 law because it deprived the governor of the church patronage.[15] But Crown officials never disallowed it, and the patronage remained under the control of the local vestries up to the Revolution. Owing their appointments to their congregations, South Carolina ministers were in no way independent. The Reverend Andrew Leslie reported in 1736 that the notion had "been zealously propagated throughout the province" that "the Clergy are a tyrannical sort of men, who study nothing so much as to enslave the Laity; that therefore they ought to be kept depending, for it is better one man should depend upon a Parish than that a whole Parish should depend upon one Man." The younger Bull expressed the same view when he wrote in the 1770's that the South Carolinians had "determined . . . not to elect their Clergy but keep them only" during good behavior, in order to insure that some clergyman's misbehavior would not "give great cause of scandal . . . to the Parish."[16]

B----p of L----n (Williamsburg, 1760), 44-47; Richard Bland, *A Letter to the Clergy of Virginia* (Williamsburg, 1760), 18; Common Sense [Richard Bland], *The Colonel Dismounted or the Rector Vindicated* ([Williamsburg], 1764), 23, 26; Landon Carter, *The Rector Detected* (Williamsburg, 1764), 14. Camm's contributions were *A Single and Distinct View of the Act, Vulgarly Entitled the Two-Penny Act* (Annapolis, 1763), *A Review of the Rector Detected: or the Colonel Reconnoitred* (Williamsburg, 1764), and *Critical Remarks on a Letter Ascribed to Common Sense* (Williamsburg, 1765). For discussion of the pamphlet warfare this affair evoked, see Glenn C. Smith, "The Parson's Cause, 1755-1765," *Tyler's Quarterly Historical and Genealogical Magazine,* 21 (1940), 140-71, 291-306. The most comprehensive and best treatment of the controversy is Morton, *Colonial Virginia,* II, 751-819. See also Joseph H. Smith, *Appeals to the Privy Council from the American Plantations* (N. Y., 1950), 607-26; Knollenberg, *Origin of the American Revolution,* 57-66, and Thad W. Tate, "The Coming of the Revolution in Virginia: Britain's Challenge to Virginia's Ruling Class, 1763-1776," *Wm. and Mary Qtly.,* 3d Ser., 19 (1962), 325-33.

15. Cooper and McCord, eds., *S. C. Statutes,* II, 239-40, 288; Labaree, ed., *Royal Instructions,* II, 484-85, 821; Bishop of London to Board of Trade, May 3, 1762, Fulham Palace MSS, South Carolina, f. 185; Glen to Board of Trade, Oct. 10, 1748, CO 5/372, ff. 80-87; Petition of Clergy to Nicholson, 1722, Papers Concerning Governorship of S. C., bMs Am 1455, Item 15, Houghton Lib.

16. Leslie to Sec. of Society, Dec. 29, 1736, B MSS, 4, f. 277, Soc. for the Prop.

By 1715 the North Carolina legislature had transferred the patronage to church offices from the governor to the vestries with the full approval of the proprietors. A law of 1704 or 1705 empowered vestries to disapprove of or displace their ministers, and another of 1715 gave each vestry authority to employ a minister of its own choosing, an arrangement continued by an act of 1741. Both the 1715 and 1741 laws violated the royal instructions and commissions giving the right of nomination to the governor, and in April 1754 the Crown disallowed the 1741 law upon the recommendation of the Board of Trade.[17] It was then left to the new governor, Arthur Dobbs, to secure the enactment of a new law to establish the church.

Between 1755 and 1762 the Lower House passed three acts to establish the church, but the Crown disallowed all of them because the House insisted that the patronage to church offices belonged to the vestries. The first of these measures, enacted in January 1755, stipulated that "care be taken to preserve the Right of presentation of Ministers to the Vestry and people the Founders and Endowers of the Churches." Dobbs accepted that stipulation at the time, but by 1759 he had come to resent the loss of church patronage and recommended the disallowance of the measure. At almost the same time the Bishop of London echoed Dobbs's sentiments, and their recommendations were largely responsible for the Crown's disallowing the act in March 1759.[18] In May 1760 and December 1762 the Lower House, insistent upon retaining for the vestries their long-enjoyed right of patronage, passed acts guaranteeing that right, only to have them both again disallowed by the Crown. Finally, in 1765 the influential Tryon persuaded the House to pass a bill that satisfied imperial authorities. The measure was silent on the question of patronage, and both Crown officials and vestries could interpret it as a confirmation of their rights to nominate ministers. In the two years after its

of the Gospel in For. Parts, London; Bull to Hillsborough, Nov. 30, 1770, to Dartmouth, Feb. 22, 1775, S. C. Pub. Recs., XXXII, 368-69, XXXV, 21-22, S. C. Arch. Dept.

17. See William Gordon to Sec. of SPG, May 13, 1709, *N. C. Col. Recs.*, I, 709; Davidson, *Establishment of Eng. Church*, 50-51; Laws, *N. C. St. Recs.*, XXIII, 6-10, 187-91; Board of Trade to King, Mar. 14, 1754, Order in Council, Apr. 8, 1754, *N. C. Col. Recs.*, V, 107-8, 116.

18. Lower House Journals, Jan. 9, 1755, *N. C. Col. Recs.*, V, 299; Laws, *N. C. St. Recs.*, XXIII, 400; Dobbs to Board of Trade, Jan. 22, 1759, Bishop of London to Board of Trade, Feb. 19, 1759, Order in Council, Mar. 3, 1759, *N. C. Col. Recs.*, VI, 5, 10-13, 15-16; Mar. 3, 1759, *Acts of Privy Council, Colonial*, IV, 408-9.

passage Tryon collated and inducted seven ministers. But the indications are that the ministers he preferred were completely acceptable to the vestries, and some vestries stubbornly insisted that the 1765 law had not deprived them of the right of choosing their ministers.[19]

Unlike the lower houses in the older colonies, the Georgia Commons seems never to have tried to deprive the Crown of its right of patronage to church offices. It established the Anglican church by statute in 1758, but did not include stipulations about the patronage. Georgia vestries did occasionally share in the choice of ministers, but as a rule the formal presentment and induction were left to governors.[20]

At some time during the colonial period all of the southern lower houses except the Georgia Commons tried to shift the patronage to church offices from the governor to the local vestries—a practice that was peculiarly American, differing greatly from the English system of church patrons nominating all ecclesiastical officers. Both the Virginia Burgesses and the South Carolina Commons succeeded in their attempts, the former by a series of laws extending back into the seventeenth century and the latter by a law of 1706. Nor did any Crown officials seriously attempt to alter these arrangements in either colony after 1720. The controversy over the Two-Penny Act in Virginia caused some dissatisfaction with the suspending clause requirement in the royal instructions but did not produce any attempt to deprive Virginia vestries of control over patronage to church offices. Under the proprietors and during the early years of royal government, the North Carolina Lower House was equally successful, but after 1750 the Crown tried to return the patronage to the governor by disallowing four successive statutes that placed it under the control of

19. Bishop of London to Board of Trade, May 3, 1762, Order in Council, June 3, 1762, Dobbs to Board of Trade, Mar. 7, 1763, Pownall to Tryon, July 2, 1764, *N. C. Col. Recs.*, VI, 714-16, 723, 970-72, 1049; Laws, *N. C. St. Recs.*, XXIII, 583-85, 660-62; Davidson, *Establishment of Eng. Church*, 56-57; Upper House Journals, May 3, 1765, *N. C. Col. Recs.*, VII, 42; Tryon to Board of Trade, Aug. 15, 1765, Board of Trade to Tryon, Nov. 29, 1765, Tryon to Bishop of London, Oct. 6, 1766, Tryon's View of Polity, 1767, *ibid.*, 105-6, 132, 261, 490; Bishop of London to Board of Trade, Mar. 1, 1766, Shelburne Papers, LIX, 1-11, Clements Lib.

20. Statutes, *Ga. Col. Recs.*, XVIII, 258-72, 568-69; Council Journals, Nov. 18, 1762, *ibid.*, VIII, 765; Upper House Journals, Jan. 24, 1763, *ibid.*, XVII, 8; Davidson, *Establishment of Eng. Church*, 72; Reba C. Strickland, *Religion and the State in Georgia in the Eighteenth Century* (N. Y., 1939), 106.

the vestries. These disallowances constituted an important source of irritation to North Carolina legislators in the early 1760's and formed a minor issue in the pre-Revolutionary years. Not until 1765 was a satisfactory settlement reached by the passage of a law that said nothing about the patronage question, making it possible for both the governor and the vestries to claim the right of nomination. In actual practice, this arrangement meant that North Carolina vestries still played a major role in choosing their ministers, despite the fact that they no longer had any legal guarantee of their right to do so. Thus, only in Georgia was the right to nominate ministers clearly left to the governor.

PART VI

THE FRUITS OF POWER:
1763-1776

*The King's majesty, by and with the advice and consent
of the lords spiritual and temporal, and commons of
Great Britain, in parliament assembled, had, hath, and
of right ought to have, full power and authority to make
laws and statutes of sufficient force and validity to bind
the colonies and people of America, subjects of the crown
of Great Britain, in all cases whatsoever.*
>—The Declaratory Act, March 1766

*The British parliament has no right to exercise author-
ity over us.*
>—Thomas Jefferson's *A Summary View
of the Rights of British America,*
>August 1774

DURING the eighteenth century the lower houses in the southern
royal colonies achieved many of the powers they had contended for.
By the end of the Seven Years' War they had supplanted the executive as the center of political authority in Virginia and the two Carolinas and were poised for a similar development in Georgia. When
Britain's new colonial policy after 1763 threatened to deprive them
of many of their powers and to bring them under the complete domination of Parliament, they met the challenge with spirited and determined opposition. The resulting stalemate culminated a decade later
in revolution and independence.

19

A New Status and a New Challenge

THE lower houses' quest for power was remarkably successful in the southern royal colonies. With the exception of the Georgia Commons, which had less than a decade of political experience behind it, they had attained a new status by the end of the Seven Years' War. Their general increase in authority had raised them from dependent law-making bodies to the center of political authority and prestige in their respective colonies. With this change in status came not only the subordination of the royal governors and councils but also a new and able group of political leaders who developed a new rationale about the constitutional position of the lower houses. Beginning in 1763 Britain's new colonial policy directly challenged their authority in many areas. They reacted violently, attempting to consolidate their hold on their various powers and further defining their relationship to the imperial government. This challenge and the lower houses' response were important factors in the unfolding Revolutionary drama.

Among the specific powers won by the lower houses during the eighteenth century those in the realm of finance were the most important. Through their power to tax, all four had won the exclusive right to frame money measures, although the upper houses in Virginia and North Carolina and the governor in Georgia could still exert some influence in preparing the calculations that formed the basis for those bills. The lower houses of Virginia and the two Carolinas had also established their authority to audit accounts of public officers;

in Georgia, the Crown's deputy auditor examined those accounts, although the Commons had won the power to review them. Further, all four bodies had assumed an extensive role in expenditures by strictly appropriating all revenues and appointing commissioners or occasionally even special supervisory committees to dispose of them. The extent of their control over public funds was demonstrated by the ability of the three older bodies to order money from the treasury without executive consent. Although none of the lower houses acquired an absolute power to issue paper money, each emitted it upon occasion prior to 1764, and Crown officials found it almost impossible to prevent such issues during emergencies. In combination, these powers brought colonial finances firmly under legislative control and provided lower houses with the means to pry still other powers away from colonial executives and imperial authorities.

In the area of the civil list the lower houses' aims were somewhat more restricted and their gains correspondingly less impressive. None of the four succeeded, in the usual textbook pattern, in making the governors and other royal officials dependent upon them for their annual salaries. However, with the exception of the Virginia Burgesses, which to atone for Bacon's Rebellion voted the Crown a perpetual fund in 1680, they managed to resist royal demands for a permanent revenue to support the civil list and thus shifted the burden of support to the imperial government. Consequently, London authorities looked to the 4½ per cent duty of Barbados and the Leeward Islands to support the governors of the two Carolinas, the quitrents to pay the other royal officials in those two colonies, and annual Parliamentary grants to defray the civil establishment in Georgia. Except for the South Carolina governor, who relied upon annual votes from the Commons for about a third of his salary, none of the royal officials in the southern royal colonies depended upon the legislatures for their official salaries. Still, the lower houses in the three older colonies had managed to bring the regulation of fees —an important part of the incomes of royal officials—under their jurisdiction.

The lower houses suffered their greatest disappointments in their efforts to win control over their compositions and proceedings. They obtained certain elements of that control with relative ease, including the basic English Parliamentary privileges of freedom of speech and debate and freedom from arrest, and the rights to determine disputed elections, expel members, determine internal procedure, and choose the speaker and other house officers except the clerk. But with other elements they were much less successful. Crown opposition prevented all except the North Carolina Lower House from securing the right to appoint the clerk, although both the Virginia Burgesses and South Carolina Commons nominated and like the Georgia Commons paid him, thus bringing him under their authority. Early in the century the lower houses in the three older colonies had exercised a free hand both in settling qualifications for members and voters and in erecting constituencies and apportioning representation. During the same period, the Carolina legislators had also placed statutory requirements upon the frequency of elections and sessions. But beginning in the late 1730's imperial officials adopted a more rigid policy. They positively refused to approve a number of colonial laws to fix either member and voter qualifications or frequency of elections and sessions, even disallowing in 1737 an existing North Carolina statute. After 1763 the Crown institutionalized this policy and at the same time forbade colonial lower houses any further exercise of their long-enjoyed power to establish constituencies and settle representation.

If the lower houses enjoyed only moderate success in their attempt to win control over their compositions and proceedings, their efforts to usurp a share of the traditional powers of the executive reaped an abundant harvest. By a resourceful use of their control over finance, they made their most significant gains in this area, extending their authority well beyond that of the British House of Commons. With the exception of the Georgia Commons, they won the power to appoint the public treasurer. On the theory that all officers concerned in collecting or handling the public's money should be supervised by the people's representatives, the South Carolina Commons insisted upon appointing all minor revenue officials as well. All four houses further encroached upon the executive's power of appointment by employing commissioners to build public works and to perform public services, selecting the public printer to handle all official printing and provide an outlet for legislative opinion through his newspaper, and naming and manipulating the agents that represented the colonies in London. In addition, the lower houses interfered in military and Indian affairs in a variety of ways. They placed statutory regulations upon the militia and participated in making military policy by appropriating all grants to specific purposes. The Virginia Burgesses and both Carolina lower houses upon several occasions appointed committees to apply military appropriations, and the two Carolina bodies even nominated people to military offices. All four houses placed legal restrictions on the Indian trade, and the South Carolina Commons and for a brief period the Virginia Burgesses assumed the direction of that trade. In addition, the South Carolina Commons and to a lesser extent the other three lower houses were able to influence Indian policy by withholding funds from projects that did not meet with their approval, although by the mid-1760's Indian diplomacy was passing to the royal superintendent of Indian affairs. In judicial matters, the lower houses in the three older colonies established the tradition that all courts should be created by statute, but the North Carolina Lower House—the only body to make the attempt— failed to fix judicial tenure during good behavior. Finally, in ecclesiastical affairs, all of the lower houses except the Georgia Commons shifted the patronage to church offices from the governors to the local vestries. This was indeed an impressive list of victories.

These specific gains were symptomatic of developments of much greater significance. To begin with, they were symbolic of a fundamental shift of the constitutional center of power in the colonies from the executive to the lower houses. They also meant that the lower houses had in a sense altered the structure of the constitution of the British Empire itself by extending the constitutions of the colonies far beyond the limitations of the instructions or fixed notions of imperial authorities. The time was ripe for a re-examination and redefinition of the constitutional position of the lower houses. With the rapid economic and territorial expansion of the colonies in the years before 1763 had come a corresponding rise in the responsibilities and prestige of the lower houses and a growing awareness among colonial representatives of their own importance, which served to strengthen their long-standing, if still imperfectly defined, impressions that colonial lower houses were miniature Parliaments entitled to the same powers in their limited spheres that the House of Commons possessed in Great Britain. Under the proper stimuli, they would carry this impression to its logical conclusion: that the lower houses enjoyed an equal status under the Crown with Parliament. Here, then, well beyond the embryonic stage, was the theory of colonial equality with the mother country, one of the basic constitutional principles of the American Revolution, waiting to be nourished by the series of crises that beset imperial-colonial relations between 1763 and 1776.

The psychological implications of this new political order were profound. By the 1750's the lower houses had developed a vigorous spirit of opposition, and their phenomenal success had generated a soaring self-confidence and a willingness to take on all comers. Called upon to operate on a larger stage during the Seven Years' War, they emerged from that conflict with an increased awareness of their own importance and a growing consciousness of the implications of their activities, at once more impatient of restraint and more tenacious of their powers and privileges. Symptomatic of these developments was the spate of bitter controversies that characterized colonial politics during and immediately after the war. Between 1750 and 1763 the Gadsden election controversy in South Carolina, the prolonged disputes between Dobbs and the Lower House in North Carolina, and the contests over the pistole fee and the Two-Penny Act in Virginia gave abundant evidence of both the lower houses' stubborn determination to preserve their authority and the failure of Crown officials in London and the colonies to gauge accurately their temper or to accept the fact that they had made important changes in the constitutions of the colonies.

With the shift of power to the lower houses also came the development in each colony of an extraordinarily able group of politicians. The lower houses provided excellent training for the leaders of four rapidly maturing societies, and the recurring controversies prepared them for the problems they would be called upon to meet in the dramatic conflicts after 1763. In the decades before Independence there appeared in the Virginia Burgesses a veritable galaxy of potential statesmen, including Thomas Jefferson, George Washington, Patrick Henry, Richard Henry Lee, Peyton Randolph, Edmund Pendleton, Richard Bland, George Wythe, George and Thomson Mason, Robert Carter Nicholas, the younger Thomas Nelson, Benjamin Harrison, John Robinson, Landon Carter, Archibald Cary, John Blair, Jr., Severn Eyre, James Mercer, Joseph Jones, and Paul Carrington. Alumni from the South Carolina Commons and the North

Carolina Lower House were perhaps equal in ability, if somewhat less conspicuous in national affairs. The former produced Christopher Gadsden, John Rutledge, Henry Laurens, Rawlins Lowndes, Peter Manigault, Charles and Charles Cotesworth Pinckney, James Parsons, Isaac Mazyck, Thomas Bee, Thomas Ferguson, Miles Brewton, and Thomas Heyward, Jr. The latter contributed Samuel Swann, John Starkey, Cornelius Harnett, Richard Caswell, John Harvey, Robert Howe, John Ashe, Maurice Moore, Joseph Hewes, Samuel Johnston, William Hooper, Alexander Martin, Abner Nash, and Isaac Edwards. Even the youthful Georgia Commons yielded some distinguished leaders, among others Noble Wymberly Jones, Archibald Bulloch, Alexander Wylly, William Young, Patrick Houston, William Ewen, Jonathan Bryan, Edward Telfair, and Samuel Elbert. These men guided their colonies through the debate with Britain, assumed direction of the new state governments after 1776, and played conspicuous roles on the national stage as members of the Continental Congress, the Confederation, and, after 1787, the new federal government. By the 1760's, then, each of the southern royal colonies had an imposing group of native politicians thoroughly schooled in the political arts and primed to meet any challenge to the power and prestige of their lower houses.

Britain's "new colonial policy" after 1763 provided just such a challenge. It precipitated a constitutional crisis in the empire, creating new tensions and setting in motion forces different from those that had shaped earlier developments. The new policy was based upon concepts both unfamiliar and unwelcome to the colonists, such as centralization, uniformity, and orderly development. Yet it was a logical continuation of earlier trends and, for the most part, an effort to realize old aspirations. From Edward Randolph in the last decades of the seventeenth century to the Earl of Halifax in the 1750's, colonial officials had envisioned a highly centralized empire with a uniform political system in each of the colonies and with the imperial government closely supervising the subordinate governments.[1] But, because

1. On this point see Charles M. Andrews, *The Colonial Period of American History*, 4 vols. (New Haven, 1934-38), IV, 368-425; Michael Garibaldi Hall, *Edward Randolph and the American Colonies, 1676-1703* (Chapel Hill, 1960); Arthur H. Basye, *The Lords Commissioners of Trade and Plantations, 1748-1782* (New Haven, 1925); Dora Mae Clark, *The Rise of the British Treasury: Colonial Administration in the Eighteenth Century* (New Haven, 1960); and Knollenberg, *Origin of the American Revolution.*

they had never made any sustained or systematic attempt to achieve these goals during the first half of the eighteenth century, there had developed a working arrangement permitting the lower houses considerable latitude in shaping colonial constitutions without requiring Crown or proprietary officials to give up any of their ideals. That there had been a growing divergence between imperial theory and colonial practice mattered little so long as each refrained from openly challenging the other. But the new policy threatened to upset this arrangement by implementing the old ideals long after the conditions that produced them had ceased to exist. Aimed at bringing the colonies more closely under imperial control, this policy inevitably sought to curtail the influence of the lower houses, directly challenging many of the powers they had acquired over the previous century and in the case of the Georgia Commons preventing it from winning new ones. To American legislators accustomed to the lenient policies of Walpole and the Pelhams and impressed with the rising power of their own lower houses, the new program seemed a radical departure from precedent, a frontal assault upon the several constitutions they had been forging over the previous century. To protect gains they had already made and to make good their pretensions to greater political significance, they thereafter no longer had merely to deal with weak governors or casual imperial administrators; they now faced an aggressive group of officials bent upon using every means at their disposal, including the legislative authority of Parliament, to gain their ends.

Beginning in 1763 one imperial action after another seemed to threaten the position of the lower houses. A variety of measures, some aimed at particular colonial legislatures and others at general legislative powers and practices, posed serious threats to powers that the lower houses had either long enjoyed or were trying to attain. But all of these matters were secondary to the question of Parliamentary taxation, the heart of the lower houses' controversies with Great Britain after 1764. Between 1764 and 1766 Parliament's attempts to tax the colonists for revenue directly challenged the colonial legislatures' exclusive power to tax, the foundation of legislative authority in America. Upon that power the lower houses had built their political fortunes. To have been required, at that late date, to share it with Parliament would have been to forfeit a century of political gains, to abandon their quest to attain real political significance, and to admit that they were subordinate to Parliament and not the miniature Houses of Commons they had long pretended to be. Such an admission would have been thoroughly antithetic to their whole pattern of development. The realization that Parliamentary taxation was a direct challenge to their political power and might eventually even lead to the abolition of colonial law-making bodies forced them to resist. To meet the challenge, they had to spell out the implications of the changes they had been making, consciously or not, in their respective governments. For the first time they had to make clear in their own minds and to verbalize what they conceived their respective constitutions in fact were or should be. In the process, the lower houses laid bare the wide gulf between imperial theory and colonial practice. Although justified by the realities of the colonial situation, their definition of their constitutional position within the empire was at marked variance with imperial ideals. The reaction of British officials was an increasing resolution to take a stricter tone with the colonies, which in turn produced among American lawmakers a heightened consciousness of the implications of the constitutional issue and a continuously rising level of expectation.

That the lower houses would vigorously oppose any attempt by Parliament to levy taxes on the colonies was revealed in the great debate over the Sugar and Stamp Acts in 1764-65. The issue was constitutional: did Parliament have the right to tax the colonies? All four southern lower houses returned a resounding no. Of the four, only the North Carolina Lower House raised the question in regard to the taxes imposed by the Sugar Act. In October 1764 in a message to Governor Arthur Dobbs prepared by a committee that included Cornelius Harnett, John Harvey, and Maurice Moore, the North Carolina representatives attacked both those taxes and the proposed stamp duties, boldly objecting to being "Burthened with new Taxes and Impositions laid on us without our Privity and Consent" and emphatically asserting "our Inherent right, and Exclusive privilege of Imposing our own Taxes."[2] Confronted with the more obvious and general threat posed by the Stamp Act, the other three houses eventually matched and improved upon this sharp denial of

2. Lower House Journals, Oct. 27, 31, 1764, *N. C. Col. Recs.*, VI, 1259, 1261.

Parliament's right to tax the colonies. In the year between First Minister George Grenville's suggestion that Parliament might levy stamp duties upon the colonies and the passage of the Stamp Act in early 1765 each of the three issued formal protests against such duties. In September 1764 the South Carolina committee of correspondence, consisting of eleven assemblymen and acting at the direction of the Commons, instructed agent Charles Garth to join with other agents to oppose the duties. The committee built its case largely upon economic grounds, offering a variety of reasons to demonstrate that the colony was unable to bear the proposed tax and raising the practical objection that Parliament simply did not and could not know what taxes South Carolinians could afford. But the committee also had reservations regarding the constitutionality of the duties. It argued that the proposed duties were inconsistent "with that inherent right of every British subject not to be taxed but by his own consent, or that of his representatives" but cautiously tempered its stand by promising to "submit most dutifully at all times to acts of Parliament." This equivocal protest did not mean that the committee was not aware of the grave portents these duties would hold for the future of American lower houses. Parliamentary taxation would not only deprive Americans of their "birthright," it clearly recognized, but also reduce them and their legislatures "to the condition of vassals and tributaries."[3] Although they differed considerably in tone, the North Carolina and South Carolina protests rested upon common assumptions: that Americans were entitled to the rights of Englishmen, that one of those was the right to be taxed only by their own representatives, that Parliament did not represent Americans, and that, therefore, only their own lower houses could tax them. Here, in essence, before the debate had really begun was the whole American case against taxation by Parliament.

It remained for the Virginia House of Burgesses to undertake a more elaborate formulation of that case. As early as July 1764 the Virginia committee of correspondence wrote agent Edward Montague protesting the Sugar Act on purely economic grounds and suggesting that the proposed stamp duties, and possibly the sugar taxes, were "contrary to Reason and Justice" and tended "to the Destruction of

3. S. C. Committee of Correspondence to Garth, Sept. 4, 1764, R. W. Gibbes, ed., *Documentary History of the American Revolution . . . in South Carolina,* 3 vols. (N. Y. and Columbia, 1853-57), I, 1-6.

the Constitution."[4]   The committee's protest was a preview of the Burgesses' action five months later.   Careful preparation and debate preceded the Burgesses' adoption on December 18, 1764, of three formal petitions to the King, Lords, and Commons against the proposed stamp duties.   Prepared by a distinguished committee headed by Peyton Randolph and including Richard Henry Lee, Landon Carter, George Wythe, Edmund Pendleton, Benjamin Harrison, Archibald Cary, and John Fleming, these petitions respectfully and dispassionately set forth the Burgesses' objections to Parliamentary taxation, amplifying the arguments put forth earlier by the North Carolina Lower House and its own and the South Carolina committees of correspondence.   Like those protests, the Virginia petitions proceeded from the assumption that Virginians held certain *"just and undoubted Rights as* Britons" and that it was *"essential to* British *Liberty that Laws imposing Taxes on the People ought not to be made without the Consent of Representatives chosen by themselves,"* categorically declaring that Virginians were not and could not *"constitutionally be represented"* in Parliament.   Going much further than the earlier protests, these petitions suggested that any attempt by Parliament to impose taxes on the colonies would be *"the Exercise of anticonstitutional Power,"* and the petition to the King offered a concise definition of the limit of Parliament's power in the colonies, claiming for Virginians *"their ancient and inestimable Right of being governed by such Laws respecting their internal Polity and Taxation as are derived from their own Consent."*   The Burgesses was claiming exclusive jurisdiction and at the same time denying Parliament's authority over not only taxation but also *"internal Polity,"* and its failure to define the phrase *"internal Polity"* made its claim all the more sweeping.   The product of a century of legislative development, this claim represented the considered opinion of the House, plainly implying that the Burgesses had the same authority over taxation and internal affairs in Virginia that Parliament had over those matters in Britain; it therefore constituted an important milestone on the road to the complete and explicit rejection of the idea that the lower houses were in any way subordinate to Parliament.[5]

4. Va. Committee of Correspondence to Edward Montague, July 28, 1764, "Proceedings of Va. Committee of Correspondence," *Va. Mag. of Hist. and Biog.,* 12 (1905), 8-14.

5. Nov. 14, Dec. 18, 1764, *Va. Burgesses Journals, 1761-65,* 256-57, 302-4.

These petitions along with an earlier one from the New York House left little doubt that American legislators were firmly opposed to Parliamentary taxation and would not accept Grenville's theory of virtual representation. On the other side of the Atlantic, Parliament was equally determined not to admit any limitations upon its legislative authority over the colonies, even refusing to consider either these petitions or other more moderate ones from the colonial agents on the grounds that petitions could not be heard against a money bill. Nor could a small but vociferous minority in both houses deter Parliament from its chosen course, and on March 22, 1765, the Stamp Act became law.

Neither the ministry nor Parliament had reckoned with the American temper. To the lower houses taxation without representation was something more than an abstract principle. They clearly saw that to admit Parliament's power to tax would eventually mean the loss of much of their political power, the end of their still vague pretensions to equality with Parliament, and their consignment to the political backwater of the empire. In the face of these stark political realities, resistance was the only course.

News of the passage of the Stamp Act reached the colonies in April, and the Virginia House of Burgesses sounded the call to opposition. Under the eloquent persuasion of Patrick Henry, the impetuous young hotspur from Hanover County, and against the better judgment of its more sober members, the Burgesses adopted a set of five resolutions on May 30 that boldly challenged Parliament's right to tax the colonies. The resolutions took almost exactly the same position as the Burgesses' petitions of the previous December but were strikingly different in both tone and form. In tone they were emphatic, in form a specific declaration of rights. But the Burgesses was breaking new ground and was still unwilling to deny explicitly Parliament's power to tax. On May 31 it rescinded the narrowly carried fifth resolution that specifically asserted that it held "the only exclusive Right and Power to lay Taxes and Imposts upon the Inhabitants of this Colony" and branded "every Attempt to vest such Power in any other Person or Persons" as "illegal, unconstitutional and unjust." Two still stronger resolutions apparently failed to pass, if they were introduced at all. A sixth declared that Virginians were not obliged to pay any tax not imposed by the Burgesses; and a seventh stated that anyone upholding the power of another agency to tax the colony would "be deemed an Enemy to this his Majesty's Colony." Although Henry had not succeeded in leading the Burgesses as far as he had originally intended, he had persuaded it to take the first, and perhaps the most important, step in opposing the Stamp Act, and his dramatic triumph was the rallying call for a general American uprising.[6]

Between May and December the Virginia resolves inspired similar protests from lower houses in eight of the other twelve colonies. Almost every American printer published the resolves in his newspaper, usually including the fifth, sixth, and seventh as well as the four the Burgesses actually passed and thereby eliciting declarations that went beyond those of the Virginia legislators. Less than ten days after Henry's victory, the Massachusetts House of Representatives sent a circular letter to the other lower houses on the continent inviting them to send delegates to a congress at New York to prepare a general and united protest against the Stamp Act. Of the southern lower houses, only the South Carolina Commons responded favorably, sending John Rutledge, Thomas Lynch, and Christopher Gadsden. Governors Fauquier in Virginia, Tryon in North Carolina, and Wright in Georgia kept their legislatures from taking similar actions simply by not calling them into session. The same tactic prevented both the North Carolina Lower House and the Georgia Commons from passing formal declarations against the Stamp Act in emulation of the Virginia Burgesses. Of course, the North Carolina body had bluntly stated its position on Parliamentary taxation the previous October, and in 1765 Representative Maurice Moore emphatically rejected the theory of virtual representation in *The Justice and Policy of Taxing the American Colonies in Great Britain, Considered* and argued that Americans should be taxed "according to their constitutional right, in their own provincial assemblies, where they are really represented."[7] Similarly, the Georgia Commons, though carefully refraining from calling "in question the Authority of parliament" in its objections

6. May 30, 1765, *ibid.*, 360. The best account of the passing of the Virginia resolves is Edmund S. and Helen M. Morgan, *The Stamp Act Crisis: Prologue to Revolution* (Chapel Hill, 1953), 88-98. The best single collection of documents on these resolves is Edmund S. Morgan, ed., *Prologue to Revolution: Sources and Documents on the Stamp Act Crisis, 1764-1766* (Chapel Hill, 1959), 45-50.

7. Maurice Moore, *The Justice and Policy of Taxing the American Colonies in Great Britain, Considered* (Wilmington, 1765), 16.

to the Stamp Act in April and July 1765 while still under the domination of Wright, eventually subscribed to the memorial and petitions
of the Stamp Act Congress in December and officially aligned itself
with the other colonies.[8]

In South Carolina the story was different. The younger Bull,
acting lieutenant governor, permitted the Commons to meet in July,
and it promptly appointed delegates to the Stamp Act Congress.
When those delegates returned to Charleston in the fall, a newly
elected Commons was on hand to welcome them. Gadsden and
Lynch in particular had played conspicuous parts in the Congress,
being largely responsible for persuading it to stand upon the broader
foundation of the rights of Englishmen instead of upon charter rights.
The South Carolina Commons displayed its appreciation by immediately ratifying the actions of the Congress and adopting on November 29 a set of resolves modeled closely after those of the Congress,
specifically declaring that the Commons was the only body representing South Carolinians and that "no Taxes ever have been or can be
constitutionally imposed on them, but by the Legislature of this
Province."[9]

By the end of 1765 all four of the lower houses in the southern
royal colonies had thus taken a common stand against Parliamentary
taxation. Each had asserted its sole right to tax its constituents.
Only the Virginia Burgesses had claimed exclusive jurisdiction over
internal polity as well, but the unanimous presumption of equality
with Parliament in matters of taxation was an important step in
developing the concept that the lower houses were co-ordinate legislatures with Parliament under the Crown. In Virginia, two leading
Burgesses, veteran pamphleteers Richard Bland and Landon Carter,
came very close to that conclusion during the Stamp Act crisis. Their
writings never had the impact nor enjoyed the popularity of those of
Daniel Dulany or John Dickinson. Two of Carter's contributions,
a letter of June 1765 to the *Virginia Gazette* and a long pamphlet of
November 1765, were never published, and both his third effort, a
letter written in September 1765 but not printed in the *Maryland
Gazette* until May 1766, and Bland's *An Enquiry, into the Rights of*

8. Ga. Committee of Correspondence to William Knox, Apr. 15, July 18, 1765,
Habersham Letters, 32, 40-41; Commons Journals, Dec. 14, 1765, *Ga. Col. Recs.*,
XIV, 315-16.
9. Nov. 26-29, 1765, S. C. Commons Journals, XXXVII, 15-31, S. C. Arch. Dept.

the British Colonies, published in March 1766, appeared too late in
the controversy to attract much attention.[10]   Nevertheless, all of these
productions are important both because they make it clear that the
Burgesses' inclusion of the phase *"internal Polity"* in its formal protests against the Stamp Act was not inadvertent and because they
contained ideas about the nature of the connection between Britain
and the colonies that were well in advance of most of their contemporaries.

Indeed, all of the arguments used by Thomas Jefferson, James Wilson, Benjamin Franklin, and John Adams in the next decade to
prove their contention that Parliament had no authority to legislate
for the internal affairs of the colonies were present, some explicitly
and others implicitly, in the writings of both Bland and Carter. Both
recognized clearly that Parliamentary taxation threatened not only
the right of American individuals to be taxed without their consent
but also the long-standing rights, privileges, and powers of colonial
lower houses.   Bland had no doubt that American acceptance of the
theory of virtual representation would degrade colonial legislatures
"even below the Corporation of a petty Borough in *England*," and
both he and Carter tried to combat that notion by asserting the
primacy of colonial legislatures in taxation and internal affairs. Building on the assumptions that the "Constitution of the Colonies" was
"established upon the Principles of *British* Liberty" and that the
colonists—though "a distinct People from the Inhabitants of *Britain*"
—inherited and were entitled to all the rights of Britons, they argued
that the right of representation was one of "the most essential" of
those rights.   Precisely because the colonists were "a distinct People"
they exercised that right not through Parliament but through their

10. Fauquier prevented the publication of Carter's first piece, which was addressed to the freeholders of Richmond County and may be found with Carter's
letter to Joseph Royle, June 3, 1765, Fairfax Papers, III, Brock Collection, Huntington Lib. His long pamphlet address to Mr. ———— in Great Britain is
an answer to the attack on the American argument that charters protected them
from Parliamentary taxation by a writer using the pseudonym William Pym in
the London *Publick Ledger,* Aug. 23, 1765. It is dated Nov. 30, 1765, and is in
the Sabine Hall Collection, Alderman Lib. His third piece, dated Sept. 1765, was
published in the *Maryland Gazette* (Annapolis), May 8, 1766. It was unsigned,
but conclusive proof of Carter's authorship may be found in his letter to Jonas
Green, Nov. 4, 1765, in the Sabine Hall Collection, Alderman Lib. On Bland's
pamphlet see J. E. Pate, "Richard Bland's Inquiry into the Rights of the British
Colonies," *Wm. and Mary Qtly.,* 2d Ser., 11 (1931), 20-28, and Clinton Rossiter,
*Seedtime of the Republic: The Origin of the American Tradition of Political
Liberty* (N. Y., 1953), 278-79.

own representative assemblies. Unlike most American writers, Bland and Carter, like the Virginia Burgesses, put as much emphasis upon internal legislation without representation as upon taxation without representation and suggested that Parliament lacked not only the power to tax but the power to legislate for the colonies. Bland claimed for Virginians the "Right . . . of directing their *internal* Government by Laws made with their own Consent," and Carter reiterated again and again that Virginians could be *"governed and taxed"* only by "Laws made with the Consent of the Majority of their own Representatives." If Parliament did not represent Americans and if only the colonial legislatures could pass laws to *"govern and tax"* them, then—though neither writer was bold enough to state the conclusion explicitly—Parliament had no authority either to tax or to legislate for the internal affairs of the colonies.

The logical corollary to this conclusion was that the colonists were equal to Britons and colonial legislatures were equal to Parliament. Both authors inferred as much, Bland in asserting that *"Rights* imply *Equality"* and Carter in rejecting any suggestion that the Virginia legislature was "but a pitiful American Assembly—Vainly forming a poor epitomé of British greatness." Finally, both Carter and Bland implied that the colonies were united with Britain only through the Crown. Bland wrote that the colonies were "distinct" states, "independent, as to their *internal* Government, of the original Kingdom, but united with her, as to their *external* Polity, in the closest and most intimate LEAGUE AND AMITY, under the same Allegiance." Carter went even further, rejecting the idea that there had to be a supreme legislature in the empire and arguing that as long as the King exercised "an actual Supremacy . . . in every Legislation," there was no "Necessity . . . for a further supremacy" in Parliament.[11] These arguments were yet too radical to gain general acceptance, but they were the logical conclusions to the propositions put forth in the debate over the Stamp Act and they indicated the direction that Americans would take in developing their constitutional position during the next decade.

Having formulated their constitutional objections in the more dignified surroundings of their legislative chambers and libraries, the

11. Bland, *An Inquiry into the Rights of the British Colonies* (Williamsburg, 1766), 4, 12, 17, 20, 22-25; *Maryland Gazette* (Annapolis), May 8, 1766; Carter to Mr. ————, Nov. 30, 1765, Sabine Hall Collection, Alderman Lib.

representatives privately joined with other Americans to translate those objections into action. Sons of Liberty organizations in every colony forced stamp distributors to resign and thus made sure that no good American would have the opportunity to forfeit his birthright. The same groups also initiated economic sanctions, enforcing informal agreements not to import British goods until the Stamp Act was repealed. Among the four southern colonies, only Georgia under the steady determination of James Wright actually witnessed the enforcement of the Stamp Act. When Parliament repealed the act on March 18, 1766, under the new Rockingham ministry, it was largely because of the ill effects of the economic sanctions upon British merchants and in no way represented any admission of the validity of American constitutional arguments. That Parliament had made no concessions on questions of principle was vividly indicated by its simultaneous passage of the Declaratory Act, which asserted its authority to legislate for the colonies "in all cases whatsoever," and by its retention of the duties, though lowered, levied by the Sugar Act.[12]

These actions were a harbinger of things to come. Still in force was the Quartering Act of 1764, amplified in 1766, requiring lower houses to furnish housing and supplies for British troops stationed in their colonies. This act involved certain basic constitutional questions, including the keeping of standing armies in colonial towns and, after 1766, the quartering of troops upon private dwellings, both without the consent of the lower houses. More important, the Quartering Act demonstrated that Parliament could through its power to legislate for the colonies indirectly tax them by forcing colonial legislatures to vote funds to comply with Parliamentary requirements.[13]

An even more direct threat was in the offing. Parliament emerged

12. Morgan and Morgan, *Stamp Act Crisis*, 180-204, 261-81. The best brief account of the Stamp Act tumults in the southern colonies is John R. Alden, *The South in the Revolution, 1763-1789* (Baton Rouge, 1957), 64-98.

13. On this point, see Apr. 14-15, 1768, *Va. Burgesses Journals, 1766-69*, 165-72. In the south, only the Georgia and South Carolina Houses were ever asked to comply with the Quartering Acts. The former finally yielded in November 1767 in the face of a royal order, but the latter flatly refused in June 1769 to provide for troops temporarily stationed in Charleston. See Abbot, *Royal Governors*, 138-43; Wright to Earl of Shelburne, Apr. 6, 1767, unpubl. Ga. Col. Recs., XXXVII, 177-90, Ga. Dept. of Arch. and Hist.; June 30, Aug. 10-19, 1769, S. C. Commons Journals, XXXVIII, 20, 136-37, 163-64, 177-79, S. C. Arch. Dept.

from the debate over the Stamp Act with the mistaken impression that the colonies objected only to internal taxes such as the stamp duties. The colonies' failure to protest the continuation of the Sugar Act after the repeal of the Stamp Act supported that notion. Accordingly, when Chancellor of the Exchequer Charles Townshend decided to try his hand at taxing the colonies in early 1767, he accepted the distinction and pushed through Parliament a revenue measure levying external duties on all glass, lead, paper, paints, and tea imported into the colonies. Calculated to produce only a relatively small revenue, these duties were quite obviously also intended to establish Parliament's right to tax the colonies. The simultaneous declaration that money collected from the duties would be used to render royal officials independent of colonial legislatures and that an American Board of Customs would be established in Boston to supervise collection of the duties and to tighten up enforcement of the navigation acts re-emphasized the ministry's intention of bringing the colonies under closer supervision.

But American lower houses recognized that the Townshend Acts, like the Stamp Act, seriously threatened their power and position and made it clear that the Townshend duties were no more acceptable than the stamp taxes, that they had denied and would continue to deny Parliament's right to levy any taxes, internal or external, upon the colonies. From an economic standpoint the new duties were less onerous to the agricultural southern colonies than to the commercial provinces in the north, and the first cries of protest came from New England and the middle colonies. From Pennsylvania between November 1767 and January 1768 came John Dickinson's famous *Farmer's Letters,* which admitted Parliament's right to levy duties to regulate the trade of the empire but denied its authority to levy any taxes for revenue purposes—a position subsequently endorsed by most of the lower houses. The first official protest came from the Massachusetts House of Representatives in February 1768 in the form of a circular letter to the other lower houses calling for a concerted defense of American rights.

Once the issue had been raised, the southern legislatures lined up with their northern counterparts at the earliest opportunity. In contrast to some of the protests from the northern colonies, where the proposal to pay royal officials from the Townshend revenues was a major issue, the southern objections concentrated on the question of Parliamentary taxation. In separate petitions to King, Lords, and Commons prepared by a committee chaired by Richard Bland and including Robert Carter Nicholas, Edmund Pendleton, Archibald Cary, John Blair, Benjamin Harrison, and Severn Eyre, the Virginia Burgesses on April 15, 1768, took a stand against the Townshend duties that was almost identical to the one it had taken three years earlier against the Stamp Act: Parliament could legislate for the empire and could *"make Laws for regulating the Trade of the Colonies"* but could not tax the colonies without their consent. In the petition to the King the Burgesses again asserted jurisdiction over internal affairs as well, claiming for Virginians *"the Enjoyment of their antient and inestimable right of being Governed by such Laws only, respecting their internal Polity and Taxation as are derived from their own Consent."* Then the Burgesses joined the Massachusetts House of Representatives at the forefront of the opposition by ordering Speaker Peyton Randolph to write the speakers in other colonies acquainting them with the Burgesses' action and emphasizing the necessity for united opposition *"to every Measure which may affect the Rights and Liberties of the* British *Colonies in* America."[14]

The other three houses took a similar stand before the end of the year. On April 12, 1768, the South Carolina Commons ordered its committee of correspondence to direct Charles Garth to join the other agents in seeking a repeal of the duties, but a more elaborate protest awaited the meeting of a newly elected House in November. Governor Lord Charles Greville Montagu greeted the new Commons with Lord Hillsborough's order forbidding American lower houses to consider the Massachusetts circular letter and requiring the dissolution of any house that approved it. But the Commons on the recommendation of a committee headed by James Parsons and including Christopher Gadsden, Charles Pinckney, John Rutledge, Thomas Lynch, and Henry Laurens defiantly and unanimously resolved on November 19 that both that letter and the one from the Virginia speaker were "founded upon undeniable Constitutional Principles," thus endorsing the stands taken in those letters. The Commons also resolved to present an address to Parliament protesting the unconstitutionality of the Townshend measures, but Montagu

14. Apr. 7, 14-15, 1768, *Va. Burgesses Journals, 1766-69*, 158, 165-74.

dissolved it before the address was finished.[15] Two weeks later, on December 2, the North Carolina Lower House pushed through an address to the Crown declaring that "Free men" could not "be legally taxed but by themselves or their Representatives," but Tryon managed to persuade the representatives to soften the tone of the document so that it did not greatly offend London officials.[16] The Georgia Commons followed suit on December 24, quietly adopting a formal petition to the Crown that placed it firmly against the Townshend Acts before a surprised Governor Wright could dissolve it.[17] All four of the southern lower houses had again taken a constitutional stand against Parliament's right to tax the colonies.

If American legislatures were resolved never to consent to Parliamentary taxation, Parliament was just as determined to assert its legislative supremacy over the colonies "in all cases whatsoever." The ministry's reply to the Virginia petitions was an additional instruction to Virginia's new governor, Norborne Berkeley, Baron de Botetourt, requiring him to inform the Burgesses that the ministry would never abandon the principles set forth in the Declaratory Act and "to discountenance and reject as null and void, every Act and Proceeding in Our Colonies, inconsistent with, and derogatory from Our said Right."[18] To make matters worse, the ministry emphasized its continued determination to enforce the Townshend Acts by dispatching four regiments of troops to Boston, the center of the protest, and by obtaining Parliament's approval to seize and send to England for trial leaders of the colonial opposition on charges of treason under an old statute of Henry VIII. These measures convinced many Americans that the cabinet and Parliament would stop at nothing to deprive the lower houses of their traditional rights and authority and to render them subordinate to the imperial government, and the lower houses promptly resorted to more drastic measures to achieve their objectives.

Singled out for special disciplinary action, the Virginia Burgesses again took the lead in the south. On orders from the ministry, Botetourt upon his arrival in October 1768 dissolved the House for calling Parliament's authority into question in its April petitions.

15. Apr. 12, Nov. 18-19, 1768, S. C. Commons Journals, XXXVII, Pt. I, 691-92, Pt. II, 9, 17-20, S. C. Arch. Dept.
16. Lower House Journals, Dec. 5, 1768, *N. C. Col. Recs.*, VII, 980-82.
17. Commons Journals, Dec. 24, 1768, *Ga. Col. Recs.*, XIV, 643-59.
18. Additional Instruction to Botetourt, Aug. 21, 1768, CO 5/1346.

But this action only made Virginia legislators even more indignant and the new House which convened in May defied both the Declaratory Act and the additional instructions by adopting a set of resolutions emphatically asserting its "sole Right of imposing Taxes on the Inhabitants of . . . *Virginia*," claiming an "undoubted Privilege" to petition the Crown for redress of grievances, and condemning the transportation of prisoners to Britain for trial. To implement their resolutions, the burgesses, meeting illegally after Botetourt had dissolved the House for its boldness, followed the example of the northern colonies and adopted the Virginia Association, an agreement pledging non-importation of taxed items, slaves, and other goods until the Townshend duties had been repealed.[19] Speaker Randolph's letter describing the burgesses' proceedings inspired the other southern colonies to act accordingly. In June South Carolina planters and artisans under the leadership of Christopher Gadsden, Thomas Lynch, and other members of the Commons also adopted a non-importation agreement, and when the Commons met in August it passed a series of resolutions similar to the Virginia ones. Georgia followed the same pattern. A group of private citizens, probably including many of those members of the Commons who were active in the local Sons of Liberty, forced its merchants to accept non-importation in September, and the Commons officially subscribed to the Virginia resolves when it convened later in the fall. Meeting at the same time, the North Carolina Lower House surprised Tryon by unanimously adopting the Virginia resolutions and, after Tryon had dissolved it, meeting extralegally to adopt non-importation.[20] Again the southern lower houses had been unanimous in claiming the exclusive right to impose taxes upon their constituents, and the fact that both the North Carolina and Georgia resolutions came after notification that the ministry would seek repeal of all the duties except the tax on tea showed their unyielding opposition to any violation of that right.

The most important contribution to the constitutional debate to come from the southern colonies during the crisis over the Town-

19. May 16, 1769, *Va. Burgesses Journals, 1766-69,* 214-15.

20. Alden, *South in Revolution,* 99-117; Aug. 17-19, 1769, S. C. Commons Journals, XXXVIII, 165-66, 174-75, S. C. Arch. Dept.; Commons Journals, Nov. 7, 1769, *Ga. Col. Recs.,* XV, 25-34; Lower House Journals, Nov. 2, 1769, *N. C. Col. Recs.,* VIII, 121-24.

shend Acts was the Reverend John Joachim Zubly's *An Humble Enquiry into the Nature of the Dependency of the American Colonies upon the Parliament of Great Britain,* published in Charleston in 1769. A Savannah minister and the unofficial chaplain to the Georgia Commons, Zubly denied the right of Parliament to tax the colonies because it "would deprive them of the rights of *Englishmen,* nay, in time, with the loss of the constitution, . . . of liberty and property altogether" and because Americans had "had their own legislatures and representatives" to tax them "for ages past." Zubly clearly recognized that the rights of individuals depended on the rights of the colonial legislatures and that Parliamentary taxation constituted an important threat to colonial legislative power. If Americans were "not to raise their own taxes," Zubly declared, "all their Assemblies become useless in a moment, all their respective legislatures are annihilated at a stroke; an act passed by persons, most of whom probably never saw, nor cared much for *America,* may destroy all the acts they ever passed, may lay every burden upon them . . . and all their civil and religious liberties . . . will, or may be at an end." Moreover, if the colonies were—as the Declaratory Act stated—dependent upon both Crown and Parliament, Parliament might be expected to take over, or at least to share, many of the traditional functions of the Crown. It could not only disallow colonial laws and hear appeals from colonial courts but also—as it had already done in the case of the New York Assembly—even "suspend, which is but another word for proroguing or dissolving (or annihilating) Assemblies."[21]

This consciousness that Parliamentary taxation could mean the eventual annihilation of the colonial legislatures caused Americans to stiffen their position. They claimed nothing they had not claimed at the time of the Stamp Act, but their claims were now firmer and more precisely and thoroughly formulated. In addition, their vision of themselves was greater than ever. Their arguments had led them increasingly to the exhilarating conclusions that they were independent of Parliamentary authority and that they were equal legislatures with Parliament under the Crown. To be sure, no southern legislator put forth a formal or explicit case for these conclusions, but the royal governors recognized that they had gained wide currency.

21. [Zubly], *An Humble Enquiry into the Nature of the Dependency of the American Colonies upon the Parliament of Great Britain and the Right of Parliament to lay Taxes on the said Colonies* (Charleston, 1769), 9-11, 20, 23, 25.

As early as June 1767 Wright wrote the Board of Trade that he had "lately discovered more than ever" among Georgia representatives "a strong Propensity to be as Considerable and Independent as they Term it, of the British Parliament . . . as any of the Northern Assemblies,"[22] and in May 1769 Botetourt warned Hillsborough "that Opinions of the Independency of the Legislature of the Colonies are grown to such a Height in this Country, that it becomes Great Britain, if she intends it, immediately to assert her Supremacy in a manner which may be felt, and to loose no more time in Declarations which irritate but do not decide."[23]

But British officials were not yet willing to accept either Botetourt's advice or the validity of American arguments. Rather, they chose a middle course. Although favorable economic conditions had softened the effects of non-importation, the prospect that a revival of trade with America would lead to even greater prosperity and the recognition that it was not good mercantilist economics to levy duties on one's own goods finally convinced the ministry to seek repeal of the Townshend duties. The only question was how to repeal the duties without appearing to have yielded to the Americans on the constitutional question. The answer, pushed through Parliament in April 1770, was to repeal all the taxes except the three-penny duty on tea, leaving that along with the 1764 duty on molasses as symbols of Parliament's right to tax the colonies. Most American legislators were probably not content with these concessions, but it was difficult to carry on the fight against token duties that did not greatly affect the economic well-being of the colonies. Particularly in the northern colonies non-importation had been hard on American merchants. One colony after another therefore abandoned the associations, and by July 1771 the whole system had collapsed. The best the patriots could do was to retain the boycott on tea.

Over the next three years unprecedented prosperity and a variety of local problems forced the constitutional question into the background, and even the boycott on tea gradually broke down.[24] But this temporary lull did not obscure the fact that the debate over taxation had ended in stalemate; neither side had made any con-

22. Wright to Board of Trade, June 15, 1767, unpubl. Ga. Col. Recs., XXVIII, Pt. II-A, 496-97, Ga. Dept. of Arch. and Hist.
23. Botetourt to Hillsborough, May 23, 1769, CO 5/1347.
24. Alden, *South in Revolution*, 110-17.

cessions on matters of principle. Parliament had not abandoned the claim expressed in the Declaratory Act to "full power and authority" over the colonies. The lower houses still adhered to the position taken during the Stamp Act crisis, claiming the same exclusive authority over taxation in the colonies that Parliament had over that matter in Britain and, in the case of the Virginia Burgesses, asserting an equal right in matters of internal polity. Any small spark might rekindle the contest. From Virginia former Burgess George Mason issued a warning in December 1770: "should the oppressive system of taxing us without our consent be continued, the flame lowered now will break out with redoubled ardor, and the spirit of opposition . . . wear a more formidable shape than ever."[25]

25. George Mason to ————, Dec. 6, 1770, in Kate Mason Rowland, *The Life of George Mason, 1725-1792*, 2 vols. (N. Y. and London, 1892), I, 148.

Tightening the Reins:
General Issues

Parliamentary taxation was not the only issue that agitated the lower houses in the southern royal colonies in the years after 1763. In an effort to tighten up colonial administration, crown officials intensified the program of centralization begun in the early 1750's by the Earl of Halifax, and the determination of the home government to take a stricter tone with the colonies was increased by the response of colonial legislatures to the Stamp Act and Townshend measures. Because imperial authorities could not accept the constitutional claims that issued from American lawmakers, the power and privileges of the lower houses were important targets of their new restrictive policy. In the period after 1760 they not only invoked the authority of Parliament to challenge these powers but also applied traditional checks such as restrictive instructions, legislative review, and the suspending clause in a way that was increasingly irksome to American legislators. A variety of measures, some aimed at particular colonial legislatures and others at general legislative powers and practices, posed serious challenges to the powers of the lower houses, threatening to undermine their position and contributing greatly to the growing tension between the mother country and the colonies. Two general measures that became important issues in all four of the southern royal colonies were the general instruction of September 1767 and the Currency Act of 1764.

The general instruction of 1767 was the culmination of a systematic attempt to restrict the lower houses' control over membership that dated back more than a quarter of a century. Throughout the middle decades of the eighteenth century Crown officials had tried to prevent the lower houses from exercising the powers to establish constituencies and apportion representation, fix the qualifications of voters and members, and regulate by law the frequency of elections and sessions. This movement had resulted in the disallowance of the North Carolina biennial act in 1737 and of three South Carolina election acts of 1745, 1747, and 1759. In the 1750's under the leadership of the Earl of Halifax, imperial authorities had sought to deprive the North Carolina Lower House of the power to erect constituencies by assigning that power exclusively to the governor and Council; they had also threatened to disallow the South Carolina triennial act of 1721 and had positively forbidden the Georgia Commons to exercise any authority over membership at the institution of royal government in Georgia. Similarly, Crown officials had refused to sanction a Virginia election act of 1762 which would have established new qualifications for voting and membership and limited the duration of the Burgesses to seven years. In September 1767 they formalized this long-standing policy in a general instruction, forbidding governors to assent to laws "by which the number of the assembly shall be enlarged or diminished, the duration of it ascertained, the qualification of the electors or the elected fixed or altered, or by which any regulations shall be established with respect thereto inconsistent with our instructions."[1] This instruction left no doubt that imperial officials now intended to enforce that policy much more vigorously.

The instruction was the immediate product of an objection in 1766 by Board of Trade counsel Matthew Lamb to a South Carolina law of 1765 establishing St. Matthew's Parish and empowering it to elect two representatives. Lamb questioned the authority of the South Carolina Commons to pass such a measure, and a year later the Crown disallowed the law and ordered the preparation of the new instruction. At first, the instruction was intended only for South Carolina, but when Crown officials discovered that similar laws were pending from Nova Scotia, New Hampshire, Massachusetts, and New York, they made it applicable to all the royal colonies on the continent except Georgia, whose governor already had a similar instruction, and Massachusetts, whose charter specifically protected it from

1. Labaree, ed., *Royal Instructions*, I, 107.

such a regulation.[2] Striking at the very heart of the lower houses'
control over membership, the instruction represented a formidable
challenge to one of the more important powers exercised by the lower
houses over the previous century and became a significant source of
irritation in all of the southern royal colonies. For the next seven
years London officials sought to enforce the terms of the instruction
rigidly.

But for a time at least the lower houses in Virginia, North Carolina, and South Carolina all found means to circumvent the restriction against new electoral districts. Before the issuance of the
instruction the South Carolina Commons had passed in May 1767 an
act to establish two new parishes, St. Luke and All Saints, empowering each to elect two representatives. Because it was a direct violation
of the instruction, Crown officials disallowed it in December 1770;[3]
but in the meantime the Commons had found an expedient that
enabled it to get around the instruction. Because the instruction had
forbidden passage of measures which enlarged or diminished the number of assemblymen but had not specifically prohibited the erection
of new electoral districts, the Commons created three new constituencies by statute, assigning each one seat that had formerly been apportioned to older parishes. London officials did not object to this
arrangement and the new parishes continued to elect assemblymen
until the Revolution.[4] Although the South Carolina Commons
managed to create new electoral districts, it could not increase the
size of its membership. This restriction created serious hardships,
preventing the Commons from extending more equitable representation to the rapidly expanding backcountry. Thus, despite the
Commons' insistence that it was "absolutely necessary to the equal
representations of the Province," the Council refused in early 1771
to pass a bill to establish several new parishes in the interior and to
increase the number of representatives from older western parishes

2. Cooper and McCord, eds., *S. C. Statutes*, IV, 230-32; Lamb to Board of Trade,
June 30, 1766, Order in Council, June 26, 1767, S. C. Pub. Recs., XXXI, 78-79,
393-94, S. C. Arch. Dept.; Labaree, *Royal Government*, 186.

3. Cooper and McCord, eds., *S. C. Statutes*, IV, 266-68; Hillsborough *et al.* to
King in Council, Nov. 21, 1770, Order in Council, Dec. 9, 1770, S. C. Pub. Recs.,
XXXII, 358-59, 431, S. C. Arch. Dept.; Nov. 14, 1770, *Board of Trade Journals
1768-75*, 211.

4. Cooper and McCord, eds., *S. C. Statutes*, IV, 298-300; Bull to Hillsborough,
July 18, 1768, S. C. Pub. Recs., XXXII, 17, S. C. Arch. Dept.

because it increased the size of the Commons.[5]   Henry Laurens thought the restriction "tyrannical" and predicted it would "make the present Generation so watchful and attentive to their true Interests, as will defeat the Ends, which the Enemies of America have in View."[6]

Unlike the South Carolina Commons, the North Carolina Lower House and the Virginia Burgesses managed for a while to increase the size of their respective memberships, largely because they erected new constituencies simply by establishing new counties. Because the establishing statutes said nothing about representation, it was less obvious that new electoral districts were being created, and several statutes from both colonies escaped the notice of Crown officials. Thus, between 1768 and 1770 the North Carolina Lower House created five new counties, and Governor William Tryon granted each of them two representatives according to the custom of the colony. But the House established no further constituencies after 1770. Tryon's successor, Josiah Martin, was more rigid in adhering to imperial policy, turning down one attempt to create a new county because it was "inconsistent" with his instructions.[7]

The Virginia Burgesses had a similar experience.   It erected five new counties by statute between 1767 and 1772 before the Board of Trade discovered what was happening. In March 1773 the Board reprimanded Governor Dunmore for having approved measures in April 1772 creating three new counties in violation of the 1767 instruction. But Dunmore feigned ignorance of the instruction, and Crown officials apparently permitted the laws to stand, for the counties in question continued to elect representatives to the end of the royal period. However, Dunmore was careful not to assent to similar statutes thereafter.[8]

The Georgia Commons did not attempt to acquire the power to erect constituencies after 1767, but it did try to force Governor James Wright to extend representation to the rapidly growing region south of the Altamaha River. By 1770 that area was already fairly well

5. Feb. 23, Mar. 8, 1771, S. C. Commons Journals, XXXVIII, 493-94, 509, S. C. Arch. Dept.
6. Laurens to John Hopton, Jan. 29, 1771, Laurens Letter Book, 1767-71, 598, Laurens Papers, S. C. Hist. Soc.
7. See Martin to Dartmouth, May 30, 1773, *N. C. Col. Recs.*, IX, 663.
8. Board of Trade to Dunmore, Mar. 2, 1773, CO 5/1369; Dunmore to Dartmouth, May 25, 1773, CO 5/1351; Hening, ed., *Va. Statutes*, VIII, 597-601.

settled and had been divided into four parishes: St. David, St. Patrick, St. Thomas, and St. Mary. When the Commons convened late in 1769, it was greeted by petitions from each of these parishes asking permission to send delegates to the Commons. Despite vigorous support from the Commons, Wright refused to grant the requests. Consequently, the Commons boldly attempted to apply pressure on Wright by exempting the four parishes from paying the annual tax because they were not *"Particularly* represented" in the legislature—an implementation of the colony's rejection of the concept of virtual representation.[9] Hillsborough approved Wright's conduct, taking the opportunity to reaffirm the Crown's policy that "the appointing what places shall send Representatives to the Assembly" was "a matter, which by the Forms and Principles of Government established for the Colony of Georgia, entirely depends upon His Majesty's Discretion." But Hillsborough also implied that Wright might justifiably extend representation to the four parishes by executive order whenever he thought it necessary—a course Wright eventually adopted, but not before the Commons had refused in 1771 to levy any taxes at all until the four parishes were represented.[10] Thus, in a sense, the Georgia Commons, by seizing the initiative in suggesting what new areas ought to be erected into constituencies, shared with the governor and Council the power to designate electoral districts. But the Commons never gained a share of the power of apportionment. It was the executive alone that decided how many representatives to assign each district.[11]

The lower houses were much less successful in their efforts to pass measures fixing either electoral qualifications or the frequency of elections and sessions after the issuance of the 1767 instruction. All of the lower houses in the southern royal colonies except the South Carolina Commons, which enjoyed the privileges of the 1721 triennial act, made such attempts after 1767, but only the Georgia Commons met with any degree of success. Because the Crown had not confirmed its septennial law of 1762, the Virginia Burgesses passed another law

9. Statutes, *Ga. Col. Recs.*, XIX, Pt. I, 161-98; Wright to Hillsborough, May 11, 1770, Feb. 28, 1771, unpubl. Ga. Col. Recs., XXXVII, 446, 520-25, Ga. Dept. of Arch. and Hist.

10. Hillsborough to Wright, July 31 and Dec. 11, 1770, Wright to Hillsborough, Oct. 8, 1770, Feb. 28, 1771, unpubl. Ga. Col. Recs., XXXVII, 462, 483, 488, 520-25, Ga. Dept. of Arch. and Hist.

11. See James Habersham to Wright, Nov. 30, 1771, *Habersham Letters*, 156-57.

with the same provisions in November 1769, but this measure, coming on the heels of the prohibiting instruction, was rejected.[12]   A similar attempt by the North Carolina Lower House in January 1771 ran afoul of Governor Tryon's veto, and two later efforts to enact a triennial law in 1773 and 1774 also failed, the first in the House and the second in the Council.[13]

Only in the case of Georgia did imperial authorities relax any of the electoral restrictions.   In May 1770 the Georgia Commons pushed through an election law to fix voter qualifications and to set the maximum duration of the legislature at three years.   Although he was sympathetic to the measure, Governor James Wright rejected it because it was contrary to his instructions and to the 1767 circular instruction.   Upon the application of both houses, however, Wright agreed to submit the measure to royal authorities for consideration. The Commons directed its agent, Benjamin Franklin, to seek imperial approval of the bill, pointing out that South Carolina enjoyed a similar law and that in many northern and West Indian colonies elections were even annual.   In justifying the law, it argued that members found it inconvenient to serve longer than three years and that many of the best qualified would not serve "if the Duration should remain undetermined by Law."[14]   Crown officials approved the bill in general and authorized Wright to consent to most parts of it, but they would not consent to the enactment of the triennial clause.   With imperial permission the Georgia Commons re-enacted the law in 1773 without the objectionable clause, although for reasons not entirely clear it does not appear to have received Wright's assent.[15]

All of these attempts by the lower houses to assert their control over membership may be taken as evidence of a fundamental dissatis-

12. Hening, ed., *Va. Statutes,* VIII, 305-17.

13. Tryon to Hillsborough, Mar. 9, 1771, *N. C. Col. Recs.,* VIII, 523; Lower House Journals, Jan. 14-15, 26, 1771, Jan. 28, 1773, Mar. 10-16, 1774, *ibid.,* VIII, 426-28, 479, IX, 457, 899-900, 917; Upper House Journals, Mar. 16, 1774, *ibid.,* IX, 855.

14. Wright to Board of Trade, July 23, 1770, unpubl. Ga. Col. Recs., XXVIII, Pt. II-B, 731-33, Ga. Dept. of Arch. and Hist.; Ga. Committee of Correspondence to Franklin, May 23, 1770, *Habersham Letters,* 82.

15. See Ga. Committee of Correspondence to Benjamin Franklin, May 23, 1770, *Habersham Letters,* 81-82; Wright to Board of Trade, July 23, 1770, Board of Trade to King, Nov. 23, 1770, Hillsborough to Wright, Dec. 11, 1770, unpubl. Ga. Col. Recs., XXVIII, Pt. II-B, 731-33, XXXIV, 604-7, XXXVII, 488, Ga. Dept. of Arch. and Hist.; Commons Journals, June 30, 1773, *Ga. Col. Recs.,* XV, 442-43; Upper House Journals, July 21, 1773, *ibid.,* XVII, 723.

faction with the general instruction of 1767. With the exception of
Parliamentary taxation, probably no other element in Britain's new
colonial policy challenged more basically or more formidably the
whole constitutional position of the lower houses. The instruction
was based on the assumptions that the lower houses were subordinate
bodies existing only by the favor of the Crown and that only the
Crown could alter the constitution of the legislature. Such assumptions were completely contrary to the reality of the colonial situation
and constituted a reaffirmation of a position that the lower houses
had much earlier come to regard as invalid. The instruction of
1767 denied that the lower houses could change even their internal
constitutions by their own actions much less the constitutions of the
colonies. Furthermore, it contradicted their argument that the right
of constituents to be represented was one of the traditional rights
of Englishmen and did not depend upon royal grace and favor.
Denying the lower houses the power to put themselves upon a firm
legal footing at the very moment they were asserting their equal
status with Parliament in questions of taxation, the regulation was
especially degrading. In Virginia Richard Henry Lee was particularly concerned about this "imperfection in the . . . constitution." "'Tis
by usage only that elections are directed and Assembly's called," he
complained to his brother Arthur in 1766; "in our code of laws not
one is to be found that directs the calling of new Assembly's, or that
appoints any time for the meeting of the representative body when
chosen." Because Virginians lacked that "one very essential security,
namely the Right of their Members being chosen and meeting in a
certain time after being dissolved, as in Britain," Lee lamented, "the
third or democratical part of our legislature is totally in the power
of the Crown" and the liberties of Virginians "on a very precarious
footing." Lee was convinced that the rights of individual Americans
would never be secure until the rights of their assemblies were firmly
established.[16] An anonymous Virginian, Phileleutheros, recommended
in 1769 that the colonies "unite" in demanding laws to limit the
duration of their legislatures. Such regulations, he declared, were
absolutely essential to "give Stability and Permanence to American
Freedom."[17] It was to secure such limitations, as well as to obtain

16. Lee to Arthur Lee, Dec. 20, 1766, Ballagh, ed., R. H. Lee Letters, I, 20-21;
Lee, State of the Constitution of Virginia, no date, Lee-Ludwell Papers, Va. Hist.
Soc.
   17. Letter of Phileleutheros, Apr. 10, 1769, Va. Misc. MSS, Lib. Cong.

both legal guarantees of their right to alter their internal constitutions and imperial recognition of their political status in the colonies, that the lower houses sought to strengthen their control over membership and opposed the instruction of 1767. Continually thwarted in their attempts, the lower houses found little consolation in the modification of the instruction in 1773 which permitted the passage of previously prohibited measures if they contained a suspending clause.[18]

Another important part of the general restrictive policy adopted by the imperial authorities after 1763 was the Currency Act of 1764.[19] Like the general instruction of 1767, it was a logical continuation of earlier policy, extending Parliament's 1751 restrictions on New England to the remaining colonies. Its passage was prompted by the continued refusal of the Virginia Burgesses to remove the legal tender stipulations from the paper money it had issued in fairly large amounts during the Seven Years' War. The subsequent depreciation of that money had caused alarm among both British merchants and colonial officials, who feared that Virginians might force their depreciated bills upon the merchants at face value in payment for sterling debts. Actually, there was little cause for such alarm. From 1757 on the Virginia General Court had repeatedly taken depreciation into account when awarding judgments for sterling debts.[20] But the Burgesses' continued insistence that the bills remain legal tender in direct defiance of a special royal instruction to the contrary, as well as the even more serious and rapid depreciation of North Carolina's paper bills, caused much uneasiness among British merchants and persuaded colonial officials to move toward a total prohibition of legal tender currency in the colonies during the early months of 1764. Agents for the six royal colonies from New York to Georgia protested against so drastic a step, arguing that each colony should be permitted some stipulated amount of paper currency to circulate as legal tender within the colony if not in payment of British debts. But the Board of

18. Labaree, ed., *Royal Instructions,* I, 107.

19. For a general discussion of the Currency Act and the colonial reaction, see Jack P. Greene and Richard M. Jellison, "The Currency Act of 1764 in Imperial-Colonial Relations, 1764-1776," *Wm. and Mary Qtly.,* 3d ser., 18 (1961), 485-518.

20. Va. Committee of Correspondence to Edward Montague, June 16, 1763, "Proceedings of Va. Committee of Correspondence," *Va. Mag. of Hist. and Biog.,* 11 (1904), 347; 12 (1905), 1-4.

Trade noted that the New England colonies had not suffered greatly from the prohibition, having solved their currency problems by establishing Crown-approved non-legal tender systems, and it contended that "inconveniences" would "arise from any further delay." Accordingly, in April 1764 Parliament passed the Currency Act to prohibit all colonies from issuing legal tender currency after September 1, 1764, and to require that all such currency then circulating be punctually retired at the time appointed by the acts of issue. The act threatened any governor who violated it with severe penalties, including a fine of £1,000 sterling, immediate dismissal, and lifetime exclusion from places of public trust.[21]

Initially, the Currency Act evoked no strong protest from any of the southern royal colonies. With the possible exception of Georgia, they had issued enough paper currency during the war to satisfy the immediate demands of commerce, and concern over the Stamp Act—passed less than three-quarters of a year later—drew their attention away from the law. But as the money issued during the war was paid into colonial treasuries for taxes and retired according to law, colonials began to complain about the want of money with which to carry on trade. As early as June 1765—less than a year after the passage of the act—Fauquier reported that "Circulating Currency" had "grown very scarce" in Virginia, so that people were "really distressed for Money of any kind to satisfy their Creditors." The situation would get continually worse, he said, as the number of bills was decreased by "burning and sinking all that are received for Taxes." A year later the South Carolina Commons listed the prohibition on legal tender currency as a major grievance and resolved to attempt to secure its repeal.[22] But it was not until after the repeal of the Stamp Act in the spring of 1766 that the southern royal colonies made a full-scale assault upon the Currency Act.

Within a year and a half after the repeal of the Stamp Act, each of the southern lower houses had petitioned against the Currency Act and sought permission to issue more legal tender currency. A petition from the Pennsylvania House in early 1766 asking repeal of the Cur-

---

21. Jan. 10-Feb. 13, 1764, *Board of Trade Journals, 1764-67*, 3-21; Danby Pickering *et al.*, eds., *The Statutes at Large from Magna Charta to the End of the Eleventh Parliament of Great Britain, Anno 1761, continued to 1806*, 46 vols. (Cambridge, Eng., 1762-1807), XXVI, 103-5.

22. Fauquier to Earl of Halifax, June 14, 1765, CO 5/1345; June 24, 1766, S. C. Commons Journals, XXXVII, 175-76, S. C. Arch. Dept.

rency Act caused the ministry to reconsider the measure, but the absence of complaints from other colonies decided it against making any changes at that time. South Carolina agent Charles Garth thought that a general protest from a number of the colonies might induce Parliament to repeal the act, and upon his suggestion the South Carolina Commons petitioned the Crown against it in November 1766. With the sinking of the wartime public orders and tax certificates, South Carolina found itself without enough currency to satisfy the requirements of internal trade, a situation complicated by the fact that over a fourth of its regular £106,500 of legal tender currency was being used in North Carolina and Georgia. The Commons was not exaggerating when it complained in its petition that the colony was "not furnished with a sufficient Quantity of Gold and Silver to answer its Demand for Money" and asserted that it was "absolutely necessary to establish a Currency as a Medium of Trade." If the amount of money in the colony continued to decline, the Commons warned, South Carolina might find itself unable to continue importing goods from Britain and be forced to set up its own manufacturing. To preclude such a development, the Commons requested the King to recommend a repeal of the legal tender prohibition and asked permission to issue an additional sum of legal tender paper equal to £50,000 sterling.[23]

After he had presented the Commons' petition to Lord Shelburne, then secretary of state for the Southern Department, Garth entertained high hopes that Parliament might repeal the Currency Act during its 1767 session. He found that Shelburne considered repeal "a very necessary Measure" and wrote the Commons in January 1767 that Shelburne had promised to "promote it to the utmost of his power." Garth's hopes rose even higher when he learned that the Committee of North American Merchants had agreed that the "Repeal of the . . . Paper Currency Act was absolutely necessary" and that a legal tender paper currency would not be prejudicial to British merchants if it were not extended to sterling debts. But by March Garth was less optimistic. He reported that the New York House's refusal to comply with the Quartering Act had made the ministry

23. Charles Garth to S. C. Committee of Correspondence, June 6, July 9, 1766, "Garth Correspondence," *S. C. Hist. and Geneal. Mag.*, 28 (1927), 232; 29 (1928), 41; S. C. Commons' petition to Crown, Nov. 28, 1766, S. C. Pub. Recs., XXXI, 300-308, S. C. Arch. Dept.

unwilling to repeal the Currency Act or, for that matter, to grant any indulgences to the colonies.   Still, Garth continued to work with the Merchants' committee and the agents for Pennsylvania, Virginia, and New York for repeal.   Indeed, Chancellor of the Exchequer Charles Townshend was willing to repeal the Currency Act as part of his American revenue plan and to permit the colonies under Crown supervision to issue paper money through loan offices in each colony if the money arising from the interest on the loans were appropriated to the Crown.   But the agents decided to withdraw their support for repeal rather than open the way for the establishment of a system that would drain more money from the colonies.   As a result, Parliament did not repeal the Currency Act, and the South Carolina Commons' application for permission to issue additional paper money was rejected.   By July 1767 Garth held out little hope for obtaining a repeal favorable to the colonies and suggested that South Carolina try to solve its money problem by establishing a non-legal tender currency.[24]

Similar applications from the other southern royal colonies met the same fate.   A petition from the Savannah merchants complaining of the scarcity of currency in the colony prompted the Georgia Commons in 1767 to propose a scheme for emitting £22,000 sterling in paper bills and to petition the Crown and both houses of Parliament for repeal of the Currency Act.   The petition had the support of both the Council and Governor Wright, although the latter thought £12,000 sterling a sufficient sum for the colony.   About the same time, the Virginia Burgesses, finding the colony in much "distress . . . for want of a sufficient circulating Medium for the Purposes of Trade and Commerce," petitioned the Crown for permission to emit £200,000, despite the Council's opposition to the proposal.   And the following January the North Carolina Lower House, discovering its colony in the same situation, joined with the Council to petition the Crown for leave to issue paper money equal in value to £75,000 sterling.[25]   The ministry refused each of these petitions in turn.   It

24. Garth to S. C. Committee of Correspondence, Jan. 31, May 17, June 6, July 5, 1767, "Garth Correspondence," S. C. Hist. and Geneal. Mag., 29 (1928), 129-30, 228-29, 296-97, 300-301.

25. Commons Journals, Feb. 4-5, 10-11, Mar. 26, 1767, Ga. Col. Recs., XIV, 427, 430-31, 434, 469-74; Wright to Shelburne, Apr. 6, 1767, unpubl. Ga. Col. Recs., XXXVII, 180-82, Ga. Dept. of Arch. and Hist.; Va. Committee of Correspondence to Montague, July 28, 1764, "Proceedings of Va. Committee of Correspondence,"

did not even bother to go through the customary formality of submitting the Georgia request to the Board of Trade, and it rejected the Virginia scheme in June 1768 because the Virginia Council had opposed it. At the same time, the Crown dismissed the North Carolina application, and Lord Hillsborough wrote Governor Tryon of the ministry's concern over the North Carolina legislature's still entertaining such a strong desire to introduce again the "pernicious Medium of a Paper Currency with a legal Tender."[26]

The ministry's action on these petitions represented a shift among colonial authorities to a very rigid policy against legal tender paper money. Lord Shelburne favored repeal of the Currency Act, and while he was in charge of American affairs the colonists had some hope of getting rid of that measure. As late as the fall of 1767 colonial agents optimistically anticipated Parliamentary reform designed to permit the colonies to issue legal tender currency in restricted quantities. But the colonies' adverse reaction to the Townshend measures in late 1767 and early 1768 and, perhaps more important, the replacement of Shelburne with Hillsborough in the American Department ended all hope of Parliamentary action. Hillsborough had shared in formulating the Currency Act and had never wavered in support of it. The ministry failed even to bring the currency issue before Parliament in 1768, despite the plethora of petitions against the Currency Act from the American colonies,[27] and by April 1768 it had adopted the doctrinaire position which imperial officials followed for the remainder of the colonial period. "This Matter," Hillsborough informed North Carolina Governor Tryon at that time, "has already received so full a Discussion at the Board of Trade, at the Privy Council, and in each House of Parliament, and so strong and unanimous a Determination that Paper Currency with a legal Tender is big with Frauds, and full of Mischief to the Colonies, and to Commerce in general that I apprehend no Consideration of a possible

---

Va. Mag. of Hist. and Biog., 12 (1904), 11; Apr. 7, 11, 1767, *Va. Burgesses Journals, 1766-69*, 115-16, 125-29; R. C. Nicholas to ————, July 16, 1773, *Wm. and Mary College Qtly.*, 1st Ser., 20 (1911), 234; N. C. legislature's petition to Crown, Jan. 16, 1768, *N. C. Col. Recs.*, VII, 681-82.

26. Board of Trade to Crown, June 10, 1768, CO 5/1346; Hillsborough to Tryon, Apr. 16, June 11, 1768, *N. C. Col. Recs.*, VII, 709, 788-89; Upper House Journals, Nov. 8, 1768, *ibid.*, 892.

27. See Henry Eustace McCulloh to John Harvey, Sept. 13, 1767, *N. C. Col. Recs.*, VII, 517; Garth to S. C. Committee of Correspondence, Jan. 27, 1768, "Garth Correspondence," *S. C. Hist. and Geneal. Mag.*, 30 (1929), 183-84.

local Inconvenience will induce a Deviation from the sound Principles of the Act of Parliament relative thereto."[28]   This unwillingness to consider "possible local Inconveniences" when they involved making exceptions to established policy is a prime example of the inflexibility which characterized British colonial policy after 1767 and which was such an important element in the Americans' decision to seek solutions to their problems outside the British Empire.

After 1768 British statesmen, for all practical purposes, institutionalized the Currency Act and adamantly refused to consider any proposals for the establishment of legal tender currencies.   In the face of this development the lower houses of Georgia, South Carolina, and Virginia abandoned their attempts to secure the repeal or the amendment of the measure.   Only the North Carolina Lower House persisted in its efforts to emit a legal tender currency, making at least three such attempts between 1768 and 1774.   In December 1768 it directed agent Henry Eustace McCulloh to seek the repeal of the Currency Act, and Governor Tryon supported the agent's application. But Hillsborough informed Tryon even before he had heard from McCulloh that "no Petition that prays for Paper Currency as a Legal Tender can meet with success," because Crown officials could not accept any measure that was contrary to an act of Parliament.   Nor did Hillsborough change his mind as a result of McCulloh's entreaties.[29] A similar attempt in 1771 with the backing of both Tryon and his successor, Josiah Martin, also failed because of the ministry's opposition, and a final effort in March 1774 disappeared amid the excitement generated by the Intolerable Acts.[30]

The same doctrinaire attitude induced imperial authorities to disallow a 1769 South Carolina statute which did not make any addition to the colony's currency but merely provided for the printing of new bills to replace the £106,500 that had been circulating for nearly forty years.   These bills had not been replaced since 1748, and many of them were lost, destroyed, or worn out.   The Commons made the

28. Hillsborough to Tryon, Apr. 16, 1768, *N. C. Col. Recs.,* VII, 709.

29. N. C. Committee of Correspondence to McCulloh, Dec. 12, 1768, *ibid.,* 878-79; Tryon to Hillsborough, Feb. 25, 1769, Hillsborough to Tryon, Mar. 1, 1769, McCulloh to N. C. Committee of Correspondence, July 4, 1769, *ibid.,* VIII, 11-12, 17-18, 65; *North Carolina Gazette* (New Bern), Nov. 16, 1769.

30. Lower House Journals, Jan. 26, 1771, Mar. 23-24, 1774, *ibid.,* VIII, 471-72, IX, 937; Martin to Hillsborough, Aug. 15, 1771, Hillsborough to Martin, Dec. 4, 1771, *ibid.,* IX, 17-18, 65.

new bills, like the old ones, legal tender. Board of Trade counsel Richard Jackson found the legal tender provision "repugnant" to the provisions of the Currency Act and, despite the objections of Charles Garth, imperial authorities disallowed the law, making the entire new issue illegal. South Carolina merchant Henry Laurens branded the disallowance "a downright Robbery." "Those Tenders in Law have been our Property for Ages past," he wrote, "and cannot with any Colour of Justice be taken from us."[31] Had not the members of the Commons personally agreed to receive those bills and had not the Commons resolved to redeem them, the disallowance might have left the colony without any legal paper money.

Imperial refusal to permit the establishment of legal tender currency forced the lower houses in the southern royal colonies to turn to other expedients to solve their want of money. The obvious solution and the one least objectionable to imperial authorities was to issue non-legal tender paper notes—a course of action recommended by Garth to the South Carolina Commons in 1767. The Currency Act did not, after all, outlaw non-legal paper tender, and as a rule imperial authorities did not object to paper money issues if they were not made legal tender. Even Lord Hillsborough had suggested in 1769 that he would not be opposed to that kind of emission.[32] Georgia was the first colony to adopt this expedient. Between March 1765 and May 1770 the Georgia Commons provided for the emission of £8,120 to pay for several important public works.[33] The South Carolina Commons voted to emit £60,000 of public orders in 1767 to build a new exchange, customs house, and watchhouse in Charleston and £70,000 in 1770 to build courthouses and jails in newly created judicial districts.[34] Similarly, the North Carolina Lower House provided for the emission of £20,000 of debenture notes in 1768 to pay the forces

31. Cooper and McCord, eds., *S. C. Statutes*, IV, 312-14; Jackson to Board of Trade, Nov. 6, 1770, Order in Council, Dec. 9, 1770, S. C. Pub. Recs., XXXII, 351, 429-31, S. C. Arch. Dept.; Nov. 14, 1770, *Board of Trade Journals, 1768-75*, 211; Garth to S. C. Committee of Correspondence, Nov. 24, 1770, "Garth Correspondence," *S. C. Hist. and Geneal. Mag.*, 33 (1932), 118-19; Mar. 1, 6-7, 1771, S. C. Commons Journals, XXXVIII, 503, 506-7, S. C. Arch. Dept.; Laurens to John Hopton, Jan. 29, 1771, Laurens Letter Book, 1767-71, 598, S. C. Hist. Soc.

32. Garth to S. C. Committee of Correspondence, July 5, 1767, "Garth Correspondence," *S. C. Hist. and Geneal. Mag.*, 29 (1928), 300-301; Hillsborough to Tryon, Mar. 1, 1769, *N. C. Col. Recs.*, VIII, 17-18.

33. Statutes, *Ga. Col. Recs.*, XVIII, 639-48, 743-48; XIX, Pt. I, 83-89, 147-51, 161-98.

34. Cooper and McCord, eds., *S. C. Statutes*, IV, 257-61, 323-26.

sent to suppress riots around Hillsboro and £60,000 in 1771 to pay
the forces sent against the Regulators.[35]   Virginia's Burgesses also
found it necessary to make two issues, putting out £10,000 in paper
bills in 1769 to meet contingent expenses and £30,000 in 1771 to
relieve planters whose tobacco had been damaged in the flood of that
year.[36]

None of these issues was *declared* legal tender and they did not,
therefore, technically violate the restrictions of the Currency Act. But
imperial officials were unable to decide whether the clauses making
such notes redeemable for taxes and public obligations did not in
fact make them legal tender, and their policy towards these emissions
was inconsistent.   In June 1771 they disallowed a Georgia measure
of 1766 and the South Carolina law of 1769 for making the bills a
tender in payment of taxes.[37]   Although they permitted the rest of
the issuing statutes to stand, they warned Dunmore in December 1771
that the Virginia emission for that year might also contravene the
Currency Act and sharply censured James Habersham in February
1772 for consenting as acting governor to one of Georgia's emissions.[38]
Habersham found this censure difficult to take, and in complaining
to Governor Wright he pointed out the crux of the currency question
and, incidentally, the weakness of much of Britain's postwar colonial
policy.   "It is easy for People in England to speculate and refine,"
he wrote, "but here we must act as *Necessity requires,* which is an
infallible Rule."   The ministry, he lamented, "do not truly understand our local Circumstances."[39]   If there were no specie in the
colony and if legal tender issues of paper were prohibited, what other

35. Laws, *N. C. St. Recs.,* XXIII, 781-83, 850-51; Tryon to Hillsborough, Jan.
10, 1769, and July 2, 1770, *N. C. Col. Recs.,* VIII, 5-6, 212; Martin to Hillsborough,
Dec. 12, 26, 1771, Apr. 12, 1772, *ibid.,* IX, 67-68, 75-77, 278.

36. Hening, ed., *Va. Statutes,* VIII, 342-48, 501; Robert Carter Nicholas to Lord
Botetourt, Dec. 30, 1769, CO 5/1348; William Nelson to Hillsborough, July 15,
1771, CO 5/1349; Hillsborough to Dunmore, Dec. 4, 1771, CO 5/1349, 173-75; William Atchison to Charles Steuert, Jan. 2, 1770, Charles Steuert Papers, 5026, f. 2,
National Library of Scotland, Edinburgh.

37. In both instances it is probable that notes issued upon the authority of the
disallowed laws continued to circulate until it was time for their retirement.
Wright to Hillsborough, Dec. 26, 1768, unpubl. Ga. Col. Recs., XXVIII, Pt. II-B,
683-84, Ga. Dept. of Arch. and Hist.; Ga. Committee of Correspondence to Garth,
May 19, 1768, *Habersham Letters,* 72-73; June 27, 1771, *Acts of Privy Council,
Colonial,* V, 319-21.

38. Hillsborough to Dunmore, Dec. 4, 1771, CO 5/1349; Jackson to Board of
Trade, June 20, 1771, unpubl. Ga. Col. Recs., XXVIII, Pt. II-B, 762-64, Ga. Dept. of
Arch. and Hist.; Board of Trade to Habersham, Feb. 1, 1772, *ibid.,* XXXIV, 621-22.

39. Habersham to Wright, Dec. 4, 1772, *Habersham Letters,* 217.

course could a colony take to satisfy the demands of trade or to meet some emergency than to issue non-legal tender certificates supported by a government promise to accept them for taxes? Habersham was not the only American who realized that it was unreasonable and impractical to expect paper money to retain its value if it was not a tender at the office that issued it. Hillsborough's erratic policy towards non-legal tender issues was understandably galling to many American leaders, and such a rigid interpretation of the legal tender restriction was completely unrealistic.

Nevertheless, these issues of paper money helped to relieve the currency shortages in the four colonies. But in no case did they supply an adequate circulating medium; at best they provided only temporary relief. None of the four lower houses issued enough bills to replace the wartime issues as they were gradually retired. South Carolina's issues were woefully inadequate, especially in view of the colony's tremendous population growth during the 1760's and 1770's. Merchant William Fyffe wrote from Georgetown in 1767 that Carolinians were "in great Difficulties . . . not having a paper Currency allowed" them, and three years later the younger Bull reported that the scarcity of money made it necessary to carry on the colony's internal commerce by credit or barter. A prolonged controversy over the Commons' right to order money from the treasury without the governor's consent prevented any further emissions after 1769, and it is significant that, when the Commons gave up trying to solve that dispute within the context of the colonial constitution and began to act unilaterally in 1774, it issued paper certificates to pay the public debt that had accumulated during the five-year deadlock.[40] Virginia's situation was little better. By 1767 only slightly more than £200,000 of the currency issued during the war was still circulating. That amount fell to less than £100,000 by 1772, and specie was as scarce as ever. These conditions prompted the Burgesses to petition the Crown in 1769 for permission to establish a copper coinage, but the scheme was a long time in receiving the approval of the ministry and was not executed until 1775, just two months before the beginning of war. The non-legal tender issues of 1769 and 1771 helped to ease the situation; but for the entire period after 1767 Virginia was

40. W. Fyffe to James Fyffe, Aug. 3, 1767, Fyffe Papers, Clements Lib.; Bull to Hillsborough, Nov. 30, 1770, to Dartmouth, May 3, 1774, S. C. Pub. Recs., XXXII, 402, XXXV, 36-40, S. C. Arch. Dept.

without an adequate money supply.[41]   Similarly, in North Carolina the total amount of old legal tender bills in circulation fell from just £58,000 in 1770 to just under £43,000 in 1772.   Although the issues of 1768 and 1770 augmented these bills considerably, the Lower House's persistent efforts to obtain permission to emit a legal tender currency and to prevent the retirement of the old bills strongly suggest that the colony's currency supply was insufficient.[42]   By the early 1770's Georgia's currency problem was probably the most serious on the continent.   Its population and commerce were expanding at a phenomenal rate, but by 1773, when Wright induced the Commons to exchange all the old bills for new ones, there was only £4,819 still circulating—considerably less than the £12,000 sterling Wright had recommended in 1767 as an adequate sum to meet the colony's currency requirements.   Nor did the addition of £800 in March 1774 to pay for defending the colony's frontiers improve the situation. Georgia remained without a sufficient medium of exchange down to the Revolution.[43]

Certainly, the Currency Act drastically curtailed the lower houses' exercise of the power to emit paper money.   They had never secured more than a highly tenuous control over that power, and the doctrinaire enforcement of the Currency Act after 1764 absolutely prevented them from issuing any legal tender paper.   Coming during a period when a growing population and an expanding trade were aggravating the chronic shortage of specie and creating a demand for even more paper currency, it could scarcely have been more untimely and probably caused a severe economic hardship on all of the southern royal colonies.   Imperial authorities did permit small issues of non-legal tender notes to meet local emergencies, but these did not fulfill the colonies' money requirements.   The ministry's paper currency policy

41. Robert Carter Nicholas to ———————, July 16, 1773, *Wm. and Mary College Qtly.*, 1st Ser., 20 (1911), 234, and to Lord Botetourt, Dec. 30, 1769, CO 5/1348; Nov. 22, 1769, *Va. Burgesses Journals, 1766-69*, 278-79; Mar. 6, 1772, *ibid., 1770-72*, 218; John Norton to John Pownall, Oct. 22, 1773, CO 5/1351; Dartmouth to Dunmore, Apr. 5, 1775, CO 5/1353.

42. Tryon to Hillsborough, July 2, 1770, Martin to Hillsborough, Jan. 30, 1772, *N. C. Col. Recs.*, VIII, 212, IX, 231-33; *S.-C. Gazette* (Charleston), Mar. 14, 1768; *Georgia Gazette* (Savannah), Sept. 28, 1768.

43. Statutes, *Ga. Col. Recs.*, XIX, Pt. I, 418-26, Pt. II, 3-8; Wright to Board of Trade, Dec. 30, 1773, Jan. 20, 1775, Jackson to Board of Trade, May 25, 1775, unpubl. Ga. Col. Recs., XXVIII, Pt. II-B, 878-80, 895, 901, Ga. Dept. of Arch. and Hist.

towards the southern colonies exhibited an almost utter callousness, driving the North Carolina Lower House to the desperate measure of illegally suspending taxes granted to retire its paper bills.[44]   In 1773, after Dartmouth had succeeded Hillsborough as head of the American Department, Parliament made a belated general concession, permitting non-legal tender emissions receivable for taxes or other public obligations.   Had the Revolution not intervened just two years later, this concession might have laid the foundation for a permanent paper money system that would have satisfied both the mother country and the colonies.   The fact remains, however, that none of the four southern colonies actually did solve its financial problem before Independence, and they may have been responsible for the citing of the Currency Act as a violation of colonial rights by the First Continental Congress in its Declaration and Resolves in October 1774.[45]

Nor should the concession of 1773 obscure the impact of the Currency Act upon the Revolutionary movement.   For a decade after its enactment, it had important psychological effects, serving as a constant reminder that the economic well-being of the colonies was subordinate to the desires of the imperial government at the same time colonial lower houses were beginning to demand equality for the colonies within the empire.   Furthermore, the stubborn refusal of imperial authorities through the late sixties and early seventies to repeal the Currency Act or to relax their rigid interpretation of what constituted legal tender currency persuaded many Americans that British officials either did not understand or were utterly unmindful of colonial problems.   It helped to convince all of the southern lower houses that they could not count on the ministry for enlightened solutions to their problems—that, in fact, they were perhaps the only bodies capable of solving them.

Neither the Currency Act of 1764 nor the general instruction of 1767 ever became issues of first magnitude in any of the southern

44. See Tryon to Hillsborough, Feb. 10, 1769, *N. C. Col. Recs.*, VIII, 10; Martin to Hillsborough, Jan. 30, 1772, to Dartmouth, Jan. 13 and Apr. 2, 1774, *ibid.*, IX, 231-33, 817-18, 960-61; Council Journals, Jan. 25, 1772, Mar. 28, 1774, *ibid.*, 228, 954-55; Lower House Journals, Mar. 24, 1774, *ibid.*, 943-44.

45. Pickering *et al.*, eds., *Statutes at Large*, XXX, 113-14; Worthington C. Ford *et al.*, eds., *The Journals of the Continental Congress, 1774-1789*, 34 vols. (Washington, 1904-37), Oct. 14, 1774, I, 71.

royal colonies. They were always secondary to Parliament's attempts to tax the colonies. Nevertheless, both constituted a serious challenge to the authority of the lower houses. The general instruction threatened their control over membership, and the Currency Act effectively curtailed their power to issue legal tender paper money and created serious economic problems. Moreover, both stood as blatant exceptions to American theories of colonial equality with the mother country, and the general instruction in particular served as a constant and vexing reminder that imperial authorities still considered colonial lower houses subordinate bodies and would never accept their pretensions to equality with the British House of Commons.

Tightening the Reins:
Local Issues

In addition to the general issues raised by Parliament's attempts to tax the colonies, the general instruction of 1767, and the Currency Act of 1764, there were a number of local issues that agitated individual colonies in the years between 1763 and 1775. Most of them arose out of attempts by Crown officials to make the political systems of the colonies conform to imperial precedents and ideals. Because those attempts were piecemeal and often *ad hoc* responses to glaring discrepancies in the practice of a particular colony, their impact rarely reached beyond the borders of that colony. The result was that almost every colony had its own peculiar grievances against the imperial government. Among the southern royal colonies important local issues arose out of attempts by royal officials to curtail powers of lower houses in both the Carolinas and to prevent the Georgia Commons from pursuing precedents established in the older colonies. Only in Virginia, where Fauquier's delicate handling of the Board of Trade's attempt to separate the offices of speaker and treasurer between 1758 and 1766 prevented the eruption of the one potentially explosive issue, were there no special issues after 1763.

In South Carolina there were two serious local issues. The less important one concerned the question of judicial tenure, which had disturbed North Carolina earlier in the decade. By the 1760's the absence of courts outside Charleston was a serious grievance to the numerous backcountry settlers who were rapidly filling up the Pied-

mont. Many had to travel more than two hundred miles to court,
and beginning in 1743 they had frequently presented the Commons
with petitions asking that courts be created for their region. For the
most part, the Tidewater-dominated Commons blandly passed over
the requests, but Glen and later the younger Bull patiently pleaded
the justice of the petitions. At Bull's urging, the Commons agreed
to a measure to set up courts at Beaufort, Georgetown, and the Con-
garees in 1765, but the Council permitted it to die. The bill fell far
short of satisfying western demands but would have improved the
situation substantially. It was the complete lack of courts or other
law enforcement agencies that was chiefly responsible for producing
the South Carolina Regulator movement after 1767—an attempt by
westerners to take law enforcement into their own hands. And it
was this movement that finally stirred the Commons to establish
courts in the backcountry. In April 1768 the entire legislature consented to a circuit court act establishing six judicial districts outside
Charleston. But this measure soon ran into difficulty with London
officials.[1]

One of the Crown's prime objections to this measure was its provision concerning judicial tenure. The South Carolina Commons
had not previously demonstrated any interest in the question, but
the Stamp Act had stimulated it to re-evaluate its whole relationship
with the mother country, and in June 1766 it listed the fact that the
colony's judges were appointed during pleasure as a grievance and
resolved to instruct Garth to co-operate with agents from other colonies to secure appointments during good behavior. "The unconstitutional appointment of our Judges during pleasure must be very
galling to us Americans," the Commons' correspondence committee
wrote Garth, "particularly so, when we find ourselves partially and
undeservedly distinguished from our happier fellow Subjects, in this
respect residing in Great Britain." Garth broached this matter with
Lord Shelburne and learned that "the great difficulty arises from the
Manner in which those officers have their Salaries." He came away
with the impression that if judges' salaries were established upon a
permanent basis Shelburne, at least, would consent to appoint them
during good behavior. Before "they are removed from a State of

1. See Smith, *South Carolina as a Royal Province*, 133-41; Cooper and McCord,
eds., *S. C. Statutes*, VII, 194-205; Wallace, *South Carolina: A Short History*, 222-
30; Bull to Board of Trade, Mar. 15, 1765, S. C. Pub. Recs., XXX, 251, S. C.
Arch. Dept.

Dependency upon the Crown," Garth wrote the committee of correspondence in November 1766, "it is also expected they should be removed from any sort of Dependency upon the People."[2]

It is not surprising, therefore, that when the Commons finally got around to passing the circuit court act in April 1768 it should make the establishment of salaries for the chief and assistant justices contingent upon the Crown's appointing them during good behavior. This proviso represented an attempt to secure an alteration in judicial tenure by complying with the stipulations Shelburne had laid down to Garth two years earlier. But Shelburne had already relinquished the American Department to Hillsborough, who was almost inflexible in interpreting British policy towards the colonies. Garth found him "extreamly averse to advising the Crown to grant the Judges Commissions during good Behaviour." The Board of Trade echoed Hillsborough's sentiments, especially because the tenure proviso was directly contrary to the royal instruction forbidding governors to assent to measures altering judicial tenure without the Crown's prior approval. After Board counsel Matthew Lamb also reported unfavorably on the tenure clause, there was little doubt that the act would be disallowed. "The Idea of the desired alteration in the Judges Commissions is," Garth lamented, "inadmissible with the *present* Ministry." He predicted that that clause would "prove fatal to the Act," and, upon the Board of Trade's recommendation, the Crown disallowed the circuit court act in September 1768.[3]

The Commons was greatly disappointed by the Crown's decision. It meant that the backcountry would still be without courts and that something had to be done immediately to replace the disallowed law. Most of the measure was perfectly satisfactory to Crown officials, and there was little question that the new law would not differ materially from the old one. But it was uncertain what the House would do about judicial tenure, for it obviously had not altered its conviction that judges should serve during good behavior. It could have simply re-enacted the old bill without providing any salaries for the assistant

2. June 24, 1766, S. C. Commons Journals, XXXVII, 175-76, S. C. Arch. Dept.; S. C. Committee of Correspondence to Garth, July 2, 1766, Garth to S. C. Committee of Correspondence, Nov. 24, 1766, "Garth Correspondence," *S. C. Hist. and Geneal. Mag.*, 28 (1927), 228-29; 29 (1928), 120.

3. Garth to S. C. Committee of Correspondence, June 16, Aug. 14, 1768, "Garth Correspondence," *S. C. Hist. and Geneal. Mag.*, 30 (1929), 217-23; Lamb to Board of Trade, July 22, 1768, Board of Trade to Crown, Sept. 15, 1768, Hillsborough to Bull, Oct. 12, 1768, S. C. Pub. Recs., XXXII, 24-25, 47-48, 51-52, S. C. Arch. Dept.

judges, thus implying that it would not pay these officials so long as they held their posts during pleasure. But two of the assistant judges, Rawlins Lowndes and George Gabriel Powell, were key members of the House and were unwilling to serve on the circuit without a salary. Their influence was great enough that they were able to persuade the majority of the House in July 1769 to provide salaries for the assistant judges *"payable out of any monies that shall be in the treasury"* without insisting that the Crown make their tenure during good behavior. Probably the House hoped—as Garth had given it good reason to hope—that it might be able to secure a change in that policy later upon a change of ministry. By giving up its demands on tenure the Commons had removed the Crown officials' main objection to the law, and when the revised measure came before them in the fall, they promptly confirmed it.

But the Commons soon had cause to regret its somewhat hasty surrender. Shortly after the Crown had confirmed the circuit court bill, Hillsborough appointed four new judges from England to fill the chief justiceship and three assistant judgeships, thus depriving Lowndes and Powell—the chief advocates of giving up the fight for judicial tenure during good behavior—and the other Carolinian assistant justice, Daniel D'Oyley, of their posts. This step did nothing to improve relations between Crown officials and the South Carolina Commons. Rawlins Lowndes complained to the Commons in October 1772 that he and his colleagues had "lately been discharged from their Offices without any cause assigned or misbehaviour imputed to them contrary to the Spirit of the English Constitution which provides for Judges holding their Commissions during good Behaviour." Three years later, in 1773, Bostonian Josiah Quincy, Jr., found the Carolina legislators still embittered over the dismissal.[4]

A far more important issue in South Carolina involved the right of the Commons to issue money from the treasury without the consent of the governor and Council, a power that the Commons had assumed in the 1740's and 1750's. Although it directly violated the

4. S. C. Committee of Correspondence to Garth, July 7, 29, 1769, Garth to S. C. Committee of Correspondence, Dec. 10, 1769, "Garth Correspondence," *S. C. Hist. and Geneal. Mag.*, 31 (1930), 60-62, 137-39; Board of Trade to King, Nov. 22, 1769, Order in Council, Nov. 29, 1769, S. C. Pub. Recs., XXXII, 113-17, S. C. Arch. Dept.; Oct. 22, 1772, S. C. Commons Journals, XXXIX, 14, S. C. Arch. Dept.; entry of Mar. 11-12, 1773, Howe, ed., "Quincy Journal," Mass. Hist. Soc., *Proceedings*, 49 (1916), 448-50.

royal instruction requiring the governor's warrant for all disbursements, this practice was quietly acquiesced in by South Carolina governors and never came to the attention of Crown officials. But in the decade after 1763, the Commons ordered money from the treasury for purposes to which the governor and Council could not consent because of their obligation to preserve the royal prerogative. In August 1765 the Commons ordered Treasurer Jacob Motte to advance £600 sterling from the public funds to defray the cost of sending three of its number—Christopher Gadsden, John Rutledge, and Thomas Lynch—to the Stamp Act Congress in New York. Neither the younger Bull nor the Council approved of that action, but neither could prevent it at the time. When the Commons appropriated a sum to repay the treasurer in the next annual tax bill, both Bull and the Council allowed it to pass "sub silentio," as Bull later remarked, rather than provoke a violent dispute by rejecting it altogether. But a similar situation four years later produced the most serious dispute in the colony's history—the Wilkes fund controversy. That controversy arose late in 1769 as an aftermath of the disturbances over the Townshend Acts. The ensuing debate was intense and so aggravated the long-standing division between the Commons and the Council that it put an end to almost all effective joint legislative action for the remaining six years of the colonial period.[5]

The affair began quietly on December 8, 1769, when the Commons during the normal course of business ordered Motte to advance £1,500 sterling out of the treasury to a committee composed of Speaker Peter Manigault and six of its leading members—James Parsons, John Rutledge, Christopher Gadsden, Benjamin Dart, Thomas Lynch, and Thomas Ferguson. The Commons ordered its committee to send the money to Great Britain to "support . . . the just and Constitutional Rights and liberties of the People of Great Britain and America." The order was issued without the consent of the governor or Council, but at the same time—as was customary in such cases—the Commons resolved to reimburse the treasurer.[6] The committee promptly executed the Commons' order by remitting bills of exchange for the

5. Aug. 2, 1765, June 27, 1766, S. C. Commons Journals, XXXVII, 97, 194, S. C. Arch. Dept.; Bull to Hillsborough, Sept. 8, 1770, S. C. Pub. Recs., XXXII, 320-30, S. C. Arch. Dept. For a detailed treatment of the Wilkes fund affair, see Jack P. Greene, "Bridge to Revolution: The Wilkes Fund Controversy in South Carolina, 1769-1775," *Jo. of So. Hist.*, 39 (1963), 19-52.

6. Dec. 8, 1769, S. C. Commons Journals, XXXVIII, 215, S. C. Arch. Dept.

money to Robert Morris, secretary to the Society of the Gentlemen Supporters of the Bill of Rights in London. That society was formed to pay the debts of the indomitable John Wilkes. Since his attack on George III's speech from the throne in *North Briton* No. 45 on April 23, 1763, Wilkes had been popularly associated with the cause of liberty, and his imprisonment for various misdemeanors in early 1768 after his return from a long exile in France touched off demonstrations in both Britain and America, where the ministry's harassment of him and Parliament's attempts to tax the colonies were viewed as part of the same general assault upon liberty. That the Commons intended its grant to be used to support Wilkes is indicated by its committee's stipulation that the money be used "for supporting such of our Fellow Subjects who by asserting the Just Rights of the People, have or shall become obnoxious to administration, and suffer from the hand of Power."[7]

Neither Bull nor the Council could allow this bold act to pass "sub silentio." Wilkes was a center of attention in London, the very nemesis of George III and the ministry, and the Commons' grant was certain to receive some play in the press and quickly come to the attention of imperial authorities. Bull wisely resolved to break the news to them himself and immediately sent Hillsborough an account of the affair. To excuse himself and to explain his inability to prevent the Commons from sending the money, he noted that from "the great religious and Civil indulgences granted by the Crown to encourage Adventurers to settle in America, the Government of the Colonies has gradually inclined more to the democratical than regal side" and that "since the late unhappy discontents and the universal extension of the Claims of the American Commons" the power of the South Carolina Commons had "risen to a great heighth." So extensive was that power, Bull reported, that the House had adopted the practice of ordering money out of the treasury by its single authority "as less liable to obstruction from the Governor or Council" to its "pursuing any favorite object."[8]

When London officials received Bull's letter they were both indignant and astonished. The Commons' audacity in voting money to

7. S. C. Committee of Correspondence to Robert Morris, Esq., Dec. 9, 1769, "Garth Correspondence," *S. C. Hist. and Geneal. Mag.*, 31 (1930), 132-33.

8. Bull to Hillsborough, Dec. 12, 16, 1769, S. C. Pub. Recs., XXXII, 132-36, S. C. Arch. Dept.

support the ministry's most violent and effective critic deeply offended them, and they were amazed to learn that the Commons had acquired the power to order money out of the treasury without executive consent. Moving with unusual alacrity, they sought an opinion from Attorney General William De Grey, who reported early in February 1770 that the Commons could not "by the Constitution" order money from the treasury without the approval of the governor and Council. The Commons' exercise of that power, he declared, was contrary to the governor's commission and instructions and could not "be warranted by the modern practice of a few years, irregularly introduced, and improvidently acquiesced in." The assumptions were that the Commons could not alter the constitution of South Carolina or acquire new powers by usage and that both royal instructions and commissions took precedence over local practice. De Grey also questioned whether the Commons could vote money for any purpose other than purely local services and whether it could divert to different purposes money already appropriated by law. He concluded that the Commons' grant to Wilkes was illegal and suggested that "preventive measures for the future . . . to protect the subject from the Repetition of such exactions" should be taken either "by the Parliament here, or by Instructions to the Governor."

The Privy Council agreed with De Grey and on April 5 formally approved an additional instruction that embodied the substance of his report. It threatened the governor with removal if he assented to any revenue measures that did not appropriate money to specific purposes and that did not expressly limit the use of that money to the services for which it was appropriated. The instruction also directed that all money bills contain a clause subjecting the treasurer to permanent exclusion from public office and a penalty triple the sum involved if he issued money from the treasury solely upon the Commons' order. On April 14 Hillsborough transmitted the instruction to Bull along with a letter expressing hope that it would prevent further abuses.[9] Far from solving the problem, however, the instruction only further aggravated an already tense political situation in South Carolina.

Indeed, while the Board of Trade was preparing the additional

---

9. Report of De Grey, Feb. 13, 1770, Orders in Council, Apr. 3, 5, 1770, Hillsborough to Bull, Apr. 14, 1770, *ibid.*, 166-81, 233-34, 241-48, 253-55; Labaree, ed., *Royal Instructions*, I, 208-9.

instruction in London, the South Carolina Council was challenging the Commons' right to order money from the treasury without executive consent. In April 1770 it objected to the Commons' inclusion of an item in the annual tax bill to repay the Wilkes grant to the treasury. Declaring that the grant was a tacit affront to "His Majestys' Government" and in no "sense honourable, fit, or decent," the Council denied that the Commons could legally appropriate money for uses that did not directly concern the colony.

In reply the Commons outlined the position it would tenaciously adhere to for the next four years. It contended, somewhat speciously perhaps, that to grant money to support "the Just and Constitutional Rights and Liberties of the People of Great Britain and America" could hardly be "disrespectful or Affrontive to His Majesty, the great patron of the Liberty and Rights of all His Subjects." The Commons also declared that the Council's insinuation that there were limitations upon its authority to appropriate money inferred that some power "other than their own Representatives" could levy taxes upon the inhabitants. That "Seditious Doctrine," the Commons declared, "must manifestly tend, to increase the Discontents and Disorder which have but too long subsisted in his Majesty's American Dominions." Upon the central point at issue—whether or not it could issue money from the treasury by its sole authority—the Commons resolved that it had always "exercised a Right of Borrowing monies out of the Treasury," which it had always "faithfully and punctually" repaid, and that no governor had ever attempted to abridge that right. Here, the Commons was arguing that it could alter the constitution of South Carolina by its own action and that local precedents, habits, traditions, and statutes were important parts of that constitution—views directly opposite from those put forth by De Grey in London just two months earlier. From this vigorous defense the Commons took the offensive by pointing out "the inconsistency and absurdity" of the Council's acting as both an upper house of the legislature and an advisory council and resolved to ask the Crown to appoint a separate upper house "composed of independent men, and men of Property." This request was the logical culmination of both the Crown's recent policy of filling the Council with placemen who were not natives of the colony and the long-standing rivalry between the Commons and the Council that had seen the Council continuously decline in status and political influence within the colony.[10]

Before the Commons met again in August, the additional instruction had reached Charleston. Anticipating the storm it would raise, Bull chose to lay it casually before the Commons rather than chance the possibility of interrupting his good relations with that body by making too great an issue of it. As a former speaker of the Commons and as a keen observer of South Carolina politics, he knew that the House was unlikely to recede from its position even in the face of a royal mandate.[11] That he had gauged the temper of the House correctly was apparent from its treatment of the instruction.

The Commons immediately adopted ten resolutions that completely defied the instruction. Declaring that the instruction was based upon "false, partial and insidious" information, the Commons denied that it had recently assumed the power to order the treasurer to advance money without consulting the governor or Council and pointed out that it had exercised that power for some time and would continue to exercise it, repaying the money later in the annual tax law. Far from being unconstitutional, therefore, the vote of funds to the Bill of Rights Society was, the Commons asserted, "agreeable to the usage and practice both ancient and Modern of the Commons House of Assembly." That assertion clearly implied that precedent and usage were important elements in the constitution of the colony and that no mandate from the Crown could supersede the practice and custom of the colony. Categorically rejecting the instruction's contention that it could grant money only for local uses, the Commons affirmed its "undoubted Right" to vote funds for whatever services it thought fit and emphasized its disapproval of the instruction's requiring an insertion of certain clauses in money bills by boldly declaring that "Ministers dictating how a Money Bill shall be framed, is an Infringement of the Privileges of this House; to whom alone it belongs to Originate and prepare the same, for the concurrence and Assent of the Governor and Council without any Alteration or Amendment whatsoever." Finally, the Commons dared to suggest that its actions

10. Apr. 7-10, 1770, S. C. Commons Journals, XXXVIII, 387-92, S. C. Arch. Dept.; Bull to Hillsborough, Apr. 15, 1770, S. C. Pub. Recs., XXXII, 256-59, S. C. Arch. Dept.

11. Bull to Hillsborough, Aug. 23, 1770, S. C. Pub. Recs., XXXIII, 316-19, S. C. Arch. Dept.

would not have been considered dangerous "if the Money borrowed had not been applied towards frustrating the unjust and unconstitutional measures of an Arbitrary and Oppressive Ministry" and declared its intention of endeavoring to obtain the withdrawal of the instruction by presenting the affair in a true light to the home officials through its London agent.[12]

But the additional instruction was not immediately withdrawn and continued, in fact, to serve as the *cause célèbre* in local politics for five more critical years. The Council repeatedly refused to pass any money bill that did not comply with the instruction, and the Commons steadfastly adhered to its determination not to abandon its power to issue money from the treasury by its sole authority, despite a number of rather clumsy attempts by Governor Lord Charles Greville Montagu to force it to do so.[13] In London the ministry twice turned down applications to revoke the instruction, although Hillsborough did agree in June 1772 to withdraw its most objectionable sections if the Commons would pass a permanent declaratory act stipulating "that no Monies in the Treasurers Hands . . . be at any Time issued by Order of any one Branch of the Legislature singly and alone."[14] But this slight concession would not satisfy the Commons, and the legislative impasse continued. Indeed, Montagu goaded the Commons into an even more determined opposition by calling the legislature to meet in Beaufort instead of Charleston and by dissolving four Houses during his eighteen-month administration from September 1771 to March 1773.[15] The *South-Carolina Gazette* complained in early 1773 that "By an unparalleled Succession of Prorogations and Dissolutions, the Inhabitants of this Province have been

---

12. Aug. 29, 1770, S. C. Commons Journals, XXXVIII, 430-33, S. C. Arch. Dept.; S. C. Committee of Correspondence to Garth, Sept. 6, 1770, "Garth Correspondence," *S. C. Hist. and Geneal. Mag.*, 31 (1930), 244-46.

13. Sept. 7, 1770, Jan. 31, Feb. 7, 9, 26, Oct. 2, Nov. 4-5, 1771, Oct. 29, Nov. 10, 1772, Mar. 19, 22, Aug. 13, 18, Sept. 8, 11, 1773, S. C. Commons Journals, XXXVIII, 453-56, 474-76, 487-88, 497-99, 543, 577-84, XXXIX, Pt. I, 20-29, Pt. II, 14, 21-22, 37-40, 48-49, 73-95, S. C. Arch. Dept.

14. Garth to S. C. Committee of Correspondence, Mar. 27, Apr. 5, 1771, June 3, 25, 1772, Board of Trade to Privy Council's Plantation Affairs Committee, Mar. 27, 1771, Garth's Memorial to Hillsborough, [June 2, 1772], "Garth Correspondence," *S. C. Hist. and Geneal. Mag.*, 33 (1932), 125-31, 238-44; Hillsborough to Montagu, July 1, 1772, S. C. Pub. Recs., XXXIII, 164, S. C. Arch. Dept.

15. Nov. 5, 1771, Oct. 29, Nov. 10, 1772, S. C. Commons Journals, XXXVIII, 579-84, XXXIX, Pt. I, 20-29, S. C. Arch. Dept.; *S.-C. Gazette* (Charleston), Apr. 16, Nov. 12, 1772, Jan. 14, 1773.

unrepresented in Assembly about three Years" and asked *"Whether this is a Grievance?* And, *if it is,* Whether it is one of *the least Magnitude?"*[16] Nor was Bull any more successful in restoring harmony after Montagu had given up and returned to Britain in the spring of 1773, for the Council's aggressive efforts to force the Commons to comply with the additional instruction in the late summer of 1773 only provoked House leaders to launch a formidable assault upon the Council's power to act in a legislative capacity.[17]

This attack resulted in an exchange of pamphlets that perhaps better than any other surviving records indicates, the wide gulf between the contending parties in the Wilkes fund controversy. To counter the Commons' appeal against the Council in Britain, Sir Egerton Leigh, councilor and attorney general in South Carolina, published in January 1774 his *Considerations on Certain Political Transactions of the Province of South Carolina.* In defending the additional instruction of April 1770 and the Council's adherence to it, Leigh argued that "Our Constitution is *derivative,* and entirely flows from the Crown." The implications of this argument were that the constitutions of the colonies were, as Leigh remarked, "wholly *ex gratia,"* that colonial lower houses owed their existence not to any inherent right of the freeholders in the colonies to be represented but only to the King's pleasure, and that they had no rights except those that were derived from the royal commissions and instructions or from the sanction of the Crown. Although he recognized that the power of the South Carolina Commons had, in practice, increased to the point at which the "due equipoise" of the constitution had been upset, he denied that this development was permanent. Contending that precedents of "new Communities" and *"Infant Societies"* were "of very little weight," he declared that the Commons could not extend its power "beyond the original views and intention of those from whom they derive their whole authority" and denied that the Commons could by the practice of a few years change the constitution of the colony or acquire new powers. Thus the Commons' claim to the power to order money from the treasury by its sole authority was untenable and the Wilkes vote was "an unconstitutional and unwarrantable stretch of Power." One of the functions of the Crown was

16. *S.-C. Gazette* (Charleston), Feb. 22, 1773.
17. Aug. 13, Sept. 8, 11, 1773, S. C. Commons Journals, XXXIX, Pt. II, 39-40, 73-95, S. C. Arch. Dept.; *S.-C. Gazette* (Charleston), Sept. 13, 1773.

to check such *"novel Invention."* Because legislative bodies were "equally liable with Individuals to be misled by passion, fancy, or caprice," they had to "have boundaries, restraints, and limitations." The additional instruction was, then, "only a *Remembrancer,*" a *"timely. Correction"* to *"check"* a "departure from the Constitution" and to point out "the proper practice." For similar reasons, Leigh argued that the Commons' claim that the Council was not an upper house was invalid. Although he conceded the Commons' point that the Council did not stand upon the same independent footing as the House of Lords, he argued that it derived its right to act as an upper house from the royal commission and instructions—the same instructions to which the Commons owed its legislative authority. That the Crown should uphold the Council's power to act in a legislative capacity was particularly important at such a critical juncture, when the "bands of our Society are now loosened, the plan of his Majesty's Government totally disordered, and the Commons are the *vortex* which swallows all the power."[18]

This pamphlet sent Leigh's old enemy, Henry Laurens, who was then in London, to gather materials with which to refute Leigh's arguments. At his urging and with financial backing and editorial help from both him and Ralph Izard, Jr., Virginian Arthur Lee prepared an *Answer,* which was published the following April.[19] Lee proceeded from entirely different assumptions and ended up with opposite conclusions. He dismissed Leigh's argument that the "Constitution and Liberties of the Provinces" were "merely *ex gratia,* flowing wholly from the Bounty of the Crown" as a doctrine that went "back somewhat more than a Century, into the Days of omnipotent Prerogative." Rather, he argued that rights were inherent, not permissive, and that South Carolinians were entitled to all of the traditional rights of Englishmen. The inference was that the existence of

18. [Sir Egerton Leigh], *Considerations on Certain Political Transactions of the Province of South Carolina* (London, 1774), 15, 18, 21-22, 25-26, 37, 42, 60.

19. On the authorship of these pamphlets and the preparation and printing of the *Answer to Considerations on Certain Political Transactions of the Province of South Carolina* (London, 1774), see Henry Laurens to John L. Gervais, Jan. 24, 1774, to James Laurens, Jan. 27, Feb. 17, Mar. 2, Apr. 13, 1774, to John Laurens, Jan. 28, Feb. 18, Apr. 8, 1774, to James Crokatt, Feb. 16, 1774, to Alexander Garden, Feb. 19, Apr. 13, 1774, Laurens Letter Book, 1772-74, 191-92, 194-96, 202, 211-21, 238-40, 261-62, 274-79, S. C. Hist. Soc.; Ralph Izard, Jr., to Edward Rutledge, May 25, 1775, A. I. Deas, ed., *Correspondence of Mr. Ralph Izard of South Carolina, from the Year 1774 to 1804* (New York, 1844), 77.

the Commons House depended not on the Crown's pleasure as expressed in the original charter to the colony or on the commission and instructions but on the fundamental and unalterable right of the freeholders of South Carolina to be represented. "The Rights and Privileges of that Commons House," Lee wrote, "spring from the Rights and Privileges of *British* Subjects, and are coequal with the Constitution. They were neither created, nor can they be abolished by the Crown." On the assumption that precedent and usage were just as important in shaping the constitution of South Carolina as they were in determining the British constitution, Lee argued in direct contrast to Leigh that "what has prevailed from the Beginning of the Colony, without Question or Controul, is Part of the Constitution." He thus implied that the South Carolina Commons, like the British House of Commons, could change the constitution by long usage not challenged by the Crown and that changes so made could not be undone by the unilateral action of the Crown. Unlike Leigh, who argued from the point of view that the constitution of the colony was static, Lee suggested that it was constantly changing. Thus, the vote to Wilkes was "not Novel" but *"constitutional in its Mode, and laudable in its Intention"* because it *"was agreeable to the Usage and Practice, both antient and modern, of the Commons House of Assembly in the Province of South Carolina."* The additional instruction was "clearly unconstitutional" and "an arbitrary and dangerous Interposition of Prerogative" because it attempted to curtail the "ancient and undoubted" power of the Commons to issue money from the treasury by its sole authority and because it violated the Commons' exclusive control over money matters by prescribing the form in which money bills should be framed. The issue was simply whether the Commons should bow to the "unconstitutional Mandate of a Minister" and "make a formal Surrender" of its "Privileges and the Rights of the People" or whether the Crown should "retract from an Attempt . . . arbitrarily to interfere in the Exercise of that which is the peculiar and incommunicable Power of the Commons."[20]

But neither of these pamphlets had any noticeable impact;[21] by

20. [Arthur Lee], *Answer*, 3, 12, 29-30, 43, 45-46, 48, 51-53, 59, 63, 101-4, 111, 120.

21. Leigh's pamphlet was not noted in the Charleston newspapers until Sept., and the *Answer* was not mentioned at all. *S.-C. Gazette* (Charleston), Sept. 19, 1774. Only 42 copies of the *Answer* sold during the first month in London. See Henry Laurens to James Laurens, May 12, 1774, to Ralph Izard, Jr., Sept. 20, 1774, Laurens Letter Book, 1772-74, 305-8, 365-68, S. C. Hist. Soc.; Laurens to

the time of their publication the storm over the Tea Act and the Coercive Acts had eclipsed both the Wilkes fund controversy and the dispute over the Council's right to act as an upper house. Crown officials, Garth reported in April 1774, were so preoccupied with "all the Measures affecting Boston" that South Carolina matters had been pushed far down the agenda.[22] Still, the Commons never abandoned its intention of getting around the additional instruction. South Carolina patriots inevitably looked at broader imperial measures in terms of their particular problems, viewing the Coercive Acts as a precedent by which the ministry could justify a law to "Cram down the Instruction of the 14th April and every other Mandate which Ministers Shall think proper for keeping us in Subjection to the Task Master who Shall be put over us."[23]

The spring of 1774 marked the beginning of the fifth successive year of deadlock between imperial authorities and the Commons over the issues raised by the additional instruction, and there was little prospect of immediate solution. Bull reported in March 1774 that the Commons still demanded as its "sine quibus non" that the £1500 sterling be replaced and that no money bills be passed in the form stipulated by the instruction, and Dartmouth and his colleagues in the ministry were unflinching in their insistence that the Commons either adhere to the instruction or pass a declaratory act stipulating that it would not issue money from the treasury solely on its own authority.[24]

Events that spring finally led to the Commons' devising a means to ignore the additional instruction altogether. Unrest among the Indians on the southern frontier made the need for defensive meas-

---

Izard, Feb. 10, 1775, "Izard-Laurens Correspondence," *S. C. Hist. and Geneal. Mag.*, 22 (1921), 1-3.

22. Garth to Committee of Correspondence, Apr. 21, 1774, Garth Letter Book, 1765-75, 171, S. C. Arch. Dept. See also Henry Laurens's remark that "the Complexion of the Times" would prevent a hearing on the dispute with the Council. To James Laurens, Feb. 5, 1774, Laurens Letter Book, 1772-74, 198-201, S. C. Hist. Soc.

23. Henry Laurens to John L. Gervais, to Thomas Savage, Apr. 9, 1774, Laurens Letter Book, 1772-74, 266, 268-73, S. C. Hist. Soc.

24. Dartmouth to Bull, Oct. 28, 1773, Jan. 8, May 4, 1774, Bull to Dartmouth, Mar. 10, 1774, S. C. Pub. Recs., XXXIII, 335, XXXIV, 2-3, 15-19, 33-34, S. C. Arch. Dept.; Henry Laurens to James Laurens, Mar. 11, 1773, to Alexander Garden, Apr. 8, 1773, Laurens Letter Book, 1772-74, 59-62, 96-97, S. C. Hist. Soc.; Garth to Committee of Correspondence, May 20, July 5, Nov. 13, 1773, Garth Letter Book, 152, 155, 157, S. C. Arch. Dept.

ures urgent. To provide some rangers to patrol the critical area, the Commons introduced a money bill without the penalties on the treasurers required by the additional instruction. It hoped that public opinion would force the Council to accept the measure and thereby admit the Commons' right to pass money bills without the objectionable clauses specified by the instructions. But the Council preferred to assume the blame for not defending the frontier rather than offend the ministry by passing a revenue measure that did not conform to the instruction. By rejecting the bill the Council gave the Commons an excuse for adopting a radical measure. Taking matters into its own hands, it proceeded to audit accounts of all public creditors to January 1, 1773, and without consulting either Bull or the Council ordered its clerk to issue certificates of indebtedness signed by him and five representatives to pay those accounts. The Commons promised to redeem the certificates the first time it succeeded in passing a tax bill, and its members as well as the Chamber of Commerce pledged to accept them as currency. The Council vigorously protested this action, and Bull prorogued the legislature; but everyone in the colony except Bull—including even the councilors—accepted the certificates. The success of this measure made the passage of a tax bill less imperative and enabled the Commons to sidestep the issues embodied in the additional instruction.[25]

Ironically, at the very time the Commons was acting unilaterally to ameliorate the colony's fiscal plight, imperial authorities were modifying the instruction. As early as June 1773 Garth had urged Dartmouth to revoke the instruction because the bonds designed by Bull in 1770 to be signed by the treasurers prevented them from applying money except by ordinance or act of all three branches of the legislature. After Montagu's resignation in the spring of 1773, Garth persuaded South Carolina's new governor, Lord William Campbell, that withdrawal of the instruction was absolutely necessary. Upon Campbell's request colonial officials omitted it from his instructions so that the South Carolina representatives would "have no longer any pretense to say that they are not left at liberty to frame their Money Bills as they think fit." At the same time, however, they inserted another instruction absolutely prohibiting Campbell to pass any bill to replace money ordered out of the treasury by the sole authority of the

25. Bull to Dartmouth, Mar. 24, May 3, 1774, S. C. Pub. Recs., XXXIV, 21-22 36-40, S. C. Arch. Dept.

Commons, thus making it clear that they were neither recognizing the Commons' power to order money from the treasury without executive approval nor consenting to the repayment of the money sent to Wilkes.[26]

That this arrangement would have satisfied the Commons is highly unlikely, but the Commons never had an opportunity either to accept or to reject it. The ministry did not inform Bull of the precise changes in the instructions, and by the time Campbell arrived in the colony in June 1775 the Wilkes fund controversy had been pushed into the background by questions of greater moment.[27] A shooting war had broken out in Massachusetts, and the Carolinians had turned their attention to the broader questions of American rights.[28] The Wilkes fund dispute ended in stalemate with neither the Commons nor Crown officials ever having yielded on the question of the Commons' right to issue money from the treasury by its single authority.

With the Wilkes fund controversy a number of earlier political developments and issues came to a culmination. The Commons' exclusive control over all financial matters had been the central issue in South Carolina politics from the introduction of royal government in 1721 until the mid-1750's. The antipathy of the Commons towards the royal instructions and the argument that they were not binding upon the legislature derived from the 1720's and had acquired increasing currency in succeeding decades. The Council had been declining in prestige and political effectiveness since the 1740's, and the denial of its legislative authority was a reiteration of an earlier suggestion.

26. Garth to Dartmouth, June 16, 1773, Dartmouth to Bull, May 4, 1774, Dartmouth et al., to Crown, June 20, 1774, ibid., XXXIII, 277-78, XXXIV, 33-34, 47-52; Labaree, ed., Royal Instructions, I, 210; Campbell to Dartmouth, Apr. 2, 1774, Dartmouth MSS, II, 306; Garth to Rawlins Lowndes, Feb. 1, 1773, to Committee of Correspondence, Nov. 13, 1773, Mar. 11, Apr. 21, July 19, 1774, Garth Letter Book, 141, 157, 165, 171-72, 178-79, S. C. Arch. Dept.; Henry Laurens to John Laurens, Apr. 8, 1774, to John L. Gervais, Apr. 9, 16, 1774, Laurens Letter Book, 1772-74, 261-62, 268-73, 283-84, S. C. Hist. Soc.; Henry Laurens to John Laurens, Apr. 19, May 10, 1774, "Laurens Correspondence," S. C. Hist. and Geneal. Mag., 4 (1903), 101, 107.

27. See Dartmouth to Bull, Dec. 10, 1774, Alexander Innes to Dartmouth, May 1, 1775, S. C. Pub. Recs., XXXIV, 222, XXXV, 92-99, S. C. Arch. Dept.; Innes to Dartmouth, May 16, 1775, Dartmouth MSS, 1270, William L. Salt Library, Stafford, Staffordshire, Eng.; Jan. 25, 1775, S. C. Commons Journals, XXXIX, Pt. II, 180-81, S. C. Arch. Dept.

28. July 11, 24, 29, 1775, S. C. Commons Journals, XXXIX, Pt. II, 293, 302-5, S. C. Arch. Dept.

The controversy also produced a constitutional impasse, making it absolutely clear that a wide and, for the moment at least, an unbridgeable gulf existed between the notions of the ministry and those of the Commons about the constitution of the empire. The ministry's shock at the Wilkes vote and its doctrinaire insistence upon adhering to the additional instruction left no doubt that British officials were firmly committed to the old imperial ideals. Despite abundant evidence to the contrary, they still insisted that the colonies were subordinate political units with constitutions fixed for all time by the charters, commissions, and instructions and with only a small measure of representative government through inferior legislative bodies that were subject to both ministerial and Parliamentary control. On the other hand, the Commons' sustained opposition revealed its intense devotion to the principle of a dynamic constitution in which as the representative part it was a central and constructive force just as the House of Commons in Britain was the dominant element in the British constitution.

Most important, the Wilkes fund controversy was instrumental in bringing South Carolina politicians to a full realization of the nature of the political challenge involved in Britain's new colonial policy. Henry Laurens correctly interpreted the broader aims of British policy and the additional instruction as a "Scheme . . . to reduce us to the State of a Country Corporation." In attempting to curtail the Commons' authority to order money from the treasury without executive consent, the ministry was challenging a power that the Commons had exercised without contest for two decades, and the additional instruction stood as a blatant symbol of the slight regard held by imperial authorities for the rights of American lower houses. The South Carolina Commons shared Henry Laurens's belief that "the Representative Body of the People in Carolina, when regularly Assembled, have and ought to enjoy all the Rights and Privileges of a free People—or in other words—all the Rights and Privileges, as a Branch of the Legislature, which are held, enjoyed and exercised by the House of Commons of Great Britain."[29] Its stubborn resistance indicated how vital those rights were to American legislators and how far they would go to preserve the political structures they had built over the previous century.

29. Henry Laurens to James Laurens, Dec. 12, 1771, Laurens Letter Book, 1771-72, 95-104, S. C. Hist. Soc.

For five crucial years beginning in December 1769 the Wilkes grant was the central issue in South Carolina politics, interrupting the normal process of government and contributing to the rise of an intense bitterness towards the ministry among South Carolina politicians. For them the description in the *Gazette* of a statue of Lord Hillsborough inscribed with the motto "Massachusetts is my wash-pot, and South Carolina my Footstool" was no idle jest. "What Shall we Say," lamented Henry Laurens in April 1774 on the eve of the modification of the instruction, "of the Injury done to a province by a Ministerial Mandate held over that province and totally Stagnating public business for four Years." In October 1774, after one of the frequent prorogations, the *South-Carolina Gazette* complained that "we *still continue* in the Situation we have been for some Years past . . . with little more than a *nominal* Legislative Representation."[30] No annual tax bill was passed in South Carolina after 1769 and no legislation at all after February 1771. For all practical purposes royal government in South Carolina broke down four years earlier than it did in any of the other colonies. There was no period of quiet in South Carolina. While the flames of revolution cooled elsewhere in the colonies after the repeal of most of the Townshend duties in 1770, the Wilkes fund controversy kept the fires of revolt burning brightly in South Carolina. Along with the fight over the location of the capital in Massachusetts and similar, less intense issues in other colonies, it stood as glaring testimony to the fact that, despite the repeal of most of the Townshend taxes, there was no relaxation in the broader objectives of the new colonial policy. With the exception of Parliamentary taxation no other issue was so important in persuading South Carolina politicians that their political fortunes would never be secure so long as they were subject to the whims of a group of politicians over whom they had no control and from whom they could expect no sympathetic treatment of their grievances.

In North Carolina, as in South Carolina, there were two important local issues in the decade after 1765. The first concerned the right of the Lower House to nominate the colonial agent. It began as an internal dispute between the House and the Council, but authorities at Whitehall eventually became involved. A continuation of a

30. Laurens to John L. Gervais, Apr. 16, 1774, Laurens Letter Book, 1772-74, 283-84, S. C. Hist. Soc.; *S.-C. Gazette* (Charleston), Sept. 6, 1773, Oct. 24, 1774.

question that had agitated the colony since 1758, when the Lower House had sought to appoint James Abercromby agent under its exclusive jurisdiction, the dispute had been temporarily settled in 1761 with the appointment of Couchet Jouvencal for a term of two years, after the House had consented to permit some councilors to sit on the committee of correspondence. But the Council's victory had proved to be a hollow one, for assemblymen on the correspondence committee continued to act without consulting Council members. When the question of Jouvencal's reappointment as agent came up in early 1764, the Council insisted that a councilor be present to constitute a quorum. But the House rejected the proviso and unilaterally appointed Jouvencal to act under the direction of a committee composed solely of representatives. Subsequent attempts to obtain a regular appointment of an agent failed in November 1764 when the Council refused to consent to the nominee of the Lower House and in May 1765 when the House, by that time resolved to exclude the Council from any share in controlling the agent, refused even to allow councilors to sit on the committee of correspondence and forced through a provision to pay Jouvencal, despite the fact that neither the governor nor the Council had consented to his appointment.

These actions caused Tryon to submit the whole matter to the Board of Trade. He protested against the House's continued exclusion of councilors from the committee of correspondence and suggested that the Board might solve the matter by refusing to receive applications "presented by the Agent, coming solely from the Assembly." The Board declined to intervene in the dispute at that point but declared that if the Lower House continued to exclude the Council from participating in the committee it would then "consider what step it may be proper for His Majesty to take."[31]

But the continued refusal of both houses to compromise made settlement of the controversy improbable. It might have been satisfactorily adjusted had the House consented to allow the Council to participate in the committee of correspondence and had it been will-

31. Lower House Journals, Nov. 15, 1764, *N. C. Col. Recs.*, VI, 1240; Upper House Journals, Nov. 19, 1764, May 18, 1765, *ibid.*, 1287-88, VII, 59-60; Tryon to Board of Trade, Aug. 15, 1765, Board of Trade to Tryon, Nov. 29, 1765, *ibid.*, VII, 107, 132-33. The Council could have prevented Jouvencal's payment by rejecting the accounts committee's report, but to have done so would have raised an even greater dispute, and the Council consented to his full payment. Upper House Journals, Jan. 15, 1768, *ibid.*, 622.

ing to make the presence of one councilor necessary for the committee to do business. But the House insisted upon the exclusive right to nominate the agent, and until the Council recognized that right it was not disposed to make any concessions. When Tryon reconvened the legislature in November 1766 for the first time since the Stamp Act troubles had begun, the Lower House ruled out all prospects for an immediate settlement by vigorously condemning the Council's stand. In "every other part of his Majesty's American Dominions, where the Constitution is similar to that of this Province," the House asserted, "the Representatives of the people enjoy the priviledges of naming an agent" and the "concurrence of the other Branches of the Legislature" is "considered as necessary only to give a sanction to such nomination." It therefore appealed to Tryon "to exert every practicable endeavour to restore the people to the exercise of their just rights and priviledges." Tryon was unwilling to admit that the governor and Council could only sanction the House's appointee but offered to consent to whomever the two houses could agree on until he had submitted the matter to the Crown for a decision. But the House despaired of ever convincing the Council to waive its claim to a share of the right of nomination and temporarily abandoned its attempt to secure a regularly appointed agent, leaving the colony unrepresented in London.[32]

The colony's affairs suffered without an agent, and it was only a question of time before the House would renew its attempts. Former North Carolina councilor Henry Eustace McCulloh began a tireless campaign in the fall of 1767 with Speaker John Harvey and other representatives to obtain the agency for himself, and his urgings were important in inducing the House to act. Hillsborough himself reiterated McCulloh's entreaties, declaring in November 1768 "that the Affairs of No. Carolina must, in some degree, necessarily suffer delay and disappointment for want of a regular Agent here."[33] But the attempt by the Lower House in December 1768 to appoint McCulloh for one year to lobby for the repeal of objectionable Parliamentary statutes met the same fate as its earlier proposals and succeeded only in reviving the old controversy. The Council again refused its con-

32. Lower House Journals, Nov. 6, 10, 1766, Upper House Journals, Dec. 1, 1766, ibid., 337, 348-49, 356.
33. See McCulloh to John Harvey, Sept. 13, 1767, to Col. Fanning, May 20, 1768, ibid., 517-18, 753-54; Hillsborough to Tryon, Nov. 15, 1768, ibid., 868.

sent because there was no provision for councilor participation in the correspondence committee, and the House again proceeded unilaterally to make the appointment.[34]

Oddly enough, McCulloh's appointment set the stage for the settlement of the controversy. Previously, when the House had appointed Abercromby and Jouvencal without the Council's concurrence, Crown officials had willingly received them and worked with them throughout their tenure in office. But they reacted quite differently to McCulloh. Hillsborough informed him "that stricter regulations had for sometime taken place in American Affairs, and that it was determined that the Assent of the Governor, Council, and Assembly, formally expressed by an Act of the whole legislature, was necessary to Invest a person with the Character of a provincial Agent," and the Board of Trade refused to consider a petition from him until he could produce "testimonials of his being authorized to act . . . as agent for the province of North Carolina." Discouraged by these rebuffs, McCulloh strongly recommended to the North Carolina correspondence committee that his appointment be changed to conform to "the mode which Government here has declared necessary." McCulloh's experience convinced the House that it was absolutely necessary to secure a regular appointment for him and put it in a mood to compromise. When the legislature met in the fall of 1769, the House brought in a bill to appoint McCulloh and offered to allow the Council to appoint some members to the committee of correspondence. The Council accepted the offer and contributed to the compromise by neither making an issue over the right of nomination nor insisting that the presence of a councilor be required for the correspondence committee to act.[35]

The stand of the imperial authorities had forced the Lower House to abandon its quest for exclusive control over the agent, but significantly, the six-year controversy had gained nothing for the Council. McCulloh's appointment was identical with that of Jouvencal—the last regular agent—in 1761. In effect, the Council had capitulated.

34. Lower House Journals, Jan. 7, 1768, Upper House Journals, Dec. 2, 5, 1768, *ibid.*, 641-42, 918, 924; N. C. Committee of Correspondence to McCulloh, Dec. 12, 1768, *ibid.*, 877-79; Tryon to Hillsborough, Feb. 25, 1769, *ibid.*, VIII, 11.

35. McCulloh to N. C. Committee of Correspondence, July 14, 1769, to John Harvey, Jan. 26, 1770, *ibid.*, 56-57, 172; Tryon to Hillsborough, Nov. 22, 1769, *ibid.*, 151; Laws, *N. C. St. Recs.*, XXV, 518; Apr. 18, 1769, *Board of Trade Journals, 1768-75*, 88.

The Lower House's right to nominate, appoint, and assume the major —almost exclusive—role in directing the agent was now unchallenged. Through its majority on the committee—the Lower House appointed five of the eight members—it still had a close control over the agent. At the end of McCulloh's appointment in 1771 the House extended it for another two years but thereafter did not renew it. McCulloh's failure to win a favorable decision on a 1773 court bill was probably the major factor in deciding the House to dispense with his services and to abandon the institution of a regular agent. The growing intensity of the controversy with Britain made it difficult for agents to function effectively, and although the House did appoint Thomas Barker and Alexander Elmsley in the spring of 1774 to secure a settlement of the court issue, many North Carolina representatives had undoubtedly come to believe with Samuel Johnston that an agent was unnecessary except "on particular occasions and for special purposes."[36]

A more important issue concerned North Carolina's right in actions for debt to attach property of foreigners, even those who had never resided in the colony. The Lower House had regularly provided for such attachments by a clause in its superior court bills without complaint from Crown officials. But in December 1770 the Board of Trade objected to the provision because it was without precedent in English common law. There was no question about the right of creditors to attach the property of absconding debtors; British creditors had long enjoyed it. But what Crown officials did object to was the attempt by North Carolina and other American colonies to extend that right to cover the effects of Britons who had never resided in the colonies. Cases involving British debtors, Crown officials insisted, should be tried in British courts, and in February 1772 the Crown issued an additional instruction to all royal governors forbidding them to assent to bills providing for the attachment of the effects of people who had never resided in the colony. When the North Carolina superior court bill expired in 1773, Governor Martin presented the Lower House with the additional instruction along with a recommendation that the superior court bill be renewed. But in preparing

---

36. Laws, *N. C. St. Recs.*, XXIII, 854; Martin to Hillsborough, Mar. 1, 1772, Elmsley to Johnston, May 17, 1774, Johnston to Alexander Elmsley, Sept. 23, 1774, *N. C. Col. Recs.*, IX, 253, 999-1000, 1071; Lower House Journals, Dec. 21, 1773, *ibid.*, 785.

the measure to continue that law, the House simply ignored the instruction and retained the attachment clause, modifying it only slightly by extending the time allowed for defendants to replevy. Martin had to reject the measure, and it appeared likely that a bitter contest would ensue. In late February he wrote Secretary of State Dartmouth of the House's proceedings and reported that he had been informed that a majority of the members had entered into "a temperate but firm resolution" to be without courts of justice rather than conform to the additional instruction. Such sentiments made it abundantly clear that the House could not be induced to accept the additional instruction, and Martin wisely abandoned the attempt.

Instead, Martin determined to transfer to London officials the odium of denying the colony the right of attachment and offered to pass the superior court bill with the attachment provision if the House would add a clause suspending the execution of the bill until it had received imperial approval. The offer represented the only positive course of action open to the House, but it acquiesced only after resolving *nemine contradicente* that the right of attaching the property of foreigners had "been long exercised by the inhabitants of this Province in common with other Provinces in America and several Trading Cities, Liberties and Franchises of Great Britain," that that right had "been found greatly beneficial to the Trade and Commerce of this Country and the security and property of Individuals," and that the House could not "by any . . . public act . . . relinquish that right without at the same time abandoning the interest of their Constituents, and the peace and happiness of this Colony." This declaration left no doubt as to the House's position. Even an adverse decision by imperial authorities would not persuade it to change its mind. But if the Lower House was determined not to yield, so also were Crown officials. They remained firm in their refusal to accept any court bill containing the controversial attachment clause and immediately disallowed the North Carolina statute.[37]

This decision virtually precluded any possibility of a satisfactory court settlement in North Carolina. To make the situation still worse, Martin, by creating courts of oyer and terminer solely by execu-

37. Martin to Dartmouth, Feb. 26, Apr. 6, 1773, *N. C. Col. Recs.,* IX, 373-74, 626-27; Lower House Journals, Mar. 6, 1773, *ibid.,* 579-81; Richard Jackson to Board of Trade, July 15, 1773, *ibid.,* 670; Laws, *N. C. St. Recs.,* XXIII, 872-92; Labaree, ed., *Royal Instructions,* I, 340; Martin to Samuel Martin, Mar. 14, 1773, Martin Papers, Add. MSS, 41361, ff. 250-51, British Museum.

tive authority, unwittingly revived the old quarrel of ten years earlier over whether or not legislative consent was necessary to establish courts. Martin thought the move a good one because the breakup of the spring legislative session had left the colony without any legally constituted courts. Inclusion of a suspending clause in the superior court bill meant that it would not go into effect until the Crown had confirmed it; and Martin had rejected two other bills to continue the old court laws six months because they would have extended the operation of the attachment provision. Martin's courts of oyer and terminer at least partially filled the void, but the Lower House rightly considered the action a serious challenge to its judicial powers. If Martin could set up one type of court without its consent, it followed that he could do the same with any other sort of court. Thus Martin would be able to establish both inferior and superior courts upon the conditions desired by Crown officials without consulting the House and, among other things, to regulate the foreign attachment clause right out of existence.

When a newly elected House convened in December, it flatly refused Martin's request for money to defray the expenses of the courts of oyer and terminer and denied that the executive could create such courts "without the aid of the Legislature of this Province." The House was equally adamant in its refusal to pass a superior court law without the foreign attachment clause. Martin officially informed the House of the Crown's disallowance of the March court law and urged it to prepare a new measure that would meet the Crown's approval. The previous August Dartmouth had made a slight concession by offering to consent to a provision permitting attachments of former residents in cases in which it was absolutely clear that the defendant had absconded to avoid paying his debt. But the Lower House found this offer completely unacceptable. Such a proviso, as an anonymous writer in the *Cape Fear Mercury* pointed out, would have frustrated the whole purpose of extending the attachment clause to Britons. That extension was not aimed primarily at absconding British debtors but at British debtors who had never resided in North Carolina and could not therefore have absconded. To have to enter proceedings against such debtors in Britain would be an expensive and unreasonable requirement, and the Lower House continued to insist that North Carolinians be guaranteed the right to attach the effects of all foreigners whether they had ever resided in the colony or not. Accordingly, the House passed a new court bill containing the old attachment clause. The Council, failing to persuade it to delete that clause, rejected the bill. Thoroughly disheartened, Martin then prorogued the House for three months to give it time to reconsider its stand, but not before it had appointed a committee to prepare addresses to the Crown asking special permission to enact the attachment clause. The House further directed the worst sort of insult at Martin by ordering the committee to seek former Governor Tryon's aid.[38]

These addresses did not have the slightest chance of success, and when the Lower House reconvened in March prospects for a settlement were remote. The situation was more acute than it had been in December because Martin's courts of oyer and terminer had ceased to function immediately upon the House's refusal to provide for their expenses, and the colony now had no judicial system whatever. Fortunately, Martin and the House did manage to agree on a one-year inferior court bill and a bill establishing the courts of oyer and terminer, thus restoring a portion of the colony's court system and ending the controversy over the governor's right to establish courts without legislative approval. In passing the oyer and terminer court bill, Martin made a significant concession to the Lower House by implicitly admitting the House's claim that its consent was necessary to establish courts. But on the question of a superior court measure the controversy over the attachment clause again resulted in deadlock. In his opening address Martin pleaded with the House to prepare a measure without that clause, but the House replied that its constituents had approved of its stand and preferred to be without courts rather than forfeit their "right of attachment." Again the House brought in a bill containing the controversial clause. This time, the Council reluctantly sided with the House, choosing to disobey the royal instructions rather than see the colony without superior courts; and Martin was left the disagreeable task of rejecting the bill.[39]

38. Dartmouth to Martin, Aug. 4, 1773, *N. C. Col. Recs.,* IX, 681; Council Journals, Mar. 16, 1773, *ibid.,* 607; Lower House Journals, Feb. 24, Dec. 9-11, 21, 1773, *ibid.,* 534, 743, 749-50, 786-88; Upper House Journals, Dec. 18, 21, 1773, *ibid.,* 721-22, 733; *Cape Fear Mercury* (Wilmington), Feb. 23, 1774, reprinted in *S.-C. Gazette* (Charleston), Mar. 14, 1774.

39. Upper House Journals, Mar. 2, 11, 16, 19, 24, 1774, *N. C. Col. Recs.,* IX, 831-34, 844, 853, 862-63, 870-72; Lower House Journals, Mar. 5, 19, 24, 1774, *ibid.,* 879-80, 928, 939-40, 946. See also John Pownall to Richard Jackson, Apr. 22, 1774, CO 5/159.

The Crown's denial of its right to enact the attachment clause remained one of the colony's most serious grievances up to the actual outbreak of hostilities with the mother country, and the controversy almost completely disrupted legislative affairs in the colony, leaving it without superior courts for the last three years before the Declaration of Independence. Of all the British restrictions in the years after 1763, North Carolinians found this one the most objectionable. Next to Parliamentary taxation probably no other issue was so important in promoting the rise of Revolutionary sentiment in that colony.

Georgia was also beset by a variety of political questions in the years after 1763 as the Commons sought to obtain many of the powers already won by the lower houses in the older colonies. By emphasizing the necessity for a strong representative assembly, the Stamp Act and other imperial measures after 1765 accelerated its development. "The assembly here are only *just now attempting* to follow the example and advice of some of their Republican spirited neighbours," Governor James Wright reported to the Board of Trade in June 1767, "and if check't at the beginning the matter will rest, and I am very hopefull everything will be set Right." But check the Commons he could not. In early 1771 he reported that it claimed *"all the Powers Laws and Customs of the Parliament of Great Britain"* and that its members were hopelessly "intoxicated with Ideas of their own Importance and Power." For the last decade before the Revolution he battled it almost to a standstill. Only his stubborn opposition prevented the Commons from reaching the final phase of legislative development during the colonial period.[40]

In the middle 1760's the Commons attempted to assert its exclusive right to nominate the London agent and in the process demonstrated its power to order money from the treasury without executive consent. It will be recalled that the Commons had established the authority of the legislature to appoint the agent in 1762. But the agent appointed at that time, William Knox, published in 1765 *The Claims of the Colonies Examined*—a tract in behalf of virtual repre-

40. Wright to Shelburne, June 15, 1767, to Hillsborough, Feb. 28, Apr. 30, 1771, unpubl. Ga. Col. Recs., XXVII, 216-17, XXXVII, 520-25, 535-38, Ga. Dept. of Arch. and Hist. For an account of Wright's role in Georgia's political development, see Abbot, *Royal Governors*, 84-183.

sentation which gave the Commons "the greatest Umbrage." Consequently, in the fall of 1765 it voted that Georgia had "no further Occasion for his Service" and chose South Carolina agent Charles Garth to present its petitions against the Stamp Act to the Crown, Lords, and Commons for a stipend of £50. It was over a year before the Commons decided to appoint a permanent replacement for Knox. In the meantime, the Commons was pleased with Garth's performance, sending him in November 1766 the £50 it had promised and an additional £54 to cover the Stamp Act solicitation. The following March the Commons attempted to push through an ordinance to appoint Garth regular agent, but the Council rejected it, sensibly arguing that with several important matters in dispute between South Carolina and Georgia Garth would be unable to serve both provinces at once. The Commons, following the example of the North Carolina Lower House, then unilaterally made the appointment and named a committee of correspondence composed solely of representatives. It directed Garth to present its request to issue more paper money and voted him a salary of £100, which it provided for in an article in the annual tax act. Objecting to paying an agent whom it had not accepted, the Council tried to induce the Commons to withdraw that article. But when the Commons refused to do so the Council accepted the bill anyway, not wishing to reject the entire tax bill.

Although the Commons had succeeded in pushing through a legal provision for Garth's payment, Wright intended to nullify that action by refusing to sign a warrant. In fact, Wright complained bitterly to home authorities and endeavored to prevent Garth's appointment from becoming effective by requesting Crown officials not to recognize him as agent. If "any Countenance is given to these kind of appointments and partial applications from the Assembly alone to the Fountain Head at one step," he warned Lord Shelburne in April 1767, "then in a very little time the assemblies in America will assume and actually take to themselves every kind of Power, make Cyphers of the Council and in some degree of His Majesties Governors too." Although they later ruled that they would not receive an agent appointed solely by the Commons, Crown officials apparently did not immediately heed Wright's warning, and Garth acted on behalf of the House in presenting its currency request and in handling a number of other matters.[41]

Another year passed before the two houses finally concluded a satisfactory agreement. Unable to persuade the Council to accept Garth, the Commons in early 1768, after Garth had notified it that he did not want the agency unless he were acceptable to the entire legislature, finally decided to appoint Benjamin Franklin instead. The Council readily consented to the Commons' new candidate, and in April Governor Wright gave his formal assent, thus putting the agency back on the original foundations erected before the Commons had dismissed Knox in the fall of 1765. By forcing the Commons to abandon Garth, the Council had in effect demonstrated its right to reject the Commons' nominee for agent. But the Commons had nominated Franklin, and Governor Wright despairingly reported that it still asserted its "Right to the Sole Appointment of an agent in the future."[42]

The one remaining bone of contention was the £100 salary the Commons had provided for Garth in the 1767 tax bill. Despite the fact that money had been legally appropriated for his payment, both Wright and the Council refused to pay Garth for over a year. When the Commons reconvened early in 1768 it stipulated in the tax bill for that year that "the Governor and Council *shall* give an order to the Treasurer . . . who *shall* Issue . . . monies . . . as appropriated and directed by . . . Law"—a stipulation intended by the Commons to serve as a *"Compulsory Clause"* to oblige Wright and the Council to issue orders for payment of all sums provided for by the tax laws.[43]

41. Commons Journals, Nov. 15, Dec. 14, 19, 1765, Nov. 10, 1766, Mar. 26, 1767, *Ga. Col. Recs.*, XIV, 293-94, 315-17, 327, 387, 473-74; Upper House Journals, Mar. 20, 1767, *ibid.*, XVII, 366-68; Ga. Committee of Correspondence to Garth, July 27, 1764, Habersham to Knox, Oct. 28, Dec. 4, 1765, to Samuel Lloyd, Sept. 5, 1767, *Habersham Letters*, 24-25, 44, 50, 58-60; Wright to Shelburne, Apr. 6, 1767, unpubl. Ga. Col. Recs., XXXVII, 182-84, Ga. Dept. of Arch. and Hist.

42. William Knox to Habersham, Feb. 4, 1768, Knox-Habersham Letters, Personal Collection of Miss Margaret McLaughlin, deposited at the Ga. Hist. Soc.; Statutes, *Ga. Col. Recs.*, XIX, Pt. I, 12-14; Commons Journals, Jan. 15, Mar. 24, 1768, *ibid.*, XIV, 497, 572-73; Upper House Journals, Feb. 4, Apr. 11, 1768, *ibid.*, XVII, 392, 448-49; Wright to Hillsborough, May 23, 30, Oct. 5, Nov. 18, 1768, Hillsborough to Wright, July 20, 1768, unpubl. Ga. Col. Recs., XXXVII, 280-82, 305, 314-15, 363, 385, Ga. Dept. of Arch. and Hist.; Wright to Board of Trade, June 8, 1768, *ibid.*, XXXVIII, Pt. II-B, 560-67; Habersham to Knox, May 7, 1768, Ga. Committee of Correspondence to Franklin, May 19, 1768, *Habersham Letters*, 64-65, 73.

43. Wright to Hillsborough, May 23, 1768, to Board of Trade, June 8, 1768,

But Wright and the Council continued to withhold Garth's salary until Hillsborough directed them to pay him. Hillsborough pointed out at the time "that in all Cases where the Legislature had judged it necessary to grant the Money under special Appropriation the Governor and Council have no . . . discretionary Power in the Disposal of it, and that their Warrant or Order for the issue of it for the Service to which it is appropriated is an Act of executive Government that follows of Course." Hillsborough's ruling meant simply that the governor and Council had no choice but to issue orders for payment of all sums appropriated by law. Following this ruling, Wright and the Council reluctantly gave in and agreed to provide for Garth's payment.[44] The whole incident stood as positive evidence of the executive's inability to prevent the Commons from ordering money from the treasury without its consent.

Franklin served as the Commons' agent for the rest of the colonial period. Between 1768 and 1773 the Georgia legislature regularly appointed him to successive one-year terms. When it came time to renew his appointment in September 1773, the Commons also brought in an ordinance to appoint Councilor Grey Elliott to act as agent during Franklin's absence, there being some possibility that Franklin might not remain in London for the full term. The Council consented to both measures, but Wright, who during his visit to England at the beginning of the decade seems to have developed serious objections to Franklin, vetoed the ordinance to name Franklin, although he did consent to Elliott's appointment. The governor's veto promptly revived the old controversy. When the incensed Commons met again in January, it immediately passed another ordinance to appoint Franklin, but the Council, following Wright's example, rejected the measure. The Commons struck back sharply, declaring "that the power of appointing an Agent . . . is a right and priviledge which is and ought to be exclusively lodged in the Representatives of the People." To implement this declaration the Commons voted to appoint Franklin by virtue of its own authority with an annual salary of £150 and selected nine of its members to act as a committee

---

unpubl. Ga. Col. Recs., XXXVII, 275-76; XXXVIII, Pt. II-B, 560-67, Ga. Dept. of Arch. and Hist.; Statutes, *Ga. Col. Recs.*, XIX, Pt. I, 113.

44. Hillsborough to Wright, July 20, 1768, Wright to Hillsborough, Nov. 18, 1768, unpubl. Ga. Col. Recs., XXXVII, 314-15, 385, Ga. Dept. of Arch. and Hist.; Statutes, *Ga. Col. Recs.*, XIX, Pt. I, 136; Knox to Habersham, Feb. 4, 1768, Knox-Habersham Letters, Ga. Hist. Soc.

of correspondence. Although it was abundantly clear that the Commons intended to make good its claim to the exclusive right to name and appoint the agent, both Wright and the Council played out their roles and tried to prevent Franklin's acting by asking Crown officials not to receive him. In May 1774 Dartmouth took a predictable stand, guaranteeing that "no person so appointed shall be received in the Character of Agent for the Province." But the conflict was never resolved, for the Commons never really needed Franklin's services. Moreover, events were already moving toward that impasse that would relegate the agent issue to the background and eventually render such an office unnecessary.[45]

The Georgia Commons also followed the lead of the older lower houses by attempting in the period after 1763 to gain the power to regulate officers' fees by statute. It began in 1765 by fixing the charges of treasurers and comptrollers appointed to collect an import duty,[46] but the vast majority of fees taken in the colony remained beyond its control. Wright wrote Shelburne in July 1767 that the Commons considered fees as "a kind of Tax on the people" and that it "looked upon those established under the authority of His Majesty's Royal Instruction as illegal." He also reported that it had "been hinted more than once that a Bill was to be prepared . . . for establishing fees," although he had "hitherto prevented any attempt of that kind." But by December 1768 Wright had altered his position. In response to Hillsborough's inquiry about necessary changes in the royal instructions, Wright questioned "whether Fees ought not rather to be Established by a Law of the Province" than by executive ordinances. Such a law, he suggested, "might be more Effectual with Respect to Punishing Such as may Presume to Exact more, or Larger Fees than are allowed."[47] Finally, in September 1773 the Commons passed a comprehensive measure covering the charges of every officer in the colony and stipulating a penalty for taking fees not allowed by law.

45. Statutes, *Ga. Col. Recs.*, XIX, Pt. I, 199-201, 249-52, 506-8; Upper House Journals, Mar. 11, 1774, *ibid.*, XVII, 777-86; Ga. Committee of Correspondence to Franklin, May 11, 1770, Habersham to James Wright, Jr., Feb. 17, 1772, *Habersham Letters*, 78, 166; Wright to Board of Trade, Dec. 30, 1773, Wright to Dartmouth, Mar. 12, 1774, Dartmouth to Wright, May 4, 1774, unpubl. Ga. Col. Recs., XXVIII, Pt. II-B, 886, XXXVIII, Pt. I, 208-11, 233, Ga. Dept. of Arch. and Hist.

46. Statutes, *Ga. Col. Recs.*, XVIII, 691-703.

47. Wright to Shelburne, July 20, 1767, unpubl. Ga. Col. Recs., XXXVII, 229-30, Ga. Dept. of Arch. and Hist.; Wright to Hillsborough, Dec. 26, 1768, *ibid.*, XXVIII, Pt. II-B, 687.

The bill contained a suspending clause and had strong support from Wright, who wrote the Board of Trade that he considered "a Provincial Law . . . the properest Method of Establishing and Regulating Publick Officers and all other Fees." The following summer Board of Trade counsel Richard Jackson reported favorably on the measure, and in December 1774 the Crown formally approved it after the Board had ruled that the "Fees, thereby established," were both "reasonable and moderate."[48] This action was significant as a reaffirmation of the imperial authorities' earlier rulings concerning North Carolina and, in effect, marked the transfer of power to establish fees to the Georgia Commons.

Less successful was the Georgia Commons' attempt to gain authority to appoint executive officers—authority exercised to some extent by all of the three older lower houses. Crown officials tried to prevent that power from falling into the hands of the Commons at the beginning of royal government by assigning all appointments to the executive. For nearly ten years the Commons had little opportunity to acquire a share of that power because the public treasurer, appointed by the governor, was the only important officer in the colony who received a salary from the public and was not appointed by officials in London. But by 1765 the volume of Georgia's commerce had increased so considerably that it became imperative to create additional offices to handle it. When the Commons began to create new executive offices, it quietly assumed the right to fill them. In March 1765 the Commons adopted a bill to impose duties on a number of articles and provided for the appointment of a waiter to assist the treasurer and comptroller in collecting the duties at Savannah and of a comptroller to handle all the tasks of collection at the rapidly rising port of Sunbury. Both offices were patterned after similar ones in South Carolina; and, although the duty law did not explicitly empower the legislature to fill them, it implied as much by specifying that the executive might fill vacancies temporarily while the legislature was not in session. The Commons then pushed through a separate ordinance appointing its nominees to the new ports. Neither Wright nor the Council apparently recognized the implication of this

48. Statutes, *Ga. Col. Recs.*, XIX, Pt. I, 359-406; Wright to Board of Trade, Dec. 30, 1773, Jackson to Board of Trade, June 11, 1774, Board of Trade to Crown, Nov. 5, 1774, unpubl. Ga. Col. Recs., XXVIII, Pt. II-B, 881-82, 890, XXXIV, 643-44, Ga. Dept. of Arch. and Hist.

measure, for both passed it without a murmur of opposition. Nor was Board of Trade counsel Matthew Lamb any more perceptive, permitting the ordinance and duty law to pass without objection. For the first time the Georgia Commons had exercised the power to make an important executive appointment by statute. When vacancies occurred in the Sunbury comptrollership in 1768 and 1770, the Commons again exercised the right of nomination without contest.[49]

Having successfully established a precedent, the Commons during the next five years extended its power of appointment by creating a number of new offices and by assuming the right to fill them with nominees of its own choice through legislative ordinances. Most of these offices were inspectorships designed to improve the colony's external commerce by maintaining the quality of Georgia exports. In March 1766 the legislature passed a measure to prevent frauds in packing meats, naval stores, and firewood for export. This bill established standard packing regulations and provided for the appointment of packers and inspectors to enforce them. That the Commons intended the power of appointment to rest in the hands of the legislature was explicit in the clause stipulating that the offices be filled "by Ordinance or otherwise of the Governor, Council, and Commons House of Assembly, in general Assembly met." Accordingly, the Commons enacted an ordinance naming inspectors to serve at Savannah and Sunbury. Originally proposed by the Council with the full support of Wright,[50] this system was so successful that the Commons extended it to cover other commodities, establishing four more groups of inspectors between 1767 and 1770. It created inspectors of lumber in 1767; tanned leather in 1768; hemp, flax, and wheat in 1770; and tobacco in 1770. Each group was usually six in number with representatives at Savannah, Sunbury, and Frederica, the tobacco inspectors also operating at Augusta. In addition, the Commons in 1770 set up the post of harbor master for Savannah to enforce uniform rates for wharf storage and other port ordinances.

49. Statutes, *Ga. Col. Recs.*, XVIII, 691-703, XIX, Pt. I, 72-73, 145-46; Commons Journals, Mar. 12-14, 1765, *ibid.*, XIV, 244-46. See Matthew Lamb's Report of Georgia Acts of 1764-65, Oct. 29, 1765, unpubl. Ga. Col. Recs., XXVIII, Pt. II-A, 402, Ga. Dept. of Arch. and Hist.; Richard Jackson to Board of Trade, Jan. 8, June 20, 1771, *ibid.*, XXVIII, Pt. II-B, 740-41, 760-62.

50. Statutes, *Ga. Col. Recs.*, XVIII, 774-80; Commons Journals, Dec. 5, 11-18, 1765, *ibid.*, XIV, 309, 314-24; Wright to Shelburne, June 15, 1767, unpubl. Ga. Col. Recs., XXXVII, 225, Ga. Dept. of Arch. and Hist.

In every case the Commons repeated the pattern established with the creation of the first inspectors, placing the power of appointment in the entire legislature but proceeding to exercise the right of nomination itself.[51] By 1770 the Commons seemingly had established its right to play the major role in appointing officers who received a salary from the public. Its patronage was extensive, including thirty inspectors, a harbor master and a waiter for Savannah, and a comptroller for Sunbury. The public treasurer was the only major office to which the executive could claim the exclusive right of nomination.

For nearly five years royal officials in both Georgia and London raised no objections to this practice,[52] but by the summer of 1770 Wright recognized that it was a serious encroachment upon his appointive powers. Characteristically, he chose not to create a major altercation by making an issue of the matter in the colony, deciding instead to try to persuade imperial authorities to take some repressive action at home. In July 1770 he complained to the Board of Trade of the Commons' "disposition to Appoint every Petty Officer by an Ordinance of the General Assembly" and pointed out that those ordinances resulted in "taking Away that Influence which the Governor would have, were all these Officers in his Appointment, and . . . Adding to the Power and Influence of the Assembly." He suggested that Crown officials might put a stop to the practice simply by disallowing one or two of the appointing ordinances and issuing him positive "directions not to Allow any more Such Appointments."[53]

But not until after Wright had visited England a year later and personally impressed colonial authorities with the seriousness of the situation did they take any repressive action. The Board of Trade reviewed the matter carefully, and upon its recommendation the Privy Council in January 1772 disallowed several of the measures by which the Commons had made appointments, ruling that it was highly improper for the Commons to have adopted the "practice of passing Laws under the name of Ordinances, for the appointment of

51. Statutes, *Ga. Col. Recs.*, XVIII, 797-99, XIX, Pt. I, 70-71, 89-93, 151-55, 204-8, Pt. II, 8-23; Commons Journals, Dec. 8-16, 1766, Mar. 8-9, 1770, *ibid.*, XIV, 395-400, IX, 146-47; Upper House Journals, Feb. 27, 1770, *ibid.*, XVII, 541; Ordinance to appoint Inspectors of Hemp, Flax, and Wheat Flour, Feb. 27, 1770, CO 5/683, f. 86.

52. Wright to Shelburne, June 15, 1767, unpubl. Ga. Col. Recs., XXXVII, 225, Ga. Dept. of Arch. and Hist.; Richard Jackson to Board of Trade, Jan. 8, June 20, 1771, *ibid.*, XXVIII, Pt. II-B, 740-41, 760-62.

53. See Wright to Board of Trade, July 23, 1770, *ibid.*, Pt. II-B, 727-31.

Persons to various executive offices in that Colony." Declaring "that such mode of appointments appears to imply a Claim in the assembly to Concurr in the choice of such officers, by which . . . [the Crown's] Constitutional Rights are improperly lessened and Impaired," the Privy Council ordered the Board of Trade to instruct Wright "not to give his assent for the future to any Laws of the like nature."[54] To enforce this order the Board prepared a formal additional instruction forbidding Wright to pass any further laws or ordinances that should "Extend to the appointment of any person or persons to any executive office or offices" and ordering him to enter the instruction on the Council journals "as a Standing Rule" and "as a Bar to any Claim, which our Assembly of our said Colony may hereafter think fit to set up, to Concur in the Nomination of persons to those offices, the appointment to which does of right belong to us, and to those Acting under our Authority." Wright had gotten what he wanted: an imperial order reaffirming the executive's exclusive right to the appointive power. And he had dealt a serious blow to the Commons' pretensions to power at little cost to his own popularity within the colony.[55]

But Wright's victory was more apparent than real because according to Georgia law the legislature still retained the right to fill all of the offices except one. Of the laws that had originally invested the right of appointment in the legislature, only the wharfage act of 1770 empowering the General Assembly to appoint the harbor master had actually been disallowed. The rest were still in force, and unless royal instructions could supersede colonial laws, a doctrine nowhere admitted by American legislators, the Commons could argue that the governor and Council could not legally fill the offices without its consent. President James Habersham, who served as acting governor until Wright's return from England in February 1773, tactfully tried to soften the blow by making no great point of the additional instruction and by not removing the Commons' nominees from their posts. Nonetheless, in view of its behavior on other questions the Commons

54. Order in Council, Jan. 15, 1772, *ibid.*, Pt. II-B, 846-49. Only four of the appointing ordinances were disallowed: those to appoint the Sunbury comptroller; harbor master; inspectors of hemp, flax, and wheat flour; and packers and inspectors of provisions, lumber, and naval stores. Also disallowed was the act empowering the legislature to appoint the harbor master.

55. Order in Council, Feb. 3, 1772, *ibid.*, Pt. II-B, 859; Council Journals, June 2, 1772, *Ga. Col. Recs.*, XII, 321-22.

might have been expected to put up a determined fight on legal grounds and even to deny the validity of the additional instruction as the South Carolina Commons was then doing in the Wilkes fund controversy. Accordingly, in March 1773 the Commons raised the issue by selecting committees to prepare ordinances to appoint a comptroller and a harbor master for Savannah in direct defiance of the additional instruction. Had either of these measures gotten out of the House, neither Wright nor the Council could have passed it without violating the instruction, and a full-scale controversy might have ensued. But the matter never formally came before them because Wright prorogued the Commons before it had given the measure its final reading.[56] Nor did the issue come up in subsequent sessions as questions of greater moment arising out of the deepening Revolutionary crisis pushed it into the background.

Thus, the legal question was never put to the test, and the additional instruction had its intended effect. The Commons did not succeed in making another such appointment during the remaining few years of royal government. But by curtailing the Commons' bid for a share of the appointive power, Crown officials had won few friends within the ranks of the Commons. Rather, they had helped to teach Georgia legislators what their counterparts in the older colonies had long known: that they could never attain great political power so long as their accomplishments could be so easily undone by the British ministry, so long as they were required to submit to government by instruction. In this small way this experience helped to push Georgia a little closer to her sister colonies in the political debate with the mother country and a little farther down the path to revolution.

The most intensive contest in Georgia involved the governor' right to reject the Commons' nominee for speaker. That contest began late in April 1771 and agitated Georgia politics for nearly twenty-one months. In 1768 Speaker Alexander Wylly incurred the displeasure of Hillsborough by writing an encouraging answer to the Massachusetts circular letter. Hillsborough ordered Wright to reject Wylly if he were again elected speaker. However, when the next

56. Habersham to Hillsborough, June 15, 1772, *Habersham Letters*, 189; Commons Journals, Mar. 12, Sept. 14-29, 1773, *Ga. Col. Recs.*, XV, 423-24, 529-37. That Wright regarded the appointment of the Sunbury collector as the governor's prerogative is indicated in "Report of James Wright on the Condition of the Province of Georgia on 20th Sept. 1773," Ga. Hist. Soc., *Collections*, 3 (1873), 173.

legislature convened Wylly was absent and the Commons chose Noble Wymberly Jones instead. Jones continued as speaker until the House was dissolved in 1771, but, probably because of his activities as leader of the Georgia Sons of Liberty, Wright considered him an unsatisfactory occupant of the post.[57]   Consequently, when the Commons again chose Jones speaker at the opening of a new General Assembly in April 1771, Wright rejected him, ordering the Commons to select another. The Commons complied by electing Archibald Bulloch, but quickly realized the folly of its acquiescence and the following day resolved "that the rejecting the Speaker, elected by the unanimous Consent of the House, is a high Breach of the Privilege of the House, and tends to subvert the most valuable Rights and Liberties of the People, and their Representatives." It further declared that it had chosen another speaker only to avoid delaying public business and that its action should not be "admitted as a Precedent." This resolution directly denied the validity of the royal instructions from which Wright derived his authority to reject the speaker and so raised his ire that he immediately dissolved the House, accusing it of insulting and attacking the King's authority and asserting that the Crown had an "undoubted right to Approve or disapprove a Speaker," which was "particularly delegated" to him.[58]

When this affair came to the attention of Hillsborough, he sided with Wright, deploring the Commons' adherence to such "unwarrantable and unconstitutional Doctrines and Principles" and ordering James Habersham, president of the Council and acting governor of Georgia during Wright's absence in England, to reject the House's first choice as speaker at the meeting of a new legislature so that the Crown might establish its right. Accordingly, when the new Commons convened in April 1772, Habersham rejected its choice as speaker, Noble Wymberly Jones. In an attempt to prevent a serious altercation, however, he informed the members privately that the action was meant to establish the Crown's right of rejection and was not intended as a personal affront to Jones. Still, the Commons refused to give in and re-elected Jones, who was again rejected by Habersham.

57. Hillsborough to Wright, Sept. 15, 1768, unpubl. Ga. Col. Recs., XXXVII, 332-33, Ga. Dept. of Arch. and Hist.; Wright to Hillsborough, Dec. 14, 1769, *ibid.*, XXVIII, Pt. II-B, 674-75. For an account of Wright's emerging distaste for Jones, see Abbot, *Royal Governors*, 146-56.

58. Commons House Journals, Apr. 24-25, 1771, *Ga. Col. Recs.*, XV, 305, 311-12; Upper House Journals, Apr. 26, 1771, *ibid.*, XVII, 650.

Elected for a third time, Jones declined so that business might not be further retarded, and the Commons selected Archibald Bulloch. Habersham readily accepted Bulloch but, upon learning that the Commons had chosen him only after Jones's refusal, demanded that the Commons expunge the record of Jones's third election from its journal. When the Commons appeared reluctant to accede to this demand, Habersham dissolved it.[59]

This dissolution set off a spirited public debate. In reply to several articles in the *Georgia Gazette* in May and June 1772 defending the Crown's right to reject the speaker, John Joachim Zubly published a pamphlet, *Calm and Respectful Thoughts on the Negative of the Crown on a Speaker Chosen and Presented by the Representatives of the People.* Zubly believed with the Commons that the "Rights and Liberties of the People, and their Representatives" took precedence over royal instructions. Denying that instructions could give the governor a right to reject the speaker, he argued that because the King could "do nothing against law or the Constitution" he could not give instructions that were "contrary to the Constitution, or derogatory to the right of the subject." The Crown's claim to a right of rejection was not only against the "spirit and design of the Constitution of a free people"; it also defied all logic. The speaker was the representative of the people, not the Crown, and, Zubly argued, if "none shall be Speaker but one that will obey orders, or . . . is agreeable to the King," he would be subject to the control of the very authority "to prevent whose too powerful influence, and restrain it within its proper bounds, is, or ought to be, the principal object of the Representatives of a free people." "To talk of a free choice, which yet may be controuled and annulled by another," Zubly reasoned, "seems inconsistent with the very nature of the choice." Assuming that the Georgia Commons possessed the same right in choosing a speaker as the British House of Commons, he pointed out that the Crown's only attempt to reject the choice of the British Commons was during the "reign of a *Stuart,* when there was a settled design against the religion and liberties of the nation." Zubly's arguments are significant both because of their denial that royal instructions

59. Hillsborough to Habersham, Dec. 4, 1771, Habersham to Hillsborough, Mar. 30, 1772, unpubl. Ga. Col. Recs., XXXVII, 552-53, 603, Ga. Dept. of Arch. and Hist.; Habersham to William Knox, Nov. 26, 1771, to Hillsborough, Apr. 30, 1772, *Habersham Letters,* 151, 174-77.

could alter the constitution of the colony and because of their suggestion of an equality between the Georgia and the British Commons. They indicate quite clearly that whatever the deficiencies in actual power of the youthful Georgia Commons, Georgia legislative leaders shared a common body of theory with their counterparts in the older colonies that was distinctly contrary to imperial ideas.[60]

Habersham's deft handling of the situation when the Commons met the next December deprived the leaders of the Commons of the opportunity to make good their pretensions, however. The Commons again elected Jones speaker, but Habersham urged his friends to induce Jones to decline the office in the interest of harmony, which he did. The Commons then chose William Young, whom Habersham readily accepted. The controversy thus ended without the issues ever having been resolved. The Crown could conceivably have claimed victory on the grounds that it had prevented Jones's serving as speaker, but it had not prevented his election. On the contrary, the Commons had twice made another choice only after Jones had declined the speakership, and it had never conceded the governor's right of rejection.[61] The Crown cannot, therefore, be said to have established its right to veto the Georgia Commons' choice for a speaker. Still, its attempt to do so constituted a very real threat to one of the cherished privileges of the Commons. The fact that the Crown was so eager to exercise that right so late in the colonial period when it had not previously done so was ample evidence that it had no intention of conceding to the Commons any great measure of political power and was probably an important factor in creating a climate of opinion in Georgia favorable to Revolution.

Separately, none of these local issues would have brought any one of the four colonies into open rebellion against the mother country, but their concentration within a short period and their association with the program of Parliamentary taxation made them appear especially grave to colonial leaders. Serious threats to fundamental powers of the lower houses were posed by the attempts to separate the offices of speaker and treasurer in Virginia before 1766, deny

60. [Zubly], *Calm and Respectful Thoughts on the Negative of the Crown on a Speaker Chosen and Presented by the Representatives of the People* (Savannah [?], 1772), 5-7, 11, 21-22, 24.

61. Habersham to Wright, Dec. 4, 1772, to Charles Pryce, Jan. 16, 1773, *Habersham Letters*, 215-18, 221.

the authority of the North Carolina Lower House to establish the right of its constituents to attach the property of non-residents in the 1770's, prevent the South Carolina Commons from ordering money from the treasury without executive consent during the Wilkes fund controversy, assert the Crown's right to reject the Commons' choice of speaker in Georgia in the early 1770's, insist that judicial tenure be during pleasure in both Carolinas in the 1760's, thwart the efforts of the North Carolina Lower House and Georgia Commons to exercise exclusive authority over the colonial agent in the 1760's and 1770's, and forbid the Georgia Commons any further exercise of the power of appointment to executive offices in 1772. Only in the attempts of the Georgia Commons to fix electoral qualifications and to gain the power to settle fees by statute did a lower house meet with any acceptance of its pretensions to greater political power. This piecemeal assault upon the power of the lower houses, becoming especially intensive after 1768 when Hillsborough as colonial secretary attempted to enforce rigidly all canons of imperial policy, appeared to American lawmakers to be a settled plot against the constitutions of the colonies. As early as December 1765 Christopher Gadsden thought he saw "the appearance of a design" in the "late attacks on different parts of the Constitution in different places . . . in New York on one point, in our province on another, in Jamaica on a third, in Maryland on several"; and two years later Richard Henry Lee expressed his suspicion that "Great Britain . . . having discovered the error of attempting our ruin, by one bold and general stroke, has, at length, fallen on a method of singly attacking the colonies, hoping that the others will quietly behold the destruction of the one."[62] After he had succeeded Hillsborough as colonial secretary in the summer of 1772, Dartmouth in the year and a half before the Coercive Acts tried to ease the situation by making some minor concessions on almost all the important issues, but in every case they were both too little and too late. By that time imperial actions over the previous decade had convinced American legislatures that nothing less than an absolute and free exercise of their rights and powers on their own terms could secure them.

62. Gadsden to Garth, Dec. 2, 1765, in Gibbes, ed., *Doc. Hist. of Rev. in South Carolina*, I, 9; Lee to ————, Mar. 27, 1768, Ballagh, ed., *R. H. Lee Letters*, I, 26-27.

The Ultimate Issue

In the process of verbalizing and defending their constitutional position after 1763, the lower houses acquired aspirations well beyond any they had had in the earlier colonial period. Parliament's attempts to tax the colonies caused them to assert their equality with Parliament in matters of taxation, and the efforts of Crown officials to tighten up colonial administration and to curtail many of the powers they had gained over the previous century led them to re-evaluate the imperial-colonial connection. They began to question the imperial concept of colonial subordination and gradually developed a fully articulated theory about their constitutional position in the empire that asserted their equality with the British House of Commons and the equality of the colonies with the mother country under the King. That theory was unacceptable to the home government, and the resulting constitutional impasse was of great importance in the decision of American leaders to seek their political fortunes outside the empire.

Among southern lower houses the debate with the mother country not only caused them to question Parliament's authority over the colonies but also accentuated their dislike for certain imperial checks upon their power. Aside from the Currency Act and various acts of Parliament to tax the colonies, most of the measures the lower houses found objectionable in the decade after 1763 came from the Crown through either the secretary of state in charge of American affairs or the Board of Trade, and the lower houses gradually came to regard as oppressive some of the traditional features of royal control over the colonies. Applied in ways that were increasingly irksome to them, the suspending clause, the Crown's right of legislative review, the royal instructions, the governor's power to dissolve them, and the theoretical equality of the royal-appointed councils in matters of legislation served as constant reminders of their subordinate status and stood as glaring contradictions to their pretensions to equality with Parliament.

Never popular with American lawmakers, the instruction requiring the insertion of a clause suspending the execution of any law "of unusual and extraordinary nature" until the Crown had approved it became a source of great annoyance within the context of the new colonial policy as the Crown began to require it in bills relating to an increasing number of areas. The Georgia Commons set forth the prevailing attitude in March 1770 when it declared that suspending clauses were of "pernicious Consequences," tending "to annihilate the Rights of any Assembly" and preventing "the execution of any Act, though ever so immediately necessary and Beneficial to the Province."[1]

Nor was the Crown's right of disallowance any more palatable. Time after time in the last quarter century of the colonial period Crown officials disallowed statutes that lower houses had thought necessary and appropriate for solving local problems. In the 1750's the Crown twice raised major political problems in Virginia by disallowing ten of the laws from the revisal of 1749 and, in 1759, the Two-Penny Act and its predecessors of 1753 and 1755. In the 1760's and 1770's the Crown disallowed badly needed court laws in the two Carolinas, bills to erect new constituencies and to replace worn-out paper bills in South Carolina, and several measures designed to give the Commons a share in appointing revenue officers in Georgia. Many began to feel with South Carolina legislator Henry Laurens that these disallowances were either "tyrannical" or "downright Robbery" or both.[2]

Another source of irritation was the royal instructions. The lower houses had early developed the doctrine that instructions were binding upon the governor and council but not upon themselves. After 1765, however, they found themselves confronted with instructions

1. Commons Journals, Mar. 14, 1770, *Ga. Col. Recs.*, XV, 152; Wright to Hillsborough, May 11, 1770, unpubl. Ga. Col. Recs., XXXVII, 444-45, Ga. Dept. of Arch. and Hist.

2. Laurens to John Hopton, Jan. 29, 1771, Laurens Letter Book, 1767-71, 598, S. C. Hist. Soc.

aimed specifically at curtailing their power, directly challenging the validity of that doctrine. Additional instructions requiring in 1768 that the Virginia Burgesses accept the principles of the Declaratory Act, in 1770 that the South Carolina Commons be deprived of the right to issue money from the treasury without executive consent, and in 1772 that the Georgia Commons be denied the right to share in selecting executive officers and that the North Carolina Lower House be forbidden to provide for the attachment of the effects of foreigners each in turn appeared as "ministerial mandates" to keep the lower houses "in Subjection."

The lower houses also found the governors' power to dissolve them especially vexing. They had never questioned the governors' right to that power prior to 1763, but in the decade after the Stamp Act governors in all four colonies made wide use of it in attempting either to prevent the lower houses from protesting violations of their rights or to punish them for not complying with imperial demands. Botetourt twice dissolved the Virginia Burgesses for protesting the Townshend Acts, once in October 1768 at the express command of the Crown and again in May 1769. For the same reason, Montagu dissolved the South Carolina Commons in November 1768, Wright the Georgia Commons in December 1768, and Tryon the North Carolina Lower House in November 1769. Between November 1771 and January 1773 Montagu dissolved the South Carolina Commons four times because it would not comply with the Crown's additional instruction during the Wilkes fund controversy; and the Georgia Commons was dissolved twice, once in April 1771 by Wright and again in April 1772 by Habersham, for disputing the governor's right to reject its choice as speaker. Such dissolutions, as Peter Timothy complained in the *South-Carolina Gazette* in early 1773, left the voters "unrepresented in Assembly" and was a *"Grievance"* of considerable *"Magnitude."*[3]

Finally, the lower houses began to question the right of the councils to serve as upper houses of the legislature, denying that twelve Crown-appointed advisors to the governor should have any legislative rights, much less the same rights as those enjoyed by the people's representatives. Unlike the peers in Britain, who held their seats in the House of Lords on a hereditary basis and could not be removed

3. *S.-C. Gazette* (Charleston), Feb. 22, 1773.

by the Crown, colonial councilors were entirely dependent upon the Crown and could be removed at pleasure. American leaders increasingly recognized that this arrangement was an important defect in the constitutions of the colonies, another instance in which those constitutions departed from the model of the mother country to the disadvantage of the colonies. As early as 1764 the North Carolina Lower House suggested that the Council should be referred to as "board" or "Council" rather than as "House," thus implying that the Lower House did not consider the Council a properly constituted legislative body.[4] Virginian Richard Henry Lee in 1769 deplored the fact that the "just equilibrium" that marked the British constitution was "totally destroyed" in Virginia "by two parts out of three of the Legislature being in the same hands." It appeared to Lee an "injudicious combination" for the Council to have "all the executive, two thirds of the legislative, and the whole judiciary powers."[5] In 1773 George Mason echoed Lee's sentiments, expressing his opinion that it was absolutely necessary that "members of the Intermediate Branch of the Legislature, should have no precarious tenure, that it should be . . . equally independent of the Crown and of the people."[6] Resentment against the Council was strongest in South Carolina. By 1774 William Henry Drayton, member of the Council and son of an old South Carolina family, was convinced that "the constitution of the present Councils in America" was "injurious to the Subject, and destructive of a free constitution of Government."[7] "Placemen dependent upon the Crown," Drayton complained, "being Strangers *ignorant* of the interests and laws of the Colonies," had been sent from England to fill the majority of seats on the Council. During the Wilkes fund controversy the Commons' resentment culminated in a denial that the Council was an upper house and a request to the Crown to appoint "a constitutional branch of Legislature . . . independent of the Council."[8]

The lower houses' distaste for these traditional features of British

4. Upper House Journals, Mar. 5-7, 1764, *N. C. Col. Recs.,* VI, 1129-33.
5. Lee to Arthur Lee, Dec. 20, 1776, Ballagh, ed., *R. H. Lee Letters,* I, 19-20.
6. Mason's Comments on the Va. Charters, 1773, Rowland, *George Mason,* I, 405.
7. Drayton, *A Letter from Freeman of South-Carolina, to the Deputies of North-America, Assembled in the High Court of Congress at Philadelphia* (Charleston, 1774), 12.
8. *Ibid.,* 9; Bull to Hillsborough, Apr. 15, Nov. 30, 1770, S. C. Pub. Recs., XXXII, 257, 371-73, S. C. Arch. Dept.

control, increased by the imperial authorities' extensive use of them
after 1765, was the product both of rising dissatisfaction with anything that put the colonies in an unequal position to Great Britain
and of a growing conviction that the lower houses knew best what
to do for their constituents and their colonies. Increasingly they
viewed anything which interfered with their freedom to adopt whatever course seemed necessary as a troublesome and impolitic restraint;
the best remedy, it was becoming more and more clear, was for them
to assume exclusive jurisdiction over local affairs.

Imperial authorities contributed to this conviction by adopting
measures that threatened the very existence of the lower houses.
Parliament's abrupt suspension of the New York Assembly in 1767
for refusing to comply with the Quartering Act, along with the
ministry's order in April 1768 to suspend the Massachusetts House of
Representatives until it had rescinded the circular letter and to dissolve any American legislature that presumed to endorse that letter,
convinced American lawmakers that Parliament and the ministry
would go to any length—even to the very destruction of representative
government in the colonies—to establish Parliament's supremacy.
After hearing of a rumored plan not to call the annual Massachusetts
Assembly in 1769, Henry Laurens wrote James Habersham that he
had "never heard of so diabolical a project in all history as that of
abandoning us 'to run into confusion for want of Assembly.' "[9]
Arthur Lee was disturbed by a parallel he thought he saw between
the attempts of Charles I to rule without Parliament and those of
the ministry "to govern the provinces of *America* without their Assemblies."[10] If Parliament and the ministry could suspend the lower
houses merely for protesting violations of traditional rights, of what
importance, constitutional or political, were they, of what value was
the power they had painstakingly built up over the previous century?
There could no longer be much doubt that the conflict was not what
it had first appeared—a simple contest over constitutional rights.
Rather, it was a struggle for existence. Very little in the way of
further provocation was necessary to bring American lawmakers to
the opinion expressed by Virginian Theodorick Bland in 1774 that

9. Laurens to James Habersham, May 25, 1769, Laurens Letter Book, 1767-71,
392, S. C. Hist. Soc.
10. Junius Americanus [Arthur Lee], *The Political Detection* (London, 1770),
19-20.

any measure depriving Americans "of their liberties, shall also deprive them of their existence."[11] The only sure hope for survival was to obtain guarantees of an equal status with Parliament and relief from the traditional checks of the Crown. But even as late as 1773 most American representatives were still reluctant to think in those terms.

The increased dissatisfaction with the various features of imperial control combined with the challenge of the new colonial policy and Parliamentary taxation to produce a strong undercurrent of discontent during the period from 1770 to 1773. Lord North's Tea Act of April 1773, intended merely to revive the sagging fortunes of the East India Company, brought that discontent surging to the surface. The act conferred on the company new trading privileges that threatened to give it a monopoly of the American tea market. It made the price of tea so cheap that many Americans interpreted it with Robert Carter Nicholas as an "arbitrary" attempt to inveigle them into paying "the odious Duty" and thereby recognizing Parliament's taxing power.[12] Such a step, Richard Henry Lee declared, would have "a direct Tendency to render Assemblies Useless and to introduce Arbitrary Government."[13] To preclude these developments Boston patriots resisted the measure by the most direct means at their disposal, dumping 342 chests of tea into Boston harbor on the night of December 16, 1773. For this rash action, Parliament undertook to make an example of Massachusetts in the spring of 1774 by passing the Coercive Acts, but succeeded only in raising colonial tempers to the boiling point. The Coercive Acts fundamentally altered the Massachusetts constitution and in so doing confirmed the worst fears of American legislators. If Parliament could change the basic fabric of a colonial constitution at will, their position was even more precarious than they had formerly supposed. And if Parliament could, as it did in the case of Quebec in May 1774, deprive a large body of Englishmen of the right of representative government, then English representative traditions amounted to little outside the home islands. By these measures, Hugh Williamson declared, "every other province was informed that nothing was sacred or secure."[14] "The *same author-*

11. Bland to Messrs. Farrel and Jones, Dec. 1, 1774, in Charles Campbell, ed., *The Bland Papers* (Petersburg, 1843), 33.
12. [Robert Carter Nicholas], *Considerations on the Present State of Virginia Examined* ([Williamsburg], 1774), 9.
13. Lee's Resolves of June 1774, Ballagh, ed., *R. H. Lee Letters*, I, 115.
14. [Hugh Williamson], *The Plea of the Colonies* (London, 1775), 15.

ity upon the *same principle*," North Carolina politician James Iredell later wrote, "might have declared the king, by his representative, sole legislative as well as executive power." "What was the case of Massachusetts Bay to-day," he warned, "might be that of New York, Pennsylvania, and any of the others to-morrow."[15]

Indeed, the Coercive Acts forced American leaders into a radical reassessment of their constitutional arguments. The question had become, as an anonymous Englishman argued, "not what the constitution was, or is, but what[,] present circumstances considered[,] it ought to be."[16] American legislators agreed with Georgia Governor James Wright that the time had come "to Settle the Line with respect to *Taxation etc* by some new mode or Constitution,"[17] but they had in mind a very different kind of settlement from Wright's. Convinced that the only security for their political fortunes was to abandon their attempts to restrict and define Parliamentary authority in America, the lower houses were now ready to follow the lead suggested by Landon Carter and Richard Bland in 1765 and 1766 and to deny Parliament's jurisdiction over them, asserting their equality under the Crown. For ten years the lower houses had been contesting Parliament's right to tax the colonies. Now they were ready to apply the same arguments against Parliament's right to legislate for the colonies. As in the case of the resistance to the Stamp Act and Townshend Acts, Virginia again took the lead among the southern royal colonies, the most elaborate and compelling statement of the new colonial position coming from the pen of a young member of the House of Burgesses from Albemarle County, Thomas Jefferson.

By the summer of 1774 Jefferson was convinced that it was necessary to make explicit what Carter and Bland had been content to leave implicit: that Parliament had no authority over the internal affairs of the colonies. In a series of resolutions adopted by a meeting of the freeholders of Albemarle County on July 26, 1774, he had declared "that the Inhabitants of the several states of British America are subject to the laws which they adopted at their first settlement, and to such others as have been since made by their respective legis-

15. James Iredell's essay on the American Revolution, June 1776, in Griffith J. McRee, ed., *Life and Correspondence of James Iredell,* 2 vols. (N. Y., 1857), I, 301.
16. [Charles Garth?], *America Vindicated from the High Charge of Ingratitude and Rebellion* (Devizes, 1774), 6.
17. Wright to Dartmouth, Aug. 24, 1774, unpubl. Ga. Col. Recs., XXXVIII, Pt. I, 304-5, Ga. Dept. of Arch. and Hist.

latures, duly constituted and appointed with their own consent; that no other legislature whatever may rightfully exercise authority over them, and that these privileges they hold as the common rights of mankind, confirmed by the political constitutions they have respectively assumed, and also by several charters of compact from the Crown."[18] Jefferson elaborated upon this direct assertion of the exclusive jurisdiction of the colonial lower houses over their respective colonies and this complete denial of Parliamentary authority over the colonies in his *Summary View of the Rights of British America,* originally intended as instructions to the Virginia delegation to the First Continental Congress and published in Williamsburg in August 1774. Proceeding from the assumption that "our properties within our own territories" should not "be taxed or regulated by any power on earth but our own," Jefferson stated his main point succintly: "the British parliament has no right to exercise authority over us." Condemning not only the various acts by which Parliament had tried to tax the colonies but all Parliamentary legislation for the colonies including the Navigation Acts, Jefferson declared that the colonies were connected with Britain only by a voluntary union under "the same common sovereign, who was thereby made the central link connecting the several parts of the empire thus newly multiplied." For "one free and independent legislature" to take "upon itself to suspend the powers of another, free and independent as itself," as Parliament did in its act to suspend the legislature of New York in 1767, was "a phaenomenon, unknown in nature, the creator and creature of it's own power." Americans could never be persuaded to believe that they held "their political existence at the will of a British Parliament."[19]

But Jefferson realized that not all the grievances of the colonies could be laid at the door of Parliament; some of them had proceeded directly from the King, and Jefferson boldly charged him with a whole series of violations of the rights of American legislatures. He protested that the King was guilty of a "wanton exercise of . . . power" by disallowing "the laws of the American legislatures" for "the most trifling reasons" long after "his ancestors, conscious of the impropriety of opposing their single opinion to the united wisdom of two houses

18. Resolutions of the Freeholders of Albemarle County, July 26, 1774, in Julian P. Boyd *et al.,* eds., *The Papers of Thomas Jefferson* (Princeton, 1950——), I, 117. 19. *A Summary View* in *ibid.,* 122-26, 135.

of parliament," had "modestly declined the exercise of this power in that part of his empire called Great Britain." Jefferson complained that the Crown had "With equal inattention to the necessities of his people here" neglected to consider colonial laws and required suspending clauses in all laws "of any moment" no matter how "immediate may be the call for legislative interposition." The King had deprived some of the colonists of their "glorious right of representation" by the instruction of 1767, dissolved representative bodies for protesting violations of their rights long after his predecessors had abandoned that power in Britain, and after such dissolutions delayed to call new elections "so that for a great length of time the legislature provided by the laws" had "been out of existence." By granting at advanced prices lands that belonged to the whole of society and not merely to him, by sending armed troops to the colonies without the consent of their legislatures, and by attempting to make the military superior to the civil power, the king had also infringed the rights of individuals. All these actions, Jefferson declared, violated rights "derived from the laws of nature," not from the "gift" of the Crown. Boldly asserting that "kings are the servants, not the proprietors of the people," Jefferson exhorted George III to no "longer persevere in sacrificing the rights of one part of the empire to the inordinate desires of another: but deal out to all equal and impartial right."[20]

At the same time Jefferson's *Summary View* was being published in Williamsburg, William Henry Drayton's *A Letter from Freeman of South Carolina* appeared in Charleston. A blueprint for the constitutional reform of the empire in which a general American congress would have taxing powers to fulfill requisitions from the Crown and local legislatures would retain full control over the internal polity of their respective colonies, Drayton's pamphlet included a list of grievances against Britain that reflected South Carolina's own peculiar experience over the previous decade and that differed in many details from those of Jefferson. Drayton, for instance, was especially concerned over the Crown's refusal to grant American judges tenure during good behavior and the dependent status of colonial councilors. Despite these differences, the arguments of the two men were strikingly similar both in tone and in general direction. Like Jefferson, Drayton saw that with Parliament's passage of the Coercive Acts the

20. *Ibid.,* 129-35.

issue was no longer simply "whether Great-Britain has a right to *Tax* America against her consent;—but, whether she has a constitutional right to exercise *Despotism* over America." Though he did not explicitly deny Parliament's jurisdiction over the colonies, Drayton strongly implied as much by denying that there was "any distinction, in the nature of a representation for the purposes of taxation or of legislation" and declaring that "the British Parliament ought not to have, and cannot of right possess any Power to Tax, or in any shape to bind American Freeholders of the British Crown." Finally, he saw, like Jefferson, that restrictions had to be placed on the Crown as well as on Parliament, suggesting that "the King's Prerogative ought not, and cannot of right, be more extensive in America, than it is by law limited in England."[21]

The general meetings or conventions—composed in most cases of the members of the lower houses and other influential citizens and meeting to elect delegates to the First Continental Congress because the royal governors would not call the lower houses into session—did not go so far as Jefferson or Drayton in defining American grievances or in suggesting limitations upon the power of the King and Parliament. Meeting early in July, a month before publication of Drayton's pamphlet, a general gathering of "the Inhabitants of South Carolina" specifically pointed out that it did not concur with the northern colonies in denying Parliament's general superintending power,[22] but it did instruct its delegates to Congress to consider not only "the grievances under which *America* labours by reason of the several Acts of Parliament that impose taxes or duties for raising a revenue" but also those "Statutes, Parliamentary Acts, and Royal Instructions, which make any invidious distinction between his Majesty's subjects in *Great Britain* and *America*"—a clear indication that South Carolinians realized that there was more at stake than simply Parliament's right to tax the colonies.[23] Similarly, the Virginia Convention's instructions to its delegates to Congress were neither so bold nor so explicit as Jefferson had recommended. They did, however, assert the equality of Americans with "their Fellow Subjects . . . in

21. Drayton, *Letter from Freeman,* 7-15, 31.
22. See the remark attributed to Rawlins Lowndes in John Drayton, ed., *Memoirs of the American Revolution,* 2 vols. (Charleston, 1821), I, 130.
23. Resolutions of the Inhabitants of South Carolina, July 6-8, 1774, in Peter Force, ed., *American Archives . . . ,* 9 vols. (Washington, 1837-53), Ser. 4, I, 525-27.

Britain" and specifically denounce the Declaratory Act as "unconstitutional." Moreover, the instructions left no doubt that Virginians were convinced that to protect the rights of the House of Burgesses some limitations had to be imposed on the authority of both the King and Parliament, declaring that the "original Constitution of the American Colonies possessing their Assemblies with the sole Right of directing their internal Polity, it is absolutely destructive of the End of their Institution that their Legislatures should be suspended, or prevented, by hasty Dissolutions, from exercising their legislative Powers."[24] Meeting in August, the North Carolina Convention went further than the South Carolina or Virginia meetings, instructing its delegates to seek "an explicit declaration and acknowledgment of our rights," to assert "our right to all the privileges of *British* subjects, particularly that of paying no taxes or duties but with our own consent," and to declare that "the Legislature of this Province have the exclusive power of making laws to regulate our internal polity, subject to his Majesty's disallowance."[25] Though the Georgia Convention, also meeting in August, did resolve to concert with the other colonies in protecting their constitutions, it alone, among the general meetings in the southern royal colonies, failed to select delegates to Congress or to suggest that it would require more to restore harmony in the empire than the repeal of the Coercive Acts and strict guarantees that Parliament would no longer tax the colonies.[26]

The First Continental Congress at Philadelphia, like the conventions in the southern colonies, did not subscribe to Jefferson's blanket indictment of the imperial government, but it was under no illusion that it could remove American grievances simply by securing an exemption from Parliamentary taxation and officially adopted the view set forth by Jefferson and by James Wilson of Pennsylvania in his *Considerations on the Nature and Extent of the Legislative Authority of Parliament* that Parliament had no authority over the colonies. Although it agreed to permit Parliament to regulate the trade of the empire for "the commercial benefits of its respective members," it claimed for Americans in its Declarations and Resolves "a free and exclusive power of legislation in their several provincial legislatures,

24. Instructions by the Va. Convention to Their Delegates in Congress, Aug. 1-6, 1774, in Boyd *et al.*, eds., *Jefferson Papers*, I, 141-42.

25. Journal of the First Provincial Convention of North Carolina, Aug. 24, 1774, Force, ed., *American Archives*, Ser. 4, I, 734-37.

26. Resolutions of Georgia Inhabitants, Aug. 10, 1774, *ibid.*, 700-701.

where their right of representation can alone be preserved, in all cases of taxation and internal polity, subject only to the negative of their sovereign, in such manner as has been heretofore used and accustomed." Congress centered its attack upon the post-1763 Parliamentary statutes applying to the colonies, citing among others the various revenue acts, the Declaratory Act, the Currency Act, the act to suspend the New York legislature, the Coercive Acts, and the Quebec Act as "infringements and violations" of colonial rights. It was much less sweeping in condemning the measures of the Crown, limiting its objections to protests against dissolving assemblies frequently for attempting "to deliberate on grievances," keeping a standing army in the colonies without the consent of colonial legislatures, and permitting the "exercise of legislative powers in several colonies, by a council appointed, during pleasure, by the crown."[27] Endorsed by general legislative gatherings in each of the thirteen colonies, including even Georgia, the Declarations and Resolves thus became the official statement of the constitutional position of the colonies.[28]

Parliament could not accept this position without giving up the principles it had asserted in the Declaratory Act of 1766 and, in effect, abandoning the traditional British theory of empire. In its address to the people of Great Britain, the First Continental Congress had professed that a return to the status quo of 1763 would satisfy the colonies. "Place us in the same situation that we were at the close of the last war," it declared, "and our former harmony will be restored."[29] But Parliament in 1774-76 was unwilling even to go that far, much less to promise them exemption from Parliamentary taxation. Besides, American legislators now aspired to much more. The Reverend William Smith, Pennsylvania loyalist, correctly charged that American leaders had "been constantly enlarging their views, and stretching them beyond their first bounds, till at length they have wholly changed their ground."[30] Edward Rutledge, young delegate from South Carolina to the First Continental Congress, was one who recognized that the colonies would not "be satisfied with a restoration of such rights only, as have been violated since the year '63, when

27. Oct. 14, 1774, Ford *et al.*, eds., *Journals of the Continental Congress*, I, 63-73.
28. Resolutions of the Ga. Commons, Jan. 1775, in Force, ed., *American Archives*, Ser. 4, I, 1156-58; Alden, *South in Revolution*, 179-80.
29. Oct. 21, 1774, Ford *et al.*, eds., *Journals of Continental Congress*, I, 89.
30. Candidus [William Smith], *Plain Truth: Addressed to the Inhabitants of America* (London, 1776), 46.

we have as many others, as clear and indisputable, that will even then be infringed."[31]   The simple fact was that Americans, no matter what their professions, would not have been content to return to the old inarticulate and undefined pattern of accommodation between imperial theory and colonial practice that had existed through most of the period between 1689 and 1763.   They now sought to become masters of their own political destinies.   Rigid guarantees of colonial rights and precise definitions of the constitutional relationship between the mother country and the colonies and between Parliament and the lower houses on American terms—that is, imperial recognition of the autonomy of the lower houses in local affairs and of the equality of the colonies with the mother country—would have been required to satisfy them.

Parliament's inadequate concessions in Lord North's Conciliatory Resolution and the outbreak of war in Massachusetts in April 1775 left little hope that the dispute could be settled within the framework of the old empire.   Thereafter, royal government rapidly deteriorated in the southern colonies as elsewhere.   By mid-summer of 1775 the lower houses had transformed themselves into provincial congresses, extralegal representative assemblies meeting against the express commands of the royal governors.   As the situation became more and more tense, each governor in turn abandoned his post for the safety of a British warship, leaving the provincial congresses in complete political control.   Preoccupied with running a war, the congresses temporarily lost sight of the constitutional question in the closing months of 1775 and the early part of 1776.   But as they began to think in terms of independence and to form independent constitutions in 1776, the old grievances against Britain were again elaborated at length to provide justification for their actions.   North Carolina and Georgia waited until later to adopt constitutions, but both the South Carolina constitution, adopted in March 1776, and the Virginia constitution, adopted the following June, contained a number of charges against the British government in which violations of the rights of the colonial lower houses were especially prominent.[32]

31. Rutledge to Ralph Izard, Jr., Oct. 29, 1774, in Deas, ed., *Izard Correspondence*, 22-23.
32. S. C. Constitution, Mar. 26, 1776, Hemphill and Wates, eds., *Extracts of S. C. Provincial Congress Journals*, 256-58; Va. Constitution, May 1776, *Ordinances passed at a General Convention of Delegates and Representatives from the Several Counties and Corporations of Virginia [May 1776]* (Richmond, 1816), 4.

Similarly, the official list of grievances in the Declaration of Independence left no doubt that the imperial challenge to the powers of the lower houses was of primary importance in the coming of the American Revolution. Of the seventeen charges against the King alone, eleven of the twelve that referred to actions or policies taken before the actual outbreak of war concerned attempts of the imperial government to curtail the authority of the lower houses. Eight of those eleven applied directly to issues which had arisen between the lower houses in the southern royal colonies and the Crown over the previous two decades.

The first and second charges, that "He has refused his assent to Laws, the most wholesome and necessary for the public good," and that "He has forbidden his Governors to pass laws of immediate and pressing importance, unless suspended in their operation till his assent should be obtained; and when so suspended, he has utterly neglected to attend them," applied respectively to the Crown's exercise of the power of disallowance and its insistence upon the inclusion of suspending clauses in all laws of an "extraordinary nature," both of which had been frequent sources of annoyance and discontent to the lower houses in all four colonies.

The fifth charge, that "He has dissolved Representative houses repeatedly, for opposing with manly firmness his invasions on the rights of the people," had also been a grievance in all four colonies; and part of the sixth charge, that "He has refused for a long time, after such dissolutions, to cause others to be elected . . . ," and the entire third charge, that "He has refused to pass other Laws for the accomodation of large districts of people, unless those people would relinquish the right of Representation in the Legislature, a right inestimable to them and formidable to tyrants only," were relevant to the Crown policies as expressed in the general instruction of 1767 forbidding passage of laws to settle the frequency of elections or to erect new constituencies.

The fourth charge, that "He has called together legislative bodies at places unusual, uncomfortable, and distant from the depository of their public Records, for the sole purpose of fatiguing them into compliance with his measures," was applicable to Montagu's calling the South Carolina Commons to meet in Beaufort in the fall of 1772 in an attempt to force the Commons to accept the royal instruction of April 1770 prohibiting the issuance of money from the treasury without executive consent during the Wilkes fund dispute.

Finally, a portion of the ninth charge, that "He has made Judges dependent upon his Will alone, for the tenure of their offices . . . ," was relevant to the Crown's disallowance of laws to establish judicial tenure during good behavior in both Carolinas during the 1760's; and the eighth charge, that "He has obstructed the Administration of justice, by refusing his Assent to Laws for establishing Judiciary powers," applied to those disallowances as well as to the Crown's refusal in the 1770's to permit the North Carolina Lower House to pass a court law that included a clause to guarantee the right of its constituents to attach the property of foreigners in suits for debt.

Five of the nine charges against the King and Parliament also involved infringements of assembly rights, and each of the five had been issues of importance. Only in South Carolina and Georgia during the late 1760's had the law "For Quartering large bodies of armed troops among us" been enforced in the southern royal colonies, but the laws "For imposing Taxes on us without our Consent" had threatened to deprive all four lower houses of their extensive financial powers, and the laws "For establishing . . . an Arbitrary government" in a "neighbouring Province" so "as to render it at once an example and fit instrument for introducing the same absolute rule into these Colonies," "For taking away our Charters, abolishing our most valuable Laws, and altering fundamentally the Forms of our Governments," and "For suspending our own Legislatures, and declaring themselves invested with power to legislate for us in all cases whatsoever" had threatened the very existence of the lower houses and the constitutions they had been building over the previous century.[33]

No analysis of the charges in the Declaration of Independence can fail to suggest that the preservation and consolidation of the rights and powers of the lower houses were the central issue in the struggle with Britain between 1763 and 1776, just as they had been the most important issue in the political life of the colonies over the previous century and a half. Between 1689 and 1763 the lower houses' contests with royal governors and imperial officials had brought them political maturity, a fair measure of control over local

33. Declaration of Independence, in Boyd *et al.*, eds., *Jefferson Papers*, I, 429-33.

affairs, capable leaders, and a rationale to support their pretensions to political significance within the colonies and in the Empire. The British challenge after 1763 threatened to render their accomplishments meaningless and drove them to demand equal rights with Parliament and autonomy in local affairs and eventually to declare their independence. In this context the American Revolution becomes in essence a war for political survival, a conflict involving not only individual rights as traditionally emphasized by historians but assembly rights as well.

APPENDIX I

Chief Executives of the Southern Royal Colonies, 1660-1776

VIRGINIA

Sir William Berkeley	1660-77
Francis Moryson (President of Council)	1661-62
Herbert Jeffries (Lt. Governor)	1677-78
Thomas Lord Culpeper	1677-83
Sir Henry Chicheley (President of Council)	1678-80
Francis, Lord Howard, fifth Baron of Effingham	1684-92
Nathaniel Bacon (President of Council)	1684
	1687
	1689-90
Francis Nicholson (Lt. Governor)	1690-92
Sir Edmund Andros	1692-98
Ralph Wormeley (President of Council)	1693
Francis Nicholson (Lt. Governor)	1698-1705
William Byrd I (President of Council)	1700
	1703
	1704
Lord George Hamilton, Earl of Orkney	1704-37
Edward Nott (Lt. Governor)	1705-6
Edmund Jenings (President of Council)	1706-10
Alexander Spotswood (Lt. Governor)	1710-22
Hugh Drysdale (Lt. Governor)	1722-26
Robert Carter (President of Council)	1726-27
William Gooch (Lt. Governor)	1727-49
William Anne Keppel, second Earl of Albemarle	1737-54
Reverend James Blair (President of Council)	1740-41
Thomas Lee (President of Council)	1749-50

Lewis Burwell (President of Council)	1750-51
Robert Dinwiddie (Lt. Governor)	1751-58
John Campbell, fourth Earl of Loudoun	1756-57
John Blair (President of Council)	1758
Francis Fauquier (Lt. Governor)	1758-68
Sir Jeffrey Amherst	1759-68
John Blair (President of Council)	1768
Norborne Berkeley, Baron de Botetourt	1768-70
William Nelson (President of Council)	1770-71
John Murray, fourth Earl of Dunmore	1771-76

NORTH CAROLINA
Albemarle

William Drummond	1663-67
Samuel Stephens	1667-69
Peter Carteret	1670-73
John Jenkins (President of Council)	1673-76
Thomas Eastchurch	1676-78
Thomas Miller (Deputy Governor)	1677
John Culpeper (elected)	1677-78
Seth Sothel	1678
John Harvey (Deputy Governor)	1679
John Jenkins (President of Council)	1679-81
Seth Sothel	1682-89

Carolina North and East of Cape Fear

Philip Ludwell	1689-91
Thomas Jarvis	1691-94
Thomas Harvey	1694-99
Henderson Walker (President of Council)	1699-1704
Robert Daniel	1704-5
Thomas Cary	1705-6
William Glover (President of Council)	1706-8
Thomas Cary (President of Council)	1708-11
Edward Hyde	1711-12

North Carolina
Proprietary

Edward Hyde	1712
Thomas Pollock (President of Council)	1712-14
Charles Eden	1714-22
Thomas Pollock (President of Council)	1722
William Reed (President of Council)	1722-24
George Burrington	1724-25
Richard Everard	1725-31

Royal

George Burrington	1731-34
Gabriel Johnston	1734-52
Nathaniel Rice (President of Council)	1752-53
Matthew Rowan (President of Council)	1753-54
Arthur Dobbs	1754-65
William Tryon	1765-71
James Hasell (President of Council)	1771
Josiah Martin	1771-75

SOUTH CAROLINA
Proprietary

William Sayle	1669-70
Joseph West (President of Council)	1670-72
Sir John Yeamans	1672-74
Joseph West	1674-82
Joseph Morton	1682-84
Richard Kyrle	1684
Robert Quary (President of Council)	1684-85
Joseph West	1685
Joseph Morton (President of Council)	1685-86
James Colleton	1686-90
Seth Sothel	1690-91
Philip Ludwell	1691-93
Thomas Smith	1693-94
Joseph Blake (President of Council)	1694
John Archdale	1694-96
Joseph Blake	1696-1700
James Moore (President of Council)	1700-1702
Sir Nathaniel Johnson	1702-8
Edward Tynte	1706-9
Robert Gibbes (President of Council)	1709-12
Charles Craven	1712-16
Robert Daniel (Deputy Governor)	1716-17
Robert Johnson	1717-19

Revolutionary

James Moore, Jr. (elected by convention)	1719-21

Royal

Francis Nicholson	1721-25
Arthur Middleton (President of Council)	1725-30
Robert Johnson	1730-35
Thomas Broughton (Lt. Governor)	1735-37

William Bull I (President of Council)	1737-38
(Lt. Governor)	1738-43
James Glen	1743-56
William Henry Lyttelton	1756-60
William Bull II (Lt. Governor)	1760-61
Thomas Boone	1761-64
William Bull II (Lt. Governor)	1764-66
Lord Charles Greville Montagu	1766-73
William Bull II (Lt. Governor)	1768
	1769-71
	1773-75
Lord William Campbell	1775

GEORGIA

John Reynolds	1754-57
Henry Ellis	1757-60
James Wright	1760-82
James Habersham (President of Council)	1771-73

APPENDIX II

Speakers of the Lower Houses in the Southern Royal Colonies 1689-1776

VIRGINIA

Arthur Allen	1686-88
Thomas Milner	1691-93
Philip Ludwell II	1695-96
Robert Carter	1696-97
William Randolph I	1698
Peter Beverley	1700-1705
Benjamin Harrison III	1705-6
Peter Beverley	1710-14
Daniel McCarty, Sr.	1715-18
John Holloway	1720-34
Sir John Randolph	1734-36
John Robinson II	1738-66
Peyton Randolph	1766-75

SOUTH CAROLINA
Proprietary

Jonathan Amory	1692-93
Ralph Izard, Sr.	1694-95
Jonathan Amory	1696-99
Job Howes	1700-1705
William Rhett, Sr.	1706-7
Thomas Cary	1707
Landgrave Thomas Smith	1707-8
James Risbee	1708-11
William Rhett, Sr.	1711-15
Thomas Broughton	1716-17

George Logan, Sr. — 1717-19
Thomas Hepworth — 1719-21

Royal

James Moore, Jr. — 1721-24
Thomas Hepworth — 1724
Thomas Broughton — 1725-27
John Fenwick — 1727
William Dry — 1728-29
John Lloyd I — 1731
William Dunning — 1731
John Lloyd I — 1731-32
Robert Hume — 1732-33
Paul Jenys — 1733-36
Charles Pinckney — 1736-40
William Bull II — 1740-42
Benjamin Whitaker — 1742-44
William Bull II — 1744-47
Henry Middleton — 1747
William Bull II — 1748-49
Andrew Rutledge — 1749-52
James Mitchie — 1752-54
Henry Middleton — 1754-55
Benjamin Smith — 1755-63
Rawlins Lowndes — 1763-65
Peter Manigault — 1765-72
Rawlins Lowndes — 1772-75

NORTH CAROLINA
Proprietary

John Porter — 1697
Edward Moseley — 1708
William Swann — 1711
Thomas Snowden — 1712
Edward Moseley — 1715-23
Thomas Swann — 1724
Maurice Moore I — 1725
John Baptista Ashe — 1726

Royal

Edward Moseley — 1731-34
William Downing — 1734-39
John Hodgson — 1739-40
Samuel Swann, Sr. — 1742-54
John Campbell — 1754-55
Samuel Swann, Sr. — 1756-61

John Ashe	1762-65
John Harvey, Jr.	1766-69
Richard Caswell, Jr.	1770-71
John Harvey, Jr.	1771-75

GEORGIA

David Douglas	1755-56
William Little	1757
David Montaight	1757-59
Grey Elliott	1760-61
Lewis Johnson	1761-64
Alexander Wylly	1764-68
Noble Wymberly Jones	1768-71
Archibald Bulloch	1771-72
William Young	1772-75

APPENDIX III

The Leaders of the Lower Houses of Assembly in the Southern Royal Colonies, 1688-1776

NOTE ON METHOD

The following tables are based on a quantitative analysis of committee assignments and include any individual who performed a significant portion of committee business at any one session for which records still exist in all four colonies between 1688 and 1776. The first column lists the names, and the second the inclusive dates of service and the constituency. Among the leaders a few always had a greater portion of committee assignments than the rest. I have designated those the first rank of leaders and the rest the second rank. Columns three and four indicate the sessions during which each leader belonged to each rank.

In preparing these tables, I have established seven categories of committees according to their relative importance and the nature of their work and, for lack of a better device, assigned numerical values to each. Five categories apply to committees appointed to handle the regular work of the legislative session. They are, in descending order of importance, standing committees, extraordinary committees, committees of the whole house, major committees, and routine committees. The standing committees and the committees of the whole house were so designated by the lower houses. I considered as extraordinary committees all those involved in determining matters of broad policy both in regard to internal affairs and to relations with the mother country, particularly during the years of crisis after 1763. The remaining committees I divided into two groups, those handling purely routine business and those concerned with matters of somewhat greater importance. The latter group I called major committees; the former, routine committees. In addition, the lower houses occasionally appointed what might be called extrasessionary committees—that is, committees created to perform legislative or sometimes even executive tasks when the legislature was not in session. They included those to correspond with the London agent and those to supervise military expenditures during the intercolonial wars. I divided them into major and minor committees.

To differentiate between the relative importance of these seven categories, I have assigned the following numerical values to the memberships and chairmanships of each: chairman, standing committee—15; member, standing committee—5; member, major extrasessionary committee—8; member, minor extrasessionary committee—6; chairman, extraordinary committee—7; member, extraordinary committee—4; chairman, committee of the whole—3; chairman, major committee—5; member, major committee—3; chairman, routine committee—3; member, routine committee—2.

I have ranked the individual representatives for each session between 1688 and 1776 by counting up their total number of committee posts in each category, assigning them the stated values for each post, and in turn adding up those values. Obviously, this system is not entirely satisfactory, but it seems to me to reflect more accurately the value of each man's committee work than would a simple quantitative tabulation of the total number of his assignments.

I have treated several short sessions of the Virginia House of Burgesses as single sessions. The three between September 24, 1696, and November 3, 1697, are referred to as *1696-97*; the three between May 13 and August 28, 1702, as *1702*; the two between October 23, 1705, and June 22, 1706, as *1705-6*; the two between April 23 and December 1, 1718, as *1718*; the three between February 20, 1746, and April 18, 1747, as *1746-47*; the three between February 14 and November 2, 1754, as *1754*; the three between May 1 and November 8, 1755, as *1755*; the two between March 25 and September 8, 1756, as *1756*; the two between April 14, 1757, and April 12, 1758, as *1757-58*; the two between September 14 and November 11, 1758, as *1758*; the two between February 22 and November 21, 1759, as *1759*; the three between March 4, 1760, and April 1, 1761, as *1760-61*; the three between November 3, 1761, and April 7, 1762, as *1761-62*; the two between October 30, 1764, and June 1, 1765, as *1764-65*; the two between November 6, 1766, and April 11, 1767, as *1766-67*; and the two between November 7, 1769, and June 28, 1770, as *1769-70*. In 1693 there were two different assemblies. The first, which met from March 2 to April 3, is referred to as *1693(1)*. The second, which met from October 10 to November 18, is referred to as *1693(2)*.

Because the South Carolina Commons met so frequently for short periods and because the governors usually permitted it to adjourn itself rather than formally proroguing it as was the custom in the other three colonies, it is not always clear where sessions begin and end. I have treated the meetings of the Commons between the following dates as sessions and have referred to them by the indicated designations: September 20 to October 15, 1692, as *1692*; January 9 to September 20, 1693, as *1693*; November 20 to 28, 1695, as *1695*; January 30 to December 5, 1696, as *1696*; February 23 to November 12, 1697, as *1697*; September 13 to November 19, 1698, as *1698*; October 30 to November 16, 1700, as *1700*; February 4 to August 28, 1701, as *1701*; January 7 to February 3, 1702, as *1702(1)*; April 1 to September 10, 1702, as *1702(2)*; January 13 to February 23, 1703, as *1703(1)*; April 15 to September 17, 1703, as *1703(2)*; January 31 to February 16, 1705, as *1705*; March 6 to April 9, 1706, as *1706*; November 20, 1706, to February 8, 1707, as *1706-7*; June 5 to July 19, 1707, as *1707*; October 22, 1707, to February 12, 1708, as *1707-8*; November 24, 1708, to February 19, 1709, as *1708-9*; April 20 to November 5, 1709, as *1709*; October 10, 1710, to March 1, 1711, as *1710-11*; May 15 to November 12, 1711, as *1711*; April 2 to December 11, 1712, as *1712*; September 22 to December 18, 1713, as *1713*; May 4 to December 18, 1714, as *1714*; February 8 to October 13, 1715, as *1715*; February 28 to August 4, 1716, as *1716*; November 13, 1716, to February 16, 1717, as *1716-17*; April 10 to December 15, 1717, as *1717*; February 3 to September 3, 1720, as *1720*; November 22, 1720, to April 28, 1721, as *1720-21*; July 27 to September 21, 1721, as *1721*; January 25 to August 4, 1722, as *1722*; November 6, 1722, to May 18, 1723, as *1722-23*; October 1, 1723, to June 16, 1724, as *1723-24*; February 23 to June 1, 1725, as *1725*; November 1, 1725, to April 30, 1726, as *1725-26*; November 15, 1726, to March 11, 1727, as *1726-27*; August 1 to September 30, 1727, as *1727*; January 31 to May 11, 1728, as *1728(1)*; July 9 to 24, 1728, as *1728(2)*; January 15 to February 21, 1729, as *1729*; January 21 to August 20, 1731, as *1731*; November 16, 1731, to March 3, 1732, as *1731-32*; November 7, 1732, to September 22, 1733, as *1732-33*; November 15, 1733, to May 31, 1734, as *1733-34*; November 8, 1734, to September 6, 1735, as *1734-35*; November 25, 1735, to July 17, 1736, as *1735-36*; November 10, 1736, to March 5, 1737, as *1736-37*; October 4, 1737, to September 18, 1738, as *1737-38*; January 16 to June 7, 1739, as *1739*; September 12, 1739, to May 10, 1740, as *1739-40*; July 15, 1740, to July 3, 1741, as *1740-41*; October 27, 1741, to July 10, 1742, as *1741-42*; September 14, 1742, to May 7, 1743, as *1742-43*; October 4, 1743, to July 7, 1744, as *1743-44*; October 2, 1744, to May 25, 1745, as *1744-45*; September 10, 1745, to June 17, 1746, as *1745-46*; September 10, 1746, to June 13, 1747, as *1746-47*; January 19 to June 28, 1748, as *1748*; March 28 to June 1, 1749, as *1749*; November 21, 1749, to May 31, 1750, as *1749-50*; November 13, 1750, to August 31, 1751, as *1750-51*; November 14, 1751, to May 16, 1752, as *1751-52*; September 26, 1752, to August 25, 1753, as *1752-53*; January 8 to September 6, 1754, as *1754*; November 12, 1754, to May 20, 1755, as *1754-55*; September 15, 1755, to May 3, 1756, as

1755-56; June 17, 1756, to July 6, 1757, as *1756-57*; October 6, 1757, to May 19, 1758, as *1757-58*; October 23, 1758, to July 14, 1759, as *1758-59*; October 4, 1759, to August 20, 1760, as *1759-60*; October 6, 1760, to January 14, 1761, as *1760-61*; March 26 to December 26, 1761, as *1761*; February 5 to September 13, 1762, as *1762*; October 25, 1762, to September 17, 1763, as *1762-63*; January 4 to October 6, 1764, as *1764*; January 8 to August 9, 1765, as *1765*; October 28, 1765, to July 2, 1766, as *1765-66*; November 11, 1766, to May 28, 1767, as *1766-67*; November 3, 1767, to April 12, 1768, as *1767-68*; November 15 to 19, 1768, as *1768*; June 15 to August 23, 1769, as *1769*; November 28, 1769, to April 11, 1770, as *1769-70*; June 5 to September 8, 1770, as *1770*; January 15 to November 5, 1771, as *1771*; April 2 to 10, 1772, as *1772(1)*; October 8 to November 10, 1772, as *1772(2)*; January 6 to 12, 1773, as *1773(1)*; March 8 to September 13, 1773, as *1773(2)*; January 11 to October 22, 1774, as *1774*; and January 24 to August 30, 1775, as *1775*.

I have also treated several short sessions of the North Carolina Lower House of Assembly as single sessions. The two between November 1, 1725, and April 13, 1726, are referred to as *1725-26*; the three between February 6 and November 15, 1739, as *1739*; the two between February 5 and August 22, 1740, as *1740*; the two between July 20, 1743, and March 8, 1744, as *1743-44*; the two between November 15, 1744, and April 20, 1745, as *1744-45*; the two between June 12 and December 5, 1746, as *1746*; the two between February 25 and October 9, 1747, as *1747*; the two between March 15, 1748, and April 14, 1749, as *1748-49*; the three between September 26, 1749, and July 10, 1750, as *1749-50*; the two between May 16 and December 14, 1757, as *1757*; the two between April 28 and December 23, 1758, as *1758*; the two between May 8, 1759, and January 9, 1760, as *1759-60*; and the five between April 24 and December 6, 1760, as *1760*. In both 1762 and 1773 there were two assemblies. The one from April 13 to 29, 1762, is referred to as Apr., 1762; that from November 3 to December 11, 1762, as Fall, 1762; that from January 25 to March 6, 1773, as Spring, 1773; and that from December 4 to 21, 1773, as Dec., 1773. In 1764 there were two long sessions of the same assembly. The first, which lasted from February 3 to March 10, is referred to as Spring, 1764; the second, which lasted from October 25 to November 27, as Fall, 1764. *1733* refers to the assembly that met from July 3 to 18, 1733. A second assembly that met from November 5 to 8, 1733, was never officially organized because it did not contain sufficient members to constitute a quorum.

The two sessions of the Georgia Commons House of Assembly in 1757 are referred to as Jan.-Feb., 1757, and June-July, 1757. The first session in 1758 is referred to as Jan.-Mar., 1758; and the two sessions between June and December 1758 as June-Dec., 1758.

THE VIRGINIA HOUSE OF BURGESSES

Name	Service and Constituency	Sessions in First Rank	Sessions in Second Rank
Acrill, William	**1736**: Charles City	1736	
Adams, Richard	1752-65: New Kent		1769-70
Alexander, John	1766-75: Stafford		1772
Allen, Arthur	1684-88: Surry	1688	
Allerton, Isaac	1668-74; 1677; 1680-82: Northumberland; 1684;1696-97: Westmoreland	1696-97	
Allerton, Willoughby	1699; 1710-14: Westmoreland		1710; 1712
Armistead, William	1692-93; 1700-06; 1712-15: Elizabeth City		1712
Aylett, William	1736-40: Westmoreland		1738
Baker, Richard	1768-71: Isle of Wight		1769-70
Ball, William	1703-14; 1720-26: Lancaster		1705-6
Banister, John	1766-68; 1769-76: Dinwiddie		1769-70; 1772; 1775
Barradall, Edward	1738-42: College of William and Mary	1740; 1742	1738
Bassett, William	1693-1702: New Kent		1695; 1696-97; 1699
Beverley, Peter	1700-14: Gloucester; 1715: College of William and Mary	1700; 1701; 1702; 1703; 1704; 1705; 1705-6; 1710; 1711-12; 1712; 1713; 1714	
Beverley, Robert	1699-1702; 1705-6: Jamestown; 1720: King and Queen	1705-6	1699; 1701; 1702
Beverley, William	1734-40: Orange; 1742-49: Essex	1744; 1746-47; 1748-49	1736; 1738; 1740; 1742
Blair, Archibald	1718; 1727-34: Jamestown; 1720-26: James City		1718; 1720; 1722; 1730; 1732
Blair, John, Sr.	1734: Jamestown; 1736-40: Williamsburg		1736; 1738
Blair, John, Jr.	1766-70: College of William and Mary	1766-67; 1769-70	1768; 1769
Bland, Richard, Sr.	1693; 1700-5: Charles City; 1705-6: Prince George		1701; 1703; 1705-6
Bland, Richard, Jr.	1742-76: Prince George	1746-47; 1748-49; 1752; 1753; 1754; 1755; 1756; 1757-58; 1758;	1761-62; 1769

Name	Service and Constituency	Sessions in First Rank	Sessions in Second Rank
		1759; 1760-61; 1762; 1763; 1764-65; 1766-67; 1768; 1769-70; 1771; 1772; 1773; 1774; 1775	
Bolling, John	1710-4; 1718; 1723-29: Henrico		1712; 1718
Bolling, Robert	1723-34: Prince George	1732	1734
Boush, Maxmillan	1710-26: Princess Anne		1715
Braxton, Carter	1761-71; 1775-76: King William	1775	1766-67
Braxton, George, Jr.	1742-49; 1758-61: King & Queen	1746-47; 1748-49	1742
Brent, George	1688: Stafford		1688
Buckner, William	1698-99; 1710-14: York		1699; 1711-12; 1712; 1713; 1714
Burwell, Carter	1742-55: James City	1754; 1755	1746-47;1748-49; 1752; 1753
Burwell, Lewis of Kingsmill	1758-74: James City		1764-65; 1766-67; 1769-70
Burwell, Nathaniel	1710-12: Jamestown; 1720: Gloucester		1720
Byrd, William, II	1696: Henrico		1696-97
Carrington, Paul	1765-76: Charlotte		1769-70; 1772; 1775
Carter, Charles of Cleve	1734-64: King George	1742; 1744· 1746-47; 1748-49; 1752; 1753; 1754; 1755; 1756; 1757-58; 1759; 1760-61	1736; 1758; 1761-62
Carter, Charles of Corotoman	1758-76: Lancaster		1769-70
Carter, Landon	1752-68: Richmond	1752; 1754; 1755; 1756; 1757-58; 1759; 1766-67	1758; 1760-61; 1762: 1764-65
Carter, Robert	1691-92; 1695-99: Lancaster	1695; 1696-97; 1699	1691; 1696
Cary, Archibald	1748-49: Goochland 1756-76: Chesterfield	1762; 1764-65; 1766-67; 1769-70; 1772; 1775	1757-58; 1758; 1760-61; 1768; 1769; 1773; 1774
Cary, Miles	1684; 1688-92; 1698-1706: Warwick; 1693: Jamestown	1691; 1693 (1); 1698; 1699; 1700; 1701; 1702; 1703; 1705-6	1704; 1705

Name	Service and Constituency	Sessions in First Rank	Sessions in Second Rank
Chiswell, John	1742-55: Hanover; 1756-58: Williamsburg		1755
Churchill, William	1691-92; 1704-5: Warwick		1691; 1692
Claiborne, Augustine	1748-53: Surry		1753
Clayton, John	1715: Jamestown; 1720-26: James City; 1727-34: Williamsburg	1720; 1722; 1728; 1730; 1732; 1734	1715
Colston, William	1692: Rappahannock; 1693; 1698-99: Richmond		1699
Conway, Edwin	1710-18; 1723-55: Lancaster	1736; 1738; 1740; 1742; 1744; 1746-47	1712; 1715; 1730; 1732; 1734; 1752
Corbin, Gawin, Sr.	1698-1705; 1718-22: Middlesex; 1715: King and Queen	1702; 1715; 1718; 1720	1703; 1704; 1705; 1722
Corbin, Gawin, Jr.	1734-40: King and Queen; 1742-47: Middlesex	1736	1738; 1744; 1746-47
Corbin, Richard	1748-49: Middlesex		1748-49
Custis, John, II	1684-86; 1693-99: Northampton	1699	1693 (1); 1693 (2); 1695; 1696; 1696-97
Dandridge, Bartholomew	1772-76: New Kent		1775
Digges, Dudley (1665-1711)	1695-97: Warwick		1696-97
Digges, Dudley (1718-90)	1752-76: York	1775	1754; 1755; 1756; 1757-58; 1769-70; 1772
Digges, William	1752-71: Warwick		1754; 1755; 1757-58; 1760-61
Duke, Henry	1692-93; 1696-97; 1699: James City		1696-97
Edwards, William	1693: Surry (?)		1693 (2)
Eskridge, George	1705-14; 1718-34: Westmoreland	1718; 1728; 1730; 1732	1710; 1712; 1713; 1734
Eyre, Littleton	1742-61: Northampton		1752
Eyre, Severn	1766-73: Northampton	1769-70	1766-67; 1772
Fitzhugh, Henry	1734-42: Stafford	1736; 1738; 1740; 1742	1734
Fitzhugh, William (1650-1701)	1677-84; 1693: Stafford		1693 (2)
Fitzhugh, William (1741-1809)	1772-76: King George		1772
Fleming, John	1756-67: Cumberland		1764-65; 1766-67

Name	Service and Constituency	Sessions in First Rank	Sessions in Second Rank
Foster, Joseph	1684; 1688; 1696; 1700-5: New Kent		1701; 1705
Fry, Joshua	1746-54: Albemarle	1753	1748-49; 1752
Goodrich, Edward	1711-18: Prince George		1715
Gray, Edwin	1769-76: Southampton		1774
Grymes, John	1718-22: Middlesex	1718	1720
Harmar, John	1742-47: Williamsburg		1742
Harrison, Benjamin, II	1677; 1680-82; 1691-92; 1697-98: Surry	1691; 1692; 1696-97; 1698	
Harrison, Benjamin, III	1703-5: James City; 1705-6: Charles City	1705-6	1705
Harrison, Benjamin, IV	1736-45: Charles City	1744	1738; 1740; 1742
Harrison, Benjamin, V	1748-76: Charles City	1769-70; 1772	1753; 1755; 1757-58; 1759; 1760-61; 1762; 1764-65; 1766-67; 1768; 1769; 1773; 1774
Harrison, Henry	1715-30: Surry	1718	1722; 1723; 1728; 1730
Harrison, Nathaniel	1699-1706: Surry		1700; 1701; 1705; 1705-6
Hartwell, Henry	1684-86; 1691-92: Jamestown	1691	1692
Harwood, William	1742-76: Warwick		1774
Hedgman, Peter	1732-40: Prince William; 1742-58: Stafford		1748-49
Henry, Patrick	1765-68: Louisa; 1769-76: Hanover	1769-70	1766-67; 1772
Hill, Edward, IV	1704-6: Charles City		1705-6
Holloway, John	1710-14: King & Queen; 1720-22; 1727-34: York; 1723-26: Williamsburg	1710; 1712; 1713; 1714; 1720; 1722; 1723; 1726; 1728; 1730; 1732	1711-12
Holt, James	1772-76: Norfolk County		1772
Jefferson, Thomas	1769-76: Albemarle		1775
Johnson, Philip	1752-58: King & Queen; 1761-65: James City		1753; 1755; 1757-58
Johnston, George	1758-65: Fairfax		1759; 1762
Jones, Gabriel	1748-53: Frederick; 1756-58; 1769-71: Augusta; 1758-61: Hampshire		1757-58; 1769-70
Jones, Joseph	1772-76: King George	1775	1772
Jones, Orlando	1715-18: King William		1715
Jones, Robert	1748-55: Surry		1748-49; 1752; 1753

Name	Service and Constituency	Sessions in First Rank	Sessions in Second Rank
Kemp, Matthew	1723-30: Middlesex	1730	1728
Lawson, Anthony	1680-82; 1688-91: Lower Norfolk; 1692: Norfolk Co.		1688; 1691
Lee, Francis Lightfoot	1758-68: Loudoun; 1769-76: Richmond		1766-67; 1775
Lee, Henry	1758-76: Prince William	1775	1766-67; 1769-70; 1772
Lee, Richard of Lee Hall	1757-76: Westmoreland		1769; 1769-70; 1774
Lee, Richard Henry	1758-76: Westmoreland	1762; 1766-67; 1769-70; 1772; 1774	1759; 1760-61; 1761-62; 1764-65; 1769; 1771; 1773
Lee, Thomas	1726-33: Westmoreland	1732	
Leigh, William	1692-1704: King and Queen	1696-97; 1699; 1700; 1702; 1703	1692; 1693 (1); 1693 (2); 1695; 1701
Lewis, William	1691-92: James City		1692
Lomax, Lunsford	1742-55: Caroline		1744; 1746-47; 1752; 1754; 1755
Ludwell, Philip, II	1695-96; 1698-99: James City; 1697: Jamestown	1695; 1696	1699
Ludwell, Philip, III	1742-49: Jamestown	1748-49	1744; 1746-47
McCarty, Daniel, Sr.	1705-6; 1715-23: Westmoreland	1715; 1718	1705; 1722; 1723
McCarty, Daniel, Jr.	1734-44: Westmoreland		1738
Marable, George	1700-6;1712-18: James City		1715
Martin, John	1730-34; 1738-40: Caroline; 1752-56: King William		1734; 1740; 1752; 1753; 1754; 1755
Mason, David	1758-76: Sussex		1774
Mason, George, II	1688-91; 1693-1702; 1705-12; 1715: Stafford		1699
Mason, Thomson	1766-71: Stafford; 1772-74: Loudoun		1766-67
Mercer, George	1761-65: Frederick		1762
Mercer, James	1762-76: Hampshire	1775	1766-67; 1769-70
Meriwether, Francis	1705-6; 1712: Essex		1705-6
Meriwether, Nicholas	1705-20: New Kent; 1722-34: Hanover	1712	1710; 1714; 1715; 1730; 1732; 1734
Milner, Thomas	1688-93: Nansemond	1688; 1691; 1692; 1693 (1); 1693 (2)	
Munford, Robert	1765-76: Mecklenburg	1775	
Nelson, Thomas (1716-87)	1745-49: York	1746-47	1748-49

Name	Service and Constituency	Sessions in First Rank	Sessions in Second Rank
Nelson, Thomas (1738-89)	1761-76: York	1775	1769-70; 1772
Nelson, William	1742-45: York	1744	1742
Nicholas, Robert Carter	1756-61: York 1766-76: James City	1756; 1757-58; 1760-61; 1769-70; 1772; 1774; 1775	1758; 1759; 1766-67; 1768; 1773
Norton, John	1749-55: York		1755
Page, John	1752-68: Gloucester		1754; 1755; 1756; 1757-58
Parke, Daniel, II	1688; 1693: James City; 1693: York; 1695: New Kent		1693 (1); 1695
Pendleton, Edmund	1752-76: Caroline	1754; 1755; 1756; 1757-58; 1760-61; 1764-65; 1766-67; 1768; 1769-70; 1772	1752; 1753; 1758; 1759; 1761-62; 1762; 1769; 1773; 1774
Power, James	1742-47: King William; 1752-58: New Kent	1754; 1755; 1756	1746-47; 1752
Pressley, Peter	1710-12; 1715-47: Northumberland		1715
Randolph, Beverley	1744-49: College of William and Mary		1746-47
Randolph, Isham	1738-40: Goochland		1740
Randolph, Sir John	1734-36: College of William and Mary	1734; 1736	
Randolph, John, Jr.	1769: Lunenburg; 1774-76: College of William and Mary		1775
Randolph, Peter	1749: Henrico		1748-49
Randolph, Peyton	1748-49; 1761-75: Williamsburg; 1752-61: College of William and Mary	1748-49; 1752; 1753; 1755; 1756; 1757-58; 1758; 1759; 1760-61; 1761-62; 1762; 1764; 1764-65; 1766-67; 1768; 1769; 1769-70; 1771; 1772; 1773; 1774; 1775	
Randolph, Richard	1727-48: Henrico	1734; 1742; 1746-47	1730; 1732; 1736; 1740; 1744
Randolph, William, I	1684-92; 1693-98; 1703-11: Henrico	1693 (2); 1695; 1696; 1696-97; 1698	1691; 1692; 1693 (1); 1705; 1705-6; 1710

Name	Service and Constituency	Sessions in First Rank	Sessions in Second Rank
Randolph, William, II	1715-26: Henrico	1726	1718; 1720; 1723
Randolph, William, III	1752-61: Henrico	1757-58	1753; 1754; 1756; 1759
Reade, Clement	1748-54; 1758-63: Lunenburg		1752; 1753; 1759
Riddick, Lemuel	1736-68; 1769-75: Nansemond		1742; 1744; 1748-49; 1752; 1755; 1764-65; 1769-70; 1772
Ring, Joseph	1684; 1691-92; 1693: York		1691
Robinson, Christopher, I	1680-82; 1685-92: Middlesex	1691	1688; 1692
Robinson, Christopher, III	1752-58: Middlesex		1753
Robinson, John, I	1710-14: Middlesex		1712
Robinson, John, II	1727-65: King & Queen	1732; 1734; 1736; 1738; 1740; 1742; 1744; 1746-47; 1748-49; 1752; 1753; 1754; 1755; 1756; 1757-58; 1758; 1759; 1760-61; 1761-62; 1762; 1763; 1764; 1764-65	
Robinson, William	1703-14: Richmond; 1720-26: Stafford; 1734: King George	1712	1705-6; 1710; 1713; 1714
Ruffin, John	1754-55: Surry		1755
Scarburgh, Charles	1680-84; 1688-91: Accomack	1691	1692
Sherwood, William	1680-84: James City; 1688; 1695-97: Jamestown	1688	1695; 1696-97
Smith, John	1685-86; 1691: Gloucester	1691	
Smith, Lawrence	1688-92: Gloucester		1691; 1692
Soane, Henry, Jr.	1710-14: James City		1713
Spicer, Arthur	1685-88: Rappahannock; 1693-96: Richmond		1688; 1693 (1)
Starke, Bolling	1769-72: Dinwiddie		1769; 1769-70
Swann, Samuel	1677; 1680-88; 1693: Surry	1693 (1)	
Tabb, Thomas	1748-58; 1761-69: Amelia		1766-67
Tayloe, John	1727-32: Richmond		1730; 1732

Name	Service and Constituency	Sessions in First Rank	Sessions in Second Rank
Tayloe, William	1695-96; 1700-2; 1705-6: Richmond		1700; 1701
Taylor, John	1693; 1696-99: Charles City		1693 (2); 1696-97; 1699
Thruston, Malachy	1692: Princess Anne; 1698: Norfolk		1692
Walker, Thomas	1752-54: Louisa; 1756-61: Hampshire; 1761-76: Albemarle		1757-58; 1764-65; 1769-70
Waller, Benjamin	1744-61: James City	1746-47; 1748-49; 1752; 1754; 1755; 1756; 1757-58; 1760-61	1744; 1753; 1758; 1759
Waller, John	1710-14; 1720-22: King William		1712; 1713
Waller, William	1742-53; 1756-60: Spotsylvania		1748-49; 1752
Washington, George	1758-65: Frederick; 1766-76: Fairfax		1769-70; 1772
Westcomb, James	1700-2: Westmoreland		1701
Whiting, Beverley	1738-55: Gloucester	1746-47; 1748-49; 1752; 1753	1744
Whiting, Thomas	1755-76: Gloucester		1775
Willis, Francis	1727-40; 1745-49: Gloucester		1732; 1734; 1738
Wilson, Willis	1693; 1696-99: Elizabeth City		1699
Wood, James	1766, 1769-76: Frederick		1775
Woodson, John	1768-76: Goochland		1772; 1774
Wormeley, Ralph	1742-64: Middlesex		1748-49
Wythe, George	1754-55: Williamsburg; 1758-61: College of William and Mary; 1761-68: Elizabeth City	1764-65; 1766-67	1754; 1755; 1759; 1760-61; 1761-62; 1762

The South Carolina Commons House of Assembly

Name	Service and Constituency	Sessions in First Rank	Sessions in Second Rank
Abercromby, James	1739-42: Prince Frederick; 1744-45: Prince George Winyaw		1739-40; 1740-41; 1741-42; 1743-44
Allen, Eleazer	1725-27: St. Philip's		1725; 1725-26; 1726-27
Allien, Richard	1721-24; 1731-33: St. Philip's	1721; 1731	1722; 1723-24; 1732-33
Amory, Jonathan	1692-95: Berkeley; 1696-98: Berkeley and Craven	1692; 1693; 1695; 1696; 1697; 1698	
Ash, John	1701-8: Colleton	1702 (2)	1703 (1)
Ashby, John	1698-1702: Berkeley and Craven; 1725-27: St. Thomas and St. Dennis		1701
Austin, George	1741-42; 1745-46; 1754-57: St. Philip's; 1749-51: St. Bartholomew	1749; 1754-55; 1756-57	1745-46; 1749-50; 1755-56
Barnwell, John	1710-11: Colleton; 1711-12: Colleton and Granville; 1717-19; 1721-24: St. Helena	1710-11; 1717; 1722; 1722-23	1712; 1721; 1723-24
Barton, Thomas	1706-7: Berkeley and Craven; 1725-27: Christ Church		1706; 1706-7
Beale, Othniel	1731-36; 1745-46: St. Philip's	1731; 1732-33; 1733-34; 1734-35; 1735-36; 1745-46	1731-32
Bee, Thomas	1762-65: St. Paul's; 1766-68: St. Peter's; 1769-71: St. Luke's; 1772-75: St. Andrew's	1772 (2); 1773 (2); 1775	1764; 1770; 1774
Bellinger, Edmund, I	1695: Berkeley; 1696-97: Berkeley and Craven	1695; 1696	
Beresford, Richard	1702-5; 1707-8; 1710-11: Berkeley and Craven; 1721-22: St. Thomas and St. Dennis	1710-11	1705; 1707-8; 1721; 1722
Blake, Joseph, Jr.	1733-36: St. Bartholomew		1733-34; 1734-35; 1735-36
Blakeway, William	1721-22: St. Bartholomew [?]	1721	1722
Bond, Jacob	1725-27; 1736-39; 1745-46: Christ Church; 1731-33: St. Helena;	1732-33; 1745-46; 1748	1725; 1726-27; 1727; 1731; 1731-32;

Name	Service and Constituency	Sessions in First Rank	Sessions in Second Rank
	1748; 1752-54: St. Thomas and St. Dennis; 1749-51: St. Bartholomew		1736-37; 1737-38; 1739; 1752-53; 1754
Boyd, John	1692-93: Craven		1692
Brewton, Miles	1765-68: St. Philip's; 1771: St. Andrew's; 1772-75: St. Michael's	1766-67; 1773 (2); 1775	1767-68; 1772 (2); 1774; 1775
Brewton, Robert	1733-39: St. Philip's; 1739-42: Christ Church; 1746: St. Thomas and St. Dennis		1734-35; 1735-36; 1736-37; 1739-40
Broughton, Nathaniel	1725-27; 1731-36: St. John's Berkeley		1732-33; 1733-34; 1734-35
Broughton, Thomas	1696-1703; 1716-17: Berkeley and Craven; 1725-27: St. Thomas and St. Dennis	1716; 1716-17; 1725; 1725-26; 1726-27; 1727	1701; 1702 (1)
Buchanan, William	1746-47: St. Bartholomew; 1751-54: Prince Frederick		1751-52
Buckly, John	1698; 1702-5: Berkeley and Craven		1698; 1703 (2)
Bull, Stephen, I	1700-1703: Berkeley and Craven	1702 (1)	1701; 1702 (2); 1703 (1)
Bull, William, Sr.	1706-8; 1716-17: Berkeley and Craven		1716
Bull, William, Jr.	1736-42; 1746-47: St. Andrew's; 1742-45: St. John's Berkeley; 1745-46; 1749: Prince William's; 1748: St. Bartholomew	1740-41; 1741-42; 1743-44; 1744-45; 1745-46; 1746-47; 1748; 1749	1739; 1739-40; 1742-43
Burnham, Charles	1695: Berkeley; 1698; 1702-3; 1706-7: Berkeley and Craven	1703 (1)	1695; 1698
Cary, Thomas	1707: Berkeley and Craven	1707	
Cattell, William, Jr.	1742-47: St. Andrew's; 1748: St. Helena	1746-47	1745-46; 1748
Cattell, William, III	1769-75: St. Andrew's		1774
Caw, David	1752-54: St. James Santee; 1755-57: St. James Goose Creek		1752-53; 1754
Champneys, John	1736-42: St. Bartholomew		1739; 1739-40; 1741-42
Chicken, George	1707-9; 1713-15: Berkeley and Craven; 1721-27: St. James Goose Creek		1721; 1722-23; 1725

Name	Service and Constituency	Sessions in First Rank	Sessions in Second Rank
Clifford, Thomas	1731-33: St. James Goose Creek		1732-33
Cochran, James, Sr.	1707-8: Colleton; 1714-17: Colleton and Granville; 1717-19: St. Paul's	1714; 1717	1715; 1716; 1716-17
Cochran, James, Jr.	1733-39: St. Bartholomew		1733-34
Cordes, Thomas, Sr.	1733-42; 1745-46; 1748: St. John's Berkeley		1735-36; 1737-38; 1741-42; 1745-46; 1748
Courtis, Daniell	1692-93; 1696-97: Colleton		1696; 1697
Crawford, Daniel	1742-45; 1748: Prince Frederick; 1746-47: St. James Santee; 1757-60: St. Philip's	1746-47	1743-44; 1744-45; 1748; 1757-58; 1758-59
Dale, Thomas	1749-50: St. Peter's		1749
Daniel, Robert	1706-7; 1708-9; 1713-15: Berkeley and Craven	1713	
Dart, Benjamin	1761-62: St. Andrew's; 1765-71: St. Michael's	1767-68; 1769; 1769-70	1762; 1765-66; 1766-67; 1768
Dart, John	1735-45; 1749-51: St. Philip's; 1753-54: St. Helena	1736-37; 1737-38; 1739; 1739-40; 1741-42; 1744-45; 1749	1735-36; 1740-41; 1743-44; 1750-51; 1751-52; 1752-53; 1754
Deas, David	1749-54: St. Philip's; 1775: St. Michael's	1751-52	1752-53; 1754; 1775
De La Conseillere, Benjamin	1713-17: Berkeley and Craven; 1717-19: St. Philip's	1714; 1716; 1716-17; 1717	1713; 1715
Delebere, John	1728-33; 1737-39: St. Helena		1728 (2); 1732-33
D'Harriette, Benjamin	1731-36: St. Philip's; 1742-45: St. John's Colleton		1733-34; 1735-36
Diston, Thomas	1716-17: Berkeley and Craven		1716
D'Oyley, Daniel	1765-68: St. Thomas and St. Dennis		1766-67; 1767-68
Drake, Jonathan	1707-8; 1716-17: Berkeley and Craven; 1717-21; 1724: St. John's Berkeley		1716; 1717; 1720; 1723-24
Drake, William	1728-33: St. John's Berkeley; 1733-36: St. James Santee; 1737-39: St. John's Colleton	1731; 1733-34	1728 (1); 1732-33; 1734-35; 1735-36; 1737-38

Name	Service and Constituency	Sessions in First Rank	Sessions in Second Rank
Drayton, Thomas	1736-42; 1748-51: St. Andrew's; 1746: St. James Goose Creek		1748; 1750-51
Dry, William	1720-21; 1725-29; 1733-36: St. James Goose Creek	1728 (1); 1728 (2); 1729	1720-21; 1725; 1725-26; 1726-27; 1727; 1733-34; 1734-35
Dunning, William	1731-32: St. Bartholomew	1731	
Edwards, John	1772-75: St. Michael's		1772 (2); 1775
Elliott, Barnard	1769-72: Prince William's		1771
Elliott, Benjamin	1765-68; 1770-75: St. Paul's		1773 (2); 1775
Elliott, William, Jr.	1728; 1731-36; 1739-45: St. Andrew's; 1748: St. Paul's		1733-34; 1748
Evance, Branfill	1746-48: St. Philip's		1746-47; 1748
Evance, Thomas	1766-71: St. James Santee; 1772: Prince William's; 1773-75: St. John's Colleton	1772 (2)	1773 (2)
Evans, George	1713-15: Berkeley and Craven	1713; 1714; 1715	
Eve, Abraham	1706-7: Colleton; 1711-15: Colleton and Granville; 1720-23: St. Paul's		1714
Eveleigh, Samuel, Sr.	1725-27: St. Philip's		1725
Eveleigh, Samuel, Jr.	1745-46: St. Philip's		1745-46
Fenwick, John	1706-7: Colleton; 1711-15: Colleton and Granville; 1720-27: St. Paul's; 1728-29: St. Philip's	1720; 1720-21; 1721; 1722; 1722-23; 1725; 1725-26; 1727	1711; 1712; 1714; 1715; 1726-27; 1728 (2); 1729
Fenwick, Robert	1700-1702; 1707-8; 1713-15: Berkeley and Craven; 1721-24: Christ Church [?]	1702 (1); 1707-8; 1714; 1715	1700; 1701; 1707; 1713; 1722-23; 1723-24
Ferguson, Thomas	1762-65: St. Andrew's; 1766-68: Prince William's; 1769-71: All Saints; 1772-75: St. Paul's		1767-68; 1769-70; 1773 (2)
Fitch, Tobias	1725-33: St. James Goose Creek	1728(1)	1727; 1729; 1731; 1732-33

Name	Service and Constituency	Sessions in First Rank	Sessions in Second Rank
Gadsden, Christopher	1757-61;1768-75: St. Philip's; 1762-68: St. Paul's	1758-59; 1759-60; 1760-61; 1761; 1762-63; 1764; 1765-66; 1768; 1769; 1769-70; 1772 (2)	1765; 1767-68; 1770; 1771; 1773 (2); 1774
Gadsden, Thomas	1762: Prince George Winyaw; 1762-65: St. Helena		1765
Gaillard, Tacitus	1749-54; 1762-65: St. James Santee; 1766-67; 1773-75: St. Matthew's; 1768: St. George Dorchester; 1769-72: St. Stephen's		1766-67
Gibbes, Robert	1692-93: Colleton		1692; 1693
Gibbon, William	1707-9; 1711-12: Berkeley and Craven; 1717-19: St. Philip's		1707-8; 1712; 1717
Glen, Thomas	1749-54: St. Helena		1749-50
Godin, Benjamin	1711-12: Berkeley and Craven	1712	1711
Golightly, Culchworth	1739-42: St. John's Colleton; 1743-45; 1748: St. Bartholomew		1744-45; 1748
Graeme, David	1755-61: Christ Church		1755-56; 1756-57; 1760-61
Graeme, James	1733: St. Helena; 1742-45: St. Philip's; 1749-51: St. George Dorchester	1742-43; 1743-44	1744-45; 1749; 1749-50; 1750-51
Grange, Hugh	1707-8; 1711-12: Berkeley and Craven		1711; 1712
Greene, Daniel	1725-27: St. Helena; 1729: St. Philip's		1725-26; 1729
Guerard, Benjamin	1765-68: St. Michael's		1765-66; 1766-67
Guerard, John, Sr.	1713-14: Berkeley and Craven		1713
Guerard, John, Jr.	1754-60: St. Philip's	1757-58; 1758-59	1754-55; 1755-56; 1756-57; 1759-60
Hall, Arthur	1711-12; 1716-17: Colleton and Granville; 1717-24: St. Paul's; 1725-27: St. Bartholomew		1717; 1726-27

Name	Service and Constituency	Sessions in First Rank	Sessions in Second Rank
Hall, Robert	1698-1702: Berkeley and Craven		1700; 1701
Henning, Thomas	1736-39: Prince Frederick		1736-37
Hepworth, Thomas	1720-21: St. John's Berkeley [?]; 1721-24: St. Paul's [?]; 1725-27: St. Helena	1720; 1720-21; 1723-24	1721; 1722; 1722-23; 1725
Herbert, John	1725-27: St. James Goose Creek		1727
Hext, Alexander	1725-36: St. Paul's; 1736-41: St. John's Colleton		1733-34; 1734-35; 1735-36; 1736-37
Hext, David	1736-39; 1742-45: St. John's Colleton; 1740-42: St. James Goose Creek; 1746: Prince Frederick; 1746-51: St. Philip's		1744-45; 1745-46; 1748; 1749; 1750-51
Heyward, Thomas, Jr.	1772-75: St. Helena		1773 (2); 1775
Hill, Charles	1717-19; 1721-24: St. Philip's	1722	1717; 1722-23; 1723-24
Holmes, Isaac	1746-48: St. Philip's; 1750-51: Prince Frederick		1746-47; 1748
Howes, Job	1696-1705: Berkeley and Craven	1696; 1697; 1698; 1700; 1701; 1702 (1); 1702 (2); 1703 (1); 1703 (2); 1705	
Hume, Robert	1725-27; 1731-33: St. Philip's	1731; 1731-32; 1732-33	1725-26
Hyrne, Edward	1716-17: Berkeley and Craven		1716
Hyrne, Henry	1728; 1736-39: St. Paul's; 1739-42; 1761: St. Bartholomew	1740-41; 1761	1736-37; 1737-38; 1739; 1741-42
Ingerson, James	1708-11: Berkeley and Craven		1710-11
Irving, James	1749-54: St. Helena	1754	1749-50; 1750-51; 1751-52; 1752-53
Izard, Henry	1742-48: St. James Goose Creek		1746-47; 1748
Izard, Ralph, Sr.	1692-95: Berkeley; 1696-1702; 1703-7; 1708-10: Berkeley and Craven	1695; 1696; 1698; 1700; 1701; 1703 (2); 1706; 1708-9; 1709	1692; 1693; 1702 (1); 1705; 1706-7; 1710-11

Name	Service and Constituency	Sessions in First Rank	Sessions in Second Rank
Izard, Ralph, Jr.	1711-13; 1716-17: Berkeley and Craven; 1717-19: St. James Goose Creek	1716; 1716-17; 1717	
Izard, Ralph, of Barton (1717-66)	1746-47; 1757-61: St. George Dorchester		1746-47
Izard, Walter, Sr.	1713-17: Berkeley and Craven; 1717-21: St. Andrew's; 1721-27: St. George Dorchester		1714; 1722; 1722-23; 1727
Jenys, Paul	1728: St. Philip's; 1729-36: St. George Dorchester	1732-33; 1733-34; 1734-35; 1735-36	1728 (2); 1729; 1731; 1731-32
Kershaw, Joseph	1769-72; 1773-75: St. Mark's		1769; 1769-71; 1771
Ladson, John	1692-95: Berkeley; 1696-97: Berkeley and Craven		1693
Lamboll, Thomas	1728: St. Paul's; 1754-60: St. Andrew's	1754-55; 1755-56; 1756-57; 1759-60	1728 (1); 1757-58; 1758-59
Langhorne, Arthur	1713-15: Berkeley and Craven		1713
Laurens, Henry	1757-61; 1765-72: St. Philip's; 1762-65: St. Michael's	1757-58; 1758-59; 1765; 1765-66; 1766-67; 1767-68; 1769; 1769-70	1759-60; 1764; 1768; 1770
Leigh, Sir Egerton	1755-60: St. Peter's		1757-58
Le Noble, Henry	1696-97; 1708-12: Berkeley and Craven		1710-11; 1712
Lewis, Maurice	1736-39: Prince Frederick	1736-37	1737-38; 1739
Lloyd, John, I	1721-27: St. Philip's; 1728-29: St. Thomas and St. Dennis; 1731-33: St. James Goose Creek	1721; 1723-24; 1725; 1725-26; 1727; 1728 (1); 1729; 1731; 1731-32; 1732-33	1722-23; 1726-27
Lloyd, John, III	1768-71: St. Michael's		1768; 1769
Logan, George, Sr.	1698-99; 1702-5; 1707-12: Berkeley and Craven; 1717-21: Christ Church	1708-9; 1717	1703 (2); 1707; 1707-8; 1709; 1710-11; 1711; 1712; 1720; 1720-21
Logan, George, Jr.	1755-57; 1761-68: St. Bartholomew		1761; 1762

Name	Service and Constituency	Sessions in First Rank	Sessions in Second Rank
Lowndes, Rawlins	1749-51: St. Paul's; 1751-54; 1757-60; 1761-68; 1769-75: St. Bartholomew	1757-58; 1762; 1762-63; 1764; 1765; 1772 (2); 1773 (1); 1773 (2); 1774; 1775	1752-53; 1754; 1759-60; 1769; 1770; 1771
Lynch, Thomas, Sr.	1717-24; 1728: Christ Church		1720; 1721; 1722
Lynch, Thomas, Jr.	1752-54; 1757-60: Prince Frederick; 1755-57; 1772: St. James Santee; 1760-72; 1773-75: Prince George Winyaw	1765; 1769; 1769-70; 1770; 1771; 1774	1756-57; 1758-59; 1765-66; 1766-67; 1767-68; 1768; 1772 (2); 1773 (2); 1775
Manigault, Gabriel	1733-35; 1745-46: St. Philip's; 1748; 1751-54: St. Thomas and St. Dennis	1745-46; 1748; 1751-52	1733-34; 1752-53; 1754
Manigault, Peter	1755-57: St. Philip's; 1757-73: St. Thomas and St. Dennis	1758-59; 1762; 1762-63; 1764; 1765-66; 1766-67; 1767-68; 1768; 1769; 1769-70; 1770; 1771; 1772 (1); 1772 (2)	1755-56; 1756-57; 1757-58; 1759-60; 1760-61; 1761; 1765
Mathewes, Anthony	1733-42: St. Bartholomew; 1746-47; 1749-51: St. John's Colleton		1736-37; 1750-51
Mazyck, Isaac	1736-42: St. Philip's; 1742-45: Prince George Winyaw; 1745-46; 1748-51: Prince Frederick; 1747; 1757-68; 1769-70: St. John's Berkeley; 1753-54: St. James Goose Creek; 1757: St. Thomas and St. Dennis	1737-38; 1739-40; 1740-41; 1741-42; 1742-43; 1743-44; 1744-45; 1745-46; 1748; 1749-50; 1750-51; 1752-53; 1754; 1757-58; 1759-60; 1762; 1765; 1765-66	1736-37; 1739; 1756-57; 1758-59; 1760-61; 1761; 1762-63; 1764; 1766-67
Michie, James	1742-45; 1752-55: St. Philip's	1742-43; 1752-53; 1754	1744-45; 1751-52; 1754-55
Middleton, Arthur	1706-7; 1708-9; 1716-17: Berkeley and Craven; 1717-21: St. James Goose Creek	1706-7; 1709; 1716; 1716-17	1706; 1708-9; 1717; 1720; 1720-21

Name	Service and Constituency	Sessions in First Rank	Sessions in Second Rank
Middleton, Henry	1742-45; 1746-48; 1754-56: St. George Dorchester	1746-47; 1754-55; 1755-56	1748
Middleton, Thomas	1742-45; 1746-48: St. James Goose Creek; 1752-54; 1756-57: St. Bartholomew; 1757-61: Prince William's; 1762: St. Michael's	1762	1756-57; 1757-58
Moore, James, Sr.	1692-93: Berkeley	1692; 1693	
Moore, James, Jr.	1706-8: Berkley and Craven; 1721-24: St. James Goose Creek [?]	1721; 1722; 1722-23; 1723-24	
Moore, Roger	1717-24: St. James Goose Creek; 1725-28: St. James Santee		1728 (1)
Morris, Samuel	1737-42: St. James Goose Creek		1739; 1739-40
Morton, John	1695-97: Colleton		1696
Motte, Jacob, Sr.	1739-43: St. Philip's		1739-40; 1740-41; 1741-42; 1742-43
Motte, John Abraham	1706-11: Berkeley and Craven	1709	1707; 1707-8; 1708-9
Moultrie, William	1761-62; 1766-68: Prince Frederick; 1762-65: St. Helena; 1768-73: St. John's Berkeley		1769-70
Nairne, Thomas	1707-8: Colleton; 1711-12: Colleton and Granville	1707; 1712	1711
Oliphant, David	1761: Prince William's; 1762-68: St. James Santee; 1769-75: St. George Dorchester		1769; 1769-70; 1772 (2)
Parris, Alexander	1703-5; 1710-15: Berkeley and Craven	1703 (2); 1710-11	1711; 1714
Parris, John	1736-39: St. Helena		1737-38
Parsons, James	1752-54: St. Paul's; 1760-75: St. Bartholomew	1764; 1765; 1765-66; 1768; 1773 (2); 1774	1751-52; 1752-53; 1754; 1761; 1762; 1762-63; 1767-68; 1769; 1769-70; 1771; 1772 (2); 1775
Pasquereau, Lewis	1706-7; 1708-9: Berkeley and Craven	1706-7; 1709	1708-9
Pawley, Percival	1721-23: St. John's Berkeley	1722	1722-23

Name	Service and Constituency	Sessions in First Rank	Sessions in Second Rank
Peterson, Richard	1708-9: Colleton		1709
Pinckney, Charles (1699-1758)	1731-33: Christ Church; 1733-41: St. Philip's	1731; 1732-33; 1733-34; 1734-35; 1735-36; 1736-37; 1737-38; 1739; 1739-40	1731-32; 1740-41
Pinckney, Charles (1732-82)	1754-60: Christ Church; 1760-61; 1768-75: St. Philip's; 1761-68: St. Michael's	1760-61; 1761; 1762; 1765; 1765-66; 1768; 1773 (2); 1775	1754-55; 1755-56; 1756-57; 1757-58; 1759-60; 1762-63; 1764; 1766-67; 1767-68; 1769; 1769-70; 1772 (2)
Pinckney, Charles Cotesworth	1769-75: St. John's Colleton	1773 (2)	1770; 1771; 1772 (2); 1774; 1775
Powell, George Gabriel	1751-57: Prince George Winyaw; 1761: St. Helena; 1769-71; 1773-75: St. David's	1751-52	1761; 1769; 1769-70; 1774
Pringle, Robert	1752-54: Prince William's; 1755-62: St. James Santee	1752-53	1754; 1756-57; 1757-58; 1758-59; 1762
Prioleau, Samuel	1728-29; 1733-36; 1739-42: St. Helena; 1731-33; 1749-51: St. Philip's; 1748: Prince William's		1732-33; 1734-35; 1735-36; 1739-40; 1741-42
Quelch, Benjamin	1708-17: Berkeley and Craven	1710-11; 1711; 1715	1712; 1713; 1714
Quintyne, Henry	1713-17: Colleton and Granville		1714
Rattray, John	1754-60: St. Helena; 1761: Prince William's	1754-55; 1755-56; 1756-57; 1757-58; 1759-60; 1761	
Raven, John	1695: Craven; 1702-5; 1707-9; 1711-17: Colleton and Granville; 1720-27: St. Paul's		1709; 1713
Rhett, William, Sr.	1706-7; 1710-15: Berkeley and Craven	1706; 1706-7; 1711; 1712; 1713; 1714; 1715	1710-11

Name	Service and Constituency	Sessions in First Rank	Sessions in Second Rank
Rhett, William, Jr.	1725-29: St. Philip's	1727; 1728 (1); 1728 (2); 1729	1725; 1725-26; 1726-27
Risbee, James	1702-7; 1708-11: Berkeley and Craven	1702 (2); 1706; 1708-9; 1709; 1710-11	1703 (2); 1706-7
Roper, William	1748; 1757-65: St. Helena; 1765-68; 1769-71: Prince William's		1748; 1762; 1764
Rutledge, Andrew	1733-42; 1748-54: Christ Church; 1746: St. John's Colleton	1733-34; 1734-35; 1735-36; 1736-37; 1737-38; 1739-40; 1749-50; 1750-51; 1751-52; 1754	1739; 1740-41; 1741-42; 1745-46; 1749; 1752-53
Rutledge, John, Sr.	1743-45: St. Paul's; 1746-50: Christ Church	1749	1743-44; 1744-45; 1746-47; 1748; 1749-50
Rutledge, John, Jr.	1761-75: Christ Church	1768; 1769; 1773 (2)	1762-63; 1764; 1765; 1765-66; 1766-67; 1767-68; 1769-70; 1770; 1771; 1772 (2); 1774; 1775
Saunders, Roger	1728-33: St. Andrew's; 1733-36: St. Bartholomew	1731-32	1731; 1732-33; 1734-35; 1735-36
Savage, John	1752-57: St. Philip's; 1761: St. Michael's	1755-56	1751-52; 1752-53; 1754; 1754-55; 1756-57; 1761
Savage, Thomas	1768-71: St. Michael's		1769; 1769-70; 1771
Saxby, George	1746; 1751-53: St. Paul's	1751-52	
Scott, William	1762-65: St. Philip's; 1765-75: St. Andrew's		1762; 1762-63
Sheed, George	1768: St. Andrew's; 1769-71: St. George Dorchester		1769
Sindry, Daniel	1703-4: Berkeley and Craven		1703 (2)
Skene, Alexander	1720-21: St. Philip's [?]		1720; 1720-21
Skirving, James, Sr.	1748; 1755-57; 1762; 1764-65: St. Bartholomew		1755-56; 1762

Name	Service and Constituency	Sessions in First Rank	Sessions in Second Rank
Smith, Benjamin	1747-48; 1751-65: St. Philip's; 1749-51: St. George Dorchester; 1766-68: St. James Goose Creek; 1769-70: St. John's Colleton	1749; 1750-51; 1754; 1754-55; 1755-56; 1756-57; 1757-58; 1758-59; 1759-60; 1760-61; 1761; 1762; 1762-63	1748; 1749-50; 1751-52; 1764; 1765
Smith, George (Son of 1st Landgrave Thomas Smith)	1698-99; 1702-3; 1707-8: Berkeley and Craven		1707
Smith, George (Son of 2nd Landgrave Thomas Smith)	1720-27; 1729: St. Andrew's	1726-27	1720-21; 1721; 1722; 1723-24; 1725-26; 1729
Smith, James Le Serurier	1702-5: Berkley and Craven	1703 (1); 1703 (2); 1705	1702 (2)
Smith, Roger	1772-75: St. Philip's		1772 (2); 1773 (2)
Smith, Landgrave Thomas (1664-1738)	1696-1703; 1707-8: Berkeley and Craven; 1726-33: St. James Santee	1707-8	1700; 1701; 1702 (1); 1703 (1); 1728 (1)
Smith, Thomas (d. 1724)	1721-24: St. James Goose Creek		1723-24
Smith, Thomas, of Broad Street (1719-90)	1751-54: St. Philip's; 1760-61: St. Paul's; 1762-65: St. Andrew's; 1769-71: St. Helena; 1772: St. James Goose Creek	1751-52; 1752-53; 1760-61	1754; 1761; 1764; 1765; 1769; 1769-70
Smith, William	1695: Berkeley; 1696-1705; 1707-9: Berkeley and Craven	1696	1695; 1700; 1703 (1); 1703 (2); 1707-8
Stevens, Robert	1696-1702: Berkeley and Craven	1696; 1698; 1702 (1)	1697; 1700; 1701
Stroud, John	1703-5; 1707-9: Berkeley and Craven	1707-8	1705
Taylor, Peter	1733-39; 1742-45; 1749-51; 1757-62: St. James Goose Creek	1736-37; 1739; 1749; 1749-50; 1750-51; 1760-61; 1761; 1762	1733-34; 1734-35; 1735-36; 1737-38; 1742-43; 1743-44; 1759-60
Thorpe, Robert	1739; 1745-46: St. Helena		1745-46

Name	Service and Constituency	Sessions in First Rank	Sessions in Second Rank
Trapier, Paul	1748; 1751-54; 1757-60: Prince George Winyaw	1751-52; 1758-59	1752-53; 1754; 1757-58
Trewin, William	1734-36: St. Bartholomew; 1736-39: St. Thomas and St. Dennis		1737-38; 1739
Trott, Nicholas	1700-1703: Berkeley and Craven	1703 (1)	1701; 1702 (1); 1702 (2)
Villepontoux, Zachariah	1749-51: St. James Goose Creek		1750-51
Waring, Benjamin, Jr.	1720-24; 1728: St. George Dorchester	1728 (1)	
Waring, Thomas	1713-17: Berkeley and Craven; 1717-19: St. Andrew's; 1728: St. George Dorchester		1728 (1)
Waties, William	1721-24; 1728-29: St. James Santee; 1731-36: St. John's Berkeley; 1748: Prince George Winyaw	1731-32	1728 (1); 1731; 1732-33; 1733-34; 1734-35
Whitaker, Benjamin	1722-27: St. Helena; 1728; 1736-45: St. Philip's	1722-23; 1723-24; 1725; 1726-27; 1728 (1); 1736-37; 1737-38; 1739; 1739-40; 1740-41; 1741-42; 1742-43; 1743-44; 1744-45	1725-26; 1727
Wigington, Henry	1702-3; 1706-8; 1711-12: Berkeley and Craven	1707; 1711; 1712	1702 (2); 1703 (1); 1706
Wilkinson, Christopher	1706-8: Colleton; 1713-17: Colleton and Granville; 1720-24: St. John's Berkeley [?]		1714; 1715; 1716; 1720; 1723-24
Williamson, William	1760-68: St. Paul's; 1768-71: St. Peter's		1769; 1771
Wragg, Samuel	1711-12; 1716-17: Berkeley and Craven; 1717-19: St. Philip's		1712; 1716; 1717
Wragg, William	1758-68: St. John's Colleton	1759-60; 1760-61; 1761; 1762; 1765	1758-59; 1762-63; 1764
Wright, John	1710-11: Berkeley and Craven		1710-11

Name	Service and Constituency	Sessions in First Rank	Sessions in Second Rank
Wright, Thomas	1740-42; 1746-47: St. Thomas and St. Dennis; 1742-45: St. John's Colleton; 1752-60; 1762-66: St. John's Berkeley		1741-42; 1742-43; 1743-44; 1746-47; 1751-52; 1762; 1765-66
Yonge, Robert	1728; 1729-33; 1746-47: St. Paul's		1728 (1); 1728 (2); 1731; 1732-33; 1746-47

THE NORTH CAROLINA LOWER HOUSE OF ASSEMBLY

Name	Service and Constituency	Sessions in First Rank	Sessions in Second Rank
Anderson, Joseph	1739; 1743-46: Chowan		1743-44
Ashe, John Baptista	1725-26: Beaufort	1725-26	
Ashe, John	1747-75: New Hanover	1754; Apr., 1762; Fall, 1762; Spring, 1764; Fall, 1764; 1765; 1775	1753; 1754-55; 1755; 1757; 1758; 1758-60; 1760; 1766; Dec., 1773; 1774
Badham, William	1734: Edenton; 1735: Chowan		1735
Baker, Blake	1760-65: Halifax County	Spring, 1764	1760; 1761; Apr., 1762; Fall, 1762; Spring, 1764
Barker, Thomas	1743-45: Bertie; 1754-60: Edenton; 1760-62: Chowan	1744-45; 1754-55; 1755; 1756; 1757	1743-44; 1758; 1760
Barrow, John	1743-54; 1760-68: Beaufort		Apr., 1762; Fall, 1762; 1766; 1767-68
Benton, Samuel	1760-68: Granville		Apr., 1762; 1766
Campbell, John	1744-45: Chowan; 1754-60; 1769-75: Bertie	1754-55; 1755	1744-45; 1758; 1770-71
Castellaw, James	1725-26; 1731-35; 1739-45: Bertie		1731; 1735
Caswell, Richard, Jr.	1754-60: Johnston; 1760-68; 1773-75: Dobbs; 1769-71: New Bern	1767-68; 1768; 1769; 1770-71; 1771; Spring, 1773	1759-60; Fall, 1762; Spring, 1764; 1766
Corbin, Francis	1760-65: Chowan		Apr. 1762; Fall, 1762; 1765
Craven, James	1740-46: Edenton		1740; 1744-45; 1746
Dawson, Henry	1766-71 (?): Northampton		1767-68; 1769
Dawson, John	1734-35; 1739-40: Bertie; 1744-45; 1747-52: Northampton	1751	1749-50
Denman, Charles	1725-26; 1731-35: Perquimans	1725-26; 1731	
DeRossett, Lewis	1747-53: Wilmington	1751	1752
Downing, William	1725-26; 1731-34: Chowan; 1735-39: Tyrrell	1733; 1735; 1736; 1739	1725-26; 1731

Name	*Service and Constituency*	*Sessions in First Rank*	*Sessions in Second Rank*
Dunn, John	1769-71: Salisbury		1770-71; 1771
Eaton, William	1746-54: Granville		1752
Edwards, Isaac	1773-75: New Bern	Dec. 1773; 1774	
Elmsley, Alexander	1762: Halifax 1762-68: New Bern	Apr. 1762; Fall, 1762	
Etheridge, John	1725-26; 1731-33; 1734-35; 1739: Currituck		1731
Everard, Sir Richard	1736-40: Bladen	1739; 1740	
Fanning, Edmund	1762; 1766-68: Orange; 1770-71: Hillsborough	1767-68; 1768; 1770-71	1766
Farris, William	1740-45: Wilmington		1740; 1744-45
Frohock, John	1760-68: Rowan County		Apr., 1762; 1766
Gray, Thomas	1770-75: Duplin		Spring, 1773
Harnett, Cornelius, II	1754-75: Wilmington	Apr., 1762; Spring, 1764; 1766; 1767-68; 1768; 1769; 1770-71; 1771; Spring, 1773; Dec., 1773; 1775	1754; 1754-55; 1759-60; 1760; 1761; Fall, 1762; Fall, 1764; 1765; 1774
Harris, Robert	1747-68: Granville		1766
Harvey, John, Jr.	1754-75: Perquimans	1757; 1758; 1766; 1767-68; 1768; 1769; Spring, 1773; Dec., 1773; 1774; 1775	1759-60; Fall, 1762; Fall, 1764; 1765; 1771
Hewes, Joseph	1766-68; 1770-75: Edenton		1766; 1767-68; 1768; 1770-71; Dec., 1773; 1774; 1775
Hodgson, John	1739-46: Chowan	1739; 1740	1743-44
Hooper, William	1773: Campbelltown; 1773-75: New Hanover	Spring, 1773	Dec., 1773; 1774
Howe, Robert	1760-62: Bladen; 1764-75: Brunswick County	1770-71; 1771; Spring, 1773; 1774	1766; 1767-68; 1768; Dec., 1773; 1775
Hunter, Thomas	1740: Pasquotank		1740
Johnston, Samuel	1754-60; 1766-75: Chowan; 1761-65: Edenton		Apr., 1762; Dec., 1773; 1774
Jones, Robert, Jr.	1754-61; 1764-65: Northampton	1754-55; 1755; 1758	1756; 1759-60; 1760; Spring, 1764
Knox, Andrew	1764-75: Perquimans		1769; 1770-71
Lane, Joel	1770-71: Johnston; 1773: Wake		1770-71

Name	Service and Constituency	Sessions in First Rank	Sessions in Second Rank
Leech, Joseph	1760-62: New Bern; 1762-65: Craven		1760; Apr., 1762; Spring, 1764
Lovick, Thomas	1734-35; 1739-40; 1744-55: Carteret		1747; 1748-49; 1749-50; 1751
Macknight, Thomas	1762: Pasquotank; 1770-75: Currituck		1770-71; Spring, 1773
Martin, Alexander	1773-74: Guilford	Spring, 1773	Dec.,1773; 1774
Maule, Patrick	1725-26: Hyde; 1733; 1735: Beaufort		1733
Montfort, Joseph	1762; 1764-65: Halifax County; 1766-74: Halifax		Apr., 1762; Spring, 1764; 1765; 1767-68
Montgomerie, John	1739-40: Tyrrell		1740
Moore, George	1743-45; 1754-62: New Hanover		1756; 1758
Moore, Maurice, I	1725: Carteret (?); 1735-40: New Hanover	1725-26	
Moore, Maurice, II	1754-60; 1762-74: Brunswick	Fall, 1764; 1771	1759-60; Spring, 1764; 1770-71
Moseley, Edward	1708; 1715-23; 1731-34: Chowan	1708; 1715-23; 1731; 1733; 1734	
Nash, Abner	1770-71: Halifax County		1770-71
Neale, Christopher	1770-71: Craven; 1773: New Bern		1770-71; Spring, 1773
Ormond, Wyriot, Sr.	1746: Bath; 1750-54: Beaufort; 1754-58: Bath	1756	1746; 1752; 1753; 1754-55
Park, Julius Caesar	1746: Pasquotank		1746
Person, Thomas	1769-75: Granville		1770-71
Polk, Thomas	1766-71; 1773-74: Mecklenberg		1770-71
Pollock, Cullen	1725-26; 1731-34: Chowan	1733	1731
Pollock, Thomas	1731: Bertie		1731
Porter, Edmund	1725-26; 1733: Chowan		1725-26; 1733
Porter, John	1697: Chowan	1697	
Rhodes, Henry	1775: Onslow		1775
Roberts, George	1735; 1740: Craven		1735; 1740
Rutherford, Griffith	1766-75: Rowan		1770-72
Smith, Thomas	1731-33; 1735; 1739; 1743-44; 1754-60; 1761-65: Hyde		1731
Snowden, Thomas	1712: ?	1712	
Starkey, Edward	1773: Onslow		Spring, 1773

Name	Service and Constituency	Sessions in First Rank	Sessions in Second Rank
Starkey, John	1734; 1739-64: Onslow	1749-50; 1751; 1752; 1753; 1754; 1754-55; 1755; 1756; 1757; 1758; 1759-60; 1760; 1761; Apr., 1762; Fall, 1762; Spring, 1764; Fall, 1764	1743-44; 1744-45; 1746; 1747; 1748-49
Swann, John	1739-51: New Hanover	1747; 1748-49; 1749-50	1743-44; 1744-45
Swann, Samuel, Sr.	1725-26; 1731-35: Perquimans; 1739-62: Onslow	1743-44; 1744-45; 1746; 1747; 1748-49; 1749-50; 1751; 1752; 1753; 1754; 1754-55; 1756; 1757; 1758; 1759-60; 1760; 1761	1735; 1739; 1740; 1755; Fall, 1762
Swann, Samuel, Jr.	1754-61; 1762-68 (?): Pasquotank		1758
Swann, Thomas	1724-26; 1731-33: Pasquotank	1724; 1731	
Swann, William	1711: ?	1711	
Vail, Jeremiah	1753-54: New Bern	1754	1753
Waddell, Hugh	1760: Rowan; 1762; 1766-68; 1770-71: Bladen		1766
Westbeer, Charles	1733; 1735: Edenton		1733
Williams, Arthur	1731-35; 1739: Bertie		1733
Williams, William	1731: Edenton; 1744-45: Pasquotank; 1754-60: Edgecombe; 1760: Bertie; 1761: Currituck		1731; 1758
Winwright, James	1725-26: Pasquotank; 1734: Carteret		1725-26

The Georgia Commons House of Assembly

Name	Service and Constituency	Sessions in First Rank	Sessions in Second Rank
Andrews, Benjamin	1769-74: St. John		1769-70; 1772-74
Barnard, Edward	1757-74: Augusta		Jan.-Feb., 1757 Jan.-Mar., 1758
Box, Philip	1768: Vernonburgh; 1769-71: Acton		1771
Bryan, Jonathan	1770-71: Ogeechee; 1771-73: Savannah		1771; 1772
Bulloch, Archibald	1768-72: Savannah	1769-70; 1770-71; 1771; 1772	1768
Butler, Elisha	1755-56: Ogeechee; 1760-64: St. Philip		1756
Clay, Joseph	1772-74: Savannah		1772-74
Crooke, Richard	1764-66: St. Philip; 1769-71: Augusta	1764-65; 1769-70	1770-71; 1771
Cuthbert, George	1755-56: Ebenezer		1755
DeVeaux, James	1755-56; 1760-64: Ebenezer; 1757-59: Halifax	Jan.-Mar., 1758	June-July, 1757; June-Dec., 1758; 1759; 1760-61; 1761; 1761-62; 1762-63; 1763-64
Douglas, David	1755-56: Augusta	1755; 1756	
Elbert, Samuel	1769-71: Ebenezer		1769-70
Elliott, Grey	1760-61: Savannah	1760-61; 1761	
Elliott, John	1755-59: Midway		June-Dec., 1758; 1759
Ewen, William	1757-72: Ebenezer	1762-63; 1764-65; 1765-66; 1766-67; 1768; 1769-70	Jan.-Mar., 1758; June-Dec., 1758; 1759; 1761; 1761-62; 1763-64; 1767-68
Farley, Samuel	1769-71: Ebenezer; 1771: St. Philip; 1772: Sea Islands; 1773-74: Savannah	1771; 1772	1769-70; 1770-71
Gibbons, Joseph	1760-61: Savannah; 1761-68: St. John		1762-63; 1765-66; 1766; 1766-67
Gibbons, William	1760-64: Acton		1761-62
Glen, John	1769-71: St. George		1770-71
Graeme, William	1769-70: St. Andrew	1769-70	
Graham, John	1760-63: Augusta	1761-62	1760-61
Gwinnett, Button	1769-71: St. John		1769-70

Name	Service and Constituency	Sessions in First Rank	Sessions in Second Rank
Houston, Sir Patrick	1764-68: Vernonburgh; 1769-71; 1772-74: St. Andrew	1765-66	1764-65; 1766-67; 1769-70; 1770-71; 1772-74
Jamieson, John	1772-74: Vernonburgh		1772-74
Johnson, Lewis	1755-56: Abercorn and Goshen; 1760-64: Savannah	1760-61; 1761; 1761-62; 1762-63; 1763-64	1755; 1756
Johnston, Andrew	1765-68: St. George		1765-66
Jones, Noble Wymberly	1755-59: Acton; 1760-61: Ebenezer 1761-74: Savannah	1764-65; 1768; 1769-70; 1770-71; 1771; 1772; 1772-74	1755; June-July, 1757; Jan.-Mar., 1758; June-Dec., 1758; 1761-62; 1762-63; 1763-64; 1766; 1766-67; 1767-68
Kennan, Henry	1761-64: Ebenezer		1761
LeConte, William	1768-71; 1772-74: St. Philip		1769-70; 1770-71; 1772; 1772-74
Little, William	1757: Ebenezer	Jan.-Feb., 1757	
McKeithen, Alexander	1761-64: Frederica	1762-63	1761-62
Martin, Clement	1755-56: Ebenezer	1755	
Milledge, John	1757-59: Vernonburgh; 1761-71: Savannah		1764-65; 1768
Montaight, David	1757-59: Ebenezer	June-July, 1757; Jan.-Mar., 1758; June-Dec., 1758; 1759	
Mulryne, John	1764-71: Sea Islands		1765-66; 1766; 1766-67; 1769-70
Netherclift, Thomas	1772-74: Augusta		1772-74
Ottolenghe, Joseph	1755-61; 1761-66: Savannah	June-July, 1757; Jan.-Mar., 1758; June-Dec., 1758; 1759; 1761-62; 1762-63; 1764-65	1763-64
Powell, James Edward	1755-56: Savannah	1755	
Rasberry, Thomas	1758-59: Savannah		Jan.-Mar., 1758

Name	Service and Constituency	Sessions in First Rank	Sessions in Second Rank
Read, James	1760-64: Ogeechee	1761; 1761-62; 1762-63	1763-64
Shruder, Thomas	1772-74: Augusta	1772-74	
Simpson, John	1765-68: Sea Islands; 1769-71: Frederica; 1772-74: St. George	1765-66; 1766-67; 1767-68; 1772-74	1766
Smith, John	1765-68: St. John	1768	1766-67
Telfair, Edward	1768: Augusta	1768	
Tennatt, Edmond	1755-56: Savannah; 1760-63: Vernonburgh	1760-61; 1761	1755; 1756; 1762-63
Vincent, Thomas	1766-68: Savannah		1766-67
Wood, Joseph	1761-64: St. George		1761; 1761-62
Wylly, Alexander	1760-64: St. George; 1764-68: Savannah	1764-65; 1765-66; 1766; 1766-67; 1767-68	1761-62; 1762-63; 1768
Yonge, Henry	1755-56; 1760-61; 1772-74: Sea Islands; 1757-59: Savannah; 1763-64: Vernonburgh	Jan.-Mar., 1758; June-Dec., 1758; 1763-64	1755; June-July, 1757; 1759; 1762-63; 1772-74
Young, Thomas	1772-74: St. Andrew		1772-74
Young, William	1768: Augusta; 1769-75: Savannah	1769-70; 1771; 1772-74; 1775	1768; 1770-71; 1772
Zubly, David	1772-74: Acton		1772-74

Bibliographical Essay

The bulk of this study is based upon printed and manuscript official records. I have treated the published official records of the southern colonies in detail in "The Publication of the Official Records of the Southern Colonies," *William and Mary Quarterly*, 3d Ser., 14 (1957), 268-80. On the imperial side, *The Calendar of State Papers, Colonial Series*, begun in 1860 by William N. Sainsbury and still in progress, contains either extracts or the full printed text of all the documents in the Colonial Office Papers from the Public Record Office. The series currently fills forty-three volumes and covers the period from 1556 to 1737. Other official collections are the *Calendar of Treasury Books and Papers*, 5 vols. (London, 1897-1903), edited by William A. Shaw; *Acts of the Privy Council of England, Colonial Series*, 6 vols. (London, 1908-12), edited by W. L. Grant and James Munro; and *Journals of the Commissioners for Trade and Plantations, 1704-1782*, 14 vols. (London, 1920-38). George Chalmers, *Opinions of Eminent Lawyers, on Various Points of English Jurisprudence, Chiefly Concerning the Colonies, Fisheries, and Commerce of Great Britain*, 2 vols. (London, 1814), is an older but still valuable collection of legal opinions on various aspects of the empire. Much of the elder Pitt's correspondence with colonial governors is included in Gertrude S. Kimball's *The Correspondence of William Pitt*, 2 vols. (New York and London, 1906); and in 1935 Leonard W. Labaree brought together in a usable form all the royal instructions in his two-volume *Royal Instructions to British Colonial Governors, 1670-1776* (N. Y. and London). Extracts and occasionally full texts of other semi-official documents may be found in the Historical Manuscripts Commission Reports. Particularly germane to this study are *The Manuscripts of the Marquess of Townshend (Eleventh Report, Appendix, Pt. IV* [London, 1887]); *The Manuscripts of the Earl of Dartmouth*, II *(Fourteenth Report, Appendix, Pt. X* [London, 1895]); and the "Manuscripts of Captain H. V. Knox," *Report on Manuscripts in Various Collections*, VI (Dublin, 1909).

Numerous official records are still in manuscript and require a fuller listing. The Public Record Office in London houses the most extensive collection, but a sizable amount will be found in state archives and in other repositories in both the United Kingdom and the United States. The largest and most valuable single collection is the Colonial Office Papers in the Public Record Office. In Class 5, volumes 13-20 contain general correspondence with officials in the colonies from 1742 to 1762; and volumes 293-357, 358-507, 636-708, and 1308-1440 respectively include most of the records of North Carolina, South Carolina, Georgia, and Virginia. Classes 323/1-23; 324/22-40, 60; and 325/1-5 are other general collections with many items relating to the southern royal colonies. Still other useful groups of documents in the Public Record Office are the Treasury Papers, Class 1/319-435, containing the correspondence of the Treasury with officials in the colonies that was not published in Shaw's *Calendar of Treasury Books and Papers*; State Papers Foreign, Class 109/68-71, consisting of abstracts of letters from American governors to the elder Pitt; and the colonial materials in the Chatham Papers, PRO 30/8, and the Egremont Papers, PRO 30/47. An excellent guide to these manuscripts is Charles M. Andrews, *Guide to the Materials for American History to 1783, in the Public Record Office of Great Britain,* 2 vols. (Washington, 1912-14).

Elsewhere in London, the British Museum houses a number of relevant documents, particularly in the Lansdowne, King's, Hargrave, and Additional Manuscripts. Important among the Additional Manuscripts are the Newcastle Papers, volumes 32686-33057, containing much of the correspondence of the Duke of Newcastle with colonial officials through the middle decades of the eighteenth century; the Hardwicke Papers, volumes 36125-36133; and the Martin Papers, volume 4136. Also in London, the Fulham Palace Manuscripts at Fulham Palace include the correspondence of the Bishop of London, head of the Anglican Church in the colonies, with the Anglican clergy, royal governors, and others in America; and the House of Lords Manuscripts at the House of Lords contain petitions from the colonies and reports from the Board of Trade. Three important semi-official collections outside London are the John Locke Manuscripts, Bodleian Library, Oxford, which have considerable material on Virginia; the Sir Robert Walpole Papers among the Cholmondeley (Houghton) Manuscripts, University Library, Cambridge, which include a few interesting documents on the colonies; and the Dartmouth Manuscripts, William L. Salt Library, Stafford. Charles M. Andrews and Frances G. Davenport, *Guide to the Manuscript Materials for the History of the United States to 1783, in the British Museum, in Minor London Archives, and the Libraries of Oxford and Cambridge* (Washington, 1908), describes most of these materials.

In this country, the South Carolina Archives Department, Columbia, has the largest single collection of unpublished official records. Among its more important treasures are the Journals of the Commons House of Assembly from 1692 to 1775 in forty-two volumes; Journals of the Council and Upper House of Assembly from 1721 to 1775 in thirty-eight volumes; South Carolina Indian Books, 1750-1765, and Journals of the Directors of the Cherokee Trade, 1762-1765, in six volumes; Treasurer's Ledgers, 1725-1775, in four volumes; and Charles Garth Letter Book, 1765-1775, in one volume. The South Carolina Archives Department also has thirty-six volumes of the Public Records of South Carolina, transcripts of the South Carolina material from the English Public Record Office. The South Carolina Historical Society, Charleston, has the Journal of the Commissioners of Fortifications, 1755-1770, and the Records of the Commissioners of the High Roads of St. John's Parish, Berkeley County, 1760-1798. The Georgia Department of Archives and History, Atlanta, houses fourteen volumes of the unpublished Colonial Records of Georgia, typescript copies of materials from the English Public Record Office. In the North Carolina Department of Archives and History, Raleigh, the Legislative Papers, 1689-1775, in eleven volumes contain a few important unpublished manuscripts. The Virginia State Library, Richmond, has the letter book of James Abercromby, which includes his correspondence as agent for North Carolina and Virginia.

A number of collections of semi-official papers are scattered through many libraries and archives in the United States. The William L. Clements Library, Ann Arbor, Michigan, is rich in such materials, housing the Sir Jeffrey Amherst, George Clinton, General Thomas Gage, William Knox, William Henry Lyttelton, Shelburne, and Sydney Papers. Particularly the Knox, Lyttelton, and Shelburne manuscripts have a wealth of valuable material on the southern colonies. In the same category, the Henry E. Huntington Library, San Marino, California, has the papers of General James Abercromby and the Earl of Loudoun; the Library of Congress, Washington, D.C., the manuscripts of Lord Wilmington; Colonial Williamsburg, Inc., Williamsburg, Virginia, the papers of William Blathwayt, Francis Nicholson, and Alexander Spotswood; Houghton Library, Harvard University, Cambridge, Massachusetts, Papers Concerning the Governorship of South Carolina; the Southern Historical Collection of the University of North Carolina Library, Chapel Hill, the William L. Saunders Papers, and the library of the College of William and Mary, the papers of Lord Dunmore.

In addition to official and semi-official records, collections of private papers, both printed and in manuscript, are important. Among the unpublished materials in the British Isles should be mentioned the microfilm collection of Arthur Dobbs Papers in the National

Library of Ireland, Dublin; Arthur Dobbs Manuscripts in the Public Record Office of Northern Ireland, Belfast; Lyttelton Manuscripts, Hagley Hall Collection, Birmingham Reference Library, Birmingham; Hobhouse Papers, Jeffries Collection, Bristol Reference Library, Bristol; American Manuscripts, Series A and B, Society for the Propagation of the Gospel in Foreign Parts, London; Charles Steuert Papers, National Library of Scotland, Edinburgh; and Laing Manuscripts, Edinburgh University Library, Edinburgh, many of which are published in Historical Manuscripts Commission, *Report on the Laing Manuscripts preserved in the University of Edinburgh,* 2 vols. (London, 1914-25); and James Glen Letter Book and Alexander Gordon Letters, Scottish Record Office, Edinburgh.

Useful materials in American libraries are the William Byrd II Letter Book, Richard Corbin Letter Book, Sir William Gooch Papers, and John Norton Manuscripts, Colonial Williamsburg, Inc.; Virginia Miscellaneous Manuscripts, Virginia Religious Papers, and Robert Beverley Letter Book, Library of Congress; Robert A. Brock Collection, Huntington Library; Thomas Nelson Letter Book, Virginia State Library; Custis Papers, John Blair Diary, Francis Fauquier Papers, Edmund Jenings II and Edmund Jenings III Letter Book, Lee-Ludwell Papers, Godfrey Pole Papers, and Edmund Randolph's Manuscript History of Virginia, Virginia Historical Society, Richmond; Thomas Pollock Letter Book, North Carolina Department of Archives and History; author's annotated copy of Anthony Stokes, *A View of the Constitution of the British Colonies in North America and the West Indies at the Time the Civil War Broke Out on the Continent of America* (London, 1783), John Carter Brown Library, Providence, Rhode Island; George Bancroft Transcripts and George Chalmers Transcripts, and William Beverley Letter Book, New York Public Library, New York City; Henry Laurens Letter Book, Historical Society of Pennsylvania, Philadelphia; Preston and Virginia Papers, Draper Collection, State Historical Society of Wisconsin, Madison; William Byrd, Eliza Lucas Pinckney, James Wright, and Georgia Papers, Duke University Library, Durham, North Carolina; Miscellaneous Manuscripts, Massachusetts Historical Society, Boston; Edward E. Ayer Manuscripts, Newberry Library, Chicago, Illinois; Sabine Hall and Richard Henry Lee Collections, Alderman Library, University of Virginia, Charlottesville; Hayes Microfilm Collection, Southern Historical Collection, University of North Carolina Library; Carter Family Papers, Library of the College of William and Mary, Williamsburg, Virginia; Fyffe Papers, Clements Library; Manigault Family Papers and Miscellaneous Manuscripts, South Caroliniana Library, University of South Carolina, Columbia; Henry Laurens Papers, South Carolina Historical Society, Charleston; and Noble Wymberly Jones

Papers, Knox-Habersham Letters, and John J. Zubly Diary, Georgia Historical Society, Savannah.

Among the more important published collections of non-official papers are *The Jefferson Papers*, ed. Julian P. Boyd *et al.* (Princeton, 1950——); *Letters of Richard Henry Lee*, ed. James C. Ballagh, 2 vols. (N. Y., 1911-14); *Writings of George Washington*, ed. John C. Fitzpatrick, 39 vols. (Washington, 1931-44); *Letters of James Murray, Loyalist*, ed. Nina Moore Tiffany (Boston, 1901); *Memoirs and Correspondence of George, Lord Lyttelton, from 1734 to 1773*, ed. Robert J. Phillimore (London, 1845); *Journal of a Lady of Quality; being the narrative of a journey from Scotland to the West Indies, North Carolina, and Portugal, in the Years 1774 to 1776*, ed. Charles M. and Evangeline W. Andrews (New Haven, 1923); "Journal of Josiah Quincy, Junior, 1773," ed. Mark A. DeWolfe Howe, Massachusetts Historical Society, *Proceedings*, 49 (1916), 424-81; *Papers relating to the History of the Church in Virginia, 1650-1776*, ed. William S. Perry (Hartford, 1870); *The Letters of the Hon. James Habersham, 1756-1775* (Georgia Historical Society, *Collections*, 6 [1906]); and the Henry Laurens Correspondence in *South Carolina Historical and Genealogical Magazine*, 3-10 (1902-9).

Pamphlets and newspapers also constitute important sources. Pamphlets are listed either in Charles Evans, *American Bibliography*, 13 vols. (Chicago, 1903-34), or Joseph Sabin, *Bibliotheca Americana*, 29 vols. (N. Y., 1868-1936). Clarence S. Brigham, *History and Bibliography of American Newspapers, 1690-1820*, 2 vols. (Worcester, Mass., 1947), is the best guide to newspapers. Other source material may be found scattered through the *Virginia Magazine of History and Biography, William and Mary Quarterly, North Carolina Historical Review, South Carolina Historical Magazine*, and *Georgia Historical Quarterly*.

The secondary literature on the political and constitutional development of the southern colonies is enormous, and only the more important works will be listed here. Certain general studies contain valuable background material. The best general treatments of colonial government are Leonard W. Labaree, *Royal Government in America* (New Haven, 1930), and Arthur Berriedale Keith, *Constitutional History of the First British Empire* (Oxford, 1930), although Evarts B. Greene, *The Provincial Governor in the English Colonies* (N. Y., 1898), is still valuable. Charles M. Andrews's *The Colonial Background of the American Revolution* (New Haven, 1931) and "The American Revolution: an Interpretation," *American Historical Review*, 31 (1926), 219-32, together provide an excellent analysis of the influence of the rise of the representative assemblies upon the coming of the American Revolution. My own interpretation is set forth briefly in "The Role of the Lower Houses of Assembly in

Eighteenth-Century Politics," *Journal of Southern History*, 37 (1961), 451-74. Wesley Frank Craven, *The Southern Colonies in the Seventeenth Century* (Baton Rouge, 1949), and John R. Alden, *The South in the Revolution, 1763-1789* (Baton Rouge, 1957), are excellent surveys that provide a good general background for any specialized study of the southern colonies. The same may be said of Carl Bridenbaugh's provocative collection of essays, *Myths and Realities: Societies of the Colonial South* (Baton Rouge, 1952), which attempts to explore the social forces that shaped southern culture in the eighteenth century. Valuable general studies that throw much light on particular aspects of the lower houses' rise to power are Leslie V. Brock, The Currency of the American Colonies, 1700-1764: A Study in Colonial Finance and Imperial Relations (unpubl. Ph.D. diss., University of Michigan, 1941); Beverly W. Bond, *The Quit-Rent System in the American Colonies* (New Haven, 1919); Mary Patterson Clarke, *Parliamentary Privilege in the American Colonies* (New Haven, 1943); Ella Lonn, *Colonial Agents of the Southern Colonies* (Chapel Hill, 1945); Verner W. Crane, *The Southern Frontier, 1670-1732* (Durham, 1928); John R. Alden, *John Stuart and the Southern Frontier* (Ann Arbor, 1944); and Elizabeth Davidson, *The Establishment of the English Church in Continental American Colonies* (Durham, 1936).

There are a number of studies of Virginia's eighteenth-century political development. Two Columbia University dissertations, Elmer I. Miller, *The Legislature of the Province of Virginia* (N. Y., 1907), and Percy Scott Flippin, *The Royal Government of Virginia, 1624-1775* (N. Y., 1919), respectively provided pioneer studies of the internal development of the House of Burgesses and the mechanics of Virginia government. Stanley M. Pargellis described the Burgesses' procedure in "The Procedure of the Virginia House of Burgesses," *Wm. and Mary Qtly.*, 2d Ser., 7 (1927), 73-86, 143-157; and Ray Orvin Hummel, Jr., in his unpublished doctoral dissertation, The Virginia House of Burgesses, 1689-1750 (University of Nebraska, 1934), carried the study of the Burgesses' institutional development considerably beyond Miller. The years since the Second World War have seen the publication of several additional works on Virginia politics. One of the most suggestive is the late Charles S. Sydnor's study of the practices and patterns of Virginia politics in the late colonial period, *Gentlemen Freeholders: Political Practices in Washington's Virginia* (Chapel Hill, 1952), which particularly emphasizes the Burgesses' role in developing the leaders of the Revolutionary generation. Interpretations of the social background of Virginia politics are Carl Bridenbaugh, *Seat of Empire: The Political Role of Eighteenth-Century Williamsburg* (Williamsburg, 1950); Daniel J. Boorstin, *The Americans: The Colonial Experience* (N. Y., 1958), 99-143; and Bernard Bailyn, "Politics and Social Structure in Virginia," *Seventeenth-Cen-*

tury America: Essays in Colonial History, ed. James Morton Smith (Chapel Hill, 1959), 90-115. Lucille Blanche Griffith's unpublished doctoral dissertation, The Virginia House of Burgesses, 1750-1774 (Brown University, 1957), has provided an interpretative account of the composition and personnel of the Burgesses in the quarter century before the Revolution, and I have offered some tentative conclusions about the structure of power within the Burgesses in "Foundations of Political Power in the Virginia House of Burgesses, 1720-1776," *Wm. and Mary Qtly.,* 3d Ser., 16 (1959), 485-506. David Alan Williams's unpublished doctoral dissertation, Political Alignments in Colonial Virginia, 1698-1750 (Northwestern University, 1959), covers the origins of political factions in the early years of the eighteenth century. In *Give Me Liberty: The Struggle for Self-Government in Virginia* (Philadelphia, 1958), Thomas Jefferson Wertenbaker has woven accounts of popular uprisings, contests of the Council with royal governors, and the Burgesses' quest for power into a tale of a struggle for liberty. Treatments of specific controversies are Glenn C. Smith's two articles, "The Affair of the Pistole Fee, Virginia, 1752-55," *Va. Mag. of Hist. and Biog.,* 48 (1940), 209-21, and "The Parson's Cause, 1755-1765," *Tyler's Quarterly Historical and Genealogical Magazine,* 21 (1940), 140-71, 291-306, and my "The Case of the Pistole Fee," "The Opposition to Lt. Gov. Alexander Spotswood, 1718," and "The Attempts to Separate the Offices of Speaker and Treasurer in Virginia, 1758-1766," *Va. Mag. of Hist. and Biog.,* 46 (1958), 399-422, 70 (1962), 35-42, 71 (1963), 11-18. Biographical studies valuable for their accounts of political developments are Leonidas Dodson, *Alexander Spotswood* (Philadelphia, 1932); Louis K. Koontz, *Robert Dinwiddie* (Glendale, Calif., 1941); Douglas Southall Freeman, *George Washington,* 5 vols. (N. Y., 1948-52); and David J. Mays, *Edmund Pendleton, 1721-1803,* 2 vols. (Cambridge, Mass., 1952). Of special importance is Thad W. Tate, "The Coming of the Revolution in Virginia: Britain's Challenge to Virginia's Ruling Class, 1763-1776," *Wm. and Mary Qtly.,* 3d Ser., 19 (1962), 323-43.

For North Carolina, two general histories, Samuel A. Ashe, *History of North Carolina,* 2 vols. (Raleigh and Greensboro, 1908-25), and R. D. W. Connor, *History of North Carolina: Colonial and Revolutionary Periods* (Chicago, 1919), provide detailed narratives of political events, but there has been a dearth of good specialized studies of either political or constitutional development. John S. Bassett, *The Constitutional Beginnings of North Carolina* (Baltimore, 1894), and Charles L. Raper, *North Carolina: A Study in English Colonial Government* (N. Y., 1904), are two pioneer studies now outdated. In the 1930's Florence Cook analyzed the procedure of the Lower House in "Procedure in the North Carolina Assembly, 1731-1770," *N. C. Hist. Rev.,* 8 (1931), 258-83, and Lawrence F. London published an excellent article on one of North Carolina's major political squabbles, "The Representation Controversy in Colonial North Carolina," *N. C. Hist. Rev.,* 11 (1934), 255-70. In the past five years three studies have made important contributions. Desmond Clarke's *Arthur Dobbs, Esquire, 1689-1765* (Chapel Hill, 1957) provides a clear narrative of the politics of Dobbs's administration, and both Alonzo T. Dill, *Governor Tryon and His Palace* (Chapel Hill, 1955), and Charles G. Sellers, Jr., "Making a Revolution: The North Carolina Whigs, 1765-1775," *Studies in Southern History,* ed. J. Carlyle Sitterson (Chapel Hill, 1957), treat aspects of the politics of the coming of the Revolution. Also useful is my "The North Carolina Lower House and the Power to Appoint Public Treasurers, 1711-1775," *N. C. Hist. Rev.,* 40 (1963), 37-53. Herbert R. Paschal, Jr., Proprietary North Carolina: A Study in Colonial Government (unpubl. Ph.D. diss., University of North Carolina, 1961), is instructive.

The politics and constitution of early South Carolina have also suffered from lack of attention by historians. Of two earlier works, Edson L. Whitney, *The Government of the Colony of South Carolina* (Baltimore, 1895), is hopelessly inadequate and David D. Wallace, *Constitutional History of South Carolina from 1725-1775* (Abbeville, S. C., 1899), is much too brief. Fortunately, there have been two good general histories in Edward McCrady's two volumes, *The History of South Carolina under the Proprietary Government, 1670-1719* (N. Y., 1897), and *The History of South Carolina under the Royal Government, 1719-1776* (N. Y., 1899), and in Wallace's more recent *The History of South Carolina,* 4 vols. (N. Y., 1934-35). Another able study is W. Roy Smith's account of the mechanics of royal government, *South Carolina as a Royal Province, 1719-1776* (N. Y., 1903). Wallace's *The Life of Henry Laurens* (N. Y., 1915) is illuminating on politics just before the Revolution, as are Robert H. Woody's "Christopher Gadsden and the Stamp Act," South Carolina Historical Association, *Proceedings,* 9 (1939), 3-12; and my "The Gadsden Election Controversy and the Revolutionary Movement in South Carolina," *Mississippi Valley Historical Review,* 46 (1959), 469-92; "The South Carolina Quartering Controversy, 1757-1758," *S. C. Hist. Mag.,* 50 (1959), 193-204; "South Carolina's Colonial Constitution: Two Proposals for Reform," *S. C. Hist. Mag.,* 52 (1961), 72-81, and "Bridge to Revolution: The Wilkes Fund Controversy in South Carolina, 1769-1775," *Jo. of So. Hist.,* 39 (1963), 19-52. Clarence John Attig, William Henry Lyttelton: A Study in Colonial Administration (unpubl. Ph.D. diss., University of Nebraska, 1958), is useful.

Until quite recently, royal Georgia was perhaps the most neglected area in the history of the colonial south, but two recent books cover the subject well. The better of these is W. W. Abbot's penetrating study, *The Royal Governors of Georgia, 1754-1775* (Chapel Hill,

1959) , though Kenneth Coleman, *The American Revolution in Georgia, 1763-1789* (Athens, 1958), contains a wealth of material. Other valuable studies are the sections on the royal period in Albert B. Saye's *New Viewpoints in Georgia History* (Atlanta, 1943) and *A Constitutional History of Georgia, 1732-1945* (Athens, 1948); E. Merton Coulter, *Wormsloe: Two Centuries of a Georgia Family* (Athens, 1955); Percy Scott Flippin's treatment of the workings of royal government in "The Royal Government in Georgia, 1752-1776," *Ga. Hist. Qtly.*, 8-13 (1924-29), *passim*; John P. Corry's "Procedure in the Commons House of Assembly in Georgia," *Ga. Hist. Qtly.*, 13 (1929), 110-27; W. W. Abbot's "A Cursory View of Eighteenth-Century Georgia," *South Atlantic Quarterly*, 61 (1962), 339-44; and my "The Georgia Commons House of Assembly and the Power of Appointment to Executive Offices, 1765-1775," *Ga. Hist. Qtly.*, 46 (1962) , 151-61.

Index

A

Abercromby, James, 246; agent for N. C. Lower House, 77-78, 99-100, 272-76, 417, 419; agent for Va. executive, 162-63, 281-83; leader of S. C. Commons, 475

Accounts, power to audit: in Great Britain, 72, 85-86, in N. C., 72-80, 85-86, in Va., 80-81, 85-86, in S. C., 82-86, in Ga., 84-86; procedure for auditing: in N. C., 73, in Va., 80-81, in S. C., 82-84, in Ga., 84-85

Acrill, William, 467

Act of Settlement. *See* Great Britain

Acts of Parliament. *See* Great Britain

Adair, James, 318

Adams, John, 370

Adams, Richard, 467

Agents, colonial, responsibilities of, 266; power to appoint: in S. C., 267-72, in N. C., 272-77, 416-20, in Va., 278-84, in Ga., 284-85, 424-28; protest Currency Act of 1764, 387

Albemarle, Earl of. *See* Keppel, William Anne

Albemarle Co., N. C., 20, 42, 174-84, 218

Albemarle Co., Va., 444-45

Albemarle Sound, 39, 40

Alexander, John, 467

Allen, Arthur, 459, 467

Allen, Eleazer, 209, 238, 475

Allen family in Va., 23

Allerton, Isaac, 467

Allerton, Willoughby, 467

Allien, Richard, 215-16, 475

All Saints Parish, S. C., 383

Allston, Joseph, 33

Altamaha River, 19; representation extended to region south of, 383-84

American Board of Customs. *See* Customs

Amherst, Sir Jeffrey, 456

Amory, Jonathan, 224, 459, 475

Amyand, Isaac, 209

Anderson, Joseph, 489

Andrews, Benjamin, 493

Andrews, Charles M., viii-ix

Andrews, William, 198, 215

Andros, Sir Edmund, 11, 26, 207-8, 455

Annapolis, Md., newspaper in, 288

Anne, Queen of Great Britain, 52, 149, 330

Anson Co., N. C., 117

Answer to Considerations on Certain Political Transactions of the Province of South Carolina (Arthur Lee), 410-11

Appointments to executive officers, power of: in Great Britain, 223; in S. C., 224-33, 249-50; in N. C., 233-43, 249-50; in Va., 243-50; in Ga., 248-49, 429-33

Archbishop of Canterbury, Thomas Tenison, 345

Archdale, John, 457

Archer's Hope Creek, Va., 261

Aristocracy, in Va., 22-26; in S. C., 32-33; in N. C., 39-41; in Ga., 45-46

Armistead, William, 467

Arrest, freedom from, for lower house members. *See* Freedom

Articles of Confederation, 362

Ash, John, 475

Ashby, John, 475

Ashby v. *White*, 193

Ashe, John, 206, 242, 362, 461, 489

Ashe, John Baptista, 42, 150, 176-77, 460, 489

Ashe family in N. C., 39-41

Ashley River, S. C., 21; settlement on, 35, 42

Assemblies. *See* Lower Houses

Assembly rights, as issues in American Revolution, ix-x, 453

Atkin, Edmund, 301

Atkin, James, 191-92

Attachment clause, controversy over in N. C., 342-43, 420-24